SECURITY
ANALYSIS
AND
PORTFOLIO
MANAGEMENT

Donald E. Fischer

University of Connecticut

Ronald J. Jordan

Certified Public Accountant

Prentice-Hall, Inc., Englewood Cliffs, New Jersey 07632

Third Edition

SECURITY ANALYSIS AND PORTFOLIO MANAGEMENT

Library of Congress Cataloging in Publication Data

FISCHER, DONALD E.
    Security analysis and portfolio management.

    Includes index.
    1. Investment analysis   2. Portfolio management.
I. Jordan, Ronald J.   II. Title.
HG4529.F57 1983   332.63'2   82-12297
ISBN 0-13-798876-1

Security Analysis and Portfolio Management, 3/E
Donald E. Fischer and Ronald J. Jordan

Editorial/production supervision by Esther S. Koehn
Interior design by Maureen Olsen and Esther S. Koehn
Cover design by Maureen Olsen
Manufacturing buyer: Ed O'Dougherty

Printed in the United States of America

10   9   8   7   6   5   4   3   2   1

ISBN   0-13-798876-1

Prentice-Hall International, Inc., *London*
Prentice-Hall of Australia Pty. Limited, *Sydney*
Editora Prentice-Hall do Brasil, Ltda., *Rio de Janeiro*
Prentice-Hall of Canada Inc., *Toronto*
Prentice-Hall of India Private Limited, *New Delhi*
Prentice-Hall of Japan, Inc., *Tokyo*
Prentice-Hall of Southeast Asia Pte. Ltd., *Singapore*
Whitehall Books Limited, *Wellington, New Zealand*

To our parents,
to Mary,
to Sheryl,
and Noah, Joshua,
and Geremy

CONTENTS

EIGHT
Company Analysis: Measuring Earnings   **197**

NINE
Company Analysis: Forecasting Earnings   **252**

TEN
Company Analysis: New Approaches
to Forecasting Earnings   **282**

part four
BOND ANALYSIS ————————————————————311

ELEVEN
Bond Analysis: Returns and Systematic Risk   314

TWELVE
Bond Analysis: Unsystematic Risk   339

THIRTEEN
Bond Management Strategies   373

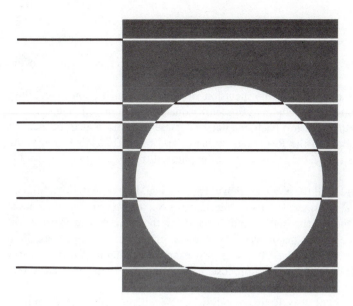

PREFACE

This book is about investing in securities. It is aimed at providing a comprehensive introduction to the areas of security analysis and portfolio management. The text approaches investing as a rational decison-making process in which the investor attempts to select a package or portfolio of securities that meets a predetermined set of goals. These investor goals are usually expressed in terms of return and the degree of uncertainty about the return or risk. More return is desirable; more uncertainty or risk is undesirable.

Special attention has been directed throughout to clarity of exposition. We have tried to make the contents as readable, understandable, and nonmathematical as possible. Only simple algebra and some elementary statistics are used in the book. For those who dread mathematics, even the algebra and the statistics are explained in lay terms.

In the past several decades the fields of security analysis and portfolio management have changed from a completely descriptive institutional body of literature to a highly formalized quantitative area of study. We have attempted to blend the best and most relevant pieces from the evolving field of endeavor into a meaningful, cohesive framework of analysis that would be of interest to the student of business and finance, the practioner in the field, and the informed investor.

The text starts with the premise that the reader had no knowledge of investmemts but some knowledge of economics and accounting. As such, it shoud serve for an introductory course in investment analysis at either the undergraduate or graduate level. The material builds in difficulty as the chapters progress. The text is designed to be followed in the presented progression; however, some users will prefer to cover Chapters 16-22 early in the course. This can be done without loss in continuity. All chapters end with comprehensive questions and/or problems that apply the material presented in the chapter.

An innovation of this work is the inclusion of a comprehensive continuing illustration of the application of the techniques of security analysis and portfolio management to a *real* stock and a *real* portfolio. Each chapter that presents tools of analysis includes an application of the tools to the Restaurant Industry and to McDonald's Corporation. This permits the reader to see the transference of explicated theory to a tangible real-life situation.

The book is divided into seven sections. Part I, The Investment Environment, contains three chapters. Chapter 1 surveys alternative investment vehicles, their more salient attributes, and the relative supply and demand for these investment types in the recent past. The functioning of major securites markets, or how an investor goes about buying and selling particular security types, is also examined (Chapter 2). Finally, the impact of differential taxes and transaction costs is explored, for these costs are a very real part of the investment decision (Chapter 3).

Part II, Framework of Risk-Return Analysis, sets forth in detail the theoretical tenants and practical dimensions of how security prices are determined and the manner in which returns are measured (Chapter 4). Equally important, we develop the notion of risk, what creates it, and techniques for stating risk in explicit quantitative terms (Chapter 5).

In Part III, Common-Stock Analysis, a detailed systematic approach to estimating future dividends and prices for common stocks is developed. The framework for the approach is an economic-industry-company analysis. The strong link between economic activity and security prices requires that the investor forecast the direction and degree of change in economic activity (Chapter 6). Key sectors of overall economic activity influence particular industries in different ways; the investor must link forecasts of economic activity to the prediction of relative movements in specific industries and analysis of selected industries (Chapter 7). From the industry level to the level of individual companies, the investor must examine and analyze factors that influence earnings, dividends, and stock prices of companies (Chapters 8-10).

Bonds and preferred stocks represent less exciting, but, nonetheless, important alternatives to common stock investing. The systematic sources of risk affecting bonds, particularly inflation, and changes in the level and structure of interest rates, are key areas in bond analysis that are examined first (Chapter 11). In addition, unsystematic risk and other nonrisk factors that influence required yields on bonds are explored in depth (Chapter 12). The final chapter in Part IV, Bond Analysis, probes specific passive and active strategies used to manage bond portfolios.

The chapters (14 and 15) in Part V, Options, examine various forms of security options that might be purchased or sold. These options represent rights to underlying common shares as well as fixed income securities.

The approach detailed in Parts III and IV is best described as *fundamental analysis.* Considerations of economic-industry-company analysis are linked in order to reach considered estimates of return and risk on individual securities. In Part VI we also develop the rationale and explore the methods employed by so-called *technical analysis* (Chapter 16). This approach concentrates on supply and demand relationships in the market and on historical price and volume relationships to predict the movement of the market as well as the movement of prices of individual securites. The last segment of Part VI is devoted to the idea of efficient markets and the theory of random walk. The efficient markets notion questions the validity of technical analysis and also raises some questions about fundamental analysis (Chapter 17).

The risk-return output of security analysis is the raw material for portfolio management. Part VII, Portfolio Analysis, Selection, and Management, deals systematically with the procedures involved in portfolio management. Using modern methods for analyzing portfolios and packaging securities in such a way as to achieve diversification of risk is· the first task to be accomplished (Chapter 18). The selection of the one best portfolio from those available to the investor is stage two of portfolio management (Chapter 19). Chapter 20 introduces capital market theory and extends the idea of diversification to include international securities. Following the analysis and selection of a portfolio, the investor must be attentive to revising it as economic conditions and the prospects for individual securities change (Chapter 21). The final chapter in the text (22) explores the ways in which an investor might place his funds in the hands of professionals for management, and how portfolios managed individually, or by others, might be evaluated for performance over time.

This edition of the text has some significant revisions which are worth noting:

1. A completely new industry and company are used as an integrating example to illustrate certain analytical aspects of security analysis. This edition examines the restaurant (fast foods) industry and a premier participant, McDonald's Corporation.

2. There are new chapters on options. These chapters examine puts and calls (including convertible securities) and the evolving interest-rate futures markets; they also discuss widely accepted trading strategies.

3. Rewritten chapters on transaction costs and taxes incorporate the latest developments in these areas.

4. An expanded chapter on accounting information exposes the reader to the very latest in areas of interest to analysts (e.g., replacement accounting, business segment reporting).

5. There is a new chapter on managing fixed income securities, including accepted passive and active strategies.

6. New material on the risks and rewards associated with international diversification is presented.

7. The revised and enlarged end-of-chapter questions and problems have had extensive class testing.

8. Additional aids to instructors in a greatly expanded teachers manual include specifics on setting up and administering a securities trading game, test banks, and suggested course outlines.

As in all large undertakings, the principals gain invaluable advice from numerous individuals. The authors are especially indebted to Richard McEnally, University of North Carolina, who has carefully reviewed every edition and provided valuable advice and encouragement. A number of practitioners have provided especially useful information and suggestions: David Marks, CIGNA Corporation; Pete Morley, Frank Russell Investment Company; Jim Vertin, Wells Fargo Investment Advisors; Jan Vanter, Stein, Roe and Fannham; Roy Burry, Kidder, Peabody and Company; Don Mazur, Dean, Witter,

Reynolds, Inc.; Ken Lynch, Travelers Corporation; Tom Hylinski, Peoples Savings Bank, and Mike Porreca, Aetna Life and Casualty. We are grateful to the Institute of Chartered Financial Analysts (ICFA) for permission to use certain questions and problems appearing on annual examinations for the designation Chartered Financial Analyst.

The manuscript was also vastly improved through the critical comments of our colleagues in academia: John Edmunds, Northeastern University; Adrian Edwards, Western Michigan University; Robert Hollinger, Kansas State University; Michael Robinson, Valparaiso University; Cathy Sherman, Michigan State University, and Tony Wingler, University of North Carolina. Deborah Pauls, and Rhonda Perry typed various versions of the manuscript with their usual good cheer and efficiency. Finally, we are indebted to Dave Hildebrand and Esther Koehn for their special efforts in getting the manuscript into production and for following through to the bound book.

We invite all those who find this book useful to share with us any observations that might serve to improve the substance and employment of the contents.

DONALD E. FISCHER *and* RONALD J. JORDAN

Stamford, Connecticut
West Hartford, Connecticut

SECURITY ANALYSIS AND PORTFOLIO MANAGEMENT

part one
THE
INVESTMENT
ENVIRONMENT

Before we begin our investigation of the ways and means of analyzing individual securities and constructing portfolios, we must understand the investment environment in which we will operate. This is the purpose of this section.

The array of investment vehicles and the participants in the investment arena represent elements worth understanding. Each type of investment has different risk and return characteristics. The participants in the investments game range from the mighty institutional investors (such as pension funds) with considerable dollar muscle to the small, individual investor of modest means. It is important to assess the shifting role and tastes of market participants across a wide spectrum. Who is in the game, and what characterizes the behavior of these participants?

Knowledge of what is available and who the buyers and sellers are must be followed by attention to how one goes about the business of buying or selling securities. It is important to know the various markets through which stocks, bonds, and options can be purchased or sold. The placing of orders to buy and sell and the markets through which this is accomplished are key decision areas in the investment process.

The final link in the investment environment is investor knowledge of the costs of investing. Investing cannot be conducted without cost. Every investor faces the real impact of transaction costs, such as brokerage commissions, and he or she must be attuned to the ever-present differences in the ways in which returns from securities are taxed. Efforts to minimize the burden of transaction costs and taxes occupy much of an investor's time and energy.

Chapter 1 presents a discussion of the differences betweeen investment and speculation, a survey of alternative investment vehicles, and a review of the supply and demand for various security forms during the last several years.

Chapter 2 presents very pertinent information about the function, structure, and operation of the major securities markets in the United States.

Chapter 3, the last chapter in this section, outlines the taxes and other transaction costs that every investor must face and should understand.

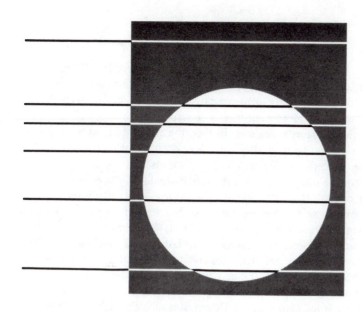

ONE

Introduction to Securities

This book is about investing in securities. Unfortunately, however, we cannot provide the toll for the easy road to riches. Security analysis and portfolio management are hard work, requiring discipline and patience, and the work is not always rewarded by exceptional returns.

None can deny that handsome returns have been reaped in the market by a variety of methods ranging from sheer genius to the occult. The unfortunate thing about most of these techniques is that they are difficult to duplicate consistently by everyone. Often they just cannot be verbalized in a way that permits systematizing.

Our approach is straightforward and consistent within a well-developed framework for decision making. We propose that investors are interested primarily in eventually selling a security for more than they paid for it. Including the receipt of interest or dividends during the time the security is held, the investor hopes to achieve a higher reward than would have been possible by simply placing the same amount of money in a savings account. This reward, or *return,* must be measured and estimated for each security being considered, with appropriate adjustments for decision-making costs.

But in seeking rewards that exceed those available on savings accounts, every investor, consciously or not, faces the very real risk that his hoped-for return will fall short of his expectations. *Risk* means the uncertainty in the probability distribution of returns. This aspect of investing in securities must also be measurable and estimated for each security being considered. The entire process of estimating return and risk for individual securities is known as *security analysis.*

This has not always been the function of security analysis in practice. Traditionally, analysts have attempted to identify undervalued securities to buy, and overvalued securities to sell. Modern-day thinking, strongly influenced by the efficient-markets hypothesis—sometimes popularly called the random-walk theory—questions the validity of or benefit to be derived from traditional security analysis. In fact, the efficient-markets hypothesis sees only indirect benefits emanating from the analyst's risk-return calculations.

Briefly stated, the concept of market efficiency means that stock prices nearly always fully reflect *all* available information. If this is so, it would be exceedingly difficult for the average investor or analyst to earn exceptional returns—particularly on a consistent basis. In fact, the only way for the analyst in such a market to achieve superior performance is by having (1) access to "secret" or "inside" information, (2) superior analytical tools, or (3) superior forecasting abilities. This last item can include everything from being able to forecast earnings per share for some future period to being able to assess the impact of technological and economic developments on the firm's future. We hope that this book will aid the reader in developing analytical ability and useful tools of analysis. For if the domestic stock markets are efficient, it is only through unique insights that the investor can achieve unusually high returns—and then, perhaps only rarely.

Securities that have return and risk characteristics of their own, in combination, make up a *portfolio*. Portfolios may or may not take on the aggregate characteristics of their individual parts. *Portfolio analysis* thus takes the ingredients of risk and return for individual securities and considers the blending or interactive effects of combining securities. *Portfolio selection* entails choosing the one best portfolio to suit the risk-return preferences of the investor. *Portfolio management* is the dynamic function of evaluating and revising the portfolio in terms of stated investor objectives.

Investment versus Speculation

Because this text deals with investments, we will begin our venture with a clear understanding of just what an investment is and what the investment process entails.

An investment is a commitment of funds made in the expectation of some positive rate of return. If the investment is properly undertaken, the return will be commensurate with the risk the investor assumes.

Generally, investment is distinguished from speculation by the time horizon of the investor, and often by the risk-return characteristics of the investments. The true investor is interested in a *good* rate of return, earned on a rather consistent basis for a relatively long period of time. The speculator seeks opportunities promising *very large* returns, earned rather quickly. The speculator is less interested in consistent performance than is the investor, and is more interested in the abnormal, extremely high rate of return than the normal, more moderate rate. Furthermore, the speculator wants to get these high returns in a short time and then seek greener pastures in other investment outlets. In this text the emphasis will be on investments and investment analysis, although speculative situations will also be considered.

The same stock can be purchased as a speculation or an investment, depending on the motivation of the purchaser. For example, AT&T—American Telephone and Telegraph—is generally considered an investment-grade security. That is, it represents a basic service in our economy, and therefore the firm and the price of its shares should grow pretty much with the economy on average over time. However, if a student of the stock market feels that AT&T, selling at $60 a share, is underpriced and is likely to rise to the mid-60s very quickly, he[1] might buy it as a speculation. He is unconcerned with AT&T's dividend or long-term growth prospects. His only concern is with its potential short-term price appreciation.

Despite his motivations, the speculator adds to the market's liquidity and depth, for he is frequently "turning over" (changing) his portfolio. Thus, his presence provides a market for securities (depth) and a wider distribution of ownership of securities (breadth), and enhances the capital markets.

Investment in securities in the *capital markets* (markets for securities with maturities over one year) is a key factor in the U.S. economy. If the economic environment is ripe and corporate management expectations are optimistic, a firm normally wishes to expand. This expansion can take the form of an enlarged physical facility, an increased sales force, or any one of a number of such factors. If conditions are appropriate, all this will eventually lead to higher earnings and higher prices for the firm's outstanding securities. Financing this expansion often comes about by gaining access to the capital markets—namely, through the sale of stocks and bonds. Investors who have earned profits, called *capital gains,* on previous investments in securities or have observed others doing this will be standing ready to finance expansions by providing funds. Thus, firms grow, jobs are provided, families prosper, and the economy grows.[2]

The Investment Process

Now that we have distinguished between investment and speculation and extolled some of the virtues of the capital markets, it becomes necessary to see how one goes about entering the investment arena.

Security Analysis

Traditional investment analysis, when applied to securities, emphasizes the projection of prices and dividends. That is, the potential price of a firm's common stock and the future dividend stream are forecast, then discounted back to the present. This *intrinsic value* is then compared with the security's current market price (after adjusting for taxes and commissions). If the current market price is below the intrinsic value, a purchase is recommended. Conversely, if the current market price is above this intrinsic value, a sale is recommended.

Although modern security analysis is deeply rooted in the fundamental concepts just outlined, the emphasis has shifted. The more modern approach to common-stock analysis emphasizes return-and-risk estimates rather than mere price and dividend estimates. The return-and-risk estimates, of course, are dependent on the share price and the accompanying dividend stream. Chapter 3 will discuss tax and commission considerations,

[1]The use of "he," "his," and so on, is only for the purpose of simplifying the exposition; it should be understood as including both sexes.

[2]Obviously, the presence of organized secondary markets, where already-issued securities are traded, facilitates and boosts investor participation, for these markets provide liquidity for the investor. These issues will be discussed in greater detail in Chapter 2.

and Chapters 4 and 5 will establish the framework of analysis for risk and return that we will be utilizing throughout the text.

Any forecast of securities must necessarily consider the prospects of the economy. As we shall see in Chapter 6, the economic setting greatly influences the prospects of certain industries, as well as the psychological outlook of the investment public. Among industries, the impact of the economy will differ, and thus it is incumbent on the analyst to be thoroughly informed about any industry peculiarities. This industry analysis will be the subject of Chapter 7. Even within industries, the outlook for specific firms will differ. A company's outlook will be related to such things as product line, production efficiency, marketing force, finances, and management capability. A recommended procedure for screening firms and their securities will be presented in Chapters 8 through 13; the analysis in these chapters will yield estimates of risk and return.

The Computer and Investment Analysis

Most of the techniques of security analysis can be applied manually by a limited number of personnel using desk calculators, but this process is feasible only for analyzing a small number of securities. For a large number, the use of a computer becomes a necessity. However, today investors can make use of home or micro computers for limited numbers of securities.

Computers can absorb many thousands of pieces of information and can make use of them as the computer program instructs. The analyst informs a programmer as to the given inputs, the required operations, and the desired format of the output. The required calculations, which might take days to perform manually, can be done by the computer in seconds. This kind of quick turnaround is invaluable to the analyst.

The computer also assists in other valuable ways. First, the analyst can vary his assumptions, resubmit the data, and observe what differences arise as a result of the changed assumptions. Second, alternative constructs can be tested on data of various companies merely by applying "canned" (already-existing) programs to data that have been collected and are stored at the computer center.[3] The results of these various constructs can be compared—often within minutes after they have been conceived. This allows the analyst to follow through immediately with various thought processes without interrupting them for several days while the data are being compiled and processed.

These advantages are realized not only by the largest research organization; individuals can lease limited amounts of time on computers, and various data banks as well, for a reasonable cost. The implication is not that all small investors can (or should) run out and lease computer time for mere pennies a day. It does mean, however, that an individual investor with the necessary know-how and a portfolio of above-average size can avail himself of more sophisticated research techniques and systems.

From time to time throughout the text, we will point out areas where computer applications are both efficient and necessary.[4]

---

[3]Services exist that provide pertinent balance-sheet, income-statement, stock-price, trading-volume, and other data on magnetic tape to subscribers. The data are regularly updated.

[4]Before turning to portfolio analysis in Chapter 18, we will examine two alternative explanations of the behavior of stock prices. Chapter 16 will present the essentials of technical analysis—a set of techniques based on a study of the patterns of share prices. Chapter 17 will discuss the theory of random walk, which denies the existence of such patterns.

We have already seen that modern security analysis differs in emphasis from traditional security analysis. The former emphasizes risk-and-return estimates; the latter emphasizes the calculation of an intrinsic value. Portfolio management is also characterized by an old and a new way of solving the portfolio problem.

Portfolios are combinations of assets. In this text, portfolios will consist of collections of securities. Traditional portfolio planning called for the selection of those securities that best fit the personal needs and desires of the investor. For example, a young, aggressive, single adult would be advised to buy stocks in newer, dynamic, rapidly growing firms. A retired widow would be advised to purchase stocks and bonds in old-line, established, stable firms, such as utilities.

Modern portfolio theory suggests that the traditional approach to portfolio analysis, selection, and management may well yield less than optimum results—that a more scientific approach is needed, based on estimates of risk and return of the portfolio and the attitudes of the investor toward a risk-return trade-off stemming from the analysis of the individual securities.

The return of the portfolio, as we shall see in Chapter 18, is nothing more than the weighted average of the returns of the individual stocks. The weights are based on the percentage composition of the portfolio. (A stock representing 10 percent of the portfolio receives a weight of .10). The total risk of the portfolio is more complex. Here we need only point out that securities when combined may have a greater or lesser risk than the sum of their component risks. This fact arises from the degree to which the returns of individual securities move together or interact. Modern portfolio-management techniques will be discussed in Chapters 18-20, and 22. More traditional timing and management techniques will be the subject of Chapter 21.

Investment Categories

Investments generally involve *real assets* or *financial assets.* Real assets are tangible, material things, like buildings, automobiles, and textbooks. Financial assets are pieces of paper representing an indirect claim to real assets held by someone else. These pieces of paper represent debt or equity commitments in the form of IOUs or stock certificates.

Among the many properties that distinguish real from financial assets, one of special interest to investors, is *liquidity*. Liquidity refers to the ease of converting an asset into money quickly, conveniently, and at little exchange cost. Real assets are generally less liquid than financial assets, largely because real assets are more heterogeneous, often peculiarly adapted to a specific use, and yield benefits only in cooperation with other productive factors. In addition, returns on real assets are frequently more difficult to measure accurately, owing to the absence of broad, ready, and active markets. Many of the concepts, techniques, and decision rules applicable to financial assets are applicable to real assets, but our principal concern in this book is with financial assets.

Financial assets can be categorized in a variety of ways. We will examine them according to their source of issuance (public or private) and the nature of the buyer's commitment (creditor or owner).

Financial assets often take the form of IOUs, issued by governments, corporations, and individuals. They call for fixed periodic payments, called *interest,* and eventual repayment of the amount borrowed, called the *principal.* Debt instruments provide interest in either of two ways. Interest is paid periodically (for example, every six months), or the securities are sold to the investor on a discount-price basis. In the latter type, the instrument is sold at a price below the eventual redemption price, and the difference between the sale price and redemption value constitutes interest. Thus, 6 percent interest is received from a debt security due in one year and redeemable for $100 by either (a) paying $100 at the start and receiving $6 interest payments or (b) paying $94.30 at the outset and receiving $100 at redemption.[5] The redemption amount is referred to as the *face, par,* or *maturity value.* The interest payment in dollars, stated as a percentage of the face, par, or maturity value, is referred to as the *nominal* or *coupon rate.* The repayment of principal is either on demand or at some future time. When the principal is paid in the future, it can be in one lump-sum payment or piecemeal payments spread over time. In all cases it is important to remember that debt instruments represent money loaned rather than ownership to the investor.

INSTITUTIONAL DEPOSITS AND CONTRACTS

Money and checking and savings accounts all represent fixed-dollar commitments that are debtlike in character. Currency is in reality a government IOU. Checking and savings accounts, referred to as *demand* and *time deposits,* are loans to banks and other financial institutions. Demand deposits bear no interest and are redeemable upon demand. Savings accounts, or time deposits, technically cannot be withdrawn without notice, although institutions normally provide this privilege. Savings accounts draw interest, and some forms, called *certificates of deposit* (CDs), have specified maturities (such as one, two, four, or six years). CDs pay higher interest than do normal savings accounts, and penalties are exacted (e.g., loss of interest) if withdrawal is made before the maturity date.

Certain types of life insurance policies build up what is called *cash surrender value.* This reserve accumulates primarily because premiums paid by policyholders normally exceed death benefits in early years. This difference is placed in reserve for later years, when death benefits exceed premiums paid. A policyholder's share of the reserve is similar to a savings account. A policy can be turned in for its cash surrender value, or money may be borrowed from the insurance company against it.

Employees who contribute to pension funds in anticipation of retirement can usually withdraw their own contributions if they leave the company before that time. Normally, during the years of employment, both the employer and the employee will contribute to the pension fund. Upon retirement, the employee receives a pension supported partly by his own and his employer's contributions. Leaving the company before retirement does not usually entitle the employee to the share contributed by his employer.

---

[5]The $5.70 difference ($100 − $94.30) is 6 percent of $94.30.

Thus, cash, demand and savings accounts, and reserves built up in insurance policies and pension funds all represent fixed-dollar commitments. Some bear interest, others do not. Maturities may run from demand to several years' duration. In all cases, however, these "investments" originate with some institution (bank, savings and loan association, insurance company, or other corporation) and are transferable to or redeemed by only the issuer. They may not have title transferred to a third party.

GOVERNMENT DEBT SECURITIES

Debt securities are issued by federal, state, and local governments. They differ in quality (risk), yield, and maturity. U.S. government securities (USGs) are among the safest and most liquid securities available anywhere. Securities of states and municipalities vary substantially in quality.

Short-Term.   Short-term government securities have maturities of one year or less. USGs include Treasury bills offered weekly at a discount, with maturities of 91 days up to three years. Government agencies, such as Federal Home Loan Banks and the Federal National Mortgage Association, frequently sell short-term, interest-bearing obligations.[6] State and local governments frequently sell short-term notes in advance of receipts from taxes and bond issues. These instruments are called *tax* or *bond anticipation notes.*

Long-Term.   The U.S. government issues Treasury notes (one- to five-year maturities) and Treasury bonds (maturities in excess of five years), which bear interest. Over 60 percent of the U.S. government securities held by individuals represent savings bonds. These securities are sold at a discounted price and can be acquired via payroll deductions through employers. Federal agencies also sell longer-term issues. States and municipalities sell long-term debt of two types: *general obligations* and *revenue obligations.* General obligations are backed by the taxing powers of the issuer, whereas revenue bonds pay interest and principal from a special revenue source. In the latter case, a toll-road bond would pay interest and principal from toll receipts. It is easy to see that revenue bonds can represent high risks if the revenue source does not meet expectations.

PRIVATE ISSUES

Private debt issues are offered by corporations engaged in mining, manufacturing, merchandising, and financing activities. As a unit, private issues run the spectrum in quality (risk) and yield, from the high quality of AT&T bonds to the defaulted securities of the Penn Central.

Short-term.   The most common short-term privately issued debt securities are *commercial paper.* Commercial paper is unsecured promissory notes of from 30 to 270 days' maturity. These securities are issued to supplement bank credit and are sold by companies of prime credit standing. *Banker's acceptances* are issued in international trade. They are of high quality, since they carry bank guarantees, and have maturities of from 90 days to one year. Large corporate time deposits in commercial banks are often

---

[6]The securities of government agencies are technically not guaranteed by the full faith and taxing powers of the U.S. government.

of certain minimum amounts for a specified time period. Unlike time deposits of individuals, these *certificates of deposit* are negotiable; that is, they can be sold to and redeemed by third parties.

Long-Term. There is a great variety of subclassifications in long-term corporate or private bonds. It may be well to remember that these subclasses merely represent modifications of the two basic promises in a debt contract: (1) to pay regular interest, and (2) to redeem the principal at maturity.

Interest is usually paid on bonds every six months. Failure to make such payments constitutes an act of default, and bondholders may seek relief from default in the courts. All interest on bonds, current and accumulated, must be paid before any dividends are distributed to shareholders. The only exception to this rule is with the *income bond,* on which interest is paid only if earnings are sufficient to permit it. These bonds often result from reorganizations and are infrequently sold to raise new capital because of the residual nature of interest payments.

We normally associate bonds with the fixed return from interest that gives them their basic appeal to investors seeking safety and regular income. However, the *convertible bond* provides the holder with an option to exchange his bond for a predetermined number of common shares at any time prior to maturity. As the cost of this option, convertible bonds usually provide lower interest (yield) than straight bonds do, since at some future time, if converted into shares, the bond might provide more current income; and/or there may be a handsome capital gain as the bond price moves up with the value of the underlying shares. Obviously, the underlying shares can prove a disappointment both in dividends and in price movement.

The promise to redeem bonds at maturity can be altered or modified by what is termed a *call feature,* provided for the benefit of the issuer (borrower). In the event that interest rates decline after the sale of a bond issue, he would want the option to accelerate the maturity (call the bonds) and replace them at a lower interest cost. Issuers are normally required to pay a penalty (premium) of one year's interest for the call privilege. Quite frequently, call privileges are given but deferred (inoperative) for a period of years.

A special form of call feature, called a *sinking fund,* is often found in bond issues for the benefit of investors. Under a sinking fund, bonds are redeemed piecemeal over the nominal maturity, very much as monthly payments amortize a home mortgage. Such payments give the investor peace of mind that the principal will be repaid, an assurance that is not inherent in the promise of a single lump-sum payment at a distant maturity date. Bonds are retired for sinking-fund purposes at a price not greater than par (plus accrued interest). Bonds are retired in the open market if market prices are below par. If market prices exceed par, bonds are redeemed by random lot. An alternative strategy to sinking-fund bonds is the *serial bond.* Serial issues are really several small bond issues carrying many maturity dates rather than a single one. Each series is redeemed as it comes due, usually at par. Rather than a single bond issue with a thirty-year maturity, we might have thirty subissues due one year apart for from one to thirty years.

To protect the return of principal and any unpaid interest in the event of adversity, bond investors often seek a lien against specific assets of the issuer. The advantage is that during liquidation, creditors with specific liens receive proceeds from the sale of those assets, up to a limit of the debt and interest owed. Otherwise, in the absence of any specific asset claim, bondholders become general or unsecured creditors sharing equally in asset distributions (after creditors with liens or secured creditors). The names attached to bonds often indicate the existence of the security and the type. Unsecured bonds are normally referred to as *debentures*. Bonds secured by real property are known as *mortgage bonds,* with first lienholders called *first-mortgage bondholders,* and so on. Personal property usually stands behind *collateral trust bonds* (bonds and stocks of other companies) and *equipment trust certificates* (railroad rolling stock, airplanes).

The types and variations of bonds available are substantial. Every investor should study the *indenture,* or bond contract, which spells out all the details behind the issue. Most investors do not examine the actual indenture, but more likely an abbreviated version found in the offering *prospectus* available for all new issues of securities sold publicly. A prospectus is a document required by law that is issued for the purpose of describing a new security issue.

Short-term or long-term loans to government and business can be bought from or sold to other investors, often via middlemen or "brokers." Thus, unlike the case with savings accounts and contract reserves, investors in these debt securities need not deal exclusively with the original issuer of the claim. This swapping of debt securities for cash and vice versa takes place through well-established markets, or exchanges.

Equities

We have just discussed investment media that represent a debtor position—that is, in which the investor in bonds or in other debt instruments is a creditor of the party issuing the debt. In this section we will discuss investment media that represent an ownership position—that is, in which the investor in stocks or certain options is an owner of the firm and is thus entitled to a residual share of profits.[7] We will divide equity ownership into two main categories, one representing indirect equity investment through institutions, and the second representing direct equity investment through the capital markets.

EQUITY INVESTMENT VIA INSTITUTIONS

Several vehicles permit an equity investment that requires less supervision than does a direct investment in common or preferred stocks. These investments involve a commitment of funds to an institution of some sort that in return manages the investment for the investor. The most common vehicle is shares of an investment company, but we will defer our discussion of this form of professionally managed portfolio to a later chapter. Several other important institutional outlets for investment dollars should be noted.

Variable Annuities. Under current federal tax laws, certain taxpayers are permitted to have certain portions of their salaries withheld by their employers for investment in a variable annuity. The great advantage of this scheme is that the amount invested in the variable annuity is not taxable to the investor until it (along with accumulated earnings on it) is withdrawn from the plan. Generally, this is during retirement, when the taxpayer is in a lower tax bracket. Quite simply, then, the *tax-sheltered variable*

---

[7]Admittedly, the holder of an option is often not an owner of the firm until he exercises his option and acquires stock.

annuity is a device for deferring the payment of federal income taxes. Although variable annuities are not always of the tax-sheltered variety (the setup is the same in all cases, though), this is the form usually thought of in discussions of variable annuities.

The equity characteristic is that the organization managing the annuity typically invests the proceeds of all the participants in the plan in a portfolio. It is called *variable* because the amount of the monthly annuity payment can vary, depending on the success of the portfolio's investments, which are mainly equities. Thus, this form of planning for retirement is not only tax-sheltered but also quite aggressive.

Insurance Policies.   Purchasing a life insurance policy could well be considered an investment. In fact, if the policy is purchased from a mutual insurance company, the insured becomes an owner of the company. The discussion of adequate life insurance coverage is a specialized area, and we recommend that the interested reader consult any basic life insurance text for further information. In this book we will assume that the investor has already made proper provisions for life insurance, savings accounts, a home, automobile, and other necessities, and is contemplating an investment with other available funds.

DIRECT EQUITY INVESTMENTS

The two main direct equity investments are common stock and preferred stocks. In addition, several options exist that, when exercised, permit the purchase of one of these types of stocks.

Common Stock.   Common stock represents an ownership position. The holders of common stock are the owners of the firm, have the voting power that, among other things, elects the board of directors, and have a right to the earnings of the firm after all expenses and obligations have been paid; but they also run the risk of receiving nothing if earnings are insufficient to cover all obligations.

Common-stock holders hope to receive a return based on two sources—dividends and capital gains. Dividends are received only if the company earns sufficient money *and* the board of directors deems it proper to declare a dividend. Capital gains arise from an advance in the market price of the common stock, which is generally associated with a growth in per-share earnings. Since earnings often do not grow smoothly over time, stock prices have historically been quite volatile over time. This fact points out the need for careful analysis in the selection of securities for purchase and sale, as well as in the timing of these investment decisions, for common stock has no maturity date at which a fixed value will be realized. We advocate the use of fundamental analysis, as outlined in later chapters.

Stock Splits.   Often one reads of a firm declaring a stock split. When this occurs, the firm ends up with more shares outstanding, which sell at a lower price and have a lower par value than the outstanding shares did previous to the split. Stock splits are frequently prompted when the company's stock price has risen to a level that corporate management feels is out of the "popular trading range." If this is so, trading volume in the shares will decrease and investor interest may subside. To overcome this, management may declare a stock split.[8]

For example, suppose ABC Corporation has 1 million shares of common outstanding. The par value is $2 per share and the current market price is $100 per share. Management may rightfully believe that the average investor wishes to deal in lots of 100 shares—round lots—and would like to buy 100 shares of ABC but cannot afford to invest $10,000 at one time. Therefore, management decides to declare a 2-for-1 split.[9] Then there will be 2 million shares outstanding, with a par value of $1 per share and a theoretical market price of $50 per share. Thus it would require only $5,000 (ignoring commissions) to purchase 100 shares of ABC for cash. Of course, earnings per share would be proportionately reduced (by half, in this case) because of the split. Splits can occur at any ratio of new-to-old shares. Several popular ratios are 2 for 1, 3 for 2, and 5 for 4.

Stock Dividends. Instead of (and sometimes in addition to) cash dividends, investors can receive dividends in the form of stock. The end result to the investor is the same as from a stock split: He receives more shares. Stock dividends are typically stated in percentage terms—such as 20 percent stock dividend, meaning a 20 percent increase in the number of shares outstanding.[10] The investor previously owning 100 shares of common would own 120 shares after the stock dividend has been paid. Instead of reducing the par value of the stock on the corporate books, as in the stock-split case, the firm in this case transfers amounts from retained earnings to the capital-stock account for par value of the newly issued stock in the case of a large stock dividend (generally over 25 percent), and transfers the market value of the shares from retained earnings to the common-stock and paid-in-capital accounts in the case of a small stock dividend. Frequently, firms will have to account for stock splits as large stock dividends. These seemingly arbitrary rules have been set up by the accounting profession.

Let us suppose that our firm, with its 1 million shares of $2-par common, declares a 3-for-2 stock split. But its accountants rule that the announced split does not meet the AICPA definition of a stock split. Therefore, the firm must account for the split as a large stock dividend (since a 3-for-2 stock split is equivalent to a 50 percent stock dividend, and 50 percent is greater than 25 percent). The only effect on the balance sheet of the firm is that the retained-earnings account is reduced by $1 million (500,000 shares × $2 par) and the common-stock account is increased by a like amount. Since dividends, both cash and stock, can be paid only out of retained earnings, the payment

---

[8]Sometimes the price of a firm's stock is very low, and management wishes to raise the prestige of the stock. One way to do this is to declare a *reverse split*. This has the opposite effect of a stock split. Fewer shares will be outstanding, but each will sell at a higher price.

[9]In conjunction with management's desire to bring the price of the stock into a more popular trading range is its desire to improve the stock's liquidity. Since more shares are outstanding after a stock split, there are more shares available for trading, and it is quite likely that there will be a wider distribution of ownership (more stockholders). These events aid in providing a fluid market in the shares of the firm. In addition, certain findings indicate that there may be an increase in price associated with some stock splits. See Eugene F. Fama, Lawrence Fisher, Michael Jensen, and Richard Roll, "The Adjustment of Stock Prices to New Information," *International Economic Review,* January 1969, pp. 1-21.

[10]A 20 percent stock dividend is equivalent to a 6-for-5 split.

of a stock dividend reduces the firm's ability to pay future dividends by the amount of par value issued. Stock splits do not have this implication.

As in the stock-split case, earnings, dividends, and theoretical share prices are proportionately reduced by the stock dividend. A 100 percent stock dividend has the same theoretical effect on these values as a 2-for-1 stock split.

Rights, Warrants, and Other Options.   Rights, warrants, and other options all represent investment media that the investor can use to acquire common stock. They differ in the lifetime over which they can be exercised, the leverage they provide the investor, and the risks they carry. Since the issues surrounding these options are somewhat intricate, we defer their full treatment to a later chapter.

Preferred Stock.   Preferred stock is said to be a "hybrid" security, because it has features of both common stock and bonds. Preferred stock is preferred with respect to assets and dividends. In the event of liquidation, preferred-stock holders have a claim on available assets before the common-stock holders. Furthermore, preferred-stock holders get their stated dividends before common-stock holders can receive any dividends. Preferred dividends are stated in either percentage-of-par or dollar terms. Thus, the issue might be known as a $6 preferred or a 6 percent preferred. If the preferred had a $100 par value, this would mean that a 6 percent preferred paid $6 per share per annum in dividends.

Thus, the dividends are fixed for preferred stocks; however, they must be declared before a legal obligation exists to pay them. The fixed characteristic is akin to that of bond interest; the declaration feature is similar to that of common-stock dividends.

Frequently, preferreds are said to be *cumulative* with respect to dividends. This means that if a quarterly dividend is passed (that is, not declared), *all* preferred dividend arrearages must be paid before *any* dividends can be paid to common-stock holders. Most companies provide that if a certain number of preferred dividend payments are missed, the preferred-stock holders may elect representatives to the board of directors in the hope that the new directors will reinstate the divdends. In addition, preferred stock sometimes, although rarely, is *participating.* This means that it can sometimes receive a double dividend—the stated dividend plus an extra dividend bonus after the common has received a dividend. Of course, as in the case of common stock, preferred stock has no maturity date.[11]

Size and Distribution of Investments

Investment, in an economic sense, refers to committing funds to capital assets. Thus, in this sense, investors are users of funds. But in finance, investing refers to the act of acquiring debt and equity instruments with savings. Thus, for us, investors are *suppliers* of funds.

Savings find their way into investments directly or indirectly. Direct investing occurs when business uses its profits to expand plant; individuals invest directly when

[11]Other possible provisions of a preferred-stock issue will be discussed in Chapter 12.

they acquire debt and equity securities through established markets for their own accounts.

Much of the savings of individuals is invested indirectly, through a complex of institutions that serve as channels through which money flows from savers to users. A common characteristic of these institutions is that they accept funds, issue deposit or contractual liabilities, and invest the funds in financial assets (debt and equity).

Financial institutions include the deposit type—commercial banks, mutual savings banks, and savings and loan associations—and the contractual type—insurance companies and pension funds. Deposit types give savers deposit accounts, and contractual institutions issue contracts as liabilities. Other institutions include investment companies that issue equity shares and, in turn, acquire debt and equity instruments of others.

In the sections that follow, we want to gauge (1) the amount of debt and equity issued and outstanding, and (2) who owns them, directly and indirectly.

Summary of Debt and Equity Outstanding

Table 1-1 shows estimates of dollar amounts outstanding in major debt and equity categories at the end of 1975 and 1980. In addition, the relative growth of each segment over the 1975-1980 period is indicated. Note that the broad sweep of change during this period masks the shift in importance that takes place from year to year. In Chapter 11 we shall see the significance of these year-to-year and intrayear flows in forecasting interest rates.

Table 1-1 does not include all sources of debt available but merely concentrates upon those that are more prominent and/or available for direct investment by individuals. Loans to consumers and business, while not insignificant, are generally institutionalized. The mortgage debt outstanding runs second only behind corporate stocks at the end of 1980. The vast majority of mortgage money is made available indirectly through financial institutions; individuals rarely invest directly in mortgages, owing to their large dollar size. Mortgages lend themselves particularly well to pooled financing through institutions.

TABLE 1-1
DATA ON OUTSTANDING LONG-TERM INVESTMENT SOURCES
(BILLIONS OF DOLLARS)

	1975	1980	Percent Change, 1975-80
Mortgages	$646	$1,163	80
Corporate securities:			
Bonds	295	524	78
Stocks*	660	1,480	124
U.S. government securities†	411	902	119
State and local government securities	209	360	72

*Amounts shown are market values. Between 1975 and 1980, the increase of $820 billion consists of $792 billion increase in market value and only $28 billion in net new issues. Thus, the percentage change attributable to net new issues is only about 3 percent.
†Includes securities of government agencies. Short-term Treasury bills included in U.S. government total.
SOURCE: Salomon Brothers, *1981 Prospects for Financial Markets* (New York: Salomon Brothers, 1981).

Principal Suppliers of Debt and Equity Funds

Investors can be classified as individuals, businesses, and government. Further subclassifications are also possible. Table 1-2 indicates the relative roles of investor groups in supporting the debt and equity instruments shown in Table 1-1. Recall that individuals provide investment funds *indirectly* via many institutions.

Commercial banks and the various nonbank institutions play mixed roles in the holding of particular kinds of investments. These differences stem largely from rules and regulations, taxation, structure of finances, and management preferences.[12] The dominant role of indirect or institutional investing is manifest in mortgages and corporate bonds. Individuals play a major role in the market for corporate stocks and securities of federal, state, and local government. In the federal securities area, perhaps 60 to 65 percent of the holdings of individuals represents savings bonds. The special tax-exempt status of state and local government securities tends to make them attractive to people in high tax brackets.

TABLE 1-2
SUMMARY OF MAJOR INVESTMENTS HELD, BY TYPE OF INVESTOR, DECEMBER 31, 1980 (ESTIMATED)

Investor Category	Investment Classification (billions of dollars)				
	Mortgages*	Corporate and Foreign		U.S. Government Securities‡	State-Local Government Securities
		Bonds	Stocks†		
Mutual savings banks	$ 99	$ 22		$ 22	$ 2
Savings and loan associations	500			43	1
Credit unions	4			10	
Life insurance companies	133	171	$ 49	16	7
Property-casualty insurance companies		26	33	23	85
Private pension funds	4	59	172	28	
State and local pension funds	10	93	52	37	3
Foundations and endowments	1	14	64	3	
R.E.I.T. and management corporations	19				
Investment companies (including money market funds)	12	7	42	16	25
Finance companies	12				
Commercial banks	259	5		162	150
Foreigners		15	106	138	
Households (direct)	120	113	955	336	83
Total §	$1,163	$524	$1,480	$902	$360

*Excludes mortgages held by federal agencies.
†Includes common and preferred stock.
‡Agencies = $290 and Treasuries = $612.
§Totals may not add due to excluding certain investor categories and/or rounding.
SOURCE: Salomon Brothers, *1981 Prospects for the Financial Markets* (New York: Salomon Brothers, 1980).

[12]For an excellent discussion of the sources of differences in investment policies of financial institutions, see Harry Sauvain, *Investment Management* (Englewood Cliffs, N.J.: Prentice-Hall, 1973), Chaps. 22-25; and H. E. Dougall and J. E. Gaumnitz, *Capital Markets and Institutions* (Englewood Cliffs, N.J.: Prentice-Hall, 1975).

Flow of New Bonds and Stocks

Table 1-3 indicates net new issuance of corporate bonds and stocks from 1975 through 1981. *Net new issuance* means the difference between brand-new cash offerings and issues retired during the year. Bonds are divided between straight debt and convertible debt.

Note how corporate bond financing has exploded, particularly in recent years. Convertible debt financing enjoyed a period of popularity in the late 1960s and then waned through the mid-1970s. There was a surge in 1980 and 1981. The amount of net new stock financing (common and preferred) in 1980 alone exceeded the aggregate of the preceding four years. To a very considerable extent, the rise in stock financing, starting in 1980 was necessary to compensate for the abundant harvest of debt financing during the 1970s. It is significant that between 1975 and 1979, net new issuance of stock aggregated a mere $16 billion. Yet in two years (1980-81), the aggregate amount doubled to $30 billion.

Table 1-1 indicated that between 1975 and 1980 alone, the market value of corporat stocks increased about $820 billion. Only $28 billion was from net new issues.

TABLE 1-3

NET NEW ISSUANCE OF CORPORATE AND FOREIGN BONDS AND STOCKS, BY YEAR, 1975-1981 (BILLIONS OF DOLLARS)

	1975	1976	1977	1978	1979	1980	1981 (est.)
Corporate bonds (net issuance): *							
Straight debt	$39.9	$41.1	$36.8	$32.9	$26.7	$37.8	$35.2
Convertible debt	.3	.3	.4	(.2)	.4	3.7	3.8
Total	40.2	41.4	37.2	32.7	27.1	41.5	39.0
Corporate stock (common and preferred) *	9.4	5.2	5.0	.5	(4.5)	12.1	18.0

*Values in parentheses mean that retirements exceeded new issuances or that a net decrease occurred in the available supply.

SOURCE: Salomon Brothers, *1981 Prospects for the Financial Markets* (New York: Salomon Brothers, 1980).

Behavior of Individuals as Investors[13]

The roles of the individual and the institution are evident in the area of investments just as in other areas of life. Table 1-2 showed the dominant direct role of individuals in total market value of stock holdings and their more modest position in the holding of corporate bonds. However, these data represent accumulated values at December 31, 1981. What is obscured is the relative shifting back and forth over time.

In Table 1-4 we portray the flow of participation by individuals in the market for bonds and stocks over time. The figures indicate a renewed interest shown in recent years by individual investors in corporate and foreign bonds. More significant, perhaps

---

[13]Some of the material in this section draws upon the *Institutional Investor Study Report of the Securities and Exchange Commission, Volume 1*, 92nd Cong., 1st sess., House Document No. 92-64, Part 1 (Washington, D.C.: U.S. Government Printing Office, 1971), Chap. 3.

startling, is the protracted period during which individuals have been, on balance, liquidating holdings on corporate stocks, which have ended up in the hands of institutions. The net aggregate liquidation by individuals totaled about $275 billion from 1975 through 1981. This is one of the bits of information that have led many to talk of the increasing institutionalization of the stock market.

TABLE 1-4
DIRECT PARTICIPATION OF INDIVIDUALS IN CORPORATE AND FOREIGN
BONDS AND CORPORATE STOCKS, 1975-1981 (BILLIONS OF DOLLARS)

	1975	1976	1977	1978	1979	1980	1981 (est.)
Bonds:							
Individuals	12.4	9.2	−2.5	−1.1	5.5	10.2	6.6
Others	27.8	32.2	39.7	33.8	21.6	31.3	32.4
Total	40.2	41.4	37.2	32.7	27.1	41.5	39.0
Stocks:							
Individuals	−6.6	−12.6	−5.7	−11.3	−27.5	−19.8	−21.8
Others	16.0	17.8	10.7	11.8	23.0	31.9	39.8
Total	9.4	5.2	5.0	.5	−4.5	12.1	18.0

Note: Negative amounts indicate net liquidation.
SOURCE: Salomon Brothers, *1981 Prospects for Financial Markets* (New York: Salomon Brothers, 1980).

In 1971, a long-awaited study by the Securities and Exchange Commission on institutional investors came to some conclusions about individuals as well. Commenting on household savings and portfolio decisions, the study said:

> In their aggregate portfolio, households have substituted for proprietors' equity, have shifted into short-term claims, and have exhibited preference for intermediated rather than direct holdings of long-term assets. They have also exhibited a willingness to disintermediate, however, if relative yields make this attractive. . . .[14]

In sum, the study is saying that individuals seem more inclined to invest money in businesses run by others than to go into business for themselves; that is, to invest through intermediaries (usually institutions) rather than directly. Further, households will invest directly in debt instruments such as bonds when interest rates become relatively more attractive than those offered by institutional arrangements such as savings accounts.

Of course, we are talking about the aggregate. Differences exist in investment behavior as a function of the age and wealth of the individual. Older and more affluent persons are likely to devote more time, attention, and money to direct stockholding. The less well-to-do will do most of their stockholding through intermediaries, via insurance and pension reserves. National Bureau of Economic Research data for 1962, for example, showed that at that time, more than 80 percent of direct stock ownership was associated with individuals whose total assets exceeded $100,000.[15]

[14]*Ibid.*, p. 89.
[15]*Ibid.*

Institutions and the Stock Market

We have seen that individuals changed from net purchasers to net sellers of corporate shares between the 1950s and the 1960s. A takedown in the total value of shares held directly by the public was the inevitable result. Nonetheless, individuals continue to account for almost 70 percent of the market value of corporate stock. The fact that institutions hold a smaller percentage of stock than individuals do masks the degree of activity, or turnover, of these institutional holdings.

SEC statistics show that between 1960 and 1968, the percentage of the dollar amount of corporate stock outstanding that individuals held stayed relatively constant—around 70 percent—even though they were net sellers during much of the period. This seems to indicate that individuals retained or purchased equities that appreciated more rapidly than those held or purchased by institutions. This observation would, in turn, seem to suggest that individuals as a group have done better than the market and better than institutions as a whole over the 1960-68 period.[16]

The SEC study of institutional investors noted a possible explanation for the relative performance of individuals and institutional investors over this period. Because of regulations and management preferences, most institutions prefer to hold the shares of large established companies with large numbers of shares outstanding. Individuals can, and often prefer to, invest in the shares of newer, smaller companies. And during the decade of the 1960s, sales, earnings, and market values of larger companies did not grow as rapidly as those of smaller firms.

The tendency of institutions to concentrate on larger, more established companies can be inferred from data on their holdings of New York Stock Exchange stocks. In 1968 about one-quarter of the market value of all New York Exchange stocks was in the hands of institutions. It is estimated that the total value of the NYSE-listed shares owned by institutions will rise to over 36 percent in 1980 and about 55 percent in the year 2000.[17]

Another factor, at least as important, in the ownership of stocks is the enormous trading activity of institutions. For example, assume that you hold 500 shares of stock and your friend owns only 100 shares. But you hold your 500 shares intact throughout an entire year, and your friend "trades" his shares, by selling and buying 100 shares of various stocks throughout the year. In investment jargon, we would say that your friend has more activity, or "turnover." Thus, while the dollar value of individual ownership of stock exceeds that of institutions by a factor of 70 to 30 percent (or 2.33 to 1), the real market impact from institutions comes from their moving more actively in and out of the stocks they do hold. In 1972, about 70 percent of the New York Stock Exchange *volume* of trading was created by institutions, while they owned only 28 percent of the market value of shares listed.[18]

---

[16]*Ibid.*, p. 124.

[17]G. L. Levy, "Outlook for the Securities Industry," a speech before the Conference of the Financial Analysts Federation, Fall 1972, reprinted in the *Wall Street Transcript,* November 27, 1972, p. 30.

[18]*Ibid.*

Risk and Reward in Securities:
A Historical Perspective

The risks and rewards available from holding various classes of securities over the period 1926-76 are vividly displayed in Figures 1-1 and 1-2.[19]

The graph in Figure 1-1 clearly indicates that among common stocks, government bonds, and treasury bills, stocks came out far ahead of others. That is, $1.00 invested in common stocks at the end of 1925 (with subsequent dividends reinvested) would have grown to $90.57 by year-end 1976. Long-term government bonds grew to only $5.44.

FIGURE 1-1
WEALTH INDICES OF INVESTMENTS IN UNITED STATES
CAPITAL MARKETS, 1926-1976

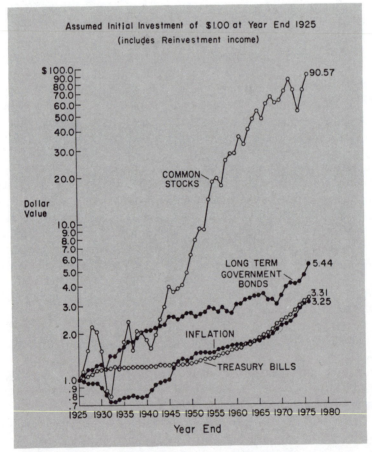

SOURCE: Roger G. Ibbotson and Rex A. Sinquefield, Chicago.
Copyright © 1977.

[19]This information on returns from various types of securities is presented in R. G. Ibbotson and R. A. Sinquefield, *Stocks, Bonds, Bill, and Inflation: The Past (1926-1976) and The Future (1977-2000)* (Chicago: Roger G. Ibbotson and Rex A. Sinquefield, 1977).

However, an examination of Figure 1-2 contrasts the variation in the return on stocks and government bonds. Notice that the lower-return governments displayed much more stability in terms of annual returns than did stocks. The average annual return and range of returns for the period 1926-76 can be summarized as follows:

Class of Security	Average Return (%)	Range of Returns: High-Low (%)
Government bills (short-term)	2.3	8.0-0
Corporate bonds (long-term)	3.9	18.4-(8.1)
Common stocks	11.4	54.0-(43.3)

Notice that there is a strong relationship between risk and return. While the average return on common stocks was 11.4% the range of returns varies from an exciting 54% to a most discouraging −43.3%. It seems clear that risk and return are inseparable!

The data presented here are historical. They may or may not be the pattern of the future. In any case it is important to note the general principle illustrated by the record: the right investment or group of investments for anyone depends upon one's preference for return relative to one's distaste for risk. No specific investment is wrong for everyone.

FIGURE 1-2
VOLATILITY OF ANNUAL RETURNS FROM UNITED STATES CAPITAL MARKETS, 1926-1976

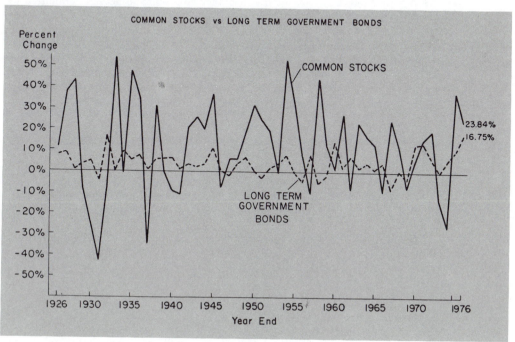

SOURCE: Roger G. Ibbotson and Rex A. Sinquefield, Chicago. Copyright © 1977.

Summary

This chapter provided a broad overview of the nature of security analysis and portfolio management. It was noted that the measurement of return and risk are the main focus of the job of the security analyst and the portfolio manager.

We explored the primary categories of securities—debt and equity instruments. We learned that debt and equity securities include a wide array of variations on the central themes of creditor and ownership interests. Finally, the size of the markets for investments and the relative participation of individuals and institutions were highlighted. The phenomenon of increasing institutionalization of the securities markets emerged quite clearly.

Questions and Problems

1. Distinguish carefully between *investing* and *speculating*. Is it possible to incorporate investment and speculation within the same security? Explain.

2. Compare briefly the traditional and modern approaches to security analysis; to portfolio management.

3. What is liquidity, and why is it so important to the efficient operation of securities markets?

4. What are the two basic promises embodied in debt contracts? Indicate examples of how each of these promises is often modified.

5. Refer to Table 1-2. Why are life insurance companies so heavily committed to mortgages and bonds, and not to common stocks?

6. Refer to Table 1-3. What are the implications of the surge in new issues of stock in the 1980-81 period?

7. Archway, Inc., stock is selling for $100 per share. At present the company pays $2 per year in cash dividends. At the most recent meeting of the board of directors, it was decided that (a) three new shares would be issued for each two shares currently outstanding, and (b) a quarterly dividend of $.48 on new shares would be declared.

    a. Is the 3-for-2 a stock split or a stock dividend? Does it make a difference what we call it?

    b. What should happen to the price per share after the 3-for-2 split, assuming that the dividend was advanced to $1.33 per year?

    c. After the 3-for-2 split and the new $.48 quarterly dividend, what is the effective percentage increase in the dividend?

8. Refer to Table 1-2. Considering the large percentage of the total corporate stock held by individuals, why is there so much fuss about the "institutionalization" of the stock market?

9. List three significant observations about the investment behavior of individuals during the past decade.

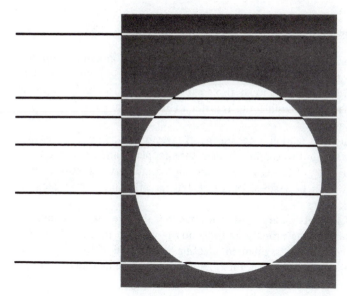

TWO

Markets for Securities

We have examined the broad universe of investment vehicles that are available. Now we are ready to focus upon the mechanism through which securities can be bought and sold.

Securities markets is a broad term embracing a number of markets in which securities are bought and sold. In this chapter the function, structure, and operations of major types of markets will be discussed, including how an individual investor goes about the business of placing any order to buy or sell, how the order is executed, and the process of settling the payment and transfer costs.

Markets and Their Functions

One way in which securities markets may be classified is by the types of securities bought and sold there. The broadest classification is based upon whether the securities are new issues or are already outstanding and owned by investors. New issues are made available in the *primary markets;* securities that are already outstanding and owned by investors are usually bought and sold through the *secondary markets.* Another classification is by maturity: Securities with maturities of one year or less normally trade in the *money market*; those with maturities of more than one year are bought and sold in the *capital market.* Needless to say, the classification system has many variations.

The existence of markets for securities is of advantage to both issuers and investors. As to their benefit to issuers, securities markets assist business and government in raising funds. In a society with private ownership of the means of production and distribution of goods and services, savings must be directed toward investment in industries where capital is most productive. Governments must also be able to borrow for public improvements. Market mechanisms make possible the transfer of funds from surplus to deficit sectors, efficiently and at low cost.

Investors also benefit from market mechanisms. If investors could not resell securities readily, they would be hesitant to acquire them in the first place, and such reluctance would reduce the total quantity of funds available to finance industry and government. Those who own securities must be assured of a fast, fair, orderly, and open system of purchase and sale at known prices.

The classification of markets we are most interested in is the one that differentiates between new and old securities—the primary and secondary markets. In recent years the secondary markets have been further fragmented, creating "third" and "fourth" markets. We will discuss each of these markets in turn. First, let us look at some factors to consider in choosing a broker.

Selecting a Broker

The investor's first step in establishing a satisfactory relationship with a broker is to choose a firm that is suitable for his needs and to select a representative of the firm with whom he can work. In practice it is hard to separate the two choices, for if one has chosen a satisfactory firm but is unhappy with the representative, it is embarrassing to shift one's account to another representative within the same firm. The brokerage firm should be a well-known and long-established institution. In selecting a firm an investor can ask for recommendations from his bank or from friends whose opinions he trusts.

Brokerage houses differ enormously in the type of clientele they attempt to build up. Some try to develop a large business with investors of modest means who are primarily interested in buying and selling odd lots; others seek wealthier customers; and still others are interested primarily in soliciting institutional business. These differences are apparent in the public advertising of brokerage firms.

The research reports of certain houses are obviously written for general public reading, while other houses turn out detailed and sophisticated evaluations aimed primarily at analysts for large institutions. Some houses emphasize mutual funds and advertise the New York Stock Exchange's monthly investment plan.

In short, while almost all brokerage firms welcome all types of investors, some houses are keyed to a particular type. In choosing a brokerage firm that will serve his needs best, an investor should try to judge the type of clientele sought by the firm in relation to the type of investor he is.

At first glance it might appear that most brokers offer about the same services. To the average investor, all firms appear equally efficient in executing orders. Differences between firms relate more to the availability of a special service that an investor may or may not want.

Most brokerage firms have research departments. The staff in these departments varies from large groups of full-time, highly competent analysts to relatively uninformed persons who process the analytical work of others and in effect turn out "second-hand" analyses. The measure of professional competence in the security analysis field is the designation "Chartered Financial Analyst" (CFA). Holders of the CFA have passed a series of three rigorous examinations on investment management decision making, and they must have had a minimum of three years' experience as a financial analyst and must possess a bachelor's degree from an accredited academic institution or the equivalent in training. An investor selecting a brokerage firm on the basis of its research department should know the size of the department and the number of CFAs on the staff. Also he should read some of their reports and compare them with similar ones published by other brokerage houses.

Many firms combine their regular brokerage business with a volume of activity as underwriters of new corporate securities. For an investor who is interested in purchasing new issues, such a house is desirable.

Many brokerage offices maintain a research library in which their customers can check on companies that interest them. If such facilities are important to an investor, he should certainly investigate their availability.

The person within the brokerage office with whom an investor will have the most contact is the registered representative. One can evaluate a representative by inquiring into his business and educational background and his investment philosophies and goals. An investor should also determine whether the representative is available at all times during business hours and should make sure that this individual is not so overburdened with other accounts that he will be unable to give the investor sufficient attention. The representative should be able to furnish the investor at all times, on reasonable notice, information on any specific company's securities.

The representative should not be the type who is always trying to sell the investor something. On the other hand, he should be aware of the securities held by the investor and should inform him of any news that is relevant to these holdings. Basically, the function of the representative is to give service and information to the investor so that the latter can make investment decisions and can have them executed properly and swiftly. A share of the responsibility for a mutually satisfactory business relationship between the two lies with the investor, for he must make his own investing philosophies and goals quite clear so that the representative will be able to offer the type of service desired.

Primary Markets

Securities available for the first time are offered through the primary securities markets. The issuer may be a brand-new company or one in business for many, many years. The securities offered may be a new type for the issuer or additional amounts of a security used frequently in the past. The key is that these secruties absorb new funds for the coffers of the issuer, whereas in the secondary markets, existing securities are simply being transferred between parties, and the issuer is not receiving new funds. After their purchase in the primary market, securities are traded subsequently in the secondary markets.

ROLE OF INVESTMENT BANKERS

Billions of dollars worth of new securities reach the market each year. The traditional middleman in the primary markets is called an *investment banker*. The investment banker's principal activity is to bring sellers and buyers together, thus creating a market.

He normally buys the new issue from the issuer at an agreed-upon price and hopes to resell it to the investing public at a higher price. In this capacity, investment bankers are said to *underwrite,* or guarantee an issue. Usually, a group of investment bankers join together to underwrite a security offering and form what is called an underwriting syndicate. The commission received by the investment banker in this case is the *differential,* or *spread,* between his purchase and resale prices. The risk to the underwriter is that the issue may not attract buyers at a positive differential.

Sales through investment bankers can take the form of a *best-efforts,* or agency, arrangement. In such a case the investment banker does not underwrite the issue but merely uses his best efforts to sell it. Any unsold securities are returned to the issuer. This best-efforts activity is mainly employed in the sale of securities of two types of issuers. New, small companies may represent too much risk for an investment banker to underwrite their securities, so he takes them only on a best-efforts basis. At the other end of the spectrum, many established and popular companies feel that their new issues will be enthusiastically received, so it would be less expensive to use a best-efforts arrangement rather than a more costly, and unnecessary, full underwriting.

Not all new issues are underwritten. Many issuers make direct sales to investor groups, with only some investment-banking services provided. For example, securities are often sold directly to institutions. This is referred to as a *private placement.* The investment banker may act only as a finder; that is, he locates the institutional buyer for a fee. Such private placements are normally restricted to bond and preferred stock issues. Common stock issues are frequently offered directly to existing shareholders, with the investment banker standing ready to sell any shares not taken by the existing shareholders. This is called a *standby* underwriting.

Thus, the investment banker is a middleman. He is paid a fee commensurate with services performed. These services can range from serving merely as a finder to assuming full market risk for the successful sale of an issue (underwriting). As a true intermediary, the investment banker brings buyer and seller together, thus creating a market.

BUYING NEW ISSUES

In the marketing of goods, we traditionally think of the marketing channel as being made up of the manufacturer, wholesaler, and retailer. In the primary markets for securities, the issuer can be thought of as the manufacturer. The investment banker serves the wholesaling function in the channel of distribution. He will locate and do business with buyers through retail outlets. These retail outlets are what we know as brokerage firms. Many investment bankers also serve as brokers and dealers; that is, they both underwrite and distribute shares to ultimate buyers.

Investors are informed of new issues in a formal way through a *prospectus,* a summary of important facts relative to the company and the securities being offered. The document is intended to ensure that potential investors are fully apprised of all important facts that may bear upon the value of the securities. In an informal sense, new issues are available only through those firms that are a part of the retail distribution group.[1]

[1]*Barron's* publishes a list of new securities planned for future offering as well as those being offered, by day, for a week ahead. The name of the principal underwriter is provided. The *New Issues Digest* is a publication that deals with the new issues market in dept.

Local brokerage firms will have "allotments" of new issues, depending upon, among other things, the size of the total issue, number of retail distributors, and degree of regional or local interest. For example, issues that are awaited with high enthusiasm are widely distributed, and one may find a participating broker in a given town with only several hundred shares available. To obtain part of a new issue locally, an investor may locate the name of the underwriter and then ascertain from him which brokers are retail distributors of that issue. The alternative means is to request that your broker keep you apprised of any new issues his firm participates in selling.

Issues that are in short supply relative to apparent demand have to be rationed by brokers. Suppose that a firm has 1,000 shares of a new issue in its office in Portland, Oregon, and customers place orders for 20,000 shares. Something has to give. Quite often another office in, say, Seattle has an allotment of 5,000 shares and orders for only 1,000. The Portland office may request the excess. Commonly, when the demand exceeds available supply, brokers will fill the requests of their best customers first. (A "best" customer is one who provides generous annual commissions.)

ATTRACTION OF NEW ISSUES

New stock issues of companies whose shares are already publicly traded are normally offered at prices very near those of the companies' existing shares. The area of the new-issues market that generates the most excitement and publicity concerns companies coming to the public market for the first time. Since these companies do not have publicly traded shares, investors and speculators are keen to test their assessment of the value of the new shares against the offering price.

The record is replete with stories of spectacular success, as well as of horror. We hear of the new issue of a fledgling computer-equipment firm that is offered at $10 a share on Monday. By Wednesday it is at $20. Within six months it has rocketed to $65. Similarly, periods of speculative excess in the new-issues market have seen the same kind of stock, risen to $65, fall to $1 almost overnight. The 1969-70 period is an example of collapse in new issues; many feel that small investors may never emotionally recover from that blow.

New issues are attractive to many because no brokerage commissions are charged to investors when these shares are purchased. The brokerage fees consist of the spread between the price paid the issuer by the investment banker and the resale price to the public. Regular commissions, however, are paid upon the sale of these shares.

Secondary Markets: The Organized Exchanges

Once new issues have been purchased by investors, they change hands in the secondary market. There are actually two broad segments of the secondary market: the organized exchanges and the over-the-counter (OTC).

The primary middlemen in the secondary markets are *brokers* and *dealers*. The distinction between the two is important. The technical difference rests upon whether the person acts as an agent (broker) or as a principal (dealer) in a transaction.

Organized exchanges are physical market places where the agents of buyers and sellers operate through the auction process. There are a number of organized exchanges. Two are truly national marketplaces, and the others are regional or local.

The largest and best-known national exchange is the *New York Stock Exchange* (NYSE). It accounts for about 80 percent of the share volume on all organized exchanges. The *American Stock Exchange* (ASE) accounts for another 10 percent of all exchange volume. Regional exchanges, located in major areas, include the Pacific, Midwest, and Philadelphia-Baltimore-Washington, and there are local exchanges in Boston and Cincinnati. These exchanges generally concentrate their efforts on securities of regional or local interest.[2]

The membership, listing activities, and functioning of organized exchanges are somewhat similar. We will focus on the NYSE because of its impact and degree of development.

WHAT SHARES ARE TRADED?

Each exchange lists certain stocks for trading. On the national exchanges, only these shares are traded. The NYSE has long enjoyed a reputation as the place where large, seasoned companies are listed for trading. Its sister exchange, the American, is identified with listing smaller and younger companies than those that qualify for the NYSE, or "Big Board."

Certain strict standards must be met and fees paid for initial and continued listing. The initial listing requirements concentrate on minimum demonstrated earnings, asset size, number of shares outstanding, and number of shareholders. Continued listing is dependent upon number of holders, number of public holders, and aggregate market value of shares.

Not all companies qualify for listing on the NYSE. Some qualify but do not wish to be listed—perhaps because they do not want wider distribution of their shares, or do not want to meet the requirements concerning disclosure of their affairs.

In any event, listing brings certain advantages to companies as well as their shareholders. Investors get reasonably full and timely information on the company, constant price quotations, and all the benefits and safeguards built into exchange requirements for continued listings. And the prestige and publicity associated with listing will have an influence on the company's future financing and its products.

MEMBERSHIP ON THE EXCHANGE

Only members of the exchange may participate in trading its listed securities on the floor of the exchange. Since 1953 the NYSE has consisted of 1,366 members. Being a member is often referred to as having a "seat" on the exchange. Seats, or memberships, are bought and sold each year, and the board of governors of the exchange must approve all such transfers of exchange membership. Over the years, seats have sold for anywhere from as low as $17,000 to a half-million dollars.

---

[2]Many also list some NYSE and/or ASE shares. This practice is referred to as *dual* or *multiple listing*. In addition, many NYSE and ASE issues are traded but not listed on local exchanges.

Members perform various functions. According to these functions, they are classified as commission brokers, floor brokers, odd-lot dealers, floor traders, and specialists.

Commission Brokers. About one-half the members of the NYSE are commission brokers, primarily concerned with executing customer orders to buy and sell on the exchange. They receive commissions for such executions. Prominent commission brokers include such firms as Merrill Lynch, Pierce, Fenner & Smith; E.F. Hutton & Co.; and Bache Halsey Stuart and Shields. Many firms have more than one membership.

Floor Brokers. When a commission broker has orders that he cannot execute personally because of their number, or because of the activity of the market, he engages the services of a floor broker. These floor brokers were once referred to as $2 brokers, because at one time they charged a fee of $2 per transaction; today this fee is considerably higher. Commissions are shared on these orders. It is easy to see that smaller commission brokers are especially prone to being swamped by an influx of orders. The floor broker, as a free-lance operator, provides a vital function in ensuring that the exchange's business is conducted rapidly and efficiently.

Odd-Lot Dealers. Trading on the floor of the exchange is conducted in round, or full lots of 100 shares. Many investors and speculators buy and sell in lots of less than 100 shares, called *odd lots*. Odd-lot trades must be executed through an odd-lot dealer who supplies commission brokers, or buys from them, any number of shares less than a round lot. Odd-lot orders account for over one-third of all orders.

Floor Traders. Some thirty members of the exchange trade for themselves; they do not engage in business for the public or for other members. These floor traders roam the floor of the exchange in search of buying and selling opportunities. One moment they may buy a stock, only to sell it shortly thereafter. A trader's profits depend upon the size and rapidity of his turnover of stock and on the accuracy of his estimate of future price movements. Traders pay no commissions and can afford to take narrower margins than others do. They are subject to a myriad of rules and regulations governing their activities, owing to their special status.[3]

Specialists. One-fourth of the membership of the exchange function as specialists. Their key role in the market mechanism will be discussed at length later in this chapter.

LISTED STOCK TABLES

The regular source of reference for basic stock price and volume information is the stock tables appearing in major newspapers throughout the country. The style and statistical information table used for stocks listed on the New York Exchange are

---

[3]In 1964 new rules and regulations were instituted to correct certain practices of traders that had come under criticism. Prior to that time, a trader could buy 100 shares of a $25 stock and sell it the same day at a profit if it rose as much as 8 cents a share. To do as well, the public would require a price rise of 68 cents. See *Report of the Special Study of the Securities Markets of the Securities and Exchange Commission, Parts I and II,* 88th Cong., 1st sess., House Document No. 95 (Washington, D.C.: U.S. Government Printing Office, 1963).

provided by the Associated Press. The format is, therefore, uniform throughout the country. Issues that have traded each day are recorded in alphabetical order and appear as shown in Figure 2-1. From this portion of the tables, let us isolate the facts for Walt Disney to explain their meaning (highlighted in Figure 2-1):

(1) 52 Weeks		(2)	(3)	(4) Yld.	(5) P-E	(6) Sales	(7)	(8)	(9)	(10) Net
High	Low	Stock	Div.	%	Ratio	100s	High	Low	Close	Chg.
67 1/8	41 1/2	Disney	1	1.9	14	481	53 1/4	52 1/2	53 1/4	+1

1. The first columns indicate both the highest and lowest closing prices at which this issue traded in the last fifty-two weeks.

2. This column briefly identifies the issue, citing its full name or abbreviated title (e.g., DrPepp is Dr. Pepper). If it is one of several preferred stocks issued by that company, some means of distinguishing this item from the others also appears. It may be a designation of "A," "B," or "C" preferred or, if the issues carry different dividend rates, that associated rate may be used instead.

3. If the company makes a dividend distribution to its stockholders, that information appears next to the corporate title or abbreviation. Thus, Disney has established a policy of paying a $1.00 per share dividend *annually*. Because of the unique character of some distributions, they appear with a footnote designation.

4. The yield is the indicated dividend (column 3) divided by the closing price of the stock. For Disney that yield is 1.9 percent (1 ÷ 53 1/4).

5. The P/E ratio, meaning price-earnings ratio, is used by some investors to gauge the relative value of a particular security. It compares the current market price of an issue to the latest 12-month earnings announcement on a per share basis. Thus, because the number 14 appears in this column and the stock is selling at about $53, simple arithmetic advises that 12-month earnings were approximately $3.80 per share (53 ÷ 14). No figure appears in this column if the issue is a preferred stock or if the company had no earnings or deficit income to report. Negative P/E ratios are meaningless.

6. Daily quantity figures are recorded only in terms of the number of round lots traded. Because the typical trading unit is 100 shares, the actual share volume is derived by adding two zeros to the number of round lots shown. Thus, a figure of 481 actually means that 48,100 shares changed hands today. One important exception to this statement concerns 10-share trading unit stocks. The quantity figure for these issues is always stated in full and is recognizable by the letter "z" preceding the volume. Sales indicated as "z100" mean, in fact, that a total of 100 shares traded today. The "x" preceding the volume figure signifies that this issue began trading ex-dividend today.

7. High refers to the highest-priced transaction for that issue this day.

8. Low refers to the lowest-priced transaction for that issue this day. Both these columns are included for the benefit of readers interested in determining the extent of the security's daily fluctuation. Note: The letter "d" next to a price is a new low for the year. If the stock had traded at a yearly high price the letter "u" would appear next to that price in the column labeled "high."

9. Close is the final sale price of that security on the exchange today.

10. Net change (Net Chg.) is the difference between *yesterday's closing price and today's closing price*. It is an indicator of daily price trend, and it enables you to determine a monetary result of trading activity on an issue you particularly favor.

FIGURE 2-1

NYSE-Composite Transactions

Wednesday, August 26, 1981

Quotations include trades on the American, Midwest, Pacific, Philadelphia, Boston and Cincinnati stock exchanges and reported by the National Association of Securities Dealers and Instinet

52 Weeks High	52 Weeks Low	Stock	Div.	Yld %	P-E Ratio	Sales 100s	High	low	Close	Net Chg.
59⅝	43¾	DelxCh	2	3.9	12	41	50⅞	50½	50⅞	+ ⅜
25	15⅝	DenMfg	1.30	5.7	9	21	22¾	22	22¾	+ ¾
31¾	17⅛	Dennys	.88	3.6	8	64	25⅜	24½	24½	− ⅛
20⅞	13⅞	Dentply	.88	6.3	9	23	14	d13¾	13⅞	.....
17	11⅞	DeSoto	1	6.9	6	28	14⅝	14½	14½	− ⅜
13⅛	10	DetEd	1.68	15.	5	868	11⅝	11½	11½	− ⅛
73	57	DetE	pf9.32	16.	..	z110	59¾	58½	58½	.....
57	44⅞	DetE	pf7.45	16.	..	z130	47	47	47	− ⅞
56	45	DetE	pf7.36	16.	..	z120	45¾	45⅛	45⅛	.....
22½	17⅞	DE pfF	2.75	16.	..	20	18	d17⅝	17⅝	− ¼
23⅜	17⅞	DE pfB	2.75	15.	..	9	18¼	18	18	− ⅛
17⅜	13¼	DetE	pr2.28	16.	..	4	14⅝	14⅜	14½	+ ⅛
35	27	Dexter	1	3.6	10	104	28½	28	28	− ⅜
14	8⅝	DiGior	.64	6.2	6	38	10⅜	10⅛	10¼	.....
26¼	18⅜	DiGio	pf2.25	10.	..	8	21⅞	21¾	21¾	− ⅛
28	18	DialCp	1.40	5.5	6	5	25½	25¼	25½	+ ¼
39⅜	31⅞	DiaInt	2.20	6.7	12	23	33⅜	32⅝	32⅝	−1
18	14¼	DiaIn	pf1.20	7.5	..	3	16	16	16	+ ¼
39⅝	27¾	DiamS	1.68	4.6	22	1427	36½	35⅜	36⅜	+1
41¾	24	Diebd s		..	15	51	36¼	36	36	.....
113¼	80¼	Digital		..	14	1427	92½	90¾	91¾	+ ⅜
11⅞	9⅞	Dilling n		..	..	42	10⅞	10¾	10¾	.....
25	13¼	Dillon	1.20b	5.8	8	26	20¾	20½	20¾	+ ⅛
67⅛	41½	Disney	1	1.9	14	481	53¼	52⅛	53¼	+1
8¼	3⅛	Divrsin		..	6	73	3⅜	3¼	3¼	.....
15¼	10¼	DrPepp	.80	6.8	9	194	11⅞	11¾	11¾	.....
33⅛	17¼	Dme g	s .16	..	..	265	24	23½	23⅝	.....
32⅜	20½	Donald	.66	2.3	16	19	29	28½	28½	− ½
12½	7⅛	DonLJ	.20	2.1	9	1166	9⅞	9¾	9¾	.....
43	30⅛	Donnly	1.28	3.5	10	34	36⅞	36½	36⅝	− ¼
31	14⅝	Dorsey	1	3.9	8	55	26	25¾	25¾	+ ⅛
64¾	45¾	Dover	1.32	2.3	12	171	57	56⅜	57	+ ⅞
39	28⅞	DowCh	1.80	6.4	7	4040	29¼	d28	28¼	−1
51⅝	24	DowJn	s .92	2.0	21	117	47	46½	46¾	+ ¾
31¾	18	Dravo	s .96	4.9	11	31	19½	19⅛	19½	+ ¼
57	34¼	Dresr	.68	1.6	11	x927	42¼	41⅜	42¼	+ ¾
16⅜	14	DrexB	1.99e	14.	..	16	14¾	14¼	14⅜	− ¼
19¾	14⅛	Dreyfs	s .40	2.4	6	43	16¾	16½	16½	− ⅜
56	36	duPont	2.40	5.6	8	2520	43⅞	42½	42⅝	− ¾
37	28⅝	duPnt	pf3.50	12.	..	4	30	30	30	− ½
46¾	37⅜	duPnt	pf4.50	12.	..	3	38	37¾	37¾	− ¾
21¼	15½	DukeP	2.04	10.	6	1196	20	19⅝	20	+ ¼
66⅜	51½	Duke	pf7.80	15.	..	z100	53	53	53	+1
24½	20¼	Duke	pf2.69	13.	..	5	20¾	20½	20½	− ½
68	54	Duke	pf8.28	15.	..	z5600	54	54	54	.....
70¼	53	DunBr	2.36	3.6	17	132	66	65	66	+1
14	11½	DuqLt	1.90	15.	7	176	12½	12¼	12⅜	.....
19⅜	14	Duq	pfA2.10	13.	..	z50	16½	16½	16½	.....
16	12½	Duq pf	2	16.	..	z220	13	12⅞	12⅞	− ⅛
16⅜	12¾	Duq	prK2.10	16.	..	5	13	13	13	+ ¼
25	21⅝	Duq pr	2.75	12.	..	z120	23¼	23¼	23¼	.....
37	23⅞	DycoP	n.10e	.4	17	24	27½	27⅛	27⅜	+ ½
13	8	DynAm	.15	1.8	3	23	8⅜	8¼	8¼	− ¼
		— E-E-E —								
48⅝	32⅜	EGG	.50	1.4	17	48	35	34⅝	35	+ ½
55⅝	39¾	E Sys	1	2.2	22	349	45	44½	45	+ ¾
22⅞	15¾	EagleP	.96	5.5	8	28	17¾	17½	17½	+ ⅛
28	15¾	Easco	1.32	5.7	8	20	23⅛	23	23⅛	+ ¼
13⅛	6⅞	EastAir		..	..	454	7⅝	7⅜	7⅝	+ ⅛
7½	2½	EAL wtO		..	..	78	4⅜	4	4	− ¼
20⅜	15½	EsAir	pf2.69	17.	..	10	15⅝	15½	15⅝	+ ⅛
20¼	16¾	EsAir	pf3.20	18.	..	35	17⅞	17⅜	17⅞	+ ¼
32½	21	EastGF	1.08	5.1	12	276	21½	d20¾	21⅜	+ ⅜
12½	10¼	EastUtl	1.60	15.	6	82	10⅞	10¾	10¾	.....
85⅜	61½	EsKod	3a	4.5	8	x2343	67¼	66	66⅛	− ⅞
41½	25¼	Eaton	1.72	5.5	11	111	31¼	30¾	31	+ ¾
17	11⅝	Echlin	.52	4.4	20	261	12	11⅞	11⅞	− ⅛
31¾	19	Eckrd	s .80	3.4	11	182	24¼	23⅝	23⅝	− ½
32¾	24	EdisBr	1.44	5.1	7	11	28	28	28	.....
28½	19⅜	Edwrd	s.60a	2.4	6	132	25¼	25	25¼	+ ⅛
29½	19¼	ElPaso	1.48	5.9	13	404	25¼	24⅝	25¼	+ ⅜
19¼	16	EPG	dpf2.35	15.	..	3	16¼	16⅛	16⅛	.....
26⅛	23⅞	EPG	pf 3.75	16.	..	1	24⅛	24⅛	24⅛	− ⅛
19⅜	12⅛	Elcor	.30	2.3	24	31	13⅛	12⅞	13	− ⅛
12⅝	6½	ElecAs		..	19	24	6¾	6½	6½	.....
29⅝	14⅝	EDS s	.60	2.4	18	38	25⅝	25⅛	25¼	− ¼

52 Weeks High	52 Weeks Low	Stock	Div.	Yld %	P-E Ratio	Sales 100s	High	low	Close	Net Chg.
26⅞	15½	GiffHill	.92	4.3	6	5	21¼	20⅜	21¼	+ ⅝
35⅝	26⅜	Gillette	2.10	7.1	8	172	29¾	29⅜	29½	− ⅛
12¼	7⅜	Ginos	.44	5.9	10	7	7⅝	7½	7½	.....
23½	14¼	GleasW	.80	5.5	5	55	14½	14½	14½	− ¼
36½	19½	GlobM	s .20	.8	13	929	25½	24⅛	24¾	− ¼
35⅜	21¼	GldNug		..	21	192	24¼	23⅞	24	+ ¼
15	9	GldWF	s .38	4.0	7	127	9⅝	9⅜	9½	+ ⅛
28⅛	20⅛	Gdrich	1.56	6.7	7	76	23⅝	23	23⅜	+ ⅜
28⅝	24½	Gdrch	pf3.12	12.	..	7	25⅜	25⅜	25⅜	.....
20¼	15	Goodyr	1.30	6.9	6	309	18⅞	18⅝	18¾	+ ⅛
31½	18	GordJw	.76	2.7	6	29	28⅞	28½	28½	− ⅛
30⅞	21⅜	Gould	1.72	6.4	13	586	26¾	26	26¾	+1
63½	43⅜	Grace	2.60	5.7	7	367	46¼	45¾	46	.....
44⅝	33⅛	Graingr	1.08	2.7	10	1364	40	39⅛	39⅜	− ¼
15	11	Granitvl	1	9.0	8	15	11⅛	11⅛	11⅛	.....
17¾	9⅜	GrayDr	.80	4.9	..	190	16¾	16¼	16¼	− ¼
7¼	3⅞	GtAtPc		..	..	229	4⅛	3⅞	4	.....
46	24¾	GtLkIn	.68a	1.9	31	15	35¾	35¾	35¾	+ ⅛
36	22⅛	GNIrn	2.50e	9.2	10	12	27¼	26½	27⅛	+ ⅞
47¾	35¼	GtNoNk	1.80	5.0	6	198	36¾	36¼	36¼	− ¼
•22	13¾	GtWFin	.88	5.9	17	1079	15¼	14⅝	14⅞	+ ⅛
20¼	12½	Greyh	1.20	7.4	5	393	16½	15⅞	16⅛	+ ¼
4¾	1¾	Greyh wt		..	..	109	3	2¾	2¾	− ⅛
11	7	GrowG	s .36	5.1	8	48	7⅜	7⅛	7⅛	− ⅛
6⅝	3¾	GthRty		..	..	3	4	4	4	.....
33⅜	22⅝	Grumm	1.40	5.8	11	127	24	23¾	24	.....
23⅞	18½	Grum	pf2.80	15.	..	29	18¾	18½	18½	− ¼
19¼	8¾	Guardl	s.32	2.0	8	17	16⅞	16⅜	16⅜	− ⅝
21⅝	14½	GlfWst	.75	4.3	4	57	17⅜	17⅛	17¼	+ ⅛
52¾	30⅝	GulfOil	2.80	7.5	7	1021	37⅜	37	37⅛	− ¼
29⅜	18¾	GulfRes	.50	2.0	13	1391	26⅛	25⅛	25⅝	−1¼
36¼	23¼	GulfR	pf1.30	4.1	..	32	32	30½	32	−1
12⅞	10⅜	GlfStUt	1.48	13.	5	687	11¼	10⅞	11¼	+ ⅜
25⅜	18⅛	GulfUtd	1.32	7.3	7	606	18¼	d18	18	− ⅛
50½	39¾	GlfU pf	3.78	9.9	..	1	38	d38	38	−2
21½	10½	Gulton	.60	5.7	26	43	10¾	10½	10½	.....
		— H-H-H —								
9½	6⅜	HMW		..	6	38	7¼	7	7¼	+ ¼
21	17	HackW	2.20	13.	12	20	17¼	d16⅞	16⅞	− ⅛
7¼	5½	Hajoca		..	14	5	6½	6½	6½	.....
31	20⅝	HallFB	1.66	7.1	9	95	23½	22¾	23⅜	+ ⅜
87	53¾	Halbtn	1.20	1.9	13	908	63⅞	53	63⅜	+ ¼
35¾	23¾	HamrP	1.68	6.3	5	170	26⅞	26⅛	26¾	− ¼
12⅞	10	HanJS	1.47a	15.	..	70	10⅜	10⅛	10⅛	.....
16¼	13⅝	HanJI	1.84a	13.	..	32	14⅛	13⅞	14	+ ¼
19⅞	11⅞	Hndlmn	1	6.8	9	55	15	14½	14¾	+ ½
34½	19	HandyH	.50	2.1	14	79	24	23	23⅜	− ⅜
38½	29	Hanna	2	5.6	7	176	36	35½	35¾	+ ½
20⅞	14	HarBJ	s 1	5.8	7	68	17½	17¼	17⅜	− ⅛
26⅜	17½	Hrlnd	s .50	2.2	15	73	23¾	23⅛	23¼	+ ¼
23¼	12⅜	Harnish	.40	3.1	5	198	13½	13	13	− ¼
32½	22¾	HarrBk	2.20	8.7	6	7	25¼	25	25¼	+ ⅛
60¼	41	Harris	.80	1.9	13	168	43¼	42¾	43	+ ¼
21⅝	16½	Harsc	s 1.10	5.6	7	1023	19⅞	19½	19½	− ⅛
24⅛	13¼	HartSM	1.12	5.4	7	42	20⅝	20¼	20⅝	+ ¼
10⅝	6⅝	HartfZd	.40	5.2	12	13	7⅞	7¾	7¾	.....
14½	12	HattSe	1.68a	14.	8	10	12⅛	12⅛	12⅛	.....
26¾	19⅜	HwllEl	2.64	12.	6	35	22⅞	22⅝	22⅞	+ ¼
13⅝	7¾	HayesA		..	..	49	8¾	8¾	8¾	.....
34½	19⅞	Hazeltn	.80	3.4	12	17	24⅛	23⅞	23⅞	− ⅜
13⅞	9½	Hecks	s .24	1.9	8	526	12¾	12⅜	12½	+ ⅛
26½	12½	HeclM	s .50	3.8	9	248	13⅜	13⅛	13¼	+ ⅛
32⅝	19⅛	Heilm	s .64	2.3	10	48	28	27¼	28	+1
59	41½	HeinzH	2.60	4.9	7	75	53¼	52¾	53¼	+ ⅜
20¾	7¾	HelenC		..	7	45	18½	18¼	18⅜	+ ⅛
27⅜	17⅞	HelirInt	1.30	6.1	6	54	21⅝	21	21¼	− ¼
54⅛	38	HelmP	.22	.5	17	624	45⅛	42¾	45	+2¼
4¾	3⅜	HemCa		..	..	2	3½	3½	3½	− ⅛
8⅝	8	HemInc	.85e	10.	..	4	8⅜	8⅜	8⅜	.....
26⅜	18	Herculs	1.32	6.1	8	249	21½	21¼	21½	+ ¼
41	22	Hershy	1.90	5.3	7	32	36	35½	35⅝	− ¼
16	7⅜	Hesston	.20	2.7	..	10	7¾	7½	7½	− ⅛
18½	12⅛	Hestn	pf1.60	13.	..	5	12¼	12¼	12¼	+ ⅛
35¼	24¾	Heublin	1.82	6.6	7	3464	27¾	27	27¾	+ ⅛
53⅞	33⅜	HewlP	s .24	.5	18	874	44½	43¾	44	− ¼
46½	28	Hexcel	.60	2.2	16	61	28⅜	d27⅝	27⅞	− ⅛

EXPLANATORY NOTES

(For New York and American Exchange listed issues)

Sales figures are unofficial.

The 52-Week High and Low columns show the highest and the lowest price of the stock in consolidated trading during the preceding 52 weeks plus the current week, but not the current trading day.

u–Indicates a new 52-week high. d–Indicates a new 52-week low.

s–Split or stock dividend of 25 per cent or more in the past 52 weeks. The high-low range is adjusted from the old stock. Dividend begins with the date of split or stock dividend.

n–New issue in the past 52 weeks. The high-low range begins with the start of trading in the new issue and does not cover the entire 52-week period.

g–Dividend or earnings in Canadian money. Stock trades in U.S. dollars. No yield or PE shown unless stated in U.S. money.

Unless otherwise noted, rates of dividends in the foregoing table are annual disbursements based on the last quarterly or semi-annual declaration. Special or extra dividends or payments not designated as regular are identified in the following footnotes.

a–Also extra or extras. b–Annual rate plus stock dividend. c–Liquidating dividend. e–Declared or paid in preceding 12 months. i–Declared or paid after stock dividend or split up. j–Paid this year, dividend omitted, deferred or no action taken at last dividend meeting. k–Declared or paid this year, an accumulative issue with dividends in arrears. r–Declared or paid in preceding 12 months plus stock dividend. t–Paid in stock in preceding 12 months, estimated cash value on ex-dividend or ex-distribution date.

x–Ex-dividend or ex-rights. y–Ex-dividend and sales in full. z–Sales in full.

wd–When distributed. wi–When issued. ww–With warrants. xw–Without warrants.

vj–In bankruptcy or receivership or being reorganized under the Bankruptcy Act, or securities assumed by such companies.

SOURCE: *The Wall Street Journal,* August 26, 1981.

Secondary Markets: The Over-the-Counter Market

The over-the-counter market (OTC) is not a central physical marketplace but a collection of broker-dealers scattered across the country. This market is more a way of doing business than a place. Buying and selling interest in unlisted stocks are matched not through the auction process on the floor of an exchange but through *negotiated bidding,* over a massive network of telephone and teletype wires that link thousands of securities firms here and abroad.

SCOPE OF MARKET

The OTC encompasses all securities not traded on national organized exchanges.[4] It is really a group of markets, each tending to specialize in certain securities. The first of these markets deals in the securities of the U.S. Treasury and government agencies. The second encompasses the trading in municipal bonds. The third is not as clear-cut but deals in listed and unlisted corporate bonds, in many preferred stocks, and in bank and insurance stocks. The fourth major market deals in unlisted stocks of manufacturing, merchandising, and miscellaneous companies. The quality of issues traded in these heterogeneous and diffuse markets ranges all the way from the highest (U.S. governments) to the lowest (small, highly speculative stocks).

Many more securities are traded over-the-counter than on the organized exchanges. Perhaps 50,000 securities, of which a third are actively traded, are traded in the OTC. However, the volume of activity in the OTC is such that only about one-third of all stock-trading activity in the United States takes place there. The OTC remains dominant in number of issues traded and dollar volume of bonds.

PARTICIPANTS

OTC activity is both wholesale and retail in character. The participants are broker-dealers. A wholesale dealer buys and sells for his own account and from or to professionals. These dealers "make markets" by standing ready to buy or sell securities. They maintain an inventory position in many securities and are actively engaged as principals in buying and selling those in which they are interested. The market here is an interdealer market, since the business transacted is only with other securities firms.

Larger OTC firms are linked by private telephone and teletype. These means of communication serve as the vehicle for buying and selling. Traders quote buy and sell prices to other dealers who call, usually without knowing whether the caller wants to buy or sell.

Individual investors deal with retail firms. For example, should you wish to buy an OTC stock, your brokerage firm might buy the stock from a wholesale dealer for its own account and resell it to you at a slightly higher price. In this case, your firm is functioning as a dealer. The other way your firm could have handled the deal would be to act as your agent in buying the stock from a wholesaler, and it would charge you a commission for its services.

---

[4]Some listed stocks are also traded over-the-counter.

PRICES AND QUOTATIONS

Buyers and sellers of listed stocks meet through brokers on the floor of an exchange and arrive at prices by the *auction* method. OTC transactions are effected within or between the offices of securities houses, prices being arrived at by *negotiation.*

Answering an inquiry as to the market on a particular security, a dealer may quote "20 bid, offered at 21." The prices quoted are "inside," or wholesale, prices at which dealers will sell to each other. The bid is the highest price the dealer will pay for the stock, and the lowest price he will sell it for (offer it) is 21.

The caller frequently asks about the size of the dealer's market. The reply indicates the number of shares the dealer is willing to buy or sell at the quoted prices. Suppose that the response is "300 shares either way" (buy or sell). The next move is up to the caller. He has instructions from his customer as to price limits. If the customer wanted 100 shares at a limit of $20.75, the broker may tell the dealer, "I will pay 20 1/2 for 100 shares." He is *negotiating* for the best price for his customer by bidding away from the offering price (21) and below his customer's limit (20 3/4). The dealer may or may not be willing to make a concession from his offering price of 21. Perhaps he will counter by paring his offering price somewhat, but not all the way to the broker's offer to buy. The dealer may counter with, "I will sell 100 at 20 5/8." The broker may accept this or negotiate further. If he accepts the price of 20 5/8, he has been able to obtain the stock for his customer below the limit and dealer's first quote.

The ultimate price to the customer will exceed 20 5/8 by the charges he must pay. If his firm acts as his agent (broker), he will pay the 20 5/8 plus the regular commission. In other cases, his firm might sell from its own inventory at a "net" price, at which a markup is involved but buried in the price. In our example above, if the shares came from the firm's inventory rather than purchase from a wholesaler, the net price might still be 20 5/8; however, it would be difficult to ascertain how much the firm marked up its own stock.[5]

NASDAQ.   In 1971 a computerized communications network called NASDAQ came into being to provide automated quotations for OTC securities.[6] Securities salesmen can get up-to-date bid and asked prices on OTC securities from a small console that is electronically connected to the NASDAQ computer. They can then contact dealers offering the best prices and negotiate a trade. This rapid centralizing of bid-asked quotes replaced a long-archaic system of "shopping around" by brokers. Under the old system an investor had no assurance that he was receiving the best price available.

Not all OTC stocks are active enough to be included in the NASDAQ system. Of those in the system, the more widely held and traded are quoted in *The Wall Street Journal* according to the bid-asked prices and volume of trading. The latter information was unavailable under the old system.

---

[5]The National Association of Securities Dealers, which supervises activities of OTC broker-dealers, suggests that a 5 percent markup is reasonable under normal conditions.

[6]This acronym, NASDAQ, stands for National Association of Securities Dealers Automated Quotations.

There are about 2200 bond issues on the NYSE, representing the debt of U.S. and foreign corporations, the U.S. government, New York City, international banks, foreign governments, and so forth. Because bonds are traded in large amounts and have special characteristics, the rules of the NYSE ordinarily permit transactions to be executed off the floor even though the issue is listed. Accordingly, bonds are handled primarily in the OTC market.

The actual buying and selling of securities is carried on by traders associated with dealer firms or with large institutions. An institutional trader becomes familiar with the dealers who make markets in the securities in which the institution is interested. By keeping close ties, the institutional trader can gauge whether the dealer is long or short, and the side of the market in which the dealer is likely to be aggressive.

An institution may have direct communications lines to the active dealers; the number of lines depends on its size. On the other hand, individual investors place orders with brokers, who transmit them to their traders for execution. The trader will probably explore the market and obtain several quotations before actually effecting a purchase or sale.

Dealer banks play an important role in the market for bonds in the U.S. government and federal agencies and for general obligations of state and local governments. In the case of U.S. government bonds, the Federal Reserve Bank of New York, which is the fiscal agent for the U.S. government and the Federal Reserve System, recognizes certain "primary dealers." By agreeing to abide by certain rules, such a dealer becomes entitled to a private line between the reserve bank's trading desk and its own. Without this direct line, which may be withdrawn if its performance is considered unsatisfactory, a dealer would be severely handicapped.

TYPES OF MARKET TRANSACTIONS

One prerequisite to successful investing in stocks is a basic understanding of the operational mechanics of the secondary securities markets. Before a security is purchased or sold, the investor must instruct his broker about the order. This means clearly specifying how the order is to be placed. Much confusion and ill will can be avoided if proper jargon, which has a widely accepted usage, is utilized.

Investors should be concerned that they get the best "execution" in market transactions. This means the best price on the buy or sell. The adroit handling of orders to buy or sell can have an appreciable effect on the rate of return that an investor realizes from the holding of a security.

There are basically two types of stock transactions—buy orders and sell orders. Sell orders can be further classified as either selling long or selling short.

Buy Orders.   Buy orders, obviously, are used when the investor anticipates a rise in prices. When he deems the time appropriate for the stock purchase, the investor enters a buy order. As will be seen shortly, there are several other determinations the investor must make besides just instructing his broker to buy XYZ common.

Sell-Long Orders.   When the investor determines that a stock he already owns (long position) is going to experience a decline in price, he may decide to dispose of it. To do this, he enters a sell-long order (generally just called a sell order). Here also, other determinations must be made to accompany the sell order.

Sell-Short Orders.   Short selling, or "going short," is a special and quite speculative variety of selling. Basically, it involves selling shares of a stock that are not owned but borrowed, in anticipation of a price decline. When and if the price declines, the executor of the short sale buys the equivalent number of shares of the same stock at the lower price and returns to the lender the stock he borrowed. On a per-share basis, the short seller profits by the difference between the sale price and the purchase price (minus taxes and commissions).

The procedure just outlined, carried out in the hope of a stock price decline, is probably the most widely used form of short selling. Furthermore, this speculative form of short selling is the stereotype of a sell-short order in the eyes of the general public. Various other uses of short selling, as well as a discussion of its technical aspects, will be presented later in this chapter.

SIZE OF ORDER

All trading in NYSE stocks occurs as either a round-lot order or an odd-lot order.

Round Lots.   When an order is considered a round lot, it is for the proper unit of trading for the particular stock, or some multiple of that unit. For most NYSE securities, the unit of trading is 100 shares.[7] Therefore, orders for 100 shares or multiples thereof, such as 300, 500, or 1,000, are considered round-lot orders.

Odd Lots.   An order for less than the unit of trading is considered an odd-lot order. Thus an order for 1, 50, or 99 shares is an odd-lot order. An order for, say, 132 shares is treated as both types of orders; the 100 shares is treated as a round lot and the 32 shares as an odd lot. Odd-lot orders carry somewhat higher costs than round lots, as we shall see in the following chapter.

PRICE LIMIT OF ORDERS

An investor can have his order executed either at the best prevailing price on the exchange or at a price he determines.

Market Orders.   Market orders are executed as fast as possible at the best prevailing price on the exchange. In the case of a buy order, the best price is the lowest obtainable price; in the case of a sell order, the highest obtainable price. When such an order is desired, the investor merely tells his broker to "buy 100 PQR at the market."

---

[7]Some relatively inactive or high-priced stocks and many preferred stocks have units of trading of 10 shares.

The obvious advantage of a market order is the speed with which it is executed. The disadvantage is that the investor does not know the exact execution price until after the fact, when his broker receives confirmation of the order execution. This disadvantage is potentially most troublesome when dealing in either very inactive or very volatile securities.

Limit Orders.   Limit orders overcome the disadvantage of the market order—namely, not knowing in advance the price at which the transaction will take place. Thus, limit orders aid in setting the boundaries of dollar risk the investor wishes to assume. When using a limit order, the investor specifies in advance the limit price at which he wants the transaction carried out. It is always understood that the price limitation includes an "or better" instruction. In the case of a limit order to buy, the investor specifies the maximum price he will pay for the stock; the order can be carried out only at the limit price or lower. In the case of a limit order to sell, the investor specifies the minimum price he will accept for the stock; the order can be carried out only at the limit price or higher.

Assume that McDonald's Corp. (symbol MCD) is currently trading at $60 per share. You want to buy the stock soon, but you want to be certain to obtain shares not much higher than the current price. You might place a limit order to buy at 60 1/2. This order will be executed only at 60 1/2 or less. In this fashion you have stated the maximum price ($60.50) you are willing to pay and thus have limited your dollar risk. Conversely, if you wanted to sell MCD or go short, you might desire to specify the minimum sale price you will accept. Therefore, your order might be "Sell MCD 59 limit." This order will be carried out only if $59 or more per share can be obtained. Thus, you would not sell at 58 3/4, but you would at 59 1/4.

Generally, limit orders are placed "away from the market." This means the limit price is somewhat removed from the prevailing price (generally, above the prevailing price in the case of a limit order to sell, and below the prevailing price in the case of a limit order to buy). Obviously, the investor operating in this manner believes that his limit price will be reached and executed in a reasonable period of time. Therein, however, lies the chief disadvantage of a limit order—that it may never be executed at all. If the limit price is set very close to the prevailing price, there is little advantage over the market order. Furthermore, if the stock is moving sharply upward or downward, to place a limit order very close to the market and risk not getting the trade off is sheer folly. On the other hand, if the limit is considerably removed from the market, the price may never reach the limit—even because of a fractional difference. And because limit orders are filled on a first-come-first-served basis as trading permits, it is also possible that so many of them are in ahead of the investor's limit at a given price that his order will never be executed. Thus, selecting a proper limit price is a delicate maneuver.

TIME LIMIT OF ORDERS

Thus far we have classified orders by type of transaction (buy or sell), by size (round lot or odd lot), and by price (market or limit). Now we examine differences stemming from the time limit placed on the order. Orders can be for either a day, a week, a month, or until canceled.

Day Orders.   A day order is one that remains active only for the trading day during which it was entered. Unless otherwise requested by the customer, brokers enter all orders as day orders. Market orders are almost always day orders, because they do not specify a particular price. One key rationale for the day order is that market, economic, industry, and firm conditions might change markedly overnight, and thus a seemingly good investment move one day might seem considerably less desirable the following day.

Week Orders and Month Orders.   Week orders expire at the end of the calendar week during which they were entered—generally, at the close of Friday's trading session. Month orders expire at the end of the last trading session during the calendar month. As the longevity of the order increases, it approaches an open order.

Open Orders.   Open orders remain in effect until they are either executed or canceled. Thus they are often referred to as GTC orders, "good-till-canceled." Frequently, open orders are used in conjunction with limit orders. When using an open or GTC order, the investor is implying that he understands the supply and demand conditions of the stock in question, and therefore feels sufficiently confident that, given enough time, his order will be executed on his terms. Open orders are regularly (monthly or quarterly) confirmed by the broker with the investor to ensure that he is aware of their continued existence.

There are several closely similar types of risks associated with open orders. First, there is the substantial risk the situation surrounding the proposed transaction has changed markedly so that the contemplated action is no longer advisable. For example, some very bullish information may be boosting the stock's price so that a limit sell order is reached. However, circumstances may have changed, and a sell order may be inappropriate and unwanted, but the investor may not have time to cancel the open order. Conversely, some very bearish news may have depressed the stock so that an open limit order to buy is activated. However, the buy may have meanwhile become completely unwarranted. Yet because of the open order and an inability to cancel it in time, the new unwanted purchase may be made. A related risk is that the investor may just forget about the open order because considerable time has passed since it was confirmed by the broker. When this occurs, the investor may (1) not want the transaction any more, or (2) be unable to pay for the stock, in the event of an open order to buy. Finally, the open order may be at a limit price just below (in the case of a buy order) or just above (in the case of a sell order) the price the stock reaches before a major move. In this event, a desired transaction is not consummated because of a fraction of a point differential. Under such circumstances, the open order is indeed penny-wise and pound-foolish.

SPECIAL TYPES OF ORDERS

In this section, several key varieties of orders will be discussed and several situations in which these orders may be desired will be outlined. The discussion will represent a number of possible situations and is not meant to be exhaustive. The Appendix at the end of this chapter lists and describes an array of types of orders available to stock traders.

Stop Orders.   A stop order may be used to protect a profit or limit a loss. In effect, a stop order is a special type of limit order, but with very important differences in intent and applications. A stop order to sell is treated as a market order when the stop price or a price below it is "touched" (reached); a stop order to buy is treated as a market order when the stop price or a price above it is reached. Thus a stop order to sell is set at a price below the current market price, and a stop order to buy is set at a price above the current market price. A few examples will help clarify the rationale of the stop order.

Suppose that you bought 100 shares of a stock at 20 and it is currently selling at 40. Thus, on paper (excluding taxes and commissions) you have a 20-point or $2,000 profit, which you wish to protect as much as possible; however, should the stock's price continue upward, you wish to maintain your long position. One way of achieving this profit protection is to enter a sell stop order at a price below 40—say, 38. Now if the price falls to 38 or below, your stop order becomes a market order, and your position will be sold out in the area of $38 per share at the best obtainable price. Let's say that you are "stopped out" at 38. In this case you would realize an 18-point or $1,800 profit (ignoring taxes and commissions). On the other hand, should the price decline to 39, then turn around and continue upward, your long position will be maintained.[8] Thus a certain level of profit is maintained. Such profit protection can also be obtained in a short sale, as you can see by thinking through the procedure for protecting a short-sale profit.

Next let us see how a short-position loss can be minimized through the judicious use of a stop order. Suppose that you shorted 100 shares of a stock at 50. However, you are a bit leery about your position; you wish to minimize a possible loss resulting from an upward movement in price, but at the same time, if the stock's price moves downward, you wish to maintain your short position. This can be achieved by entering a buy stop order at a price above the current 50 (where you went short)—say, at 52. Now if the price rises to 52 or above, your stop becomes a market order, and your short will be covered at the best obtainable price, say, 52. Then your loss will be two points, or $200, rather than considerably more. On the other hand, if the price goes to 51 and then goes down, or just declines from 50, your short position will remain intact.

There are several possible dangers in the use of stops. First, if the stop is placed too close to the market, the investor might have his position closed out because of a minor price fluctuation, even though his idea will prove correct in the long run. On the other hand, if the stop is too far away from the market, the stop order serves no purpose. Second, because stop orders become market orders only after the proper price level has been reached, it is possible that the actual transaction will take place some distance away from the price the investor had in mind when he placed the order. (One reason may be a prior accumulation of orders.) In summary, then, stop orders may be useful if used wisely by a generally knowledgeable investor; however, they cannot rectify basically bad investment decisions, and, poorly placed, they can close out good investment positions.

Stop-Limit Orders.   The stop-limit order is a device to overcome the uncertainty connected with a stop order—namely, that of not knowing what the execution price will be after the order becomes a market order. The stop-limit order gives the investor the advantage of specifying the limit price: the maximum price he will pay in the case of a stop limit to buy, or the minimum price he will accept in the case of a stop limit to sell.

---

[8]In such a situation, you might raise your stop to "lock in" a larger profit.

Therefore, a stop-limit order to buy is activated as soon as the stop price or higher is reached, and then an attempt is made to buy at the limit price or lower. Conversely, a stop-limit order to sell is activated as soon as the stop price or lower is reached, and then an attempt is made to sell at the limit price or higher. For example, suppose that you are long 100 shares of a stock at 40 and wish to protect most of a profit you currently have. You could enter a stop limit to sell at 38. If and when the stock reaches 38 or below, your order is activated, and an attempt is made to sell at 38 or above. But nothing below 38 will be accepted.[9]

The obvious danger is that the order may not be executed in a down market because you have quibbled about a small amount and the end result may well be a substantially greater loss. Thus, the investor using stop-limit orders must exercise even greater caution than the investor utilizing stop orders. However, if things work out as planned, the stop-limit order to sell will be very effective. The reader should work through the mechanics of a stop-limit order to buy.

Discretionary Orders.   As the name implies, the discretionary order permits the broker leeway in the filling of a customer's order. This leeway can be complete, in which case the broker decides everything from the security to the price to the direction of the order—that is, buy or sell. In the case of a limited discretion account, the broker decides only the timing and price of the transaction. This type of order is frequently used when the investor goes on vacation and does not want to follow and worry about his investments. Obviously, an investor giving his broker any type of discretion must have great faith in the broker's ability, his judgment, and the time at his disposal.

ORDER EXECUTION

Once the investor instructs his broker about his order, a chain of events is set off. Without going into complete detail on every step, let us trace the process. In the discussion, the reader should note the key role played by the specialist in the proper functioning of the NYSE.

First, let us trace a round-lot order to buy 100 shares of McDonald's. The investor calls his broker to determine the current price of McDonald's stock. In addition, he wants to know the high and low prices for the day, and the price on the last trade. The broker would also give the bid and asked prices. The bid represents the highest offer to buy that the specialist has received, and the asked represents the lowest offer to sell.

The broker checks his stock-quote machine, and he reports back that MCD (McDonald's) is quoted at "60 to a quarter." This means that the investor would probably pay 60 if he put in a market order immediately. If this seems appropriate, the market order is placed. The written order is then wired to the New York office of the brokerage firm.[10] From there it is phoned to a clerk of the firm on the floor of the NYSE. The clerk notifies a member partner of the firm (only members—those having seats—are entitled to execute orders) via an annunciator board system—huge boards on which each member can be paged via his assigned number. The member then returns to

---

[9]The stop and limit may be placed at different prices. In our example, you could specify 38 stop, 37 limit. This means you will sell at 37 or above.

[10]This procedure would be followed regardless of where the investor was located.

his clerk (or if he is too busy, he sends an exchange employee) to pick up the orders. Next he goes to the location on the floor at which MCD is traded. (Each stock is assigned to a specialist at a particular U-shaped trading post.) There he checks with the specialist to ascertain the current bid and asked prices of MCD, and he executes the buy order at the best obtainable price. This frequently occurs through face-to-face contact with another member partner representing another investor. They "auction" with each other through offers to buy and sell and reach a mutually satisfactory transaction price. This is called a *double-auction process*. It should be observed that buyer bought from seller. One party dealt with another party. The NYSE has provided a place and apparatus that allowed agents of buyers and sellers to meet and transact business.

After the trade is consummated, the brokers note the transaction and with whom it was made, an exchange reporter notes the transaction for reporting on the ticker, and the phone clerks reverse the order-placing process so that the investor is notified how his buy of 100 shares of MCD at the market was executed. This entire process (including the appearance of the trade on the ticker) occurs within minutes of the initial phone call by the investor to his broker.

ROLE OF THE SPECIALIST

The most attractive and important feature of a stock exchange listing is marketability at fair and reasonable prices. Toward this objective, one category of members has been delegated with responsibility for ensuring that each listed stock experiences an "orderly succession of prices." These members are known as *specialists*. Each stock issue traded on an exchange is assigned a specialist to supervise and conduct an equitable market for that security. To perform this function, a specialist is obliged to act in a dual capacity—as agent and as principal.

The specialist in a particular security normally receives orders to buy or sell when a firm's commission house or two-dollar brokers are unable to execute them immediately. Usually, this means that the specialist receives orders away from the current price levels of that issue. Such orders include limit orders to buy and stop orders to sell at prices below the prevailing market level, as well as limit orders to sell and stop orders to buy at prices above the prevailing market level. The specialist then enters them in a book maintained as a constant reminder to satisfy these instructions if and when market conditions favor their execution. When able to execute an order, the specialist may charge and receive a floor brokerage fee for this service as can any two-dollar broker. The brokerage fee is negotiated between the specialist and the firm for whom that order was executed.

Many specialists in stocks that are popular with the public earn a substantial portion of their income acting in this riskless agency capacity. However, there is no assurance that:

1. The customers' instructions can ever be satisfied.
2. These orders will not be canceled just prior to execution.
3. Sufficient quantities of customers' orders will be given to the specialist for execution.

In fact, the specialist's book is often empty of customers orders on the side of the quotation or at the time when they are needed most to maintain depth and price continuity. It is especially important at this time for the specialist to act as a dealer.

The specialist is encouraged to buy and sell for a personal account and risk in order to maintain marketability and an orderly succession of prices. The specialist is expected to personally bid or offer when the public is reluctant to do so and thus provide continuous two-sided markets in all quotations.

The exchanges do not expect the specialist to act as a barrier in a rising market or as a support in a falling market. The specialist must merely try to keep these rises and declines equitable and consistent. Because of the variable facts influencing supply and demand for individual stocks, a specific formula for an orderly market cannot be defined.

To maintain the market a specialist usually purchases stock at a higher price than anyone else is willing to pay. For example, let us assume that a stock has just sold at 55. The highest price anyone is willing to pay is 54 1/4 (the best bid), and the lowest price at which anyone is willing to sell is 55 1/4 (the best offer). The specialist, acting as a dealer for his own account, may now decide to bid 54 3/4 for 100 shares, making the quotation 54 3/4-55 1/4, which narrows the spread between the bid and offer prices to 1/2 point. Now, if a prospective seller wishes to sell 100 shares at the price of the best bid, the specialist will purchase his stock at 54 3/4. By doing this, the specialist not only provides the seller with a better price, but also maintains better price continuity, since the variation from the last sale is 1/4 of a point.

Here, on the other hand, is an example of how the specialist may sell stock for his own account to maintain a market. Let us assume that with the last sale in a stock at 62 1/4 the best bid is 62 and the best offer 63, the specialist offers 500 shares at 62 1/2 for his own account, changing the quotation to 62-62 1/2. A buyer enters the market and buys the stock from the specialist. Thus, the buyer purchased the stock 1/2-point cheaper than would have been the case without the specialist's offer, and again, better price continuity and depth have been maintained.

In his efforts to maintain an orderly market, sometimes a specialist makes both the best bid and best offer in a stock for his own account. Many times, when the specialist does not have sufficient stock in his inventory, he will sell "short" to maintain a market. In doing this, he must observe all the rules and regulations governing short selling.

Obviously, a single, specific formula cannot be applied to markets in individual stocks to determine whether they are fair and orderly. What is considered fair and orderly in one stock may be regarded as completely inadequate in another. It depends on such things as market conditions, price level of the stock, normal volume of transactions, number of outstanding shares, and how widely the stock is distributed. This can prove to be an expensive public service. If only sell orders prevail, and the specialist continually bids for stock, albeit at consecutively lower prices, there is no way for him to deal profitably. However, professional traders, including specialists, realize that prices do not fall continuously, even in bear markets, nor, on the other hand, do they rise continuously in bull markets. Prices of securities do, in fact, fluctuate as speculators, traders, and investors attempt to gain advantage of what they consider to be attractive values. This fluctuation enables specialists to trade out of their positions as they satisfy both supply and demand in a market-making capacity. They do not always have an opportunity to trade profitably. They often incur losses to keep their stock positions at manageable levels and still provide equitable prices for the public.

As a legally recognized market-maker, a specialist enjoys certain financing and tax advantages not available to most investors. The specialist is privileged to maintain both a specialty (trading) account and an investment account for each assigned stock. By keeping these positions physically separate and distinct, the specialist can:

1. Take advantage of favorable long-term capital gains rates for profits established in an investment account.
2. Arrange financing for securities in the speciality account exempted from the restrictive provisions of the Federal Reserve Board's Regulation U. Generally, this means that the specialist can obtain credit in amounts up to 90 percent of the market value of the security pledged.

A specialist may also repurchase stocks sold at a loss within the past 30 days and still be able to use that loss to offset profits in calculating taxable income. That privilege, known as a *wash sale,* is denied to most investors under the Internal Revenue Code.

On the other hand, the government does not grant specialists any privileges to provide a tactical advantage over competing brokers in the trading crowd. Specialists must observe the unique rules about executing short sales for themselves or for customers in the same manner as do all other members. This means that when selling short, they too must sell shares short at least 1/8 point above the previous different-priced transaction. Just like everyone else, a specialist cannot depress the price of a stock when selling it short.

The New York Stock Exchange realizes that the specialist's vantage point in the marketplace provides information that could prove to be personally profitable if the specialist were permitted to use it. Because the contents of his book are generally unavailable to anyone else except NYSE officials, the specialist alone knows how many orders and shares are entered at prices just away from the prevailing quotation—orders that may serve as support or resistance levels. The specialist alone knows of the presence of stop orders and their memorandum price levels—orders that may accentuate price volatility if activated. Consequently, although the NYSE urges specialists to maintain personal trading relative to total volume in each assigned security, it must be done under restrictive regulations to avoid prejudicing the public interest.

Because of their key function in maintaining fair and orderly markets, specialists are required to submit to the Exchange—about eight times a year—details of their dealings for unannounced one-week periods selected at random by the Exchange. These figures and studies of price continuity, spreads in quotations and depth are examined carefully by the Exchange to determine the specialist's effectiveness in maintaining fair and orderly markets.

In addition, the Exchange maintains an on-line price surveillance program based on trading data obtained from the Exchange's computers which run the stock ticker. This program monitors all trades reported on the ticker throughout the market session. When the price movement of a stock exceeds pre-set standards, the computer prints the symbol, time, and price of the transaction on a teletypewriter machine in the Exchange's surveillance section. The surveillance section retrieves from the computer's memory bank the chronological sequence of sales, which is then carefully examined.

If there is no apparent cause for the fluctuation, the surveillance section alerts a trading floor official in the area where the stock is traded. The official will then speak to the specialist to determine if a problem exists.

SHORT SELLING

Technical Aspects of a Sell-Short Order. Most neophytes involved in the stock market tend to think that the only way to make money is to buy a stock that is subsequently expected to rise in price. In other words, if stocks in general are expected to decline in price the best way to behave is to stay out of the market. However, astute speculators use the technique of *short selling* to capitalize on *downward* movement in stock prices. The Federal Reserve Board requires short-selling customers to deposit 50 percent of the net proceeds of such sales with the brokerage firm effecting those transactions. It is from this deposit that all marks to the market, cash dividends, interest obligations, and so on are deducted.

This relationship for a short sale in which the net proceeds amount to $10,000 is shown in Figure 2-2.

FIGURE 2-2
SHORT SALE WITH NET PROCEEDS OF $10,000

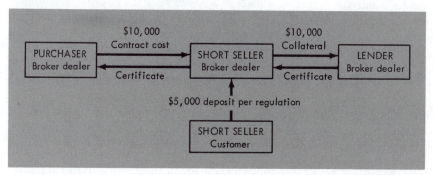

Note that short-selling broker-dealer organization has use of the $5,000 cash deposit from its customer free of charge. It may use this deposit to finance other customers' debit balances in their margin accounts or segregate it in a special bank reserve account. In effect, whenever any customer sells short, the broker-dealer organization enjoys somewhat of a financial advantage as a result. Fundamentally, a short sale is the sale of a security that is not owned at the time of the transaction. The short sale necessitates the purchase of the security by the seller some time in the future to eliminate the deficiency.

Obviously, people sell short to make money. They hope that their purchase expense will be lower than their sale proceeds; thus, the difference becomes their profit. If expenses are greater than proceeds, the difference represents their loss. A short sale is really not an unusual investment practice in today's markets. Typically, investors buy a security first and subsequently sell it. What is so strange if they merely reverse this procedure to take advantage of market conditions?

Selling short is sometimes maligned because of its implication of illegality (selling something not owned). However, this is a basic premise of business, not confined solely to the securities industry. Any time a manufacturer is awarded a contract for merchandise that is not immediately available, to be delivered on a future date at a fixed price, that concern is selling the merchandise short. It is speculating that it will be able to produce those goods for less money than the contract price of sale.

People selling short in the securities market are, to be sure, creating an artificial supply. But at the same time, they are also satisfying an aggressive demand and thereby moderating the otherwise violent effect that demand would have upon price.

The short sellers' usefulness is best demonstrated when they are needed most. During periods of falling prices, when there is a scarcity of ordinary demand, the people who are already short represent a built-in buying interest because they must eventually cover (purchase) their short position. This demand serves to cushion the depression of a bear market just as the original sale cushioned the optimism of a bull market.

One key requirement in executing a short sale is worthy of note for those who sense that short sellers can drive down the price of the stock through successive short sales (which thereby increases the supply of stock). The Securities Exchange Act of 1934 requires that the short sale occur at a price higher than the preceding sale, or at the same price as the preceding sale if that took place at a higher price than a preceding *different* trade price. For example, if the seller wants to go short at 42 and the preceding trade was at 41 3/4, there is no problem. However, if he wants to go short at 42 and the preceding trade took place at 42, he can do so only if the last preceding *different* trade price before a 42 trade was below 42, such as 41 7/8. Thus, the 42 trade was an "uptick." If the previous different price was above 42, such as 42 1/8, no short sale can take place, because the 42 trade was a "downtick." Thus, we say that a short can take place only on either an "uptick" or a "zero tick" (no price change) that follows an "uptick."[11] This is called a "zero plus tick" or "zero uptick." This regulation militates against successively lower prices instigated by a series of shorts.

EXAMPLE.   Assume that the following are successive prices involving a specific stock. The time sequence is numbered 1-12:

(1)	(2)	(3)	(4)	(5)	(6)	(7)	(8)	(9)	(10)	(11)	(12)
50	50 1/2	51	51	51	48	49	49 1/2	51	50	50	51 1/2

Legitimate short sales may take place at time-sequence points (2), (3), (7), (8), and (9) following the "uptick" rule, and at points (4), (5), and (12) under the "zero plus tick" rule. We cannot tell about price (1), since no prior prices are given.

Short-sale transactions are ever mindful of protecting the lender's rights and privileges. First, the lender is entitled to cash collateral, equivalent at all times to the market value of the shares loaned. For example, suppose that 100 shares of a stock were sold

---

[11]If a "zero tick" follows a series of "zero ticks," the records must be traced back to determine if a previous trade at a different price was an "uptick" or a "downtick." An "uptick" is required to execute a short sale.

short at $50. The lender is entitled to receive the $5,000 in proceeds as collateral for the loan. Moreover, as the price of the shares rises or falls subsequent to the short sale, this collateral must be adjusted. Should the shares rise from $50 to $52, say, it is necessary for the borrower to advance an additional $200 to the account of the lender. Similarly, if the stock falls from $50 to $48, the lender must remit $200 to the borrower. This process is referred to as "marking-to-the-market." The lender always has a 100 percent collateralized loan.

Should the lender decide to sell his shares, another lender must be found if the short seller intends to maintain his short position. This is frequently a simple book-keeping transfer. Thus, shares can be borrowed with no time limit. The lenders simply change.

The lender is entitled to all the privileges of ownership even though physical possession of certificates has been surrendered. The short seller is ultimately responsible also for protection of the lender's interest in the receipt of interest or dividend payments as well as voting rights. The borrower must send the lender a check in the amount of any interest or dividends paid by the issuing corporation since such payments are now being made directly to a new holder of record (the party buying the shares from the short seller).

Short selling cannot create more votes than actually exist. If the lender insists on casting a proxy, the seller's broker merely allows the use of another, more disinterested customer's right.

Short selling is risky. It should be noted that the most that can be lost (ignoring taxes and commissions) on a buy (going long) is the sum paid. The loss is limited to 100 percent of the investment. However, there is no such finite limit on the loss that can be sustained on a short sale, for theoretically, the stock's price can continue to rise indefinitely. As a practical matter, an investor can prevent this occurrence by the judicious use of stop orders, which we will discuss in a later section of this chapter. This also points out the very speculative nature of this form of short-sell order, and why it is recommended for use only by more sophisticated investors.

Other Major Uses of Sell-Short Orders. There are several uses of sell-short orders that have come to be called short sales "against the box." These are situations in which the investor going short already has a long position in the same stock. The "box" in the expression refers to the fact that the stock certificate is, so to speak, in his safe deposit box.

Shorting against the box can be used for tax purposes, for hedging or insurance purposes, and for convenience in delivery of the actual shares. In the first instance, the investor may want to avoid earning any more capital gains in a given tax year. By shorting against the box, he can guarantee a certain profit and postpone taxes for a year. For example, assume that you own 100 shares of JKL with a December market price of $30 per share. Your cost was $20 per share; thus your profit (ignoring taxes and commissions) is $1,000. However, you would rather earn the $1,000, and be taxed on it, in the following year. So you go short JKL at $30 in December. The following year, perhaps in January, you deliver the JKL shares you own long and close out the short position. Thus both positions (short and long) are closed, the $1,000 profit is retained, and the taxes are deferred to the next year.

Suppose that you have a $1,000 profit from a long position in 100 shares of MNO; however, it is December, and for tax reasons you do not wish to take your profit in this calendar year. Assume that MNO is now trading at 60. You can short 100 MNO against the box. If MNO rises to 70 next year, you will profit an additional $1,000 on the long position. Conversely, if MNO drops to 50, your $1,000 profit on the short position will be offset by a loss of the same amount in the original long position (again ignoring transaction costs). The merit of this technique is simply that your $1,000 profit has remained intact and yet has been transferred into a more favorable tax year. Bear in mind, however, that this technique does not allow you to extend a short-term gain into a long-term gain.

This technique can also be used to hedge or ensure a position about which the investor is unsure and insecure. Suppose that you own MNO but feel it may decline from its current level. On the other hand, for some reason you do not want to sell out your position. One way of handling this dilemma is to short the security against the box. If the stock's price declines, as was thought possible, the profit on the short position will exactly offset the loss on the long position (ignoring commission and taxes). Thus, you have ensured or hedged yourself against the decline. Conversely, if the stock's price rises, the gain on the long position will be offset exactly by the loss on the short (again ignoring commission and taxes). Obviously, if you knew what was going to happen and had no qualms about closing out your position, this technique would not be necessary, for in both cases profits would have been greater without the short. In the former case, an outright sale followed by a new long position at a lower price would have increased profits, and in the latter case, merely maintaining the long position would have increased profits.

Finally, shorting against the box can be used to facilitate delivery of securities.[12] For example, you are out of town on a business trip or vacation and wish to dispose of one of your holdings, but you will be unable to get the stock certificate to your broker within the allotted time. You can call your broker, sell the stock against the box at the current price, thus ensuring the desired sale price, and deliver your stock (held long in your safe deposit box) upon return from your trip.

Margin Trading

FINANCING AND SETTLEMENT

Securities purchased can be paid for in cash, or a mix of cash and some borrowed funds. Conservative investors use borrowed funds sparingly, often as a convenience. For example, an investor might wish to buy securities before his tax refund or other cash arrives to pay for them, or he may simply want to avoid taking money out of the bank for a while. Buying with borrowed funds permits him to buy at a good price at a good time. Most users of borrowed funds in the securities markets, however, are more interested in stretching their buying power and getting more bang for the buck.

The borrowing of money from a bank or a broker to execute a securities transaction is referred to as using *margin*. When an investor buys on margin, he simply borrows money from his broker to buy securities. When he sells short on margin, he borrows the

---

[12]This feature can also be used in conjunction with a highly specialized variety of arbitraging— that is, simultaneously carrying on transactions in the same security in different markets.

money to guarantee that he will be able to buy back the securities that he also borrowed and sold. The amount that an investor can borrow is determined by Regulation T of the Federal Reserve Board. Regulation T permits brokers to lend up to 50 percent of the value of stocks or convertible bonds acquired or sold short by customers, 70 percent for corporate bonds and about 90 percent for U.S. government securities. In stockmarket parlance, the cash paid by the customer is the customer's margin. Thus, if an investor buys shares worth $10,000 and puts up $7,000 in cash, his margin is $7,000, or 70 percent of the value of the shares acquired. At all times the customer's margin can be calculated as:

$$\text{Margin } (\%) = \frac{\text{Customer's equity}}{\text{Market value of securities}}$$

Again, when we indicated the permissible limits on borrowing for bonds, we could have said that the margin requirement was 30 percent for corporate bonds and 10 percent for U.S. governments.

After the initial transaction takes place, the Federal Reserve no longer concerns itself with the investor's margin. The effect of fluctuating market prices on the customer's margin is largely regulated by stock exchanges and the generally more restrictive policies of brokerage firms themselves. The New York Stock Exchange requires that the customer maintain an equity of 25 percent of the market value of all securities in the account, although most brokers actually require equity of 30 percent. *Equity* is simply the market value of the customer's portfolio less margin debt, or the market value of any securities that were sold short. The Federal Reserve requirements are referred to as the initial margin requirement and the exchange and/or brokers' guidelines are called *maintenance requirements.* Now that we know most of the nomenclature and the rules, let's see how it all works.

Assume, for example, that you buy 1,000 shares of a $20 stock (net cost $20,000) and you deposit $10,000 (50 percent of $20,000) to meet the initial requirement. At this point your margin account shows a market value of $20,000 and a loan balance (called a *debit balance*) of $10,000. The equity in the account stands at $10,000. With a $20,000 market value, the exchange requires that equity must be at least $5,000, or 25 percent of $20,000. So far, so good; the account more than conforms to the minimum maintenance rule (25 percent).

CUSTOMER'S ACCOUNT

Stock	$20,000	Debt	$10,000
		Equity	10,000

$$\text{Margin} = \frac{10,000}{20,000} = 50\%$$

Now suppose that the stock falls. Gradually, it moves down to $17. Where are we now?

Stock	$17,000	Debt	$10,000
		Equity	7,000

$$\text{Margin} = \frac{7,000}{17,000} = 41.1\%$$

Note that all the shock of the falling price must be absorbed by the customer's equity since the debt has not been repaid. Also, the lender's (broker's) stake is rising since the borrowed funds represent a larger part of the total value of the shares. The broker's risk is rising.

The maintenance margin of 30 percent will be reached under the following conditions:[13]

$$\text{Market value of securities} = \frac{\text{Loan (\$)}}{1 - \text{Maintenance margin (\%)}}$$

$$= \frac{(\$10,000)}{(1 - .30)}$$

$$= \$14,286 \text{ or } \$14.28/\text{share}$$

Another way of saying the same thing is to note that the maintenance margin is reached when the market value of the stock is equal to 1.4286 times the amount of the loan. So, at a price per share of $14.28 we have

Stock	$14,286	Debt	$10,000
		Equity	4,286

$$\text{Margin} = \frac{4,286}{14,286} = 30\%$$

If the maintenance margin falls below 30 percent, the broker will send a maintenance margin call (*margin call*) requiring that the customer supply additional funds in cash or securities in two to five days. Otherwise, the securities in his account will be sold and cash used to repay the outstanding margin loan.

Suppose that the stock hits $13. Then we have

Stock	$13,000	Debt	$10,000
		Equity	3,000

$$\text{Margin} = \frac{3,000}{13,000} = 23\%$$

To lift the margin to the 30 percent maintenance level requires equity of 30 percent of $13,000 or $3,900. This means that an additional $900 in cash and/or securities must be advanced ($3,900 − $3,000).

It is important to remember that the maintenance requirement applies to the market value of all securities in a customer's account. You could buy shares that would plummet into worthlessness without receiving a single margin call. How so? As long as cash and securities are kept in the account equal to 1.4286 times the amount of the loan, you are okay.

Margin calls represent instances in which the investor has already lost 60 percent of his equity. The reason such calls are feared is that borrowing has been done heavily on

---

[13]For short sales the maintenance margin is reached when

$$\text{Market value of securities} = \frac{\text{Initial proceeds} + \text{Initial margin (\$)}}{1 + \text{Maintenance margin (\%)}}$$

losing stocks. Frequently, the investor lacks backup resources since he may be at the limit. His equity melts away.

The other side of the coin is simple enough. Suppose that the stock rises. Let's say that it moves from $20 to $25.

Stock $25,000   Debt $10,000
                     Equity   15,000

$$\text{Margin} = \frac{15,000}{25,000} = 60\%$$

What happens? First, equity has risen from $10,000 to $15,000 or 50 percent against a mere 25 percent increase in the price of the stock. This is the magic lure of using margin in the first place. Moreover, the investor now has additional borrowing power. He can borrow another $5,000 to buy stock without depositing another dime of his own. This brings the situation to the following:

Stock $30,000   Debt $15,000
                     Equity   15,000

His equity is now at the required 50 percent under Regulation T.

There is risk attached to any kind of speculative borrowing that is designed to enhance the borrower's return significantly. To appreciate this risk-return relationship, let us assume the original parameters of our example: 1,000 shares purchased at $20 using 50 percent margin. Let us add a hypothetical cost of borrowing at 15 percent on margin loans. What are the results of using margin versus not using margin at some assumed price levels? Taxes and commissions are ignored to simplify matters.

	NO MARGIN		
	Price = $15	*Price = $23*	*Price = $25*
Proceeds	$15,000	$23,000	$25,000
Cost	−20,000	−20,000	−20,000
Net proceeds	(5,000)	3,000	5,000
Equity	20,000	20,000	20,000
Return on equity	(25%)	15%	25%

	50% MARGIN		
	Price = $15	*Price = $23*	*Price = $25*
Proceeds	$15,000	$23,000	$25,000
Cost	−20,000	−20,000	−20,000
Interest	−1,500	−1,500	−1,500
Net proceeds	(6,500)	1,500	3,500
Equity	10,000	10,000	10,000
Return on equity	(43%)	15%	35%

The message is clear. As long as the stock rises at least 15 percent (the cost of the borrowing) or above $23 the returns are enhanced by using margin. The returns at $25 are 25 percent without and 35 percent with margin. But look out! You will lose 25 percent of your money if the stock falls to $15, without the help of margin. Borrowing 50 percent of the money at 15 percent causes you to lose almost half your funds (43 percent). There can be more bang for the buck with margin . . . provided that things work out.

The extent of the magnification of profits and losses can be quantified. The magnification factor is the reciprocal of the margin, or 1/margin (%):

Margin (%)	Magnification Factor
100	1.00
80	1.25
75	1.33
60	1.67
55	1.82
50	2.00
40	2.50
33	3.00
25	4.00

Delivery

Securities transactions end with funds passing to the seller and securities to the buyer. The custom is to settle funds and securities transfers by the fifth business day (that is, Saturdays, Sundays, and holidays excluded) following the day of the trade. For example, a transaction that takes place on Wednesday would be settled by Wednesday of the following week. These settlements are called *regular-way* settlements.

Two other settlement forms are used frequently. *Cash contracts* are used when the seller requires his money quickly, or with the expiration of tax years, conversion options, and rights. Cash contracts call for same-day delivery, and the price will probably be less than the regular-way price. In the case of expiration of a tax year, an investor might wish to use this settlement option on, say, December 30 to take advantage of a tax loss before year-end. *Seller's option* gives the seller, at his option, up to sixty days to deliver.

Institutional Investors and Changing Markets

Need for Changes

The growth in size and activity of institutional investors had produced increasing pressures on the securities markets. The fixed commission structure, membership requirements, and auction process of the organized exchanges have shown great incompatibility with the nature and needs of institutional investors.

The fact remains that organized exchanges account for two-thirds of all stock-trading activity. Moreover, the NYSE accounts for two-thirds of all exchange share volume. The impact of the NYSE is even more substantial when one considers that the kinds of stocks that are of interest to institutional investors are virtually monopolized by the NYSE.

The growing size and needs of institutional investors have increasingly come up against exchange rules, regulations, and other rigidities. The result has been the effort of institutional investors to circumvent the floor of the NYSE, primarily to avoid paying the normal commissions.

For many, many years, NYSE commission rates were fixed. Volume discounts were not allowed, the commission on a 5,000-share order was fifty times that of a 100-share order. Institutions bought and sold most stocks they held in large blocks and thus paid high commissions. To overcome these constraints, certain institutional investors employed several strategies. First, because NYSE member firms were prohibited from trading or executing orders off the floor of the exchange except with special permission, institutions began to buy and sell through nonmembers who made markets in listed shares at markups below the NYSE commission schedule. The nonmember firms would accommodate institutions either as dealer-wholesalers or as agents, matching buys and sells between institutions off the floor in much the same way specialists do on the floor. These dealers traded only with big institutions, not with the public. This activity became known as the *"third" market.*

The need for a third market has essentially disappeared because of two events. First, in 1975 the SEC required that all commissions be negotiated. This brought volume discounts into full bloom. Second, in 1979 the SEC established a rule that any stock not already being traded on an exchange can be traded off board by member firms as well as on the floor.

The second strategy was for many institutions to try to obtain seats on the NYSE and other exchanges, thus eliminating commissions. Some sought and obtained seats on regional exchanges, but the NYSE forbids institutional membership. Attempts at mergers with member firms were similarly thwarted.

A third strategy developed whereby institutions bought and sold directly with each other, completely bypassing the exchange and broker-dealer services. This is known as *"fourth"-market* activity. Several privately owned fourth-market organizations have developed, each operating differently, in which block traders deal with each other through varied communications networks.

The key is to find one institution to trade with another. The Instinet System, developed by International Networks Corporation, allows subscribers to trade in any listed stock via a cathode-ray-tube display that is connected with a central computer. Subscribers submit limit buy and sell orders for any stock in the system. Orders are thus accessible to all subscribers. The system permits subscribers to communicate anonymously in haggling over price or quantity. Commissions, charged only if a transaction is consummated, average about 30 percent of typical exchange rates.[14] This is but one example of private fourth-market activity.

---

[14]R. R. West, "Institutional Trading and the Changing Stock Market," *Financial Analysts Journal,* May-June 1971, pp. 22-23.

INSTITUTIONALIZATION OF THE MARKET

Possibly the most important development in the postwar period has been the gradual domination of the stock market by institutions.

The expanding role of institutions in the securities markets has had several important consequences, including a shift in the site of much trading from the floor of the exchange to the third market and the regional exchanges, the erosion of the minimum commission rate system (discussed in Chapter 3), and the development of special trading patterns.

FRAGMENTATION OF THE MARKET

The relatively liberal rules of the regional exchanges and the latitude permitted third-market dealers have attracted institutional business. As a result, the exchange market has been fragmented. The efficiency of the auction system is impaired by the dissipation of orders to different channels.

Fragmentation not only means less business to the NYSE but also causes the floor to become a poorer market. There was and is a real possibility that this deterioration will accelerate. Worsening of the floor as a market and the improvement of other markets would give institutions more reason to execute orders elsewhere. To avert this possibility, the NYSE has sought legislative or SEC sanction to require securities that meet specified standards to trade on the floor. Such a provision is bitterly opposed by the third-market firms, since it would mean the end of their activities.

NEW TRADING PATTERNS

While the NYSE developed substantially to meet the needs of individual investors, other sectors of the market, especially the block positioners, thrived by responding to the needs of institutional trading. This type of business requires a considerable amount of capital and a willingness to risk it. That willingness, in turn, depends upon the ability of the trader to determine what other blocks of a given stock might appear on the market and who might be interested in accumulating a position.

Some specialists are capable of handling large orders as well as a block positioner can. Others are less proficient, either because their capital is inadequate or because they are reluctant to commit their capital to risky positions. Institutional traders soon learned that using these less-qualified specialists meant poor executions, and they arranged their transactions off the floor even if the block finally crossed on the floor. Sometimes, to avoid the participation of a specialist, the block was brought to a regional exchange. As a result of the inroads of block positioners, even able specialists found that they were not seeing all the orders, and they began to fear that the appearance of an unexpected block would depress the price of the stock in which they had a position. This situation added to the difficulty of making a good market.

INSTITUTIONAL MEMBERSHIP

The minimum-commission rate system contributed to the fragmentation of the markets and to the drive for a central market. It also abetted institutional interest in stock exchange membership. In part, this interest arose because of the desire of the financial institutions and brokerage firms to diversify. By acquiring a broker-dealer affiliate that did a public business, for example, an insurance company or investment adviser would not only broaden its own activity but also provide a new source of capital to the broker-dealer.

In part, also, the interest reflected a desire to reduce the costs of brokerage. Thus the institution might acquire a *shell broker*—that is, a broker who became a member of a regional exchange solely to get back some of the brokerage commissions paid by the parent to other brokers. At times, this recapture was effected through a circuitous route whereby the affiliate referred its parent's order to a dual member who executed the transaction on the NYSE, then directed a predetermined amount of commissions on unrelated transactions to the affiliate, which finally rebated part or all of the commissions to the parent.

Efforts Toward a Central Market

Because of the problems that the securities markets encountered in recent years, a general agreement arose that change was necessary. The SEC was concerned that trading barriers prevented the markets from serving the best interests of the investor; the NYSE saw fragmentation as a threat to its dominance; the regional exchanges wanted freedom to build local impact; and third-market dealers complained about rules that limited their ability to trade with NYSE members. Eventually, these conflicting views came together under the concept of a *central market.*

The term *central market system* refers to a system of communications by which the various elements of the marketplace, be they exchanges or over-the-counter markets, are tied together. It also includes a set of rules governing the relationships that will prevail among market participants.

The central market is intended to allow investors to buy or sell shares at the then best possible price wherever a stock may be traded. The heart of the system is a set of communications linkages consisting of a computer-reporting mechanism, a composite quotation arrangement for displaying the bids and offers of all qualified market makers in listed securities, and a central repository for limit orders. Progress has been slow because of disputes among the interested parties and because of uncertainty regarding the specifics of the new rules.

Tying the several stock markets together into a national market is a matter of setting up mechanisms that will allow a participant in one market to gain access to the facilities of another market. Those facilities include order price and quantity information, order routing, execution, reporting, and clearing and settlement. The separate markets limit access to one another's facilities at present, but some links are in place, and more appear to be in the offing. And the feasibility of linking the markets increases as each becomes more completely automated internally.

CONSOLIDATED INFORMATION

The best known vehicle for providing market information probably is the NYSE ticker. But today's consolidated tape is a far cry from the old ticker. The Big Board's full consolidated tape immediately prints all trades of its listed stocks on participating markets—these being the two exchanges in New York (Big Board and American) and the four regionals (Boston, Midwest, Pacific, and Philadelphia), along with the Cincinnati Stock Exchange, the National Association of Securities Dealers, and Instinet. Trades of stocks listed on other exchanges also are reported promptly and automatically, and over-the-counter transactions are reported through NASDAQ.

Information on the latest trade, however, is only one part of the picture. For trading purposes the really vital information is in the quotes. The trader has to know at what prices a quantity of stock is being bid or offered. In the past, up-to-date bid and offer information would be available only from the local exchange specialist for listed stocks, and only for one exchange. In 1978, however, with the advent of the consolidated quotation service, bid and offer prices from the various registered exchanges were brought together for display on a single screen. The specialist or broker could look at this screen to see where the best price was to be had and, if the best price was in another market, he could communicate with that market. Since 1979, NASD over-the-counter quotes have been listed in the consolidated service along with the exchanges quoted.

ORDER ROUTING AND EXECUTION

The reason for consolidating information is to make trading in other markets not only possible but as easy as possible. It is a way of reducing the information cost of getting the best trade. But some of that gain may be lost if market participants are not able to route their orders to the preferred market and get them executed efficiently.

At the New York Stock Exchange, the Designated Order Turnaround (DOT) system, inaugurated in 1976, allows a firm to transmit smaller routing orders directly to the specialist at his trading post on the floor, bypassing the floor booth. Upon execution, the specialist sends confirmation of the trade back to the member firm office over the same data link that brought it in. DOT orders now participate in about 45 percent of all Big Board trades, and that percentage is expected to rise. At the American Stock Exchange, a similar but less comprehensive system—Post Execution Reporting (PER)—handles routing of market orders and odd lots (less than 100 shares). These routing systems represent a considerable saving in floor brokerage.

The NYSE and AMEX routing systems are just that—internal routing systems. The Philadelphia Stock Exchange and the Pacific Stock Exchange both use systems that not only route but also execute orders. The Philadelphia Automated Communication and Execution (PACE) system, which handles about 20 percent of Philadelphia's total equity share volume, automatically executes orders under 400 shares at the better of the prices available in Philadelphia and on the Big Board, and it does so without levying a floor brokerage fee or a specialist fee on any order. Although some market observers fear that regional automated execution systems may introduce a certain amount of fragmentation and keep some bids and offers from meeting, the users apparently find them to be highly cost-effective.

INTERMARKET TRADES

For years the industry heard a great deal of discussion about what form the national market should take—whether it should build on then-current organizations or start over from scratch. But even while that discussion was going on, the exchanges were working at a trading system that would help to reduce regional fragmentation. Extension of this system to NASDAQ subscribers and others is highly likely.

One prototype is the Intermarket Trading System (ITS). This system provides brokers and market makers with an electronic link for transmitting buy or sell orders from one exchange to another after seeing the bids and offers in all markets. So, for example, a floor broker at the NYSE who takes an order to a trading post can look at the ITS television monitor mounted over the post and see the last trade price, the local bid and offer spread, and the best prices available in all the other markets. And if the price displayed on the Midwest or Pacific exchange, say, is better than the Big Board price, he can communicate across country and make a trade. Further, ITS trades require no extra clearing and settlement procedures. In short, ITS allows market centers to compete in certain stocks, regardless of location, by using a central computer to store bid and offer prices.

The second possible form is an electronic system similar to the Cincinnati Stock Exchange. Unlike the traditional face-to-face trading on other exchanges, in the Cincinnati Stock Exchange all buying and selling is done through the computer. Brokers simply enter their orders through terminals located in their offices, and then, trades are automatically confirmed. In place of the specialist system, the Cincinnati computer automatically logs limit orders and executes them when prices hit the predetermined level.

Critics of the ITS have noted that the system does not guarantee that orders are routed to the market with the best price. Many times NYSE brokers ignore, as they have the right to do, better quotes elsewhere. Also, time delays occur with the ITS which are due to its separation from the composite quotation system. Consequently, during times of heavy trading, brokers avoid using ITS. Supporters of the Cincinnati's electronic exchange believe that elimination of exchange floors and manual trading methods can provide substantial savings to investors. Furthermore, the Cincinnati system automatically executes limit orders which would save brokers the fees now paid to specialists. Nevertheless, only forty-six securities now trade on the Cincinnati system. With the exception of Merrill Lynch, who accounts for more than half of Cincinnati's trading, many brokers are reluctant to trade on the Cincinnati system due to its low volume. However, a proposed linkage of the Cincinnati Exchange to the ITS could dramatically improve the acceptance of the Cincinnati Exchange.

National limit order protection has encountered the least amount of progress. The SEC proposed a system that would electronically pool and display limit orders from all markets. This central file would provide nationwide limit order protection by treating all limit orders on a simple time and price priority basis, regardless of where the limit orders were placed. An example of such a system, known as a *central limit order book* (CLOB), is the Cincinnati Stock Exchange. However, a nationwide CLOB does not exist. There now is no assurance that a customer's limit order on one exchange will be executed when the specified price is reached on another exchange. The composite quotation system only provides the highest bid and the lowest ask prices from each of the exchanges. Furthermore, the existing ITS system does not store or execute limit orders.

There are several advantages to the CLOB. First, the system could easily and automatically impose execution priorities according to price and time. The computer would provide a clear record for regulating the participating dealers. Second, the CLOB encourages effective competition by allowing any qualified dealer to submit price quotes. Third, investors' transaction costs would be reduced by eliminating fees and physical inefficiencies associated with manually operating the book on exchange floors.

FUTURE DEVELOPMENTS

In the longer run, the exact shape of the future market remains far from certain. Nevertheless, the trend of recent developments has outlined the general shape of the market during the 1980s and beyond.

The growing trading volume of the 1980s will simply demand more automation. The mythical 100-million-share day will soon become a reality. As more trades are executed by computer, many of the current paperwork snarls will disappear.

As part of the trend to reduce the costs of paperwork, stock certificates will be eliminated. An electronic funds transfer system will automate the settlement mechanism. A majority of the brokerage business will be concentrated among a few large, full-service firms. Mergers of brokerage firms have signaled a more capital-intensive industry. Capital is needed for the new dealer opportunities in a national market system environment.

Eventually, there will be a twenty-four-hour global market. The large, multinational firms such as IBM, Sperry Rand, and General Motors are each listed on more than ten exchanges around the world. Ultimately, there might be a single universal financial marketplace that trades stocks, options, bonds, futures, and commodities.

The National Market System is no longer a vague, abstract concept. Key elements have already been established, providing benefits to investors. The record of progress includes lower brokerage commission rates; increasing automation of trading which provides the ability to handle more trading volume; intense cost-consciousness and cost-effectiveness among brokerage firms; and new technologies that eliminate many barriers to competition. Given the conflict of interests among different market participants, the optimal rate of change is debatable. But above all the discussion of the ultimate trading mechanism, the essential characteristic of the National Market System is a system based on equitable principles of trade that will reduce costs of transacting for investors.

Summary

In this chapter we have explored the securities markets, both their nature and mode of operation. We reviewed the distinction between primary and secondary markets and discussed in some depth the inner workings of the main secondary market, the New York Stock Exchange, as well as the OTC markets. In the process, we explored the various types of orders available to an investor and their advantages and disadvantages, as well as the mechanics of paying for and receiving stocks.

Questions and Problems

1. Why is it necessary to maintain a liquid secondary market in securities in the United States?

2. Discuss the functions of commission brokers, floor brokers, and odd-lot dealers.

3. The New York Stock Exchange is often used as an example of a competitive market because of the direct confrontation of buyers and sellers. Discuss this statement.

4. How does the OTC market differ from the organized exchanges?

5. It has been said that short selling is an uncomfortable maneuver for most investors, whereas they are quite comfortable going long. Why should this be so?

6. Under what circumstances would you be inclined to place a limit order to buy?

7. What are some possible disadvantages of limit orders?

8. Suppose you have a friend who says that when he finds a stock he would like to buy, he selects an appropriate price and places an open or GTC order. What advice, if any, would you give him?

9. Suppose that you are generally bearish on the market. In particular you feel that the craze over home insulation (due to the energy crisis) has caused the price of Sterling Fiberglas to move ahead too far to $60.

    a. If you shorted 100 shares of Sterling, what sort of order(s) might it be appropriate to use? Why?

    b. Suppose that you shorted 100 shares of Sterling in March at $60 using the margin limit (cost of borrowing, 10 percent):

        (1) Would your order be executed if the immediate last price of the stock was $60? Why?

        (2) At what price on the stock would a 25 percent maintenance margin be reached if the initial margin was 50 percent?

        (3) If you "covered" four months later at $51, how much better (worse) would you do being on 50 percent margin as opposed to 100 percent margin?

    c. Suppose that you owned 100 shares of the stock "long" at a cost of $55. What are two reasons why you might go "short" at $60?

10. The following represents a consecutive series of prices (hypothetical) during part of a trading day in ABC shares:

A	B	C	D	E	F	G	H	I	J	K	L
250	250.5	251	251	250	248	249	249.5	252	250	250	251

    a. Indicate by letter reference those prices at which short sales would be permitted (ignore "A").

    b. Why would someone "long" 100 shares of ABC consider shorting 100 shares at, say, $251?

11. What are three possible uses of "shorting against the box"?

12. Answer each question below, given the following information: You have $100,000 to invest in a single stock. The initial margin limit is 40 percent. The maintenance margin is set at 25 percent. Funds can be borrowed from your broker at 10 percent per annum (ignore commissions and taxes).

    a. How may dollars in securities could you buy if margined to the limit?

    b. Suppose that you bought $20,000 of Disney stock, borrowing $10,000 from your broker. You sell Disney at the end of six months for $22,000. What is the annual rate of return on your equity?

13. How is a stop order different from a limit order?

14. How can an investor use a stop order to protect a short-sale profit?

15. Since each stock is assigned to only one specialist on the NYSE, the specialist has a monopoly; therefore, the specialist function as it currently exists cannot be efficient. Do you agree?

16. How does the operation of the OTC differ from the operation of the NYSE with respect to order execution?

17. Is trading on margin a good idea? Explain.

18. If margin requirements are 40 percent and an investor has $6,000 on deposit with his broker, how much stock can he purchase?

19. Suppose that you used $10,000 to purchase $15,000 in stocks (non-dividend payers). The $5,000 needed is borrowed from a broker at 10 percent. Six months later you sell out at $20,000 (debt has not been reduced). Demonstrate the effect of margining on your rate of return.

APPENDIX

Types of Orders

MARKET ORDER. An order to buy or sell at the most advantageous price obtainable after the order is represented in the trading crowd.

LIMIT, LIMITED, OR LIMITED PRICE ORDER. An order to buy or sell a stated amount of a security at a specified price, or at a better price, if obtainable after the order is represented in the trading crowd.

ALL OR NONE ORDER. A market or limited price order that is to be executed in its entirety or not at all.

ALTERNATIVE OR EITHER/OR ORDER. An order to do either of two alternatives—e.g., sell (buy) at a limit price or sell (buy) on stop.

AT THE CLOSE ORDER. A market order to be executed at or as near the close as practicable.

AT THE OPENING ORDER. A market or limited price order to be executed at the opening of the stock or not at all.

BUY "MINUS" ORDER. A market or limited price order to buy a stated amount of a stock provided that the price is not higher than the last sale if the last sale was a "minus" or "zero minus" tick, and is not higher than the last sale minus the minimum fractional change in the stock if the last sale was a "plus" or "zero plus" tick.

DAY ORDER. An order to buy or sell which, if not executed, expires at the end of the trading day on which it was entered.

DO NOT REDUCE (DNR) ORDER. A limited order to buy or a stop limit order to sell a round lot or odd lot or a stop order to sell an odd lot that may not be reduced by the amount of an ordinary cash dividend on the ex-dividend date.

FILL OR KILL ORDER. A market or limited price order to be executed in its entirety as soon as it is represented in the crowd and if not so executed is to be treated as canceled.

GOOD TILL CANCELED (GTC) OR OPEN ORDER. An order to buy or sell that remains in effect until executed or canceled.

IMMEDIATE OR CANCEL ORDER. A market or limited price order to be executed in whole or in part as soon as such order is represented in the trading crowd; the portion not executed is to be treated as canceled.

NOT HELD ORDER. A market or limited price order marked "not held," "disregard tape," "take time," or any such qualifying notation.

ORDER GOOD UNTIL A SPECIFIED TIME. A market or limited price order to be represented in the trading crowd until a specified time, after which such order or any portion not executed is to be canceled.

PERCENTAGE ORDER. A market or limited price order to buy (sell) a stated amount of a specified stock after a fixed number of shares in that stock have traded.

SCALE ORDER. An order to buy (sell) a security specifying the total amount to be bought (sold) and the amount to be bought (sold) at specified price variations.

SELL "PLUS" ORDER. A market or limited price order to sell a stated amount of a stock provided that the price is not lower than the last sale if the last sale was a "plus" or "zero plus" tick, and is not lower than the last sale plus the minimum fractional change in the stock if the last sale was a "minus" or "zero minus" tick.

STOP ORDER (ODD LOTS ONLY). An order to buy (sell) which becomes a market order when a transaction in the security occurs at or above (below) the stop price after the order is represented in the trading crowd.

STOP LIMIT ORDER. A buy (sell) order executable at the limit price or better when a transaction in the security occurs at or above (below) the stop price after the order is represented in the trading crowd.

SWITCH OR CONTINGENT ORDER. An order for the purchase (sale) on one stock and the sale (purchase) of another stock at a stipulated price difference.

TIME ORDER. An order that will become a market or limited price order at a specified time.

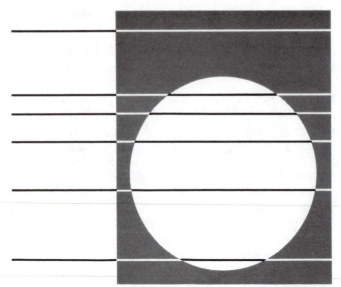

THREE

Costs of Investing in Securities

Investment and speculation are not carried on without cost. There are *direct costs*, such as commissions, interest paid on borrowed funds, and taxes, and *indirect costs*, such as federal estate and gift taxes. Finally, there are *implicit costs*, such as the investor's time in seeking out and evaluating investment opportunities (and worrying about them after purchase) and deciding what to sell, as well as the implicit cost of money tied up in an investment.[1]

These various direct transaction costs are the topic of this chapter. We shall attempt to provide general relationships between tax law, commission structure, and the investment process. Investors and speculators should appreciate the complexities of the transaction-cost environment and know when to seek expert advice—or at the very least, take transaction costs into account when contemplating an investment or speculative action.

Direct Commissions and Transfer Taxes

When an investor buys and sells securities, his transaction costs involve direct costs stemming from the transaction—brokerage commissions and transfer taxes—and costs stemming from the completion of a transaction cycle—a buy and a sell order in the same

[1]It has been vividly noted elsewhere that frequent buying and selling—high turnover—is expensive not only in dollars but also in undermining the quality of decisions. The more frequent the buy and sell decisions, the greater the strain on the quality of analysis and the judgment in making choices. Hence, transaction costs come in many forms. See C. D. Ellis, *Institutional Investing* (Homewood, Ill.: Dow Jones-Irwin, 1971), Chap. 7.

security. These latter costs will be discussed in conjunction with the personal income tax, in a later section of this chapter. First, we will consider the brokerage costs and transfer taxes associated with stock transactions.

Direct transaction costs can cut deeply into profits. In fact, if the profit (in either dollars or percentage) is relatively small, these costs can change it into a net loss. Such a situation is most likely to occur with a speculator who is constantly switching positions in order to capitalize on minor price fluctuations.

Regular Commissions

Prior to March 1972 all investors in the stock market would pay a standard commission per "round" lot, that is, lots of 100 shares. In March 1972 this commission structure was changed. The new structure required all investors to continue to pay the same commission per round lot on dollar amounts up to $300,000; but on amounts above $300,000, the commission would be reached by negotiation. This commission structure continued until May 1, 1975, when all fixed commission rates were abolished. All commissions became negotiated commissions on May 1, 1975.

The idea behind a competitive or negotiated rate structure was to increase competition among the brokerage houses. However, an SEC study has shown that the actual brokerage rates for small investors actually rose by 2 percent from April 1975 to March 1976. During the same period the commission rates for the large institutions operating in the market decreased by 23 percent. In fact, some big institutions have been able to negotiate discounts of as much as 85 percent. It has been reported that the typical small investor pays a regular commission of about 51 cents per share while large institutions pay a commission of between 10 and 12 cents per share.[2]

Discount Brokers

With the new era of fully negotiated commissions, the discount broker assumed a role in the stock market. Discount brokers do not charge the same commissions as the larger retail brokerage firms such as Merrill Lynch, Pierce, Fenner & Smith or Bache Halsey Stuart. These discount commission brokers provide fewer services than do the better-known, larger firms. For example, the discount brokers frequently provide no research support or little if any investment advice. The customer merely phones the discount broker and places an order. In other words, the discount broker is best for an investor who makes his own investment decisions about *what* to buy or sell and *when* to buy or sell it. The discount brokers are not set up to give investment advice to the customer. The discounts offered can range anywhere from 10 to 50 percent off the commissions that the better-known retail brokerage firms would charge. In fact, the discount might even be greater than 50 percent for a very large order.[3] Table 3-1A shows what some major discount brokers charge for trades of 100, 500, 1,000, and 2,500 shares of stock at various prices. Table 3-1B shows what some major full-service brokers charge for similar trade. One can very readily see how large the discounts can be.

---

[2]What You Should Know about Discount Stock Brokers," *Consumer Reports*, October 1976, pp. 588-91.

[3]The discounters claim that this can be as much as 80 percent. See "Discount Brokers Do What They Advertise, Three 'Investors' Find," *The Wall Street Journal*, April 5, 1977, p. 1.

It should be pointed out that these discount houses, aside from not providing investment advice, often quote rates based upon a required minimum amount of business per year. They often charge extra for such services as delivery of stock certificates, placing limit orders, or placing an order on one of the major stock exchanges.

TABLE 3-1A
DISCOUNT SHOPPING GUIDE
WHAT TEN MAJOR DISCOUNT BROKERS CHARGE

Discount Brokers	Price per Share	Total Commission on Number of Shares Traded			
		100	500	1,000	2,500
Charles Schwab & Co.	$ 10	$30.00	$ 66.00	$ 87.00	$132.00
	30	54.00	102.00	147.00	225.00
	50	66.00	132.00	207.00	264.99
	100	87.00	207.00	225.00	452.97
Quick & Reilly	10	30.00	52.38	117.49	210.53
	30	30.00	127.73	219.95	209.45
	50	39.72	178.99	149.78	238.96
	100	44.40	222.00	224.30	470.26
Fidelity Brokerage Services	10	33.00	64.00	84.00	149.00
	30	48.00	114.00	144.00	286.50
	50	64.00	149.00	224.00	N
	100	84.00	224.00	374.00	N
Source Securities Inc.	10	30.00	75.00	115.00	175.00
	30	30.00	120.00	175.00	280.00
	50	30.00	126.00	215.00	380.00
	100	30.00	126.00	226.00	466.00
Rose & Co.	10	20.00	69.56	128.16	174.88
	30	25.00	110.00	200.00	279.20
	50	25.00	110.00	200.00	312.50
	100	25.00	110.00	200.00	312.50
Andrew Peck Associates Inc.	10	39.50	62.50	82.50	132.50
	30	39.50	62.50	82.50	132.50
	50	39.50	62.50	82.50	132.50
	100	39.50	62.50	82.50	132.50
Brown & Co.	10	29.00	45.00	65.00	117.50
	30	32.00	60.00	95.00	122.50
	50	33.00	65.00	105.00	137.50
	100	33.00	65.00	105.00	137.50
Muriel Siebert & Co.	10	25.00	53.35	96.12	170.00
	30	26.95	116.12	179.95	235.00
	50	35.75	162.69	199.70	300.00
	100	40.36	181.64	261.68	310.00
Tradex Brokerage Service	10	35.00	45.00	75.00	137.50
	30	35.00	95.00	115.00	225.00
	50	35.00	130.00	145.00	287.50
	100	45.00	162.50	220.00	475.00
William Aronson & Co.	10	40.00	42.68	64.09	N
	30	40.00	92.89	119.97	N
	50	40.00	130.15	149.97	N
	100	40.00	149.74	206.55	N

N, negotiated rate.
SOURCE: *Financial World*, February 1, 1981, p. 28.

TABLE 3-1B
FULL-SERVICE SHOPPING GUIDE
WHAT THREE FULL-SERVICE FIRMS CHARGE

Full-Service Brokers	Price per Share	Total Commission on Number of Shares Traded			
		100	500	1,000	2,500
Merrill Lynch, Pierce,	$ 10	$36.85	$137.76	$251.66	$ 512.29
Fenner & Smith	30	69.44	266.21	461.85	667.93
	50	87.00	372.45	575.34	667.93
	100	87.00	460.00	575.34	667.93
E.F. Hutton & Co.	10	34.00	135.00	240.00	497.50
	30	66.00	255.00	442.00	760.00
	50	81.00	355.00	548.00	1,017.30
	100	85.00	425.00	791.00	1,662.50
Shearson Loeb Rhoades	10	34.75	143.75	252.50	512.00
	30	69.85	269.25	469.00	809.50
	50	97.00	377.50	581.00	1,089.50
	100	97.00	485.00	861.00	1,789.50

SOURCE: *Financial World*, February 1, 1981, p. 29.

Odd-Lot Differential

Odd lots generally consist of orders for fewer than 100 shares. Such transactions are generally carried out through odd-lot brokers on the floor of the exchange. Because of the involvement of this additional middleman, the cost of executing odd-lot orders is more expensive than the cost of round-lot orders.

Odd-lot brokers charge a fee known as an odd-lot differential for their service. For New York Stock Exchange securities, this differential is 12 1/2 cents per share, or one-eighth of a "point" (dollar). This per-share charge is added to the actual purchase price of the stock in the case of a buy order, and subtracted from the actual sales price in the case of a sell order. Thus, if an odd lot is purchased at $12 per share, the investor will pay 12 1/8 in addition to the normal brokerage commissions. Conversely, if an odd lot is sold at $12 per share, the investor will receive 11 7/8 minus normal brokerage commissions and transfer taxes. Some firms, such as Merrill Lynch, executed orders "in house" at prevailing bid and asked prices without the odd-lot differential.

Transfer Taxes

The state of New York imposes a tax on the *seller* of stocks. It varies according to the price of the stock and the place of residence of the seller; however, the maximum rate is only 5 cents per share. Thus the state transfer tax generally does not play a material role in the investment decision, but it is a cost nonetheless.

The federal government has not imposed a stock transfer tax since 1965, but the SEC does assess a fee on *securities sold*, also levied only on the seller. This fee is 1 cent for each $500 or fraction thereof of transaction value. Thus, if 100 shares of a $9 stock are sold, the SEC fee would be 2 cents in total.

After the direct transaction costs have been paid, the investor must still face up to paying federal taxes on his profits, although he gets tax relief on any losses sustained. Federal taxes are the next topic to be examined.

Federal Personal Income Tax

Our major concern in discussing federal taxes will be their impact upon individuals as investors. First, let us briefly note the general procedure for tax calculations; then we shall see how the amount of tax is affected by dividends, capital gains provisions, and various tax shelters that are available under the current tax laws.[4]

Tax Return Procedure

The first step in calculating the tax liability is to derive *gross income*—wages, salaries, interest, rent, net capital gains, and so on. Interest on municipal bonds, social security benefits, and other such items are specifically excluded from gross income. The second step is to arrive at *adjusted gross income*, determined by subtracting from gross income such items as business expenses and moving expenses. Adjusted gross income is then reduced by allowable deductions—medical expenses, charitable contributions, state and local taxes, and interest paid, or else a "zero bracket amount." In addition to the above mentioned deduction, taxpayers are allowed to claim personal exemptions for dependents. For each taxpayer and those persons supported financially by the taxpayer, a personal deduction of $1,000 is allowable. Thus, for a married couple with three dependent children, the total allowable personal deduction is $5,000 ($1,000 × 5) on a joint tax return.

Let us assume that a married couple with two children are attempting to calculate their taxable income. The husband earns $30,000 in salary and the wife $11,000. There is no other income. Excess itemized deductions total $2,000. Taxable income would be calculated as follows (assuming a joint return):

Adjusted gross income	$41,000
Less:	
Excess deduction	−2,800
Personal exemptions	−4,000
Taxable income	$34,200

The income tax owed is based on taxable income.

Special Features of the Tax Laws for Investors

Investors receive favorable tax treatment in a number of their investment dealings. In this section we will explore the main areas of preferential tax treatment. If the investor is aware of these areas, he is better able to plan his investment policies and management decisions so that, if possible, his taxes may be minimized.

---

[4]The provisions outlined in this chapter are based on the U.S. tax laws as of mid-1981. Unfortunately, tax laws change frequently by congressional action or are applied and interpreted differently based on recent court decisions.

TABLE 3-2
INDIVIDUAL INCOME TAX RATE SCHEDULES

SCHEDULE X—Single Taxpayers

TAXABLE INCOME		TAX	
Not over $2,300		—0—	
Over—	But not over—		of the amount over—
$2,300	$3,400	14%	$2,300
$3,400	$4,400	$154+16%	$3,400
$4,400	$6,500	$314+18%	$4,400
$6,500	$8,500	$692+19%	$6,500
$8,500	$10,800	$1,072+21%	$8,500
$10,800	$12,900	$1,555+24%	$10,800
$12,900	$15,000	$2,059+26%	$12,900
$15,000	$18,200	$2,605+30%	$15,000
$18,200	$23,500	$3,565+34%	$18,200
$23,500	$28,800	$5,367+39%	$23,500
$28,800	$34,100	$7,434+44%	$28,800
$34,100	$41,500	$9,766+49%	$34,100
$41,500	$55,300	$13,392+55%	$41,500
$55,300	$81,800	$20,982+63%	$55,300
$81,800	$108,300	$37,677+68%	$81,800
$108,300		$55,697+70%	$108,300

SCHEDULE Y—Married Taxpayers and Qualifying Widows and Widowers

Married Filing Joint Returns and Qualifying Widows and Widowers

TAXABLE INCOME		TAX	
Not over $3,400		—0—	
Over—	But not over—		of the amount over—
$3,400	$5,500	14%	$3,400
$5,500	$7,600	$294+16%	$5,500
$7,600	$11,900	$630+18%	$7,600
$11,900	$16,000	$1,404+21%	$11,900
$16,000	$20,200	$2,265+24%	$16,000
$20,200	$24,600	$3,273+28%	$20,200
$24,600	$29,900	$4,505+32%	$24,600
$29,900	$35,200	$6,201+37%	$29,900
$35,200	$45,800	$8,162+43%	$35,200
$45,800	$60,000	$12,720+49%	$45,800
$60,000	$85,600	$19,678+54%	$60,000
$85,600	$109,400	$33,502+59%	$85,600
$109,400	$162,400	$47,544+64%	$109,400
$162,400	$215,400	$81,464+68%	$162,400
$215,400		$117,504+70%	$215,400

Married Filing Separate Returns

TAXABLE INCOME		TAX	
Not over $1,700		—0—	
Over—	But not over—		of the amount over—
$1,700	$2,750	14%	$1,700
$2,750	$3,800	$147.00+16%	$2,750
$3,800	$5,950	$315.00+18%	$3,800
$5,950	$8,000	$702.00+21%	$5,950
$8,000	$10,100	$1,132.50+24%	$8,000
$10,100	$12,300	$1,636.50+28%	$10,100
$12,300	$14,950	$2,252.50+32%	$12,300
$14,950	$17,600	$3,100.50+37%	$14,950
$17,600	$22,900	$4,081.00+43%	$17,600
$22,900	$30,000	$6,360.00+49%	$22,900
$30,000	$42,800	$9,839.00+54%	$30,000
$42,800	$54,700	$16,751.00+59%	$42,800
$54,700	$81,200	$23,772.00+64%	$54,700
$81,200	$107,700	$40,732.00+68%	$81,200
$107,700		$58,752.00+70%	$107,700

SCHEDULE Z—Unmarried Heads of Household (including certain married persons who live apart (and abandoned spouses))

TAXABLE INCOME		TAX	
Not over $2,300		—0—	
Over—	But not over—		of the amount over—
$2,300	$4,400	14%	$2,300
$4,400	$6,500	$294+16%	$4,400
$6,500	$8,700	$630+18%	$6,500
$8,700	$11,800	$1,026+22%	$8,700
$11,800	$15,000	$1,708+24%	$11,800
$15,000	$18,200	$2,476+26%	$15,000
$18,200	$23,500	$3,308+31%	$18,200
$23,500	$28,800	$4,951+36%	$23,500
$28,800	$34,100	$6,859+42%	$28,800
$34,100	$44,700	$9,085+46%	$34,100
$44,700	$60,600	$13,961+54%	$44,700
$60,600	$81,800	$22,547+59%	$60,600
$81,800	$108,300	$35,055+63%	$81,800
$108,300	$161,300	$51,750+68%	$108,300
$161,300		$87,790+70%	$161,300

SOURCE: *Federal Tax Course,* Prentice-Hall Editorial Staff (Englewood Cliffs, N.J.: Prentice-Hall, 1982).

CORPORATE DIVIDENDS

An investor is permitted to exclude from gross income the first $100 in dividends he has received during the year.[5] In the case of a joint return, if both parties had dividend income, *each* can exclude up to $100, for a maximum exclusion of $200. However, if the wife earned $40 in dividends and the husband earned $160, only $140 could be excluded on a joint return (the wife's $40 plus the husband's $100); the husband is not entitled to his wife's unused $60 of dividend exclusion.

To ensure maximum exclusion, a husband and wife (1) should hold some stock jointly, or (2) should divide ownership of their stock in such a way that each earns at least $100 in dividends. Dividends earned above the $100-per-person exclusion are taxed as ordinary income. In addition special exclusion is available for certain utility stock dividends which are reinvested in the utility rather than being received in cash by the investor.

REGULATED INVESTMENT COMPANY DIVIDENDS

Dividends received from regulated investment companies, more commonly called mutual funds, also qualify for special treatment. If they pay out at least 90 percent of their investment income, these funds are not taxed on these earnings, and they can avoid corporate taxation. The advantage to the investor is that the distributions he receives are treated for his tax purposes as though *he*, not the fund, actually made the transaction. Thus, if part of the distribution of mutual-fund investment income stems from long-term capital gains earned by the fund, the investor can treat that portion of his dividend as a long-term capital gain. (We shall see shortly that this is quite a boon to the investor.) Furthermore, that portion (if any) of the distribution the investor receives that is not the result of a long-term gain still often qualifies for the $100-per-person dividend exclusion. Of course, any gain or loss realized on the price of the mutual-fund shares themselves is treated as a capital gain or loss upon sale of the shares.

INTEREST ON GOVERNMENT BONDS

Interest received on municipal bonds is free of federal income taxes and is therefore not included in gross income. Thus, many wealthy individuals invest in municipal bonds, receive regular interest payments, and pay no federal income taxes on them.[6]

Series E, F, and J bonds of the U.S. government are sold on a discounted basis. For example, a Series E bond purchased for $75 will be worth $100 at maturity. The $25 difference is interest earned. Normally, taxpayers report their income on a cash basis; that is, income is reported for tax purposes as received. But taxpayers investing in U.S. government bonds of Series E, F, and J have an option in reporting the interest earned on these bonds. They can elect to wait until maturity and then report the total increase in value—in our example, $25—in that year as interest income; or they can elect to report each year's increase in value (interest) as it is earned. Electing one method or the other depends on the expected future tax bracket.

[5]This statement applies to cash dividends. Stock dividends are generally taxable not when received but rather when they are sold (if sold at a gain). (See the capital gains section of this chapter.) In addition, some dividends received from public utilities and mutual funds are tax-free and thus need not be counted toward the dividend exclusion.
[6]Some states, however, levy taxes on interest earned on municipal bonds.

Series H bonds are current-income bonds; the interest is paid to the investor semi-annually, rather than accumulated. Income tax must be paid on this interest in the year it is received. Therefore, the Series E, F, and J bonds have a tax advantage over Series H.

INTEREST INCOME

For the tax shares 1982-84 a taxpayer must report all interest income with the exception of the all-saver tax-exempt savings certificates, which will be discussed shortly. After 1984, investors will be able to enjoy 15 percent of net interest income up to $3,000 ($6,000 for joint tax returns) tax-free. Net interest income is computed by adding up interest which is earned on savings and subtracting all interest paid on loans except for mortgages and business debts. If the interest earned should exceed the interest which has been paid, the taxpayer may exclude 15 percent of this difference. For example, if the taxpayer is married and files a joint return and has received $1,000 in interest income and has paid $500 of interest on loans, the taxpayer's exclusion would be $75, that is, 15 percent of the $500 excess of interest income over interest paid.

Beginning in October 1981, investors will have an option to purchase an all-saver tax-exempt saving certificate. This option will remain open, at this writing, until the end of December 1982. Banks, savings and loans institutions, and credit unions will offer certificates that pay 70 percent of the one-year Treasury bill yield. The interest up to $1,000 for a single return or $2,000 for couples filing joint returns will be tax-free.

CAPITAL GAINS AND LOSSES

Current capital gains provisions in U.S. tax law furnish individual taxpayers with a number of ways of being taxed at lower rates than those shown in our tax table. Generally, capital gains stem from the increased value of capital (property). To the investor, this could mean anything from a rise in the price of a stock to the sale of cattle above the purchase price. After outlining the general framework of the capital gains tax provisions, we will show specific investment situations that can qualify for this favorable treatment.

Transactions qualify for either long-term or short-term capital gains treatment. In the case of securities, the criterion is a twelve-month holding period, after which the gain is considered long term. Short-term capital gains are treated as ordinary income; 40 percent of long-term capital gains is added to other income and regular tax rates are applied to this sum. This is the normal procedure for calculating the tax impact of long-term capital gains. However, the reader should be aware that there is an alternative minimum tax computation which can be performed under certain circumstances and thereby reduce the tax impact of capital gains. However, since the provisions of this alternative minimum tax is so complex they are beyond the scope of this text and, therefore, we will not address this issue. Inasmuch as 60 percent of net capital gains which are long-term are not taxed, and since the maximum individual income tax rate is 50 percent, the effective maximum capital gains tax rate is 20 percent—namely, 50 percent times 40 percent.

When capital losses are incurred, they may be offset against capital gains of the same tax year. If there are more short-term losses than short-term gains, the excess short-term capital loss may be offset against ordinary income up to a limit of $3,000. But excess *long-term* losses can be offset against ordinary income only on a two-for-one basis. That is, it takes $2,000 of excess long-term capital loss to offset $1,000 of ordinary income. However, the total capital loss (long-term plus short-term) may not exceed

$3,000 in a given year. Any unused losses may be carried forward any number of years, and the losses retain their original character; that is, short-term capital loss carryforwards are treated as short-term capital losses in future tax years, and long-term capital loss carryforwards remain long-term capital losses in future tax years.

EXAMPLE 1. An investor who earns $10,000 sells one stock held for fifteen months for a $2,000 profit. He sells another stock held for one month for $3,000 profit. Overall, $3,800 is added to his income. This is calculated as follows:

40% of long-term gain	$ 800
100% of short-term gain	3,000
Added to income	$3,800

EXAMPLE 2. An investor who earns $20,000 sells one stock held for a year and a half for a $3,000 profit, and sells another stock held for two months for a $2,000 loss. In this case, $400 is added to his income, calculated as follows:

Long-term gain	$3,000
Minus short-term loss	2,000
Excess long-term gain	$1,000
Minus 60% of long-term gain	600
Added to income	$ 400

If the short-term loss had been $5,000, the excess short-term loss would have been $2,000. All of this amount could be used to reduce ordinary income in the current year.

EXAMPLE 3. If an investor realized a net short-term gain of $4,000 and a net long-term loss of $5,000, $500 would be deducted from ordinary income. This is calculated as follows:

Short-term gain	$4,000
Minus long-term loss	5,000
Net long-term loss	$1,000

But since only 50 percent of long-term loss is deductible from ordinary income, the deduction would be $500. Also, there is no carryforward. If the long-term loss had been $3,000 in the above example, $1,000 (net short-term gain) would be added to ordinary income.

If an investor incurred net short-term losses of $4,500 and net long-term losses of $800, he would first deduct $3,000 of net short-term loss, the maximum loss that can offset income in a given year. The remaining $1,500 of short-term loss and $800 of long-term loss would be carried forward, retaining their identity.

Figure 3-1 summarizes the process for determining the net amount of capital gains and losses for the tax year. In addition, the tax treatment of the net amount of short- and/or long-term capital gains (losses) is specified.

FIGURE 3-1
TAXATION OF CAPITAL GAINS AND LOSSES

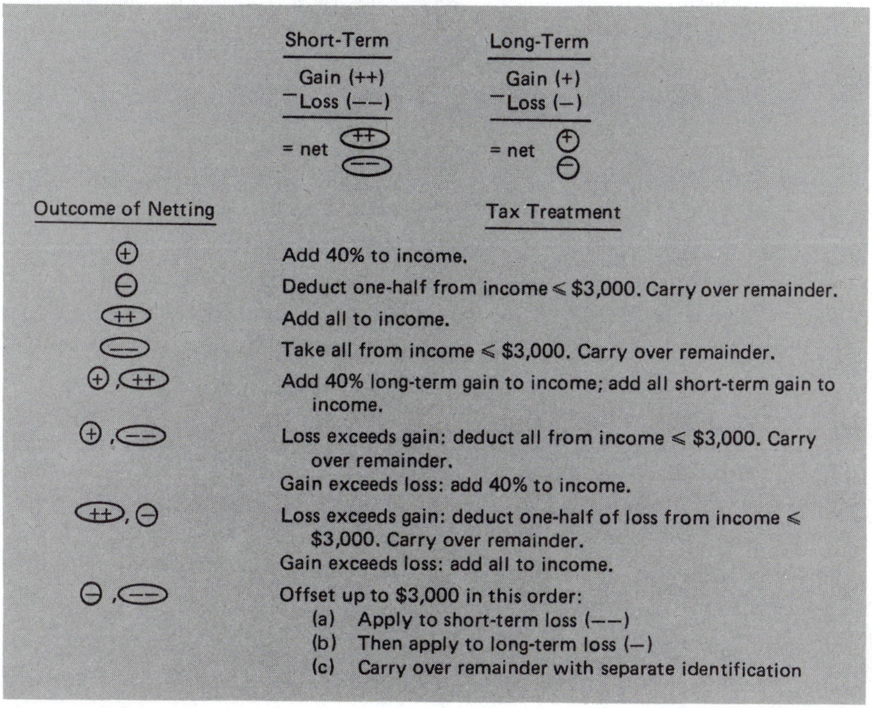

Corporate Securities. If corporate securities are held for more than twelve months, they qualify for long-term capital gain (or loss) treatment. Thus, if corporate management follows a policy of paying little or no dividends, it aids the investor in minimizing his tax burden. This is so because dividends (above the $100 exclusion) are taxed as ordinary income, whereas profits from increased share prices are taxed as capital gains. And these increased share prices usually result from increasing company earnings, which in turn follow from, among other sources, reinvestment of earnings that were not paid out as dividends. If the stock has been held for more than twelve months, this means that the investor receives a tax shelter in the form of a long-term capital gain.[7]

[7]Small Business Investment Corporation stocks (SBICs) provide an even greater boon to investors. Gains on SBIC shares are taxed as capital gains, but losses on such shares are fully deductible without limit as ordinary losses (against ordinary income).

Short Sales.   In the normal stock transaction, the investor buys a security in the hope that its price will advance. When he sells, if his hope is realized, he has a profit. If the stock has been held for more than twelve months, the profit is taxed as a long-term capital gain. If the stock has been held for less than twelve months, the profit is taxed as a short-term capital gain. However, recall that in a short sale the procedure is reversed. First the investor or speculator sells, hoping the stock's price will decline, then he buys. If he is right, the purchase will be at a lower price than the sale and he will make a profit. From a tax standpoint, he has not held the stock at all, irrespective of the minimum of twelve months. Therefore, any gains from short selling are taxed as short-term capital gains, and losses are treated as short-term capital losses.

Wash Sales.   Investing is a risky business. Occasionally, investors make mistakes. That is, stocks purchased long occasionally decline rather than advance in price. When this occurs, if the stock has not yet been sold, unrealized losses, or "paper losses" as they are often called, result. If the investor still believes in the stock's potential, he wants to maintain his position; but at the same time, he would like to get the tax benefit resulting from a capital loss. The way of solving this dilemma is to sell the stock, thereby establishing a tax loss, and at the same time buy a like amount of the same stock at the same price, thereby maintaining a position. Unfortunately, current tax law would disallow the loss on such a transaction—which is called a *wash sale*. In fact, if "substantially identical" stock is purchased within thirty days of the sale (before or after), the tax loss will not be allowed. Normally, "substantially identical" means the stock of the same company, or a security convertible into the stock. Sale of a stock in one industry and the purchase of a stock of a different firm in the same industry within thirty days does not constitute a wash sale. Thus, the sale of Ramada Inns and the purchase of Holiday Inns shares would not be a wash sale.

Put and Call Options.   Later in this text we will devote a chapter to options. Here, it is our purpose only to point out the main tax implications of put and call options.

A *call option* is an option to purchase shares at a given price from the option writer. A *put option* is an option to sell shares at a given price to the option writer. The tax problem with options can be summarized rather briefly. The buyer of an option realizes a short-term or long-term gain or loss just as with stocks if he sells the option or lets it expire. If a call is exercised, the price he paid for it is added to the exercise price to determine the cost of the stock he acquires. His holding period on the stock begins on the day he exercises, and the holding period of the call is not added to the holding period of the stock.

The writer of an option receives a premium. This premium is "held in suspense" until the option transaction is consummated. The termination of the option, by expiration, causes the premium to be subject to treatment as a short-term capital gain. Termination by repurchase results in a short-term gain or loss. Exercise of the option results in a short-term or long-term gain or loss depending upon how long the writer has held the stock. If the option position is terminated with a closing purchase, the profit or loss realized is the difference between the premium of the option sold and the price paid for the closing option. Such profit or loss is reported as a short-term capital gain or loss. This rule does not apply to options written by broker-dealers in the ordinary course of their trade or business. Gain or loss from such transactions is to be treated as ordinary gain or loss.

Retirement Planning for the Investor.   Investors, whether they are self-employed or employees, can set aside a prescribed amount of money each year for their retirements. An employed investor may make a tax-deductible contribution of $2,000 to an *individual retirement account* (IRA). Such a contribution together with whatever return is earned on that investment accumulates tax free until the investor withdraws this sum of money at retirement cr age 59 1/2. Should the investor withdraw this money earlier, there are substantial penalties.

Self-employed investors may contribute for their retirements to what is commonly referred to as a *Keogh plan.* Under a Keogh plan a self-employed individual may contribute up to 15 percent of earned income up to a maximum of $15,000 dollars. As in the IRA plan, Koegh contributions accumulate tax free until the monies are withdrawn. There are numerous investment vehicles available to the taxpayer for accumulating monies in either an IRA plan or a Keogh plan; however, the investment vehicle must be such that it is approved by the IRS.

Tax Shelters

Throughout this text we will be placing most of our emphasis on traditional types of securities: stocks, bonds, and options. However, in this chapter since we are dealing with the subject of income taxes it is necessary to pause and consider a very widely used set of investments which supposedly will reduce the income for investors. This group of securities is generically referred to as *tax shelters*. Our view is, however, that a tax shelter should be evaluated as any other investment would be evaluated. The fact that because of the way the investment is constructed this investment may also reduce the investors' taxes is merely an additional advantage when evaluating the investment worth of the tax shelter itself. For if the investors were to purchase a tax shelter which turned out to be a total loss to the investor, he unfortunately would end up with a much larger tax deduction than he had originally anticipated. Therefore, it is necessary to evaluate the tax shelter as a potentially good or potentially bad investment.

There are many areas of tax-sheltered investments. However, we will briefly consider three principal areas. They are real estate, oil and gas drilling, and equipment leasing. Other less widely used tax shelter areas include art works, cattle feeding, cattle or horse breeding, book publishing, coal mining, and vehicle leasing.

REAL ESTATE TAX SHELTERS

In real estate tax shelters as in most types of tax shelters the investor invests his money by purchasing a limited partnership interest in a partnership. In a normal real estate partnership structured as a tax shelter the investor purchases a percentage participation in a commercial building, or apartment complex, or a shopping center. In exchange for this interest he receives his pro rata share of depreciation, mortgage interest, property taxes, and other expenses incidental to the operation and management of real estate. The anticipation is that these expenses will at least initially exceed the income of the underlying property. Since the arrangement is structured as a partnership, each partner will then be able to deduct his pro rata share of the losses incurred by the partnership. The anticipation is that several years down the line either the project will be refinanced at a higher price than it was originally purchased for so that the investors will be able to recover their investment, or the property will be sold at a substantial profit. The hope is that the profit at least in part will be taxed at favorable capital gains rates rather than ordinary income tax rates.

OIL AND GAS DRILLING

Another major form of tax-sheltered or tax-favored investment is drilling for oil and or natural gas. Current tax laws permit a very generous deduction for items classified as intangible drilling costs. The Congress has seen fit to encourage the development of new oil and gas discoveries in the United States and therefore has created the deductibility of this category of expense incurred in the search for new oil and gas. Furthermore, when oil or gas is discovered, a portion of the revenues derived from such discoveries is sheltered by depletion allowances. In simple terms depletion represents for wasting natural resources the counterpart of depreciation for fixed assets. In effect the owner of the limited partnership interest is allowed to deduct a percentage of either the cost of the well or a percentage of the dollar value of oil revenue produced from the well over a period of time as prescribed in the revenue code. The result of this depletion allowance is to reduce the amount of taxable income received by the investor. Needless to say, drilling for oil and gas is a risky business. It is particularly risky if the drilling is being conducted in a new area in which little if any previous drilling or exploration has taken place. Obviously, the closer the drilling program is in proximity to previous successful drilling efforts, the less risky the potential investment is.

EQUIPMENT LEASING

In equipment leasing tax shelters the investor is buying a particular piece of equipment or vehicle such as a computer, an airplane, a railroad car, or piece of manufacturing equipment. He is purchasing either the entire unit or a pro rata share of that unit. Because he is purchasing tangible personal property, he is allowed to deduct his share of the investment tax credit, which is a direct reduction of his tax bill. This is differentiated from a deduction which is merely a reduction from income in the amount of the expense. Then this difference is used to calculate the tax. Therefore, a tax credit is much more beneficial to a taxpayer than is a tax deduction. In addition to this bonus we call the investment tax credit, the investor is allowed to deduct his portion of ownership costs, including but not limited to his share of the depreciation. The investor, through a broker of some sort, then arranges for the leasing of his asset to a bona fide lessee. This company is then obligated to pay the investor a stipulated rent over a period of time for the use of the equipment. The hope is that at some time in the future the equipment can be resold by the original purchaser and the net result will be that he will have generated substantial amounts of cash flow during the lease period plus ultimately recapturing a good portion of his investment or perhaps all of his investment after the lease expires plus a profit. The risk in this type of venture is that the equipment is not going to be leased out all the time in a profitable transaction.

CAVEATS TO A POTENTIAL TAX SHELTER INVESTOR

In the preceding sections we have outlined very briefly three popularly used tax shelter vehicles. It should be observed, however, that this has been merely an introduction to an extremely complex area. As a general rule one might say that tax shelter investments involve the use and understanding of some of the most complicated sections of the Internal Revenue Code, and thus any potential investor contemplating dabbling in this area should do so only after he has carefully had the deal examined by a knowledgeable tax expert such as an accountant or an attorney. To compound the difficulties of analysis of these types of investments the investor should realize that there are almost innumerable ways in which the entire transaction can be constructed. That is to say, the organizer or syndicator of such a tax shelter has considerable latitude as to the kinds of fees and the way the investment will be financed. This type of latitude can cause what appeared to be very similar type deals to yield ultimately very, very different economic returns to potential investors. The investor needs to examine very carefully every detail of the transaction in order to evaluate properly the economic worthiness of such an investment.

Our discussion of taxes has undoubtedly convinced the reader that this subject is no easy one to master. However, it was our intention to expose the investor to key aspects of our federal tax system affecting personal income tax, in order that he may be better able to plan with tax considerations in mind and to know when to seek competent tax advice.

Other Costs of Investing

Other costs of investing are often overlooked by investors. First, there are opportunity costs. Investors spend time analyzing possible investments and then spend time monitoring and worrying about them after they are made. These are very real opportunity costs, because the investor is sacrificing the satisfaction he could receive or money he could earn in alternative activities that he could engage in if he were not investing or worrying. Furthermore, when money is committed to an investment, the investor with limited capital (which is most of us!) forgoes alternative returns that he would earn elsewhere, such as interest earned on a savings-bank account. In addition, when securities are bought on margin, interest is paid on the borrowed funds. Even though the interest is deductible on the investor's income tax return—subject to limitations—this too should be treated as a very real cost of investing.

Summary

In this chapter we have examined the various transaction costs that must be considered in any investment decision. These include brokerage costs, transfer taxes, and personal income taxes. We observed that all these will reduce the return an investor realizes—particularly an investor with a short time horizon (less than twelve months). In the next chapter these costs will be incorporated explicitly into a generalized framework for security analysis with the emphasis on common stocks.

Questions and Problems

1. A married couple receives $170 in corporate dividends. Assuming that the husband owns stock representing $90 of the dividends, his wife owns stock representing $80 of the dividends, and the couple files a joint return, how much of the dividends can the couple exclude from their income?

2. If an investor receives $10,000 in interest on municipal bonds and files his tax return as a single person, how much of this interest will be subject to income taxes?

3. A married investor earned $60,000 and had $20,000 of long-term capital gains. Calculate his taxes (assume no deductions), using both capital gains computational methods and the tax-rate schedule.

4. If an investor has a $1,600 long-term loss, how much can he offset against his regular income? Is there a carryforward? If so, how much?

5. If an investor has a $1,600 short-term loss, how much can he offset against his regular income? Is there a carryforward? If so, how much?

6. If an investor has a $1,600 long-term gain, how much is added to his regular income? If he has a $1,600 short-term gain, how much is added to his regular income? If he has both these gains, how much is added to his regular income?

7. If an investor has a $2,000 long-term gain and a $500 short-term loss, how much is added to his regular income?

8. If an investor has a net short-term gain of $2,000 and a net long-term loss of $4,000, how much would be deducted from ordinary income? Is there a carryforward?

9. It is near the end of the 1981 tax year. Each item listed below represents the result of security transactions already completed in 1981. For each case, indicate what type(s) of "paper" gains or losses might be turned into "realized" gains or losses in order to minimize taxes. Indicate your reasons in each case. (Treat each case separately.)
- a. Realized long-term gain
- b. Realized long-term loss (no short-term gains available)
- c. Realized net short-term gain and net long-term loss
- d. Realized short-term loss

10. For each of the following, state the amount of the *tax paid* by a single person in the 30 percent tax bracket (treat each separately): (1) $1,000 capital gain from a short sale (stock bought on 4/1/80 and sold on 1/4/81); (2) $180 received in dividends: $90 from common stocks, $90 from preferred stocks; (3) $500 in interest from Toledo, Ohio, Sewer Bonds; (4) 5 percent stock dividend on Revlon shares (added shares held by investor rather than sold).

11. Ms. Quinn is figuring taxes for 1981. She discovered that she lost $4,000 on Xerox shares held for four months. In addition, she has a profit of $7,000 on IBM shares held from February until December 1981, and a loss of $10,000 on Chrysler common sold this year and purchased in 1979. These transactions have already been completed in 1981. She now has her eye on a paper profit of $6,000 on Disney which was purchased just three months ago.
- a. Is it better to take the profit on Disney now for tax purposes? Why?
- b. What would be added to (subtracted from) her taxable income for 1981 if Disney were sold now, given the other completed transactions?

12. Following are a series of hypothetical security transactions:

Code	Security	Date Bought	Date Sold	Gain (Loss)
A	Dow Chemical	9/81	10/81	$(6,000)
B	Xerox	4/80	6/81	(8,000)
C	General Motors	1/79	5/81	6,000
D	IBM	6/72	2/81	6,000
E	Xonics	3/73	4/81	2,000

For any *two* cases below, fill in the required information:

Transactions	Which?: "Net" Gain (Loss)	Short-Term? or Long-Term?	Amount Added to (+) or Deducted from (−) Taxable Income	Amount of Carryover
(1) A + B				
(2) B + C				
(3) A + E				
(4) A + B + C				

13. Assume that auto stock prices have suffered recent setbacks, and Investor C wants to take a tax loss he has on General Motors. However, he feels that this industry is due for a large rebound. What should he do?

14. How might you evaluate a "tax shelter?"

15. Jane Whitney is attempting to plan tax strategies relative to her securities holdings in December 1981. She is considering various positions in stocks in which she has "paper" (unrealized) gains and losses.

Security	Date Acquired (Sold)	Cost	Market Value 12/81
Union Carbide	2/81	$30,000	$24,000
American Airlines	11/80	25,000	17,000
General Electric	12/79	15,000	19,000
Texaco	(3/81)	20,000	16,000

All positions are long except Texaco, which is a short sale. GE and Texaco shares were purchased or sold on 50 percent initial margin at broker loan rates of 12 percent. All other shares were purchased for cash.

She has the following questions she would like you to answer (treat each question separately).

      a. Is it smart to sell both GE and Carbide in 1981 or Union Carbide and Texaco? Why?

      b. Suppose that Texaco is covered. What other stock is the best candidate for sale if only one were to be eliminated? Explain.

      c. Which stocks should be sold if her goal were to sell the largest number of stocks and end up with a "zero" impact on taxable income and no carryover? (Ignore the effects of margin interest).

      d. What is the impact in 1981 if both Union Carbide and American Airlines are sold?

APPENDIX

Year-End Tax Strategies

This Appendix provides a series of steps that might be helpful in planning year-end tax savings strategy. But you should remember that the investment incentive for holding or selling a stock is a crucial matter and that saving on taxes is an extra and not the end point of investing.

Near the end of the tax year you should consider what have been your realized gains and losses from completed transactions. Next check to see what your "paper" gains and losses are. Then you might consider the following transactions if your completed security transactions show:

LONG-TERM GAIN. You might avoid taking any losses this year and pay capital gains tax on these gains. If you want to realize losses, sell securities giving long-term losses.

SHORT-TERM GAIN. You might realize losses to offset these gains that would be taxed at ordinary income tax rates. Sell securities giving long-term losses to offset these gains.

LONG-TERM LOSS. You might consider realizing gains that would be offset by these losses. Sell securities giving short-term gain. Net long-term capital losses in excess of short-term capital gain are subject to this limitation: Only 50 percent of the net long-term loss is deductible from up to $3,000 of ordinary income. Therefore, to take full advantage of the loss, it is advisable to realize short-term gains. If you do not have short-term gains, you might consider selling a stock having a paper long-term gain with an immediate repurchase of the stock. The gain is offset by the loss; on the repurchase, you get an increased tax basis. Wash sale rules do not apply to profitable sales.

SHORT-TERM LOSS. You might consider realizing short-term gains, to offset these losses. In planning the extent of your sales, note that short-term losses up to $3,000 may be deducted in full from ordinary income.

NET SHORT-TERM GAIN AND NET LONG-TERM GAIN. You might sell securities giving short-term loss not in excess of the short-term gain.

NET LONG-TERM GAIN AND NET SHORT-TERM LOSS. You might sell securities giving short-term gain up to the amount of short-term loss.

NET SHORT-TERM GAIN AND NET LONG-TERM LOSS. If the long-term loss is equal to the short-term gain, you might consider no further transactions, as the loss eliminates the gain. If short-term gain exceeds the net long-term loss, you might sell securities to realize long-term loss to the extent of the excess. If the long-term loss exceeds the short-term gain, you might sell securities to realize short-term gain up to the extent of the excess loss.

part two
FRAMEWORK
OF RISK-RETURN

There are many motives for investing. Some people invest in order to gain a sense of power or prestige. Often the control of corporate empires is a driving motive. For most investors, however, their interest in investments is largely pecuniary—to earn a return on their money. However, selecting stocks exclusively on the basis of maximization of return is not enough.

The fact that most investors do not place available funds into the one, two, or even three stocks promising the greatest returns suggests that there must be other considerations besides return in the selection process. Investors not only like return, they dislike risk. Their holding of an assortment of securities attests to that fact.

To say that investors like return and dislike risk is, however, simplistic. To facilitate our job of analyzing securities and portfolios within a risk-return context, we must begin with a clear understanding of what risk and return are, what creates them, and how they should be measured.

Chapter 4 examines the theoretical tenets that explain what determines the value of a security, or what it is worth, and also explores the manner in which return is measured.

Chapter 5 looks into what creates risk, and it provides a quantitative measure of risk. We examine those forces that are largely uncontrollable, external, and broad in their effect upon securities—risks referred to as systematic in nature—and the controllable, internal factors somewhat peculiar to certain industries and/or firms—referred to as elements of unsystematic risk. Our search for a suitable quantification of risk will encompass the notion of risk premiums and the notion that risk refers to the variation in rates of return. The chapter concludes with a historical look at return-and-risk measures for broad groups of stocks and bonds.

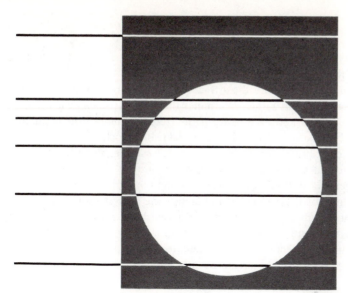

Security Returns and Valuation

The ultimate decisions to be made in investments are (1) what securities should be held, and (2) how many dollars should be allocated to each. These basic decisions are normally made in two steps. First, estimates are prepared of the return and risk associated with available securities over a forward holding period. This step is known as *security analysis*. Second, return-risk estimates must be compared in order to decide how to allocate available funds among these securities on a continuing basis. This step is composed of *portfolio analysis, selection,* and *management*. In effect, security analysis provides the necessary inputs for analyzing and selecting portfolios. Parts Two through Four of this text cover security analysis, and Part Seven examines portfolios.

Security analysis is built around the idea that *investors are concerned with two principal properties inherent in securities: the return that can be expected from holding a security, and the risk that the return that is achieved will be less than the return that was expected*. The primary purpose of this chapter is to explore the notion of security values and to focus upon return and how it is measured. Chapter 5 will examine risk in holding securities—what risk is and how it is measured.

Approaches to Valuation

There are essentially three main schools of thought on the matter of security price evaluation. Advocates are normally classified as (1) fundamentalists, (2) technicians, and (3) efficient markets advocates—although few people would fit neatly into any one of the three categories. Let us try to compare these different perspectives in summary form before going into detail on them in the subsequent text.

The *fundamentalist* does not measure the attractiveness of a stock by the changeable standards of the marketplace, but rather determines the price at which he is willing to invest and then turns to the market place to see if the stock is selling at the required price. The fundamental analyst focuses on the "intrinsic" value of a stock.

This intrinsic value (equilibrium price) depends on the earnings potential of the security. The earnings potential of the security depends in turn on such fundamental factors as quality of management, outlook for the industry and the economy, and so on.

Through a careful study of these fundamental factors the analyst should, in principle, be able to determine whether the actual price of a security is above or below its intrinsic value. If actual prices tend to move toward intrinsic values, the attempting to determine the intrinsic value of a security is equivalent to making a prediction of its future price; and this is the essence of the predictive procedure implicit in fundamental analysis.

Fundamentalists argue that, at any time, the price of a security is equal to the discounted value of the stream of income from the security; that in the main, the price is a function of a set of anticipated returns and anticipated capitalization rates corresponding to future time periods. Prices change as anticipations change, and a major source of altered anticipation is new information. Where we have something less than complete dissemination of information, the actual price of a security is generally away from its theoretical value. Fundamentalists would buy the stock if its market price is below its theoretical value, or sell the stock if the price exceeds underlying value. For so-called fundamentalists, such matters as earnings, dividends, asset values, and management are the basic ingredients in determining underlying security values.

Technical analysis endeavors to predict future price levels of stocks by examining one or many series of past data from the market itself. The basic assumption of all the chartist or technical theories is that history tends to repeat itself; that is, *past patterns of price behavior in individual securities will tend to recur in the future.* Thus, the way to predict stock prices (and, of course, increase one's potential gains) is to develop a familiarity with past patterns of price behavior in order to recognize situations of likely recurrence.

Technical analysis stands on the assumption that the value of a stock is primarily dependent upon supply and demand, having very little to do with intrinsic value. Underlying supply and demand are influenced by rational and irrational forces. Information, moods, opinions, and guesses (good and bad) as to the future all intermix. The result is price movement that follows trends for appreciable lengths of time. Changes in trend represent shifts in the supply-demand balance. However caused, these shifts are detectable sooner or later in the action of the market itself.

Technicians assess supply-demand strength through a variety of tools, generally in the form of charts wherein price and volume relationships are compared. Consensus and reinforcement from varied indicators serve as the basis for price predictions.

Efficient market advocates are at least directly at odds with the technician.[1] They

---

[1] Certain strong forms of the random-walk theory challenge fundamental analysis also. These issues will be discussed in Chapter 17.

argue that one cannot forecast future stock prices on the basis of past history alone. To random-walk theorists, technical analysis borders on the occult, and technicians enjoy the same stature as palmists or tea-leaf readers. Efficient market advocates contend that securities markets are perfect, or at least, not too imperfect. In such a market, security prices should reflect all the information available to market participants and all price changes should be independent of any past history about a company that is generally available to the public. The major complaint is aimed at the technician who tries to predict future price movements solely from the historical record.

In sum taken in their strongest forms, fundamentalists say that a security is worth the present value (discounted) of a stream of future income to be received from the security; technicians contend that price-trend data should be studied for their own sake, independent and regardless of the underlying data; random-walk theorists say that a share of stock is generally worth whatever it is selling for.

Chapters 6 through 13 deal with the approach normally associated with modern fundamental security analysis. Chapters 16 and 17 will compare and contrast the ideas of technical analysis and random walk.

Fundamental Approach to Valuation

Investments provide satisfaction to the holder in both financial and nonfinancial ways. A person may own a house and some paintings because they give him or her pleasure. Someone may own stock for prestige and/or control. The importance of nonmonetary motives is undeniable, but such benefits are very difficult to measure accurately. *Satisfaction* and *return* in this chapter refer to money motives.

Security returns come from two sources: (1) regular receipts in the form of dividends or interest, and (2) changes in capital invested. Individual securities differ in the total amount of return afforded, as well as in the relative amounts provided from the two sources.

Value and Time

Money has a "time value." A dollar now is worth more than a dollar a year from now, since we could put the dollar now in a bank at 5 percent interest, and have $1.05 in a year. For different securities, future benefits may be received at different times. Even when the amount of future payments is the same, differences in the speed of their receipt may create differences in value. The time value of money suggests that earlier receipts are more desirable than later receipts, even when both are equal in amount and certainty, because earlier receipts can be reinvested to generate additional returns before later receipts come in. The force operating is the principle of compound interest.

An initial investment or input of any kind can grow over time. The terminal value V_n, can be seen in general as

$$V_n = P(1 + g)^n \tag{4.1}$$

where:

$$V_n = \text{ending or terminal value}$$

$$n = \text{number of compounding periods}$$

$$g = \text{rate of compounding (\%)}$$

$$P = \text{initial value}$$

Thus, for example, a dollar placed in the bank at 5 percent interest will grow to $1.05 at the end of a year, since $V_n = \$1(1 + .05)^1 = \$1.05$. At the end of two years, we will have $1.1025,

$$V_n = \$1(1 + .05)^2 = 1.1025$$

since the $1.05 earned in the first year will earn an additional $.0525 in interest. We can deal quite easily with amounts other than $1.00. Suppose that we place $6.22 in the bank today at 5 percent interest. What will the terminal value be at the end of three years?

$$V_n = \$6.22(1 + .05)^3$$
$$= \$6.22(1.1576)$$
$$= \$7.20$$

COMPOUNDING PERIODS WITHIN ONE YEAR

In the illustration set forth thus far the example has been for returns that were received once a year or annually. If the interest rates are calculated for periods of time within one year a simple relationship can be followed, utilizing the principles already set forth. For compounding within one year, we simply divide the interest rate by the number of compoundings within a year and multiply the annual periods by the same factor. For example, in our first equation for compound interest we had the following:

$$V_n = P(1 + g)^n$$

This was for annual compounding. For semiannual compounding we would follow the rule just set forth. The equation would become

$$V_n = P\left(1 + \frac{g}{m}\right)^{nm} \tag{4.1A}$$

where m is the number of compoundings during a period.

We may apply this in a numerical illustration. Suppose that we wish to know how much $1,000 at a 6 percent interest rate would accumulate to over a five-year period. The answer is $1,338 [$1,000 $\times$ (1.06)^5]. Let us apply semiannual compounding. The equation would appear as follows:

$$V_n = \$1,000 \left(1 + \frac{.06}{2}\right)^{(5)(2)}$$

Thus, the new expression is equivalent to compounding the $1,000 at 3 percent for ten periods. The compound interest (Table 4-1) for 10 years shows that the interest factor would be 1.344. Our equation would, therefore, read

$$V_n = \$1,000(1 + .03)^{10}$$
$$= \$1,344$$

It will be noted that with semiannual compounding the future sum amounts to $1,344 as compared with the $1,338 we had before. Frequent compounding provides compound interest paid on compound interest, so the amount is higher. Thus we would expect that daily compounding, as some financial institutions advertise, or continuous compounding, as is employed under some assumptions, would give somewhat larger amounts than annual or semiannual compounding. But the basic ideas are unchanged.

Present values can be thought of as the reverse of compounding or future values. The formulation for present value can be achieved from Equation 4.1 by (1) dividing both sides of the equation by $(1+g)^n$, and (2) dropping the subscript n from V_n:

$$P = \frac{V}{(1+g)^n} \tag{4.2}$$

For example, how much should we deposit in the bank today at 5 percent interest in order to have $2 one year hence?

$$P = \frac{\$2}{(1+.05)^1}$$
$$= \$1.9048$$

Referring back to compounding, let us see whether $1.9048 will indeed grow to $2 in one year at 5 percent.

$$V_n = \$1.9048\,(1+.05)^1$$
$$= \$2.00$$

Equations 4.1 and 4.2 describe the future and present values of *single sums*. In other words, we can determine from Equation 4.1 the future value of a single lump sum invested initially and permitted to compound for a number of periods. Similarly, Equation 4.2 tells us the present value of a single sum to be received at some terminal point in the future. Tables 4-1 and 4-2 summarize future and present values of a single payment of $1 for a sample of various values of g and n.

TABLE 4-1
COMPOUND SUM OF $1

Year	1%	2%	3%	4%	5%	6%	7%	8%	9%	10%
1	1.010	1.020	1.030	1.040	1.050	1.060	1.070	1.080	1.090	1.100
2	1.020	1.040	1.061	1.082	1.102	1.124	1.145	1.166	1.188	1.210
3	1.030	1.061	1.093	1.125	1.158	1.191	1.225	1.260	1.295	1.331
4	1.041	1.082	1.126	1.170	1.216	1.262	1.311	1.360	1.412	1.464
5	1.051	1.104	1.159	1.217	1.276	1.338	1.403	1.469	1.539	1.611
6	1.062	1.126	1.194	1.265	1.340	1.419	1.501	1.587	1.677	1.772
7	1.072	1.149	1.230	1.316	1.407	1.504	1.606	1.714	1.828	1.949
8	1.083	1.172	1.267	1.369	1.477	1.594	1.718	1.851	1.993	2.144
9	1.094	1.195	1.305	1.423	1.551	1.689	1.838	1.999	2.172	2.358
10	1.105	1.219	1.344	1.480	1.629	1.791	1.967	2.159	2.367	2.594
11	1.116	1.243	1.384	1.539	1.710	1.898	2.105	2.332	2.580	2.853
12	1.127	1.268	1.426	1.601	1.796	2.012	2.252	2.518	2.813	3.138
13	1.138	1.294	1.469	1.665	1.886	2.133	2.410	2.720	3.066	3.452
14	1.149	1.319	1.513	1.732	1.980	2.261	2.579	2.937	3.342	3.797
15	1.161	1.346	1.558	1.801	2.079	2.397	2.759	3.172	3.642	4.177

TABLE 4-2
PRESENT VALUE OF $1

Year	1%	2%	3%	4%	5%	6%	7%	8%	9%	10%
1	.990	.980	.971	.962	.952	.943	.935	.926	.917	.909
2	.980	.961	.943	.925	.907	.890	.873	.857	.842	.826
3	.971	.942	.915	.889	.864	.840	.816	.794	.772	.751
4	.961	.924	.889	.855	.823	.792	.763	.735	.708	.683
5	.951	.906	.863	.822	.784	.747	.713	.681	.650	.621
6	.942	.888	.838	.790	.746	.705	.666	.630	.596	.564
7	.933	.871	.813	.760	.711	.665	.623	.583	.547	.513
8	.923	.853	.789	.731	.677	.627	.582	.540	.502	.467
9	.914	.837	.766	.703	.645	.592	.544	.500	.460	.424
10	.905	.820	.744	.676	.614	.558	.508	.463	.422	.386
11	.896	.804	.722	.650	.585	.527	.475	.429	.388	.350
12	.887	.788	.701	.625	.557	.497	.444	.397	.356	.319
13	.879	.773	.681	.601	.530	.469	.415	.368	.326	.290
14	.870	.758	.661	.577	.505	.442	.388	.340	.299	.263
15	.861	.743	.642	.555	.481	.417	.362	.315	.275	.239

There are cases in which *periodic* sums are invested or received. Such periodic sums, or series of payments, are called *annuities*. Figure 4-1 shows a graphic illustration of the future value of an annuity. Notice that we are now dealing with compound sums; early payments are compounding and then compounding again. Thus, the future or terminal value of $1 deposited each year for three years (rather than once only at the beginning) at 6 percent is $3.184. Since the third payment is made at the end of the third year, it does not earn interest. In contrast, the future (compounded) value of $1 invested one time only at 6 percent will in three years equal $1(1 + .06)^3$, or $1.191.

FIGURE 4-1
GRAPHIC REPRESENTATION OF COMPOUND SUM OF ANNUITY

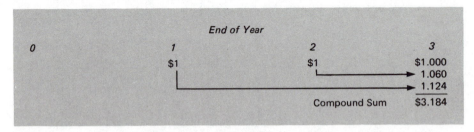

FIGURE 4-2
GRAPHIC REPRESENTATION OF PRESENT VALUE OF ANNUITY

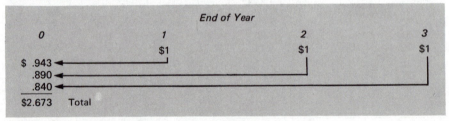

Figure 4-2 shows the present value of an annuity.[2] The present value of a series of payments of $1 received at the end of each of the next three years at a rate of 6 percent is $2.673. This contrasts with the present value of a single payment at the end of the third year at 6 percent, which is $P = \$1(1+.06)^3 = \$.840$. Tables 4-3 and 4-4 show a sample future and present values of annuities of $1 where g and n are varied.[3]

TABLE 4-3
SUM OF AN ANNUITY OF $1 FOR *N* YEARS

Year	1%	2%	3%	4%	5%	6%	7%	8%	9%	10%
1	1.000	1.000	1.000	1.000	1.000	1.000	1.000	1.000	1.000	1.000
2	2.010	2.020	2.030	2.040	2.050	2.060	2.070	2.080	2.090	2.100
3	3.030	3.060	3.091	3.122	3.152	3.184	3.215	3.246	3.278	3.310
4	4.060	4.122	4.184	4.246	4.310	4.375	4.440	4.506	4.573	4.641
5	5.101	5.204	5.309	5.416	5.526	5.637	5.751	5.867	5.985	6.105
6	6.152	6.308	6.468	6.633	6.802	6.975	7.153	7.336	7.523	7.716
7	7.214	7.434	7.662	7.898	8.142	8.394	8.654	8.923	9.200	9.487
8	8.286	8.583	8.892	9.214	9.549	9.897	10.260	10.637	11.028	11.436
9	9.369	9.755	10.159	10.583	11.027	11.491	11.978	12.488	13.021	13.579
10	10.462	10.950	11.464	12.006	12.578	13.181	13.816	14.487	15.193	15.937
11	11.567	12.169	12.808	13.486	14.207	14.972	15.784	16.645	17.560	18.531
12	12.683	13.412	14.192	15.026	15.917	16.870	17.888	18.977	20.141	21.384
13	13.809	14.680	15.618	16.627	17.713	18.882	20.141	21.495	22.953	24.523
14	14.947	15.974	17.086	18.292	19.599	21.051	22.550	24.215	26.019	27.975
15	16.097	17.293	18.599	20.024	21.579	23.276	25.129	27.152	29.361	31.772

TABLE 4-4
PRESENT VALUE OF AN ANNUITY OF $1

Year	1%	2%	3%	4%	5%	6%	7%	8%	9%	10%
1	0.990	0.980	0.971	0.962	0.952	0.943	0.935	0.926	0.917	0.909
2	1.970	1.942	1.913	1.886	1.859	1.833	1.808	1.783	1.759	1.736
3	2.941	2.884	2.829	2.775	2.723	2.673	2.624	2.577	2.531	2.487
4	3.902	3.808	3.717	3.630	3.546	3.465	3.387	3.312	3.240	3.170
5	4.853	4.713	4.580	4.452	4.329	4.212	4.100	3.993	3.890	3.791
6	5.795	5.601	5.417	5.242	5.076	4.917	4.766	4.623	4.486	4.355
7	6.728	6.472	6.230	6.002	5.786	5.582	5.389	5.206	5.033	4.868
8	7.652	7.325	7.020	6.733	6.463	6.210	5.971	5.747	5.535	5.335
9	8.566	8.162	7.786	7.435	7.108	6.802	6.515	6.247	5.995	5.759
10	9.471	8.983	8.530	8.111	7.722	7.360	7.024	6.710	6.418	6.145
11	10.368	9.787	9.253	8.760	8.306	7.887	7.499	7.139	6.805	6.495
12	11.255	10.575	9.954	9.385	8.863	8.384	7.943	7.536	7.161	6.814
13	12.134	11.348	10.635	9.986	9.394	8.853	8.358	7.904	7.487	7.103
14	13.004	12.106	11.296	10.563	9.899	9.295	8.745	8.244	7.786	7.367
15	13.865	12.849	11.938	11.118	10.380	9.712	9.108	8.559	8.060	7.606

[2]The mathematically inclined will note that the future value of an annuity (sum of an annuity) is described as

$$\frac{(1+i)^n - 1}{i} \times \text{Amount}$$

and the present value of an annuity is described as

$$\frac{1-(1+i)-n}{i} \times \text{Amount}$$

[3]More extensive present- and future-value tables appear at the end of the book.

We now have the rudiments for talking about the future or present value of a single lump-sum payment or a series of payments.

Bond Valuation

The powerful tools of compounding and discounting can assist us in building a theoretical framework of valuation for bonds and stocks. Bond values are reasonably easy to determine. As long as a bond is not expected to go into default, the expected return is made up of annual interest payments plus the principal amount to be recovered at maturity or sooner.

Let us take an example of a five-year bond with a principal value of $1,000, bearing a nominal rate of interest (coupon) of 8 percent. Our concepts of present value of a single sum and of a series of payments can assist us in determining the value of the bond. Let us assume that the investor wishes to purchase this bond for a required rate of 8 percent. What should he be willing to pay for a series of five $80 interest payments (annuity) and a single sum of $1,000 at the end of the fifth year?

The present value of the interest-payment stream of $80 per year for five years is as follows:

$$P = \frac{\$80}{1 + .08} + \frac{\$80}{(1 + .08)^2} + \frac{\$80}{(1 + .08)^3} + \frac{\$80}{(1 + .08)^4} + \frac{\$80}{(1 + .08)^5} = \$319$$

The present value of the principal at maturity (end of year 5) is $1,000/(1 + .08)^5 = $681. Thus, the total value of the bond is $319 + $681, or $1,000. In other words, a $1,000 bond is worth $1,000 today if the nominal rate and the required rate of interest are equal. The $1,000 value is a composite of $319 of interest payments and $681 of principal.

In general, the value of a bond can be determined from

$$V = \left(\sum_{n=1}^{N} \frac{I_n}{(1 + i)^n} \right) + \frac{P_N}{(1 + i)^N} \qquad (4.3)$$

where:

V = value of bond

I = annual interest ($)

i = required rate of interest (%)

P = principal value at maturity

N = number of years to maturity

It is easy to see that while bonds carry a promise to maintain a constant dollar interest payment to maturity, I, and pay a fixed principal at maturity, P, the number of years to maturity, N, and the required rate of interest, i, can vary.

Table 4-5 contains extracts from a book of bond tables. Bond-yield tables are used by analysts to determine exact yield or return, according to Equation 4.3. The tables are constructed for a given coupon rate—in this case, 6 percent—and indicate the return corresponding to particular combinations of time to maturity and coupon rate. These tables assume semi-annual compounding since bond interest is normally paid every six months. From the table, one can determine a bond's value, or the price (V) necessary to achieve a particular required return (i), or, given a price in the market, the associated return.

TABLE 4-5
TABLES OF BOND YIELDS AT 6 PERCENT

MATURITY PRICE	2¼ YEARS	2½ YEARS	2¾ YEARS	3 YEARS	3½ YEARS	4 YEARS	4½ YEARS	5 YEARS
75	20.38	19.03	17.89	16.98	15.53	14.45	13.61	12.95
76	19.69	18.41	17.32	16.45	15.07	14.05	13.25	12.62
77	19.02	17.79	16.77	15.94	14.63	13.65	12.90	12.29
78	18.35	17.19	16.22	15.44	14.19	13.26	12.55	11.97
79	17.70	16.60	15.68	14.94	13.76	12.88	12.20	11.66
80	17.06	16.02	15.15	14.45	13.34	12.51	11.86	11.35
81	16.42	15.45	14.63	13.97	12.92	12.14	11.53	11.05
82	15.80	14.88	14.11	13.49	12.51	11.77	11.20	10.75
83	15.19	14.33	13.60	13.03	12.10	11.41	10.88	10.45
84	14.58	13.78	13.11	12.57	11.70	11.06	10.56	10.16
85	13.99	13.24	12.61	12.11	11.31	10.71	10.24	9.87
86	13.40	12.71	12.13	11.66	10.92	10.36	9.93	9.59
87	12.82	12.19	11.65	11.22	10.54	10.02	9.63	9.31
88	12.25	11.67	11.18	10.79	10.16	9.69	9.33	9.04
89	11.69	11.16	10.72	10.36	9.79	9.36	9.03	8.76
90	11.14	10.66	10.26	9.94	9.42	9.03	8.74	8.50
90½	10.86	10.41	10.03	9.73	9.24	8.87	8.59	8.36
91	10.59	10.17	9.81	9.52	9.06	8.71	8.45	8.23
91½	10.32	9.92	9.58	9.31	8.88	8.55	8.30	8.10
92	10.05	9.68	9.36	9.11	8.70	8.40	8.16	7.97
92½	9.79	9.44	9.14	8.90	8.52	8.24	8.02	7.84
93	9.52	9.20	8.92	8.70	8.35	8.08	7.88	7.71
93½	9.26	8.96	8.70	8.50	8.17	7.93	7.74	7.59
94	9.00	8.72	8.49	8.30	8.00	7.77	7.60	7.46
94½	8.74	8.49	8.27	8.11	7.83	7.62	7.46	7.33
95	8.48	8.25	8.06	7.90	7.66	7.47	7.32	7.21
95¼	8.35	8.14	7.95	7.81	7.57	7.39	7.26	7.15
95½	8.22	8.02	7.85	7.71	7.49	7.32	7.19	7.08
95¾	8.10	7.91	7.74	7.61	7.40	7.24	7.12	7.02
96	7.97	7.79	7.63	7.51	7.32	7.17	7.05	6.96
96¼	7.84	7.68	7.53	7.42	7.23	7.09	6.99	6.90
96½	7.72	7.56	7.42	7.32	7.15	7.02	6.92	6.84
96¾	7.59	7.45	7.32	7.22	7.06	6.94	6.85	6.78
97	7.47	7.34	7.22	7.13	6.98	6.87	6.78	6.72
97¼	7.34	7.22	7.11	7.03	6.90	6.80	6.72	6.66
97½	7.22	7.11	7.01	6.94	6.81	6.72	6.65	6.60
97¾	7.09	7.00	6.91	6.84	6.73	6.65	6.59	6.53
98	6.97	6.88	6.80	6.75	6.65	6.58	6.52	6.47
98¼	6.85	6.77	6.70	6.65	6.57	6.50	6.45	6.41
98½	6.72	6.66	6.60	6.56	6.49	6.43	6.39	6.35
98¾	6.60	6.55	6.50	6.47	6.40	6.36	6.32	6.30
99	6.48	6.44	6.40	6.37	6.32	6.29	6.26	6.24
99¼	6.36	6.33	6.30	6.28	6.24	6.21	6.19	6.18
99½	6.24	6.22	6.20	6.19	6.16	6.14	6.13	6.12
99¾	6.12	6.11	6.10	6.10	6.08	6.07	6.06	6.06
100	5.99	6.00	6.00	6.00	6.00	6.00	6.00	6.00
100¼	5.87	5.89	5.90	5.91	5.92	5.93	5.94	5.94
100½	5.75	5.78	5.80	5.82	5.84	5.86	5.88	5.88
100¾	5.64	5.67	5.70	5.72	5.76	5.79	5.81	5.82
101	5.52	5.57	5.60	5.63	5.68	5.72	5.75	5.77
102	5.04	5.14	5.21	5.27	5.37	5.44	5.49	5.54
103	4.58	4.71	4.82	4.91	5.05	5.16	5.24	5.31
104	4.12	4.30	4.44	4.56	4.75	4.89	5.00	5.08
105	3.66	3.88	4.06	4.21	4.44	4.62	4.75	4.86
106	3.21	3.47	3.68	3.86	4.14	4.35	4.51	4.64

MATURITY PRICE	13½ YEARS	14 YEARS	14½ YEARS	15 YEARS	16 YEARS	17 YEARS	18 YEARS	19 YEARS
75	9.29	9.21	9.15	9.08	8.97	8.88	8.79	8.72
76	9.13	9.06	9.00	8.94	8.83	8.74	8.65	8.58
77	8.97	8.91	8.85	8.79	8.69	8.60	8.52	8.45
78	8.82	8.76	8.70	8.65	8.55	8.46	8.39	8.33
79	8.67	8.61	8.55	8.50	8.41	8.33	8.26	8.20
80	8.52	8.47	8.41	8.36	8.28	8.20	8.14	8.08
81	8.38	8.32	8.27	8.23	8.15	8.07	8.01	7.96
82	8.23	8.18	8.14	8.09	8.02	7.95	7.89	7.84
83	8.09	8.05	8.00	7.96	7.89	7.83	7.77	7.72
84	7.95	7.91	7.87	7.83	7.76	7.70	7.65	7.61
85	7.82	7.78	7.74	7.70	7.64	7.58	7.54	7.49
86	7.68	7.65	7.61	7.58	7.52	7.47	7.42	7.38
87	7.55	7.52	7.48	7.45	7.40	7.35	7.31	7.27
88	7.42	7.39	7.36	7.33	7.28	7.24	7.20	7.17
89	7.29	7.26	7.24	7.21	7.17	7.13	7.09	7.06
90	7.17	7.14	7.12	7.09	7.05	7.02	6.98	6.96
90½	7.11	7.08	7.06	7.04	7.00	6.96	6.93	6.91
91	7.04	7.02	7.00	6.98	6.94	6.91	6.88	6.85
91½	6.98	6.96	6.94	6.92	6.88	6.85	6.83	6.80
92	6.92	6.90	6.88	6.86	6.83	6.80	6.78	6.75
92½	6.86	6.84	6.82	6.81	6.78	6.75	6.72	6.70
93	6.80	6.78	6.77	6.75	6.72	6.70	6.67	6.65
93½	6.74	6.72	6.71	6.69	6.67	6.64	6.62	6.61
94	6.68	6.67	6.65	6.64	6.61	6.59	6.57	6.56
94½	6.62	6.61	6.59	6.58	6.56	6.54	6.52	6.51
95	6.56	6.55	6.54	6.53	6.51	6.49	6.47	6.46
95¼	6.53	6.52	6.51	6.50	6.48	6.46	6.45	6.44
95½	6.51	6.49	6.48	6.47	6.46	6.44	6.43	6.41
95¾	6.48	6.47	6.46	6.45	6.43	6.41	6.40	6.39
96	6.45	6.44	6.43	6.42	6.40	6.39	6.38	6.37
96¼	6.42	6.41	6.40	6.39	6.38	6.36	6.35	6.34
96½	6.39	6.38	6.37	6.37	6.35	6.34	6.33	6.32
96¾	6.36	6.35	6.35	6.34	6.33	6.31	6.30	6.30
97	6.33	6.33	6.32	6.31	6.30	6.29	6.28	6.27
97¼	6.31	6.30	6.29	6.29	6.27	6.27	6.26	6.25
97½	6.28	6.27	6.26	6.26	6.25	6.24	6.23	6.23
97¾	6.25	6.24	6.24	6.23	6.22	6.22	6.21	6.20
98	6.22	6.22	6.21	6.21	6.20	6.19	6.19	6.18
98¼	6.19	6.19	6.18	6.18	6.17	6.17	6.16	6.16
98½	6.17	6.16	6.16	6.15	6.15	6.14	6.14	6.13
98¾	6.14	6.13	6.13	6.13	6.12	6.12	6.12	6.11
99	6.11	6.11	6.10	6.10	6.10	6.10	6.09	6.09
99¼	6.08	6.08	6.08	6.08	6.07	6.07	6.07	6.07
99½	6.05	6.05	6.05	6.05	6.05	6.05	6.05	6.04
99¾	6.03	6.03	6.03	6.03	6.02	6.02	6.02	6.02
100	6.00	6.00	6.00	6.00	6.00	6.00	6.00	6.00
100¼	5.97	5.97	5.97	5.97	5.98	5.98	5.98	5.98
100½	5.95	5.95	5.95	5.95	5.95	5.95	5.96	5.96
100¾	5.92	5.92	5.92	5.92	5.93	5.93	5.93	5.93
101	5.89	5.89	5.90	5.90	5.90	5.91	5.91	5.91
102	5.78	5.79	5.79	5.80	5.81	5.81	5.82	5.82
103	5.68	5.69	5.69	5.70	5.71	5.72	5.73	5.74
104	5.57	5.58	5.59	5.60	5.62	5.63	5.64	5.65
105	5.47	5.48	5.50	5.51	5.53	5.54	5.56	5.57
106	5.37	5.38	5.40	5.41	5.43	5.45	5.47	5.49

SOURCE: *Bond Yield Tables*, Pub. No. 254 (Boston: Financial Publishing Co., copyright 1971), pp. 52-53.

For example, a required rate of return of 8% for a five-year, 6 percent, $1,000 bond suggests a price of 92.[4] Using the table of present values to solve for the price of 92 ($30 every six months at 4 percent semi-annually):

$$V = \frac{\$30}{1 + .04} + \frac{\$30}{(1 + .04)^2} + \frac{\$30}{(1 + .04)^3} + \frac{\$30}{(1 + .04)^4} + \frac{\$30}{(1 + .04)^5} + \cdots + \frac{\$30}{(1 + .04)^{10}} + \frac{\$1,000}{(1 + .04)^{10}}$$

$$= \$918.92$$

Since the $30 interest payments are similar to an *annuity*, and the principal value of the bond at maturity is a *single sum*, we can see that bond tables are themselves built by using Tables 4-2 and 4-4, noting that they are constructed using semiannual compounding (as stated earlier). Thus:

Present value of single sum of $1,000 principal received at the end of five years at 4% (Table 4-2) = $1,000(.6756) =	$675.60
Present value of annuity of $30 per year for five years at 4% (Table 4-4) = $30(8.1109) =	243.32
Present value of bond	$918.92

The same 8 percent required return for a 15-year maturity suggests a price of between 82 and 83. An appreciation for the availability of these tables develops quickly when one attempts the long way of calculation for a bond with a long maturity.

The general availability of calculators with power functions makes it far easier to do these calculations in minutes without tables. These instruments have become a necessary part of the tool kit of all serious students of investments.

Figure 4-3 shows the sensitivity of maturity to changes in the required rate of interest. The long-term bond is a 6 percent perpetuity,[5] the short-term bond is a five-year, 6 percent issue (see Table 4-5). Notice that the longer the maturity of a bond, the greater its price change relative to a given change in the required rate of interest. This differential response between long- and short-term bonds always holds true. Historically, short-term interest rates have fluctuated more frequently and to a greater magnitude than long-term rates; however, Figure 4-3 suggests that long-term bond prices fluctuate to a greater extent than do short-term bond prices.

---

[4]92 means 92 percent of par. For a $1,000 par bond, the price is thus $920.
[5]A perpetuity is a bond that never matures. Such a bond pays interest indefinitely.

FIGURE 4-3
VALUE OF LONG-TERM AND SHORT-TERM BOND AT VARYING INTEREST RATES

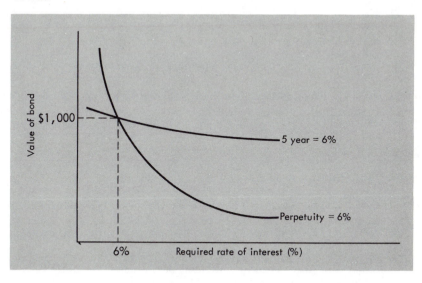

Preferred-Stock Valuation

When the term to maturity approaches infinity, as it would in the case of a perpetuity (a security that never matures), interest is paid indefinitely. Equation 4.3 becomes

$$V = \frac{I}{i} \tag{4.4}$$

Since most preferred stocks entitle their owners to regular fixed dividends similar to interest payments, they are in fact like perpetuities. Although preferreds are often retired, this is not the usual case. The value of a preferred stock can thus be thought of in terms of Equation 4.4, where $I = D$, D signifying annual dividend payments rather than interest payments. Suppose a preferred stock paying annual dividends of $6 was sold in 1955. This preferred today, given market conditions, should be yielding 10 percent. What is it worth today?

$$V = \frac{D}{i}$$
$$= \frac{\$6}{.10} = \$60$$

The absence of a maturity in preferred stock lends perpetuity aspects to this security form. The result is greater value or price fluctuation in preferreds vis-à-vis bonds as a class.

Substituting price in the market for value, it is possible to determine the yield or return. Assume that a $6 preferred stock is selling in the market for $75. The yield or return is

$$\$75 = \frac{\$6}{i}$$

$$.080 = i$$

Thus, given the annual income flow, it is possible to determine value given the required yield or return; or it is possible to determine the yield or return given the market price.

Common-Stock Valuation

The use of present-value theory by bond and preferred-stock investors is well established.[6] The valuation task is relatively straightforward, because benefits are generally constant and reasonably certain. Perpetuities, or infinite life securities with constant dividend receipts, are the normal case in dealing with straight preferred stock. Bonds represent constant income flows with a finite, measurable life.

Common-stock valuation is different, because earnings and dividend streams are uncertain as to the timing of receipt and the amount of the dividend. The value of a common stock at any moment in time can be thought of as the discounted value of a series of uncertain future dividends that may grow or decline at varying rates over time. The more theoretical present-value approach to common-stock valuation will be compared with the more traditional and pragmatic capitalization or multiplier approach in the next several sections.

Present-Value Approach

ONE-YEAR HOLDING PERIOD

It is easiest to start with common-stock valuation where the expected holding period is one year. The benefits any investor receives from holding a common stock consists of dividends plus any change in price during the holding period. Suppose that we buy one share of the Olsen Co. at the beginning of the year for $25. We hold the stock for one year. One dollar in dividends is collected, and the share is sold for $26.50. The rate of return achieved is the composite of dividend yield and change in price (capital gains yield). Thus, we get

$$\text{Dividend yield} = \frac{D}{P} = \frac{\$1}{\$25} = .04$$

$$\text{Capital gains yield} = \frac{\$26.50 - \$25.00}{\$25} = .06$$

---

[6]Present-value models of stock price determination have a long and abundant history in the literature, going back to the early thoughts of J. B. Williams, *The Theory of Investment Value* (Amsterdam: North-Holland, 1964).

The total rate of return achieved is .04 + .06 = .10, or 10 percent. How might we express this same notion in terms of present values? Thus:

$$P_0 = \frac{D_1}{1+r} + \frac{P_1}{1+r} \qquad (4.5)$$

where:

D_1 = dividend to be received at the end of year 1

r = investor's required rate of return or discount rate

P_1 = selling price at the end of year 1

P_0 = selling price today

Therefore:

$$\$25 = \frac{\$1.00}{1+r} + \frac{\$26.50}{1+r}$$

Will r = .10 balance the equation? At a required rate of return of 10 percent, the dividend is worth \$.909 today (see Table 4-2),[7] the selling price has a present value of \$24.091 (\$26.50 × .909). The combined present value is \$.909 + \$24.091 = \$25.00.

Should a rate of return of 15 percent have been required, the purchase price would have been too high at \$25. (The \$1 dividend is assumed fixed, and the selling price of \$26.50 remains constant.) To achieve a 15 percent return, the value of the stock at the *beginning* of the year would have had to be

$$P_0 = \frac{\$1.00}{1+.15} + \frac{\$26.50}{1+.15}$$
$$= \$.87 + \$23.04$$
$$= \$23.91$$

An alternative approach would be to ask the question, At what price must we be able to sell the stock at the *end* of one year (if the purchase price is \$25 and the dividend is \$1) in order to attain a rate of return of 15 percent?

$$\$25 = \frac{\$1.00}{(1+.15)} + \frac{P_1}{(1+.15)}$$

$$\$25 = \$0.87 + .87P_1$$

$$\$24.13 = .87P_1$$

$$\$27.74 = P_1 \text{ (selling price)}$$

---

[7]Dividends are generally received quarterly. Our example assumes receipt once each year, at the end of the year.

MULTIPLE-YEAR HOLDING PERIOD

Consider holding a share of the Olsen Co. for five years. In most cases the dividend will grow from year to year. To look at some results, let us stipulate the following:

g = annual expected growth in earnings, dividends and price = 6%

e_0 = most recent earnings per share = $1.89

d/e = dividend payout (%) = 50%

r = required rate of return = 10%

P = price per share

P/E = price-earnings ratio = 12.5

N = holding period in years = 5

Given these stipulations, the present value of a share of stock can be determined by solving the following equation:

$$P = \left(\sum_{n=1}^{N} \frac{[(e_0)(d/e)] \ (1 + g)^n}{(1 + r)^n} \right) + \left(\frac{(P/E)[(e_0)(1 + g)^N]}{(1 + r)^N} \right) \tag{4.6}$$

This imposing formula says, "Sum the present value of all dividends to be received over the holding period, and add this to the present value of the selling price of the stock at the end of the holding period to arrive at the present value of the stock."

Let us write out the string of appropriate numbers. Since the current earnings per share (e_0) are $1.89 and the dividend payout (d/e) is 50 percent, the most recent dividend per share is e_0 times d/e, or $1.89 times 50 percent, or $.943. This was stipulated in the beginning of the problem. After one year, the dividend is expected to be $.943 times $(1 + g)^1$, where g = .06. So the first year's dividend will be $1. The process is repeated for years 1 through 5 as follows:

Dividend Year 1	Dividend Year 2	Dividend Year 3	Dividend Year 4	Dividend Year 5
$ .943(1.06)^1	$ .943(1.06)^2	$9.43(1.06)^3	$ .943(1.06)^4	$ .943(1.06)^5
$1.00	$1.06	$1.12	$1.19	$1.26

The values of $(1.06)^t$ are found conveniently in Table 4-1. The next step is to discount each dividend at the required rate of return of 10 percent. Thus:

$$\frac{\$1.00}{(1.10)^1} + \frac{\$1.06}{(1.10)^2} + \frac{\$1.12}{(1.10)^3} + \frac{\$1.19}{(1.10)^4} + \frac{\$1.26}{(1.10)^5}$$

The values for the string $(1.10)^t$ can also be found in Table 4-1. The string of fractions reduces to

$$\frac{\$1.00}{1.10} + \frac{\$1.06}{1.21} + \frac{\$1.12}{1.333} + \frac{\$1.19}{1.464} + \frac{\$1.26}{1.611}$$

The sum of the numbers above is

$$\$.909 + \$.876 + \$.844 + \$.813 + \$.783 = \$4.225$$

Thus, the present value of the stream of dividends is equal to $4.225 over the five-year period if the required rate of return is 10 percent and the dividends grow at a rate of 6 percent per year. Although the number of dollars of dividends is $5.63, their present value is only $4.225 as indicated, since the dividends grow at only 6 percent and the investor requires a 10 percent rate of return.

The price of the stock at the end of the holding period (year 5) is the last part of our equation. Let us assume that the current price of the stock is $25, forecasted earnings per share (e_1) are $2.00 [$1.89(1.06)] and the price-earnings ratio (P/E) is 12.5. Holding P/E at 12.5, the earnings, expected to grow at 6 percent per year, should amount to $2.68 [$1.89(1.06)^6] for year six. Thus:

$$\begin{aligned} \text{Selling price at the} \\ \text{end of year 5} \quad &= (12.5)[(\$1.89)(1.06)^6] \\ &= \$33.45 \end{aligned}$$

The present value of the selling price is $33.45/(1.10)^5$, or $20.78. Adding the present value of the stream of dividends to the present value of the expected selling price of the stock yields $4.22 + $20.78 or $25.00.

Notice that throughout this explanation, the variables g, d/e and P/E are estimated by the analyst or investor. The current price of the stock (P) and current earnings (e_0) are observed. Equation 4-6 is solved for the rate of return (r). Let us illustrate our efforts up to now with a real-world example.

EXAMPLE: McDONALD'S STOCK.   Let us estimate the return on McDonald's stock as an investment to be held for five years. McDonald's operates the largest "fast-food" restaurant system in the country. Assume that its common stock can be purchased at the beginning of 1981 for $60. A thoroughgoing analysis of expected future earnings, dividends, and price-earnings ratio (P/E) has provided the following predictions:

Year	Earnings per Share	Dividends per Share
1981	$ 6.35	$ .95
1982	7.30	1.30
1983	8.45	1.70
1984	9.70	2.20
1985	11.10	2.80

It is estimated that at the end of 1985, the stock will sell for 11 times 1985 earnings. Given the estimated earnings in 1985 of $11.10, the forecast selling price at the end of the fifth year is $122 ($11.10 × 11).

What rate of return would equate the flow of dividends and the terminal price shown above back to a current market price of $60? Alternatively stated, what yield or return is required on an investment of $60 in order that an investor may withdraw dividends each year as indicated above and be able to remove a final balance of $122 at the end of five years?

In effect, we want to find the rate of return that will solve the following:

$$\$60 = \frac{\$.95}{1+r} + \frac{\$1.30}{(1+r)^2} + \frac{\$1.70}{(1+r)^3} + \frac{\$2.20}{(1+r)^4} + \frac{\$2.80}{(1+r)^5} + \frac{\$122}{(1+r)^5}$$

where r is the rate of return. Calculating the rate that will solve the equation is a somewhat tedious task, requiring trial-and-error computation. One rate is tried, and if it fails to work, we must try others. Let us turn the equation into columnar form and try some discount rates.

Year	Receipt	16% Present-Value Factor	Present Value
1	$ .95	.862	$ .82
2	1.30	.743	.97
3	1.70	.641	1.09
4	2.20	.552	1.21
5	2.80	.476	1.33
5	122.00	.476	58.07
			$63.49

At 16 percent, this stream of receipts has a present value of $63.49, not the $60 the market is asking. This suggests that the discount rate is more than 16 percent. In order to achieve lower present values of the stream of payments, present-value tables suggest higher discount rates. Using 18 percent, the present-value results are:

Year	Receipt	18% Present-Value Factor	Present Value
1	$ .95	.847	$ .80
2	1.30	.718	.93
3	1.70	.609	1.03
4	2.20	.516	1.13
5	2.80	.437	1.22
5	122.00	.437	53.31
			$58.42

We are close! The yield is really about 17 percent per annum. The investor must decide if 17 percent is a satisfactory return for him, given his alternative investment opportunities and his attitude toward risk in holding McDonald's stock.

What happened to earnings? We instinctively feel that earnings should be worth something, whether they are paid out as dividends or not, and wonder why they do not appear in the valuation equation. In fact, they do appear in the equation but in the correct form. Earnings can be used for one of two purposes: they can be paid out to stockholders in the form of dividends or they can be reinvested in the firm. If they are reinvested in the firm they should result in increased future earnings and increased future dividends. To the extent earnings at any time, say time t, are paid out to stockholders, they are measured by the term D_t and to the extent they are retained in the firm and used productively they are reflected in future dividends and should result in future dividends being larger than D_t. To discount the future earnings stream of a share of stock would be double counting since we would count retained earnings both when they were earned and when they, or the earnings from their reinvestment, were later paid to stockholders.

CONSTANT GROWTH

The simplest extension of what we have been doing assumes that dividends will grow at the same rate (g) into the indefinite future. Under this assumption the value of a share of stock is

$$P = \frac{D(1+g)}{1+r} + \frac{D(1+g)^2}{(1+r)^2} + \frac{D(1+g)^3}{(1+r)^3} + \cdots + \frac{D(1+g)^N}{(1+r)^N} + \cdots$$

Where N approaches infinity this equation collapses simply to

$$P = \frac{D_1}{r-g} \qquad (4.7)$$

This model states that the price of a share of stock should be equal to next year's expected dividend divided by the difference between the appropriate discount rate for the stock and its expected long-term growth rate. Alternatively, this model can be stated in terms of the rate of return on a stock as

$$r = \frac{D_1}{P} + g \qquad (4.8)$$

The constant-growth model is often defended as the model that arises from the assumption that the firm will maintain a stable dividend policy (keep its retention rate constant) and earn a stable return on new equity investment over time.

How might the single-period model be used to select stocks? One way is to predict next year's dividends, the firm's long-term growth rate, and the rate of return stockholders require for holding the stock. The equation could then be solved for the theoretical price of the stock that could be compared with its present price. Stocks that have theoretical prices above their actual prices are candidates for purchase; those with theoretical prices below their actual price are candidates for sale.

Another way to use the approach is to find the rate of return implicit in the price at which the stock is now selling. This can be done by substituting the current price, estimated dividend, and estimated growth rate into Equation 4.7 and solving for the discount rate that equates the present price with the expected flow of future dividends.

If this rate is higher than the rate of return considered appropriate for the stock, given its risk, it is a candidate for purchase.

Let us illustrate the use of the single-period model with a simple example. BOQ stock is selling for $90 a share. Earnings are $4.00 per share with a $2.00 dividend. Analysts are estimating BOQ's long-term growth rate at 12 percent and its dividend payout rate at 50 percent. If we assume that 14 percent is an appropriate discount rate for BOQ, we would compute a theoretical price of

$$P = \frac{2.00}{.14 - .12} = \$100$$

While BOQ's stock would seem to be undervalued selling at $90 a share, notice the sensitivity of this valuation equation to both the estimate of the appropriate discount rate and the estimate of the long-term growth rate. For example, if BOQ's growth rate was estimated to be 9 percent rather than 12 percent, its theoretical price would be 40 percent as large or $40.

It seems logical to assume that firms which have grown at a very high rate will not continue to do so into the infinite future. Similarly, firms with very poor growth might improve in the future. While a single growth rate can be found that will produce the same value as a more complex pattern, it is so hard to estimate this single number, and the resultant valuation is so sensitive to this number that many analysts have been reluctant to use the constant growth model without modification.

TWO-STAGE GROWTH

The most logical further extension of the constant growth model is to assume that a period of extraordinary growth (good or bad) will continue for a certain number of years, after which growth will change to a level at which it is expected to continue indefinitely. Firms typically go through life cycles; during part of these cycles their growth is much faster than that of the economy as a whole. Automobile manufacturers in the 1920s and computer and manufacturers of hand calculators in the 1970s are examples.

A hypothetical firm is expected to grow at a 20 percent rate for ten years, then to have its growth rate fall to 4 percent, the norm for the economy. The value of the firm with this growth pattern is determined by the following equation:

Present price = PV of dividends during above normal growth period
+ Value of stock price at end of above normal growth period
discounted back to present

$$P_0 = \sum_{t=1}^{N} \frac{D_0(1 + g_s)^t}{(1 + r_s)^t} + \frac{D_{N+1}}{r_s - g_n} \frac{1}{(1 + r_s)^N} \qquad (4.9)$$

where:

g_s = above-normal growth rate

g_n = normal growth rate

N = period of above-normal growth

Consider a firm whose previous dividend was $1.92 ($D_0$ = $1.92), with the dividend expected to increase by 20 percent a year for ten years and thereafter at 4 percent a year indefinitely. If stockholders' required rate of return is 9 percent, what is the value of the stock? On the basis of the calculations in Table 4-6, the value is $138.19, the present value of the dividends during the first ten years plus the present value of the stock at the end of the tenth year.

TABLE 4-6
CALCULATING THE VALUE OF A TWO-STAGE GROWTH STOCK

Assumptions:
a. Required rate of return = 9%.
b. Growth rate is 20% for ten years, 4% thereafter (g_s = 20%, g_n = 4%, and N = 10).
c. Last year's dividend was $1.92 ($d_0$ = $1.92).

Step 1. Find the present value of dividends during the rapid-growth period.

End of Year	Dividend $1.92(1.20)^t$	PVIF = $1/(1.09)^t$	PV
1	$ 2.30	.917	$ 2.11
2	2.76	.842	2.32
3	3.32	.772	2.56
4	3.98	.708	2.82
5	4.78	.650	3.11
6	5.73	.596	3.42
7	6.88	.547	3.76
8	8.26	.502	4.15
9	9.91	.460	4.56
10	11.89	.422	5.02

$$\text{PV of first ten years' dividends} = \sum_{t=1}^{10} \frac{d_0(1+g_s)^t}{(1+r_s)^t} = \underline{\underline{\$33.83}}$$

Step 2. Find the present value of the year 10 stock price.
   a. Find the value of the stock at the end of year 10:

$$p_{10} = \frac{d_{11}}{r_s - g_n} = \frac{\$11.89(1.04)}{.05} = \$247.31$$

   b. Discount p_{10} back to the present:

$$PV = p_{10}\left(\frac{1}{1+r_s}\right)^{10} = \$247.31(.422) = \$104.36$$

Step 3. Sum to find the total value of the stock today:

$$p_0 = \$33.83 + \$104.36 = \$138.19$$

MULTIPERIOD RATES OF RETURN

The concept of a one-period rate of return can easily be extended to produce multiperiod returns. For example, the return from holding a stock for one year can be visualized as the product of a series of 12-monthly (one-period) rates of return.

To illustrate the calculation of a multiperiod rate of return, suppose that you lent out $6,000 over a four-year period at annual interest rates of 8 percent in the first year, 9 percent in the second, 10 percent in the third, and 11 percent in the fourth. Interest was compounded annually, so that each year was, in effect, a single-period investment.

At the end of the first year, for example, the principal grew from $6,000 to $6,480, that is, to $6,000 (1 + .08). This terminal sum was then reinvested at 9 percent in the second year to produce $7,063.20, that is, $6,480 (1 + .09). After four years of compounding, the original investment of $6,000 has grown to $8,313.39. In more general terms, if C_0 is the original investment cash flow and C_T is the terminal realized cash flow, C_T is related to C_0 by the following equation:

$$C_T = C_0(1 + R_1)(1 + R_2) \cdots (1 + R_T)$$

where the R's are the one-period realized rates of return earned in the various periods.

How do we go about finding the realized multiperiod rate of return implied by the growth of C_0 to C_T over period T? The answer is

$$R = \sqrt[T]{(1 + R_1)(1 + R_2) \cdots (1 + R_T)} - 1 \qquad (4.10)$$

As this formulation suggests, the realized multiperiod rate is an average of the realized one-period rates of return. More specifically, it is the geometric average of the one-period rates that span the life of the investment.

For example, in the case of the four-year investment of $6,000 made at realized annual rates of 8 percent in the first year, 9 percent in the second, and so on, we have

$$R = \sqrt[4]{(1.08)(1.09)(1.10)(1.11)} - 1 = .0949$$

The realized geometric mean return will equal the arithmetic average of the one-period rates of return if these rates remain constant over the period T. This being the case, the simpler arithmetic average can be used as an approximation of the more complex geometric mean in cases in which the variability of the one-period rates is slight. For instance, in the $6,000 four-year loan example discussed above, the arithmetic average rate of return, 9.5 percent, just above the geometric mean return.

Where there is substantial period-to-period variability, however, the arithmetic and geometric versions of the rate of return will produce significantly different results. This point is nicely illustrated in Table 4-7, which shows the prices and one-period realized rates of return for a non-dividend-paying common stock. As the table reveals, the arithmetic average rate of return approximates 4 percent per year, while the geometric mean, which takes into account the period-to-period compounding of the principal available at the beginning of each period, is, obviously, zero.

TABLE 4-7
RETURNS OF A HYPOTHETICAL STOCK

Year	Closing Price	One-Year Return (%)
1	$100	—
2	120	+20
3	80	−33
4	100	+25

Arithmetic average return $= \dfrac{+20 - 33 + 25}{3} = 4\%$

Geometric average return $= \sqrt[3]{(1.20)(.67)(1.25)} - 1.0 = 0\%$

Holding-Period Yield

One of our principal tasks throughout the remainder of the text will be to estimate return and risk for both securities and portfolios over a forward holding period. The holding period, or elapsed time between the purchase and sale of a security, could be any amount of time, from our hour to a decade, or longer. The *holding-period yield* will be defined as the percentage dividend or interest yield plus percentage capital-appreciation yield over the holding period—or:

$$\text{Stock HPY} = \frac{D_1 + (P_1 - P_0)}{P_0} \tag{4.11}$$

$$\text{Bond HPY} = \frac{I_1 + (P_1 - P_0)}{P_0} \tag{4.12}$$

where:

HPY = expected holding-period yield

D_1 = expected dividends over holding period

I_1 = expected interest over holding period

P_0 = current security price

P_1 = expected security price, end of holding period

These equations say that the holding-period yield is the sum of the dividend or interest yield and the capital-appreciation yield.

The Capitalization or Multiplier Approach

Judging from current practice, the capitalization or multiplier approach to valuation still holds the preeminent position. A survey of practicing analysts indicated that 75 percent of them preferred simple multiplier techniques.[8] Present-value techniques were preferred by only about 6 percent. The underlying reasons for ignoring present-value formulas seem to lie in (1) severe earnings-forecasting limitations, and (2) the influence of sharply increased competition on short-range performance.

The multiplier is a shortcut computation to find the present value. The analyst estimates earnings per share for the year ahead. He divides this figure into the current market price of the stock, and the result is an earnings multiplier. The terms *multiplier* and *price-earnings ratio* (P/E) are used interchangeably. Thus:

$$\text{Earnings multiplier} = \text{P/E ratio} = \frac{\text{Current market price}}{\text{Estimated earnings per share}} \tag{4.13}$$

The multiplier, or P/E, is primarily determined by the riskiness of the firm and the rate of growth in its earnings. High multipliers are associated with high earnings growth. The Dow Jones Industrial Average might sell in the range 9 to 11 P/E. It represents a cross section of stocks with average risk and growth prospects. McDonald's may sell at

---

[8]R. A. Bing, "Survey of Practitioners' Stock Evaluation Methods," *Financial Analysts Journal*, 26, No. 2 (May-June 1971), 55-60.

a P/E of 11, because of its high rate of earnings growth. American Telephone and Telegraph Co. may sell at a P/E of 9, because of average growth.

The analyst seeks various rules of thumb for selecting an appropriate price-earnings ratio that can be applied to a company's earnings to determine value for its shares. The resulting price is compared with current market prices to assess bargains or overpriced stocks. For example, if Standard Oil of California is expected to earn $6 per share next year and normally sells at a P/E of 8, the analyst might conclude that a fair price at present is $48. If the stock is currently selling for $40, it is undervalued; if it is selling for $55, it is over-priced (overvalued).

The determination of the current P/E on a stock must be followed by a standard of comparison, taken from the historical record of the stock in question. The analyst may ascertain the median or mean P/E for a stock, as well as its range over time. More weight can be given to the recent past. This provides boundaries within which the P/E should fall (range) and indicates whether the stock is tending to sell at the upper limits of expectation (high end of P/E range) or lower limits. Industry P/E's provide some guidelines; however, different companies in the same industry frequently carry quite different P/E's.

Statistical Approaches to P/E

Still another approach to valuation is to take the broad determinants of common stock prices—earnings, growth, risk, time value of money, and dividend policy—and to measure these and weigh them together in some manner to form an estimate of the P/E ratio. One way to do this is to use statistical analysis to define the weights the market places on a set of determinants of common stock prices.

From our earlier discussion of constant growth models, we can easily convert the model from a price to a price-earnings form:

$$P = \frac{D}{r-g} \quad \text{and} \quad P/E = \frac{D/E}{r-g}$$

The relationship that exists in the market at any point in time between price or price-earnings ratios and a set of specified variables can be estimated using regression analysis. Figure 4-4 presents the relationship between P/E ratios and forecasted growth for a sample of stocks as of the end of 1971. Each point in the diagram represents the P/E ratio and forecasted growth rate for a company as of the end of 1971. The straight line is fitted statistically and its equation is given by

Price/Earnings = 4 + 2.3 (growth rate in earnings)

The usual technique of relating price or price-earnings ratios to more than one variable is directly analogous to this. Called multiple regression analysis, it finds that linear combination of a set of variables that best explains price-earnings ratios.

One of the earliest attempts to use multiple regression to explain price-earnings ratios, which received wide attention, was the Whitbeck-Kisor model. We could have said, equally well, that Whitbeck and Kisor set out to measure the relationship of the P/E on a stock to dividend policy, growth, and risk. They obtained estimates of earnings growth rates, dividend payouts, and the variation (standard deviation) of growth rates from a group of security analysts. Then, using multiple regression analysis to define the average relationship between each of these variables and price earnings ratios, they found (as of June 8, 1962) that

$$
\begin{aligned}
\text{Price-earnings ratio} \quad &= 8.2 \\
&+ 1.50 \quad \text{(earnings growth rate)} = g \\
&+ .067 \quad \text{(dividend payout rate)} = D/E \\
&- .200 \quad \text{(standard deviation in growth} \\
& \text{rate or a proxy for risk} \\
& \text{affecting } r)
\end{aligned}
$$

This equation represents the estimate at a point in time of the simultaneous impact of the three variables on the price-earnings ratios. The numbers represent the weight that the market placed on each variable at that point in time. The signs represent the direction of the impact of each variable on the P/E ratio. We might take some comfort from the fact that the signs are consistent with what theory and common sense would lead us to expect: the higher growth, the higher dividends (growth held constant), and the lower risk, the higher the P/E ratio. The equations tell us that on average a 1 percent increase in earnings growth is associated with a 1.5-unit increase in the P/E ratio, a 1 percent increase in the dividend payout ratio is associated with a .067-unit increase in the P/E ratio, and a 1 percent increase in the standard deviation of growth is associated with a .2-unit decrease in the P/E ratio.

FIGURE 4-4
P/E RATIOS VERSUS GROWTH RATES

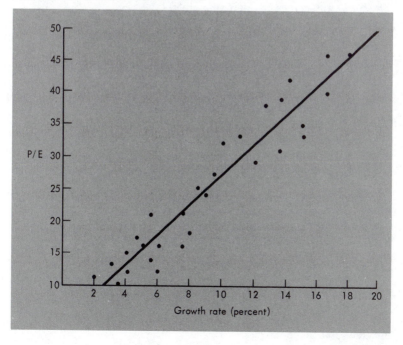

An equation such as this can be used to arrive at the theoretical P/E ratio for any stock. Simply by substituting the forecasted earnings growth rate, dividend payout ratio, and risk for the stock on the right-hand side of the equation, one arrives at a theoretical P/E ratio. We can illustrate this. Assume that we have a stock whose growth was forecast at 12 percent, its dividend payout ratio was 50 percent, and its standard deviation in growth rate was about 5. Substituting these numbers in the expression for price earnings ratios presented above, we get a theoretical P/E ratio of 28.55. Many people advocate buying stocks with theoretical P/E ratios above their actual P/E ratios, and selling short stocks with theoretical prices below their market P/E ratio. Many models like this have appeared in print.

The ability of cross-sectional regressions actually to distinguish winners from losers is questionable. As forecasting devices these models are plagued by instability in the regression coefficients. The coefficients are extremely sample sensitive—that is, the results are partially dependent upon the sample selected (time period and companies).

Summary

This chapter focused on the fundamental approach to the determination of the value of a security, and how to calculate return on a security. The central idea that a security is worth the discounted present value of all future income that flows from it enabled us to discuss the theory behind what a stock or a bond *should* sell for. The value of a preferred stock or a bond is easier to calculate than the value of a common stock, since the latter is likely to provide income flows whose timing and amount are more uncertain. Bond interest and preferred dividends are fixed by contract. Bond tables were introduced to facilitate the valuation process.

We saw the method for determining the present worth or value of a share of common stock when the holding period is one year or a number of years. The multiplier or P/E approach to stock valuation was explored briefly, since it is preeminent in use today by practicing security analysts.

Questions and Problems

1. a. At an annual rate of compounding of 8 percent, how long does it take a given sum to double? triple? quadruple?

b. How do you explain the results in part (a)?

2. Which amount is worth more at 16 percent: $1,000 today or $2,100 after five years?

3. How much should you be willing to pay today for an annual cash payment of $10,000 to be received forever if your required rate of return is 9 percent?

4. Duker Electronics has a 6 percent, $100 par value bond outstanding that is due in ten years. The firm also has a $6 preferred stock outstanding.

a. What is the present value of each security if the required rate of return on these securities in the marketplace is 8 percent?

b. How do you account for the differences in value determined in part (a)?

5. Why is it more difficult to determine the value of a common stock as opposed to finding the value of a bond?

6. Tasty Fast Foods, Inc., stock is currently selling for $35 per share. The stock is expected to pay a $1 dividend at the end of the next year. It is reliably estimated that the stock will sell for $37 at the end of one year.

   a. Assuming that the dividend and price forecasts are accurate, would you pay $35 today for the stock to hold it for one year if your required rate of return were 12 percent?

   b. Given the present price of $35 and the expected dividend of $1, what would the price have to be at the end of one year to justify purchase today if your required return were 15 percent?

7. Consult *Value Line, Moody's*, or other investment services to determine price and dividend data for American Telephone and Telegraph Company and McDonald's Corporation. If you had purchased each stock at the average of its high and low prices in 1974 and sold each stock at the average price in 1978 what rate of return would you have earned on each stock (before transaction costs and taxes)? Assume that dividends paid each year are collected in one payment at the end of the year.

8. You have just made some forecasts for Standard Oil Company of Ohio. It is determined that you want to buy 450 shares today with the intention of selling out at the end of five years (at which time you will retire to Bermuda). You estimate that SOHIO will pay $1.35 per share in dividends each year into the foreseeable future and that, at the end of the five-year holding period, the shares could be sold for $55. What would you be willing to pay today for these shares if your required return is 10 percent per annum?

9. Lenn Industries paid a cash dividend on its stock of $2.00 per share last year. The earnings and dividends of the company are expected to grow at an annual rate of 12 percent indefinitely. Investors expect a rate of return on Lenn's shares of 14 percent. What is a fair price for this company's shares?

10. The Spirer Co. has common shares outstanding which had a dividend last year of $1.50. Investors have traditionally required a rate of return on these shares of 20 percent. Forecasts suggest that earnings and dividends on the stock will grow at a rate of 15 percent over the next five years and at a rate of 10 percent thereafter. What is the present value of the stock?

11. Refer to the Whitbeck-Kisor price-earnings model in the chapter. A stock has been observed that sells currently at a P/E of 20. The company's earnings grow at 10 percent per year with a dividend payout equal to 50 percent of earnings. The standard deviation in the growth rate of earnings over the past five years has been about 15 percent. Is this stock a bargain? Why or why not?

12. White Tire and Rubber Company and Orange Computers, Inc., shares are presently at $50 and $100, respectively. Annual dividends over the next year are expected to be $1.00 for White and $4.00 for Orange on projected earnings of $2.50 for White and $6.00 for Orange. White's earnings and dividends are expected to grow at 15 percent per annum into the foreseeable future; Orange's earnings and dividends are expected to advance 12 percent per year. These analysts have estimated the following equally likely prices one year ahead on the two stocks: White, $55 or $60, and Orange, $108 or $116.

   a. Examine the risk-return of each stock. Pick one stock for purchase now for a one-year holding period. Support your choice.

   b. Which stock appears the most undervalued for long-term holding if investors require a 16 percent return on both stocks? Why?

13. My-Lady, Inc., a manufacturer of women's high-fashion apparel, is expected to earn $1.00 per share next year and pay a dividend of $.25 per share. Earnings and dividends are expected to grow into the foreseeable future at 10 percent per annum. Investors are judged to require a return of 15 percent per annum on the company's stock.

   a. What is the theoretical *value* of this stock?

   b. What would the theoretical *price-earnings ratio* be for this stock if, other things equal, required returns by investors were only 12 percent?

Other things equal: (1) indicate whether each of the following events (treat each separately) would tend to cause the price of My-Lady, Inc., stock to *rise, fall,* or remain *unchanged*; and (2) state *why*.

    c. An increase in total debt relative to equity financing

    d. A merger with Hi-Scent Flavors & Fragrances, a large maker of men's cosmetics

    e. A decline in the dividend from $.25 to $.20

APPENDIX

Three-Stage Growth

The two-stage model assumed that during the initial period, earnings would continue to grow at some constant rate. At year N the second period started and growth was assumed to drop instantly to some "steady-state" value. Normally, the change to a new long-term growth rate would not occur instantly; rather, it would occur over a period of time. Thus, a logical extension is to assume a third stage or period. The resultant model would assume that in period one, growth is expected to be constant at some level. It is necessary to forecast both the level of growth and the duration of period one. During period two, the growth changes from its value in period one to a long-run steady-state level. It is necessary to forecast both the duration of period two and the pattern of change in growth. Although it is possible to use various patterns of change in growth, it is common to assume that the change is linear or straight-line. The third and final period is the period of steady-state growth. For example, if the duration of the transition period is ten years, the initial growth rate 20 percent, and the final steady-state growth rate 6 percent, the annual decline in the growth rate would be 1.4 percent $[(20 - 6)/10]$. Once a firm reaches steady-state growth, it will have whatever growth is deemed appropriate.

As we move from a constant growth model to a three-period growth model, we increase the number and the complexity of the inputs that must be provided while, hopefully, picking up some information. If growth patterns are overly simplified, insufficient information will be provided by the forecasts. If they are made too complex, the forecasts are likely to be inaccurate. The trade-off between complexity and manageability will have to be made on the basis of one's forecasting skills.[9]

The practical application of these ideas to common stocks has been greatly facilitated by tables composed of numerous combinations of underlying factors, such as earnings and dividend growth rates, growth duration, and required rate of return. One early example is a set of tables introduced by Molodovsky, May, and Chottiner. We will look at these tables now.

---

[9]Among the earliest stock tables were those of S. E. Guild, *Stock Growth and Discount Tables* (Boston: Financial Publishing Company, 1931), p. 163. Other tables not discussed here are those of W. S. Bauman, *Estimating the Present Value of Common Stocks by the Variable Rate Method* (Ann Arbor: Bureau of Business Research, University of Michigan, 1963).

Molodovsky, May, and Chottiner use price-earnings in their calculations and they use a built-in relationship between the growth rate and dividend payout ratio, determined through statistical analysis.[10] The assumed pattern of growth is shown in Figure 4-5. Notice a high but constant growth rate for the initial period (segment A), followed by a transitional period during which the growth rate will decline to zero (segment B). Zero growth is then extended infinitely (segment C).

FIGURE 4-5
PATTERN OF EARNINGS GROWTH EVALUATED BY
MOLODOVSKY-MAY-CHOTTINER TABLES

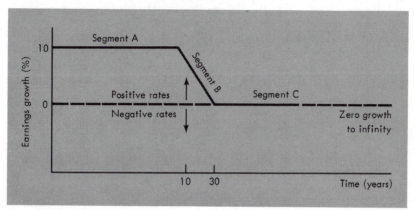

Referring to Table 4-8, which is an extract from the Molodovsky-May-Chottiner tables, let us use an example. RST Co. earnings are expected to grow at 10 percent a year for the next ten years. Thereafter, the rate of growth will decline to zero over a twenty-year period. Earnings will then stabilize at zero growth (from year 31 on). The investor seeks a 9 percent rate of return. In Table 4-8, the initial growth rate of 10 percent is found in the right-hand column. Finding 10 in the "Years Constant Growth" column, read across to the column marked "20" for years of diminishing growth. The table number is 22.9. This is the price-earnings ratio most appropriate to current earnings. The interpretation is that if current earnings are at $3.00, the stock is worth about $68.70 ($3 X 22.9).

The tables we have analyzed are attempts to put present-value theory into operational form. The main difficulty in application lies in the problems inherent in forecasting (1) rates, (2) duration, and (3) pattern of growth of earnings or dividends of a stock for a long period ahead. The problem of the complex calculations required to evaluate virtually limitless possibilities for growth rates and their duration has been solved by programs available for hand-held calculators.[11]

---

[10]Nicholas Molodovsky, Catherine May, and Sherman Chottiner, "Common Stock Valuation: Theory and Tables," *Financial Analysts Journal*, 20 (March-April 1965), 104-23.
[11]R. J. Fuller, "Programming the Three-Phase Dividend Discount Model," *The Journal of Portfolio Management*, Summer 1979, pp. 28-32.

TABLE 4-8
INVESTMENT VALUES OF NORMAL EARNINGS OF $1 AT 9 PERCENT RETURN

Projected Earnings Growth Rate

5.0%
Years Diminishing Growth

Years Constant Growth	2	4	6	8	10	12	14	16	18	20
2	8.6	8.9	9.2	9.5	9.8	10.0	10.2	10.4	10.6	10.8
4	9.4	9.7	9.9	10.2	10.4	10.7	10.9	11.1	11.3	11.4
6	10.1	10.3	10.6	10.8	11.0	11.3	11.5	11.6	11.8	12.0
8	10.7	11.0	11.2	11.4	11.6	11.8	12.0	12.2	12.3	12.5
10	11.3	11.5	11.8	12.0	12.2	12.3	12.5	12.7	12.8	13.0
12	11.9	12.1	12.3	12.5	12.7	12.8	13.0	13.1	13.3	13.4
14	12.4	12.6	12.8	13.0	13.1	13.3	13.4	13.6	13.7	13.8
16	12.9	13.1	13.2	13.4	13.5	13.7	13.8	14.0	14.1	14.2
18	13.3	13.5	13.7	13.8	13.9	14.1	14.2	14.3	14.4	14.5
20	13.7	13.9	14.0	14.2	14.3	14.4	14.6	14.7	14.8	14.9
22	14.1	14.3	14.4	14.5	14.7	14.8	14.9	15.0	15.1	15.2
24	14.5	14.6	14.7	14.9	15.0	15.1	15.2	15.3	15.4	15.4
26	14.8	14.9	15.0	15.2	15.3	15.4	15.5	15.5	15.7	16.0
28	15.1	15.2	15.3	15.4	15.5	15.6	15.7	15.8	15.9	16.0
30	15.4	15.5	15.6	15.7	15.8	15.9	16.0	16.0	16.1	16.2

6.0%
Years Diminishing Growth

Years Constant Growth	2	4	6	8	10	12	14	16	18	20
2	8.8	9.2	9.5	9.9	10.2	10.5	10.8	11.1	11.4	11.6
4	9.7	10.1	10.4	10.8	11.1	11.4	11.6	11.9	12.1	12.4
6	10.6	10.9	11.3	11.6	11.9	12.1	12.4	12.7	12.9	13.1
8	11.4	11.7	12.1	12.3	12.6	12.9	13.1	13.4	13.6	13.8
10	12.2	12.5	12.8	13.1	13.3	13.6	13.8	14.1	14.3	14.5
12	12.9	13.2	13.5	13.8	14.0	14.3	14.5	14.7	14.9	15.1
14	13.7	13.9	14.2	14.4	14.7	14.9	15.1	15.3	15.5	15.7
16	14.3	14.6	14.8	15.1	15.3	15.5	15.7	15.9	16.1	16.2
18	14.9	15.2	15.4	15.6	15.9	16.0	16.2	16.4	16.6	16.8
20	15.5	15.8	16.0	16.2	16.4	16.6	16.8	16.9	17.1	17.2
22	16.1	16.3	16.5	16.7	16.9	17.1	17.3	17.4	17.6	17.7
24	16.6	16.8	17.0	17.2	17.4	17.6	17.7	17.9	18.0	18.2
26	17.1	17.3	17.5	17.7	17.9	18.0	18.2	18.3	18.4	18.6
28	17.6	17.8	18.0	18.1	18.3	18.4	18.6	18.7	18.8	19.0
30	18.1	18.2	18.4	18.6	18.7	18.8	19.0	19.1	19.2	19.3

7.0%
Years Diminishing Growth

Years Constant Growth	2	4	6	8	10	12	14	16	18	20
2	9.0	9.4	9.9	10.3	10.7	11.1	11.4	11.8	12.1	12.5
4	10.1	10.5	10.9	11.3	11.7	12.1	12.5	12.8	13.1	13.4
6	11.1	11.6	12.0	12.4	12.7	13.1	13.4	13.8	14.1	14.4
8	12.2	12.6	13.0	13.4	13.7	14.1	14.4	14.7	15.0	15.3
10	13.2	13.6	13.9	14.3	14.7	15.0	15.3	15.6	15.9	16.2
12	14.1	14.5	14.9	15.2	15.6	15.9	16.2	16.5	16.8	17.0
14	15.1	15.4	15.8	16.1	16.4	16.7	17.0	17.3	17.6	17.9
16	15.9	16.3	16.6	17.0	17.3	17.6	17.9	18.1	18.4	18.6
18	16.8	17.1	17.5	17.8	18.1	18.4	18.6	18.9	19.2	19.4
20	17.6	18.0	18.3	18.6	18.9	19.1	19.4	19.7	19.9	20.1
22	18.4	18.7	19.0	19.3	19.6	19.9	20.1	20.4	20.6	20.8
24	19.2	19.5	19.8	20.1	20.3	20.6	20.8	21.1	21.3	21.5
26	19.9	20.2	20.5	20.8	21.0	21.3	21.5	21.7	22.0	22.2
28	20.6	20.9	21.2	21.5	21.7	21.9	22.2	22.4	22.6	22.8
30	21.3	21.6	21.9	22.1	22.4	22.6	22.8	23.0	23.2	23.4

8.0%
Years Diminishing Growth

Years Constant Growth	2	4	6	8	10	12	14	16	18	20
2	9.1	9.7	10.2	10.7	11.2	11.7	12.1	12.5	13.0	13.4
4	10.4	11.0	11.5	12.0	12.4	12.9	13.4	13.8	14.2	14.6
6	11.7	12.2	12.7	13.2	13.7	14.1	14.6	15.0	15.4	15.8
8	13.0	13.5	14.0	14.5	14.9	15.4	15.8	16.2	16.6	17.0
10	14.2	14.7	15.2	15.7	16.1	16.5	17.0	17.4	17.8	18.1
12	15.4	15.9	16.4	16.8	17.3	17.7	18.1	18.5	18.9	19.3
14	16.6	17.1	17.6	18.0	18.4	18.9	19.3	19.7	20.0	20.4
16	17.8	18.3	18.7	19.2	19.6	20.0	20.4	20.8	21.1	21.5
18	18.9	19.4	19.8	20.3	20.7	21.1	21.5	21.9	22.2	22.6
20	20.1	20.5	21.0	21.4	21.8	22.2	22.6	22.9	23.3	23.6
22	21.2	21.6	22.0	22.5	22.9	23.2	23.6	24.0	24.3	24.7
24	22.2	22.7	23.1	23.5	23.9	24.3	24.7	25.0	25.4	25.7
26	23.3	23.7	24.2	24.6	24.9	25.3	25.7	26.0	26.4	26.7
28	24.4	24.8	25.2	25.6	26.0	26.3	26.7	27.0	27.4	27.7
30	25.4	25.8	26.2	26.6	27.0	27.3	27.7	28.0	28.3	28.6

Projected Earnings Growth Rate

9.0%
Years Diminishing Growth

Years Constant Growth	2	4	6	8	10	12	14	16	18	20
2	9.3	9.9	10.5	11.1	11.7	12.3	12.8	13.3	13.9	14.4
4	10.6	11.2	11.8	12.4	13.0	13.5	14.1	14.6	15.1	15.6
6	11.9	12.5	13.1	13.7	14.2	14.8	15.3	15.9	16.4	16.9
8	13.1	13.7	14.3	14.9	15.5	16.1	16.6	17.1	17.7	18.2
10	14.4	15.0	15.6	16.2	16.8	17.3	17.9	18.4	18.9	19.4
12	15.7	16.3	16.9	17.5	18.0	18.6	19.1	19.7	20.2	20.7
14	16.9	17.5	18.1	18.7	19.3	19.9	20.4	20.9	21.5	22.0
16	18.2	18.8	19.4	20.0	20.6	21.1	21.7	22.2	22.7	23.3
18	19.5	20.1	20.7	21.3	21.8	22.4	22.9	23.5	24.0	24.5
20	20.7	21.3	22.0	22.5	23.1	23.7	24.2	24.7	25.3	25.8
22	22.0	22.6	23.2	23.8	24.4	24.9	25.5	26.0	26.5	27.0
24	23.3	23.9	24.5	25.1	25.6	26.2	26.7	27.3	27.8	28.3
26	24.5	25.1	25.8	26.3	26.9	27.5	28.0	28.5	29.1	29.6
28	25.8	26.4	27.0	27.6	28.2	28.7	29.3	29.8	30.3	30.8
30	27.1	27.7	28.3	28.9	29.4	30.0	30.5	31.1	31.6	32.1

10.0%
Years Diminishing Growth

Years Constant Growth	2	4	6	8	10	12	14	16	18	20
2	9.5	10.2	10.9	11.6	12.3	12.9	13.6	14.2	14.8	15.4
4	11.2	11.9	12.6	13.3	14.0	14.7	15.3	16.0	16.6	17.3
6	13.0	13.7	14.4	15.1	15.8	16.5	17.2	17.8	18.5	19.1
8	14.8	15.5	16.2	16.9	17.7	18.3	19.0	19.7	20.4	21.0
10	16.6	17.3	18.1	18.8	19.5	20.2	20.9	21.6	22.3	22.9
12	18.4	19.2	19.9	20.7	21.4	22.1	22.8	23.5	24.2	24.9
14	20.3	21.1	21.9	22.6	23.4	24.1	24.8	25.5	26.2	26.9
16	22.2	23.0	23.8	24.6	25.3	26.1	26.8	27.5	28.2	28.9
18	24.2	25.0	25.8	26.6	27.3	28.1	28.8	29.6	30.3	31.0
20	26.1	27.0	27.8	28.6	29.4	30.2	30.9	31.7	32.4	33.1
22	28.2	29.0	29.8	30.7	31.5	32.3	33.0	33.8	34.5	35.3
24	30.2	31.1	31.9	32.8	33.6	34.4	35.2	36.0	36.7	37.5
26	32.3	33.2	34.1	34.9	35.7	36.6	37.4	38.2	38.9	39.7
28	34.5	35.4	36.2	37.1	37.9	38.8	39.6	40.4	41.2	42.0
30	36.6	37.6	38.4	39.3	40.2	41.0	41.9	42.7	43.5	44.3

11.0%
Years Diminishing Growth

Years Constant Growth	2	4	6	8	10	12	14	16	18	20
2	9.7	10.5	11.3	12.1	12.8	13.6	14.4	15.1	15.9	16.6
4	11.6	12.5	13.3	14.1	14.9	15.7	16.5	17.2	18.0	18.8
6	13.6	14.5	15.3	16.2	17.0	17.8	18.6	19.5	20.3	21.1
8	15.7	16.6	17.5	18.4	19.2	20.1	20.9	21.8	22.6	23.4
10	17.9	18.8	19.7	20.6	21.5	22.4	23.3	24.1	25.0	25.9
12	20.1	21.1	22.0	23.0	23.9	24.8	25.7	26.6	27.5	28.4
14	22.4	23.4	24.4	25.4	26.3	27.3	28.2	29.2	30.1	31.0
16	24.9	25.9	26.9	27.9	28.9	29.9	30.9	31.8	32.8	33.8
18	27.4	28.4	29.5	30.5	31.5	32.6	33.6	34.6	35.6	36.6
20	29.9	31.0	32.1	33.2	34.3	35.4	36.4	37.5	38.5	39.5
22	32.6	33.8	34.9	36.0	37.1	38.2	39.3	40.4	41.5	42.6
24	35.4	36.6	37.8	38.9	40.1	41.2	42.4	43.5	44.6	45.7
26	38.3	39.5	40.8	42.0	43.2	44.3	45.5	46.7	47.8	49.0
28	41.3	42.6	43.8	45.1	46.3	47.6	48.8	50.0	51.2	52.4
30	44.4	45.7	47.0	48.3	49.6	50.9	52.2	53.4	54.7	55.9

12.0%
Years Diminishing Growth

Years Constant Growth	2	4	6	8	10	12	14	16	18	20
2	9.9	10.8	11.7	12.5	13.4	14.3	15.2	16.1	17.0	17.9
4	12.0	13.0	13.9	14.9	15.8	16.7	17.7	18.6	19.5	20.5
6	14.3	15.3	16.3	17.3	18.3	19.3	20.3	21.3	22.2	23.2
8	16.7	17.8	18.8	19.9	20.9	22.0	23.0	24.1	25.1	26.2
10	19.3	20.4	21.5	22.6	23.7	24.8	25.9	27.0	28.1	29.2
12	22.0	23.2	24.3	25.5	26.6	27.8	29.0	30.1	31.3	32.5
14	24.8	26.1	27.3	28.5	29.7	31.0	32.2	33.4	34.7	35.9
16	27.8	29.1	30.4	31.7	33.0	34.3	35.6	36.9	38.2	39.5
18	31.0	32.4	33.7	35.1	36.5	37.8	39.2	40.6	42.0	43.3
20	34.4	35.8	37.2	38.7	40.1	41.6	43.0	44.5	45.9	47.4
22	37.9	39.4	40.9	42.5	44.0	45.5	47.0	48.6	50.1	51.6
24	41.6	43.2	44.8	46.4	48.1	49.7	51.3	52.9	54.5	56.1
26	45.6	47.3	49.0	50.7	52.4	54.1	55.8	57.5	59.2	60.9
28	49.7	51.5	53.3	55.1	56.9	58.7	60.5	62.3	64.1	65.9
30	54.1	56.0	57.9	59.8	61.7	63.6	65.5	67.4	69.3	71.2

SOURCE: Nicholas Molodovsky. "Common Stock Valuation: Theory and Tables," *Financial Analysts Journal*, 20, No. 2 (March-April, 1965), 122.

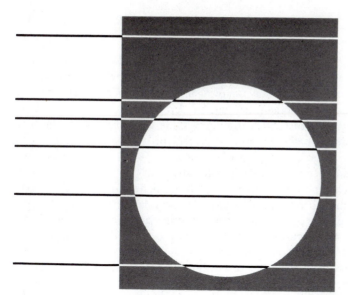

FIVE

Risk in Holding Securities

Risk in holding securities is generally associated with the possibility that *realized* returns will be less than the returns that were *expected*. The source of such disappointment is the failure of dividends (interest) and/or the security's price to materialize as expected.

Our goals in this chapter are (1) to examine what it is that creates risk, and (2) to provide a quantitative measure of risk.[1]

What Creates Risk?

Forces that contribute to variations in return—price or dividend (interest)—constitute elements of risk. Some influences are external to the firm, cannot be controlled, and affect large numbers of securities. Other influences are internal to the firm and are controllable to a large degree. In investments, those forces that are uncontrollable, external, and broad in their effect are called sources of *systematic* risk. Conversely, controllable, internal factors somewhat peculiar to industries and/or firms are referred to as elements of *unsystematic* risk.

Systematic risk refers to that portion of total variability in return caused by factors affecting the prices of all securities. Economic, political, and sociological changes are

---

[1]The words "risk" and "uncertainty" are used interchangeably. Technically, their meanings are different. *Risk* suggests that a decision maker knows the possible consequences of a decision and their relative likelihoods at the time he makes that decision. *Uncertainty*, on the other hand, involves a situation about which the likelihood of the possible outcomes is not known.

sources of systematic risk. Their effect is to cause prices of nearly all individual common stocks and/or all individual bonds to move together in the same manner. For example, should it become apparent that the economy is moving into a recession and that corporate profits will shift downward, stock prices may decline across a broad front. Nearly all stocks listed on the New York Stock Exchange move in the same direction as the New York Stock Exchange Index. On the average, 50 percent of the variation in a stock's price can be explained by variation in the market index.[2] In other words, about one-half the total risk in an average common stock is systematic risk.[3]

Unsystematic risk is the portion of total risk that is unique to a firm or industry. Such factors as management capability, consumer preferences, labor strikes, and the like cause unsystematic variability of returns in a firm. Unsystematic factors are largely independent of factors affecting securities markets in general. Since these factors affect one firm, they must be examined for each firm.

Firms with high systematic risk tend to be those whose sales, profits, and stock prices follow the level of economic activity and the level of the securities markets closely. These companies include most firms that deal in basic industrial goods and raw materials. In the industrial chain, we might find that industries related to automobile manufacture take on high systematic risk (steel, rubber, glass, and so on).

Higher proportions of unsystematic risk are found in firms producing nondurable consumer goods. Examples include suppliers of basic necessities such as telephone, light and power, and foodstuffs. Sales, profits, and stock prices of these companies do not depend as much upon the level of economic activity or the stock market.

Systematic and unsystematic risk can be subdivided. Systematic risk for bonds as a group is normally identified with interest-rate risk; for stocks, with market risk. For securities in general, purchasing-power risk is pervasive. Unsystematic risk, or risk unique to an industry or firm, includes business and financial risks.

Systematic Risk

Market Risk

It is not uncommon to find stock prices falling from time to time while a company's earnings are rising, and vice versa. The price of a stock may fluctuate widely within a short span of time even though earnings remain unchanged. The causes of this phenomenon are varied, but it is mainly due to a change in investors' attitudes toward equities in general, or toward certain types or groups of securities in particular. Variability in return on most common stocks that is due to basic sweeping changes in investor expectations is referred to as *market risk*.

Market risk is caused by investor reaction to tangible as well as intangible events. Expectations of lower corporate profits in general may cause the larger body of common stocks to fall in price. Investors are expressing their judgment that too much is being paid

[2]B. F. King, "Market and Industry Factors in Stock Price Behavior," *Journal of Business*, January 1966, pp. 139-90. Since King's study, other researchers have found that the market effect has declined in importance. However, King's work did pick up this approaching trend.
[3]Systematic risk/Total risk = Systematic risk (%).

for earnings in the light of anticipated events. The basis for the reaction is a set of real, tangible events—political, social, or economic.

Intangible events are related to market psychology. Market risk is usually touched off by a reaction to real events, but the emotional instability of investors acting collectively leads to a snowballing overreaction. The initial decline in the market can cause the fear of loss to grip investors, and a kind of herd instinct builds as all investors make for the exit. These reactions to reactions frequently culminate in excessive selling, pushing prices down far out of line with fundamental value. With a trigger mechanism such as the assassination of a president, virtually all stocks are adversely affected. Stocks in a particular industry group can be hard hit when the industry goes "out of fashion."

This discussion of market risk has emphasized adverse reactions. Certainly, buying panics also occur as reactions to real events. However, investors are not likely to think of sharp price advances as risk.

Two other factors, interest rates and inflation, are an integral part of the real forces behind market risk and are part of the larger category of systematic or uncontrollable influences. Let us turn our attention to interest rates. This risk factor has its most direct effect on bond investments.

Interest-Rate Risk

Interest-rate risk refers to the uncertainty of future market values and of the size of future income, caused by fluctuations in the general level of interest rates.

The root cause of interest-rate risk lies in the fact that as the rate of interest paid on U.S. government securities rises or falls, there is a rise or fall in the rates of return demanded on alternative investment vehicles, such as stocks and bonds issued in the private sector. In other words, as the cost of money changes for nearly risk-free securities (U.S. governments), the cost of money to more risk-prone issuers (private sector) will also change.

Investors normally regard U.S. government securities (USGs) as coming closest to being risk-free. The interest rates demanded on USGs are thought to approximate the "pure" rate of interest, or the cost of hiring money at no risk. Changes in rates of interest demanded on USGs will permeate the system of available securities, from corporate bonds down to the riskiest common stocks.

Interest rates on USGs shift with changes in the supply and demand for government securities. For example, a large operating deficit experienced by the federal government will require financing. Issuance of added amounts of USGs will increase the available supply. Potential buyers of this new supply may be induced to buy only if interest rates are somewhat higher than those currently prevailing on outstanding issues. Should rates on USGs advance from, say, 9 to 9 1/4 percent, investors holding outstanding issues that yield 9 percent will notice a decline in the price of their securities. Since the rate of 9 percent is fixed by contract on these "old" USGs, a potential buyer would be able to realize the competitive 9 1/4 percent rate only if the present holder "marked down" the price. As the rate on USGs advances, they become relatively more attractive and other securities become less attractive. Consequently, bond purchasers will buy governments instead of corporates. This will cause the price of corporates to fall and the rate on corporates to rise. Rising corporate bond rates will eventually cause preferred and common stock prices to adjust downward as the chain reaction is felt throughout the system of security yields. (The exact nature and extent of this markdown process and the relationships between rates, prices, and maturity will be explored in Chapter 11.)

Thus there is a rational structure of security yields that is highly interconnected. Shifts in the "pure" cost of money will ripple through the structure. The direct effect of increases in the level of interest is to cause security prices to fall across a wide span of investment vehicles. Similarly, falling interest rates precipitate price markups on outstanding securities.

In addition to the direct, systematic effect on all security prices, there are indirect effects on common stocks. First, lower or higher interest rates make the purchase of stocks on margin (using borrowed funds) more or less attractive. Higher interest rates, for example, may lead to lower stock prices because of a diminished demand for equities by speculators who use margin. Ebullient stock markets are at times propelled to some excesses by margin buying when interest rates are relatively low.

Second, many firms finance their operations quite heavily with borrowed funds. Others, such as financial institutions, are principally in the business of lending money. As interest rates advance, firms with heavy doses of borrowed capital find that more of their income goes toward paying interest on borrowed money. This may lead to lower earnings, dividends, and share prices. Advancing interest rates can bring higher earnings to lending institutions whose principal revenue source is interest received on loans. For these firms, higher earnings could lead to increased dividends and stock prices.

Purchasing-Power Risk

Market risk and interest-rate risk can be defined in terms of uncertainties as to the amount of current dollars to be received by an investor. *Purchasing-power risk* is the uncertainty of the purchasing power of the amounts to be received. In more everyday terms, purchasing-power risk refers to the impact of inflation or deflation on an investment.

If we think of investment as the postponement of consumption, we can see that when a person purchases a stock, he has forgone the opportunity to buy some good or service for as long as he owns the stock. If, during the holding period, prices on desired goods and services rise, the investor actually loses purchasing power. Rising prices on goods and services are normally associated with what is referred to as *inflation*. Falling prices on goods and services are termed *deflation*. Both inflation and deflation are covered in the all-encompassing term *purchasing-power risk*.

Generally, purchasing-power risk has come to be identified with inflation (rising prices); the incidence of declining prices in most countries has been slight. The most widely recognized sources of inflation are rising costs of production and excess demand for goods and services relative to their supply. In the vocabulary of economics, these types of inflation are called *cost-push* and *demand-pull*.

Demand-pull inflation is traceable to unfilled demand when the economy is at a full-employment level of operations. At this level, supply cannot be readily increased in the short run until the labor force or production expands. With demand high and increasing, available goods and services are allocated by price increases that bring supply and demand into equilibrium by forcing out some of the demand.

Cost-push inflation stems from increasing costs of production. As raw material and wage costs rise, producers attempt to pass along these increased costs through higher prices. In an environment where many labor contracts are up for renewal and workers feel their wages are lagging in comparison to prices, a spiral can be set off—wage increases followed by price increases, and so on.

Since we described purchasing-power risk as generally associated with price changes on goods and services, the question remains as to what specific price changes we should be concerned with as a measure of inflation (or deflation). The most common measure used on the level of prices on goods and services is the *consumer price index*. This index uses a "market basket" of goods and services for an average American family—including food, shelter, and a variety of services from medical to laundry—and prices them on a continuous basis. The *wholesale price index* measures the general price level associated with raw materials used in the manufacture of finished products. The record of inflation in recent years according to these indexes is shown in Table 5-1.

TABLE 5-1
PRICE INDEXES

Year	Wholesale Price Index (1967 = 100)	Consumer Price Index (1967 = 100)	Rate of CPI Inflation (%)
1967	100.0	100.0	—
1968	102.5	104.2	4.2
1969	106.5	109.8	5.3
1970	110.4	116.3	5.9
1971	112.9	121.2	4.2
1972	119.8	125.3	3.4
1973	134.7	133.1	6.2
1974	160.1	147.7	11.0
1975	174.9	161.2	9.1
1976	182.9	170.5	5.8
1977	194.2	181.5	6.4
1978	209.3	195.4	7.6
1979	235.5	217.4	11.2
1980	268.5	235.8	8.5

SOURCE: *Federal Reserve Bulletin.*

Rational investors should include in their estimate of expected return an allowance for purchasing-power risk, in the form of an expected annual percentage change in prices. If a cost-of-living index begins the year at 100 and ends at 103, we say that the rate of increase (inflation) is 3 percent [(103 − 100)/100]. If from the second to the third year, the index changes from 103 to 109, the rate is about 5.8 percent [(109 − 103)/103]. Referring to Table 5-1 we note that a market basket of goods and services that cost the average consumer $100 in 1967 rose to $170 in 1976. Using compound interest tables, we can see that the annual compound rate of inflation was about 6 percent between 1967 and 1976.

The necessity to adjust expected return for anticipated price changes can be seen in a simple example. Suppose that you lend $100 today for a promise to be repaid $105 at the end of the year. The rate of interest is 5 percent. However, assume that prices over the next year are expected to advance 6 percent (index from 100 to 106). The $105 received at the end of the year has a purchasing power of only 94 percent of

$105, or $98.70. You must charge a rate of 11 percent in the beginning (5 percent, plus 6 percent expected inflation) to allow for this.

Just as changes in interest rates have a systematic influence on the prices of all securities, both bonds and stocks, so too do anticipated purchasing-power changes manifest themselves. If annual changes in the consumer price index or other measure of purchasing power have been averaging steadily around 3 percent, and it appears that prices will spurt ahead by 4 1/2 percent over the next year, required rates of return will adjust upward. This process will affect government and corporate bonds as well as common stocks.

Market, purchasing-power, and interest-rate risk are the principal sources of systematic risk in securities; but we should also consider another important category of security risks—unsystematic risks.

Unsystematic Risk

Unsystematic risk is that portion of total risk that is unique or peculiar to a firm or an industry, above and beyond that affecting securities markets in general. Such factors as management capability, consumer preferences, labor strikes, and so on can cause unsystematic variability of returns for a company's stock. Since these factors affect one industry and/or one firm, they must be examined separately for each company.

The uncertainty surrounding the ability of the issuer to make payments on securities stems from two sources: (1) the operating environment of the business and (2) the financing of the firm. These risks are referred to respectively as *business risk* and *financial risk*. They are strictly a function of the operating conditions of the firm and the way in which it chooses to finance its operations. Our intention here will be directed to the broad aspects and implications of business and financial risk. In-depth treatment will be the principal goal of later chapters on analysis of the economy, the industry, and the firm.

Business Risk

Business risk is a function of the operating conditions faced by a firm and the variability these operating conditions inject into operating income and expected dividends. In other words, if operating earnings are expected to increase 10 percent per year over the foreseeable future, business risk would be higher if operating earnings could grow as much as 14 percent or as little as 6 percent than if the range were from a high of 11 percent to a low of 9 percent. The degree of variation from the expected trend would measure business risk.

Business risk can be divided into two broad categories: external and internal. *Internal business risk* is largely associated with the efficiency with which a firm conducts its operations within the broader operating environment imposed upon it. Each firm has its own set of internal risks, and the degree to which it is successful in coping with them is reflected in operating efficiency.

To a large extent, *external business risk* is the result of operating conditions imposed upon the firm by circumstances beyond its control. Each firm also faces its own set of external risks, depending upon the specific operating environmental factors that it must deal with. The external factors, from cost of money to defense-budget cuts to higher tariffs to a downswing in the business cycle, are far too numerous to list in detail, but the most pervasive external risk factor is probably the business cycle. The sales of some industries (steel, autos) tend to move in tandem with the business cycle, while the sales of others move countercyclically (housing). Demographic considerations can also influence revenues through changes in the birthrate, or the geographical distribution of the population by age group, race, and so on. Political policies are a part of external business risk; government policies with regard to monetary and fiscal matters can affect revenues through the effect on the cost and availability of funds. If money is more expensive, consumers who buy on credit may postpone purchases, and municipal governments may not sell bonds to finance a water-treatment plant. The impact upon retail stores, TV manufacturers, and producers of water purification systems is clear.

Among other things, the nature of general economic conditions will influence the level of revenues. This is an external influence or risk. But, from an internal-risk standpoint, how can a firm adjust to the business cycle? If we segregate costs of operation into fixed and variable costs, we see that as revenues change, if fixed costs absorb a large percentage of total costs, the firm will have difficulty curtailing expenses and production during declines in the economy; and it may also be sluggish to respond as demand surges upward. Such a firm would have large internal business risks relative to its ability to respond to changing business conditions. On the other hand, if total revenues come from a diversified list of products, it is possible that the products are not equally vulnerable to the business cycle to the same degree or at the same time. To this extent, internal risk is reduced by spreading the cycle effects over multiple products or product lines.

The extent to which a change up or down in total revenues leads to more or less than proportionate changes in earnings before interest and taxes (EBIT) is an indication of internal business risk. If a decline in revenue from one product line can be offset by an increase in another, leaving total revenue virtually unchanged, the firm is using product diversification to protect it against business risk. Downward pressures on revenues can also be minimized in EBIT via cost and production cutbacks and other evidences of operating skill on the part of management.

Financial Risk

Financial risk is associated with the way in which a company finances its activities. We usually gauge financial risk by looking at the capital structure of a firm. The presence of borrowed money or debt in the capital structure creates fixed payments in the form of interest that must be sustained by the firm. The presence of these interest commitments—fixed interest payments due to debt or fixed dividend payments on preferred stock—causes the amount of residual earnings available for common-stock dividends to be more variable than if no interest payments were required. Financial risk is avoidable risk to the extent that managements have the freedom to decide to borrow or not to borrow funds. A firm with no debt financing has no financial risk.

By engaging in debt financing, the firm changes the characteristics of the earnings stream available to the common-share holders. Specifically, the reliance on debt financing, called *financial leverage*, has at least three important effects on common-stock holders.[4]

---

[4]Debt financing is also referred to as *trading on the equity*, because by its use the company is able to acquire a larger amount of assets than equity contributed by owners.

Debt financing (1) increases the variability of their returns, (2) affects their expectations concerning their returns, and (3) increases their risk of being ruined.

Let us assume we have two identical companies, in the very same line of business and selling to the same types of customers, differing only with respect to the mix of their financing. One company, Careful, Inc., is financed entirely with 1 million shares of common stock, sold initially at $20 per share. The other company, Daring Co., is financed half with common stock (500,000 shares sold at $20 per share) and half with debt ($10 million) bearing interest at 5 percent. Each company has $20 million in assets, expected to yield earnings of $1 million, or 5 percent of total assets. We will assume that there are no corporate income taxes.

The earnings of $1 million can easily be converted into a per-share figure for each company. Careful, Inc., earns $1 per share on 1 million shares. Daring pays $500,000 in interest ($10 million × 5 percent), and the remaining $500,000 provides $1 in earnings for each of the 500,000 shares outstanding. At this point, both firms enjoy earnings per share of $1. There appear to be no effects of financial leverage on the stockholders' returns.

Let us consider the effects on both companies of a very good year for business and a very bad year for business, when earnings go up 50 percent in one case and down 50 percent in the other, as in Table 5-2.

TABLE 5-2
EARNINGS UNDER ALTERNATIVE RETURN ON ASSET ASSUMPTIONS

	Good Year	Bad Year
Assumed rate of return on assets	7 1/2%	2 1/2%
Operating earnings	$1.5 million	$.5 million
Earnings per share:		
Careful, Inc.	$1.50	$.50
Daring Co.	$2.00	$.00

Recall that originally each company earned $1 per share. Thus, a 50 percent rise in earnings (from $1 million to $1.5 million) causes a 50 percent rise in earnings per share for Careful, Inc., and a 100 percent rise for Daring Co. In the latter case, the effect is magnified because the bondholders receive only 5 percent on their money no matter how well or how poorly the company does. Thus, the shareholders of a levered company like Daring get a good deal of action from even small changes in operating earnings. Conversely, a 50 percent decrease in earnings (from $1 million to $500,000) causes the earnings per share of Careful to fall 50 percent (from $1 to $0.50), but Daring's earnings per share fall from $1 to zero, a 100 percent drop. It should be easy to see that when operating earnings fall to $500,000, there is only a 2 1/2 percent return on assets, and since bondholders still get their 5 percent, the difference is, in effect, taken from the pockets of shareholders. Leverage is a two-edged sword!

The significance is that not only does this fixed-return borrowed capital enhance the return to shareholders or reduce it substantially but the variation in returns for the owners of shares in companies with borrowed funds (levered firms) exceeds the variation for stockholders in unlevered firms. This variance in returns is what we refer to when we discuss financial leverage or financial risk. To the extent that firms have the freedom to choose how they will be financed, we say that financial leverage or financial risk is an *avoidable* risk, within the power of management to control.

The risk of shareholders' being ruined can be seen quite simply. Should even small negative rates of return on assets persist for a number of years in a row, stockholders' equity can be wiped out. Careful, Inc., shows a positive earnings per share of $.50 when the rate of return on assets is 2 1/2 percent, but Daring shows zero earnings per share at this level. Then what happens if the rate of return on the assets is zero percent? Careful earns zero on a per-share basis, whereas Daring *loses* $.50 per chare, or $500,000 (the amount of interest owed).

Negative rates of return can have even more dramatic effects than those already suggested. For example, a negative 4 percent return on assets is magnified into a negative 22 percent loss for Daring Co. A few years like this and equity can be literally wiped out. The risk of bankruptcy is an increasing function of the degree of financial leverage or financial risk.

Thus, we think of business risk as concerned with that zone of the income statement between revenues and EBIT; financial risk can be seen in that zone between EBIT and EBT (earnings before taxes).

If the underlying revenue, cost, and EBIT pattern of a firm is somewhat erratic (that is, has some degree of business risk), then the use of borrowed funds (financial risk) may magnify the impact of the eventual earnings and dividends carried through to the shareholders. In the example above, borrowed money has caused underlying volatility of rate of return on equity to be magnified or intensified. Such magnification can be disastrous in bad years like 1972, or beneficial in good years like 1971. To the extent that borrowed funds in the capital structure inject such magnification, real or imagined, bondholders and stockholders perceive greater risk (financial risk) atop existing business risk. As a result, interest payments, earnings, and, therefore, dividends take on a greater degree of uncertainty.

There are other, more exact measures of leverage and financial risk, as well as insights into its impact, which will be explored later in our examination of analysis of the firm. Suffice it to say here that all the risks we have mentioned combine to cause returns from securities to vary. The separate risk forces may move in tandem or at cross-currents in causing variations in returns for individual securities or classes of securities. For example, while rising interest rates are depressing the price of bonds and stocks in general, favorable developments in business risk may tend to cushion the blow in specific industries and companies. Now let's take a look at some ways of quantifying risk.

Assigning Risk Allowances (Premiums)

One way of quantifying risk and building a required rate of return (r) would be to express the required rate as being made up of a riskless rate plus compensation for individual risk factors previously enunciated, or as

$$r = i + p + b + f + m + o$$

where:

    i = real interest rate (riskless rate)

    p = purchasing-power-risk allowance

    b = business-risk allowance

    f = financial-risk allowance

    m = market-risk allowance

    o = allowance for "other" risks

The first step would be to determine a suitable riskless rate of interest. Unfortunately, no investment is risk-free. The return on U.S. Treasury bills or an insured savings account, whichever is relevant to an individual investor, can be used as an approximate riskless rate. Savings accounts possess purchasing-power risk and are subject to interest-rate risk of income but not principal. U.S. government bills are subject to interest-rate risk of principal. The riskless rate might be 8 percent.

Using the rate on U.S. government bills and assuming that interest-rate-and-risk compensation is already included in the USG bill rate, Figure 5-1 depicts the process of building required rate of return for alternative investments.

To quantify the separate effects of each type of systematic and unsystematic risk would be next to impossible, because of overlapping effects and the sheer complexity involved. In the remainder of the chapter we shall examine some proxies for packaging into a single measure of risk all those qualitative risk factors taken together that perhaps cannot be measured separately.

Stating Predictions "Scientifically"

Security analysts cannot be expected to predict with certainty whether a stock will increase or decrease in price, and by how much. The amount of dividend income may be subject to more or less uncertainty than price in the estimating process. The reasons are simple enough. There is not enough understanding of political and socioeconomic forces to permit predictions that are beyond doubt or error.

This existence of uncertainty does not mean that security analysis is valueless. It does mean that analysts must strive to provide not only careful and reasonable estimates of return but also some measure of the degree of uncertainty associated with these estimates of return. Most important, the analyst must be prepared to quantify the risk that a given stock will fail to realize its expected return.

The quantification of risk is necessary to ensure uniform interpretation and comparison. Verbal definitions simply do not lend themselves to analysis. A decision on whether to buy stock A or stock B, both of which are expected to return 10 percent, is not made easy by the mere statement that there is only a "slight" or "minimal" likelihood that the return on either will be less than 10 percent. This sort of vagueness should be avoided. Although whatever quantitative measure of risk is used will be at most only a proxy for true risk, such a measure provides analysts with a description that facilitates uniform communication, analysis, and ranking.

FIGURE 5-1
BUILDING A REQUIRED RATE OF RETURN

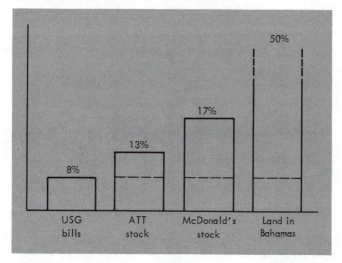

Pressed on what he meant when he said that stock A would have a return of 10 percent over some holding period, an analyst might suggest that 10 percent is, in a sense, a "middling" estimate or a "best guess." In other words, the return could be above, below or equal to 10 percent. He might express the degree of confidence he has in his estimate by saying that the return is "very likely" to be between 9 and 11 percent, or perhaps between 6 and 14 percent.

A more precise measurement of uncertainty about these predictions would be to gauge the extent to which actual return is likely to differ from predicted return—that is, the dispersion around the expected return. Suppose that stock A, in the opinion of the analyst, could provide returns as follows:

Return (%)	Likelihood
7	1 chance in 20
8	2 chances in 20
9	4 chances in 20
10	6 chances in 20
11	4 chances in 20
12	2 chances in 20
13	1 chance in 20

This sounds a little like weather forecasting. We have all heard the phrase "a two-in-ten chance of rain." This likelihood of outcome can be stated in fractional or decimal terms. Such a figure is referred to as a *probability*. Thus a "two-in-ten chance" is equal to 2/10, or .20. A likelihood of "four chances in twenty" is 4/20, or .20. When individual events in a group of events are assigned probabilities, we have a *probability distribution*. The total of the probabilities assigned to individual events in a group of events must always equal 1.00 (or 10/10, 20/20, and so on). A sum less than 1.00 indicates that events have been left out. A sum in excess of 1.00 implies incorrect assignment of weights or the inclusion of events that could not occur. Let us recast our "likelihoods" into "probabilities."

Return (%)	Probability
7	.05
8	.10
9	.20
10	.30
11	.20
12	.10
13	.05
	1.00

Based upon his analysis of economic, industry, and company factors, the analyst assigns probabilities subjectively. The number of different holding-period yields to be considered is a matter of his choice. In this case, the return of 7 percent could mean "between 6 1/2 and 7 1/2 percent." Alternatively, the analyst could have specified 6 1/2 to 7 and 7 to 7 1/2 percent as two outcomes, rather than just 7 percent. This fine tuning provides greater detail in prediction.

Security analysts use the probability distribution of return to specify expected *return* as well as *risk*. The expected return is the weighted average of the returns. That is, if we multiply each return by its associated probability and add the results together, we get a weighted-average return, or what we will call the expected average return.

(1) Return (%)	(2) Probability	(1) × (2)
7	.05	.35
8	.10	.80
9	.20	1.80
10	.30	3.00
11	.20	2.20
12	.10	1.20
13	.05	.65
	1.00	10.00%

The expected average return is 10 percent. The expected return lies at the center of the distribution. Most of the possible outcomes lie either above or below it. The "spread" of possible returns about the expected return can be used to give us a proxy of risk. It is possible for two stocks to have identical expected returns but quite different "spreads" or dispersions, and thus different risks. Consider stock B:

(1) Return (%)	(2) Probability	(1) × (2)
9	.30	2.7
10	.40	4.0
11	.30	3.3
	1.00	10.0%

Stocks A and B have identical expected average returns of 10 percent. But the spread for stocks A and B is not the same. For one thing, the range of outcomes from high to low return is wider for stock A (7 to 13). For B, the range is only 9 to 11. However, a wider range of outcomes does not necessarily imply greater risk; the range as a measure of dispersion ignores the relative probabilities of each of the outcomes.

The spread or dispersion of the probability distribution can also be measured by the degree of variation around the expected return. The deviation of any outcome from the expected return is

$$\text{Outcome} - \text{Expected return}$$

Since outcomes do not have equal probabilities of occurrence, we must weight each difference by its probability:

$$\text{Probability} \times (\text{Outcome} - \text{Expected return})$$

For purposes of computing a *variance*, we will square the deviations or differences before multiplying them by the relative probabilities:

$$\text{Probability} \times (\text{Outcome} - \text{Expected return})^2$$

The value of the squaring can be seen in a simple example. Assume three returns—9, 10, and 11 percent—each equally likely to occur. The expected return is thus (9%) .33 + (10%) .33 + (11%) .33 = .10. Since 10 percent is the expected return, the other values must lie equally above and below it. If we took an average of the deviations from 10 percent, we would get:

$$\text{Weighted deviation} = .33 \times (9 - 10) = -.33$$
$$= .33 \times (11 - 10) = +.33$$

The sum of the deviations or differences, multiplied by their respective probabilities, equals + .33 + (−.33), or zero. Squaring the differences eliminates the plus and minus signs to give us a better feel for the deviation. The variance is the weighted average of the squared deviations, with each weighted by its probability.

Table 5-3 shows the calculation of the variance for stocks A and B. The larger variation about the expected return for stock A is indicated in its variance relative to stock B (2.1 versus .6). Also shown is the *standard deviation*, the square root of the variance. Its usefulness will be examined shortly.

TABLE 5-3
CALCULATION OF VARIANCE AND STANDARD DEVIATION
FOR TWO STOCKS, A AND B

Stock A				Stock B			
(1)	(2)	(3)	(4)	(5)	(6)	(7)	(8)
Return Minus Expected Return	Difference Squared	Probability	(2) × (3)	Return Minus Expected Return	Difference Squared	Probability	(6) × (7)
7 − 10 = −3	9	.05	.45				
8 − 10 = −2	4	.10	.40				
9 − 10 = −1	1	.20	.20	9 − 10 = −1	1	.30	.30
10 − 10 = 0	0	.30	.00	10 − 10 = 0	0	.40	.00
11 − 10 = +1	1	.20	.20	11 − 10 = +1	1	.30	.30
12 − 10 = +2	4	.10	.40				
13 − 10 = +3	9	.05	.45				
		1.00	2.10			1.00	.60
Variance			2.10				.60
Standard deviation			1.45				.77

If we pause to reflect upon the significance of Table 5-3, we might notice that variance measures variability in *both* directions around the expected return. However, it might be more meaningful to think of risk from the mean downward. That is, can we really feel there is risk associated with returns *above* the expected return of 10 percent? Using only the negative deviations from the mean would give us what is called the *semivariance*. But wait. The deviations on either side of the mean are symmetrical, or balanced. The semivariance would be half the variance, for the probability distribution and the deviations below the mean are the mirror image of those above the mean. Hence, where there is this symmetry, the variance serves just as well as the semivariance. Let's compute semivariance for stock A and see if it is half the variance, or 1.05.

Whereas the variance was calculated by squaring each difference from the mean, multiplying the answer by the related probability, and summing the resulting amounts, the semivariance performs the same manipulations only for differences *below* the mean:

(1) Return Minus Expected Return	(2) Difference Squared	(3) Probability	(4) (2) × (3)
7 − 10 = −3	9	.05	.45
8 − 10 = −2	4	.10	.40
9 − 10 = −1	1	.20	.20
Semivariance			1.05

The *semideviation* would be the square root of the semivariance. However, few distributions of returns are sufficiently different from symmetrical to warrant use of the semivariance or semideviation. Further, our assumption of advance predictions is that expected returns will turn out to be approximately symmetrically distributed. Therefore we will use the variance and standard deviations as risk surrogates throughout this text in all cases. The expected return and variance or standard deviation will be used in forming estimates for all securities.

In general, the expected return, variance, and standard deviation of outcomes can be shown as:

$$R = \sum_{i=1}^{n} P_i O_i \tag{5.1}$$

$$\sigma^2 = \sum_{i=1}^{n} P_i (O_i - R)^2 \tag{5.2}$$

$$\sigma = \sqrt{\sigma^2} \tag{5.3}$$

where:

R = expected return

σ^2 = variance of expected return

σ = standard deviation of expected return

P = probability

O = outcome

n = total number of different outcomes

The variability of return around the expected average is thus a quantitative description of risk. Moreover, this measure of risk is simply a proxy or surrogate for risk, since other measures could be used. The total variance is the rate of return on a stock around the expected average that includes both systematic and unsystematic risk.

Dividing Risk into Systematic and Unsystematic Components

For the purpose of analyzing stocks, systematic risk is defined as the part of total variability that is correlated with the variability of the overall stock market. Unsystematic risk, in turn, is the remaining portion of total variability, that is, the part that, by definition, does not correlate with the variability of stock prices in general.

To analyze the riskiness of common stocks in terms of systematic and unsystematic components requires a model of the returns-generating process. Based on empirical testing, the following model has become widely accepted:

$$R_s = a + \beta_s R_M + e \tag{5.4}$$

where R_s represents the return on the security in the period, a is the estimated return on the security when the market as a whole is stationary, β_s is a measure of the systematic volatility of the security, about which we will have more to say below, R_M is the return on the market index, and e is a random-error term embodying all of the factors that together make up unsystematic return. In essence, Equation 5.4 says that the return on any stock is related to the return on the market index in a linear fashion. It is commonly referred to as the *market model*.

A somewhat more intuitive idea of what the model says can be obtained with the help of a graphical presentation. Figure 5-2 presents a picture of the returns-generating model for two common stocks. The stock 1 line, referred to as stock 1's *characteristic line*, cuts across the vertical axis at a_{s1}, thus implying that the estimated return on this stock is equal to a_{s1} when the return on the market index is zero. Similarly, the vertical intercept of the stock 2 characteristic line designates the estimated return on stock 2 when the market is stationary, that is, a_{s2}. As the market returns varies from zero, however, the estimated return on both stocks changes: specifically, both move up and down with the market, but at different rates. Stock 1 tends to be the more responsive of the two, having a β_{s1} of .9, while stock 2 is less responsive, with a β_{s2} of .3.[5] In other words, stock 1 tends to move up and down systematically with the market at a rate that is 90 percent as volatile as the market, while stock 2's market correlated movements are only 30 percent as volatile as the market.

FIGURE 5-2
CHARACTERISTIC LINE AND BETA COEFFICIENT

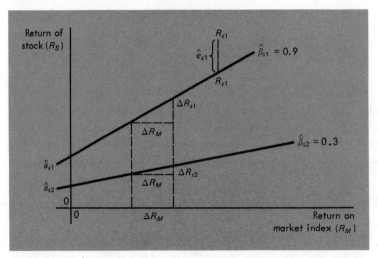

To understand how e comes into the analysis, we need to look at the actual return earned on stock 1 in a specific period, for example R_{s1}. Note that this return is somewhat above the stock 1 characteristic line, implying that stock 1 did better than might have been estimated strictly on the basis of the return on the market index during the period, that is, better than $\hat{R}_{s1}$. How do we explain this? The answer is that we explain it in terms of the factors that together make up the random error term, e. In other words, we say that the non-market-related factors (random error term) produced that portion of stock 1's return above what would have been estimated strictly on the basis of the market return during the period, that is, above R_{s1}. Algebraically, then,

$$e_{s1} = R_{s1} - \hat{R}_{s1} \qquad (5.5)$$

[5]Note in Figure 5-2 that for a change of ΔR_M, stock 1's return changes by ΔR_{s1}, whereas stock 2's return changes by only ΔR_{s2}.

The errors occur either because we do not include all of the pertinent variables that influence the asset's rate of return, or because the data used to calculate the line of best fit are not "clean."

If all the observations were exactly on the characteristic line, a change in the rate of return on the market would fully explain a change in the rate of return on the single asset. But all the points are not, in fact, on the line. So the line of best fit represents the average relation that will exist between changes in the market's rate of return and the rate of return on the asset. The goodness of fit depends on how spread out the points are from the line itself. In Figure 5-3(a) the points are very close to the line, and we could have a great deal of confidence in its ability to tell us what the relationship really is. In Figure 5-3(b) they diverge considerably from the line, and we would have less confidence in it.

FIGURE 5-3
THE GOODNESS OF FIT OF CHARACTERISTIC LINES

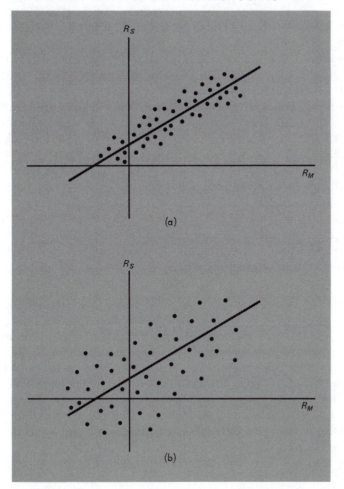

Having introduced the empirical model of the returns generating process, we are ready to consider the analysis of risk in terms of its systematic and unsystematic components. From Equation 5.2 it should be clear that the total variance of the return on stock, $\sigma^2(R_s)$, is equal to the sum of the variances associated with the various terms on the right-hand side. Of course, because a is a constant, its variance is zero; thus we are left with the following expression:

$$\sigma^2(R_s) = \beta_s{}^2 \sigma^2(R_M) + \sigma^2(e_i) \tag{5.6}$$

where $\sigma^2(R_M)$ and $\sigma^2(e_i)$ stand for the variances of the market and unsystematic components of the return, respectively.

Earlier we said that beta was a measure of a security's systematic volatility. By focusing on Equation 5.6, the reason for this statement should become clear. In effect, the first term on the right-hand side, $\beta^2 \sigma^2(R_M)$, represents that portion of total return variance that is related to the market (i.e., the systematic risk). But since $\sigma^2(R_M)$ is nothing more than the market variance itself, it is $\beta_i{}^2$ (i.e., the square of β_i) that is the operational and dominant factor in determining the size of the term. Hence, beta is an index of the systematic risk on a stock; by definition, $\sigma^2(e_i)$ is a measure of the unsystematic risk.

What determines the size of a stock beta? It is dependent on how rapidly and consistently a stock's return moves up and down with the market, on the extent to which its returns vary and are correlated with market returns.

Because the systematic risk of various securities differs due to their relationships with the market, ranking them by their beta coefficients is equivalent to ranking by systematic risk. High-beta securities are frequently referred to as high-risk securities. More specifically, securities with a beta coefficient larger than 1 are more volatile than the overall market, while those with betas smaller than 1 are less risky than the market. The beta coefficient of the market index is, by definition, 1.

The importance of beta coefficients is not limited to common stocks. They are a general measure of undiversifiable risk—a measure that is applicable to all risky assets. Although extensive estimates of beta coefficients are not readily available for most preferred stocks and bonds, they are probably substantially lower than stock betas, thereby implying smaller systematic risks relative to common stocks.

Range of Betas

Estimated beta coefficients for almost all NYSE- and AMEX-listed common stocks are readily available from investment services and brokerage houses. Table 5-4, for example, presents *Value Line*'s estimated beta coefficients for a selected group of common stocks covering a range of betas. Because of differences in the method of calculating returns, the particular index used to represent a measure of market returns, the length of the assumed holding period, and the particular time period selected for estimation, beta coefficients can vary somewhat by source. Further detail on the exact calculation of *a*, *b*, and *e* will unfold in Chapter 18.

TABLE 5-4

BETA COEFFICIENTS OF A SELECTED GROUP OF COMMON STOCKS
ESTIMATED BY VALUE LINE

Rubbermaid, Inc.	0.75	Hewlett-Packard	1.15
Southeast Public Service	0.45	Anheuser-Busch	0.90
Tonka Corp.	1.30	Dunkin' Donuts	1.25
Tootsie Roll, Inc.	0.85	Hershey Foods	0.70
Union Corp.	1.20	MCI Communications	1.50
U.S. Steel	1.00	McDonald's Corp.	1.05
Witter (Dean) Reynolds	1.55	Penn Central Corp.	1.40
Zayre Corp.	1.40	Tandy Corp.	1.45
American Express	1.10	Wendy's Int'l, Inc.	1.30
Boston Edison	0.60	Avon Products	0.90
Cessna Aircraft	1.20	Bank of New York	0.75
Church's Fried Chicken	1.20	Gillette	0.80
Eastman Kodak	1.05	Standard Oil (California)	1.05
GCA Corp.	1.85	Atlantic City Electric	0.55
Greyhound Corp.	0.85	Chase Manhattan Corp.	1.00

SOURCE: *The Value Line Investment Survey*, July 31, 1981.

Risk-Return: Stocks versus Fixed Income Securities

A significant recent study of rates of return on common stocks and bonds was conducted by Roger G. Ibbotson and Carol L. Fall.[6] They concluded that the annual compounded rate of return and the risk (standard deviation of returns) for selected investment vehicles over the period 1947-78 was as given in Table 5-5.

TABLE 5-5

U.S. CAPITAL MARKET TOTAL ANNUAL RETURNS, 1947-1978

	(1) Compound Return (%)	(2) Standard Deviation (%)
Common Stocks		
New York Stock Exchange	10.16	17.73
Over-the-counter market*	12.63	21.79
Fixed-income corporate securities		
Preferred stocks	2.92	9.20
Long-term corporate bonds	2.21	6.72

*National Quotation Bureau Industrial Index.

SOURCE: R.G. Ibbotson and C.L. Fall, "The United States Market Wealth Portfolio," *The Journal of Portfolio Management*, Fall 1979, pp. 82-92.

The higher returns and risks from common stock versus preferred stocks and corporate bonds is as we might expect.

However, while, for example, long-term corporate bond returns are about one-fifth of NYSE returns, their risk is only about half as much. The roughly similar return-to-risk relationship for NYSE and OTC stocks is interesting.

[6]R. G. Ibbotson and C. L. Fall, "The United States Market Wealth Portfolio," *The Journal of Portfolio Management*, Fall 1979, pp. 82-92.

To reemphasize the meaning of risk and return, let us take a closer look at the OTC results. Recall that when rates of return are normally distributed, about two-thirds of our results should occur between plus or minus one standard deviation of the mean (average) return and about 95 percent within two standard deviations. For OTC stocks we would expect annual returns to be somewhere between −9 and +34 percent two out of three times (12.63 ± 21.79), and between −30 and +56 percent 9 1/2 out of 10 times. The layman's translation of these statistics will help to characterize the kind of "game" this is. What we are saying is that one could expect to earn a return between −30 and +56 percent investing in OTC stocks over nine out of ten years. However, we can't tell anything about the positive and negative return sequence. That is, we could have two years of negative returns followed by nineteen years of positive returns. Needless to say, a series of negative returns of sufficient size could put you out of the "game" prior to the hoped-for string of positive results!

Fortunately, history tells us that three or more years of back-to-back negative returns has been unlikely. Table 5-6 shows NYSE and OTC rates of return by year. Note,

TABLE 5-6
COMMON STOCKS: RATE OF RETURN (%)

Year	NYSE	OTC
1947	3.30	2.07
1948	2.32	−3.04
1949	20.21	16.26
1950	29.95	29.22
1951	20.95	15.72
1952	13.32	6.52
1953	.37	3.29
1954	50.53	50.40
1955	25.26	18.88
1956	8.62	15.33
1957	−10.70	−12.16
1958	44.27	48.34
1959	12.87	9.53
1960	.60	.99
1961	27.17	36.28
1962	−9.38	−12.36
1963	21.33	24.44
1964	16.29	25.87
1965	13.92	33.15
1966	−8.96	.90
1967	26.96	56.38
1968	12.78	23.02
1969	−9.85	1.67
1970	1.40	−12.54
1971	15.89	40.65
1972	17.92	34.07
1973	−16.97	−22.88
1974	−26.85	−38.50
1975	37.73	37.48
1976	26.27	15.17
1977	−4.89	14.74
1978	7.40	14.31

SOURCE: R.G. Ibbotson and C.L. Fall, "The United States Market Wealth Portfolio," *The Journal of Portfolio Management,* Fall 1979, pp. 82-92.

however, the plight of an investor in OTC stocks who entered the "game" in 1973 and exited at the end of 1974. A whopping 61 percent loss. Ouch!

Table 5-7 is a matrix which measures how closely the rates of return are correlated on various types of securities. The strongest possible co-movement measure would be 1.00. This suggests that rates of return move in exact unison; when the return on one security is positive (negative), the return on the other is also positive (negative). Moreover, the size of the returns closely correspond, as well as the direction (plus or minus).

TABLE 5-7
SECURITY RETURNS CORRELATION MATRIX
(1947-1978)

	NYSE	OTC	Preferred Stock	Corporate Bonds
NYSE	1.00			
OTC	.876	1.00		
Preferred stock	.371	.178	1.00	
Corporate bonds	.282	.120	.894	1.00

SOURCE: R.G. Ibbotson and C.L. Fall, "The United States Market Wealth Portfolio," *The Journal of Portfolio Management*, Fall 1979, pp. 82-92.

The strong correlation between NYSE and OTC stocks is clear (.876), as is that of preferred stocks and corporate bonds (.894). The relatively weak co-movement of returns on preferred stocks and common stocks (.371 and .178) and most important between bonds and common stocks (.282 and .120) are noteworthy.

Summary

The risk associated with holding common stocks is really the likelihood that expected returns will not materialize. Should dividends or price appreciation fall short of expectations, the investor is disappointed. The principal sources behind dividend and price-appreciation uncertainties are forces and factors that are either controllable or not subject to control by the firm.

Uncontrollable forces, called sources of systematic risk, include market, interest-rate, and purchasing-power risks. Market risk reflects changes in investor attitudes toward equities in general that stem from tangible and intangible events. Tangible events might include expectations of lower corporate profits; intangible events might be overreaction to lower expected profits and the resultant panic selling. Interest-rate risk and purchasing-power risk are associated with changes in the price of money and other goods and services. Increases in interest rates (the price of money) cause the prices of all types of securities to be marked down. Rising prices of goods and services (inflation or purchasing-power changes) have an adverse effect on security prices, since the postponement of consumption through any form of investment means less "real" buying power in the future.

The principal sources of unsystematic risk affecting the holding of common stocks are business risk and financial risk. Business risk refers to changes in the operating environment of the firm and how the firm adapts to them. Financial risk is related to the debt-and-equity mix of financing in the firm. Operating profits can be magnified up or down, depending upon the extent to which debt financing is employed and under what terms.

The various sources of risk in holding common stocks must be quantified so that the analyst can examine risk in relationship to measures of return employed in Chapter 4. A reasonable surrogate of risk is the variability of return. This proxy measure in statistics is commonly the variance or standard deviation of the returns on a stock around the expected return. In reality, the variation in return *below* what is expected is the best measure of risk, but we saw that since the distribution of returns on stocks is nearly normal in a statistical sense, the semideviation or semivariance below the expected value need not be calculated.

Questions and Problems

1. Identify the risks normally associated with the following terms: (a) investor panic, (b) cost-of-living, (c) labor strikes, (d) increased debt/equity ratios, (e) product obsolescence.

2. Of those risks normally associated with the holding of securities, (a) what three risks are commonly classified as systematic in nature? (b) what risks are most prevalent in holding common stocks?

3. Show in tabular form a frequency distribution of the sums obtained by tossing a pair of dice.

4. Show a simple example using probabilities where two securities have equal expected returns but unequal variances or risk in returns.

5. A stock costing $100 pays no dividends. The possible prices that the stock might sell for at the end of the year and the probability of each are:

End-of-Year Price	Probability
$ 90	.1
95	.2
100	.4
110	.2
115	.1

  a. What is the expected return?
  b. What is the standard deviation of the expected return?
  c. What is the semideviation of the expected return?

6. Cite recent examples of political, social, or economic events (market risk) that have excited (a) the stock market, and (b) stocks in a specific industry, to surge ahead or plummet sharply.

7. Mr. Calvert has analyzed a stock for a one-year holding period. The stock is currently selling for $10, but pays no dividends, and there is a fifty-fifty chance that the stock will sell for either $10 or $12 by year-end. What is the expected return and risk if 250 shares are acquired with 80 percent margin? Assume the cost of borrowed funds is 10 percent. (Ignore commissions and taxes.)

8. What is the significance to an investor of a stock with the following specifications: expected return = .10, variance = .10, semivariance (below the mean) = .01?

9. Stocks Q and R do not pay dividends. Stock Q currently sells for $50 and R for $100. At the end of the year ahead there is a fifty-fifty chance that Q will sell for either $61 or $57 and R for either $117 or $113. Which stock, Q or R, would you prefer to purchase now? Why?

10. Determine dividends paid and the high and low prices on shares of IBM from *Value Line, Moody's Handbook of Common Stocks*, or other sources. Assuming the IBM was bought and sold each year from 1972 through 1978 at the average of the high-low price and that dividends for the year were collected, calculate, for the years 1972 through 1978, (a) the average annual holding-period yield, and (b) the standard deviation of the annual returns.

11. An investor has a normal required rate of return of 9 percent, which includes expectations of an annual rate of inflation of 4 percent. How much should he be willing to pay for a stock that pays no dividends and is expected to sell for $30 at the end of the year, if he intends to hold the stock until year-end? What if inflation expectations change to 3 percent?

12. Russo Corporation has been in the business of distributing national brands of swimming pools for many years. Recently the owner's son has been encouraging his father to increase the size of the business by 50 percent through distributing a complete line of ski equipment and accessories. In what ways would the expansion alter the business risk associated with the operation of Russo Corporation as merely a swimming-pool distributor?

13. Financial risk or leverage in the case of individuals is normally associated with margin trading, or increasing one's ability to purchase securities by borrowing money. Investor A has analyzed a stock for a one-year holding period. There is a fifty-fifty chance that the stock, currently selling at $10, will sell for $9 or $12 by year-end. The investor can borrow on 50 percent margin from his bank at 9 percent per annum. (Ignore taxes and transaction costs.)

      a. What are the investor's expected holding-period yield and risk if he buys 100 shares and does not borrow from his bank?

      b. What are expected yield and risk if he buys 200 shares, paying half the cost with borrowed funds at 9 percent per annum?

part three
COMMON-STOCK
ANALYSIS

Analytical Framework for Common Stocks

The primary motive for buying a stock is to sell it subsequently at a higher price. In many cases, dividends will be expected also. Dividends and price changes are the principal ingredients in what investors regard as return or yield.

If an investor had impeccable information and insight about dividends and stock prices over subsequent periods, he would be well on his way to great riches. But the real world of investing is full of political, economic, social, and other forces that we do not understand sufficiently to permit us to predict anything with absolute certainty. Forces intermix and flow at cross-currents. Nothing is static.

For the security analyst, what primary influences will determine the dividends to be paid on a stock in the future and what the stock price will be in the future are the ultimate questions to be answered. A logical systematic approach to estimating future dividends and stock price is indispensable.

The framework we will be using is the economic-industry-company approach, or the E-I-C framework.

Economic and Industry Analysis

King observed that, on the average, over half the variation in a stock's price could be attributed to a market influence that affects all stock-market indexes, such as the Dow Jones Industrial Average or the Standard & Poor's 500 Stock Index.[1] But stocks are also subject to an industry influence, over and above the influence common to all stocks. King noted that this industry influence explained, on the average, about 13 percent of the variation in a stock's price. In sum, about two-thirds of the variation in the prices of stocks observed in King's study was the result of market and industry influences or factors. King actually examined only about sixty companies, so it is dangerous to extrapolate from this small sample to a generalization about *all* stocks.

[1] B. F. King, "Market and Industry Factors in Stock Price Behavior," *Journal of Business,* 39 (January 1966), 139-90.

However, although the amount of variation in a stock's price attributable to the market may be more or less than the percentage observed by King, the impact of a common market influence is obviously something to be contended with.

The significance of these conclusions seems to be that in order to estimate stock price changes, an analyst must spend more than a little time probing the forces operating in the overall economy, as well as influences peculiar to industries he is concerned with. A failure to examine overall economic and industry influences is a naive error, that of assuming that individual companies follow their own private paths in a vacuum.

It is important to predict the course of the national economy because economic activity affects corporate profits, investor attitudes and expectations, and ultimately security prices. An outlook of sagging economic growth can lead to lower corporate profits, a prospect that can engender investor pessimism and lower security prices. Some industries might be expected to hold up better, and stock prices of companies in these industries may not decline as much as securities in general. The key for the analyst is that overall economic activity manifests itself in the behavior of stocks in general—or the stock market, if you will. This linkage between economic activity and the stock market is critical.

Investing is a business of relative changes. When the economic outlook is assessed, along with the direction of changes in the overall market for stocks, the analyst must realize that even though industry groups and/or individual companies may find it difficult to "buck the trend," they do not necessarily respond to the same degree. For example, it is widely assumed that heavy-goods industries fare worse in economic recessions than do consumer-goods industries. Heavy-goods industries include automobiles (and related industries such as rubber, steel, glass) and machinery. Consumer-goods and service industries include utilities (telephone, power), food, and banks. Recessions or expansions in economic activity may translate into falling or rising stock markets with different *relative* price changes among industry groups.

For the analyst, industry analysis demands insight into (1) the key sectors or subdivisions of overall economic activity that influence particular industries, and (2) the relative strength or weakness of particular industry or other groupings under specific sets of assumptions about economic activity.

Chapter 6 considers how the analyst goes about forecasting the direction and degree of change in economic activity. Chapter 7 links the forecast of economic activity to the prediction of *relative* movements in specific industries and analysis of selected industries.

Company Analysis

Estimating dividends and price changes for individual stocks must be preceded by sound economic and industry analysis. Without these, the King study shows, an analyst is looking at only a third of the story.

The most immediately recognizable effect of economic and industry influences on a specific company is probably the impact on revenues. The sales of some industries (steel, autos) tend to move in tandem with the business cycle; others (food, telephone, utilities) are relatively immune from the cycle; still others (such as housing) move countercyclically. From the viewpoint of the individual company, adjustments to changes in the general business cycle can be different from those of the industry in general. Product mix and pricing peculiar to specific firms can cause total revenues to respond more or less to broad economic and industry impact. Diversified product lines, for example, make it possible for a company to spread cyclical effects.

Revenue changes in firms in the same industry with identical product mix and pricing policies may lead to different relative changes in costs. As we saw in Chapter 5, a company in which fixed costs absorb a large percentage of total costs may have difficulty curtailing expenses during economic declines, and responding as demand increases. A firm with a large proportion of its total costs variable may respond better, both up and down. In the end, the latter firm may show better earnings (revenue minus costs). The relationship of revenues and expenses to economic and industry changes, and the resulting earnings, is the focal point of the company analysis.

Earnings and Stock Price Changes

Many factors are responsible for producing revenue and in turn converting revenue into earnings. However, in the final analysis, stock price changes and dividends paid are to some degree governed by what happens to earnings. This connection between earnings and stock price is very much analogous to the connection between what a piece of equipment is worth and the earnings it is expected to produce. The exact nature of the earnings-stock price relationship is somewhat complex, and other factors affect the price of a stock. Chapters 8, 9, and 10 will examine factors at the company level influencing stock prices and dividends. For the time being we want to paint some broad strokes.

The current price of a stock will, in some measure, reflect market expectations of earnings. Stocks of companies with prospects for superior earnings growth will sell at higher prices relative to earnings than will those of slower-growing companies. For example, companies G and H are in the same industry. Both have just reported earning $1 per share. Stock G sells for $15 and stock H for $30. Investors are paying $15 in price for each $1 of current earnings for G; they are paying $30 in price for each $1 of current earnings for H. Analysts often refer to this relationship as the price-earnings ratio, or simply the "P/E."

The principal reason for the differences in P/E ratios (15 for G and 30 for H) can be traced to the fact that investors *expect* earnings to grow more rapidly for H than G. Unanticipated changes in earnings should result in an adjustment of the stock price. Should earnings exceed expectations, stock prices should rise. Prices should fall if earnings are below expectations. Numerous studies have been made on why stocks sell at different P/E ratios. The results tend to suggest that at any moment in time, P/E ratios differ between firms according to differences in projected earnings growth and variations in the rate of earnings growth. Higher P/E's are associated with more rapid earnings growth and less variation (greater stability) in the rate of that growth over time.

Knowledge of what determines P/E's is essential. We can use this information to determine an expected selling price for a stock at the end of the holding period. In effect, applying an estimated P/E to a forecast of earnings at the end of the holding period allows the analyst to determine the expected selling price:

$$P_1 = (P/E)_1(E_1)$$

where

P_1 = stock price, end of holding period

$(P/E)_1$ = price earnings ratio, end of holding period

E_1 = estimated earnings, end of holding period

The P/E ratio used at the end of the holding period will embody expectations of *future* earnings growth and stability, beyond the holding period. In subsequent chapters we will explore P/E ratios and alternative means for estimating end-of-holding-period price.

Earnings and Dividends

The remaining element of return an analyst must estimate is the dividend. Stocks pay all kinds of dividends, from $0 on up. However, it is possible that three stocks paying $0, $1, and $2 in current dividends will all sell for $40. This suggests that dividends being paid *now* are not all that is important to investors.

It is quite common to speak of the percentage of its reported earnings that a company pays in dividends. The *dividend payout ratio* is calculated by dividing annual dividends by current annual earnings. Hence, a company that earns $3.00 per share and pays $1.20 in dividends is said to have a 40 percent payout ratio ($1.20/$3.00). Companies sometimes pay dividends in excess of current earnings. Although this practice cannot be sustained for long, it can occur if the firm expects the earnings picture to improve in the near future. In such cases the payout ratio exceeds 100 percent. Dividend payments when earnings are zero or below provide payout ratios that lack quantitative significance.

The dividend paid by a company in a given quarter or year is strongly tied to earnings. However, the dividend paid in absolute dollar terms or relative to current earnings does not necessarily reflect current earnings alone, but past and expected future earnings as well.

Many corporations recognize two fairly clear notions about the reaction of investors to dividends. First, absolute dollar levels, once established, are reduced only when it is clear that declining earnings will not recover. Second, declining stock prices are associated with reduction in absolute dollar dividends.

The most positive effects on stock price seem to lie in maintaining a "target" payout ratio over time. Over time, companies will display payout patterns that can assist the analyst in making predictions of holding-period dividends. By and large, the payout ratio that emerges over the years depends to a large extent upon the expected return on new investment opportunities generated in the firm and the need for earnings retention as a source of financing these opportunities.

Auto and rubber are examples of industries that pay out a low percentage of earnings. Their earnings are typically unstable, and their reluctance to use borrowed money to any great extent means that they must rely heavily on equity financing. Earnings retention provides a big assist in this area. The air-transport and office-equipment industries are also known for low dividend payouts, but for other reasons. Their rate of expansion of assets is so great that they retain earnings to support the use of debt. Air-transport companies face the double problem of cyclical growth. This means that while earnings trend upward over time, nonetheless they fluctuate widely. Often these companies use stock dividends instead of cash dividends in the face of heavy internal cash needs and unstable earnings.

Relatively high payout industries include in their ranks those whose rate of return on reinvested earnings is low. In other words, they are not expanding dramatically, and/or the amount of expansion they engage in does not require that large proportions of earnings be retained. The tobacco and paper industries are examples of high-payout industries.

The analyst's job is particularly difficult in those situations where a company does not follow a regular dividend policy. This subject will be pursued again in Chapter 10. Let us now begin our analysis of common stocks with the economic analysis.

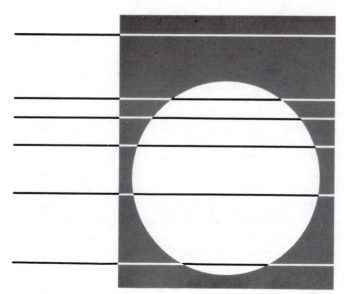

Economic Analysis

Timing is of critical importance in the investment process. It is not enough to know *what* to buy or sell; one must also know *when*. In order to facilitate a logical approach to the overall investment decision-making process (which includes knowing both *what* to buy and *when* to buy), in the next few chapters we will examine the role of the economic, industry, and company factors. Our purpose is to see how this information is relevant to the investment decision. However, first it is necessary to see how this economy-industry-company (E-I-C) approach fits into the framework established in Chapters 4 and 5.

We have noted that an investor in common stocks should be concerned with the return-and-risk characteristics of the securities under consideration. The expected return for a holding period of one year is determined by adding the price change that the investor expected to occur during the year to the dividends to be received, and dividing this sum by the price at the beginning of the year. A useful risk surrogate, we found, is the standard deviation of previous one-year-holding-period returns. The E-I-C framework provides a useful, logical means for arriving at the dividend and price change.

In brief, the analyst focuses first on the broad picture—the expected future economic environment during his one-year time horizon—in order to detect any probable emerging patterns. Such variables as the forecast of gross national product (GNP) and its key components, personal consumption, investment, government expenditures, and net exports, must be understood. In addition, monetary and fiscal policy, the outlook for corporate profits, and interest rates would be considered. From this analysis, the security analyst attempts to forecast which industries are likely to perform best in such an economic environment.[1] With this base, the E-I-C analysis continues to explore in depth the selected "good performers" among the universe of all domestic industries. After the industry analysis, the companies that the analyst feels will do best in the industries are explored in great detail. Company analysis culminates in a forecast of terminal price and dividends.

Before an investor commits funds in the market, he must decide if the time is right to invest in securities at all; and if so, he must then decide which type of security to purchase under the circumstances.[2] Thus, he must decide whether to purchase common stocks, options, preferred stocks, bonds, or some combination thereof. In this chapter we will explore the relevance of broad economic variables such as national income and defense expenditures to the investor or analyst considering the purchase of common stocks. In the process, we will place major emphasis on the techniques most frequently employed by business economists as they go about their business of short-term economic forecasting. These are important for the security analyst or investor to know, because he will be utilizing much of the output of the economists' efforts as a basis for his own opinion about the impending economic environment. In this respect, the analyst can better evaluate economic forecasts if he has at least some knowledge of alternative economic forecasting tools—not only the techniques but also their advantages and shortcomings. The techniques we will examine and evaluate include the use of surveys, key economic indicators, diffusion indexes, econometric model building, and the opportunistic model building. First, let us discuss the relationship of economic forecasting to the stock-investment decision more fully.[3]

Economic Forecasting and the Stock-Investment Decision

If an investor purchases the stock of an automobile manufacturer that is selling near an all-time high, and shortly thereafter the automobile workers go on strike for a long period of time, the investor will surely suffer a large paper loss on his investment. Certainly, if the investor had waited until the strike was close to being settled, other things being equal, his purchase price would have been considerably lower and his

---

[1]Frequently, the analyst or investor has in mind an industry that he is seriously considering as an investment opportunity. Here, the E-I-C framework is of value. The approach here is to determine first which economic variables are critical to the success of the industry. After forecasting these variables, he proceeds to the industry and company analyses. Both approaches will be utilized in a comprehensive example at the end of this chapter.

[2]Obviously, timing (which we consider to include both the *what* and *when* issues) is of critical importance not only in a purchase decision but also in the sell decision; however, in order to ease the explanation of the relevant factors, we will restrict our discussion to the purchase question, and leave it to the reader to adapt the methodology discussed in the text to the sell decision.

Furthermore, as an adjunct to the timing issue, the economic forecast of the analyst can be compared with the overall market's behavior as reflected in stock prices. If the analyst's expectations are markedly different from the apparent consensus market forecast, an investment action may be warranted. The reader should recall that if one accepts the efficient-market hypothesis, this will occur only in rare instances—and then for the good only if the investor analyst is particularly astute and skillful.

[3]Throughout this chapter we should keep in mind that the exact cause-and-effect relationships between macroeconomic variables and the stock market are not known. However, we know that they are related, and thus the economic environment must be considered.

potential capital gains greatly enhanced. In analyzing the economy, a careful analyst would have considered the potential impact of an impending automobile workers' strike.

However, there is yet another important reason for considering the economic environment before taking an investment action. As we have seen, research has discovered that approximately half the variability in stock prices is explained by the movement of the overall market. In investment jargon, this common or market effect is known as systematic risk. Furthermore, it is intuitively appealing to reason that the total market or some index of market performance is related to overall economic performance. That is, the success of the economy will utimately include the success of the overall market.[4] For without a positive and healthy economic environment, corporations in general will find it difficult to flourish over time, and investors' holding-period returns will suffer. This in turn will adversely affect an index of overall stock-market performance.

Above and beyond these broad, general relationships, we should observe that future prospects of many specific industries and firms will be tied to future developments in specific economic series, because profits are based on key economic factors. For example, labor-intensive industries will be tied to labor costs and conditions, most firms involved with transforming material and producing a final product will be tied to the costs of raw materials, savings and loan associations will be affected by the course of interest rates and the demand for mortgages, and leisure-products firms will be affected by the availability of leisure time and consumer disposable income.

Thus, we see the importance of relating economic phenomena to security price movements. To equip the security analyst and investor better for this undertaking, we will, in the next few sections, discuss several commonly used forecasting techniques, with major emphasis on the sources of this information, their potential usefulness to the analyst, and their limitations.

Forecasting Techniques

Short-Term Versus Long-Term Economic Forecasts

First, let us define some terms in the manner in which a business forecaster uses them. When he speaks of a *short-term forecast*, he is generally referring to one covering a period of up to three years, although frequently he means a much shorter period, such as a quarter or several quarters. An *intermediate forecast* refers to a three- to five-year period ahead. And finally, a *long-term forecast* refers to a period more than five years, and frequently ten or more years, in advance. These definitions are those of the business forecaster; but we must understand the different usage generally employed by a security analyst.

To a security analyst, a *short-term forecast* is related to the current U.S. tax law, which says that assets held for less than twelve months are liable for short-term tax

---

[4]Notwithstanding this, we will observe shortly that an index of 500 common-stock prices is classified as a leading indicator, with a median lead time of four months. However, it is still possible for individual economic components, such as disposable income, population, expenditures on defense, and income distribution by age group, to lead corporate sales, earnings, and the stock prices of certain industries and companies. Furthermore, if business conditions can be forecast far enough ahead, even in a general fashion, they will lead stock prices, thus *leading a leading indicator.*

treatment, and the *long-term forecast* with those assets held for twelve months and a day or more, which are treated as long-term assets for tax purposes. The next logical step is to reconcile these very different definitions of the economist and the analyst and show how they in fact fit together very nicely.

We noted in an earlier chapter that one of the differences between investment and speculation is the time horizon of the individual in question. That is, the speculator is interested in very short-term holds of securities (short-term in both a tax sense and a forecasting sense) in order to realize quick capital gains; on the other hand, the investor is interested in situations that will yield adequate returns in both dividends and capital gains for their risk class over a period of several years. However, we also observed earlier that even in the true investment situation, the investor or analyst must constantly review each security's performance both in an absolute sense and in a relative sense—relative to the market. Furthermore, he must regularly observe the state of the stock market, the money and capital markets, and the economy in general in order to ascertain if basic economic conditions have changed sufficiently to warrant his changing his investment strategy. This is another reason for viewing the macroeconomic picture—namely, to detect the relatively most attractive industries at a given moment. Thus, even for the pure investor with a long time horizon, we see that this long period is broken into several short-term periods. In other words, his initial long-term forecast can be broken down into a series of short-term forecasts that are constantly reviewed and revised. Therefore we will focus on a one-year horizon throughout our analysis.

In this chapter we will discuss only short-term forecasting techniques, realizing that when these various short-term forecasts are put side by side, they constitute a check for consistency with an independently arrived-at long-term forecast.[5]

Alternative Techniques of Short-Term Business Forecasting

Central to all forecasting techniques is an understanding of the national income and product accounts, which summarize both the receipts and the expenditures of all segments of the economy, whether government, business, or personal. These macro-economic accounts taken together measure the total of economic activity in the United States over some specified period of time. By definition, the total of the final expenditures must equal the total of the receipts in the economy. This total quantity is known as the *gross national product*, or GNP for short. Thus, to give it a formal definition, GNP is the *total value of the final output of goods and services produced in the economy*. The various approaches we are about to discuss are used in conjunction with forecasting GNP for short periods in advance, as well as for forecasting various components of GNP over similar periods of time.

It would be of no small interest to an analyst to have knowledge in advance of impending moves, particularly in those components of GNP that are most closely related to the industry or firm he is investigating. For example, if the analyst were considering a defense-oriented company or the defense industry, he would be much interested in a forecast of federal expenditures for defense. If he were examining a consumer-oriented firm, he would undoubtedly be very interested in a forecast of disposable personal

---

[5]For a discussion of an approach to long-term forecasting, see John P. Lewis and Robert C. Turner, *Business Conditions Analysis* (New York: McGraw-Hill, 1967).

income and per capita real GNP. (Real GNP is GNP adjusted for price-level changes.) Certainly, forecasts of the rate of population growth, the rate of GNP growth, and thus the rate of growth in per capita GNP would also be important to a consumer-oriented firm's future prospects.

FIGURE 6-1
ACTUAL AND POTENTIAL GROSS NATIONAL PRODUCT

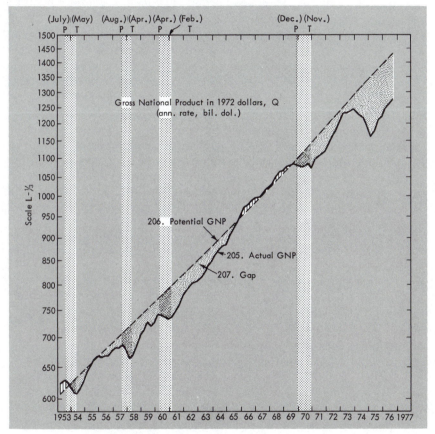

Current data for these series are shown on page 95. Trend line of 3.5 percent per year (intersecting actual line in middle of 1955) from 1st quarter 1952 to 4th quarter 1962, 3.75 percent from 4th quarter 1962 to 4th quarter 1965 and 4 percent from 4th quarter 1965 to 3rd quarter 1975. See special note on page 95.

SOURCE: U.S. Department of Commerce, *Business Conditions Digest*, October 1976.

Figure 6-1 depicts the economy's historical performance as reflected by the actual levels of GNP obtained versus the potential levels of GNP obtainable by the economy.[6] Information such as that contained in the chart is useful as a broad gauge of the eco-

---

[6]Potential GNP is defined as the level of GNP the economy could obtain assuming a 4 percent unemployment rate.

nomy's performance and can thus be used most directly in analyzing basic industries in the economy, and also as a benchmark in evaluating whether progress is being made on schedule toward an intermediate or long-term forecast level of GNP. When actual GNP is below potential GNP, such as in 1970-72, this period represents an underutilization of capacity probably brought on by unemployment in excess of 4 percent. If the forecaster or analyst has predicted an upturn in economic activity, then in time the gap between actual and potential GNP should begin to close. If this does not happen, perhaps it is time for the analyst to reconsider his forecast! In Figure 6-1 it can be seen that this gap closed almost entirely during 1973.

The matter of business forecasting is rather complex and quite specialized. As a result, it is not likely that the security analyst or investor will be called upon to make his own complete forecast of the entire economy, or for that matter a complete forecast of any individual sector in the economy. Nonetheless, it will undoubtedly be necessary for him to use, in his decision-making process concerning securities, economic forecasts or information that a business forecaster uses as a starting point; and thus, it is a prerequisite to knowledgeable and successful investing that he be able to understand and evaluate economic inputs and forecasts that are furnished to him.

To this end, we will next turn our attention to a brief review of major reputable approaches to short-term business forecasting. Our purpose will not be to turn the reader into a professional forecaster, but rather to equip him with the knowledge of the sources of this type of information and to help him understand the value, advantages, and limitations of these approaches.

ANTICIPATORY SURVEYS

Perhaps the most logical place to start a forecast is to ask prominent people in government and industry what their plans are with respect to construction, plant and equipment expenditure, and inventory adjustments, and to ask consumers what their future spending plans are. To the extent that these various entities plan and budget for expenditures in advance and adhere to their intentions, surveys of intentions constitute a valuable input in the forecasting process.[7] Table 6-1 contains a summary of the sources, uses, and timing of key forecasting information, including the sources of key survey results. These sources provide valuable insights to the analyst from people who ought to know.

Inasmuch as we are living in a decentralized economy (that is, an economy in which economic decisions are made by individual entities rather than dictated to them by a centralized government), it is necessary that a survey of intentions be based upon elaborate statistical sampling procedures. Furthermore, adequate facilities must be provided for the processing and tabulation of the results of the questionnaires. As a result, the use of surveys in forecasting is of recent vintage when compared with several of the other approaches we will discuss shortly; and because of this lack of history of performance, each forecaster must decide for himself the relative usefulness of the various surveys for his purposes. That is, the analyst must decide which surveys over-

---

[7]For a more complete discussion of the survey approach to forecasting, see Morris Cohen, "Surveys and Forecasting," in William F. Butler, Robert A. Kavesh, and Robert B. Platt, eds., *Methods and Techniques of Business Forecasting* (Englewood Cliffs, N.J.: Prentice-Hall, 1974).

TABLE 6-1

SOURCES AND USES OF KEY FORECASTING INFORMATION

Component of GNP	Type of Information	Source and Date	Uses of the Information
Federal government spending	1. President's budget message to Congress.	Newspapers carry summaries in January. Also published by government.	Provides the most important information on federal expenditures for the next fiscal year, starting on July 1. Is subject to revision by Congress.
	2. Summary of the budget message.	*The Budget in Brief* (Government publication in January).	Presents a summary of the budget message.
	3. Review of the economic situation with emphasis on the federal budget.	President's *Economic Report* (Government publication in late January).	Presents an interpretation of the budget and its economic implications.
	4. Review of the economic situation with emphasis on the federal budget.	*Midyear Budget Review* (Government publication in August).	Presents a review of the federal spending program for the current fiscal year, reflecting congressional revisions of the budget.
	5. Reports on congressional action on presidential spending plans.	Newspapers and weekly magazines throughout the sessions of Congress.	Provides information on the success or failure of the President's program in Congress, as well as predictions of future plans both of the President and Congress.
State and local government spending	1. Data on the levels of state and local government spending in recent periods.	The national income accounts in the *Survey of Current Business* (monthly).	The usual procedure is to extrapolate the recent trend into the future, with possible revisions based on newspaper reports on expedited programs or on financial difficulties.
Investment in plant and equipment	1. Surveys of intentions to invest.	McGraw-Hill Book Company (*Business Week* in November); also Department of Commerce and SEC (*Survey of Current Business*, November, March, and other issues).	These surveys provide excellent information in business investment plans for the coming year (or quarter). The past record of these surveys is good for most periods.
	2. New orders for durable goods.	*Survey of Current Business* (monthly).	Since orders usually lead actual production and sales, this series provides suggestions on future changes in investment.
	3. Nonresidential construction contracts (F.W. Dodge Index).	*Survey of Current Business* (monthly) and *Business Conditions Digest* (monthly).	Since construction awards should normally lead actual construction, this series suggests potential changes in the building of factories, office buildings, stores, etc.
Residential construction	1. Family formation.	Intermittent projections by the Bureau of the Census.	Provides information of a key segment of the potential market for new housing.
	2. Residential construction contracts awarded or housing starts.	*Survey of Current Business* (monthly) and *Business Conditions Digest* (monthly).	Provides an indication of potential changes in housing construction before those changes take place.

TABLE 6-1 (cont.)

Component of GNP	Type of Information	Source and Date	Uses of the Information
Residential construction (cont.)	3. Mortgage terms and ease of securing loans (down payments, interest rates, monthly payments).	Newspapers provide intermittent reports. *Federal Reserve Bulletin* (monthly).	Information on the terms on FHA, VA, and regular mortgages indicates the financial restraints on the purchase of new homes.
	4. Vacancy rate.	Bureau of Labor Statistics.	Indicates the extent of saturation of the housing market.
	5. Home-building survey.	*Fortune* magazine (monthly).	Indicates developments in residential construction.
Inventory investment	1. Ratios of inventories to sales on the manufacturing, wholesaling, and retailing levels (requires computations involving series on inventories and series on sales).	*Survey of Current Business* (monthly).	Indicate whether inventories are high or low in relation to a "normal" ratio. Must be interpreted with caution in the light of recent changes in final sales and the attitude of businessmen toward inventories.
	2. Manufacturers' inventory expectations.	*Survey of Current Business* (monthly).	Indicate extent to which businessmen expect to expand or contract inventories.
	3. Inventory surveys.	*Fortune* magazine (monthly).	On the basis of sales expectations and assumed inventory-sales ratios, estimates amount of inventory change.
Consumer durable goods	1. Surveys of consumers' intentions to spend and save (including intention to buy automobiles).	Survey Research Center, University of Michigan and Federal Reserve Board. *Federal Reserve Bulletin* (quarterly).	Indicates intentions to purchase durable goods. There is considerable correlation between these intentions and actual purchases.
	2. Rate of housing construction.	*Survey of Current Business* (monthly).	The building of new houses has an important influence on sales of furniture and appliances.
	3. Installment credit outstanding (in relation to the disposable personal income).	*Federal Reserve Bulletin* (monthly).	A high level of installment credit already outstanding may mean a lower willingness to incur new debt or a lower willingness to lend.
	4. Buying-plan surveys.	National Industrial Conference Board *Business Record.*	Suggests potential changes in the purchase of consumer goods.
	5. Projected consumer outlays on durable goods and housing.	*Consumer Buying Indicators* (quarterly).	Covers surveys of plans of consumers to purchase automobiles, appliances, furniture, and housing.
Nondurable consumer goods and services	1. Regression lines relating the past consumption of nondurable goods and services to the past disposable personal income.	Past issues of the *Survey of Current Business* provide the necessary data. Special articles in the *Survey of Current Business* review findings on such relationships.	Past relationships to disposable personal income show considerable stability, though the rate of sales to income rises in recession.
Comprehensive collection of indicators	1. Charts covering most of the best known indicators.	*Business Conditions Digest* (monthly).	A compact collection of charts covering indicators of income, production, prices, employment, and monetary conditions.

SOURCE: W.W. Haynes, *Managerial Economics: Analysis and Cases* (Dallas: Business Publications, Inc., 1969), pp. 131-33.

estimate and which underestimate the actual observed results, so that he can determine how the survey results need to be adjusted before inclusion in his individual forecast. This leads us to a most important point—that survey results should not be thought of as forecasts in themselves, but rather as a consensus that the forecaster can use in framing his own forecast.

Perhaps the greatest shortcoming of intention surveys is that the forecaster has no guarantee that the intentions will be carried out into final action. For this reason, the survey approach is most reliable for short-term forecasts that are continually monitored. External shocks such as strikes, political turmoil, or government action can cause sudden changes in intentions. But to the extent that intentions do become translated into final action, this survey approach provides a most valuable insight to the business investor.

Despite the shortcomings of anticipatory surveys, a great plus is their abundance and easy availability even to a noninstitutional investor. To name only three (see Table 6-1), *Fortune, Business Week*, and the *Survey of Current Business* are key sources of survey results and are publications that many investors either subscribe to or can easily consult at a local library.

BAROMETRIC OR INDICATOR APPROACH

Another forecasting tool is the barometric or indicator approach.[8] It has its foundations in work pioneered by Wesley C. Mitchell, Arthur F. Burns, and Geoffrey H. Moore, at the National Bureau of Economic Research (NBER). Currently, the U.S. Department of Commerce, following the NBER, has published in its *Business Conditions Digest* data on over 100 cyclical indicators, classified according to cyclical timing and economic process. In Table 6-2 we see a cross-classification of these indicators by economic process and timing. For example, there are ten series dealing with production and income of which two are leading indicators of business cycle peaks and eight are coincident indicators.

Table 6-2 demonstrates that the cyclical-timing classification is either leading, roughly coincident, or lagging. The leading indicators are those time series of data that historically reach their high points (peaks) or their low points (troughs) in advance of total economic activity; the roughly coincident indicators reach their peaks or troughs at approximately the same time as the economy; and finally, the lagging indicators reach their turning points after the economy has already reached its own. The NBER has painstakingly examined historical data going back in some cases as far as 1870, in order to ascertain which economical variables have led, lagged after, or moved together with the economy. In order to facilitate the use of the indicator approach, the NBER has developed a "short list" of indicators, consisting of twelve leading, four roughly coincident, and six lagging indicators. This short list is summarized graphically in Figure 6-2. The reader is urged to study Figure 6-3 so that he can fully appreciate the vast amount of information contained in Figure 6-2, which is representative of the kind of material contained in a typical issue of *Business Conditions Digest*. For example, indicator 1, the average workweek in manufacturing, is recorded in hours and plotted

---

[8]For a fuller treatment of this complex subject, see Julius Shiskin and Leonard H. Lempert, "Indicator Forecasting," in Butler, Kavesh, and Platt, *Methods and Techniques of Business Forecasting.* Shiskin and Lempert cite a number of excellent NBER sources of information.

TABLE 6-2

CROSS-CLASSIFICATION OF CYCLICAL INDICATORS BY ECONOMIC PROCESS AND CYCLICAL TIMING

A. Timing at Business Cycle Peaks

Economic Process / Cyclical Timing	I. EMPLOYMENT AND UNEMPLOYMENT (18 series)	II. PRODUCTION AND INCOME (10 series)	III. CONSUMPTION, TRADE, ORDERS, AND DELIVERIES (13 series)	IV. FIXED CAPITAL INVESTMENT (18 series)	V. INVENTORIES AND INVENTORY INVESTMENT (9 series)	VI. PRICES, COSTS, AND PROFITS (17 series)	VII. MONEY AND CREDIT (26 series)
LEADING (L) INDICATORS (62 series)	Marginal employment adjustments (6 series) Job vacancies (2 series) Comprehensive employment (1 series) Comprehensive unemployment (3 series)	Capacity utilization (2 series)	New and unfilled orders and deliveries (6 series) Consumption (2 series)	Formation of business enterprises (2 series) Business investment commitments (5 series) Residential construction (3 series)	Inventory investment (4 series) Inventories on hand and on order (1 series)	Stock prices (1 series) Commodity prices (1 series) Profits and profit margins (7 series) Cash flows (2 series)	Money flows (3 series) Real money supply (2 series) Credit flows (4 series) Credit difficulties (2 series) Bank reserves (2 series) Interest rates (1 series)
ROUGHLY COINCIDENT (C) INDICATORS (23 series)	Comprehensive employment (1 series)	Comprehensive output and real income (4 series) Industrial production (4 series)	Consumption and trade (4 series)	Backlog of investment commitments (1 series) Business investment expenditures (5 series)			Velocity of money (2 series) Interest rates (2 series)
LAGGING (Lg) INDICATORS (18 series)	Duration of unemployment (2 series)			Business investment expenditures (1 series)	Inventories on hand and on order (4 series)	Unit labor costs and labor share (4 series)	Interest rates (4 series) Outstanding debt (3 series)
TIMING UNCLASSIFIED (U) (8 series)	Comprehensive employment (3 series)		Trade (1 series)	Business investment commitments (1 series)		Commodity prices (1 series) Profit share (1 series)	Interest rates (1 series)

B. Timing at Business Cycle Troughs

Economic Process / Cyclical Timing	I. EMPLOYMENT AND UNEMPLOYMENT (18 series)	II. PRODUCTION AND INCOME (10 series)	III. CONSUMPTION, TRADE, ORDERS, AND DELIVERIES (13 series)	IV. FIXED CAPITAL INVESTMENT (18 series)	V. INVENTORIES AND INVENTORY INVESTMENT (9 series)	VI. PRICES, COSTS, AND PROFITS (17 series)	VII. MONEY AND CREDIT (26 series)
LEADING (L) INDICATORS (47 series)	Marginal employment adjustments (3 series)	Industrial production (1 series)	New and unfilled orders and deliveries (5 series) Consumption and trade (4 series)	Formation of business enterprises (2 series) Business investment commitments (4 series) Residential construction (3 series)	Inventory investment (4 series)	Stock prices (1 series) Commodity prices (2 series) Profits and profit margins (6 series) Cash flows (2 series)	Money flows (2 series) Real money supply (2 series) Credit flows (4 series) Credit difficulties (2 series)
ROUGHLY COINCIDENT (C) INDICATORS (23 series)	Marginal employment adjustments (2 series) Comprehensive employment (4 series)	Comprehensive output and real income (4 series) Industrial production (3 series) Capacity utilization (2 series)	Consumption and trade (3 series)	Business investment commitments (1 series)		Profits (2 series)	Money flow (1 series) Velocity of money (1 series)
LAGGING (Lg) INDICATORS (40 series)	Marginal employment adjustments (1 series) Job vacancies (2 series) Comprehensive employment (1 series) Comprehensive and duration of unemployment (5 series)		Unfilled orders (1 series)	Business investment commitments (2 series) Business investment expenditures (6 series)	Inventories on hand and on order (5 series)	Unit labor costs and labor share (4 series)	Velocity of money (1 series) Bank reserves (1 series) Interest rates (8 series) Outstanding debt (3 series)
TIMING UNCLASSIFIED (U) (1 series)							Bank reserves (1 series)

SOURCE: U.S. Department of Commerce, *Business Conditions Digest,* January 1981.

FIGURE 6-2

CYCLICAL INDICATORS

COMPOSITE INDEXES AND THEIR COMPONENTS

Chart A1. Composite Indexes

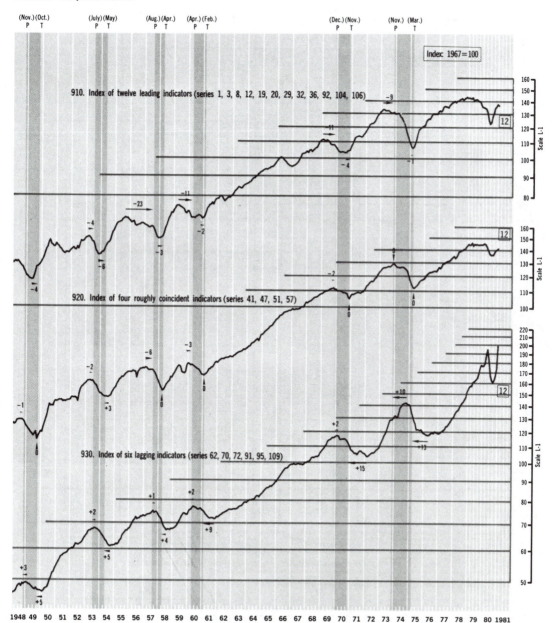

FIGURE 6-2 (cont.)

CYCLICAL INDICATORS

COMPOSITE INDEXES AND THEIR COMPONENTS—Continued

Chart A1. Composite Indexes—Continued

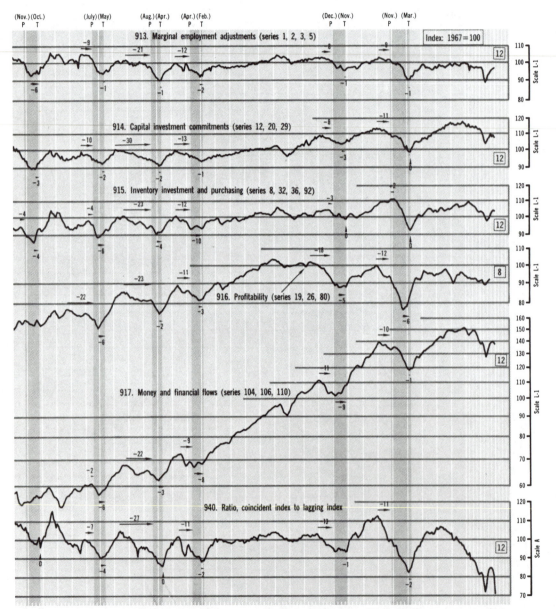

1948 49 50 51 52 53 54 55 56 57 58 59 60 61 62 63 64 65 66 67 68 69 70 71 72 73 74 75 76 77 78 79 80 1981

[1] This series is a weighted four-term moving average (with weights 1.2.2.1) placed on the terminal month of the span.

FIGURE 6-2 (cont.)

I
A

CYCLICAL INDICATORS

COMPOSITE INDEXES AND THEIR COMPONENTS—Continued

Chart A2. Leading Index Components

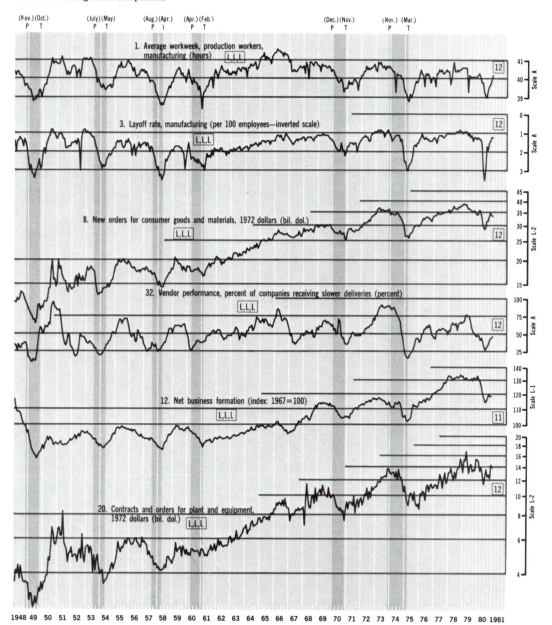

1948 49 50 51 52 53 54 55 56 57 58 59 60 61 62 63 64 65 66 67 68 69 70 71 72 73 74 75 76 77 78 79 80 1981

Current data for these series are shown on pages 61, 64, 65, and 66.

FIGURE 6-2 (cont.)

I A CYCLICAL INDICATORS

COMPOSITE INDEXES AND THEIR COMPONENTS—Continued

Chart A2. Leading Index Components—Continued

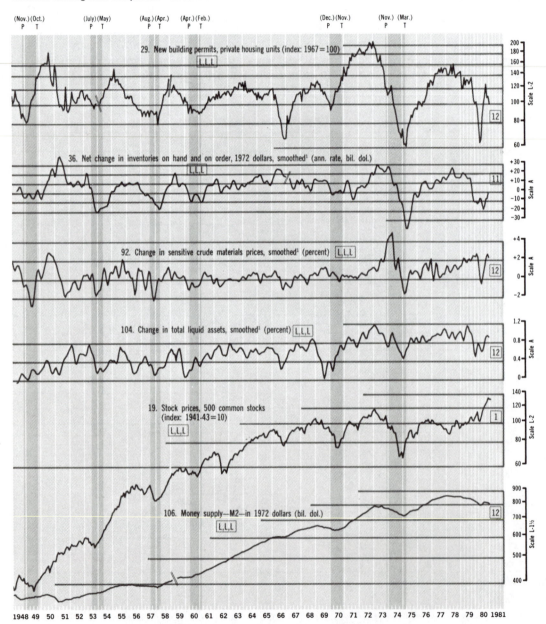

FIGURE 6-2 (cont.)

CYCLICAL INDICATORS

COMPOSITE INDEXES AND THEIR COMPONENTS—Continued

Chart A3. Coincident Index Components

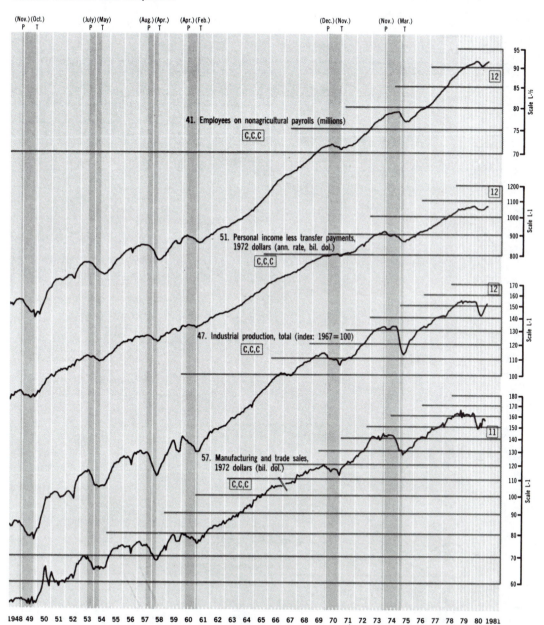

FIGURE 6-2 (cont.)

CYCLICAL INDICATORS

COMPOSITE INDEXES AND THEIR COMPONENTS—Continued

Chart A4. Lagging Index Components

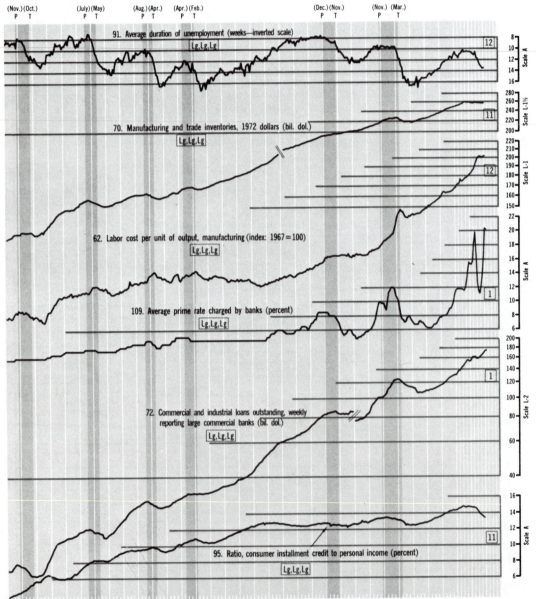

SOURCE: U.S. Department of Commerce, *Business Conditions Digest,* January 1981.

FIGURE 6-3

HOW TO READ CHARTS

Peak (P) of cycle indicates end of expansion and beginning of recession (shaded area) as designated by NBER.

Solid line indicates monthly data. (Data may be actual monthly figures or moving averages.)

Broken line indicates actual monthly data for series where a moving average is plotted.

Solid line with plotting points indicates quarterly data.

Parallel lines indicates a break in continuity (data not available, extreme value, etc.).

Solid line indicates monthly data over 6- or 9-month spans.

Broken line indicates monthly data over 1-month spans.

Broken line with plotting points indicates quarterly data over 1-quarter spans.

Solid line with plotting points indicates quarterly data over various spans.

Diffusion indexes and rates of change are centered within the spans they cover.

Solid line indicates percent changes over 3- or 6-month spans.

Broken line indicates percent changes over 1-month spans.

Solid line with plotting points indicates percent changes over 3- or 4-quarter spans.

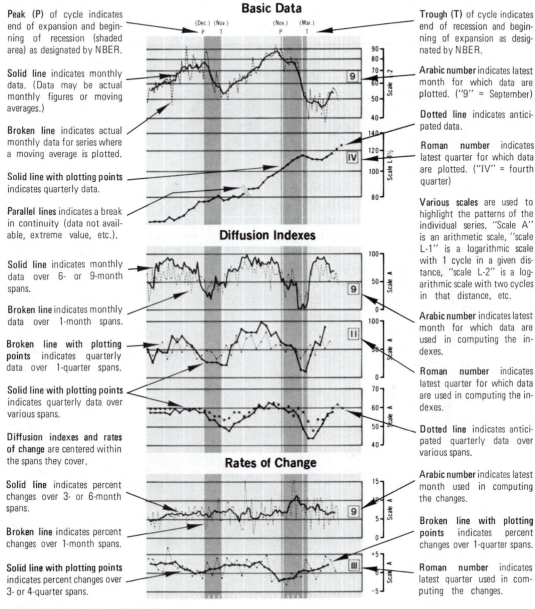

Basic Data

Diffusion Indexes

Rates of Change

Trough (T) of cycle indicates end of recession and beginning of expansion as designated by NBER.

Arabic number indicates latest month for which data are plotted. ("9" = September)

Dotted line indicates anticipated data.

Roman number indicates latest quarter for which data are plotted. ("IV" = fourth quarter)

Various scales are used to highlight the patterns of the individual series. "Scale A" is an arithmetic scale, "scale L-1" is a logarithmic scale with 1 cycle in a given distance, "scale L-2" is a logarithmic scale with two cycles in that distance, etc.

Arabic number indicates latest month for which data are used in computing the indexes.

Roman number indicates latest quarter for which data are used in computing the indexes.

Dotted line indicates anticipated quarterly data over various spans.

Arabic number indicates latest month used in computing the changes.

Broken line with plotting points indicates percent changes over 1-quarter spans.

Roman number indicates latest quarter used in computing the changes.

HOW TO LOCATE A SERIES

1. See ALPHABETICAL INDEX—SERIES FINDING GUIDE at the back of the report where series are arranged alphabetically according to subject matter and key words and phrases of the series titles, or—

2. See TITLES AND SOURCES OF SERIES at the back of the report where series are listed numerically according to series numbers within each of the report's sections.

SOURCE: U.S. Department of Commerce, *Business Conditions Digest.*

on an arithmetic scale, "scale A." The workweek dropped to a low during 1960, rose to nearly 42 hours a week during 1966, trended downward until 1970, started upward again, and then started declining in 1974.

Perhaps an explanation of the economic rationale behind the indicator approach will be helpful. For example, the rationale for the average workweek of production workers in manufacturing being expressed in hours is that before aggregate business activity picks up, the length of the workweek of production workers will increase. That is, before a company goes out and hires new workers, they will offer overtime to their present workers and thus utilize them more intensively. So we see that a leading indicator may be leading because it measures something that foreshadows a change in productive activity.

Figure 6-4 shows the relationship between leading indicators and industrial production, as well as the percent of leading indicators expanding. The ability of the leading indicators to signal changes in production well in advance is particularly in evidence in early 1974 and again in early 1975.

The indicator approach is most valuable in suggesting the *direction* of a change in aggregate economic activity; however, it tells us nothing of the magnitude or duration of the change. Table 6-3 contains a summary of the performance of the "short list" of indicators. The ratings can take on a value of 0 to 100, based on the six major criteria contained in the table. Notice that the highest score of the leading indicators was 81, stock prices. Most other scores among the leading indicators were in the 60s. This would indicate that forecasting based solely on leading indicators is a hazardous business.

There are several other difficulties with these techniques, which are excellently summarized by Lewis and Turner:

> Even with respect to indicating direction of change, the National Bureau's barometric technique encounters some difficulties. The leading series are subject to a number of wiggles, and many of the turns in them prove after the fact to have been false signals of turns in general business activity. Thus, it requires, in addition to the month or so needed to collect data, at least another two or three months' confirmation time before an apparent change of course in the leading series can be regarded as significant, and this, of course, greatly diminishes the one unique advantage the technique has. Moreover, there are frequent differences among the leading series themselves. Some signal a turn, then others do not.[9]

To overcome the last objection noted by Lewis and Turner, the diffusion-index approach has been developed.

DIFFUSION INDEXES

There are two main categories of diffusion indexes.[10] The first and broadest category is of those that combine several indicators into one measure in order to measure the strength or weakness in the movements of these particular time series of data. Therefore, this type of diffusion index is a composite or consensus index. A diffusion

[9]Lewis and Turner. *Business Conditions Analysis*, p. 376.

[10]For a more complete discussion of this topic, see Albert T. Sommers, "Diffusion Indexes," in William F. Butler and Robert A. Kavesh, *How Business Economists Forecast* (Englewood Cliffs, N.J.: Prentice-Hall, 1966).

FIGURE 6-4

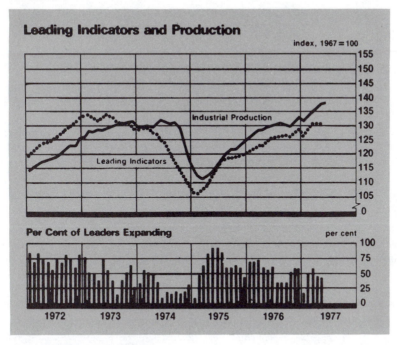

Leading Indicators and Production

index, 1967 = 100

Industrial Production

Leading Indicators

Per Cent of Leaders Expanding

per cent

1972   1973   1974   1975   1976   1977

All data are seasonably adjusted.

SOURCE: Board of Governors of the Federal Reserve System, U.S. Department of Commerce, Harris Bank.

index of the short list of leading indicators is an example of this type. Since there are twelve leading indicators, the diffusion index would be stated as a percentage of the total. For example, if four of the twelve series move up in one month, the diffusion index would be .333, or 33 percent. If, in the next month, six series moved up, the index would be .50, or 50 percent. The forecaster would need to interpret the index relative to levels of the index in the past. Certainly a move from 30 to 50 percent in the index of leading indicators would be a good indication of the future. If, in the next month, the diffusion index rose again, this would be an even stronger confirmation of a period of economic advance.

The second and more narrow type of diffusion index has been constructed by the National Bureau of Economic Research in order to measure the breadth of the movement within a particular series. Specifically, an indicator, whether leading, lagging, or coincident, is a summary measure compiled from statistics representing a cross section of the economy, so that in one figure is summarized the results of many different occurrences—for example, if an indicator refers to all production, it is a summation of many different industries. The more narrow diffusion index examines under a micro-scope the data going into the series, so that the forecaster can get a feel for the inner workings of the particular indicator. To follow through with the example just cited, the diffusion index will tell the forecaster how many industries within the indicator had experienced upturns, how many had had downturns, and how many had not changed at all.

TABLE 6-3
SHORT LIST OF INDICATORS: SCORES AND TIMING CHARACTERISTICS

Classification and Series Title (1)	First Business Cycle Turn Covered (2)	Average Score (3)	Scores, Six Criteria						Timing at Peaks and Troughs				
			Economic Significance (4)	Statistical Adequacy (5)	Conformity (6)	Timing (7)	Smoothness (8)	Currency (9)	Business Cycle Turns Covered (10)	Leads (11)	Rough Coincidences* (12)	Lags (13)	Median Lead (−) or Lag (+) in Months (14)
Leading indicators (12 series)													
1. Avg. workweek, prod. workers, mfg.	1921	66	50	65	81	66	60	80	19	13	4(2)	2	−5
30. Nonagri. placements, BES	1945	68	75	63	63	58	80	80	10	8	4(0)	1	−3
38. Index of net business formation	1945	68	75	58	81	67	80	40	10	8	3(1)	0	−7
6. New orders, durable goods indus.	1920	78	75	72	88	84	60	80	20	16	7(1)	0	−4
10. Contracts and orders, plant and equipment	1948	64	75	63	92	50	40	40	8	7	2(0)	1	−6
29. New building permits, private housing units	1918	67	50	60	76	80	60	80	22	17	5(1)	1	−6
31. Change in book value, mfg. and trade inventories	1945	65	75	67	77	78	20	40	10	9	2(1)	0	−8
23. Industrial materials prices	1919	67	50	72	79	44	80	100	21	13	9(4)	2	−2
19. Stock prices, 500 common stocks	1873	81	75	74	77	87	80	100	44	33	14(2)	5	−4
16. Corporate profits after taxes, Q	1920	68	75	70	79	76	60	25	20	13	11(4)	2	−2
17. Ratio, price to unit labor cost, mfg.	1919	69	50	67	84	72	60	80	21	17	10(1)	3	−3
113. Change in consumer installment debt	1929	63	50	79	77	60	60	40	14	11	4(0)	1	−10

Roughly coincident indicators
(7 series)

41. Employees in nonagri. establishments	1929	81	75	61	90	87	100	80	14	6	12(6)	2	0
43. Unemployment rate, total (inv.)	1929	75	75	63	96	60	80	80	14	4	8(3)	6	0
50. GNP in constant dollars, expenditure estimate, Q	1921	73	75	75	91	58	80	50	17	7	9(3)	3	−2
47. Industrial production	1919	72	75	63	94	38	100	80	21	9	13(9)	3	0
52. Personal income	1921	74	75	73	89	43	100	80	19	10	12(2)	5	−1
816. Mfg. and trade sales	1948	71	75	68	70	80	80	40	8	4	6(4)	0	0
54. Sales of retail stores	1919	69	75	77	89	12	80	100	21	5	7(1)	6	0

Lagging indicators (6 series)

502. Unempl. rate, persons unempl. 15+ weeks (inv.)	1948	69	50	63	98	52	80	80	8	1	5(1)	6	+2
61. Bus. expend., plant and equip., Q	1918	86	75	77	96	94	100	80	20	2	16(5)	13	+1
71. Book value, mfg. and trade inventories	1945	71	75	67	75	66	100	40	10	2	7(0)	8	+2
62. Labor cost per unit of output, mfg.	1919	68	50	70	83	56	80	80	21	0	1(0)	14	+8
72. Comm. and indus. loans outstanding	1937	57	50	47	67	20	100	100	12	1	6(0)	7	+2
67. Bank rates, short-term bus. loans, Q	1919	60	50	55	82	47	80	50	21	2	5(1)	15	+5

*Rough coincidences include exact coincidences (shown in parentheses) and leads and lags of three months or less. Leads (lags) include leads (lags) of one month or more. The total number of timing comparisons, which can be less than the number of business cycle turns covered by the series, in the sum of the leads, exact coincidences, and lags. Leads and lags of quarterly series are expressed in terms of months.

SOURCE: Geoffrey H. Moore and Julius Shiskin, *Indicators of Business Expansions and Contractions* (New York: National Bureau of Economic Research, 1967), p. 68.

The diffusion indexes have another important attribute. They tend to lead the indicator that is being analyzed by the index (although, unfortunately, the lead times of the various diffusion indexes are variable); and thus the diffusion indexes themselves can be thought of as a special kind of leading indicator.[11]

Unfortunately, these diffusion indexes are not without their problems. First, they are complex, in a statistical sense, to calculate; and second, even though they tend to eliminate some of the irregular moves evidenced in the indicators themselves, they are unable to eliminate them entirely. Nonetheless, the combination of the indicator approach, diffusion indexes, and judgment becomes an extremely powerful tool in the hands of a skillful forecaster.

MONEY AND STOCK PRICES

In recent years the monetarist notion of economics has grown increasingly more popular.[12] Although not universally accepted, this monetary theory in its simplest form states that fluctuations in the rate of growth of the money supply are of utmost importance in determining GNP, corporate profits, interest rates, and, of interest to us, stock prices. Monetarists contend that changes in the growth rate of the money supply set off a complicated series of events that ultimately affect share prices. In addition, they maintain that these monetary changes lead stock price changes: "Changes in monetary growth lead changes in stock prices by an average of about 9 months prior to a bear market and by about 2 or 3 months prior to bull markets."[13] These lead times are averages and are based on historical data. It cannot be said whether these average relationships can and will persist for future periods.

Research in the area of monetary theory has led many analysts, both economic and security, to consider changes in the growth rate of the money supply when preparing their forecasts. However, some contemporary thinking states that the stock market leads changes in the money supply.

ECONOMETRIC MODEL BUILDING

Econometrics is the field of study that applies mathematical and statistical techniques to economic theory. As such, it is the most precise and scientific of the approaches we have discussed thus far, because, in applying this technique the user is forced to specify in a formal mathematical manner the practice relation between the independent and dependent variables. Thus, in using econometrics, the forecaster must quantify precisely the relationships and assumptions he is making. Naturally, one of the key advantages of this approach is that the forecaster must think through clearly all the interrelationships of the economic variables; and for his reward he is yielded a forecast that gives him not only direction but magnitudes. In short, his method yields him a precise figure; even so, however, his forecast is not better than his underlying under-

[11]David H. McKinsley et al., *Forecasting Business Conditions* (New York: American Bankers Association, 1969).

[12]This section draws from Beryl W. Sprinkel, *Money and Markets: A Monetarist View* (Homewood, Ill.: Richard D. Irwin, 1971).

[13]*Ibid.*, p. 221.

standing of economic theory, his application of it, the quality of his data input, and the validity of his assumptions.[14]

Econometric model building involves the specification of a system of simultaneous equations containing both endogenous and exogenous variables. *Endogenous variables* are those determined by the system of equations; *exogenous variables* are those determined outside the system of equations. Therefore, at least one equation is needed to determine a forecast value of each endogenous variable. Values of the exogenous variables are predetermined.

Generally speaking, the well-known econometric models, such as the FRB-MIT (Federal Reserve Board/Massachusetts Institute of Technology), the Michigan, the Pennsylvania, and the Brookings models, are extremely complex; that is, they contain many equations. Their results, both new and revised, are reported regularly in the financial press, such as the *Wall Street Journal.*

Some of the problems with the econometric approach are these: (1) Large computer facilities and vast amounts of clerical and programming support are needed to maintain and update the system. (2) Frequently, the overall forecast is more reliable than the individual components of the forecast. (This is because errors tend to cancel themselves out in the overall forecast.) (3) Because of the vast amounts of data that must be collected, processed, and prepared for inclusion in the model, there are delays in making the results available to the public. Needless to say, this time lapse is potentially more troublesome to the security analyst than to the business forecaster. (4) Generally, these models are useful only for very short-term forecasts.

However, as stated earlier, the beauty of this approach is that it yields a blueprint of the economic system that is based on precisely stated factors that can then be used to yield a definite forecast figure.

OPPORTUNISTIC MODEL BUILDING

Opportunistic model building (or GNP model building, sectoral analysis, or any other of the often-used titles for this approach) refers to the most eclectic and perhaps most widely used forecasting method.[15] The forecaster using this approach draws from any and all of the methods already discussed in his quest for an accurate economic forecast. Its similarity to other approaches lies in its use of the national accounting framework to achieve a short-term forecast; its difference arises from its great flexibility and reliance on informed judgments. Perhaps this method can best be appreciated by understanding how it is applied in practice.

Initially, the forecaster must hypothesize total demand, and thus total income, during the forecast period. Obviously, this will necessitate assuming certain environmental decisions, such as war or peace, political relationships among various groups in

---

[14]For a fuller treatment of this approach, the reader is urged to read John G. Myers, "Statistical and Econometric Methods Used in Business Forecasting," in Butler, Kavesh, and Platt, *Methods and Techniques of Business Forecasting*; and Daniel B. Suits, "Forecasting and Analysis with an Econometric Model," *American Economic Review*, March 1962.

[15]Much of the material in this section parallels the discussion contained in two classics in this area of study: William F. Butler and Robert A. Kavesh, "Judgmental Forecasting of the Gross National Product," in Butler, Kavesh, and Platt, *Methods and Techniques of Business Forecasting*; and Lewis and Turner, *Business Conditions Analysis*, particularly Chaps. 17-24. The interested reader is encouraged to refer to these works for a fuller treatment of this fascinating subject.

the economy, any imminent tax changes, the rate of inflation, and the level of interest rates. After this work has been done, the forecaster begins building a forecast of the GNP figure by estimating the levels of the various components of GNP. That is, he must fill in the numbers for consumption expenditures, gross private domestic investment, government purchases of goods and services, and net exports.

Generally, the forecaster will begin with the easiest figure to come by and work toward the most complex. He usually begins with an estimate for the government sector, broken down into federal expenditures and state and local expenditures, with the federal portion being further broken down into defense and nondefense expenditures. The various government publications, including the federal budget itself and the *Annual Economic Report of the President*, provide very useful sources of information for the forecaster. Further insight can be gained in conversations with key government employees. State and local expenditures can be arrived at rather simply, merely by extrapolation of past data, because they have risen by a fairly stable percentage year after year.

Gross private domestic investment is broken down into business expenditures for plant and equipment, residential construction, and changes in the levels of business inventories. Many of the sources of both corporate and consumer surveys cited earlier in Table 6-1 are very useful starting points in forecasting each of these three figures. The most difficult to forecast accurately is the change in business inventories; this figure changes drastically over the business cycle.

The next sector to be forecast is that of net exports. This is a particularly hard number to come by, for the forecaster must consider not only domestic but also international, political, and foreign economic problems.

The last sector to forecast in opportunistic model building is the personal consumption factor. Traditionally, this sector is subdivided into three components: durable goods minus automobiles, automobiles, and nondurable goods and services. This sort of breakdown allows the forecaster to find any stable relationships between economic variables, such as between disposable income and expenditures on nondurables. Inasmuch as durables and automobiles tend to fluctuate vigorously over the business cycle, it is best for the forecaster to analyze these components separately. Here too, the surveys mentioned in Table 6-1 provide a valuable source of information.

After the forecaster has acquired totals for these four major categories, he adds them together to come up with his GNP forecast. However, his work is not yet completed, for he must then test this total for consistency with an independently arrived at *a priori* forecast of GNP, as well as test the overall forecast for internal consistency. The former consistency check might necessitate his retracing some of his steps in order to bring the two forecasts into line with each other. Thus, he may have to approximate successively the various subcategories, as well as the final estimate of GNP. The internal consistency check arises because of the interrelatedness of the GNP accounts. For example, consumption by individuals implies a level of savings that affects business investment, which further affects productive activity and thus incomes, which will once again affect savings. While these circular effects take place, other factors such as interest rates, unemployment, and inflation will be affected. Thus, it is necessary for the forecaster to ensure in the light of all these relationships that both his total forecast and his subcomponent forecast make sense and fit together in a reasonable economic fashion.[16]

In short, opportunistic model building employs all the aforementioned techniques, plus a vast amount of judgment and ingenuity, in what has been described as

> an effort to build a view of the short-run business outlook that is compre-
> hensive, that is as quantitatively precise as the state of our knowledge
> permits, that is internally consistent, that draws upon rather than sidesteps
> all the pertinent insights of modern aggregative economics but, at the same
> time, does not make a fetish of theoretical rigor. Instead, the technique
> seeks to exploit any and all evidences of business prospects that may come
> to hand. It is particularly distinguished from pure econometric model build-
> ing by its heavy use of data concerning the advance plans and commitments
> of certain spending groups, and it retains a sizable place for judgment and
> freehand adjustments.[17]

This versatile approach to forecasting is at once the greatest asset to opportunistic model building and its greatest liability, for with the advantages that accrue to the economist by mobilizing a variety of forecasting tools and adding judgment come the aforementioned weaknesses of these techniques. Unfortunately, although the weaknesses can be lessened through selective combination, they cannot be entirely eliminated. Notwithstanding the possible shortcomings of business forecasting, the analyst must still consider and incorporate economic data in his investment decision-making process. Several key sources that summarize forecasts of key research organizations, banks, and economists are the Federal Reserve Bank of Philadelphia's "Predictions for 19-," published in January of each year, and the Federal Reserve Bank of Richmond's "Business Forecasts," published in February of each year. In addition, the *New York Times* and the *Wall Street Journal*, among others, publish many forecasts as they are released.

Potential Usefulness of Economic Forecasts

It should be obvious to the reader by now that this chapter has presented a number of interesting paradoxes. Perhaps the most interesting is that we attempted initially to get a handle on future stock price behavior by predicting economic behavior. However, we learned that stock prices are in fact one of the leading indicators for the market taken as a whole. Therefore, this poses a bit of a dilemma if we are attempting to forecast the stock market using the economy. We have a problem because the stock market itself is a leading indicator of the economy. There are, however, several ways out of this chicken-and-egg type of situation. First, we can attempt to estimate aggregate economic activity far into the future, that is, attempt to forecast the economy far enough into the future so that it will be before even the stock price series is able to forecast the economy. A second possibility would be to develop an economic series that leads the economy by a period of time longer than the stock prices themselves lead the economy. In effect, the leading indicator approach as well as the use of money supply statistics have been attempts at achieving this very objective.

---

[16]Another method of checking for this internal consistency is to forecast what the distribution of incomes will be—between wages, interest, salaries, etc.—under his forecast level of GNP and the various subclassifications, and check to see if these relationships make economic sense.

[17]Lewis and Turner, *Business Conditions Analysis*, p. 571.

Accuracy of Short-Term Economic Forecasts

It is interesting to see how short-term forecasters have fared in their undertaking. The NBER has studied this issue and has discovered that shorter-term forecasts of three to six months are more accurate than forecasts approximately one year in advance. In other words, forecast errors go up as the length of the prediction period increases. In addition, their studies indicate that the total forecasts tend to be more accurate than the subcomponent forecasts.[18]

By now, at least two key points are apparent about economic forecasting: (1) It is an extremely arduous and difficult process, even for specialists; and (2) because of this, an analyst must critically evaluate such forecasts and not accept them blindly.

An Illustration of an Economic Analysis

In order to understand more clearly the E-I-C framework, in the next several chapters we will apply the techniques discussed in these chapters to the same continuous example. For analysis purposes, we will examine the restaurant industry and McDonald's Corporation, because this industry and company are widely known and contain a variety of areas of analytical interest. In this section we will attempt to analyze economic data relevant to this industry in order to ascertain if the expected economic environment will be favorable for the restaurant industry in general and for the fast-food sector of the industry in particular.

The forecasts of business conditions of any given year are by themselves difficult to construct. But the year 1982 presented even more problems because of the impending impact of President Reagan's new economic program and the possible effects of the major tax changes brought about by the Economic Recovery Tax Act of 1981. To compound the difficulties further, we have to consider the continuing worries about the rate of inflation; uncertainty as to the future course of already very high interest rates; the international monetary and political situations; and prospect of a large federal budget deficit. In addition to the aforementioned problem areas, the fast-food sector of the restaurant industry and McDonald's in particular are also affected by the forecast of beef prices. This in turn is affected by grain and weather conditions for grain and their impact on the growing of herds of cattle. This particular dependence on beef prices is caused by the fact that beef products such as hamburgers are the mainstay of McDonald's limited menu.

Disposable Income Demographic Factors and Demand

Most forecasts of GNP for 1982 anticipate continued increases. Inasmuch as disposable income is a function of gross national product it, too, is expected to rise. We further forecast that the rate of inflation will decrease to about 10 percent. Of course if real output remains constant and inflation continues at 10 percent, this will lead to

[18]Victor Zarnowitz, *Appraisal of Short-Term Economic Forecasts* (New York: NBER Occasional Paper 104, 1967); and Jacob Mincer, ed., *Economic Forecasts and Expectations* (New York: NBER Studies in Business Cycles No. 19, 1969).

a rise in GNP and disposable income of 10 percent. However, we expect that because of the recently enacted cuts that disposable income and in turn discretionary income will rise. This should auger well for the food-away-from-home industry.

Since World War II, the demand for food consumed away from home has escalated significantly more than the demand for food consumed at home for the same period. This trend, when combined with other demand factors, provided an excellent environment for large increases of sales for fast-food restaurants. However, during 1979 and 1980 the growth of total demand for food consumed away from home slowed sharply, and in fact several sources believe that the demand for food consumed away from home actually contracted in recent periods. There are several key factors which affect the amount of discretionary income which is spent on products furnished by members of this industry.

We expect that disposable income and consumer discretionary spending will increase in the early 1980s; however, we feel that the rate of increase will be slower than it has been in recent years. Furthermore, we expect that because of inflation the portion of nondiscretionary items will make up a larger portion of consumer overall spending. We further expect that the differential between the cost of eating a meal at home and the cost of eating that same meal away from home will widen during the 1980s. Obviously, this will make eating away from home a greater luxury because of its greater relative cost. We feel that this will arise because of the more rapid price inflation of such factors as labor, energy, and fixed costs of operating restaurants which impact much more greatly on restaurants than they do on the preparation of meals at home.

Another relevant factor relating to demographics is the fact that there has been a rapid rate of increase in the past in the proportion of the labor force accounted for by women. We do not expect that this dramatic rate of change in the number of women employed in the labor force will continue in the near future, and therefore the rate of demand from this sector of the labor force will slow down. In addition, the size of the younger sectors in the population has been increasing in recent years; however, this teen market, if you will, will grow at a slower rate in the period ahead, and therefore this will be a negative influence on demand for this type of industry. Furthermore, this teen sector of the market is becoming the 20- to 30-year age bracket of the population, and this sector of the population requires a greater diversity in the eating experiences when they dine out than the teen sector does. This element of the population desires a wider choice of menu and a more intriguing type of decor to make eating out more of an experience than does the teen sector of the population. This in part will lead to some decrease in the rate of increase of meal sales of the fast-food sector of the market.

Other Economic Factors

Two somewhat related factors that must be considered, particularly regarding industries that are building new physical facilities, such as restaurants, are construction costs and interest rates. These can be significant influences in expanding industries because they cut into profits and therefore affect earnings per share, dividends, and share prices. Inflationary pressures will continue to increase construction costs in terms of material used in construction and in terms of the wages of workers in the construction trades, which are highly unionized. Should construction costs continue to rise, and should firms in the industry still want to expand their physical plant, these additional costs will affect future profits. Furthermore, the high rates of interest will cut deeply into profits of firms that need to borrow money to finance the new construction.

We further expect that in 1982 the price of beef will level off. This should counter-act some of the negative influences cited in the preceding paragraph, inasmuch as beef, as has already been said, is the mainstay of the fast-food sector of the industry and in particular McDonald's menu. The energy crisis experienced several years ago should not drastically affect this industry in 1982 because gasoline prices are expected to remain level or perhaps even decrease a little. Furthermore, the bulk of McDonald's sales are in restaurants located near large population centers. Therefore, one does not have to drive very far to eat at McDonald's and therefore even should a gasoline problem develop, which we do not anticipate, the influence on McDonald's should be minor and perhaps even slightly positive.

On balance, 1982 looks like a neutral or perhaps slightly positive year for the economy and the restaurant industry, particularly the fast-food sector of the industry. In the next chapter we will examine this industry in some detail, as we continue toward our goal of price, dividend, and earnings estimates of McDonald's Corporation.

Summary

In this chapter we assessed the importance of short-time economic forecasting in the decision-making process surrounding the purchase of common stocks. In order to understand and appreciate the forecasting task, we discussed and critically evaluated several major economic forecasting techniques—anticipatory surveys, indicators, diffusion indexes, econometric models, and opportunistic model building. All these techniques have distinct advantages as well as disadvantages, but on balance they have been success-ful for forecasts up to a few quarters in advance. For the security analyst or investor, the anticipated economic environment, and therefore the economic forecast, is important for making decisions concerning both the timing of an investment and the relative invest-ment desirability among the various industries in the economy.

In the next chapter we will continue our efforts to forecast price and dividend information for our holding-period-return calculations by discussing and applying useful techniques of industry analysis.

Questions and Problems

1. Compare and contrast the survey, indicator, and econometric approaches to short-term forecasting.

2. Of what importance is the concept of "potential GNP"? What industries do you suppose would be most affected by the gap between actual and potential GNP? Why?

3. What is *opportunistic model building?*

4. Would you suppose that GNP forecasts for next year prepared by major universities, banks, and research organizations would be quite similar? Why, or why not? Get three major GNP forecasts for next year and see.

5. What economic factors do you think most directly affect defense-oriented industries and thus would be most important to forecast properly?

6. What economic factors would you be most interested in forecasting if you were an analyst investigating major consumer durable-goods sales for next year?

7. If you were told that more families than ever before would have second cars next year and that the expected lives of cars had increased, which industries do you suppose would benefit most?

8. It has often been said that common stocks are a good "hedge against inflation." Why do you suppose people think this way? Are you inclined to agree or disagree with this sentiment?

9. What does indicator 19 in Figure 6-2 mean to you?

10. If you were designing an equation to forecast corporate capital spending for an econometric model, what variables do you suppose would be useful in explaining the level of corporate capital spending?

11. How might one classify industries within a business cycle framework?

12. a. What are three examples of key leading economic indicators (excluding stock prices)?

    b. What is the rationale for the use of diffusion indexes to accompany forecasts using leading indicators?

13. What is the significance of a diffusion index with a large, positive reading?

14. The "cumulative" nature of business cycles suggests that various sectors of the economy react to changes in economic conditions to produce revivals and recessions in aggregate economic activity. Suppose that Congress passed a public works program totaling $4 billion. This program would create a net addition to government spending with no offsetting increase in taxes or decrease in other previously scheduled government spending. Assuming that the economy is in the *initial* stages of recovery, indicate the sectors of the economy and the components of GNP that would be most immediately affected and describe their reaction.

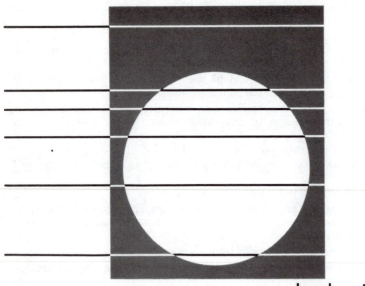

SEVEN

Industry Analysis

The analyst with an economic forecast that he has developed from scratch, or a set of figures that he has developed from forecasts prepared by others, is now ready to apply this information to an appropriate industry. Before demonstrating this, however, let us look at some definitions of an industry.

Alternative Industry Classification Schemes

Webster's Dictionary defines an *industry* as "a department or branch of a craft, art, business, or manufacture." And more specifically:

[A] group of productive or profit-making enterprises or organizations that have a similar technological structure of production and that produce or supply technically substitutable goods, services, or sources of income.[1]

Although at first glance these definitions seem neat and clear-cut, this is not so in reality. First, it may seem desirable to break industries down by their products; however, defining a product is no easy chore.

[1]*Webster's Third New International Dictionary* (Springfield, Mass.: Merriam, 1966), pp. 1155-56.

Industry Classification By Product

Are glass containers in the same industry as metal containers? Is steel in the same industry as aluminum? Is a fast-food chain in the same industry as a chain of restaurants?

In one sense, a container is a container, and the substance from which it is constructed should not cause the product to appear in a separate industry for an industry analysis; however, the firms producing these different products might be very dissimilar in the other products that they produce.[2] Between the steel and aluminum industries, the economics, technology, and refinements are so substantially different that it is advisable to analyze them as separate industries. And there are also substantial differences between the mode of operation in a limited-menu, fast-food, take-out type of restaurant and that of a limited-menu, sit-down type or a legitimate full-menu restaurant.

By now it should be clear that pinpointing an industry is not easy, and the investigator needs to have a clear goal in mind so that he can properly classify firms into industries for his specific purpose. For example, if the goal were to reach an estimate of sales for the industry, the analyst might want to consider similar products and products that could be substituted for the item in question (glass containers for metal, or aluminum containers for steel). But if he were calculating comparative costs of the industry, he might consider only those firms with similar manufacturing processes, for only such a comparison would be meaningful. For instance, the analyst might compare the costs of one candy producer with those of another candy producer but not with those of a toy manufacturer.

Industry classification by product does not present a terribly acute problem for the astute analyst when he is classifying firms with basically one product or a homogeneous group of products. The problem does worsen considerably, however, when he deals with a firm that has a diversified product line. Unfortunately, in this day and age the latter case is the rule rather than the exception. Our illustration later in this chapter will serve to highlight this problem.

SIC Classification

In order to provide an organized reporting framework for the vast amount of data collected by the federal government, the Standard Industrial Classification (SIC) was developed. The following passage from the *Census of Manufacturers* describes the organization of this system.[3]

> Structure of the Standard Industrial Classification.—The basic classification system employed in the economic censuses is the Standard Industrial Classification (SIC). The SIC was developed for use in the classification of establish-

---

[2] In an antitrust case, the Supreme Court prevented the merger of Continental Can (metal containers) with Hazel-Atlas Glass (glass containers), on the grounds of a possible lessening of competition. Thus a key issue in this case was the delineation of the container industry.

[3] *Census of Manufacturers* (Washington, D.C.: U.S. Government Printing Office).

ments by type of activity in which engaged. It covers the entire field of economic activities subdivided as follows:

Industrial Division		Major Groups
A	Agriculture, forestry, and fisheries	01-09
B	Mining	10-14
C	Contract construction	15-17
D	Manufacturing	19-39
E	Transportation, communication, electric, gas, and sanitary services	40-49
F	Wholesale and retail trade	50-59
G	Finance, insurance, and real estate	60-67
H	Services	70-89
I	Government	91-94
J	Nonclassifiable establishments	99

Below the major-group level, the SIC provides for three-digit groups and finally for four-digit industries:

> Structure of the SIC Manufacturing Division.—For the manufacturing division, the 21 2-digit SIC Major Groups (19 to 39) are subdivided into 149 3-digit SIC Groups (191 to 399) and into 422 4-digit industries (1911 to 3999).[4]

For example, under "Manufacturing," major group 20 is "Food and kindred products," industry group 202 is "Dairy products," and industry 2023 is "Condensed and evaporated milk."

A sample page of the Census of Manufacturers is shown in Figure 7-1. This table contains comparative data on industry classifications regarding the number of firms, number of employees, number of production workers, value of shipments, new capital expenditures, and so on. This information is useful in detecting changing industrial patterns and developments over time, such as expansion or contraction.

Although the Census provides valuable information to the industry analyst, it is not without its drawbacks. For example, the methodology employed in classifying firms into the various categories is not consistent over the entire spectrum of the U.S. economy.[5]

Industry Classification According To Business Cycle

Another way of classifying industries is in a cyclical framework, that is, by how they react to upswings and downswings in the economy. The general classifications in this framework are growth, cyclical, defensive, and cyclical-growth.

Growth industries are generally characterized by expectations of abnormally high rates of expansion in earnings, often independent of the business cycle. Frequently,

---

[4]*Ibid.*

[5]The discussion surrounding these issues is highly complex and beyond the realm of this text; however, the interested reader is referred to a fine treatment of the material in Joe S. Bain, *Industrial Organization* (New York: John Wiley, 1968), pp. 129-49.

this type of situation is associated with a major change in the state of technology or an innovative way of doing or selling something. In the early part of the twentieth century, industries such as automobiles and airplane manufacturing were considered the growth groups. In the 1940s, 1950s, and 1960s, the growth industries were associated with photography, color television, computers, drugs, office equipment, and sophisticated communications equipment. In recent years the growth industries have dealt with such things as soft contact lenses, genetic engineering, and computer-aided design systems.

Cyclical industries are considered to be those most likely to benefit from a period of economic prosperity, and most likely to suffer from a period of economic recession. We shall see later in this chapter that consumer and manufacturer durables, such as refrigerators and drill presses, are the type of products that characteristically benefit most, relatively, from an economic boom and suffer most in a recession. This is because their purchase can be postponed until personal financial or general business conditions improve. These industries, then, are considered cyclical.

Defensive industries are those, such as the food-processing industry, hurt least in periods of economic downswing. We will see later that consumer nondurables and services, which in large part are those items necessary for people's existence—such as food and shelter—are products in defensive industries. Defensive industries often contain firms whose securities an investor might hold for income. Defensive stocks might even be considered countercyclical, because their earnings might very well expand while the earnings of cyclical stocks are declining.

The investment press and brokerage firms have coined yet another classification, that of *cyclical-growth industries*. Obviously, these possess characteristics of both a cyclical industry and a growth industry. An example in this classification would be the airline industry. Airlines, according to some, grow tremendously, then go through periods of stagnation and perhaps even decline, and then resume their growth—often because of changes in technology, such as the introduction of a new type of aircraft, like the B747 or the DC10.

The Economy and the Industry Analysis

In the preceding chapter we saw how various techniques could be brought to bear upon the investment decision. Specifically, we observed how various approaches could be used to forecast components of GNP, and we noted that for the investment decision it was often as significant to predict the direction of any change in these sectors as it was to predict their actual level. Perhaps an example or two would help to highlight this concept.

When the GNP is growing, unemployment is relatively low (4 to 5 percent), and the general economic climate is optimistic; an economic forecast based upon any of the approaches already discussed would probably show high and increasing levels of expenditures on consumer durables, inventory, and plant and equipment. Since business is buoyant and it is generally expected that this will continue, businessmen accumulate inventory in anticipation of still higher sales levels, and they also increase their capacity through plant and equipment expenditures. At the same time, on the consumer's side of the market, individual households are experiencing high levels of personal discretionary

FIGURE 7-1

General Statistics for Establishments, by Industry Specialization and Primary Product Class Specialization: 1972

This table presents selected statistics for establishments according to their degree of specialization in products primary to their industry. The measures of plant specialization shown are (1) industry specialization—the ratio of primary product shipments to total product shipments, primary plus secondary, for the establishments; and (2) product class specialization—the ratio of the largest primary product class shipments to total product shipments.

primary plus secondary, for the establishment. See the appendix for method of computing these ratios. Statistics for establishments with specialization ratios of less than 75 percent are included in total lines but are not shown as a separate class. In addition, data may not be shown, for some industries, product classes, or specialization ratios for various reasons: e.g. to avoid disclosure of individual company data.

Industry or product class code	Industry or product class by percent of specialization	Establishments (number)	All employees		Production workers			Value added by manufacture (million dollars)	Cost of materials (million dollars)	Value of shipments (million dollars)	Capital expenditures new (million dollars)
			Number (1,000)	Payroll (million dollars)	Number (1,000)	Man-hours (millions)	Wages (million dollars)				
3991	**BROOMS AND BRUSHES**										
	ENTIRE INDUSTRY	450	17.5	118.5	14.2	26.8	79.5	235.5	204.9	438.3	13.0
	ESTABLISHMENTS WITH 75% OR MORE SPECIALIZATION	425	14.5	99.4	11.7	22.2	65.5	191.8	180.9	370.3	10.9
39911	**BROOMS**										
	(PRIMARY PRODUCT CLASS OF ESTABLISHMENT)	65	2.7	14.2	2.2	3.9	10.1	28.0	28.5	56.5	1.0
	ESTABLISHMENTS WITH 75% OR MORE SPECIALIZATION	46	1.7	8.6	1.3	2.2	6.2	15.2	15.8	31.2	.4
39912	**PAINT AND VARNISH BRUSHES**										
	(PRIMARY PRODUCT CLASS OF ESTABLISHMENT)	45	4.2	30.7	3.4	6.5	19.8	65.5	65.0	128.3	4.9
	ESTABLISHMENTS WITH 75% OR MORE SPECIALIZATION	39	3.8	28.0	3.0	5.9	18.0	59.4	57.5	114.5	4.7
39913	**OTHER BRUSHES**										
	(PRIMARY PRODUCT CLASS OF ESTABLISHMENT)	102	9.2	65.3	7.5	14.3	43.9	124.7	95.7	220.1	5.9
	ESTABLISHMENTS WITH 75% OR MORE SPECIALIZATION	86	6.9	48.4	5.6	10.7	32.0	84.8	78.1	162.4	4.1
3993	**SIGNS AND ADVERTISING DISPLAYS**										
	ENTIRE INDUSTRY	3287	49.8	415.9	37.5	68.3	261.9	760.8	447.0	1198.0	29.8
	ESTABLISHMENTS WITH 75% OR MORE SPECIALIZATION	3246	47.6	400.3	35.8	65.4	252.1	744.0	413.0	1147.6	28.6
39931	**LUMINOUS TUBING AND BULB SIGNS**										
	(PRIMARY PRODUCT CLASS OF ESTABLISHMENT)	298	10.3	98.6	7.4	14.0	64.1	167.2	87.4	250.8	7.2
	ESTABLISHMENTS WITH 75% OR MORE SPECIALIZATION	243	9.1	87.8	6.6	12.4	57.0	150.6	79.7	226.8	6.2
39932	**NONELECTRIC SIGNS AND ADVERTISING DISPLAYS**										
	(PRIMARY PRODUCT CLASS OF ESTABLISHMENT)	627	20.0	172.0	14.9	28.0	105.7	292.1	202.7	490.3	10.7
	ESTABLISHMENTS WITH 75% OR MORE SPECIALIZATION	549	17.1	147.6	12.7	24.0	91.1	258.5	159.7	414.6	9.1
39933	**ADVERTISING SPECIALTIES**										
	(PRIMARY PRODUCT CLASS OF ESTABLISHMENT)	167	7.3	54.4	5.5	10.0	34.2	106.1	65.3	169.9	3.1
	ESTABLISHMENTS WITH 75% OR MORE SPECIALIZATION	144	6.5	48.5	4.9	8.8	30.7	94.6	59.4	152.6	2.4
3995	**BURIAL CASKETS**										
	ENTIRE INDUSTRY	515	14.8	109.3	11.8	22.6	72.0	210.3	183.7	391.9	8.8
	ESTABLISHMENTS WITH 75% OR MORE SPECIALIZATION	510	14.7	108.1	11.7	22.4	71.4	208.4	181.6	387.9	8.8

Code	Industry / Category	Establishments	Col2	Col3	Col4	Col5	Col6	Col7	Col8	Col9	Col10
39951	METAL CASKETS, COFFINS, LINED, TRIMMED (ADULT)										
	(PRIMARY PRODUCT CLASS OF ESTABLISHMENT)	148	8.6	64.2	6.7	12.9	40.3	127.4	109.8	236.1	5.2
	ESTABLISHMENTS WITH 75% OR MORE SPECIALIZATION	75	5.3	40.9	4.1	7.6	24.9	91.0	68.4	158.9	3.7
39952	WOOD CASKETS, COFFINS, LINED, TRIMMED (ADULT)										
	(PRIMARY PRODUCT CLASS OF ESTABLISHMENT)	68	2.5	17.4	2.0	4.0	12.2	31.2	28.5	59.0	.9
	ESTABLISHMENTS WITH 75% OR MORE SPECIALIZATION	21	1.2	8.4	1.0	2.0	6.2	13.9	9.6	22.9	.5
39933	OTHER CASKETS AND COFFINS AND METAL VAULTS										
	(PRIMARY PRODUCT CLASS OF ESTABLISHMENT)	42	2.1	17.7	1.8	3.4	13.0	30.9	26.5	57.1	1.5
	ESTABLISHMENTS WITH 75% OR MORE SPECIALIZATION	35	1.9	16.2	1.6	3.0	11.9	28.3	24.3	52.2	1.4
3996	HARD SURFACE FLOOR COVERINGS										
	ENTIRE INDUSTRY	20	5.8	59.4	4.6	9.7	44.7	212.0	135.2	342.3	14.0
	ESTABLISHMENTS WITH 75% OR MORE SPECIALIZATION	19	(D)	(D)	(D)	(D)	(D)	(D)	(D)	(D)	(D)
3999	MANUFACTURING INDUSTRIES, NEC										
	ENTIRE INDUSTRY	3368	65.3	432.1	51.6	94.9	281.1	900.3	654.0	1 539.9	40.3
	ESTABLISHMENTS WITH 75% OR MORE SPECIALIZATION	3270	55.5	357.6	44.6	81.7	236.8	768.4	559.2	1 311.7	33.8
39991	CHEMICAL FIRE EXTINGUISHING EQUIPMENT AND PARTS										
	(PRIMARY PRODUCT CLASS OF ESTABLISHMENT)	25	4.2	40.4	2.7	5.4	24.5	83.8	84.6	163.2	3.3
	ESTABLISHMENTS WITH 75% OR MORE SPECIALIZATION	22	(D)	(D)	(D)	(D)	(D)	(D)	(D)	(D)	(D)
39992	COIN-OPERATED AMUSEMENT MACHINES										
	(PRIMARY PRODUCT CLASS OF ESTABLISHMENT)	10	3.0	22.9	2.7	5.2	17.0	42.8	28.6	69.6	.9
	ESTABLISHMENTS WITH 75% OR MORE SPECIALIZATION	9	(D)	(D)	(D)	(D)	(D)	(D)	(D)	(D)	(d)
39993	MATCHES										
	(PRIMARY PRODUCT CLASS OF ESTABLISHMENT)	20	3.7	26.2	3.1	6.3	20.5	57.9	25.0	81.9	2.4
	ESTABLISHMENTS WITH 75% OR MORE SPECIALIZATION	20	3.7	26.2	3.1	6.3	20.5	57.9	25.0	81.9	2.4
39994	CANDLES										
	(PRIMARY PRODUCT CLASS OF ESTABLISHMENT)	65	5.4	30.9	4.2	7.5	19.4	57.5	50.7	106.7	3.3
	ESTABLISHMENTS WITH 75% OR MORE SPECIALIZATION	58	4.4	24.9	3.5	6.3	16.7	42.5	43.8	85.7	2.4
39995	LAMP SHADES										
	(PRIMARY PRODUCT CLASS OF ESTABLISHMENT)	54	2.2	12.4	1.8	3.5	8.7	19.2	16.7	35.6	.3
	ESTABLISHMENTS WITH 75% OR MORE SPECIALIZATION	52	(D)	(D)	(D)	(D)	(D)	(D)	(D)	(D)	(D)
39996	FURS, DRESSED, AND DYED										
	(PRIMARY PRODUCT CLASS OF ESTABLISHMENT)	83	2.1	14.6	1.8	3.2	11.3	24.4	18.2	42.4	.4
	ESTABLISHMENTS WITH 75% OR MORE SPECIALIZATION	83	2.1	14.6	1.8	3.2	11.3	24.4	18.2	42.4	.4
39997	UMBRELLAS, PARASOLS, AND CANES										
	(PRIMARY PRODUCT CLASS OF ESTABLISHMENT)	29	1.3	8.5	.9	1.7	4.6	16.6	26.0	40.9	.3
	ESTABLISHMENTS WITH 75% OR MORE SPECIALIZATION	27	(D)	(D)	(D)	(D)	(D)	(D)	(D)	(D)	(D)
39999	OTHER MISCELLANEOUS FABRICATED PRODUCTS, NEC										
	(PRIMARY PRODUCT CLASS OF ESTABLISHMENT)	504	23.5	164.3	18.4	34.7	103.0	384.6	253.8	632.3	17.6
	ESTABLISHMENTS WITH 75% OR MORE SPECIALIZATION	460	19.9	139.7	15.7	29.1	88.1	331.6	220.1	545.2	15.6

(D) Withheld to avoid disclosing figures for individual companies.

SOURCE: *Census of Manufacturers* (Washington, D.C.: U.S. Government Printing Office).

income (income available for luxuries), and they are free to spend some of this money on such things as residential housing, automobiles, and other consumer durables. Indeed, if prior economic periods had been far less booming than those just described, expenditures on various durables, having been postponed, could now become exaggerated.

It would be desirable at such a time to buy securities of firms in industries most likely to benefit from these purchasing patterns. As you will recall in the opportunistic-model-building approach, the forecaster would arrive at specific estimates of the broad categories we have just mentioned. It is easy to see how such an economic forecast can be helpful, not only in selecting industries that will benefit in a period of general economic prosperity but also in selecting those that will benefit in periods when only certain sectors of the economy are expanding. Much academic research has substantiated the importance of sound industry analysis to successful investment analysis. Examples of the latter type would be defense industries in a period when the federal government is boosting the economy through large national-defense expenditures, and also those industries that will be hurt least during a period of economic downswing—such as those producing food, something that is always necessary.

Another way of gauging the economy's performance with special regard to specific industry classifications is to examine regularly the statistics contained in the monthly *Federal Reserve Bulletin*. By examining the behavior of the various series over time, the analyst can gain insights to important economic developments in many industries and important industry subsectors. For example, in the table from the *Federal Reserve Bulletin* that is reproduced in Figure 7-2, note the relative growth in consumer goods versus equipment since the base year of 1967. During the period from 1967 to November 1976, the index for consumer goods grew from 100 to 138.9, a 38.9 percent increase. During the same period, the equipment index grew only from 100 to 116.6, a 16.6 increase. In addition, the pace of construction contracts has grown tremendously since 1967. The possible benefit of investment in consumer-oriented industries and construction-related industries during the late 1960s and through the mid-1970s can be seen even from this superficial kind of supplemental analysis.[6]

Key Characteristics in an Industry Analysis

In an industry analysis, there are any number of key characteristics that should be considered at some point by the analyst. In this section we will enumerate and discuss several of these key characteristics: past sales and earnings performance, the permanence of the industry, the attitude of government toward the industry, labor conditions within the industry, the competitive conditions as reflected in any barriers to entry that might exist, and stock prices of firms in the industry relative to their earnings.

Past Sales And Earnings Performance

One of the most effective steps in forecasting is assessing the historical performance of the industry in question. Certainly, two factors with a central role in the ultimate success of any security investment are sales and earnings; therefore, in order to gain a

[6]Meaningful analysis of much of the information contained in the *Federal Reserve Bulletin* requires comparison with earlier time series and great familiarity with the behavior of these series.

FIGURE 7-2

SELECTED BUSINESS INDEXES (1967 = 100, EXCEPT AS NOTED)

Period	Industrial production								Capacity utilization in mfg. (per cent of 1967 output)	Construction contracts	Nonagricultural employment—Total[1]	Manufacturing[2]		Prices[4]		
		Market						Industry				Employment	Payrolls	Total retail sales[3]	Consumer	Wholesale commodity
	Total	Products					Materials	Manufacturing								
		Total	Final													
			Total	Consumer goods	Equipment	Intermediate										
1955	58.5	56.7	55.4	59.0	50.4	61.6	61.3	58.2	87.0	....	76.9	92.9	61.1	59	80.2	87.8
1956	61.1	59.9	58.6	61.2	55.3	64.4	62.9	60.5	86.1	....	79.6	93.9	64.6	61	81.4	90.7
1957	61.9	61.2	60.4	62.7	57.5	64.4	62.8	61.2	83.6	....	80.3	92.2	65.4	64	84.3	93.3
1958	57.9	58.7	57.6	62.1	51.5	62.9	56.6	56.9	75.0	....	78.0	83.9	60.3	64	86.6	94.6
1959	64.8	64.5	63.2	68.1	56.5	69.5	65.3	64.1	81.6	....	81.0	88.1	67.8	69	87.3	94.8
1960	66.2	66.3	65.3	70.7	58.0	69.9	66.1	65.4	80.1	68.6	82.4	88.0	68.8	70	88.7	94.9
1961	66.7	67.0	65.8	72.2	57.3	71.3	66.2	65.6	77.3	70.2	82.1	84.5	68.0	70	89.6	94.5
1962	72.2	72.3	71.4	77.1	63.7	75.7	72.1	71.5	81.4	78.1	84.4	87.3	73.3	75	90.6	94.8
1963	76.5	76.4	75.5	81.3	67.5	79.9	76.7	75.8	83.5	86.1	86.1	87.8	76.0	79	91.7	94.5
1964	81.7	80.9	79.8	85.8	71.4	85.2	82.9	81.0	85.7	89.4	88.6	89.3	80.1	83	92.9	94.7
1965	89.8	88.2	87.6	92.6	80.7	90.6	92.4	89.7	89.5	93.2	92.3	93.9	88.1	90	94.5	96.6
1966	97.7	95.9	95.9	97.3	94.0	96.2	100.7	97.9	91.1	94.8	97.1	99.9	97.8	97	97.2	99.8
1967	100.0	100.0	100.0	100.0	100.0	100.0	100.0	100.0	86.9	100.0	100.0	100.0	100.0	100	100.0	100.0
1968	106.3	106.2	106.2	105.9	106.5	106.3	106.5	106.4	87.0	113.2	103.2	101.4	108.3	109	104.2	102.5
1969	111.1	110.3	109.6	109.8	109.3	112.9	112.5	111.0	86.2	123.7	106.9	103.2	116.6	114	109.8	106.5
1970	107.8	106.9	105.3	109.0	100.1	112.9	109.2	106.4	79.2	123.1	107.7	98.1	114.1	119	116.3	110.4
1971	109.6	108.5	106.3	114.7	94.7	116.7	111.3	108.2	78.0	145.4	108.1	94.2	116.7	130	121.2	113.9
1972	119.7	118.0	115.7	124.4	103.8	126.5	122.3	118.9	83.1	165.3	111.9	97.6	131.5	142	125.3	119.8
1973	129.8	127.1	124.4	131.5	114.5	137.2	133.9	129.8	87.5	179.5	116.8	103.2	149.2	160	133.1	134.7
1974	129.3	127.3	125.1	128.9	120.0	135.3	132.4	129.4	84.2	169.7	119.1	102.1	157.1	171	147.7	160.1
1975	117.8	119.3	118.2	124.0	110.2	123.1	115.5	116.3	73.6	166.0	116.9	91.4	151.0	186	161.2	174.9
1975—Nov.	123.5	123.8	122.3	131.1	110.0	129.3	123.1	122.7	}76.8	148.0	117.8	92.4	158.9	192	165.6	178.2
Dec.	124.4	124.9	123.5	132.3	111.5	129.3	123.3	123.6		137.0	118.1	93.0	162.3	198	166.3	178.7
1976—Jan.	125.7	126.0	123.9	133.1	111.2	133.6	125.3	125.2	}79.0	183.0	118.7	94.0	165.9	197	166.7	179.3
Feb.	127.3	127.4	125.3	134.9	112.1	135.3	127.3	127.0		170.0	119.0	94.3	165.4	201	167.1	179.3
Mar.	128.1	128.1	126.4	136.1	112.9	134.9	128.2	127.9		185.0	119.4	94.9	167.4	204	167.5	179.6
Apr.	128.4	128.0	126.3	136.1	112.9	134.7	129.2	128.5		189.0	119.9	95.5	166.1	205	168.2	181.3
May	129.6	128.9	127.3	137.4	113.5	135.0	130.6	129.6	}80.2	205.0	119.8	95.4	170.7	202	169.2	181.8
June	130.1	129.5	127.6	137.8	113.8	135.9	131.1	130.2		187.0	119.8	95.3	171.6	206	170.1	183.1
July	130.7	129.8	127.6	136.8	114.9	137.6	132.2	131.0		184.0	120.2	*95.2	173.2	205	171.1	184.3
Aug.	131.3	130.3	128.3	137.5	115.7	137.8	133.0	131.6	}80.8	162.0	120.4	*95.2	175.9	209	171.9	183.7
Sept.	130.9	130.0	127.5	136.2	115.5	139.0	132.4	130.7		164.0	120.8	96.1	177.7	207	172.6	184.7
Oct.	130.4	129.6	127.3	136.5	114.7	138.3	131.7	129.9		237.0	120.6	95.0	175.9	209	173.3	185.2
Nov.	132.0	131.5	129.5	138.9	116.6	139.2	133.0	131.7			121.0	95.6	179.3	212	....	185.6

▲ Revised data for 1955–62, comparable to the revised data beginning 1963 shown below, will be published later.
[1] Employees only: excludes personnel in the Armed Forces.
[2] Production workers only. Revised back to 1973.
[3] F.R. index based on Census Bureau figures.
[4] Prices are not seasonally adjusted. Latest figure is final.
NOTE.—All series: Data are seasonally adjusted unless otherwise noted.

Capacity utilization: Based on data from Federal Reserve, McGraw-Hill Economics Department, and Dept. of Commerce.
Construction contracts: McGraw-Hill Informations Systems Company, F.W. Dodge Division, monthly index of dollar value of total construction contracts, including residential, nonresidential, and heavy engineering.
Employment and payrolls: Based on Bureau of Labor Statistics data; includes data for Alaska and Hawaii beginning with 1959.
Prices: Bureau of Labor Statistics data.

SOURCE: *Federal Reserve Bulletin*, December 1976.

perspective from which to forecast, it is helpful to look at the historical performance of sales and earnings.

One important factor the analyst might uncover is that the history of the industry is very short. This finding alone might make him more cautious about a commitment in this industry, because the industry may not have proved its ability to weather a variety of economic growth prospects, the opportunity of getting in on the ground floor might be a paramount consideration.

The historical record of the industry is crucial for yet another reason—namely, the calculation of both average levels and stability of performance in both sales and earnings, including growth-rate calculations. Even though past average levels or past variability may not be repeated in the future, the analyst needs to know how this industry has reacted in the past. With knowledge and understanding of the reasons behind past behavior, he is better able to assess the relative magnitudes of perform-ance in the future.[7]

---

[7]We saw in Chapter 4 how the mean and variance forecasts are important outputs of security analysis and inputs to portfolio analysis. Briefly, the analyst forecasts the future level and stability of the firm's earnings, prices, and return. We will use the mean and standard deviation of return to reflect the anticipated level and stability of the security's performance.

A related factor that the analyst must also consider is the cost structure of the industry—that is, the relation of fixed to variable costs. The higher the fixed-cost component, the higher the sales volume necessary to achieve the firm's breakeven point. Conversely, the lower the relative fixed costs, the easier it is for a firm to achieve and surpass its breakeven point.

Permanence

Another important factor in an industry analysis is the relative permanence of the industry. Permanence is a phenomenon related to the products and technology of the industry, whereas the historical record just discussed deals with the behavior of the numbers without regard to the factors that underlie them. If the analyst feels that the need for this particular industry will vanish in an extremely short period of time, it would seem foolish to invest funds in the industry. Sometimes an industry fades from the scene because of a replacement industry that eliminates or diminishes the need for the original industry. Certainly the rise of the automobile caused a decline in the importance of the carriage and the buggy whip, the growth of popularity of margarine hurt the demand for butter, and so on. In this age of rapid technological advance, the degree of permanence of an industry has become an ever more important consideration in industry analysis.

The Attitude Of Government Toward The Industry

It is important for the analyst or prospective investor to consider the probable role government will play in the industry. Will it provide support—financial or otherwise? Or will it restrain the industry's development through restrictive legislation and legal enforcement? For example, if the government feels that foreign competition is too severe for a particular domestic industry, it can impose restrictive import quotas and/or tariffs that would tend to assist the domestic industry. Conversely, if the government feels the domestic industry is becoming too independent, it can remove any barriers currently existing and thus aid foreign competition. Furthermore, government can aid selected industries through favorable tax legislation, such as the investment tax credit, which especially aids industries with large capital output.

As government becomes more influential in attempting to regulate business and to advocate consumer protection, the permanence of the industry might well be affected—not in that government interference will necessarily drive it out of business, but in that profits of the industry can be substantially lessened. Sometimes an industry declines in importance because of legal restrictions that are placed upon it.

Labor Conditions

As unions grow in power in our economy, the state of labor conditions in the industry under analysis becomes ever more important. That is, if we are dealing with a very labor-intensive production process or a very mechanized capital-intensive process where labor performs crucial operations, the possibility of a strike looms as an important factor to be reckoned with. This is particularly true in industries with large fixed costs, for fixed costs such as rent and insurance continue even when production is curtailed. Should a strike occur in such an industry, the large fixed costs would cut deeply into profits earned before and after the strike. An example of such an industry would be steel manufacturing.

In a labor-intensive industry, the variable costs would undoubtedly dominate the fixed costs; however, even here, the loss of customer goodwill during a long strike would probably more than offset the possible advantages of low fixed costs. That is, customers would find other suppliers, and even the low fixed costs might be difficult for the firm to cover.

Competitive Conditions

Another significant factor in industry analysis is the competitive conditions in the industry under study. One way to determine the competitive conditions is to observe whether any barriers to entry exist. Bain speaks of three general types of barriers: (1) a product-differentiation edge that forestalls the entry of competition, (2) absolute-cost advantages, and (3) advantages arising from economies of scale.[8]

Product-differentiation advantages generally arise when buyers have a preference for the products of established firms or industries, such as in patent medicines and breakfast cereals. Because existing firms or industries have such an advantage, a new entrant is not likely to be able to charge as high a price as they do. Furthermore, a new entrant would probably have to expend large sums of money on sales and promotion expenses in order to procure an acceptable sales level.

By absolute-cost advantages, we refer to the fact that established firms or industries are able to produce and distribute their products at any level of production or distribution at a lower cost than any new entrant can. These advantages arise from such things as patents, ownership of resources or other key raw materials, and easier access to necessary equipment, funds, or management skills. With this combination of circumstances, it can be seen that the established firms are likely to have considerably wider profit margins than their newer competition.

Economics of scale are found in industries in which it is necessary to attain a fairly high level of production in order to obtain economically feasible levels of cost— such as in producing automobiles. A firm attempting to break into such an industry would, under normal circumstances, have to obtain a significant share of the market if it expects to have a competitive cost structure relative to existing firms.

The investment implication when examining an industry that has significant barriers to entry should be clear to the reader. An analyst or prospective investor would like to see that the industry in which he is considering investment seems to be well protected from the inroads of new firms; if the industry were protected by product differentiation, not only would it be difficult for new firms to enter it but it would also be exceedingly difficult for new industries to develop in competition with the market currently owned by the existing industry.

Industry Share Prices Relative To Industry Earnings

Having evaluated the various characteristics of past sales and earnings, industry permanence, government attitude, labor conditions, and industry competitive conditions, the analyst must ultimately reach a considered investment decision. However,

[8]Bain, *Industrial Organization*, p. 255.

even if all indications are that the industry has very favorable future prospects, this does not necessarily imply that funds should be committed to it immediately. A decision to purchase is not made based only on the current status and future prospects, but also on the current prices of securities in the industry, their risk, and the returns they promise.

At this point we will refer to only the price consideration. If the price is very high relative to future earnings growth, these securities might not be a wise investment. Conversely, if future prospects are dim but prices are low relative to a fairly level future pattern of earnings, the stocks in this industry might well be an attractive investment. Frequently, when an industry develops because of technology or some other such reason, investors become overzealous in their desire to purchase securities of firms in this new industry. Thus, these share prices are bid to very high levels, with the consequence that the P/E ratio soars. So it can be seen that the "market psychology" can be a crucial factor in both raising prices to exorbitant levels and depressing prices to unreasonable levels, depending on how the market evaluates the industry's future prospects.

Restaurant Industry Example

Following the order of presentation, let us determine the key characteristics of the restaurant industry.

1. *Past sales and earnings performance.* Table 7-1 contains selected past sales and earnings performance data as compiled by Standard & Poor's in their industry survey of the restaurant industry. It should be noted in the table that only selected companies are included in this series of data. However, S&P believes that these companies are representative of the industry as a whole.

It can be seen that sales of the industry as defined by S&P have grown dramatically since 1972, almost a fourfold increase. A similiar trend is evident in operating income. This trend would even be more dramatic had the series been extended back into the 1950s and 1960s. However, even with this selected period from 1972 to 1979 it should be obvious that this has been a growth industry.

2. *Permanence of the industry.* Eating away from home has existed for many years, obviously. The restaurant industry and in particular the fast-food industry, however, is relatively new, having experienced its greatest growth in the post-World War II period. As long as people continue to be sociable creatures and desire a change of pace, eating away from home will be a habit which persists. Furthermore, as both husband and wife continue to work, the need to eat out occasionally will continue to persist. Obviously, the need to eat away from home is a necessity for travelers for both pleasure and business. The eating-away-from-home habit has spread to foreign countries as well. As members of the restaurant industry and fast-food industry expand into foreign markets, the permanence and growth of the industry will be further advanced.

3. *The attitude of government.* There has been little government intervention in the industry when compared with most industries. This in part is caused because the restaurant industry is relatively free from issues which cause political controversy. The fast-food sector of the industry in particular is staffed in large part by young, minimum-wage workers and is therefore not generally encumbered by unions, union restrictions, and potential labor law problems. The industry to date has been relatively free of anti-trust vulnerability. There has been little involvement of federal authorities in the area of pricing policies and to date there has been no significant involvement relative to pollution. The only potential governmental interference which might be foreseen would

TABLE 7-1

PAST SALES AND EARNINGS PERFORMANCE

Restaurant Companies

The companies used for this series of per share data are: Church's Fried Chicken (added 11-16-77); Denny's Inc.; Gino's Inc.; Howard Johnson (deleted 6-25-80); Marriott Corp.; McDonald's Corp.; and Pizza Hut (added 3-3-76 and deleted 11-16-77).

		1972	1973	1974	1975	1976	1977	1978	1979
Sales		11.66	15.01	17.76	21.27	26.32	29.59	34.81	42.31
Operating income		1.79	2.31	2.72	3.52	6.34	5.24	6.46	7.72
Profit margins (%)		15.35	15.39	15.32	16.55	24.09	17.71	18.56	18.25
Depreciation		0.39	0.51	0.63	0.80	0.95	1.14	1.50	1.82
Taxes		0.61	0.79	0.90	1.16	1.44	1.70	2.03	2.22
Earnings		0.68	0.90	1.00	1.24	1.62	1.92	2.32	2.82
Dividends		0.03	0.04	0.04	0.05	0.11	0.16	0.28	0.40
Earnings as a % of sales		5.83	6.00	5.63	5.83	6.16	6.49	6.66	6.67
Dividends as a % of earnings		4.41	4.44	4.00	4.03	6.79	8.33	12.07	14.18
Price	—High	42.03	41.73	28.29	27.51	30.86	25.35	30.07	28.87
	—Low	23.37	22.07	11.80	12.41	23.96	18.71	22.71	21.32
Price-earnings ratios	—High	61.81	46.37	28.29	22.19	19.05	13.20	12.96	10.24
	—Low	34.37	24.52	11.80	10.01	14.79	9.74	9.79	7.56
Dividend yield (%)	—High	0.13	0.18	0.34	0.40	0.46	0.86	1.23	1.88
	—Low	0.07	0.10	0.14	0.18	0.36	0.63	0.93	1.39
Book value		4.52	5.47	6.41	7.51	9.53	10.94	12.83	14.94
Return on book value (%)		15.04	16.45	15.60	16.51	17.00	17.55	18.08	18.88
Working capital		0.74	0.82	0.68	0.94	0.97	0.78	0.74	0.28
Capital expenditures		1.97	2.92	3.58	3.67	3.89	3.92	5.09	6.57

SOURCE: Standard & Poor's *Industry Surveys* (New York: Standard & Poor's Corporation).

be in the form of local zoning restrictions relative to the construction of more buildings and the form that these buildings and related signs may take.

4. *Labor conditions.* While labor costs in the fast-food subsector of the industry are high as a percentage, the level of wage rates is notoriously low. As has already been stated, the vast majority of the workers at the fast-food restaurants are paid at minimum-wage rates. As of this date the federal government does not have a raise in the minimum-wage rate scheduled for the year 1982. If this materializes, it would be the first year since 1973 that the minimum-wage rate has not been raised. This should aid profit margins for this sector of the restaurant industry.

5. *Competitive conditions.* Because of the high returns on investment as evidenced in Table 7-1, and because of the abundant opportunities for rapid physical expansion, the fast-food sector of the restaurant industry has experienced rapidly escalating, intensified domestic competition. Thus one could characterize this industry as being increasingly competitive. This has caused the key chains to launch massive advertising and marketing campaigns to maintain and hold their shares of the market and perhaps to increase their shares of the market. In addition, promotional gifts, contests, and prizes have been initiated to lure customers.

In addition to the large advertising and promotional expenditures, the companies have been forced to upgrade continually the decor of the facilities, maintain extremely fast service, and provide good value for the customer's money. Also because of the availability of the facilities, the member firms have attempted to expand their menus so as to achieve utilization of their facilities throughout the day and evening. Traditionally, these establishments have catered to a lunch business; however, several key member firms in this industry have now introduced a breakfast menu and are now attempting also to increase dinner business by introducing new varieties of beef dishes, such as a beef steak sandwich, and to introduce chicken dishes into their menu. Obviously, in expanding menus while attempting to maintain profit margins, the various chains will need to intensify their advertising and marketing campaigns and will cause an already competitive industry to become even more competitive.

The large chains which dominate the industry benefit from a perceived product differentiated from individual industry units that are not affiliated with a national chain. They attempt to guarantee uniform quality and uniform service throughout all members of the chain in both company-owned and franchised restaurants. Furthermore, the large chains have an additional advantage because of highly trained management teams which help achieve operating economies and effectuate efficient food delivery systems.

6. *Industry share prices relative to industry earnings.* The restaurant industry has enjoyed rapid growth in earnings, as can be seen from examining Table 7-1. As a result of this rapid rise in earnings the P/E multiples during the 1970s have also been high. This can also be seen by examining the price-earnings ratios line of Table 7-1. The growth rates of individual member firms of this industry can be seen by examining Table 7-2. This table shows the percentage change year to year of earnings for the years 1976-79 and the five-year growth rate for this same period. It should be observed in Table 7-2 that in the late 1970s the growth rate in earnings for many member firms was in fact negative and for other firms the growth rate declined. It can be seen, for example in the case of McDonald's Corporation, that the growth rate has dropped from 26.4 percent in 1976 to 16 percent for the year 1979. It is perhaps for this reason that the P/E multiples for this industry have consistently been dropping. It can be seen in Table 7-1, for example, that in 1972 the P/E multiples ranged from a low of 34 to a high of approximately 62, while in 1979 the range in P/E multiples was 7.56 to 10.24. Thus we see that this industry has undergone a rapid transformation in terms of growth and in terms of downward valuation in P/E multiples. Thus, a prospective investor in this industry needs to be sensitive to the price vulnerability of this industry's stocks, should this rate of growth continue to decline. The investor should be careful not to be overly optimistic in establishing a high P/E multiple.

Overall the outlook for the fast food sector of the restaurant industry for the 1980s is mildly optimistic.

Industry Life Cycle

Thus far in this chapter, we have discussed a number of pertinent factors that should be considered in an industry analysis. A framework within which we can place many of these considerations is known as the *industry life-cycle theory*.[9] The life of an industry can be separated into the pioneering stage, the expansion stage, the stagnation stage, and the decay stage.[10] These stages are illustrated graphically in Figure 7-3 on page 180.

Pioneering Stage

The pioneering stage is typified by rapid growth in demand for the output of the industry. In fact, in this earliest stage, demand not only grows but grows at an increasing rate. As a result, there is a great apparent opportunity for profits, and thus venture

[9]This theory is generally attributed to Julius Grodinsky. See Grodinsky, *Investments* (New York: Ronald Press, 1953), pp. 64-89.
[10]For convenience, we will combine the stagnation and decay stages and refer to them as the *stabilization stage*.

TABLE 7-2
YEAR-TO-YEAR EARNINGS GROWTH

Company Food Service (Restaurant)	1976	1977	1978	1979	5-Year Growth (%)
Chart House	30.7	5.1	5.8	15.6	18.9
Chock Full O'Nuts	NM	NM	NM	43.8	NM
Church's Fried Chicken	59.6	37.3	35.9	29.3	37.0
Collins Food Intl.	60.4	20.5	20.0	7.9	NM
Denny's Inc.	42.3	30.4	18.0	3.3	*25.0
Dunkin' Donuts	32.4	24.5	21.3	12.5	*27.0
Frisch's Restaurants	12.4	−3.0	45.1	−14.6	10.1
Gino's Inc.	−34.3	−15.4	52.4	−110.9	NM
Hardee's Food System	180.0	52.4	29.7	32.5	NM
Host International	NM	24.7	32.1	31.4	19.1
Jerrico Inc.	159.0	2.0	−14.6	28.4	*38.0
Marcus Corp.	9.5	13.6	11.2	−2.9	10.4
Marriott Corp.	41.3	17.2	50.4	30.8	*24.0
McDonald's Corp.	26.4	24.5	19.0	16.0	*23.0
Morrison Inc.	13.8	20.2	13.4	5.5	18.9
Pizza Inn	−7.3	10.7	−28.6	2.9	3.4
Ponderosa System	57.1	193.9	42.3	−2.2	*44.0
Sambo's Restaurants	31.3	5.6	−68.9	NM	NM
Shoney's Inc.	41.0	21.8	22.4	22.0	*26.0
Steak n Shake	19.2	−11.4	−39.1	NM	NM
Valle's Steak House	−15.1	40.9	−30.8	−58.6	NM
Victoria Station	3.5	20.1	−32.7	−137.8	NM
Wendy's International	142.9	107.4	64.5	−0.4	NA

NM, not meaningful; NA, not available.
*Approximately.
SOURCE: Standard & Poor's *Industry Surveys* (New York: Standard & Poor's Corporation).

capital comes into the industry. As large numbers of firms attempt to capture their share of the market, there arises a high business mortality rate; many of the weaker firms that are attempting to survive in this new industry are eliminated, and a lesser number of firms survive the initial phases of the pioneering stage. Firms are eliminated in part because of price competition, heavy losses resulting from startup costs, and generally hard nonprice competition stemming from such things as attempts to develop a brand name, a differentiated product, or a market edge as a result of product image that has been created.

Many firms are lured into the industry as a result of profit opportunities, and they compete vigorously with each other. The result is a constant shifting of the relative positions of the firms in the industry. Thus, it is difficult at this stage for the analyst to select those firms that will remain on top for some time to come. Even if the analyst has the ability to recognize an emerging industry in the pioneering stage, he will probably not invest at this point in the industry's development, because of the great risks involved and because of the tremendous difficulty in selecting the survivors. However, the astute analyst will not even consider investment in the industry in the pioneering stage but will rather observe the industry's maturity and will wait for the expansion stage before he commits funds.

FIGURE 7-3
INDUSTRIAL LIFE CYCLE

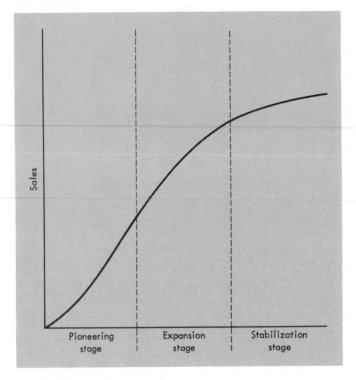

Expansion Stage

The expansion stage is characterized by the appearance of the firms surviving from the pioneering stage. These few companies continue to get stronger, both in share of the market and financially. Their competition in the expansion stage usually brings about improved products at a lower price. These firms continue to expand, but at a more moderate rate of growth than the one they experienced in the pioneering stage. As a result, these now stronger, steadier, more efficient firms become more attractive for investment purposes. While they are still growing, they have the aura of stability about them. In fact, in the expansion stage, many companies establish the precedent of paying dividends, making them an even more desirable investment.

Stabilization Stage

The growth of the industry, which had moderated in the expansion stage, begins at some point to moderate even further, and perhaps even begins to stagnate. In other words, the ability of the industry to grow appears to have been lost. Sales may be increasing at a slower rate than that experienced by competititve industries or by the overall economy. Grodinsky refers to a possible explanation of this transition as "latent obsolescence":

> Latent Obsolescence—While an industry is still expanding, economic and financial infection may develop. Though its future is promising, seeds of

decay may have already been planted. These seeds may not germinate, and the industry may remain strong. If the seeds do germinate, the latent decay becomes real. These seeds may be described as "latent obsolescence," because they may not become active, and they are the earliest signs of decline. Such factors must be examined and interpreted by the investor.[11]

Symptoms of latent obsolescence include changing social habits, high labor costs, changes in technology, and stationary demand.

The investment implication as these events take place is to dispose of one's holdings as soon as the industry begins to pass from the expansion stage to the stabilization stage, for after the transition becomes general knowledge, the stock's price may be depressed. However, an industry may only stagnate intermittently before resuming a period of growth (e.g., airlines, in the view of some analysts)—thus starting a new cycle by, say, the introduction of a technological innovation or a new product. Thus, it is crucial for the investor or analyst to monitor industry developments constantly.

Although our exposition of the industry life-cycle theory seems to imply that it is easy to detect which stage of development an industry is in at any point in time, this is not necessarily so, for often the transition from one stage to the next is slow and unclear, making it detectable only by careful analysis. Nonetheless, this approach is useful in a somewhat crude way, and at the same time it gives the analyst insight into the apparent merits of investments in a given industry at a given time. In fact, one investment advisory service states, "In judging the probable future trend of an individual stock it is therefore more important to project the trend of its industry group than to project the trend of the general market. . . ."[12]

Despite the intuitive attractiveness of the industry life-cycle framework, it should be noted that it is only a *general* framework, and therefore, exceptions to the stereotype presented here will be met in practice. The analyst must be careful not to attempt to force all situations encountered in practice into the pioneering, expansion, and stabilization molds as outlined here. Furthermore, the investment-policy implications mentioned in conjunction with the foregoing analysis serve as only a general guideline. Due heed must be paid to the current price of the security relative to its future earnings prospects.

Techniques for Evaluating Relevant Industry Factors

Thus far in this chapter, we have discussed the role of relevant industry factors in the investment decision-making process. At this point we should turn our attention to the techniques for analyzing this information and to the readily available sources of it.[13]

[11]Grodinsky, *Investments*, pp. 71-72.

[12]George A. Chestnutt, Jr., *Stock Market Analysis: Facts and Principles* (Greenwich, Conn.: Chestnutt Corporation, 1971), p. 12.

[13]One key input to the analyst is gained from visits with managements of firms in the industry under study. Sometimes this involves traveling to the various corporate headquarters; sometimes the company officials come to the analysts, via talks to groups of analysts at regularly scheduled luncheons of Financial Analysts societies, held in major cities across the United States. Information gained from exposure to management is extremely valuable to the analyst. The sources of information discussed in this section supplement such personal contacts and are often the only sources available to the analyst or investor.

End-Use And Regression Analysis

End-use analysis, or product-demand analysis, as it is sometimes called, refers to the process whereby the analyst or investor attempts to diagnose the factors that determine the demand for the output of the industry. Determining such demand is clearly crucial, since, in a single-product firm, units demanded multiplied by price will equal sales revenue. In the process, the analyst hopes to uncover the relationships that "explain" demand, thereby enabling him to forecast industry sales more accurately. Frequently, such variables as GNP, disposable income, per capita consumption, price elasticity of demand, and per capita income are powerful *explanatory variables*. If this is the case and certain basic assumptions are upheld, linear regression analysis and correlation analysis can be useful techniques.[14]

Briefly stated, simple linear regression analysis mathematically fits a line to a series of points on a scatter diagram, and correlation analysis permits us to measure the "goodness of the fit." Perhaps a simple illustration will help clarify the advantages of these techniques. Figure 7-4 shows a hypothetical scatter diagram, and Figure 7-5 shows this same scatter diagram with three regression lines, *AB, CD*, and *EF*, fitted to the data.

Merely "eyeballing" the data contained in Figure 7-4 is not a very scientific way of analyzing it. Actually, two different persons might interpret the significance of the

FIGURE 7-4
SCATTER DIAGRAM

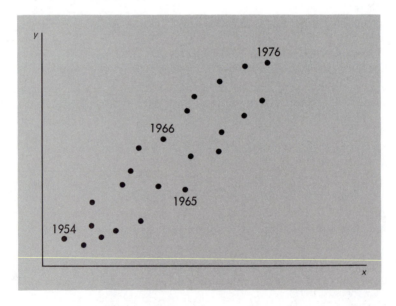

[14]For a detailed treatment of the assumptions underlying regression analysis and correlation analysis, see any comprehensive statistics or econometrics text, such as J. Johnston, *Econometric Methods* (New York: McGraw-Hill, 1963).

FIGURE 7-5
SCATTER DIAGRAM WITH A FITTED REGRESSION LINE

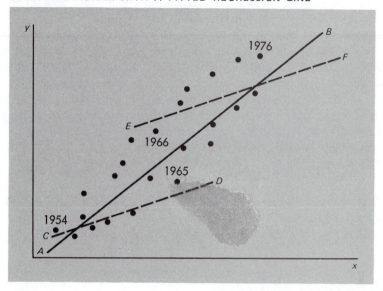

data quite differently. The next step up in sophistication would perhaps be to fit a line freehand to the data; however, this too is subjective and lacks the necessary rigor. Fortunately, there exists a technique known as the "method of least squares," which allows us to base the fitted line on the simple equation $y = a + bx$, the equation of a straight line.[15] You will recall that y is generally the dependent variable, x is the independent variable, a is the y intercept, and b is the slope of the line. For example, y might be machine production or sales, and x might be industrial production. Each point would represent the figures for both variables for a particular period, such as a year.

Most computer installations own "canned" (ready-to-use) regression programs for the interested user. These programs normally furnish the user at least such output as a, b, the mean of the independent and dependent variables, and some correlation measures of the "goodness of fit" and the "explanatory" powers of the independent variable.

We can undoubtedly imagine many uses of this statistical technique in industry analysis, such as regressing industry sales against time; industry sales against a key macroeconomic variable like GNP, personal income, or disposable income; and industry earnings over time. Figure 7-6 is an excerpt from a Standard & Poor's *Industry Surveys*; specifically, a portion of a basic analysis of the machinery industry. It contains a diagram with a fitted regression line. In this case, the y, or dependent variable, is machinery

---

[15]The reader interested in the mechanics of this technique, as well as in correlation analysis, should read one of the many statistics texts available.

production, and the x, or independent variable, is U.S. industrial production as measured by the Federal Reserve Board Index of Industrial Production. Such an application of regression analysis is common in industry analyses.

Sometimes the analyst will not be satisfied with the results of a simple linear regression analysis and will feel that two, three, or more variables would much better be able to "explain" the variability of the dependent variable. In such an instance, the analyst will use multiple regression analysis (an extension of simple linear regression analysis). In this technique, the dependent variable is regressed against several independent variables. For example, if we were attempting to forecast the sales of the power-lawn mower industry, we might use disposable income, expected rainfall, and the number of single-unit residential homes as independent variables.

PROBLEM AREAS IN REGRESSION ANALYSIS[16]

First, we can observe three distinct regression lines that have been fitted to the data contained in Figure 7-5. There are three because three different time periods were used to calculate the least-squares regression line—the period 1954-65 for line *CD*, the

FIGURE 7-6
ANALYSIS OF THE MACHINERY INDUSTRY

With the economy extending an upturn that began in the spring of 1975, concern is mounting that the continuing lag in capital spending could restrict a more sustained recovery. Consideration is also being given to a possible re-emergence of shortages of industrial capacity and basic materials, similar to those that occurred in 1973 and early 1974. Such shortages would, of course, likely lead to a rekindling of inflation.

The latest Commerce Department survey on plant and equipment spending projects a 6.5% increase in 1976 outlays, a gain that would be more than offset by higher prices. The most recent MCGRAW-HILL Economics Department survey of business indicates that spending will advance 13% in 1976 and that businessmen expect a 9% increase in capital goods prices, resulting in a 4% pickup in the real volume of plant and equipment spending. Other independent estimates point to gains in real outlays on the order of 3% to 5%. The MCGRAW-HILL study pointed out that some 50% of planned 1976 expenditures of $127.3 billion were slated for expansion, with the remainder going for modernization. While such outlays for expansion represent a larger share of investment dollars, compared with 1975, the significant spending on modernization (including safety and environmental requirement outlays) indicates a cautious concern for overexpansion.

With U.S. industry operating at less than 75% of capacity in the 1976 first quarter, there would appear to be considerable slack yet to be taken up before additional facilities are required. This idle capacity, much of it representing obsolete or otherwise unusable equipment, is

expected to fall to 20% by year end, a level that usually triggers a surge in spending. Further, the continuing abatement in the rate of inflation, coupled with the growing strength of the consumer sector, could well provide the necessary impetus for businessmen to step-up their spending plans before too long.

Additional encouragement should come from the healthier prospects for financing investment. Recent increases in corporate cash flow—profits plus depreciation—have been substantial; many businesses could finance much higher capital spending rates internally.

Industrial production, earnings, and capital expenditures					
	Indexes of Production			Corp. Profits	Cap. Consumption Allow.	Total Profits & Allow.'
	Indus-trial	Durable Mfrs.	Machinery			
Year	1967=100			Billions of Dollars		
1975	113.7	105.7	112.8	71.2	78.3	149.5
R1974	124.8	120.7	128.1	79.5	78.3	157.8
1973	125.6	122.0	125.8	R68.7	R69.0	R137.7
1972	115.2	108.4	107.5	R54.7	R65.4	R120.1
1971	106.8	99.4	96.2	R44.3	R60.6	R104.9
1970	106.6	101.4	100.3	R37.0	R55.1	R92.1
1969	110.7	110.0	106.8	R43.8	R49.4	R93.2
1968	105.7	105.5	101.9	R46.2	R44.4	R90.6
1967	100.0	100.0	100.0	46.6	R40.4	R87.0
1966	97.9	99.0	98.6	49.9	36.7	R86.6

R - Revised.
Sources: Department of Commerce, Federal Reserve Board.

---

[16]The reader should be cautioned that these are not the only potential problem areas.

FIGURE 7-6 (Cont.)

Outside capital costs are lower, although still above historical averages, and the increased cash flow should restrict interest rate increases, as fewer firms have to borrow. Finally, the surge in stock prices has made the equity market an attractive capital source.

Should a major improvement in capital spending lag behind the consumer sector of the economy by more than the usual 18 months or so, a form of cushion exists now that was not available to soften the capacity and material shortages of a few years ago. With the economies of most major European countries recovering at a much slower pace than that of the U.S., it is possible that domestic shortages could be eased by imports.

Orders expected to rise

New orders for nonelectrical machinery should be up substantially in 1976, with the bulk of the gain coming in the second half. According to MCGRAW-HILL, machinery orders spurted 27% in the first quarter of 1976, versus the comparable year-earlier period. While the domestic orders index after the first quarter was one-third ahead of the year-earlier level and the export orders index was up 22%, at 209 the total index was still some 5% below the August 1974 peak of 220. Nonetheless, the broadening recovery, combined with modest rates of price increases, suggests a significant advance in over-all profits this year and a more rapid rise in capital investment.

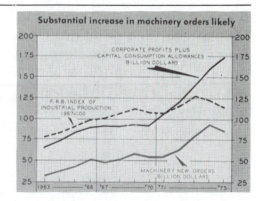

For individual components of the broad machinery category, outlays for pollution control equipment and services are expected to be maintained at relatively high levels. Construction and material handling equipment manufacturers should benefit from the stepped-up economic pace, with increased housing starts sparking a mild recovery in smaller equipment sales, offsetting a possible decline in shipments to energy-related areas. Indications are that electric utilities will be advancing new plant additions, boding well for power equipment producers.

Expenditures for new equipment by U.S. business
(In millions of dollars)

Industry	1966	1967	1968	1969	1970	1971	1972	1973	1974	1975	E1976
Manufacturing	26,990	26,690	28,370	31,680	31,950	29,990	31,350	38,010	46,010	47,950	51,850
Durable goods industries	13,990	13,700	14,120	15,960	15,800	14,150	15,640	19,250	22,620	21,840	22,930
Primary iron and steel	2,170	2,310	2,270	2,130	2,000	1,700	1,570	2,050	2,120	3,030	2,750
Primary nonferrous metals	860	900	1,090	1,100	1,240	1,080	1,180	1,670	2,330	2,280	2,180
Electrical machinery & equip.	1,190	1,240	1,780	2,030	2,270	2,140	2,390	2,840	2,970	2,310	2,530
Machinery, except electrical	2,860	2,950	2,840	3,440	3,470	2,800	2,900	3,420	4,420	4,500	5,090
Motor vehicles & equipment	1,930	1,660	1,360	1,650	1,590	1,510	1,830	2,280	2,700	2,060	2,410
Transportation equipment, excluding motor vehicles	1,090	1,090	1,120	1,110	840	620	700	853	800	920	800
Stone, clay & glass products	910	730	860	1,070	990	850	1,200	1,490	1,440	1,420	1,600
*Other durable goods	2,980	2,830	2,820	3,440	3,410	3,450	3,870	4,960	5,100	4,380	4,550
Nondurable goods industries	13,000	13,000	14,250	15,720	16,150	15,840	15,720	18,760	23,390	26,110	28,920
Food and beverage	1,390	1,410	2,210	2,590	2,840	2,690	2,550	3,110	3,250	3,260	3,920
Textile	1,130	890	530	630	560	610	730	770	840	660	760
Paper & allied products	1,500	1,640	1,320	1,580	1,650	1,250	1,380	1,860	2,580	2,950	3,330
Chemical & allied products	2,990	2,880	2,830	3,100	3,440	3,440	3,450	4,460	5,690	6,250	6,670
Petroleum and coal	4,420	4,650	5,250	5,630	5,620	5,850	5,250	5,450	8,000	10,510	11,630
Rubber	420	490	980	1,090	940	840	1,080	1,560	1,470	1,000	1,120
†Other nondurable goods	1,140	1,040	1,130	1,100	1,110	1,150	1,270	1,560	1,550	1,480	1,490
Mining	1,470	1,420	1,630	1,860	1,890	2,160	2,420	2,740	3,180	3,790	3,880
Railroad	1,980	1,530	1,450	1,860	1,780	1,670	1,800	1,960	2,540	2,550	2,080
Transportation other than rail	3,440	3,880	4,150	4,190	4,260	3,260	3,920	4,070	4,120	5,020	4,150
Public utilities	8,410	9,880	10,200	11,610	13,140	15,300	17,000	18,710	20,550	20,140	23,240
‡Commercial, communications, and other	18,360	18,250	21,970	24,350	26,690	28,820	31,960	34,250	36,010	33,340	34,860
††Total	60,630	61,660	67,760	75,560	79,710	81,210	88,440	99,740	112,400	112,780	120,060

Note: Data exclude expenditures of agricultural business and outlays charged to current account. *Includes fabricated metal products, lumber products, furniture & fixtures, instruments, ordnance, and miscellaneous manufacturers. †Includes apparel & related products, tobacco, leather & leather products, and printing & publishing. ‡Includes trade-service, finance, and construction. ††—Detail may not add to totals because of rounding. E–Estimated.
Sources: Securities & Exchange Commission, Department of Commerce.

SOURCE: Standard & Poor's *Industry Surveys* (New York: Standard & Poor's Corporation).

period 1966-76 for line *EF*, and the period 1954-76 for line *AB*. Thus, the selection of beginning and end points is critical in determining the line that will be fitted to the data. This fact is always true when any determinants underlying the variables themselves change significantly over time. In the example, some sort of underlying shift occurred during 1965-76 that affected this industry—such as a change in consumer tastes, technology, or economic or tax environment. *In selecting beginning or end points, it is important that basic conditions were similar in the base and end-point years, as well as in the interim.*[17]

A second problem area involves the nature of the relationship the analyst is measuring. The technique we are discussing here assumes a *linear* relationship as opposed to a nonlinear one, such as a curvilinear relationship, in which the points lie along a curve rather than a straight line. To the extent that this is not a valid assumption, the results of the regression analysis may at best be somewhat misleading, and at worst they will be totally meaningless.

The third and last problem to be discussed here involves the interpretation of the results of the adjunct correlation analysis. It is possible for two series of data to be highly correlated—that is, to go up and down pretty much together—and yet to be not at all causally related. For example, it is possible that for some time period, rainfall and the stock market might be highly correlated; however, we would be wrong in asserting that rainfall caused the market to go up and a drought spelled disaster for the market. If this were true, the best training for security analysis would be to study meteorology! Therefore the analyst should not just blindly strive for high correlation. The variables should appear to be related in a significant *economic* sense as well as in a *statistical* sense before he jumps to conclusions about probable causation.

Input-Output Analysis

Input-output analysis can be thought of as a way of getting inside demand analysis or end-use analysis. This technique, which is reflected in an input-output table, reflects the flow of goods and services through the economy, including intermediate steps in the production process as the good proceeds from the raw-material stage through final consumption. Thus input-output analysis observes patterns of consumption at all stages— not just the consumption of final goods—in order to detect any changing patterns or trends that might indicate the growth or decline of industries.

Basically, an input-output table is a matrix consisting of rows and columns of identically coded industries. Reading down a column tells us what the required inputs for the industry in the column head were from all the industries. Conversely, reading across a row tells us what the output (from the industry in the left-hand column) to each industry was, including intra-industry sales.

Table 7-3 is an excerpt from an actual input-output table. We can see in row 1 that the livestock and livestock-products industry sold $26,322 million worth of goods in

---

[17]Frequently, in an effort to partially overcome this problem of the appropriate time period, analysts forecast from a base period to an end period rather than from a discrete point to a discrete point. That is, to continue the example, the period average for 1954-56 would be used as the base and the period 1974-76 as the end period. However, even this is only a minimum compensation and does not completely overcome the problem. That can be achieved only by selecting a stable, but meaningful, period.

TABLE 7-3
INPUT-OUTPUT TABLE

Interindustry Transactions, 1958
(In millions of dollars at producers' prices)

For the distribution of output of an industry, read the row for that industry.
For the composition of inputs to an industry, read the column for that industry.

	1 Livestock and live-stock products	2 Other agricultural products	Intermediate outputs, total	Final Demand — Personal consumption expenditures	Final Demand — Gross private fixed capital formation	Final Demand — Net inventory change	Final Demand — Net exports[3]	Final Demand — Federal Government purchases	Final Demand — State and local government purchases	Final Demand — Total final demand	Total
1. Livestock & Livestock Products	4,153	1,705	23,565	2,111	---	601	38	−3	11	2,758	26,322
2. Other Agricultural Products	6,600	703	17,624	2,429	---	428	1,813	1,073	27	5,770	23,395
3. Forestry & Fishery Products	---	---	1,257	281	---	19	30	−137	(*)	104	1,451
4. Agricultural, Forestry & Fishery Services	493	878	1,563	---	---	20	3	45	−68	1	1,564
5. Iron & Ferroalloy Ores Mining	---	---	1,227	---	---	−23	41	---	---	18	1,245
6. Nonferrous Metal Ores Mining	---	---	1,155	---	---	−32	4	192	61	163	1,319
7. Coal Mining	6	1	2,120	201	---	−22	332	---	---	831	2,752
8. Crude Petroleum & Natural Gas	---	---	10,865	---	---	−40	28	---	---	−12	10,852
9. Stone and Clay Mining and Quarrying	1	67	1,583	17	---	4	23	10	−12	41	1,624
10. Chemical & Fertilizer Mineral Mining	---	28	485	---	---	−1	55	11	12	78	563
11. New Construction	---	---	---	1	36,957	---	2	3,388	12,069	52,416	52,410
12. Maintenance & Repair Construction	234	377	12,455	---	---	---	---	1,081	3,339	4,420	16,875
13. Ordnance & Accessories	3	3	2,136	158	---	84	17	2,270	4	2,533	4,669
14. Food & Kindred Products	2,964	---	17,536	45,759	---	248	1,298	53	272	47,620	65,165
15. Tobacco Manufactures	---	---	1,284	4,250	---	−26	436	---	(*)	4,661	5,945
16. Broad & Narrow Fabrics, Yarn & Thread Mills	---	7	10,008	712	---	−104	210	50	9	878	10,886
17. Miscellaneous Textile Goods & Floor Coverings	6	27	1,690	743	45	−27	46	4	1	812	2,502
*	*	*	*	*	*	*	*	*	*	*	*
I. Intermediate Inputs, Total	17,298	11,573	---	290,069	62,392	−1,491	2,206	53,594	40,564	447,334	447,344
V.A. Value Added	9,024	11,822	---								---
T. Total	26,322	23,395	---								---

SOURCE: U.S. Government Printing Office.

1958. The inputs to this industry can be read by going down column 1. We see that most of the raw material comes from the livestock and livestock-products industry itself and from the other-agricultural-products group (see rows 1 and 2). Note that the row total must equal the column total for a given industry classification—in this case, $26,322 million.

This technique, because of technical difficulties, is more appropriate for an intermediate or long-term forecast than for a short-term forecast. However, despite these shortcomings of the input-output technique, it has been said that "the system presents the most incisive look at an economy's industrial structure yet accomplished. . . ."[18]

External Sources of Information for Industry Analysis

Federal Government

Figures 7-1 and 7-2 showed examples of information published by the government that can be useful during the industry phase of the analysis. It is well worth the time to thumb through the *Census of Manufacturers, Federal Reserve Bulletins,* and *Survey of Current Business* in order to appreciate more fully the wealth of information, helpful in the economic as well as industry analysis, available in these government sources. Many private services use these government-furnished data as an input to their own security-analysis efforts.

Investment Services

There are many investment services available to furnish the investor or analyst with valuable industry and corporate information. The ones we shall single out in this section are perhaps the best known.[19]

STANDARD & POOR'S

Standard & Poor's regularly covers a number of different industries in two ways: a basic analysis and a current update of the basic analysis. The basic analysis provides an in-depth report on all facets of the industry and the firms comprising the industry. A revised basic analysis is published approximately every year. The current update, entitled *Current Analysis and Outlook*, is published roughly every quarter. An index to the Standard & Poor's *Industry Surveys* is reproduced in Figure 7-7. As can be seen, the index contains the dates of the latest current and basic analyses, as well as page references.

Figure 7-6 showed part of a basic analysis. Standard & Poor's also publishes the *Security Price Index Record*, containing indexes of the Standard & Poor's groupings, which are helpful when performing an industry analysis.

[18]Howard B. Bonham, Jr., "The Use of Input-Output Economics in Common Stock Analysis," *Financial Analysts Journal,* January-February 1967, p. 27. For a fuller treatment of input-output analysis, see this article, and also D. A. Hodes, "Input-Output Analysis: An Illustrative Example," *Business Economics,* Summer 1965, p. 37; Wassily W. Leontief, "The Structure of the U.S. Economy," *Scientific American,* April 1965, pp. 25-32; and Anne P. Carter, "The Economics of Technological Change," *Scientific American,* April 1966, pp. 25-31.

[19]*The Wall Street Journal, Barron's,* the *Commercial and Financial Chronicle,* and *Predicasts* are among other key sources of investment information.

FIGURE 7-7

index to surveys

STANDARD & POOR'S INDUSTRY SURVEYS
Standard & Poor's is a subsidiary of McGraw-Hill, Inc.

Dates of latest surveys

IN VOLUME 1

Subject Guide

VOLUME 1 CONTAINS PAGES A THROUGH L
VOLUME 2 CONTAINS PAGES M THROUGH U

SOURCE: Standard & Poor's *Industry Surveys* (New York: Standard & Poor's Corporation, July 31, 1981).

THE VALUE LINE

The Value Line also publishes industry data, but in a considerably more condensed form than does Standard & Poor's. Figure 7-8 is a typical *Value Line* industry report. Such a report is followed by separate pages of data for each major firm in the industry. Note that along with descriptive material, the report contains a summary of mutual-fund activity in the shares of firms in the industry, and a graph of the relative strength of the industry's share prices compared to the *Value Line* index of 1,500 stocks.

On a weekly basis, *The Value Line* ranks the probable market performance of industries over the next twelve months, and in the case of individual stocks, their probable performance over the next twelve months and the next three to five years. Figure 7-9 on page 192 contains *Value Line's* industry rankings in September 1981.

FORBES

The early-January issue of *Forbes* contains its "Annual Report on American Industry." This report includes a number of rankings of profitability, growth, and stock-market performance of over 700 U.S. corporations. Of interest here are its rankings of major industry groupings, from which the analyst can see the industry groups that appear to be on the move.

TRADE PUBLICATIONS

Virtually every major U.S. industry has at least one trade association, which in its publications reports much data pertaining to the industry it represents. The analyst can locate these sources, as well as references to various industries in other publications, by checking the *Business Periodicals Index* and the *Science and Technology Index*, as well as secondary sources already mentioned in this chapter.

CHESTNUTT CORPORATION

The Chestnutt Corporation provides an excellent service that compiles a number of interesting barometers of industry performance, as well as the performance of individual securities. Among the interesting data reported by Chestnutt are graphs and commentaries such as the graph in Figure 7-10, page 193, which points up strongly the importance of sound industry analysis.

FUNK AND SCOTT INDEX

The Funk and Scott Index of Corporations and Industries provides a valuable indexing service for the investor or analyst seeking published industry and company information. This service, published monthly, lists articles appearing in more than seven hundred trade and business publications. Funk and Scott index this information by Standard Industrial Classification (SIC) and by company name. The researcher can then consult the various cited articles and obtain information on the industry, company, or competition of the firm under investigation.

FIGURE 7-8

Most chains' customer counts weakened in late 1981; we expect further slippage in the current quarter, possibly continuing into the spring.

Costs, however, are in great shape. Soft hamburger and chicken prices are widening gross margins. The absence of an increase in the minimum wage this year—for the first time since 1973—is another plus for profit margins.

Thus, despite little in the way of price increases, earnings ought to hold up relatively well in the months ahead.

We continue to favor the industry's stocks for their year-ahead performance potential. Seven of the 16 issues under review are timely commitments. Note that we've discontinued coverage of *Sambo's Restaurants* because of the chain's bankruptcy (see Final Supplement elsewhere in this Edition).

fact, couponing and other special promotions may actually reduce average checks in the months ahead. Where will profit growth come from if customer counts are soft and menu prices aren't rising?

Expansion Pace Separates Winners From Losers

Take a look at individual company reports on the next few pages to get an idea of the range of capital spending budgets, and their direction. Several companies have stopped expanding because of a combination of high capital costs and a need to improve the performance of existing units before opening new ones. Profit growth will be tough to come by in 1982 for most of these companies.

Some fast feeders are still expanding relatively rapidly; *Shoney's* and *Jerrico* are the best examples among established companies. While nowhere near the growth rates of the '60s and early '70s, these chains are adding stores to their systems at rates of roughly 15% a year. Not only does that ensure a degree of earnings growth in 1982, but it also wins the companies market share relative to those that aren't expanding.

Long-Term Concerns Mounting

Competition is clearly heating up, and not merely for cyclical reasons. Saturation of the marketplace with fast food outlets will never be a literal reality, but the trend in that direction is undeniable.

The recent increase in the birth rate could evolve into a big negative; if it results in a flattening, or even a reversal, in the trend toward greater labor force participation by women, an important engine of the fast food industry's growth in the '70s will be removed. With the number of two-income families on the wane at the same time that there are more mouths to feed, consumers could increasingly opt for the supermarket rather than *McDonald's*.

Finally, President Reagan's economic program is designed to boost investment at the expense of consumption. Budget cuts will hurt lower-income families disproportionately, and they're a key part of the industry's customer base. (*Church's Fried Chicken* seems especially vulnerable in this regard.) We're concerned that dollars that normally would have flowed into fast feeders' coffers will be transferred to the investment and defense sectors to a greater degree than seems to be expected.

Timely Stocks

Fast food equities are risky—none rank higher than 3 (Average) for Safety. But they'll probably perform relatively well over the next 12 months; earnings won't fall apart, as they may in many other industries. *McDonald's* and *Collins* are top-ranked for Timeliness, while *Chart House*, *Denny's*, *Horn & Hardart*, *Shoney's*, and *Wendy's* rank Above Average.   *T.W.P./P.F.*

COMPOSITE STATISTICS: FAST FOOD SERVICE INDUSTRY

1977	1978	1979	1980	1981	1982	© Arnold Barnhard & Co., Inc.	84-86 E
4043.9	5013.9	5811.9	6538.9	*7550*	*8600*	Sales ($mill)	*13500*
18.2%	18.4%	18.0%	17.9%	*18.0%*	*18.5%*	Operating Margin	*18.0%*
138.1	179.2	224.3	268.3	*300*	*340*	Depreciation ($mill)	*490*
267.8	329.2	364.4	396.0	*480*	*580*	Net Profit ($mill)	*875*
47.5%	46.7%	43.8%	43.5%	*45.0%*	*44.0%*	Income Tax Rate	*42.0%*
6.6%	6.6%	6.3%	6.1%	*6.4%*	*6.7%*	Net Profit Margin	*6.5%*
56.1	69.2	7.2	d50.0	*d40.0*	*d50.0*	Working Cap'l ($mill)	*d75.0*
1071.8	1457.8	1852.3	1947.8	*1950*	*1950*	Long-Term Debt ($mill)	*2200*
1347.1	1639.6	1901.7	2213.7	*2700*	*3175*	Net Worth ($mill)	*5100*
12.9%	12.7%	11.9%	11.9%	*12.5%*	*13.5%*	% Earned Total Cap'l	*13.5%*
19.9%	20.1%	19.2%	17.9%	*18.0%*	*18.5%*	% Earned Net Worth	*17.0%*
18.0%	17.7%	16.2%	14.7%	*14.5%*	*14.5%*	% Retained to Comm Eq	*13.5%*
9%	12%	16%	18%	*18%*	*19%*	% All Div'ds to Net Prof	*20%*
11.3	11.3	9.2	8.2	Bold figures are Value Line estimates		Avg Ann'l P/E Ratio	*13.0*
8.9%	8.9%	10.9%	12.2%			Avg Ann'l Earn's Yield	*7.7%*
.8%	1.1%	1.7%	2.1%			Avg Ann'l Div'd Yield	*1.5%*

Near-Term Softness Likely

Sales trends in the restaurant industry tend to correlate well with trends in consumers' disposable income. As unemployment rose and incomes slipped last fall, fast food volumes weakened. Concern among employed consumers that they'd be next to lose their jobs didn't help. These factors will continue to depress restaurant headcounts in the months ahead. Industry sales were relatively strong in early 1981, too, so year-to-year comparisons may make unpleasant reading in the first quarter.

Costs: Under Control

The outlook for the industry's two biggest expenses—food and labor—is quite favorable. Livestock markets have continued to weaken in the face of predictions of strengthening. Supplies of meat haven't contracted the way analysts expected, and the economy's downturn is taking the edge off demand. With consumer food budgets under pressure, we expect meat to remain abundant in early 1982. Even a modest runup in beef and chicken prices later in the year would leave most fast feeders' gross margins in relatively good shape.

Labor expense takes over 20¢ of every fast food sales dollar. Many of the industry's workers earn the minimum wage. Wages of those who don't generally rise in tandem with the minimum. This year will be the first since 1973 without a federally mandated hike in the minimum wage. That represents a major cost savings for these labor-intensive companies.

In the absence of pressure on costs, the industry is foregoing menu price hikes. *McDonald's*, the premier fast feeder, plans no price increases before midyear (its last was in late 1980). Most other chains are freezing prices, too, in an effort to hold on to hard-pressed customers. In

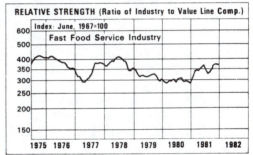

RELATIVE STRENGTH (Ratio of Industry to Value Line Comp.)
Index: June, 1967=100
Fast Food Service Industry
(600, 500, 400, 350, 300, 250, 200, 150)
1975 1976 1977 1978 1979 1980 1981 1982

FIGURE 7-9

THE VALUE LINE
Investment Survey

Part 1
Summary
&
Index

Sept. 18, 1981

File at the front of the Ratings & Reports binder. Last week's Summary & Index should be removed.

TABLE OF SUMMARY-INDEX CONTENTS

The Median of Estimated **PRICE-EARNINGS RATIOS** of all stocks with earnings	The Median of **ESTIMATED YIELDS** (next 12 months) of all dividend paying stocks under review	The Estimated Median **APPRECIATION POTENTIAL** of all 1700 stocks in the hypothesized economic environment 3 to 5 years hence
7.2	**5.1%**	**160%**

26 Weeks Ago*	Market Low 12-23-74*	Market High 12-13-68*	26 Weeks Ago*	Market Low 12-23-74*	Market High 12-13-68*	26 Weeks Ago*	Market Low 12-23-74*	Market High 12-13-68*
8.3	4.8	19.0	4.5%	7.8%	2.7%	90%	234%	18%

*Estimated medians as published in The Value Line Investment Survey on the dates shown.

ANALYSES OF INDUSTRIES IN ALPHABETICAL ORDER WITH PAGE NUMBER

Numeral in parenthesis after the industry is rank for probable performance (next 12 months).

PAGE	PAGE	PAGE	PAGE
*Advertising (90) 1817	Drug-Ethical (52) 1258	Insurance-Life (76).............1187	*Publishing (15)....................1784
Aerospace/Diversified (71) 551	Drug-Proprietary (32)............. 345	Insurance-Property/Cas. (18)... 638	Railroad (13) 304
Agric. Equip./Diversified (93) ..1434	Drugstore (5) 769	Investment Company (35) 2092	Railroad Equipment (89) 602
Air Transport (43)..........1140,251	Dual Fund (11) 2112	Iron Ore (50)......................1213	Railroad/Resources (78) 1236
Aluminum (72) 1213	Electrical Equipment (44)........1001	Lead, Zinc, & Min. Mtls. (87)..... 622	Real Estate (55) 678
Apparel (14) 1601	Electric Utility-Cent. (56) 701	Machinery (59).....................1301	REIT (33) 669,1167,2051
Auto & Truck (74).................. 101	Electric Utility-East (61).......... 178	Machinery-Const. (70)...........1358	*Recreation (51) 1751
Auto Parts-OEM (65) 793	Electric Utility-West (57) 1720	Machine Tool (60) 1342	Retail-Special Lines (24) 1700
Auto Parts-Replacement (34) 111	Electronics (79)....................1036	Manu. Housing/Rec. Veh. (16) ..1565	Retail Store (22) 1647
Bank (19) 391,2001	Fast Food Service (7)............. 313	Maritime (31) 297	Savings & Loan (91) 1151
Bank (Midwest) (54)............... 650	Finance (58).......................2058	Medical Services (3)..............1129	Sec. Brokerage (37) 352,1179
Bank (Southwest)(1)............... 650	Food Processing (45) 1451	Metal Fabricating (63) 582	Shoe (2) 1688
Brewing (68).......................1550	Food Wholesalers(26)............1532	Metals & Mining-Gen'l (85) 1213	Soft Drink (6).......................1547
Broadcasting (17) 380	Foreign Stocks (40) 819	Multiform (30) 1377	Steel-General (9)................... 609
Building (53) 851	Gold/Diamond(S. A.) (—)......1203	Natural Gas (62) 459	Steel-Integrated (29)..............1418
Canadian Energy (77) 445	Gold (No. American)(86).........1213	*Newspaper (4).....................1807	Steel-Specialty (49)...............2119
Cement (82) 913	Grocery (20).......................1509	Office Equip. & Supp.(69)........1114	Sugar (67).........................1541
Chemical-Basic (36) 1243	Health Care/Hosp.(39) 214	*Oilfield Services (28).............1846	Telecommunications (23) 750
*Chemical-Diversified (84)........1891	Home Appliance (64).............. 142	Packaging & Cont. (38) 954	Textile (42).........................1627
Chemical-Specialty (66)........... 514	*Hotel/Gaming (48)................1771	Paper & Forest Prods. (81)....... 924	Tire & Rubber (8) 129
*Coal/Uran./Geothermal (88) ...1878	Household Products (21)......... 979	Petroleum-Integrated (83)........ 401	Tobacco (25) 331
Computer/Data Proc. (75) 1081	Industrial Services (12)...........361	*Petroleum-Producing (47) .241,1825	Toiletries/Cosmetics (10)........ 804
Copper (92) 1213	Insurance-Diversified (41)......2068	Precision Instrument (80)......... 154	Toys & School Supplies (73) 781
Distilling (46)...................... 340			Trucking/Trans Lease (27)........ 277

*Reviewed in this week's edition.

In three parts: This is Part I, the Summary & Index. Part II is Selection & Opinion. Part III is Ratings & Reports. Volume XXXVI, No. 51.

Published weekly by ARNOLD BERNHARD & CO., INC. 711 Third Avenue, New York, N.Y. 10017.

For the confidential use of subscribers. Reprint by permission only. Copyright 1981 by Arnold Bernhard & Co., Inc.

SOURCE: *Value Line Investment Surveys* (New York: Arnold Bernhard & Co., September 18, 1981).

FIGURE 7-10

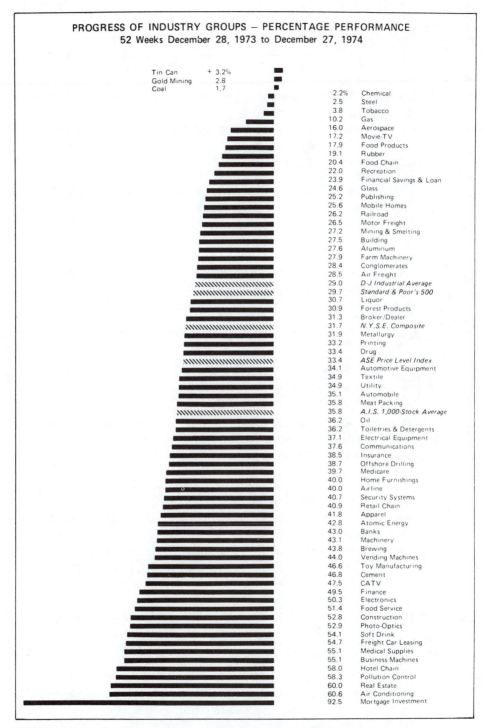

PROGRESS OF INDUSTRY GROUPS – PERCENTAGE PERFORMANCE
52 Weeks December 28, 1973 to December 27, 1974

Tin Can	+ 3.2%
Gold Mining	2.8
Coal	1.7

2.2%	Chemical
2.5	Steel
3.8	Tobacco
10.2	Gas
16.0	Aerospace
17.2	Movie-TV
17.9	Food Products
19.1	Rubber
20.4	Food Chain
22.0	Recreation
23.9	Financial Savings & Loan
24.6	Glass
25.2	Publishing
25.6	Mobile Homes
26.2	Railroad
26.5	Motor Freight
27.2	Mining & Smelting
27.5	Building
27.6	Aluminum
27.9	Farm Machinery
28.4	Conglomerates
28.5	Air Freight
29.0	*D-J Industrial Average*
29.7	*Standard & Poor's 500*
30.7	Liquor
30.9	Forest Products
31.3	Broker/Dealer
31.7	*N.Y.S.E. Composite*
31.9	Metallurgy
33.2	Printing
33.4	Drug
33.4	*ASE Price Level Index*
34.1	Automotive Equipment
34.9	Textile
34.9	Utility
35.1	Automobile
35.8	Meat Packing
35.8	*A.I.S. 1,000-Stock Average*
36.2	Oil
36.2	Toiletries & Detergents
37.1	Electrical Equipment
37.6	Communications
38.5	Insurance
38.7	Offshore Drilling
39.7	Medicare
40.0	Home Furnishings
40.0	Airline
40.7	Security Systems
40.9	Retail Chain
41.8	Apparel
42.8	Atomic Energy
43.0	Banks
43.1	Machinery
43.8	Brewing
44.0	Vending Machines
46.6	Toy Manufacturing
46.8	Cement
47.5	CATV
49.5	Finance
50.3	Electronics
51.4	Food Service
52.8	Construction
52.9	Photo-Optics
54.1	Soft Drink
54.7	Freight Car Leasing
55.1	Medical Supplies
55.1	Business Machines
58.0	Hotel Chain
58.3	Pollution Control
60.0	Real Estate
60.6	Air Conditioning
92.5	Mortgage Investment

SOURCE: *American Investors Service*, published by Chestnutt Corporation, Box 2500, Greenwich, CT 06830.

Throughout this chapter we have enumerated a number of relevant quantifiable and nonquantifiable factors, and have alluded to others, that should be considered when performing an industry analysis. Now let us point out several additional considerations: the composition of the industry's population, the distribution of income and wealth among the population, any evolving buying habits of consumers, and foreign and domestic production competition. These pieces of information are not always easy to come by, but the analyst who takes the trouble to develop *all* necessary information will find it worth his efforts.

We observed earlier that the market psychology is an important, if at times seemingly irrational, factor that must be dealt with in an industry analysis. That is to say, within a short period of time, an industry's relative attraction as an investment opportunity can change from an extremely desirable, conservative, undervalued situation to a highly risky, potentially overpriced situation. As an example of the market's enthusiasm—an enthusiasm that developed almost overnight—take the industries and companies connected with the Wankel engine. This was so evident that the *Wall Street Journal* featured a story on the "hot" Wankel stocks. It started by saying:

> Here are four ways to make your corporation's stock bound up. 1. Rename your company "The Wankel Works." 2. Announce you have just received a contract to make a screw that might be used in Wankel engines. 3. Announce that you have just hired scientists to look into Wankel engine research. 4. Announce that the clerk in your shipping room has a brother-in-law who is thinking about buying a car that has a Wankel engine.[20]

When this kind of fervor hits the market, it takes a cool analyst to discern whether the potential growth prospects of the industry have been fully discounted or whether the growth warrants purchase in the midst of such an uproar. In other words, even the best of growth situations can be bought at too high a price and thus bring a low or negative return to the investor. And even low- or no-growth industries, when bought at a very low price, can bring respectable returns. This situation arises because the market seems to value highly industries on the verge of tremendous growth in earnings, and to value low those industries that have already achieved their growth and have stabilized. That is, stocks on the verge of growth generally sell at high P/E ratios, and stocks that have come to the end of their growth pattern generally sell at low P/E ratios.

Table 7-4 shows the proportions of securities held by investment companies in various industries at various dates. Note that seven industries represented about 80 percent of the dollar value of the "favorite fifty" securities at the end of 1976. Observe too that the importance of motor holdings declined over the five-year period reported in the table, and the oil and natural gas industry holding grew in importance over the same period.

Before we continue our illustration of the application of industry-analysis techniques, it is necessary to place the importance of an industry analysis in the proper perspective. Its benefits can be fully realized only if it occurs along with a properly conceived economic analysis and company analysis.

[20]*The Wall Street Journal*, June 15, 1972, p. 1.

TABLE 7-4

SUMMARY OF FAVORITE FIFTY BY INDUSTRY
(DOLLAR VALUE OF STOCKS BY INDUSTRY TO
TOTAL DOLLAR VALUE OF FAVORITE FIFTY) (PERCENT)

	12/31/76	9/30/76	12/31/75	12/31/71
Oil and natural gas	25.3	25.1	22.9	14.9
Office equipment	20.4	20.4	18.7	17.4
Chemicals and drugs	11.6	14.7	16.2	7.9
Leisure	6.0	6.5	7.6	8.3
Utilities	7.2	6.5	5.4	4.8
Motors	5.7	5.5	4.4	8.0
Paper and printing	3.7	2.5	2.6	0.0
Miscellaneous	20.1	18.8	22.2	38.7
	100.0	100.0	100.0	100.0

SOURCE: *Vickers Guide to Investment Company Portfolios.* Copyright © 1977 by Vickers Associates, Inc. REPRODUCTION HEREOF PERMITTED ONLY ON WRITTEN PERMISSION FROM VICKERS ASSOCIATES, INC., THE COPYRIGHT OWNERS. As reprinted in *Barron's*, March 7, 1977, p. 9.

A good economic analysis informs the investor about the propriety of a current stock purchase, regardless of the industry in which he might invest. If the economic outlook suggests purchase at this time, the economic analysis along with the industry analysis will aid the investor in selecting the proper industry in which to invest. Nonetheless, knowing when to invest and in which industry to invest is not enough. It is also necessary to know which companies in which industries should be selected. We turn our attention to this topic in the ensuing three chapters.

Summary

In this chapter we first discussed alternative industry-classification schemes, observing that different schemes are appropriate for different purposes. Next, we observed how the economic analysis could best be meshed with the industry analysis. Key characteristics of the industry that the analyst needs to consider include the past sales and earnings performance of the industry, its permanence, the attitude of government toward the industry, labor conditions prevalent in the industry, industry competitive conditions, and the industry P/E levels. We illustrated this part of the analysis with an extended example using the fast food industry. The concepts of an industry life cycle, end-use analysis, regression analysis, and input-output analysis were explained. Finally, we noted some sources of industry information and then continued our fast food industry analysis.

Questions and Problems

1. If you were attempting to forecast the sales of the candy industry, what classification scheme would you use?

2. What is a cyclical industry?

3. Of what value is the past sales and earnings performance of an industry in forecasting the future prospects of the industry?

4. What domestic industries do you suppose will decline in importance in the next decade? Why?

5. Why do you suppose only four automobile manufacturers in the United States almost completely dominate the auto industry?

6. How high would industry share prices have to go relative to industry earnings before you would decide that the shares were overpriced for investment purposes? Explain.

7. Of what use is the industry-life-cycle approach to an industry analyst?

8. How would you go about forecasting the sales of domestically produced beer next year? What variables are most important in determining the demand for beer?

9. Based on the latest Standard & Poor's *Basic Analysis* of the aerospace industry, would you recommend stock purchases in the group? Why?

10. What industries were most widely held by mutual funds as of the end of 1976?

11. The analysis of sales growth is generally the starting point in estimating earning power potential for an industry (and firms therein). Further, on a perspective basis, it is common to look at an industry from an industrial-life-cycle point of view.

    a. Assume that two companies in an industry have identical rates of sales growth. Why might an analyst nevertheless consider the sales record of one superior to that of the other?

    b. Which stage of the industrial life cycle is the most attractive from an investment point of view?

12. What are the three most critical variables one might "track" in forecasting the outlook for the fast food industry?

13. What are two major problem areas in using regression analysis for evaluating relevant industry factors in investment decision making?

Company Analysis: Measuring Earnings

We are now ready to translate economic and industry assessments into judgments about holding-period yields for specific companies. The next three chapters will demonstrate how an analyst estimates return and risk for specific stocks. This chapter examines the nature and sources of relevant information about companies that is required to make judgments about return and risk. Chapters 9 and 10 will demonstrate how to translate that information into expectations about holding-period yields.

Introduction

Many pieces of information influence investment decisions. Investors need to know the characteristics of various investment alternatives and must keep informed on the institutions and markets where they are available. Up-to-date information is required on the status of and trends in the economy, particular industries, and firms.

The United States is a nation known for an abundance of widely available and rapidly disseminated information of almost every sort imaginable. This flood of information creates problems for the investor; he must continuously sample, sift, and sort messages and events for "good" information. Success in investing will be largely dependent on (1) discovering new and credible information rapidly and in more detail than others do, and (2) applying superior judgment so as to ascertain the relevance of the information to the decision at hand. *The true test of an analyst's worth lies in his ability to develop a system of security analysis that couples original insight and unique ways of forming expectations about the prospects for individual companies.* Varied public and private sources of information must be analyzed.

Superior judgment comes from the capacity to take information and (1) see given relationships more clearly, or (2) perceive more interrelationships. Judgment depends pretty much upon one's store of knowledge and experiences. The task of security analysis is largely a matter of sifting, sorting, and rearranging data on markets, the economy, industries, and firms. Applying various tools of analysis to the data, the investor formulates expectations and judgments about the alternatives open to him.[1]

This chapter is concerned with two broad categories of information: internal and external. Internal information consists of data and events made public by firms concerning their operations. It mainly takes the form of interim and annual reports to shareholders, and public and private statements of the officers and managers of the firm. The principal information sources generated internally by a firm are its financial statements. The analyst does not, of course, limit inquiry to information provided by accountants; ingenious and competent analysts sample widely from many kinds of information.

External sources of information are those generated independently outside the company. They provide a supplement to internal sources by (1) overcoming some of the bias inherent in company-generated information, and (2) providing information simply not found in the materials made available by companies themselves.

Internal Information

The Key Role Of Financial Statements

An overwhelming weight is placed by analysts and investors on the information contained in the financial statements of firms. One critical reason for this reliance lies in the vouchsafed nature of the statements, since their form and content is controlled under a variety of rules, regulations, and statutes.[2] The vast majority of these statements are attested to by independent auditors. In sum, investors tend to accept financial statements as the closest thing to complete credibility in information available to them. In the private and public statements of company officers, there is little chance of corroborating what is said. Very often the true significance of such pronouncements is clouded by some degree of enthusiasm and loyalty.

Financial Statements As Proxies Of Real Processes

Accounting is a proxy that has been developed for representing *real* processes and *real* goods. Accounts and statements are devices created to summarize certain types of information about real corporate goods and processes.[3]

---

[1] R. G. E. Smith, "Uncertainty, Information and Investment Decision," *Journal of Finance*, March 1971, pp. 73-77.

[2] For an excellent short monograph on accounting, written for analysts, see J. A. Mauriello, *Accounting for the Financial Analyst*, rev. ed., C.F.A. Monograph Series (Homewood, Ill.: Richard D. Irwin, 1971).

[3] Michael Keenan, "The State of the Finance Field Methodology Models of Equity Valuation: The Great SERM Bubble," *Journal of Finance*, May 1970, pp. 257-58.

As such, these statements, to a large extent, form the basis for action by investors, potential investors, creditors, and potential creditors of the corporation. Because of this, it is critical for analysts to understand in a general way how these statements are prepared so that they can better interpret the statements' true meaning. A good beginning point for investment analysis and ultimately investment decision making is to be aware of the historical record of the firm in a financial sense. This historical record of the firm's earnings and financial position can often give the analyst insight into the inner workings of the firm and thus assist him in projecting the future. This investigation of the past is a vital first step taken by the investment analyst.

Someone once said, however, that accounting statements are like the tips of icebergs: What you see is interesting, but what you do not see is significant! A good investment analyst must judge financial statements as they meet the tests of (1) correctness, (2) completeness, (3) consistency, and (4) comparability.

Correctness, or accuracy, is normally established through the presence or absence of an "unqualified" auditor's certification. Nearly all public corporations retain public accounting firms to audit and certify the fairness of financial statements. Unaudited statements are not necessarily inaccurate or fraudulently prepared; they simply lack the intrinsic credibility of audited statements accompanied by the signed opinion of a CPA.

Completeness is a matter of disclosure. Inasmuch as accounting is only a proxy of real goods and processes, it cannot and does not pretend to tell everything. Many, many bits of information about a business were never intended to be incorporated in established financial reports and statements. The Securities and Exchange Commission (SEC), the American Institute of Certified Public Accountants (AICPA), and the Financial Accounting Standards Board (FASB) have worked together, and at times at odds, in dealing with the matter of fuller disclosure. The vital emphasis placed upon financial statements by analysts and investors, always hungry for more and better information, is creating increasing pressure for making more and more information available in different forms.[4]

Auditors are charged with the primary responsibility of ensuring that changes in reporting over time are justified and brought to the attention of the public. *Consistency* is vital in making comparisons of the performance of a firm over time. Data constructed differently at various points in time lack meaningful continuity unless reconciled prior to analysis.[5]

No area of accounting information has created more debate and difficulties for the analyst than *comparability*. Using audited financial statements for a firm, most of the time an analyst can work toward more complete and consistent information on

---

[4]Many have suggested that the form' of the income statement should be changed to assist analysis. Traditional expense breakdowns do not explain dynamic changes in costs as volume changes. Fixed and variable cost division would be more informative for marginal analysis. Other cost segregations used by managements could also help investors. For an interesting and stimulating book on financial reporting, see Arthur Andersen & Co., *Objectives of Financial Statements* (New York: Arthur Andersen & Co., 1972).

[5]A discussion of the treatment of accounting changes is found in U.S. General Accounting Office, *Outline of Opinions of the Accounting Principles Board* (Washington, D.C., 1971) pp. 81-91. This pamphlet is an excellent summary of Accounting Principles Board Opinions on various accounting subjects. See also recent pronouncements of the Financial Accounting Standards Board.

his own. However, investment decision making involves comparing alternatives—or, as it were, *comparing the data derived from the financial statements of different firms*. The problem: Are the financial statements of different firms prepared under the same ground rules? Is it valid to make choices between two companies on the basis of financial information if the information is not generated on a uniform basis?

Accounting for revenue, costs, and profits is not done under a set of rigid rules whereby each event and transaction, regardless of the firm, is handled in one way only. To the extent that accounting provides options in handling certain transactions, comparability diminishes.

One set of accounting rules in the name of uniformity is perhaps an unrealistic ideal. Highly flexible accounting practices have grown up over the years, to recognize the wide diversity of circumstances within American business. However, from an analyst/investor point of view, the need for uniformity is obvious, since investment decisions are the product of comparative analysis of data for the determination of relative values.

In the following pages we shall examine the principal financial statements made public by corporations. Our goal is neither to teach accounting nor to cover every one of the many areas of interest in financial reporting. We do want to focus on critical problem areas—the sources of an analyst's difficulties in interpreting financial statements. A good analyst must train himself to understand the kinds of flexibility permitted in accounting and the effects of this flexibility on his interpretation of what he sees. Further, an analyst must learn to rely upon the *total* impact of all financial statements taken as a unit over time. The auditor's opinion is a critical part of the financial statements, as are the notes to the statements. In short, the prudent analyst will look at the statements "taken as a whole" and will understand how the major statements are interrelated. There is danger in looking at single figures on individual statements in an isolated year. Finally, and perhaps most important, reported financial data (especially reported earnings) need to be examined carefully and to be interpreted in the light of other generally available information.

The results of our exploration into financial statements should enable the analyst to work with the interrelationships contained in the various statements in forming expectations about earnings, dividends, and stock prices.

Operating Results: The Income Statement

Three major financial statements make up the backbone of internal information available to the analyst: the statement of income and retained earnings, the balance sheet, and the statement of changes in financial position. Accompanying notes to these statements are also crucial and are no less important than the statements themselves.

In the early 1900s, security analysts placed primary emphasis on the evaluation of the corporation's balance sheet. In fact, it would not be unfair to say that emphasis was almost exclusively placed on the financial strength or weakness of the company. As the years went by, this emphasis on the evaluation of the balance sheet began to shift toward an emphasis on the income statement. This shift continued until the early

1970s. Again it would not be unfair to say that in these years major emphasis was placed on earnings and earnings per share as reflected in the income statement. The growth rate of these earnings was also of vital importance to the analyst. However, in the mid-1970s it became apparent that looking at the income statement and the earnings figures to the detriment of the balance sheet was not a prudent thing to do any longer. And so, today analysts look very closely at both the balance sheet and the income statement as well as the statement of changes in financial position. This last statement is becoming increasingly popular to the analyst because it very nicely connects the income statement and balance sheet.

In the sections that follow we will discuss each of these statements—namely, the statement of income and retained earnings, the balance sheet, and the statement of changes in financial position. Our discussion will point out certain trouble spots which the security analyst should be aware of when examining these various statements. Since these trouble spots are often very complex to analyze—even for a trained accountant— we strongly feel that an analyst should realize that these problem areas exist so that he will at least proceed with caution and will be aware of potential pitfalls in any analysis. With this general warning, let us proceed with our analysis of these statements.

INCOME-STATEMENT FORMAT

The Accounting Principles Board has suggested the format shown in Table 8-1 for a statement of income and a statement of retained earnings. The income statement provides an analysis of significant factors that have contributed to and affected the earnings for the period. The statement of retained earnings bridges the gap between the income statement and the position statement (balance sheet), in the sense that the net income on the income statement is reflected in the retained-earnings part of the stockholders' equity on the balance sheet. The usual changes in retained earnings are the net income or loss for the period, dividends declared, and corrections of net income for prior periods.

The income statement is a key financial statement by which analysts judge management's performance. It is used perhaps more than any other statement in attempting to assess the future. Past earnings reported on the income statement are very often used as a base for predicting future performance. Thus a major job for the analyst is to probe principal areas of the income statement to assess their impact on earnings.

The nature of a company is a principal determinant of the extent to which a particular item is likely to have significance with respect to earnings. For example, the choice of depreciation method has considerable impact upon the earnings of an airline, which has almost all its assets in equipment. The choice of depreciation method is less significant, although not unimportant, for a bank, since most bank assets are in securities and loans. The analyst is forced to examine almost every item of revenue, expense, and resulting earnings on the income statement. Elements of the statement of retained earnings, particularly charges for prior periods, should be investigated. Let us address ourselves to some *major problem areas* on the income statement and statement of retained earnings.

TABLE 8-1

ILLUSTRATIVE COMPARATIVE STATEMENT OF INCOME
AND STATEMENT OF RETAINED EARNINGS

Statement of Income
Years Ended December 31, 19X0 and December 31, 19X1

	19X0	19X1

Net sales (net of trade discounts, returns, and allowances)
Other income (e.g., rents, interest, dividends, royalties)
Costs and expenses:
    Cost of goods sold (cost of merchandise sold during period)
    Selling expenses (creating sales, storing goods, and delivery,
        including depreciation)
    Administration and general expenses (administering overall
        activities, including depreciation)
    Financial management expenses (interest on borrowed money)
    Other deductions (items extraneous to primary operations)
    Income tax (federal, state, and local)
Income before extraordinary items (per share: 19X0:
        19X1:   )
Extraordinary items, less applicable income tax (per share:
        19X0:   ; 19X1:   ) (usually, nonrecurring and not
        related to primary operating activity of the business)
Net income (per share: 19X0:   ; 19X1:   )

Statement of Retained Earnings
Years Ended December 31, 19X0 and December 31, 19X1

	19X0	19X1

Retained earnings at beginning of year:
    As previously reported (on prior-period balance sheet)
    Adjustments (corrections of income reported in prior periods;
        e.g. settlements of law and tax suits, and for carelessness or
        imprudence in valuing assets at end of earlier periods)
    As restated
Net income (last line of statement of income)
Cash dividends on common and preferred stock (shown separately)
Retained earnings at end of year

EARNINGS FROM REGULAR OPERATIONS

The analyst must recognize that earnings from regular, normal operations reflect the major thrust of a business, and so these earnings should be segregated from earnings (or losses) resulting from infrequent, unusual, or nonrecurring events. Since earnings from these regular, normal operations are more apt to be continuing for some reasonable period, their separate disclosure is important to the analyst in judging and forecasting the future. Obviously, the assumption is made that these recurring types of transactions are a better base on which to build or forecast than nonrecurring or infrequent types of transactions. However, as can be seen in Table 8-1, so-called extraordinary gains or losses do sometimes occur in the operations of a business. Fortunately, however, the accounting profession has specifically defined how these items are to be treated in the financial statements.[6]

Extraordinary items need to arise from material transactions that are both unusual in nature and occur infrequently in the operating environment of the business. The *environment* of the business would include such things as the characteristics of the industry in which the firm operates, the geographic location of the facilities of the corporation, and the role of governmental regulations in this corporation's affairs. As can be seen, this definition very narrowly defines what can properly be called an extraordinary item. For example, a loss resulting from an earthquake in certain sections of California might not be considered an extraordinary item; however, damage caused by an earthquake in Connecticut would be considered an extraordinary item. As was shown in Table 8-1, the extraordinary item would be listed separately and would be listed net of any income tax effects.

Accounting Principles Board (APB) *Opinion No. 30* also deals with the problem of properly disclosing information related to disposals of certain major segments of the business. Any income or loss from such discontinued operations must also be separately disclosed in the financial statements. If a corporation in the same year had normal operations, had extraordinary items, and disposed of a segment of its business, there would be three different income figures disclosed in the income statement. The first would probably be labeled "income from continuing operations." Then there would probably be a separate section for the discontinued operations, which would lead to another income figure labeled "income before extraordinary items." Finally, there would be a section for disclosing the extraordinary items, which would lead to a final figure labeled "net income." Therefore, the analyst must be careful to select the proper income figure to use as a basis for any forecast.

THE MATCHING PRINCIPLE

Accounting is based upon many "rules of the road" called *generally accepted accounting principles*. An important rule applied to income statements that concerns the analyst is what accountants call the *matching principle*. In simple terms, the matching principle requires that expenses be reflected in the same period as the revenues to which they are related. Various accounting methods have been devised, some rather scientific and others somewhat arbitrary, for matching costs and revenues. The utility of accounting information to the investment analyst is impaired if (1) expenses and revenues are improperly matched, or (2) methods employed are switched over time.

The process of matching costs and revenues is only approximate and often yields to expediency. Do we really know the rate at which a machine depreciates? In what order did inventory really flow out of the plant? Will a particular expenditure benefit this period alone, or several future periods? If several periods, how many? Judgment in prorating expenses and recognizing revenues is needed within clearly drawn guidelines.

[6]Accounting Principles Board, *Opinion No. 30*, "Reporting the Results of Operations—Reporting the Effects of Disposal of a Segment of the Business, and Extraordinary, Unusual and Infrequently Occurring Events and Transactions" (New York: AICPA, 1973).

Let us examine some key statement areas in which the matching problem creates difficulties in analysis.

Intangibles.   Many assets are developed or purchased that lack a physical or tangible character. Some, such as patents, copyrights, and franchises, have limited life by law. Others, such as goodwill, trademarks, and secret processes or formulas, have an indeterminate life. In the past, some companies have written off intangibles immediately; others have set them up with no amortization; still others have written them off over lives determined by expediency.

Accounting Principles Board (APB) *Opinion No. 17* has helped to clarify the ground rules for recording and amortizing intangibles. In essence, it says that purchased intangibles are to be set up at cost and amortized on a straight-line basis over *estimated* useful lives not to exceed forty years. And the *Opinion* specifies certain factors to consider in estimating useful life.

Pension Costs.   Every company pension plan requires accounting for past, present, and future costs. Prior to the publication of APB *Opinion No. 8*, accounting for pension costs could be utilized to smooth profits. Some companies would treat pension costs on a cash rather than an accrual basis; that is, they would make annual contributions into the fund based upon profits. Low profits would call for modest pension-fund contributions, and vice versa. Under *Opinion No. 8*, an accrual rather than a cash basis is required for pension-fund accounting.

However, accountants still differ on how pension costs are to be computed. This argument centers on determination of the amount of contribution and accrual necessary to account properly for past, present, and future service costs. Accounting for pension costs is still in transition, and the analyst is advised to probe notes to financial statements and other sources to uncover details on a company's pension-accounting policies.

IMPLICATIONS OF INVENTORY COSTING METHODS

Two areas that deserve special attention are accounting for inventories and fixed assets. For the majority of businesses, these items amount to a major slice of total expenses during an accounting period.

Goods available for sale during the year either are sold or remain in inventory. Accountants generally subtract a value for ending inventory from goods available for sale in order to arrive, indirectly, at the cost of what was sold.

Accounting convention permits placing a value upon inventory in any of a number of ways. The most widely known methods are LIFO (last-in, first-out) and FIFO (first-in, first-out). LIFO assumes that the last units produced are the first sold; FIFO assumes that older units are sold first. There are no problems created by either method when prices remain the same, period to period. The difficulty arises when prices change.

LIFO assesses recent costs against sales and includes earlier costs in inventory. During periods of rising prices, the effect is to diminish profits and create a low carrying value for inventory. The result is deferral of income taxes. FIFO assesses sales with costs in the order of their origin. The cost of earlier units is charged against sales, and inventory includes recent purchases. Inventory is valued near current market value. When prices rise, profits are higher than with LIFO. The result is that taxes are paid as profits are reported, unlike LIFO, where taxes are deferred until inventory is liquidated.

Consider the following example: Grinnell Co. buys a product at the prevailing market price and sells it at a price 10 cents higher. The purchase price remains constant during the year. Assume that no expenses other than the cost of goods sold are incurred during the year. Let us see the effects of LIFO and FIFO inventory valuation upon (1) reported earnings, and (2) the position statement:

Units of beginning inventory (cost = $.50)	1,000	
Units purchased during year (cost = $.75)	1,000	
Units sold (at $.85)	1,000	

	LIFO		FIFO	
Sales		$850		$850
Cost of sales:				
Beginning inventory	$ 500		$ 500	
Purchases	750		750	
Goods available for sale	$1,250		$1,250	
Less: Ending inventory:				
LIFO: (1,000 at $.50)	$ 500			
FIFO: (1,000 at $.75)			$ 750	
Total cost of sales		$750		$500
Pre-tax profits		$100		$350
Taxes (50%)		$ 50		$175
Ending inventory		$500		$750

Rising purchase prices caused profits to be three and one-half times larger under FIFO, and on the position statement, FIFO inventory is 50 percent larger. The resulting numbers would be altered if prices and/or total sales were changed.

Most analysts would agree that during periods of advancing prices, LIFO provides a more conservative statement of income, with earnings less distorted and patterns more easily identified, whereas FIFO tends to overstate earnings. Conversely, during periods of falling prices, the effects on the position and income statements would be the opposite.

So choice of inventory valuation method is important to the analyst, depending as it does upon the movement of prices and the nature of the industry. Firms that have large proportions of total assets devoted to inventories can affect reported earnings through the inventory method chosen. Other things being equal, firms prefer smoothed profits rather than fluctuating profits. Smoothed profits tend to produce level share prices. LIFO permits smoothing of income, while FIFO accentuates ups and downs. The analyst should be aware of the quite different effects of LIFO and FIFO on earnings, taxes, and the carrying value of inventory as price levels change.

If the results for Grinnell Co. under FIFO and LIFO depicted results for two different firms with equal operating results and dissimilar inventory valuation methods, it is easy to see that the company using FIFO enjoys three and one-half times the pre-tax profits of its counterpart. However, the LIFO company pays less than one-third the taxes of the FIFO company. Which company is economically better off?

DEPRECIATION ACCOUNTING

Net income reported on the financial statements can be affected by depreciation accounting. Depreciation recognizes that an asset will be exhausted at some point. In general, fixed assets are charged off against revenues they help create. From an analytical point of view, a problem arises in the rate at which a fixed asset is written off. Moreover, in the same firm, not all assets are depreciated on the same basis, and shifts in rate of charge-off take place over time.

The amount of annual charge for depreciation depends primarily upon the original cost of the asset, its estimated useful life, and its estimated salvage value at the end of its useful life. Fixed assets are depreciated under accounting convention on the basis of use or the basis of time. When depreciation is based upon the passage of time, so-called straight-line and/or accelerated bases of depreciation can be employed.

The straight-line method writes off depreciation uniformly over the useful life. The accelerated method recognizes that assets do not depreciate equally year by year. More likely, the value of services from a fixed asset declines at an irregular rate. In other words, accelerated depreciation would permit the charge-off to be larger in the beginning and become progressively smaller.

Among the more significant benefits of this kind of charge-off is the delay in tax payments. For example, larger write-offs in the beginning reduce taxable income and, correspondingly, taxes. In later years the smaller depreciation charges result in higher taxable income, and therefore higher taxes, than with the straight-line method. Unless tax rates change appreciably over time, the *total* tax bill is the same under both methods of depreciation. However, considering the "time value" of money, accelerated depreciation affords a relative advantage over straight-line because tax payments are postponed.

In the straight-line method, the annual charge for depreciation would be calculated as

$$\text{Straight-line depreciation} = \frac{\text{Original cost} - \text{Estimated salvage}}{\text{Estimated useful life}}$$

Accelerated methods do not permit the firm to write off any more depreciation in the aggregate than does the straight-line; the rate of write-off is simply accelerated. A popular method is the declining-balance method.[7] Double-declining balance allows a charge-off of twice the straight-line rate the first year. In the second year, this doubled rate is repeated, not on original cost but on the "declining balance" (original cost less first year's depreciation), and so on. By this method, the asset is never completely written off, but the tax laws permit switching to straight-line whenever the company wishes. The only limitation is that total depreciation may not exceed the original cost of the asset.

Let us see the impact of using normal and accelerated depreciation in a common example. A company acquires $300,000 in new equipment with an estimated life of five years and no salvage value. Annual depreciation under straight-line would be 1/5, or 20

---

[7]Sum-of-the-years'-digits is another popular accelerated method. The digits in the estimated useful life are added together to get a denominator (e.g., 5 years is $1 + 2 + 3 + 4 + 5 = 15$). First year's charges are 5/15, second year's are 4/15, and so on.

percent. Declining-balance would permit 2/5, or 40 percent of undepreciated original cost each year:

Year	Straight-Line Depreciation	Double-Declining-Balance Depreciation
1	$ 60,000	$120,000
2	60,000	72,000*
3	60,000	43,200
4	60,000	32,400†
5	60,000	32,400
Total	$300,000	$300,000

*40% ($300,000 − $120,000) = $72,000.
†The company reverts to straight-line depreciation here. During the fourth year, accelerated depreciation would be $25,920. Reversion to straight-line provides larger depreciation.

The different effects upon pre-tax profits should be obvious. If tax rates remain unchanged, taxes will be the same in the aggregate; however, they are postponed under accelerated depreciation (declining-balance).

Not all companies use the same method of computing depreciation, nor are estimates of useful life and salvage value uniform. All this is further complicated by frequent changes in depreciation guidelines by Congress and the tax authorities. The result is great difficulty for the analyst in comparing data for a single company over time, as well as in comparing companies.

PROVISION FOR INCOME TAXES

The matching principle requires that income taxes be offset against related income, or that tax savings be offset against a related loss. Thus, in Table 8-1, income taxes related to operating income are shown separate from taxes related to extraordinary items. Just as ordinary and extraordinary income are offset by appropriate taxes, ordinary and extraordinary losses would be offset by taxes that are refundable.

During years when a loss is shown and no prior-year income is available, the tax savings could be utilized in offsetting possible income in future years. Such tax savings are, however, contingent upon future earnings and are noted in footnotes to the financial statements rather than being carried as contingent assets. Should future periods produce net income, this income is reduced by appropriate taxes, and the carryover savings from prior years is shown in the income statement as extraordinary income. This procedure avoids clouding the true picture of earnings.

Certain items are treated differently on the financial statements and in the tax returns of companies. The tax expense shown on the income statement conforms to the income reported on the statements, rather than to the income reported to the tax authorities. For example, it is both legal and quite common to use accelerated depreciation on tax returns and straight-line on the financial statements. The result is that tax savings now from accelerated depreciation will be offset by higher taxes in later years. It is customary to set up a long-term or deferred tax liability for the savings, which is converted into a current liability in the future period in which the later tax is due.

Referring to our earlier example involving depreciation, recall that we contrasted depreciation under straight-line and declining-balance for new equipment costing $300,000 with a useful life of five years and no salvage value. Let us see what the tax effects would be:

Year	(A) Straight-Line Depreciation on Statements	(B) Declining-Balance Depreciation on Tax Return	(C) Added Taxes or (Savings) at 50% Rate Using (B)
1	$ 60,000	$120,000	($30,000)
2	60,000	72,000	(6,000)
3	60,000	43,200	8,400
4	60,000	32,400	13,800
5	60,000	32,400	13,800
Total	$300,000	$300,000	

Assume that net income before depreciation and taxes in year 1 was $500,000. The tax rate is 50 percent. Using accelerated depreciation on the tax return results in a tax bill of $190,000 [1/2($500,000 − $120,000)]. Straight-line depreciation on the income statement for stockholders reporting would result in taxable income of $220,000 [1/2(500,000 − $60,000)]. To "normalize" the effect of the difference between the tax expense shown ($220,000) and taxes actually owed ($190,000), a $30,000 deferred liability would be shown on the balance sheet. In year 2, the difference between tax expense and taxes owed would be $6,000. The deferred tax liability account at the end of year 2 would be $36,000 ($30,000 + $6,000). Between year 3 and the end of year 5, the deferred tax liability would reduce to zero.

EARNINGS PER SHARE

In order to determine earnings per share, the analyst must first calculate the number of common shares outstanding, as follows. First, the number of shares issued is reduced by the number of treasury shares; these are common stock sold at one time but subsequently repurchased by the company, often with the intention of reissue. Second, a weighted average is used when stock transactions involving asset accounts have taken place during the period. For example, if 1 million shares are outstanding at the beginning of the period, and 200,000 shares are sold July 1 (midyear) for cash (an asset), the weighted-average number of shares would be 1.1 million [1 million + 1/2(200,000)].[8]

Third, when stock transactions take place that do *not* involve assets, such as stock dividends or splits, the new number of shares is treated as being effective from the beginning of the year. For example, 1 million shares are outstanding. In November a 20 percent stock dividend is declared. The weighted-average number of shares at year-end would still be 1.2 million.

Once we have determined the number of common shares outstanding, it is customary to translate net income after taxes into a per-share-of-ownership equivalent,

[8]200,000 shares sold April 15 would be outstanding for 8 1/2 months, or about 7/10 of a year. Weighted-average total shares would be 1 million plus 140,000, or 1,140,000.

in order to compare firms on a common size basis. Firms A and B may each have earnings of $1 million. However, if A has 1 million shares outstanding and B has only 500,000, firm A would have earnings per share of $1, and B of $2.

The increasing use of securities that are convertible into common shares and of stock options through warrants creates the overhang, or contingent creation of new common shares, as conversion privileges, warrants, or other options are exercised. The existence of such contingent shares is now being recognized in financial reporting by the calculation of two supplementary earnings-per-share figures. One is called *primary earnings* per share, the other *secondary* or *fully diluted earnings* per share. Primary earnings per share reflects the assumption that all options and warrants are exercised, but reflects convertible securites *only* if at the time of issuance their value by the market was mostly due to the conversion privilege. For example, if a convertible bond issue is sold at a price that yields investors 6 percent to maturity while similar bonds without conversion rights are selling to yield 10 percent, it might be said that the convertible bonds were purchased more for their option feature than as straight bonds. The other EPS figure, fully diluted or secondary earnings per share, assumes that *all* options, warrants, and convertibles were turned into stock. In effect, secondary earnings would represent the most conservative statement of EPS and would be less than or equal to primary earnings per share.

For the analyst, it is important to recognize (1) that there are multiple earnings-per-share figures, and (2) that secondary earnings per share represent the most reasonable statement of earnings, taking into account all contingent shares. Below are shown abbreviated statements for 197X for a company with convertible bonds and preferred stock outstanding. Regular earnings per share are shown.

Income Statement		Balance Sheet	
Operating income	$4,200,000	4% convertible bonds (convertible	
Interest expense	400,000	into 500,000 shares of common)	$10 million
Earnings before taxes	$3,800,000		
Taxes (50%)	1,900,000	5% preferred (convertible into	
Net income	$1,900,000	500,000 shares of common)	$ 5 million
Preferred dividends	250,000		
Earnings to common	$1,650,000	Common (1,600,000 shares)	$ 8 million
EPS	$1.03		

If we assume that the preferred at the time of issue was *not* sold mainly because of the conversion option but the bonds were, then primary earnings per share would be:

Operating earnings		$4,200,000
Taxes (50%)		2,100,000
Net income		2,100,000
Preferred dividends		250,000
Earnings to common		1,850,000
Shares:		
Bonds	500,000	
Common	1,600,000	
		2,100,000 shares
EPS		$.88

Fully diluted or secondary earnings per share (all convertibles assumed converted) would be:

Operating earnings		$4,200,000
Taxes (50%)		2,100,000
Earnings to common		2,100,000
Shares:		
Bonds	500,000	
Preferred	500,000	
Common	1,600,000	2,600,000 shares
EPS		$.81

INTERIM EARNINGS REPORTS

Quarterly reports to stockholders are an effort to provide disclosure of the continuous nature of corporate developments. The Financial Analysts Federation surveys reveal that the majority of investment analysts regard interim data of equal or greater importance than annual data. In the main, quarterly reports are used by analysts to update and adjust projections of future performance. However, there are problems in using these reports.

Quarterly reports are generally not audited. This creates problems with respect to outside, independent control over proper matching of revenues and expenses. Income can be "managed" by not segregating nonrecurring income, or by cutting off sales and related costs at different times. The brief time period involved in quarterly reports creates problems of proper estimation and proration of many items that are difficult enough to assess on an annual basis. Shortened time periods lead to more arbitrary period allocations. Further, interim reports do not contain information on changes in accounting methods and retroactive adjustments.

The usual interim or quarterly financial report is a very abbreviated earnings statement and balance sheet. The analyst would no doubt have more confidence in interim data if full and complete statements (including a funds statement) were provided, with an auditor's certification.[9]

OTHER TOPICS

There are several other key areas in income statement analysis with which the analyst should be familiar. However, these topics also have a profound influence on the balance sheet, and we will therefore defer the discussion of these recent developments in financial statement analysis and deal with them in a separate section later in this chapter. The topics that will be discussed include accounting for foreign currency transactions, reporting the financial results of various segments of a business enterprise, reporting replacement cost data, and, finally, reflecting changing price levels in the financial statements. Let us now turn our attention to the balance sheet.

Financial Position: The Balance Sheet

The level, trend, and stability of earnings are powerful forces in the determination of security prices. This *flow* of earnings is depicted on the income statement. The *stock* of assets and the claims to those assets that provide the fuel for those earnings are shown

---

[9]See L. J. Seidler and W. Benjes, "The Credibility Gap in Interim Financial Statements," *Financial Analysts Journal*, 23 (September-October 1967), 109-15.

on the balance sheet. The balance sheet shows, at a given point in time, the assets, liabilities, and owners' equity in a company. It is the analyst's primary source of information on the financial strength of a company.

Assets include properties and rights to properties, both tangible (such as buildings) and intangible (such as patents and goodwill). Liabilities are debts that are payable on demand or over specified future periods. They are evidenced by simple invoices or rather lengthy legal documents, such as mortgages. The equity of stockholders represents the excess of assets over liabilities at the balance-sheet date.

Modern accounting principles dictate the basis for assigning values to assets. Liability values are set by contracts. When assets are reduced by liabilities, the "book value" of stockholders' equity can be determined. This book value invariably differs from current value in the marketplace, since market value is dependent upon the earning power of assets, and not their cost or value in the accounts.

THE COST PRINCIPLE

For the most part, the accounting concept of conservatism requires that assets be carried at original or historical cost when they are first acquired. During subsequent time periods, they may be valued at cost or market, whichever is lower.

Income-statement and reported-earnings problems can stem from the rate at which assets are written off against related revenues, a matter we discussed under inventory and depreciation accounting. In addition, the framework of historical cost does not make reference to the changing purchasing power of the dollar. When inflation occurs, historical-dollar accounting can be unrealistic and deficient.

First, the income statement fails to express all items in dollars of the same purchasing power. For example, revenues closely represent current dollars, whereas FIFO inventory costing would represent "old" dollars. Needless to say, over time interperiod comparability is destroyed.

Second, assets and stockholders' equity reflect an admixture of items shown in dollars of different purchasing power. For example, FIFO inventory procedures might tend to show inventories in near-current dollars, but fixed assets may be worth many times their carrying value. These distortions in asset groups are similarly reflected in the stockholders'-equity section of the balance sheet. The erosion of the purchasing power of the dollar affects measurements using the balance sheet and influences "real" earning power.

BALANCE-SHEET FORMAT

Table 8-2 illustrates a balance-sheet format. It is in *account form*, with assets on the left side of the page and liabilities and stockholders' equity on the right side. Total assets equals total liabilities plus stockholders' equity.[10]

Discussion of other problems the analyst faces in using the balance sheet will be explored in the analysis of fixed-income securities in Chapter 12.

[10]The *report form* lists assets, deducts liabilities, and establishes stockholders' equity. The increasingly popular *modified report form* lists current assets and deducts current liabilities to establish working capital; long-term assets are added and long-term liabilities deducted from working capital to ascertain equity.

TABLE 8-2
BALANCE SHEET

December 31, 19X0 and December 31, 19X1

Assets	Liabilities and Equity
Current assets:	Current liabilities:
Cash and securities	Accounts payable
Receivables	Accrued wages
Inventories	Taxes payable
Prepaid expenses	Long-term liabilities:
Permanent investments:	Long-term notes
Investments in other companies	Bonds payable
Realty held for investment	Stockholders' equity:
Fixed tangible assets:	Capital stock
Buildings	Additional paid-in capital
Land	Retained earnings
Machinery and equipment	
Furniture and fixtures	
Fixed intangible assets:	
Goodwill	
Patents	
Deferred charges to expense:	
R&D expenses	
Organization costs	
Total assets	Total Liabilities and Equity

NOTES TO FINANCIAL STATEMENTS

Most accounting statements deal with rather arbitrary cutoff points in time.[11] Thus *accounting statements cannot be considered complete* without parenthetical references and notes that not only clarify the data in the body of the statements but also introduce new information not conveniently admissible within the statements proper.

Quite often, valuation bases for assets are shown next to the item caption or in footnotes. Parenthetical references should be examined to note where assets have been pledged and the related liability secured.

Footnotes to the balance sheet often show many of the following items of importance to the analyst.[12]

1. Contingent liabilities for taxes, dividends, and pending lawsuits.
2. Particulars on options outstanding, leases, loans, and other financing arrangements.
3. Changes in accounting principles and techniques, including bases of valuation, and the dollar effect on income.
4. Facts of importance occurring between the balance-sheet date and date of submission of statements that might have a material effect on the statements. Examples include refinancing, proposed mergers, and changes in capitalization.

The analyst will find a wealth of information in these parenthetical references and footnotes that can shed light on the company under analysis.

---

[11]Calendar and fiscal years are based upon custom and operating convenience.
[12]Mauriello, *Accounting for the Financial Analyst*, p. 35.

Statement of Changes in Financial Position

This statement discloses all important aspects of a company's financing and investing activity between the beginning and the end of the accounting period. It is a condensation of how activities have been financed and how the financial resources have been used.

The basic ingredients for the statement of changes in financial position come from the balance sheet, income statement, statement of retained earnings, and certain other supplementary data. Table 8-3 shows very simple income and position statements, and Table 8-4 is a statement of changes in financial position prepared from Table 8-3 for the Douglas Corporation. Certain detail on transactions not found directly in the income statement or balance sheet is required to prepare the statement of changes in financial position. This information is shown in Table 8-4 but cannot be traced directly to Table 8-3.

The statement of changes in financial position displays changes in working capital, as well as changes traced to noncurrent assets, long-term liabilities, and stockholders' equity. Let us examine Table 8-4. There are two main subdivisions in the statement: sources (of financing) and applications (investing activity). The first major source of financing is income for the period. Notice that ordinary and extraordinary income are shown separately (items A and K). Net losses would be applications, not sources. Next, added back to (item B) or deducted from (item G) operating income are items that did not use (or provide) working capital or cash during the period. Depreciation and amortization are the principal income-statement items not requiring cash outlay in the current period that are added back to income before extraordinary items. Working-capital changes not constituting a use of cash during the current period can be determined by comparing the changes in each current asset and current liability account (components of working capital) between the present and prior balance sheets. In general, to income before extraordinary items:

Add:	Subtract:
Decreases in current-asset accounts (item E)	Increases in current-asset accounts (item H)
Increases in current-liability accounts (item F)	Decreases in current-liability accounts (item I)
Extraordinary gains (net of tax) (item K)	Extraordinary losses (net of tax) (item K)

The effects of other financing and investing activities, in addition to working capital or cash provided from operations, include:[13]

1. Outlays for purchase and receipts from sale of long-term assets (items P, M)
2. Conversion of debt or preferred stock to common stock (items O, Q)
3. Issuance, redemption, assumption, and repayment or repurchase of long-term debt or stock (item N)
4. Dividends or other stockholder distributions (except stock dividends or splits) (item R)

[13]Accounting Principles Board, *Opinion No. 19*. See U.S. General Accounting Office, *Outline of Opinions of the Accounting Principles Board*, pp. 76-80.

TABLE 8-3
SIMPLIFIED INCOME AND COMPARATIVE BALANCE SHEETS
(THOUSANDS OF DOLLARS)

Douglas Corporation
Income Statement
Year Ended 12/31/X1

Net sales	$1,000
Expenses (including taxes)	775
Net income	$ 225
Dividends paid	100
Transferred to retained earnings	$ 125

Douglas Corporation
Comparative Balance Sheets
December 31, 19X0 and December 31, 19X1

	19X1	19X0	Change
Assets:			
Current assets:			
Cash	$ 150	$ 120	+30
Receivables	150	200	−50
Inventories	200	180	+20
Total current assets	$ 500	$ 500	
Tangible fixed assets:			
Plant and equipment	$1,935	$1,700	+235
Less: Accumulated depreciation	(500)	(350)	+150
Net tangible fixed assets	$1,435	$1,350	+ 85
Total assets	$1,935	$1,850	
Liabilities and stockholders' equity:			
Current liabilities:			
Accounts payable	$ 150	$ 125	+25
Accrued taxes and wages	35	105	−70
Total current liabilities	$ 185	$ 230	
Long-term liabilities:			
Nonconvertible bonds	$ 300	$ 295	+ 5
Convertible bonds	150	200	−50
Total long-term liabilities	$ 450	$ 495	
Stockholders' equity:			
Capital stock	$ 170	$ 150	+ 20
Additional paid-in capital	580	550	+ 30
Retained earnings	550	425	+125
Total stockholders' equity	$1,300	$1,125	
Total liabilities and stockholders' equity	$1,935	$1,850	

In general, proceeds received from these types of activities are "sources"; outlays are called "applications." A conversion of debt or preferred to common stock would be shown as both a source and an application, in order to cancel one event against the other.

TABLE 8-4

DOUGLAS CORPORATION: STATEMENT OF CHANGES IN FINANCIAL POSITION (THOUSANDS OF DOLLARS)

Item				
	Sources:			
	Operations:			
A	Income before extraordinary items			$225
B	Add: Income-statement items not requiring outlay of cash in current period:			
C	Depreciation	$150		
D	Changes in working-capital elements that constitute a *source of cash* in current period:			
E	Decrease in receivables	$ 50		
F	Increase in accounts payable	25	$225	
G	Less: Changes in working-capital elements that constitute *use of cash* in current period:			
H	Increase in inventories	$ 20		
I	Decrease in accrued wages	70	$ 90	135
J	Cash provided from operations of the period exclusive of extraordinary items			$360
K	Gain or loss associated with extraordinary items (net of applicable income tax)			0
L	Cash provided from operations			$360
M	Proceeds from sale of fixed assets			100
N	Proceeds from issuance of bonds			5
O	Issuance of common stock through conversion of bonds			50
				$515
	Applications:			
P	Purchase of fixed assets			$335
Q	Conversion of bonds to common stock			50
R	Payment of dividends			100
				$485
S	Net increase in cash during year			$ 30

Notes:

1. *Sources* of cash normally identified with decreases in asset accounts and increases in liabilities and equities. *Uses* of cash are: + assets and − liabilities and equity.

2. Working capital equals current assets minus current liabilities. Working capital, 19X0 = $500 − $230 = $270; 19X1 = $500 − $185 = $315. Change in working capital is +45 ($315 − $270).

USE OF STATEMENT BY ANALYST

The statement of changes in financial position discloses clearly and individually the significant financing and investing activities of the company during an accounting period, giving the analyst an overall view of the financial management of a company and its policies. Some of the questions the statement may help to answer are:[14]

1. Where did profits go?
2. Why were dividends not larger (or smaller)?
3. How were dividends possible in the face of a net loss for the period?
4. Why are current assets down and net income up?

[14]Mauriello, *Accounting for the Financial Analyst*, p. 90.

5. How did the company finance plant expansion?
6. How was debt retirement accomplished?
7. What became of the proceeds of the new bond issue?
8. How was the increase in working capital financed?

Comparing statements over the past provides insight into patterns that may or may not be followed in the years ahead. The statement of changes in financial position is a valuable supplement to the balance sheet and income statement. The analyst should probe it thoroughly.

Consolidated Financial Statements

Very often, certain operating units of a parent company are not owned 100 percent. That is, the voting common stock is shared with third parties, often other companies. Where 50 percent or more of the voting common stock is held by the parent company, the company held is referred to as a *subsidiary*. Less than 50 percent control results in an *affiliated* company. An *associated* company is a company owned jointly by two other companies.

A holding company may own anywhere from a small fraction up to 100 percent of another company. Where the percentage of ownership exceeds 50 percent, accountants strongly recommend that company statements be consolidated. Although there are certain refinements in the process, consolidation means adding the statements of the companies together. The portion of the equity that is not owned by the consolidator, or holding company, is shown as a "minority-interest" liability on the balance sheet. Net income on the statement of income is reduced by the portion accruing to minority interests.

Where ownership of voting common stock is between 20 and 50 percent, the accounting profession adopts the view that the holding company has effective control of dividend policy of the subsidiary. Thus the initial cost of the investment in the subsidiary stock is shown separately as a long-term investment under Assets on the holding company's balance sheet. As time passes, the investment account is adjusted upward for the holding company's share of subsidiary profits, and downward for its share in subsidary losses and for dividends received. This is referred to as the *equity method* of accounting for subsidiaries. For ownership of less than 20 percent, if it can be shown that the holding company and the affiliate are two separate units and that effective control is not exercised by the holding company, then the *cost method* of accounting for subsidiaries is permitted. The investment in affiliate shares is shown at cost on the balance sheet. Dividends received are treated as income.

The essential difference between the cost and equity methods is that the former does not generally adjust the investment up and down for profits and losses, less dividends. More significantly, on the income statement only dividends received are shown, and not the parent's portion of total income. This latter provision can lead to abuses, by which dividend declarations by subsidiaries or affiliates can be regulated to affect the parent's earnings. The following example illustrates the use of the *equity method* of accounting for subsidiaries.

EXAMPLE. The Melicher Co. purchased 40 percent of the voting common stock of the Rush Corp. one year ago, at a cost of $5 million. At that time, Melicher's balance sheet showed "Investments in affiliates, $5,000,000." During the past year, Rush had after-tax earnings of $250,000. It declared dividends on common shares of $100,000. The holding company's share of profits and dividends is $100,000 and $40,000 respectively. Melicher would show the net difference between its share of profits and dividends received, $60,000, as an addition to its investment account. The account would now show a total of $5,060,000. The reason for netting profits and dividends received can be seen in another way. Rush Corp. will show an increase in its assets and retained earnings of $150,000, or after-tax earnings of $250,000 less dividends of $100,000 paid. Melicher's share of these assets and retained earnings is 40 percent, or $60,000.

The Auditor's Opinion

Investors and investment analysts look to an independent certified public accounting firm to attest to the financial statements we have been discussing. The CPA, after he has conducted his examination, renders an opinion on the financial statements. An example of the general wording of an auditor's typical "unqualified" opinion follows:

> We have examined the balance sheet of RJJ Corporation as of December 31, 198X, and the related statements of income and retained earnings and changes in financial position for the year then ended. Our examination was made in accordance with generally accepted auditing standards, and accordingly included such tests of the accounting records and such other auditing procedures as we considered necessary in the circumstances.
>
> In our opinion, the aforementioned financial statements present fairly the financial position of the RJJ Corporation and the results of its operations and the changes in its financial position for the year then ended, in conformity with generally accepted accounting principles applied on a basis consistent with that of the preceding year.

This unqualified opinion, which would generally be addressed to the board of directors of the corporation, often is mistakenly taken as a *guaranty* from the CPA that the statements are 100 percent accurate. This is *not* true. You will note that the third word in the opinion is "examined." This simply means that the auditor has reviewed the content of the statements rather than that he has prepared or guaranteed these statements. Furthermore, the opinion goes on to say that the examination was conducted in accordance with certain prescribed auditing standards and that the auditor performed those tests he considered necessary. Thus the reader is made aware of the existence of specific rules that auditors must follow, and the fact that the auditor *does* exercise subjective opinion in judgment. Nonetheless, the fact that the auditor does issue this type of opinion should give some consolation to the reader that these statements and notes have been subjected to stringent external review.

When circumstances do not permit the issuance of such an unqualified opinion as that discussed in the preceding paragraph, the auditor has a number of other types of opinions that he can issue. The board of directors of the corporation or its auditing committee, however, would usually prefer that the auditor issue an unqualified opinion, and they therefore tend to cooperate with the auditor in every way possible so that he can issue this type of opinion.[15]

We have already discussed many key accounting conventions or *generally accepted accounting principles*. These rules become "generally accepted" in two main ways: (1) by authoritative pronouncements from such bodies as the Financial Accounting Standards Board (FASB) and the Securities and Exchange Commission (SEC), and (2) by widespread usage and custom among respected certified public accountants.

We will now discuss some new reporting requirements which the accounting profession feels are necessary in order to better inform the investment community.

Key Changes in Generally Accepted Accounting Principles Affecting Investment Analysis

In the sections that follow we will briefly describe several major recent developments and changes in generally accepted accounting principles. The reader should understand that these are merely some of the changes that have occurred that affect the financial statements. However, we believe we have selected those specific changes whose effect will be most widely felt in the investment community.

ACCOUNTING FOR FOREIGN CURRENCY

In 1981 the Financial Accounting Standards Board restated standards of financial accounting and reporting for the translation of foreign currency transactions and foreign currency financial statements.[16] The FASB felt that because of the U.S. dollar devaluations and the institution of "floating" exchange rates, there was a need for the development of standards reflecting these financial dealings.

FINANCIAL REPORTING FOR SEGMENTS OF THE BUSINESS ENTERPRISE

In December 1976, the Financial Accounting Standards Board issued its *Statement of Financial Accounting Standards No. 14, Financial Reporting for Segments of a Business Enterprise.*[17] The FASB recognized that businesses have continually broadened their base of operations into various industries, foreign countries (as noted in the preceding section), and various markets within countries. The FASB felt that it was necessary for financial statements to include information about the corporation's business as it occurred in different industries, in different countries, and to various major customers when the firm issues a *complete* set of statements that present financial position, and so forth. *Statement No. 14*, perhaps more than any other statement that the FASB has issued to date, reflects the accounting profession's growing awareness of the need for various types of information for various reasons—particularly among the investment community. It is of considerable interest to students of the securities markets to

---

[15]The reader who is interested in learning more about the other types of possible opinions should consult the AICPA's *Statements on Auditing Standards* (New York: AICPA, 1977), or any basic auditing textbook.

[16]Financial Accounting Standards Board, *Statement of Financial Accounting Standards No. 52, Foreign Currency Translation*, (Stamford, Conn.: FASB, 1981).

[17]Financial Accounting Standards Board, *Statement of Financial Accounting Standards No. 14, Financial Reporting for Segments of a Business Enterprise* (Stamford, Conn.: FASB, 1976).

note the wording the FASB used in explaining why it had issued *No. 14*:

> Financial statement users point out that the evaluation of risk and return is the central element of investment and lending decisions—the greater the perceived degree of risk associated with an investment or lending alternative, the greater is the required rate of return to the investor or lender. If return is defined as expected cash flows to the investor or creditor, the evaluation of risk involves assessment of the uncertainty surrounding both the timing and the amount of the expected cash flows to the enterprise, which in turn are indicative of potential cash flows to the investor or creditor. Users of financial statements indicate that uncertainty results, in part, from factors unique to the particular enterprise in which an investment may be made or to which credit may be extended. Uncertainty also results, in part, from factors related to the industries and geographic areas in which the enterprise operates and, in part, from national and international economic and political factors. Investors and lenders analyze factors at all of those levels to evaluate the risk and return associated with an investment or lending alternative.
>
> Information contained in an enterprise's financial statements constitutes an important input to that analysis. Financial statements provide information about conditions, trends, and ratios that assist in predicting cash flows. In analyzing an enterprise, a financial statement user often compares information about the enterprise with information about other enterprises, with industrywide information, and with national or international economic information in general. Those comparisons are helpful in determining whether a given enterprise's operations may be expected to move with, against, or independently of developments in its industry and in the economy within which it operates.
>
> The broadening of an enterprise's activities into different industries or geographic areas complicates the analysis of conditions, trends, and ratios and, therefore, the ability to predict. The various industry segments or geographic areas of operations of an enterprise may have different rates of profitability, degrees and types of risk, and opportunities for growth. There may be differences in the rates of return on the investment commitment in the various industry segments or geographic areas and in their future capital demands.[18]

The principal disclosure requirements of *Statement No. 14* are sales and revenue, operating profit or loss, and identifiable assets. Information relating to these specific items must be identified with specific industry segments. This required information must be presented in the body of the financial statement, or in its footnotes, or in a separate schedule that is clearly an integral part of the financial statements. The following example is taken from FASB *No. 14* and indicates what this new information and notes for this new information should look like.[19]

To be identified as a recordable segment, an industry segment must be significant to the business as a whole. An industry segment must be recorded separately if it satisfies one or more of the following tests:

1. Its revenue (including both sales to unaffiliated customers and intersegment sales or transfers) is 10 percent or more of the combined revenue (sales to unaffiliated customers and intersegment sales or transfers) of all of the enterprise's industry segments.

[18]*Ibid.*, pp. 27-28.
[19]*Ibid.*, pp. 53-56.

2. The absolute amount of its operating profit or operating loss is 10 percent or more of the greater, in absolute amount, of:

   a. The combined operating profit of all industry segments that did not incur an operating loss, or

   b. The combined operating loss of all industry segments that did incur an operating loss.

3. Its identifiable assets are 10 percent or more of the combined identifiable assets of all industry segments.[20]

Clearly, the impact of FASB *No. 14* on financial statement users will be monumental. This new information will greatly assist analysts not only in examining and understanding the past performance of the business as a whole but also in forecasting the future. While consolidated information is important, understanding the makeup of this consolidated information as defined in FASB *No. 14* will greatly benefit the investment community.

REPLACEMENT COST DATA AND ACCOUNTING FOR PRICE-LEVEL CHANGES

Throughout this chapter we have noted that accountants typically report information based upon historical cost. This means that the cost—particularly of items like fixed assets—is evidenced by purchase orders, contracts, and canceled checks. This objectively verifiable information is part of the data that allow the CPA to present an opinion such as that illustrated earlier in this chapter. Nonetheless, in the face of continued inflation, accountants, investors, and others have become troubled by the

EXHIBIT A
X COMPANY
CONSOLIDATED INCOME STATEMENT
YEAR ENDED DECEMBER 31, 1977

Sales		$4,700
Cost of sales	$3,000	
Selling, general, and administrative expense	700	
Interest expense	200	3,900
		800
Equity in net income of Z Co. (25% owned)		100
Income from continuing operations before income taxes		900
Income taxes		400
Income from continuing operations		500
Discontinued operations:		
Loss from operations of discontinued West Coast division (net of income tax effect of $50)	70	
Loss on disposal of West Coast division (net of income tax effect of $100)	130	200
Income before extraordinary gain and before cumulative effect of change in accounting principle		300
Extraordinary gain (net of income tax effect of $80)		90
Cumulative effect on prior years of change from straightline to accelerated depreciation (net of income tax effect of $60)		(60)
Net income		$ 330

[20]*Ibid.*, p. 10.

EXHIBIT B

X COMPANY

INFORMATION ABOUT THE COMPANY'S OPERATIONS IN
DIFFERENT INDUSTRIES YEAR ENDED DECEMBER 31, 1977

	Industry A	Industry B	Industry C	Other Industries	Adjustments and Eliminations	Consolidated
Sales to unaffiliated customers	$1,000	$2,000	$1,500	$ 200		$ 4,700
Intersegment sales	200		500		$(700)	
Total revenue	$1,200	$2,000	$2,000	$ 200	$(700)	$ 4,700
Operating profit	$ 200	$ 290	$ 600	$ 50	$ (40)	$ 1,100
Equity in net income of Z Co.						100
General corporate expenses						(100)
Interest expense						(200)
Income from continuing operations before income taxes						$ 900
Identifiable assets at December 31, 1977	$2,000	$4,050	$6,000	$1,000	$ (50)	$13,000
Investment in net assets of Z Co.						400
Corporate assets						· 1,600
Total assets at December 31, 1977						$15,000

See accompanying note.

Note:
The Company operates principally in three industries, A, B and C. Operations in Industry A involve production and sale of (describe types of products and services). Operations in Industry B involve production and sale of (describe types of products and services). Operations in Industry C involve production and sale of (describe types of products and services). Total revenue by industry includes both sales to unaffiliated customers, as reported in the Company's consolidated income statement, and intersegment sales, which are accounted for by (describe the basis of accounting for intersegment sales).

Operating profit is total revenue less operating expenses. In computing operating profit, none of the following items has been added or deducted: general corporate expenses, interest expense, income taxes, equity in income from unconsolidated investee, loss from discontinued operations of the West Coast division (which was a part of the Company's operations in Industry B), extraordinary gain (which relates to the Company's operations in Industry A), and the cumulative effect of the change from straight-line to accelerated depreciation (of which $30 relates to the Company's operations in Industry A, $10 to Industry B, and $20 to Industry C). Depreciation for Industries A, B, and C, respectively, was $80, $100, and $150. Capital expenditures for the three industries were $100, $200, and $400, respectively.

The effect of the change from straight-line to accelerated depreciation was to reduce the 1977 operating profit of Industries A, B, and C, respectively, by $40, $30, and $20.

Identifiable assets by industry are those assets that are used in the Company's operations in each industry. Corporate assets are principally cash and marketable securities.

The Company has a 25 percent interest in Z Co., whose operations are in the United States and are vertically integrated with the Company's operations in Industry A. Equity in net income of Z Co. was $100; investment in net assets of Z Co. was $400.

To reconcile industry information with consolidated amounts, the following elim-
inations have been made: $700 of intersegment sales; $40 relating to the net change
in intersegment operating profit in beginning and ending inventories; and $50 inter-
segment operating profit in inventory at December 31, 1977.
     Contracts with a U.S. government agency account for $1,100 of the sales to
unaffiliated customers of Industry B.

SOURCE: Copyright © by Financial Accounting Standards Board, High Ridge Park,
Stamford, Connecticut 06905, U.S.A. Reprinted with permission. Copies of the
complete document are available from the FASB.

exclusive use of historical costs. This is particularly so with respect to the reporting of
depreciation. If a firm depreciates based on historical cost, some contend that the
firm will be understating expenses and overstating income. Why? Because the replacement cost of the asset is considerably higher than the book value of the asset. Therefore
the firm's financial position and earnings are not adequately reflected merely be reporting historical cost.

To overcome this objection, the Financial Accounting Standards Board in 1979
issued FASB *Statement No. 33* which requires certain large public companies to dis-
close the effects of changing prices as a supplement to a firm's basic financial statements
which use historical cost.[21]

Earlier, the Securities and Exchange Commission felt that even though generally
accepted accounting principles did not yet require disclosure of price-level adjusted
statements or the recasting of historical cost figures, this information was still necessary
for readers of financial statements. Therefore in 1976 the SEC, in its *Accounting Series
Release 190*, required disclosure of the replacement cost of fixed assets, inventories,
and certain other selected accounts. These figures, together with the explanation of how
these amounts were arrived at, must be included in the 10-K report which is filed
annually with the SEC. This supplementary report must be filed by approximately one
thousand of the largest corporations in the United States.

In general, the affected corporations are quite averse to this additional required
filing.[22] The accounting profession has recently issued a statement of auditing standards
for this "unaudited" replacement cost information.[23]

Published Financial Forecasts

In recent years, analysts and regulatory agencies have been pressing to have
accounting statements and annual reports provide greater utility to investors. It has been
suggested, for instance, that companies provide forecasts of future operations in annual
reports, alongside traditional historical information. The primary item, of course, that
investors would like projected or forecast are earnings for the year ahead.[24] The merits,
legalities, and ethics of such a move will no doubt take some time to resolve.

[21]Financial Accounting Standards Board, *Statement of Financial Accounting Standards No. 33,
Financial Reporting and Changing Prices* (Stamford, Conn.: FASB, 1979).
     [22]See "Inflation Accounting in SEC-Ordered Test Irks Many Companies," *The Wall Street
Journal*, May 23, 1977, p.1
     [23]AICPA, *Statement on Auditing Standards, No. 18, Unaudited Replacement Cost Informa-
tion.*
     [24]The 1972 Annual Report of Fuqua Industries, Inc., was one of the earliest attempts to
incorporate forecasts of future operations into an annual report.

Officially Filed Information

Public companies are required to file certain information with the Securities and Exchange Commission. In the main, public companies are those listed on the organized securities exchange and traded over-the-counter that meet certain size tests (assets and number of shareholders). These filings take the form of periodic reports, proxies, financial statements, and other information.

Three periodic reports must be filed with the SEC: Form 8-K reports various events as they occur—acquisition and disposition of assets, changes in securities (amounts), defaults on senior securities, issuance of options, revaluation of assets, and other material events. Form 10Q is a quarterly report containing financial information in summary form. Form 10-K is an annual report containing certified financial statements and certain detailed supporting schedules not normally seen in annual reports provided to the public. These financial statements include notes on the basis for computing depreciation and certain details on leases, funded debt, management stock options, and inventory classification, among other items.

These periodic reports provide expanded information for analysts and investors. They are available from private firms that have reproduced the reports on microfilm or microfiche, and from the SEC itself. Reproduction, handling, and postage costs must be considered.[25]

External Information

External sources that the analyst can turn to for basic company information are prepared by investment services and brokerage firms. Three of the major services, to which even the novice investor will often turn for valuable information, are Standard & Poor's, Moody's, and the *Value Line.*

Figure 8-1 is taken from a portion of a Standard & Poor's *Current Analysis of the Office Equipment, Systems, and Services Industry.* Note that it contains paragraphs on several of the industry participants, as well as a summary of key financial data. These current analyses update and supplement the S&P basic analysis of the industry. Figure 8-2 is a report taken from the Standard & Poor's *Stock Reports.* This report concerns a firm on the New York Stock Exchange, but S&P also publishes similar reports on all American Stock Exchange firms and selected over-the-counter securities. These reports contain a recommendation, a report on the firm's operation and recent developments, information on the firm's financing, and pertinent share-price data, as well as other financial data. New reports are issued for this loose-leaf service at frequent intervals.

Moody's *Handbook of Common Stocks,* published quarterly, contains approximately the same type of information as the S&P *Stock Reports.* A reproduction from Moody's is shown in Figure 8-3 on page 229.

The *Value Line Investment Survey,* in conjunction with the *Industry Reports,* lists excellent one-page summary sheets of member firms. As can be seen in Figure

---

[25]For example, a complete 10-K report may be fifty pages in length and cost anywhere from 10 to 25 cents per page, excluding postage and other handling charges.

8-4, these reports are abundant in extremely valuable information. Along with information similar to that contained in Moody's and Standard & Poor's (although contained in a different format), the *Value Line* projects key income-statement data several years in advance, computes betas (the measure of relative responsiveness of the stock's price to the market, to be examined in Chapter 19), and provides an insider index (which measures insiders' decisions to buy the stock relative to their decisions to sell), historical growth rates, and *Value Line* ratings on performance, income, and safety. The use and significance of these ratings are explained by *Value Line* in Figure 8-5 on page 231.

In addition to these easily accessible services (most libraries subscribe to them), there is another source that all interested investors can obtain in some form from a stockbroker: Standard & Poor's *Stock Guide* and *Bond Guide*. Both these guides are published monthly and contain key skeletal information on all listed stocks and bonds and many unlisted securities. The *Stock Guide* provides a brief statement of the nature of the firm's business, selected accounting information, and selected price data on the stock. The *Bond Guide* contains many other items of interest and information on the firm's business, key bond provisions, investment-times-interest-earned ratios, the amount of debt outstanding, the S&P bond rating, and price data on the various bond issues of the firm. Figures 8-6 and 8-7 contain examples of the pages from these guides that contain data on McDonald's Corporation. See pages 232 through 234.

Certainly an investment decision should not be based on such sketchy data. Their use is primarily to act as a screening device for the investor. He may decide that the firm is so unappealing to him that it's not even worth a trip to the library for more research information. On the other hand, the security may look interesting, and worthy of some research. At the library, after consulting the sources already mentioned, the investor may decide to probe still further. To aid him, we recommend the use of the *Wall Street Journal Index*, the *Business Periodicals Index*, and the *Funk and Scott Index of Corporations and Industries*.[26]

The annual *WSJ Index* contains an alphabetical listing of firms mentioned in the *Wall Street Journal* during the year. Under the firm's name are listed key words from the title of the story, plus documentation concerning the issue, page, and column in which the story appeared. The interested investor can then go to the sources and read up on the company.

The *Business Periodicals Index* provides an alphabetical listing by key word, industry, and company of all stories carried by major business publications that are covered by the index. From it, researchers can readily locate much information on the industry, firm, and firm's products in which they are interested, for they can track down the stories and read up on almost all published data they need to know.

The *F&S Index* provides a similar but more specific kind of service. It indexes data on companies, products, and industries from over 750 publications—many of them specialized trade journals. Furthermore, this information is accessible numerically by SIC classification as well as alphabetically by company name. The SIC classification is useful because researchers will find references to all firms in that particular classification in one place. Using the alphabetical listing, they can zero in on firms of particular interest to them, regardless of the SIC classification.

---

[26]All three indexing services publish monthly supplements to their annual volumes.

FIGURE 8-1

COMPUTER SERVICES

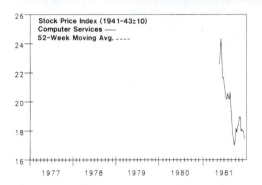

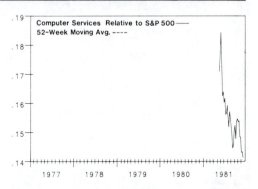

Stock price activity of the S&P computer services index (added to the S&P 500 in May 1981), has continued an unfavorable trend that started in June 1981. From 1978 through its peak this past June, the index had more than tripled. Since then, however, market performance has lagged the S&P 500, as the market has generally reacted negatively to high-P-E technology issues. The price-earnings ratio of the index has fallen from a high of 21 in the second quarter of 1981, to its present 16 times estimated 1981 earnings. ■

INDUSTRY MARKET INDICATORS						
	—Earns. Per Share—			—*P-E Ratios—		
				1981	1981	
	1979	1980	E1981	High	Low	12-30-81
500 Composite	14.86	14.82	15.43	8.95	7.31	7.93
400 Industrials	16.29	16.11	16.80	9.35	7.50	8.15
Office & Bus. Equip.	99.90	108.67	107.87	11.35	8.23	9.05
Office & Bus. Equip. (excl. IBM)	29.51	27.20	28.25	10.89	7.80	8.06
Computer Services	0.97	1.11	1.32	18.44	12.88	13.17

E-Estimated. *Based on est. 1981 earnings.

SCOREBOARD			
Stock Price Indexes	1-1-81	12-30-81	% Change
500 Composite	135.76	122.30	−9.9
400 Industrials	154.45	136.85	−11.4
Office & Bus. Equip.	1,212.02	976.50	−19.4
Office & Bus. Equip. (excl. IBM)	304.91	227.83	−25.4
¹Computer Services	20.34	17.38	−14.6

¹1978 = 10.

Computervision Corporation (CVN)

Computervision produces interactive graphic systems used in computer aided design and computer aided manfacturing (CAD/CAM). These systems include both hardware and software and enable users to increase productivity, improve product yields, and shorten the cycle for developing new products by automating certain highly complex and repetitive design and manufacturing processes. Computervision is unique in that it produces its own computers: competitors generally buy theirs from established manufacturers in order to concentrate their effort on software. However, Computervision's approach appears to be a strength because it permits the company to upgrade its products easily, and may create some synergy in the production of total systems. Industry estimates place the company's market share between 35% and 40%; its nearest competitors, Applicon (to be acquired by Schlumberger Ltd.), Calma (a division of General Electric), and Intergraph Corp. each are believed to hold less than 15% of the market.

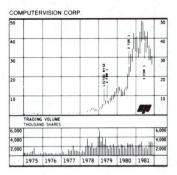

COMPUTERVISION CORP.

Following several years of exceptional growth, revenues are expected to increase at rates approximating 40% annually through 1982—slower than in past years, but strong nevertheless. Growth should be aided by continuing demand and the recent introduction of several new products. Margins, however, may come under pressure from the slowdown in revenue growth and an increasing amount of lower margin, defense-related revenues. Earnings for 1982 should rise to $1.60 a share, from the $1.30 estimated for 1981.

Although the shares (32½, NYSE) may face some further consolidation, we regard them as an attractive commitment for long-term capital appreciation. ■

FIGURE 8-1 (cont.)

*STATISTICS OF COMPANIES IN THE OFFICE EQUIPMENT INDUSTRY

Italicized entry shows addition or name change since last issue.	No. of Months	INTERIM OPERATING DATA — §Sales 1980	§Sales 1981	§[3]Net Income 1980	§[3]Net Income 1981	[3]Earns. $ Per Sh. 1980	[3]Earns. $ Per Sh. 1981	**ANNUAL EARNINGS — ††Year Ends	$ Per Share 1979	$ Per Share 1980	$ Per Share E1981	$ DIVS. PER SH. [4]Paid 1981	$ DIVS. PER SH. ¶Indic. Rate	Book Value — Per Share	[1]Wkg. Cap. Net — Per Share	[1]Wkg. Cap. "Net" Net	12-30-81 Price	1981 Price Range High Low	†Price Earns. Ratio	†Yields %
COMPUTER MANUFACTURERS																				
★ Amdahl Corp.	39 Wks.	286.3	319.1	8.6	20.5	0.47	1.00	Dec.	1.02	1.83	1.50	0.40	0.40	15.08	9.25	7.54	29⅝	46 -23⅝	20	1.4
Burroughs Corp.	9 Sept.	2,108.1	2,387.9	150.7	86.0	3.65	2.07	Dec.	7.45	1.99	3.50	2.60	2.60	51.22	14.59	5.96	34⅜	55⅜-27⅛	10	7.6
● Computer Automation	3 Sept.	18.2	16.3	0.1	0.2	0.07	0.10	June	d2.13	2.30	0.81	Nil	Nil	14.01	14.06	10.87	10	19½- 9¼	12	Nil
Control Data	9 Sept.	1,997.7	2,242.8	67.8	88.8	3.22	3.35	Dec.	3.43	4.14	4.50	0.47	0.50	38.35	14.81	11.77	34⅞	42½-30	8	1.4
Cray Research	9 Sept.	44.1	61.7	8.5	10.2	0.68	0.74	Dec.	0.63	0.85	1.25	Nil	Nil	6.32	4.00	3.09	36⅝	48⅜-28	29	Nil
Data General	12 Sept.	653.9	736.9	54.7	40.9	5.20	3.85	Sept.	4.82	5.20	3.85	Nil	Nil	36.42	39.47	27.10	53⅞	68⅜-40½	14	Nil
Datapoint Corp.	3 Oct.	98.7	126.5	10.3	10.9	0.57	0.54	July	1.47	1.90	2.45	Nil	Nil	10.17	10.91	4.20	50⅝	67½-38¾	21	Nil
Digital Equipment	3 Sept.	654.4	839.4	56.2	88.8	1.17	1.60	June	4.10	5.45	6.70	Nil	Nil	49.31	37.90	36.28	86⅛	113¼-80¼	13	Nil
Electronic Associates	39 Wks.	31.7	33.4	1.3	0.6	0.47	0.21	Dec.	0.67	0.62	...	Nil	Nil	6.27	4.82	4.50	6¾	9⅜- 4⅜	...	Nil
Four Phase System	9 Sept.	143.8	168.1	3.9	5.3	0.75	0.95	Dec.	3.29	1.06	1.25	Nil	Nil	21.02	7.88	-1.53	39½	45¾-18⅛	32	Nil
Honeywell Inc.	9 Sept.	3,487.9	3,784.6	146.1	153.7	6.57	6.79	Dec.	10.95	12.57	11.20	3.20	3.40	82.72	43.67	14.11	70½	114½-69	6	4.8
Int'l. Bus. Machines	9 Sept.	18,408.0	20,077.0	2,329.0	2,227.0	3.99	3.80	Dec.	5.16	6.10	5.80	3.44	3.44	29.63	4.76	-1.74	57¼	71½-48⅜	10	6.0
● Magnuson Computer	9 Sept.	20.7	25.6	1.3	d2.8	0.31	d0.57	Dec.	d1.49	0.54	...	Nil	Nil	5.52	2.54	2.23	11⅛	45¾- 9¾	...	Nil
NCR Corp.	9 Sept.	2,238.1	2,387.9	136.7	118.1	5.11	4.37	Dec.	8.78	9.51	8.40	2.15	2.20	61.54	38.68	26.94	43¾	75½-39¼	5	5.0
Prime Computer	9 Sept.	182.3	265.2	21.2	27.1	0.73	0.91	Dec.	0.64	1.07	1.30	Nil	Nil	4.37	4.66	2.52	24	49¼-17¼	18	Nil
Sperry Corp.	6 Sept.	2,542.2	2,608.2	139.4	45.8	3.45	1.10	Mar.	7.60	7.68	5.10	1.88	1.92	56.19	26.93	8.31	35	65⅝-29½	7	5.5
● Tandem Computers	12 Sept.	109.0	208.4	10.7	26.5	0.35	0.72	Sept.	0.20	0.35	0.72	Nil	Nil	5.65	4.92	4.86	27¾	34½-20½	39	Nil
★ Wang Laboratories	3 Sept.	156.3	236.9	11.9	18.0	0.21	0.30	June	0.59	1.00	1.36	0.10½	0.12	7.81	7.26	1.55	33¼	45⅝-24	24	0.4
PERIPHERAL EQUIPMENT AND SUBSYSTEMS																				
Centronics Data Comp.	3 Sept.	31.5	29.0	0.9	d2.7	0.15	d0.44	June	3.10	3.01	d4.08	0.30	Nil	7.81	6.64	-2.46	13	244¼- 6½	...	Nil
Data Terminal Systems	9 Sept.	98.0	89.0	4.3	d7.2	0.85	1.28	Jan.	1.91	d0.58	...	Nil	Nil	7.68	9.74	4.09	10¾	18½- 6⅜	...	Nil
★ Dataproducts Corp.	6 Sept.	125.4	129.3	7.8	4.1	1.03	0.47	Mar.	1.01	2.27	...	0.30	0.30	19.90	15.38	11.62	20½	44½-18¼	...	1.5
Mohawk Data Sciences	6 Oct.	156.4	156.2	8.9	2.9	0.79	0.22	Apr.	1.53	1.53	...	Nil	Nil	11.22	...	-4.34	14½	28⅞-10⅞	...	Nil
Recognition Equipment	12 Oct.	113.1	131.5	4.9	d8.2	0.82	d1.34	Oct.	0.43	0.82	d1.34	Nil	Nil	10.21	11.08	3.90	6½	17½- 5¾	...	Nil
Storage Technology	9 Sept.	418.5	643.9	31.4	50.4	1.23	1.72	Dec.	1.58	1.76	2.25	Nil	Nil	8.75	8.15	0.41	35⅞	40⅜-17¾	16	Nil
Telex Corp.	6 Sept.	91.0	97.9	2.8	4.9	0.22	0.39	Mar.	0.08	0.64	...	Nil	Nil	4.29	...	-5.83	6⅜	9⅜- 4¼	...	Nil
SOFTWARE AND EDP SERVICES																				
● Anacomp	3 Sept.	24.1	26.6	1.3	1.5	0.15	0.17	June	0.60	0.77	0.88	0.10⅜	0.12	3.25	6.11	0.44	12⅛	18½-11¼	14	1.0
Automatic Data Process	3 Sept.	126.1	153.6	9.0	11.0	0.29	0.33	June	1.11	1.31	1.51	0.39½	0.44	7.23	-0.14	-2.14	25¼	31¾-23⅜	17	1.7
Computer Sciences	26 Wks.	278.5	297.6	13.1	6.9	0.96	0.51	Mar.	1.70	1.82	1.50	Nil	Nil	6.20	3.97	0.99	13	24⅜-11¼	9	Nil
● COMSHARE Inc.	3 Sept.	20.5	20.3	1.0	0.9	0.27	0.19	June	1.31	1.10	0.92	Nil	Nil	7.23	2.72	0.74	7⅛	17 - 7⅛	8	Nil
Cordura Corp.	9 Sept.	19.2	21.5	2.4	3.4	0.54	0.74	Dec.	0.57	0.90	...	0.52	0.60	2.04	1.08	1.07	7⅞	13½- 5¾	...	7.6
Electronic Data Systems	3 Sept.	104.8	122.2	8.6	10.6	0.31	0.39	June	0.91	1.06	1.39	0.56	0.60	5.56	1.64	0.73	24	29⅝-16¼	17	2.5
● Reynolds & Reynolds	12 Sept.	210.3	212.2	11.0	7.1	2.33	1.51	Sept.	3.15	2.33	1.51	1.08	1.08	16.48	5.36	3.20	19¾	24¼-16¼	13	5.5
Tymshare, Inc.	9 Sept.	177.1	221.3	15.0	16.1	1.47	1.37	Dec.	1.53	1.81	1.80	Nil	Nil	12.49	5.18	3.59	28½	57¾-23⅛	16	Nil
COPYING																				
AM International	12 July	689.1	652.7	26.1	d101.9	0.47	d26.71	July	1.07	0.47	d26.71	0.07	Nil	25.81	3.12	-6.02	4	16⅞- 3⅜	...	Nil
Dennison Mfg.	9 Sept.	360.5	415.5	14.7	20.0	1.53	2.03	Dec.	2.72	2.42	...	1.30	1.30	18.17	12.25	6.66	22	25 -15⅝	...	5.9
Nashua Corp.	9 Sept.	492.8	492.1	14.5	7.5	3.10	1.60	Dec.	5.75	4.60	...	1.52½	1.60	33.66	19.48	9.95	17¾	28 -16⅝	...	9.0
SCM Corp.	3 Sept.	474.5	461.0	17.7	9.7	1.82	1.02	June	4.98	5.55	5.80	1.85	2.00	52.19	38.79	12.57	22	31⅝-21⅞	4	9.1
Savin Corp.	6 Oct.	211.8	246.7	5.9	d6.4	0.87	d1.10	Apr.	4.35	d0.52	...	Nil	Nil	14.02	17.14	-12.17	8	15¼- 7	...	Nil
Xerox Corp.	9 Sept.	5,968.6	6,409.5	471.1	290.8	5.58	5.81	Dec.	6.69	7.33	7.10	3.00	3.00	42.92	19.27	8.92	40½	64 -37⅜	6	7.4
OTHER EQUIPMENT & SUPPLIES																				
Amer. Business Prods.	9 Sept.	139.6	154.2	6.2	5.2	1.65	1.39	Dec.	1.92	2.15	...	0.48	0.48	12.67	7.27	3.73	12¾	16⅝-10½	...	3.8
Barry Wright	9 Sept.	91.3	106.9	7.3	8.8	0.97	1.08	Dec.	1.02	1.32	...	0.36	0.40	7.74	4.36	4.03	18¼	23⅜-13¾	...	2.2
Bell & Howell	9 Sept.	457.0	507.5	11.9	7.3	2.12	1.30	Dec.	3.01	3.41	...	0.96	0.96	31.97	28.34	17.78	19⅛	30⅝-16½	...	5.0
[6]*Computervision Corp.*	9 Sept.	135.0	194.4	15.8	26.4	0.62	0.96	Dec.	0.52	0.90	1.30	Nil	Nil	...	...	...	32½	49⅜-26⅛	25	Nil
★ Duplex Prods.	12 Oct.	197.8	221.0	10.7	9.5	2.89	2.49	Oct.	3.06	2.89	2.49	0.60	0.68	13.64	12.09	8.92	13⅛	16 -11¾	5	5.2
Ennis Business Forms	9 Nov.	63.4	66.7	3.5	4.6	1.90	2.43	Feb.	2.60	3.11	...	0.68	0.72	13.29	10.07	6.22	20½	22¾-14½	...	3.5
GF Business Equipment	9 Sept.	129.0	128.9	1.1	0.3	0.41	0.09	Dec.	d0.17	0.80	...	0.10	0.10	16.41	13.12	6.04	3⅝	7½- 3⅜	...	2.8
Lanier Business Prods.	3 Aug.	57.6	66.4	3.7	2.3	0.25	0.16	May	1.18	1.70	...	0.31	0.34	6.45	6.87	4.38	18¼	23 -13⅛	11	1.9
Moore Corp. Ltd.	9 Sept.	1,328.6	1,381.6	77.8	83.1	2.78	2.97	Dec.	3.72	3.95	...	1.76	1.80	23.72	14.29	10.87	33⅜	38⅝-28¾	...	5.4

SOURCE: *Current Analysis of the Office Equipment, Systems, and Services Industry* (New York: Standard & Poor's Corporation, January 1982).

FIGURE 8-2

McDonald's Corp.

1447K

NYSE Symbol MCD Put & Call Options on CBOE

Price	Range	P-E Ratio	Dividend	Yield	S&P Ranking
Oct. 26'81	1981				
67¼	70¼-48⅜	11	1.00	1.5%	A–

Summary

McDonald's has become the dominant force in the fast-food restaurant industry through its aggressive expansion and merchandising programs. Sales and earnings have risen rapidly in recent years and the uptrend is likely to continue at a worthwhile, though more moderate pace.

Current Outlook

Earnings for 1982 should increase some 15% from the $6.60 a share estimated for 1981.

The quarterly dividend is expected to continue at $0.25.

The long-term uptrend in sales should continue in 1982, aided by further expansion in the U.S. and abroad, menu diversification and increased prices. Despite industry projections of higher beef prices in early 1982, margins should be maintained, benefiting from MCD's flexible pricing policy. Strong internal generation of funds could moderate the company's financing costs.

Total Revenues (Million $)

Quarter:	1981	1980	1979	1978
Mar.	562	493	419	363
Jun.	650	563	489	431
Sep.	668	589	520	452
Dec.		570	510	427
		2,215	1,938	1,672

Revenues for the nine months to September 30, 1981 rose 14%, year to year. Improved margins at company-owned units, particularly during the first quarter, led to a 21% rise in net income. Share earnings were $5.02, versus $4.19.

Common Share Earnings ($)

Quarter:	1981	1980	1979	1978
Mar.	1.28	1.06	0.90	0.77
Jun.	1.88	1.54	1.32	1.11
Sep.	1.87	1.59	1.37	1.18
Dec.		1.30	1.10	0.95
		5.49	4.68	4.00

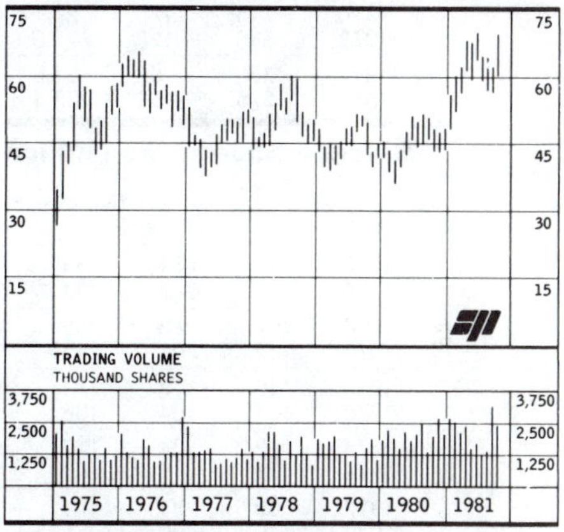

75
60
45
30
15
TRADING VOLUME
THOUSAND SHARES
3,750
2,500
1,250
1975 1976 1977 1978 1979 1980 1981

Important Developments

Jul. '81—During the 1981 second quarter MCD added 93 restaurants, including the first in Denmark. The worldwide restaurant total at June 30 was 6,418 (versus 5,951 a year ago), of which 5,333 were in the U.S. and 1,085 were in 29 other countries and territories. Another 160 restaurants, including 106 in the U.S., were under construction at June 30.

Jul. '81—The company said that it was planning to open two additional units in Denmark, bringing the total there to three. One unit, in Aalborg, was scheduled to open by 1981 year-end and the other, in Odense, was slated to open in 1982.

Jul. '81—McDonald's was testing a biscuit breakfast entree at about 1,000 units in the southeastern United States.

Next earnings report due in late January.

Per Share Data ($)

Yr. End Dec. 31	1981	1980	1979	1978	1977	[1]1976	[2]1975	[2]1974	[1]1973	[1]1972
Book Value	**NA**	26.66	21.95	18.58	14.85	12.14	9.59	7.63	5.94	4.51
Earnings	**NA**	5.49	4.68	4.00	[3]3.37	2.72	2.17	1.70	1.31	[3]0.94
Dividends	**0.95**	0.74	0.51	0.32	0.17½	0.07½	Nil	Nil	Nil	Nil
Payout Ratio	**NA**	13%	11%	8%	5%	3%	Nil	Nil	Nil	Nil
Prices—High	**70¼**	52	51⅞	60½	53⅜	66	60½	63¼	76⅞	77⅜
Low	**48⅜**	36¼	39¼	43⅞	37¾	48¾	26¾	21¼	44⅛	37
P/E Ratio—	**NA**	9-7	11-8	15-11	16-11	24-18	28-12	37-13	59-34	82-39

Data as orig. reptd. Adj. for stk. div(s). of 100% Jun. 1972. **1.** Reflects merger or acquisition. **2.** Reflects merger or acquisition and accounting change. **3.** Ful. dil.: 3.36 in 1977, 0.93 in 1972. NA-Not Available.

Standard NYSE Stock Reports
Vol. 48/No. 210/Sec. 10

November 2, 1981

Standard & Poor's Corp.
25 Broadway, NY, NY 10004

FIGURE 8-2 (cont.)

1447K

McDonald's Corporation

Income Data (Million $)

Year Ended Dec. 31	Revs.	Oper. Inc.	% Oper. Inc. of Revs.	Cap. Exp.	Depr.	Int. Exp.	Net Bef. Taxes	Eff. Tax Rate	Net Inc.	% Net Inc. of Revs.
1980	2,184	575	26.3%	410	113	102	403	45.1%	221	10.1%
1979	1,912	483	25.2%	459	92	83	345	45.3%	189	9.9%
1978	1,644	423	25.7%	357	75	69	313	48.0%	163	9.9%
1977	1,384	363	26.2%	309	62	59	267	48.8%	137	9.9%
¹1976	1,156	283	24.5%	231	46	42	217	49.3%	110	9.5%
²1975	926	229	24.7%	225	37	38	172	49.5%	87	9.4%
²1974	715	170	23.7%	237	26	26	135	50.2%	67	9.4%
¹1973	583	122	21.0%	180	19	11	101	48.7%	52	8.9%
¹1972	380	82	21.6%	114	12	6	69	47.8%	36	9.5%
¹1971	275	62	22.4%	55	9	9	48	46.1%	26	9.4%

Balance Sheet Data (Million $)

Dec. 31	Cash	Current Assets	Current Liab.	Ratio	Total Assets	Ret. on Assets	Long Term Debt	Common Equity	Total Cap.	% LT Debt of Cap.	Ret. on Equity
1980	113	234	333	0.7	2,643	8.8%	970	1,141	2,251	43.1%	21.1%
1979	141	247	274	0.9	2,354	8.8%	966	952	2,025	47.7%	21.6%
1978	157	243	252	1.0	1,953	9.0%	783	796	1,651	47.4%	22.6%
1977	132	208	215	1.0	1,645	9.3%	688	643	1,385	49.7%	23.4%
1976	116	176	171	1.0	1,284	9.3%	497	525	1,073	46.3%	23.3%
1975	101	154	136	1.1	1,069	9.0%	444	414	897	49.5%	23.2%
1974	82	124	112	1.1	853	9.1%	354	331	709	49.8%	22.7%
1973	77	110	87	1.3	624	9.8%	235	261	510	46.0%	22.4%
1972	59	81	71	1.1	422	9.6%	117	199	327	35.7%	21.4%
1971	40	90	55	1.6	319	9.1%	101	133	244	41.5%	21.3%

Data as orig. reptd. **1.** Reflects merger or acquisition. **2.** Reflects merger or acquisition and accounting change.

Business Summary

McDonald's Corp. operates, licenses and services the world's largest chain of fast-food restaurants. At 1980 year-end, there were 5,213 units in 50 states and Washington, D.C., plus 1,050 abroad, including 366 in Canada, 268 in Japan, 133 in Germany, 116 in Australia and 167 in 22 other countries or territories.

1980	Revs.	Profits
United States	80%	85%
Canada	11%	9%
Other	9%	6%

Units in operation at year end were:

Operated by—	1980	1979	1978	1977
Company	1,608	1,547	1,406	1,338
Franchisees	4,302	3,927	3,573	3,184
Affiliates	353	273	206	149
Total	6,263	5,747	5,185	4,671

The restaurants offer a substantially uniform menu featuring hamburgers, fries, fish sandwiches, beverages and desserts; most also serve breakfast. Averge revenue per unit was roughly $1,000,000 in 1980. Under current agreements, franchise fees paid to McDonald's generally amount to 11.5% of sales.

Employees: 117,000.

Dividend Data

Dividends were initiated in 1976.

Amt. of Divd. $	Date Decl.	Ex-divd. Date	Stock of Record	Payment Date
0.20	Feb. 18	Feb. 24	Mar. 2	Mar. 15'81
0.25	May 5	May 13	May 19	Jun. 3'81
0.25	Jul. 1	Jul. 28	Aug. 3	Aug. 17'81
0.25	Oct. 13	Oct. 27	Nov. 2	Nov. 17'81

Finances

During 1980, McDonald's increased its long-term bank credit lines to $300 million, from $175 million. At year end, this credit had been used for loans of $50 million at the agent bank's prime rate of 20.5%, and for a Deutsche Mark loan equivalent to $75 million at 11.1%.

Capitalization

Long Term Debt: $882,926,000.

Common Stock: 40,301,002 shs. (no par). About 12% owned by R. A. Kroc. Institutions hold some 72%. Shareholders: 22,950.

Office—McDonald's Plaza, Oak Brook, Ill. 60521. Tel—(312) 887-3200. Chrmn & CEO—F. L. Turner. Pres—M. R. Quinlan. VP-Secy—D. P. Horwitz. VP-Treas—R. B. Ryan. Investor Contact—S. Vuinovich. Dirs—R. J. Boylan, R. A. Kroc, D. G. Lubin, G. Newman, M. R. Quinlan, E. H. Schmitt, A. P. Stults, R. N. Thurston, F. L. Turner, D. B. Wallerstein. Transfer Agent—American National Bank & Trust Co., Chicago. Registrar—Northern Trust Co., Chicago. Incorporated in Delaware in 1965.

Information has been obtained from sources believed to be reliable, but its accuracy and completeness are not guaranteed.   J.P.G.

SOURCE: Standard N.Y.S.E. Reports, 44, No. 27 (New York: Standard & Poor's Corporation, November 2, 1981).

FIGURE 8-3

MC DONALD'S CORPORATION

LISTED	SYM.	LTPS♦	STPS♦	IND. DIV.	REC. PRICE	RANGE (1981)	YLD.
NYSE	MCD	84.1	116.1	$1.00	61	70 - 48	1.6%

INVESTMENT GRADE. RAPID GROWTH HAS BEEN ACHIEVED IN BOTH REVENUES AND EARNINGS.

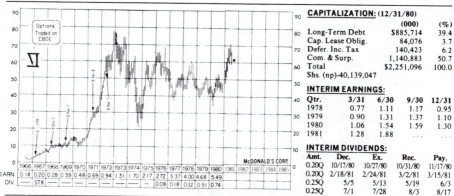

CAPITALIZATION: (12/31/80)

	(000)	(%)
Long-Term Debt	$885,714	39.4
Cap. Lease Oblig.	84,076	3.7
Defer. Inc. Tax	140,423	6.2
Com. & Surp.	1,140,883	50.7
Total	$2,251,096	100.0
Shs. (np)-40,139,047		

INTERIM EARNINGS:

Qtr.	3/31	6/30	9/30	12/31
1978	0.77	1.11	1.17	0.95
1979	0.90	1.31	1.37	1.10
1980	1.06	1.54	1.59	1.30
1981	1.28	1.88	...	...

INTERIM DIVIDENDS:

Amt.	Dec.	Ex.	Rec.	Pay.
0.20Q	10/17/80	10/27/80	10/31/80	11/17/80
0.20Q	2/18/81	2/24/81	3/2/81	3/15/81
0.25Q	5/5	5/13	5/19	6/3
0.25Q	7/1	7/28	8/3	8/17

BACKGROUND:

McDonald's develops, licenses, leases and services a nationwide system of drive-in self-service restaurants. All units are similar in design and serve a standardized menu of low priced food. As of 12/31/80, there were 4,302 units operated by licensees, 1,608 units operated by the Company and 353 units operated by affiliates. Outside of the U.S. there are 1,050 units in operation in Canada, Australia, Japan, Europe, Central America and the Caribbean. Revenues in 1980 were derived from: Company owned units sales, 77%; licensed restaurants, 22% other, 1%. Independent operators normally lease on a 20-year basis with rental derived as a percentage of sales, with a minimum fixed rent.

RECENT DEVELOPMENTS:

Earnings per share for the second quarter of 1981, amounted to $1.88 vs. $1.54 a year ago. Net income increased 23% to $76.2 million. Revenues rose 15%. For the first half of 1981 earnings per share were $3.16 vs. $2.60. Net income was up 22% to $127.8 million. Revenues increased 15%. System-wide sales, sales by all Company-owned, franchised and affiliated restaurants, gained 18% to $3.43 billion for the first half of 1981. During the second quarter, 93 restaurants were opened.

PROSPECTS:

Continued gains in earnings are expected. Anticipated increases in beef prices will be moderated by the inclusion of chicken items on the menu in all restaurants. Efforts such as the "Build a Big Mac" promotion should help to boost sales. A new free-standing restaurant building has been introduced. These buildings are somewhat smaller and more standardized, and result in lower contruction costs and shorter construction periods. Expansion outside the United States will continue.

STATISTICS:

YEAR	GROSS REVS. ($mill.)	OPER. PROFIT MARGIN %	NET INCOME ($000)	WORK CAP ($mill.)	SENIOR CAPITAL ($mill.)	SHARES (000)	EARN. PER SH $	DIV PER SH·$	DIV. PAY %	PRICE RANGE	P/E RATIO	AVG YIELD %
71	276.3	20.3	25,798	34.4	104.7	37,526	0.69	Nil	–	39 - 14¾	38.9	–
a72	385.2	19.6	36,225	9.9	120.3	38,651	0.94	Nil	–	77⅜ - 37	60.8	–
a73	592.2	18.8	51,992	22.5	230.9	39,529	1.31	Nil	–	76⅞ - 44⅛	46.2	–
74	729.0	22.2	67,396	11.5	348.5	39,690	1.70	Nil	–	63¼ - 21¼	24.9	–
75	941.5	21.9	86,881	18.0	428.4	40,015	2.17	Nil	–	60½ - 26¾	20.1	–
76	1,175.9	21.8	110,052	5.1	490.0	40,515	2.72	0.08	3	66 - 48¾	21.1	N.M.
77	1,406.1	21.7	136,696	d6.7	687.9	40,425	3.37	0.18	5	53⅜ - 37¾	13.5	0.4
78	1,671.9	22.9	162,669	d8.5	782.8	40,505	4.00	0.32	8	60½ - 43⅞	13.0	0.6
79	1,937.9	21.5	188,608	d27.6	966.1	40,199	4.68	0.51	11	51⅞ - 39¼	9.7	1.1
80	2,215.5	22.3	220,893	d98.7	960.8	40,139	5.49	0.74	14	52 - 36¼	8.0	1.7

♦Long-Term Price Score — Short-Term Price Score; see page 4a. Adjusted for stock splits: 3-for-2, 6/71 and 2-for-1, 6/72. a-Incl. acquisitions.

INCORPORATED:	TRANSFER AGENT(S):	OFFICERS:
March 1, 1965 – Delaware	American National Bank & Trust Co., Chicago, Ill.	Sen. Chmn.
PRINCIPAL OFFICE:	Royal Trust Co., Toronto, Can.	R.A. Kroc
McDonald's Plaza		Chmn. & Ch. Exec. Off.
2111 Enco Drive		F.L. Turner
Oak Brook, Ill. 60521	**REGISTRAR(S):**	Pres. & Ch. Adm. Off.
Tel: (312) 887-3200	Northern Trust Co., Chicago, Ill.	E.H. Schmitt
	Montreal Trust Co., Toronto, Can.	Exec. V.P., Secy. & Gen. Counsel
ANNUAL MEETING:		D.P. Horwitz
First Monday in May	**INSTITUTIONAL HOLDINGS:**	Vice Pres. & Treas.
NUMBER OF STOCKHOLDERS:	No. of Institutions : 395	R.B. Ryan
23,400	Shares Held : 28,081,673	

SOURCE: *Moody's Handbook of Common Stocks* (New York: Moody's Investor Service, Inc., Fall, 1981).

FIGURE 8-4

McDONALD'S CORP.

| NYSE-MCD | RECENT PRICE | 65 | P/E RATIO | 9.3 (Trailing: 10.3 / Median: 21.0) | EARN'S YLD | 10.8% | DIV'D YLD | 1.8% | 328 |

High	8.1	11.2	14.8	15.5	38.9	77.4	76.9	63.3	60.5	68.5	53.4	60.5	51.9	52.0
Low	2.3	5.6	8.1	9.2	14.8	37.1	44.1	21.3	26.8	48.8	37.8	43.9	39.3	36.3

Target Price Range — 240 / 180 / 150 / 120 / 90 / 60

Insider Decisions 1981
	A	S	O	N	D	J	F	M	A	M	J	J	A	S	O
to Buy	0	0	0	0	0	0	0	0	0	0	0	0	0	0	0
to Sell	0	0	0	1	0	1	0	6	5	1	0	1	0	0	0

20.0 × "Cash Flow" p sh

2-for-1 split
3-for-2 split
2-for-1 split
2-for-1 split

42 / 30 / 24 / 18 / 15 / 12 / 9

Options Trade On CBO

Relative Price Strength

72.9 / 48.4

| 1984 | 1985 | 1986 |

Jan. 8, 1982 Value Line

TIMELINESS	1	Highest
(Relative Price Performance Next 12 Mos.)		
SAFETY	3	Average
(Scale: 1 Highest to 5 Lowest)		
BETA 1.05	(1.00 = Market)	

1984-86 PROJECTIONS
	Price	Gain	Ann'l Total Return
High	295	(+355%)	47%
Low	195	(+200%)	33%

Institutional Decisions
	3Q'80	4Q'80	1Q'81	2Q'81	3Q'81
to Buy	77	61	81	68	82
to Sell	86	75	79	90	64
Hldg's(000)	26531	26523	26392	26638	26404

Percent shares traded: 6.0 / 4.0 / 2.0

© Arnold Bernhard & Co., Inc.

1966	1967	1968	1969	1970	1971	1972	1973	1974	1975	1976	1977	1978	1979	1980	1981	1982	1983		84-86E
1.35	1.59	2.81	4.01	5.22	7.41	9.97	14.98	18.37	23.53	29.02	34.78	41.28	48.21	55.19	62.60	71.70		Revenues per sh	110.50
.18	.25	.37	.51	.65	.93	1.23	1.77	2.34	3.10	3.90	4.82	5.77	6.84	8.18	9.60	11.10		"Cash Flow" per sh	17.40
.15	.20	.28	.39	.49	.69	.94	1.31	1.70	2.17	2.72	3.37	4.00	4.68	5.49	6.55	7.65		(A)Earnings per sh	12.25
--	--	--	--	--	--	--	--	--	--	.10	.15	.32	.51	.74	.95	1.15		(B)Div'd Decl'd per sh	2.50
.41	.47	.45	1.24	1.40	1.47	2.97	4.64	5.93	5.59	5.68	7.46	8.74	10.89	10.23	10.00	10.50		Cap'l Spending per sh	15.25
.68	.81	1.10	1.46	2.84	3.55	5.14	6.61	8.33	10.35	12.97	15.91	19.66	23.69	28.42	34.00	40.50		(C)Book Value per sh	66.25
31.67	31.67	31.67	32.27	36.99	37.53	38.65	39.53	39.69	40.01	40.51	40.43	40.51	40.20	40.14	40.35	40.45		(D)Common Shs Outst'g	40.75
15.1	23.6	31.8	29.1	26.1	40.1	59.8	48.9	25.5	22.4	21.3	13.8	12.6	9.6	8.3	9.4	Bold figures are		Avg Ann'l P/E Ratio	20.0
6.6%	4.2%	3.2%	3.4%	3.8%	2.5%	1.7%	2.0%	3.9%	4.5%	4.7%	7.2%	8.0%	10.4%	12.1%	10.7%	Value Line estimates		Avg Ann'l Earn's Yield	5.0%
										.2%	.3%	.6%	1.1%	1.6%	1.5%			Avg Ann'l Div'd Yield	1.0%

CAPITAL STRUCTURE as of 9/30/81
Total Debt $975.8 mill.   Due in 5 Yrs $625 mill.
LT Debt $927.6 mill.   LT Interest $90.0 mill.
Incl. $84.1 mill. capitalized leases.
(LT interest earned: 6.7x; total interest coverage: 6.4x)   (41% of Cap'l)

Leases, Uncapitalized Annual rentals $58.5 mill.

Pension Liability None in '80 or '79

Pfd Stock None

Common Stock 40,321,503 shs. (59% of Cap'l)

385.2	592.2	729.0	941.5	1175.9	1406.2	1671.9	1937.9	2215.5	2525	2900		Revenues ($mill)	4500
22.6%	21.9%	25.0%	25.9%	25.9%	27.1%	26.7%	26.0%	27.1%	27.5%	27.0%		Operating Margin	26.5%
11.6	18.0	25.4	37.3	48.1	58.1	70.9	86.5	107.4	122	140		Depreciation ($mill)	210
36.2	52.0	67.4	86.9	110.1	136.7	162.7	188.6	220.9	265	310		Net Profit ($mill)	500
47.8%	48.7%	50.2%	49.5%	49.3%	48.8%	48.0%	45.3%	45.1%	45.0%	45.0%		Income Tax Rate	43.0%
9.4%	8.8%	9.3%	9.2%	9.4%	9.7%	9.7%	9.7%	10.0%	10.5%	10.7%		Net Profit Margin	11.1%
9.9	22.4	11.5	17.9	5.1	d6.7	d8.5	d27.6	d98.7	d125	d140		Working Cap'l ($mill)	d200
117.0	234.6	353.5	444.0	496.6	687.9	782.8	966.1	969.8	950	925		(E)Long-Term Debt ($mill)	1000
201.9	262.0	330.5	414.3	525.4	643.1	796.3	952.2	1140.9	1385	1650		Net Worth ($mill)	2700
12.3%	11.2%	11.7%	12.2%	12.8%	12.5%	12.4%	11.9%	12.7%	13.5%	14.0%		% Earned Total Cap'l	15.0%
17.9%	19.9%	20.4%	21.0%	21.0%	21.3%	20.4%	19.8%	19.4%	19.0%	19.0%		% Earned Net Worth	18.5%
18.1%	19.9%	20.4%	21.0%	20.2%	20.3%	18.8%	17.7%	16.8%	16.5%	16.0%		% Retained to Comm Eq	14.5%
1%	--	--	--	4%	4%	8%	11%	13%	14%	15%		% All Div'ds to Net Prof	20%

CURRENT POSITION
($mill)
	1979	1980	9/30/81
Cash Assets	140.7	112.8	52.3
Receivables	56.6	66.7	63.8
Inventory (FIFO)	17.8	20.8	20.1
Other	31.6	33.6	34.1
Current Assets	246.7	233.9	170.3
Accts Payable	127.9	126.4	107.5
Debt Due	78.0	99.0	48.2
Other	68.4	107.2	127.8
Current Liab.	274.3	332.6	283.5

ANNUAL RATES
of change (per sh)	Past 10 Yrs	Past 5 Yrs	Est '78-'80 to '84-'86
Revenues	28.0%	20.5%	15.0%
"Cash Flow"	29.5%	23.5%	16.5%
Earnings	28.5%	22.5%	17.0%
Dividends	--	--	30.0%
Book Value	32.0%	24.0%	20.0%

QUARTERLY REVENUES ($ mill.)
Cal-endar	Mar. 31	June 30	Sept. 30	Dec. 31	Full Year
1978	363.2	430.5	451.5	426.7	1671.9
1979	418.5	485.9	519.6	510.3	1937.9
1980	493.4	562.9	589.1	570.1	2215.5
1981	562.1	650.0	668.1	644.8	2525
1982	625	735	780	760	2900

EARNINGS PER SHARE (A)
Cal-endar	Mar. 31	June 30	Sept. 30	Dec. 31	Full Year
1978	.77	1.11	1.18	.94	4.00
1979	.90	1.32	1.37	1.09	4.68
1980	1.06	1.54	1.59	1.30	5.49
1981	1.28	1.88	1.87	1.52	6.55
1982	1.45	2.15	2.20	1.85	7.65

QUARTERLY DIVIDENDS PAID (B)
Cal-endar	Mar. 31	June 30	Sept. 30	Dec. 31	Full Year
1978	.05	.05	.09	.09	.32
1979	.09	.14	.14	.14	.51
1980	.14	.20	.20	.20	.74
1981	.20	.25	.25	.25	.96
1982					

BUSINESS
McDonald's Corporation licenses and operates a chain of 6,536 self-service restaurants throughout the U.S., Canada and overseas under the name "McDonald's." Outlets serve a standardized menu of a few low-priced foods. About 70% of units are operated by independent licensees; 5% by overseas affiliates. Company does not sell equipment, food, or supplies to franchisees. Labor costs, 22% of sales; advertising and promotion, 4.5%. '80 deprec. rate: 4.0%. Has 110,000 employees; 23,000 shareholders. Insiders own 13% of common stock. Chrmn.: F.L. Turner. Pres.: E.H. Schmitt. Inc.: Delaware. Address: 1 McDonald's Plaza, Oak Brook, Illinois 60621.

Profit margins continue to improve. Soft beef costs and the first sign of life in customer traffic since 1978 helped Big Mac to a 19% earnings gain last year, we estimate. In 1982, the minimum wage won't rise—for the first time in almost a decade—and beef prices aren't likely to spurt upward. These factors ought to keep margins plump, despite probable customer count softness and the absence of menu price hikes (at least in the first half). We expect earnings to advance another 17% or so this year. McDonald's shares are still top-ranked for year-ahead performance. **But the first-quarter earnings comparison could be a disappointment,** because last year's results were bolstered by good weather, the "Build A Big Mac" promotion, and price increases.

The chopped steak sandwich is off the menu. Sales in test markets had dropped to unacceptable levels because of consumer dissatisfaction with the product and its relatively high price. New chicken products and "McRib" (a barbecued pork sandwich) are the remaining items in McDonald's new-products stable; how well they go over with consumers could well be the key to generating higher customer counts this year and next.

Don't worry about the absence of working capital. Inventory turnover is very high. Receivables are low, too, since fast food is a cash business. The company is doing a better job of stretching out payments to suppliers and Uncle Sam. McDonald's manages its cash efficiently enough to comfortably operate without working capital—thus leveraging up returns on equity.

The company is now essentially self-financing. Internally generated "cash flow" just about covers capital spending and dividend requirements. That's a plus for conservative investors, but it means that returns on equity may fall short of potential levels. Despite less leverage, we expect McDonald's growth rate and returns on investment to continue to compare favorably with those of the average U.S. company. That will help produce a considerably higher P/E ratio by mid-decade, in our view.   T.W.P./P.F.

Restated Revenues (and Operating) Margins) by Business Line
	1978	1979	1980	1981
Company Store	1290.6 (16.9%)	1495.2 (16.6%)	1697.8 (16.1%)	1925 (17.5%)
Licensed Store	352.9 (86.5%)	416.6 (85.8%)	486.6 (84.7%)	570 (85.0%)
Other	28.4 (100.0%)	26.1 (100.0%)	31.1 (100.0%)	30.0 (100.0%)
Company Total	1671.9 (33.0%)	1937.9 (32.6%)	2215.5 (32.7%)	2525 (33.5%)

Before unallocated corporate expenses.

(A) Based on avg. shs. outst'g. Next egs. rep't due late Feb. Est'd constant-dollar egs./sh.: '80, $4.40.
(B) Next div'd meet'g about Feb. 17.
Goes ex about Feb. 23. Approx. div'd payment dates: Mar. 15, June 3, Aug. 15, Nov. 15. Stock div'd: 2%, '67.
(C) Incl. intangibles. In '80: $70.7 mill.
$1.76/sh.
(D) In mill, adj. for stock splits & div'ds.
(E) Incl. capital leases as of 1977.

Company's Financial Strength	A
Stock's Price Stability	75
Price Growth Persistence	25
Earnings Predictability	100

SOURCE: "McDonald's Corp.," *Value Line Investment Surveys* (New York: Arnold Bernhard & Co., January 8, 1982).

FIGURE 8-5

HOW TO SELECT STOCKS FOR YOUR PORTFOLIO

To select a suitable common stock by the Value Line Method, proceed as follows:

FIRST: Decide on the degree of risk you are willing to assume All stocks involve risk But some are safer, that is to say, less risky, than others.

Risk is measured by the characteristic volatility of the stock's price around its own long term trend The narrower the band of fluctuation around trend, the safer the stock; the wider the band, the less safe, or the riskier.

Stocks ranked 1 (highest) for Safety are relatively the least volatile

Stocks ranked 2 (above average) are less safe than the 1's but safer than stocks ranked 3 (average), 4 (below average) or 5 (lowest)

Stocks ranked 5 (lowest) are the riskiest, or least safe

Stocks ranked 4 are riskier than average but not so risky as those ranked 5 (lowest)

Those ranked 3 are of average safety (i e, risk)

SECOND: Pick out from among the stocks with acceptable Safety Ranks those whose current dividend yields appear attractive to you You can select by referring to the weekly Summary Index of this Service where all 1550 stocks monitored by Value Line are listed in alphabetical order together with their recent prices, dividend yields, Safety Ranks and Performance Ranks. On the first page of the Summary Index you will find the average yield of all dividend-paying stocks. It will serve as a reference point.

Dividend yield may be desirable for some persons, not for others Where there is a division of interest, as in a trust which may distribute only the dividend income to beneficiaries, reserving capital growth for the remaindermen, dividends obviously are important Furthermore, many conservative investors shrink as a matter of habit from "invading principal", including appreciation of principal For them, dividend income is the only true income. On the other hand, to the investor in a high tax bracket, as well as the investor who looks to "total return" (which is the sum of dividend payments and capital appreciation) dividend yield may appear to be the less important portion of return. High dividend yields generally signal low appreciation potential because they indicate that the market foresees relatively little further dividend growth in the future For the vast majority of stocks over a long period of years, capital appreciation has far outweighed the dividend as a factor in total return

THIRD: Having picked a list acceptable in terms of safety and current yield, cull out from that list the stocks ranked 1 (highest) and 2 (above average) for Performance in the next 12 months. Select one of these and hold it until its rank falls to 3 (average) or lower (4 or 5) Then sell and replace it with another stock ranked 1 or 2 culled from a list that then also offers an acceptable Safety Rank and yield The policy of selling as soon as a stock falls to a Performance rank of 3 or lower may be too rigidly aggressive for all accounts Capital gains tax liability and brokerage expense should be taken into account; and where stocks sell extremely low in relation to their 3 to 5 year appreciation potentiality, performance within the next 12 months might reasonably be assigned a lesser weight in the judgment of some investors. Still the general rule is worth observing: when buying, concentrate on stocks ranked 1 or 2 for Performance in the next 12 months; when selling take aim at stocks ranked 4 or 5 for Performance When a stock falls to a rank 3 (average) for Performance in the next 12 months, bear in mind that in the coming year it will probably perform no better, but no worse either, than the average of all 1550 stocks.

SOURCE: "How to Select Stocks for Your Portfolio," *Value Line Investment Surveys*, 29, No. 19 (New York: Arnold Bernhard & Co., February 15, 1974).

FIGURE 8-6
STANDARD & POOR'S STOCK GUIDE

STANDARD & POOR'S CORPORATION

140 Mas-McQ

INDEX	Ticker Symbol	STOCKS NAME OF ISSUE (Call Price of Pfd. Stocks) Market	Com. Rank. & Pfd. Rating	Par Val.	Inst.Hold Cos	Inst.Hold Shs. (000)	PRINCIPAL BUSINESS	1960-79 High	1960-79 Low	1980 High	1980 Low	1981 High	1981 Low	Aug. Sales in 100s	Aug 1981 High	Aug 1981 Low	Aug 1981 Last	% Div. Yield	P-E Ratio
1	MSE	Massey-Ferguson Ltd. ..¹NY,B,M,P,Ph	C	No	15	874	Farm & ind'l mchy:engines	37⅞	8	17⅛	3¼	5⅝	2½	8039	2⅞	2½	2⅝		d
2	MCI	MassMutual Corp Inv. ....NY,M	...		9	140	Closed-end mgmt invest co	25⅜	11¼	11⅛	3¼	9⅝	8⅛	837	16⅝	8½	16⅝	15.5	d
3	MCV	MassMutual Inc¹⁵ ....NY,M	...		6	63	Closed-end mgmt invest co		9¼	11½	8¼	9⅜	8⅛	940	9¼	8½	8⅞	15.3	
4	MML	MassMutual M&R Inv ....NY,M	...	No	26	1170	Real estate investment trust	33¼	7¾	14½	10¾	14½	12¾	1136	14	12¾	13	13.5	7
5	MDEC	Matagorda Drill & Expl ......NY,M	NR	2¢	11	121	Contract drilling & sv,o&g	21		21	4½	17	5	1251	15	5	5ʙ		
6	MTL	Materials Research ....AS	B+	No	20	738	Sputtering, zone refining eq	16½	⅝	36¼	2¼	15½	15¼	2158	21⅝	15	15⅞	0.8	15
7	MATH	Mathematica Inc ....AS	B	10¢	3	42	Research & services for govt	17¾	2	18	6	18⅛	12	130	15¼	12⅜	12⅞ ʙ	1.6	13
8	MAGC	Mathematical Applic Gr ......AS	NR	5¢	5	31	Computer svs: image simulat	17¾	⅜	28	6¾	27⅛	15	535	20	18⅝	19⅛ ʙ		
9	MAX	Matrix Corp. ....AS	NR	1¢	14	622	Medical instr'ts:sound sys	10	⅜	26½	8¾	31⅝	15⅝	1287	24½	20⅜	21⅜ ʙ		27
10	MTRX	Matrix Science ....N	NR	1¢	14	400	Electrical connectors-defense					28⅝	15	1579	25½	20⅞	21⅜ ʙ		16
11	MC	Matsushita El IndADR ...NY,B,M,P,Ph		⁵⁷	41	5111	Japan mfr consumer elec eq	35⅜	2¼	43¾	23⅜	82½	39	6112	82¼	69¾	71	0.5	15
12	MAT	Mattel, Inc ....NY,B,M,P,Ph	B	1	46	677	Toys,dolls,cars:circus show	52¼	3¾	12¾	4	10⅝	7½	12232	9¼	6⅞	7¾	3.9	d
13	WS	Wrrt(Purch 1 com at $4) ..NY,P			9¼	3½		juvenile books and games	9¼	3½	12¾	1¼	7½	½	2705	6⅞	5	5		
14	Pr	$2.50 cm Cv A Pfd(⁴⁰27½)vtg ..NY,P	NR		20	888	hobby products: films	28⅜	21⅛	36⅝	19¾	26⅜	20	7757	24	20	20¾ ʙ	12.0	
15	MAUI	Maui Land & Pineapple ....N	B	No	20	885	Canned pineapple: resort	39	5	34½	21	36½	28¾	101	30½	29½	29½ ʙ	1.7	d
16	MTY	Maul Technology⁴² ....AS	B	No	3	358	Glass cont'r mchy: metal fab	18¾	1⅝	5⅞	1⅝	7⅝	4½	1669	7⅝	7	7⅝	2.7	6
17	MAXC	Maxco Inc ....AS	NR	1	1	21	Material handl'g eq: dstr	8¾	⅞	4⅞	⅞	4⅞	2¾	966	3¾	2⅜	2⅜ ʙ		d
18	MAXN	Maxon Indus ....N	D	10¢	1		Refuse collection vehicles	14	⅞	10	5½	8½	2¼	108	2¾	2	2⅜ ʙ		2
19	MA	May Dept Stores ......NY,B,C,M,P,Ph	A+	1⅔	140	14957	Large department store chain	45⅜	10⅝	28	18	32	23¾	3894	28⅞	26½	26½ ʙ	6.4	6
20	MAYP	May Petroleum ....N	A	5¢	43	2251	Oil & gas explor & devel	14¾	1½	44	12¾	41	26¾	5689	37¼	31½	32¼ ʙ		31
21	MYFR	Mayfair Super Mkts ....N	B-	No	7	128	⁷Foodtown supermkts.N.J	4¼	¾	2½	1⅛	2¾	1¼	27	1⅞	1⅞	1⅞		5
22	MAYF	Mayflower Corp ....N	B-	No	8	837	Moving/storage:transp eq	10⅝	4¾	10¼	4¼	9¾	7	323	8⅝	7ʙ	8⅛	8.6	5
23	MOIL	Maynard Oil ....N	B-	10¢			Drill'g:oil/gas explor/dev	17⅞	1¼	24¼	11½	20⅞	11¾	2458	16⅝	12¼	12¾ ʙ		12
24	MJW	Mays, (J.W.) ....NY,B,M	B-				Apparel dept stores,NY area	32⅜	2¾	3⅜	2¾	5⅜	3	254	4½	3¾	3⅜ ʙ		d
25	MYG	Maytag Co ....NY,B,M	A	2⅛	124	4834	Home laundry eq:dishwasher	46¾	7¾	29½	21¾	30	23¾	2209	28¾	26¾	26¾	17.9	9
26	MCA	MCA Inc ....NY,M,P,Ph	A	No	150	10530	Filmed entert:records,retail	55⅜	4¼	57¾	44¾	59	42½	3444	49⅞	43⅞	45	3.3	11
27	MCCRK	McCormick & Co⁷⁵ ....N	B+	No	37	2676	Spices, flavoring, tea, mixes	33½	1ᵇ	32¼	16	22	16⅜	4807	19¼	16⅞	17⅝ ʙ	3.6	11
28	MOGC	McCormick Oil & Gas ....AS	NR	10¢		100	Oil & gas explor & prod'n			28¾	⅞	24¾	15¾	5582	24¼	15¾	20¼ ʙ		
29	MDE	McDermott Inc. ....NY,B,C,M,Ph	B+	1	201	23507	Offshore oil & gas constr	31⅛	2⅞	46⅝	19⅝	41½	27	14610	40⅝	34½	36⅜	4.4	9
30	Pr A	$2.20cmCvA Pfd(⁷²33.45)1/2vtg ..NY	BBB		50	2862	steam gen eq:tubular goods	35¾	2¾	47¼	21¼	41¼	28¾	1711	40⅛	35	36¾	6.0	
31	Pr B	$2.60 cm B Pfd(⁷²32.25)1/2vrg ..NY,Ph	BBB	No	9	168	Fast food restaurant:franch'g	32⅛	23	27½	1⅛	22⅝	17	724	18⅛	17	14.9	
32	MCD	McDonald's Corp. ....NY,B,C,M,P,Ph,Tc	A	No	389	28452	Jet aircraft: space: missiles	77⅜	1⅛	57¾	36¼	70¼	48⅜	9992	64⅝	57⅝	57⅝ ʙ	1.7	9
33	MD	McDonnell Douglas ....NY,B,C,M,P,Ph	A	No	152	12910	Asphalt paving:construction	45	2⅞	57¾	25¼	49¾	30⅝	606	37⅝	30½	30⅝ ʙ	3.5	6
34	ME	McDowell Enterprises⁷⁵ ......AS	B+	No			Oil & gas expl & prod'r	15⅜	1½	3⅜	2⅝	13⅝	6⅝	2826	8½	7	13⅞ ʙ	1.9	14
35	MCFE	McFarland Energy ....N	NR	1	101	207		15⅜	1½	7¾	2¾	23½	12¾		16½	13⅞			
36	MGR	McGraw-Edison ....NY,B,C,M,Ph	B+	1	101	6068	Electric eq:util,appl,ind'l	46¾	11⅜	38¾	20¾	51	20	3389	42½	39¾	41⅛	4.4	9
37	MHP	McGraw-Hill ....NY,B,M,P,Ph	*	1	183	11664	Books:educ/info svs:publ:TV	56½	5⅜	46¾	24¼	56	24¾	4356	50¾	46	49¾ ʙ	3.6	13
38	M	$1.20 cm Cv Pref (40)vtg ....NY	**	10	4		fin'l svs:magazines:film	91¼	12¾	67	5⅜	90½	68				40¼ ʙ	1.6	
39	MP	McIntyre Mines NY(1⁵),M,P,Ph,Mc,Tc	B+	No	26	394	Coal mining: Falconbridge inv	179¾	17¼	89	35¾	66¾	44¼	322	55	44¼	44⅞ ʙ		
40	MKN	McKeon Liquidating ....AS,P	Liq				Assets sold	40	1	9¾	2⅜	9⅝	4¾		5¼	4½	45⅝ ʙ		
41	MLN	McLean Trucking ....NY,M,P	B	50¢	30	1763	Mtr freight common carrier	28⅜	1¼	14¾	7¾	11¾	7⅜	2052	9¾	8	8⅝	3.7	d
42	MLX	McLouth Steel ....NY,M,Ph	C	2½	174		Flat rolled steel, mainly auto	41⅝	7¾	12¾	5½	18⅜	5	1061	7⅞	6⅝	6¾		4
43	MMC	McM Corp ....N	NR	1	5	267	Casualty,life,health insur	17¾	1¾	16¼	4¼	14⅛	8	308	11⅜	10⅛	10⅝ ʙ	2.4	4
44	MME	McNeil Corp ....NY,M	A	No	5	244	Prod'n support sys:service eq	30¼	6¾	18⅜	11¾	16¼	11¾	272	15⅛	14¼	14¼ ʙ	6.3	6
45	MCQ	McQuay-Perfex ....N	A+	1	26	142	Air cond'g: refrig, heating eq	18⅞	2¾	15¼	7¾	17¼	13	1166	15	13	13¾ ʙ	6.0	6

Uniform Footnote Explanations—See Page 1. Other: ¹Mc,Tc. ²Ph. ⁴⁶Mc,Tc. ⁵¹Restated from d$0.16. ⁵⁵◻$0.45,78. ⁵⁶◻$0.07,'77.
²⁷Ph. ⁵¹◻$5.23,'79. ⁵⁵△$4.20,'80. ⁶◻ʳ,6-15-82, scrip to $25 in'86. ⁶¹Includes 0.2M shr ESOP. ⁶²Private group plans merger, $9.
⁴⁴◻$0.10,'77. ⁶³◻$0.13,'78. ⁶⁴◻$0.04,'79. ⁶⁵◻$0.19,'80. ⁴⁷◻$0.13,'79. ⁶⁸△$0.13, 79. Each ⁷⁰Non-vtg. ⁷◻$2.07,'81.
⁷²Fr.4-1-83,scale to $31¼ in'89. ⁷³From 4-1-83,scale to $31¾ in'87. ⁷⁴△$0.50,'80. ⁷⁷Hughes Capital plan offer,$12. ⁷⁷Liquidat'g divd. ⁷⁸In liquid'n. ⁷⁹△$0.14,'78.
⁴⁰◻$0.28,'79. ★&P is a sub of McGraw-Hill: common not ranked, pfd not rated

FIGURE 8-6 (Cont.)

COMMON AND PREFERRED STOCKS

A full-page reproduction of a page from Standard & Poor's *Stock Guide*, showing columnar data for common and preferred stocks (index numbers 1–45). Major column groups include: Index, Cash Divs. Ea. Yr. Since, Dividends (Latest Payment, Ex. Div., Total Ind. Rate, Paid 1980), Financial Position (Cash & Equiv., Curr. Assets, Curr. Liabs., Balance Sheet Date), Capitalization (Long Term Debt, Pfd., Com.), Earnings—$ Per Shr. (Years 1977–1981, Last 12 Mos.), and Interim Earnings or Remarks (Period, 1980, 1981).

SOURCE: *Stock Guide* (New York: Standard & Poor's Corporation, September 1981).

Stock Splits & Divs By Line Reference Index [1] REVERSE 1-for-2, '81. [2] 5-for-4, '78. [3] 3-for-1, '80. [4] 4-for-3, '81. [5] 3-for-2, '80. [6] 5-for-4, '79. [7] 4-for-3, '80. [8] 3-for-1, '80. [9] 3-for-2, '80. [10] 10%, '78, '80. [11] 10%, '81. [12] 6-for-5, '78. [13] 3-for-2, '80. [14] 10%, '76, '77, '78. [15] Adj to 3%, '79. [16] 2-for-1, '77. [17] 2-for-1, '77. [18] Adj for 3%, '79. [19] 5-for-4, '77, '78. [20] 5-for-4, '77, 4-for-3, '79. [21] 10%, '81. [22] 43-for-2, '78.

FIGURE 8-7
STANDARD & POOR'S BOND GUIDE

CORPORATE BONDS

Title-Industry Code & Co. Finances (In Italics) / Individual Issue Statistics / Exchange	Ind / Interest Dates	Chgs. 1977 / S&P Quality Rating	Eligible	Times Earn. 1978 / Bond Form	1979 / Legality (C t, M a, N H, N J, N Y)	Yr. End	Cash & Eqv / Redemption Provisions: Refund Earliest/Other	Current Assets (Million $) / Call Price: For S.F.	Liabs	Date / Call Price: Regular	L. Term Debt (Mil $) / Out-st'd'g (Mil $)	Debt % Prop / Underwriter Firm	Underwriter Year	Interim Period / Price Range 1960-78 High	1960-78 Low	Interim Times Earn. 1979 / Price Range 1979 High	Interim Times Earn. 1980 / 1979 Low	1980 High	1980 Low	Mo. End Price Sale(s) or Bid	Curr Yield	Yield to Mat.
Magnavox Co	*24f*	*Now North Amer Phillips,see*																				
SF Deb 4¾s '86	Fa15	NR	X	R	- - - ✓-		....	100		100¼	11.2	M5	'65	101⅛	58	79¼	65	68	50¼	50¼	9.45	20.85
Maine Yankee Atomic Pwr.	*72*	*1.72*		*1.74*	*1.71*	*Dc*	*0.21*	*12.5*	*17.0*	*9-80*	*134*	*50.1*		*9 Mo Sep*		*1.71*	*1.63*					
• 1st A 9.10s 2002	Mn	A	X	R	- - ✓- -		....	100.95		106.87	56.3	M5	'70	111	81	95½	74	84	61¼	s62¼	14.62	15.04
• 1st B 8½s 2002	Mn	A	X	R	- - ✓- -		....	101.10		106.72	38.5	S1	'71	109½	76	92⅛	74¾	74	59½	60⅝	14.02	14.51
• 1st C 7⅝s 2002	Mn	A	X	R	- - ✓- -		....	100.91		106.38	10.8	B9	'73	100⅞	70⅝	85⅛	77	71½	55¾	55	13.86	14.48
Mallory (P.R.)	*17a*	*Assumed by Dart Indus, see*																				
• SF Deb 8⅞s '96	mS15	A	X	R	- - ✓- -		[1]103.655	[2]100		106.787	30.0	F2	'76	103	99	No Sale		No Sale		^99	8.96	8.99
• SF Deb 9⅛s 2003	Jd15	A	X	R	- - ✓- -		[3]104.312	[3]100		107.762	20.0	F2	'78	99½	98¼	97	95	74	65	66½	13.72	14.06
Manufacturers Hanover[4]	*10a*	*1.14*		*1.11*	*1.08*	*Dc*					*966*			*6 Mo Jun*		*1.09*	*1.06*					
• Notes 7.60s '81	mS	AAA	X	R	✓✓✓- -		....	....		[5]100	50.0	S1	'74	102⅝	88	96¾	87	98½	89⅝	94.312	8.06	15.94
• Notes 8⅜s '82	jD	AAA	X	R	✓✓✓- -		....	....		[6]100	125	M5	'75	105	91½	97¾	88½	98⅝	84	s91	9.20	13.66
Notes 10¼s '83	Mn	AAA	X	R	- - ✓- -		....	....		NC	100	G2	'80	....	....	....	....	101	93	93	11.02	13.74
• [7]Cv Flt'g Rt Nts[8] 12.35s '87	Mn	AAA	X	R	- ✓✓- -		....	....		[9]100	150	B9	'79	....	....	100¾	92⅜	101½	88⅝	s89⅜	13.82	....
• SF Deb 8⅛s 2004	Ms	AAA	X	R	✓✓✓- -		....	[10]100		[11]104.42	100	S1	'74	101⅝	80	88½	72	77⅜	60	s60⅜	13.46	13.87
• SF Deb 8⅛s 2007	fA15	AAA	X	R	✓✓✓- -		....	[12]100		[13]104½	150	S1	'77	100½	84	90½	72¼	81	57⅝	s59½	13.66	13.92
Manufacturers Hanover Tr.	*10*	*Subsid of Mfrs Hanover,see*																				
• Cap Deb 8½s '85	Jd	NR	X	R	- - ✓- -		....	....		NC	75.0	M5	'75	105¼	94⅜	97	84¼	93	80⅞	81⅛	10.48	14.33
MAPCO Inc[14]	*73d*	*2.96*		*3.54*	*3.67*	*Dc*	*108*	*379*	*219*	*9-80*	*406*	*59.3*		*9 Mo Sep*		*3.28*	*3.52*					
• Sub SF Deb 10¾s '99	Ao15	BB	Y	R	- - - - -		....	[15]100		110.04	75.0	B4	'79	....	....	103¼	90	92	77	77⅝	13.85	14.20
[16]*Maple Leaf Mills*[17]	*27*	*2.03*		*2.17*	*1.72*	*Dc*	*4.72*	*113*	*59.5*	*6-80*	*82.6*	*119*		*6 Mo Jun*		*1.52*	*1.10*					
◆Sub SF Deb 11s '98	MDc 31	B	Y	R	- - - - -		[18]....	[19]100		[20]103	26.0	T1	'78	100¼	92	99¼	79	95½	76	84	13.10	13.36
Marathon Oil Co.	*49d*	*3.25*		*2.93*	*3.68*	*Dc*	*N/A*	*1597*	*1457*	*9-80*	*997*	*31.4*		*9 Mo Sep*		*4.11*	*3.72*					
• SF Deb 4⅜s '87	Ao	AA	X	CR	- ✓✓- -		....	100.09		101.16	26.2	F2	'62	103⅛	60	85⅛	82¼	83	73¼	s73¼	5.97	10.21
• SF Deb 8½s 2000	Fa	AA	X	R	- ✓✓- -		....	100		104.95	76.2	F2	'70	112⅛	86½	92½	78½	82½	61	66	12.88	13.49
• SF Deb 8½s 2006	mN	AA	X	R	- ✓✓- -		[21]104.80	[22]100		106.72	250	F2	'76	104¼	90½	92	79½	80	65⅞	^79	10.76	10.95
• Notes 7.65s '83	mN	AA	X	R	- ✓✓- -		....	....		[23]100	150	F2	'76	103⅞	91	94½	85⅝	94¼	81	s85½	8.95	13.85
• Notes 10¼s '87	jJ15	AA	X	R	- - ✓- -		....	....		[24]100	200	F2	'80	....	....	....	....	100	87	s89⅜	11.47	12.66
[25]*Marcor Inc.*[26]	*58h*	*1.51*		*1.43*	*1.17*	*Dc*	*113*	*1601*	*1523*	*9-80*	*1160*	*89.7*		*9 Mo Sep*		*1.42*	*d5.00*					
• Sub Deb 6½s '88	aO15	BBB	X	R	- - - - -		....	....		102.45	269	Exch	'68	89⅝	65	81	68½	74	59⅝	s60⅝	10.72	15.26
Marine Midland Banks	*10a*	*1.04*		*1.04*	*1.04*	*Dc*					*344*			*9 Mo Sep*		*1.04*	*1.04*					
Deb [27]8⅛s '94	Ao	NR	X	R	✓- - - -		....	....		102⅞	60.0	F2	'69	103	73	82¼	68½	72	53¾	60	13.54	15.21
• Deb 7⅝s 2003	Ms	NR	X	R	✓- - - -		....	....		[28]104.58	50.0	F2	'73	100	70	79	65¼	69	52¾	s54¼	14.06	14.61
(Corp) Deb [29]5s '89	jJ15	NR	X	CR	- - ✓- -		....	....		100¾	60.0	F2	'64	100⅝	55⅞	66½	51	68½	43	51	9.80	15.48
[30]*Martin Marietta Alum*[31]	*5*	*4.59*		*7.19*	*9.86*	*Dc*	*9.12*	*284*	*111*	*6-80*	*137*	*37.3*		*6 Mo Jun*		*10.70*	*8.31*					
• SF Deb 9⅜s '96	Jd15	A-	X	R	- - - - -		[32]104⅜	100		104⅞	39.0	K5	'71	111	81	95½	85½	87¼	63	71½	13.11	13.89
Martin Marietta Corp	*17*	*6.77*		*10.79*	*15.93*	*Dc*	*157*	*819*	*635*	*9-80*	*127*	*12.7*		*9 Mo Sep*		*17.93*	*31.50*					
SF Deb 5⅞s '92	Ao15	AA-	X	R	- - ✓✓-		....	100		102.20	17.5	B9	'67	99¾	65	72	57	61½	45	52	11.30	14.68
Maryland Cup Corp.	*16c*	*3.97*		*3.97*	*3.31*	*Sp*	*3.35*	*177*	*69.5*	*6-80*	*84.9*	*50.3*		*9 Mo Jun*		*2.95*	*2.67*					
• SF Deb 5.80s '92	Fa	A	X	R	- - ✓- -		....	100		102.03	6.70	L5	'67	100	65½	No Sale		No Sale		50	11.60	15.26
Maryland National	*10a*	*1.19*		*1.17*	*1.15*	*Dc*					*71.4*			*9 Mo Sep*		*1.17*	*1.14*					
• Notes 8s '86	jD15	A	X	R	- - ✓- -		....	....		[33]100	35.0	G2	'76	101½	90½	92½	76	86⅜	68	74	10.81	14.62
Masco Corp	*13g*	*5.85*		*5.14*	*3.80*	*Dc*	*141*	*473*	*124*	*9-80*	*315*	*139*		*9 Mo Sep*		*4.13*	*3.01*					
• SF Deb 8⅞s 2001	Jd	A	X	R	- - ✓✓-		[34]104.19	[35]100		106.70	75.0	S6	'76	106	98	98	98	80	80	67	13.25	13.72
• Notes 12¼s '85	Mn	A	X	R	- - ✓- -		....	....		[36]100	100	S6	'80	....	....	....	....	104	96½	96	12.76	13.48
[37]*Massachusetts Electric*[38]	*72a*	*2.33*		*2.74*	*2.94*	*Dc*	*60.1*	*75.1*	*160*	*9-80*	*190*	*41.7*		*12 Mo Sep*		*2.94*	*2.53*					
1st F 5s '91	jJ	A	X	CR	✓✓✓✓✓		....	101.10		102.43	17.5	M5	'61	106	55	67⅜	59⅛	62¾	47⅛	53⅝	9.32	13.28
1st G 4⅜s '92	mS	A	X	CR	✓✓✓✓✓		....	100.42		101.95	60.0	F2	'62	102½	49⅛	61⅛	53	56	41¾	47½	9.21	13.34
1st H 4⅝s '93	jD	A	X	CR	✓✓✓✓✓		....	101.52		102.98	10.0	M5	'63	102⅞	50	60¾	52½	55⅜	41⅜	46¼	10.00	13.51
1st I 5¾s '96	Ms	A	X	CR	✓✓✓✓✓		....	101.47		103.95	10.0	H2	'66	103¾	57⅝	67¼	57⅜	60⅝	46	50	11.50	13.61

Uniform Footnote Explanations—See Page 1. Other: [1]Fr 9-15-86. [2]Fr 9-15-82. [3]Fr 6-15-88. [4]See Mfrs Hanover Tr & Ritter Fin'l. [5]Fr 3-1-81. [6]Fr 7-1-82. [7]Conv into 8 3/8% Deb'09 thru 4-30-86. [8]To 4-30-81,then 1/2% above T-Bill rate,etc. [9]Fr 5-1-86. [10]Fr 3-1-85. [11]Fr 3-1-84. [12]Fr 8-15-88. [13]Fr 8-15-87. [14]See Mid-Amer Pipeline. [15]Fr 4-15-89. [16]Subsid of Canadian Pacific Enterprises. [17]Was Norin Corp. [18]Redeem at 100 by death. [19]Fr 1-31-89. [20]Fr 1-31-83. [21]Fr 11-1-86. [22]Fr 11-1-87. [23]Fr 11-1-81. [24]Fr 7-15-84. [25]Subsid of Mobil Corp. [26]See Container, Montg Ward. [27]Incr 1/2% 1-1-75. [28]Fr 3-1-83. [29]Incr fr 4 1/2% 1-1-75. [30]Was Harvey Aluminum. [31]Subsid Martin Marietta Corp. [32]Fr 6-15-81. [33]Fr 12-31-83. [34]Fr 6-1-86. [35]Fr 6-1-87. [36]Fr 5-1-83. [37]Contr by New Eng Elec Sys. [38]See Worcester Cty Elec.

SOURCE: *Bond Guide* (New York: Standard & Poor's Corporation, December 1981).

Summary

Armed with economic and industry forecasts, the analyst is ready to look at the shares of specific companies.

Company information is generated internally and externally. The principal source of internal information about a company is its financial statements. The analyst must screen quarterly and annual reports of income, financial position, and changes in financial position, in order to assure himself that such statements are correct, complete, consistent, and comparable. The use of accounting reports can be influenced by options to treat certain transactions in different ways. Further, accounting statements taken as a whole over time can reveal critical information to the trained eye that is not seen by casual analysis of specific statements in isolation, or for only a single year.

Our examination of financial statements highlighted the income statement, statement of retained earnings, balance sheet, and statement of changes in financial position. We saw the continuing importance attached to the income statement as the most prominent source of evidence regarding management performance, particularly in reference to earnings.

Many popular and widely circulated sources of information about companies emanate from outside, or external, sources. These sources provide supplements to company-generated information by overcoming some of its bias, such as public pronouncements by its officers. External information sources also provide certain kinds of information not found in the materials made available by companies themselves.

Questions and Problems

1. What four major tests must financial statements meet to have utility for investment analysis?

2. What advantages and disadvantages would probably accompany a move toward complete uniformity in accounting, where every transaction, regardless of the firm, is handled in one way only?

3. In what ways will a company behave differently with respect to its accounting if it chooses to concentrate on (a) maximizing earnings, or (b) minimizing taxes?

Prepare a table similar to the one shown on page 207, using sum-of-the-years'-digits depreciation. How do you account for any differences in the pattern of added taxes or savings? Which method would you advocate, declining-balance or SYD?

5. Distinguish between primary and secondary earnings per share. Why is such a distinction important to a common-stock investor?

6. With all the concern shown for the income statement, of what significance to an investor is the book value of assets and the amount of debt on the balance sheet?

7. Refer to the financial statements of McDonald's Corporation, in the Appendix to this chapter. What specific insights into company operations are offered by examining the consolidated statement of changes in financial position for the year ended December 31, 1980, that are not readily seen on the balance sheet and income statement for the same period?

8. The Rush Co. example in the text highlighted accounting for a subsidiary in which Melicher Corp. held only 40 percent of the voting stock. What changes would occur on the balance sheet of Melicher if it owned 70 percent of the stock of Rush?

9. What are some significant bits of investment information about a company that are not normally found in standard financial statements?

10. What does an auditor's "unqualified" opinion really mean?

11. In what ways, if any, will FASB *No. 14* prove useful to investors or security analysts?

APPENDIX

Financial Review

The following pages show financial highlights, statements, and historical statistics for McDonald's Corporation and its consolidated subsidiaries. This information is provided so that the reader may note key items on the statements that were mentioned in Chapter 8. Further, these statements and statistics will serve as part of the basic data for use in subsequent chapters.

FIGURE 8-8
McDONALD'S CORPORATION ANNUAL REPORT FOR 1980

McDonald's Corporation and Subsidiaries consolidated statement of income

		Years ended December 31, 1980	1979	1978	1977	1976
				(In thousands of dollars, except per share data)		
Revenues	Sales by Company-owned restaurants	$1,697,767	$1,495,216	$1,290,621	$1,097,434	$ 923,197
	Revenues from franchised restaurants	486,577	416,637	352,928	286,773	233,224
	Other revenues—net	31,119	26,082	28,342	21,941	20,015
	Total revenues	2,215,463	1,937,935	1,671,891	1,406,148	1,176,436
Costs and expenses	Company-owned restaurants—					
	Food and paper	660,869	602,647	518,686	429,519	359,755
	Payroll	384,133	333,818	289,836	242,098	205,740
	Rent	21,758	18,628	16,135	13,402	11,233
	Depreciation and amortization	60,886	51,177	43,342	35,661	29,453
	Other operating expenses	289,374	241,063	204,544	173,950	139,699
		1,417,020	1,247,333	1,072,543	894,630	745,880
	Expenses directly applicable to revenues from franchised restaurants—					
	Rent	27,791	23,725	19,986	16,408	13,914
	Depreciation and amortization	46,510	35,276	27,543	22,454	18,593
		74,301	59,001	47,529	38,862	32,507
	General, administrative and selling expenses	230,702	214,501	175,658	149,818	132,473
	Interest expense— Total interest charges	102,401	82,863	68,968	59,368	52,841
	Less amounts capitalized	11,554	10,271	5,632	3,326	2,769
		90,847	72,592	63,336	56,042	50,072
	Total costs and expenses	1,812,870	1,593,427	1,359,066	1,139,352	960,932
Income before provision for income taxes		402,593	344,508	312,825	266,796	215,504
Provision for income taxes		181,700	155,900	150,156	130,100	106,324
Net income		$ 220,893	$ 188,608	$ 162,669	$ 136,696	$ 109,180
Net income per share of common stock		$5.49	$4.68	$4.00	$3.37	$2.69
Dividends per share	Declared	$ .74	$ .51	$ .32	$ .15	$ .10
	Paid	$ .74	$ .51	$ .32	$.175	$.075

The Financial Comments beginning on page 34 are an integral part of the consolidated financial statements.

FIGURE 8-8 (cont.)

McDonald's Corporation and Subsidiaries consolidated balance sheet

Assets		December 31, 1980	1979
		(In thousands of dollars)	
Current assets	Cash	$ 37,611	$ 47,081
	Certificates of deposit	26,671	64,201
	Short-term investments, at cost, which approximates market	48,569	29,408
	Accounts receivable	55,247	48,369
	Notes receivable	11,473	8,206
	Inventories, at cost, which is not in excess of market	20,848	17,798
	Prepaid expenses and other current assets	33,521	31,667
	Total current assets	233,940	246,730
Other assets and deferred charges	Notes receivable due after one year	66,776	48,968
	Investments in and advances to affiliates	13,080	14,145
	Miscellaneous	31,733	29,377
	Total other assets and deferred charges	111,589	92,490
Property and equipment	Property and equipment, at cost	2,706,696	2,331,870
	Less accumulated depreciation and amortization	479,548	386,933
	Net property and equipment	2,227,148	1,944,937
Intangible assets, net		70,692	69,849
	Total assets	$2,643,369	$2,354,006

The Financial Comments beginning on page 34 are an integral part of the consolidated financial statements.

FIGURE 8-8 (cont.)

		December 31, 1980	1979
Liabilities and stockholders' equity		*(In thousands of dollars)*	
Current liabilities	Notes payable	$ 60,207	$ 33,735
	Accounts payable	126,389	127,906
	Income taxes	57,054	27,222
	Other accrued liabilities	50,216	41,201
	Current maturities of long-term debt	38,756	44,243
	Total current liabilities	332,622	274,307
Long-term debt	Long-term debt	885,714	875,809
	Obligations under capital leases	84,076	90,314
	Total long-term debt	969,790	966,123
Security deposits by franchisees		59,651	54,633
Deferred income taxes		140,423	106,777
Stockholders' equity	Common stock, no par value— Authorized—100,000,000 shares Issued—40,614,568 shares in 1980 and 40,605,771 shares in 1979	4,516	4,515
	Additional paid-in capital	94,023	93,508
	Retained earnings	1,063,080	871,918
		1,161,619	969,941
	Less treasury stock, at cost—475,521 shares in 1980 and 407,080 shares in 1979	20,736	17,775
	Total stockholders' equity	1,140,883	952,166
	Total liabilities and stockholders' equity	$2,643,369	$2,354,006

FIGURE 8-8 (cont.)

McDonald's Corporation and Subsidiaries consolidated statement of changes in financial position

	Years ended December 31, 1980	1979	1978	1977	1976
					(In thousands of dollars)
Source of working capital	Operations— Net income	$220,893	$188,608	$162,669	$136,696	$109,180
	Items not involving working capital:					
	Depreciation and amortization	119,848	96,967	79,831	65,387	53,717
	Deferred income taxes	31,090	24,178	13,945	10,089	11,828
	Other—net	5,341	1,450	(457)	(7)	(2,525)
	Total from operations	377,172	311,203	255,988	212,165	172,200
	Issuance of common stock on exercise of options	751	584	4,719	690	2,604
	Long-term debt additions	408,709	506,937	312,066	156,632	130,599
	Property and equipment disposals (gains and losses included in operations)	19,383	18,682	16,976	14,825	14,602
	Security deposits by franchisees	6,486	8,059	7,236	6,735	5,470
	Other	20,881	24,135	22,085	20,663	11,152
	Total source of working capital	833,382	869,600	619,070	411,710	336,627
Use of working capital	Property and equipment additions	410,457	437,754	354,095	301,636	233,127
	Non-current assets of businesses purchased	12,760	52,399	7,833	21,869	6,132
	Notes receivable due after one year	29,806	30,741	19,425	11,134	14,704
	Long-term debt reductions	401,929	321,611	215,052	64,298	80,680
	Cash dividends	29,731	20,516	12,949	6,073	4,021
	Treasury stock purchases	3,320	13,633	1,416	5,096	885
	Other	16,484	11,974	10,110	9,015	8,627
	Total use of working capital	904,487	888,628	620,880	419,121	348,176
Decrease in working capital		$(71,105)	$(19,028)	$ (1,810)	$ (7,411)	$(11,549)
Changes in elements of working capital	Increase (decrease) in current assets:					
	Cash and certificates of deposit	$(47,000)	$ 29,680	$ 33,466	$ 3,715	$ 6,992
	Short-term investments	19,161	(45,582)	(9,205)	12,481	6,562
	Accounts and notes receivable	10,145	7,478	5,995	10,863	4,411
	Inventories	3,050	3,466	1,920	1,295	1,433
	Prepaid expenses and other current assets	1,854	8,230	3,212	3,548	388
		(12,790)	3,272	35,388	31,902	19,786
	Increase (decrease) in current liabilities:					
	Accounts and notes payable	24,955	21,392	17,085	29,765	22,770
	Income taxes	29,832	(5,779)	(2,918)	(4,129)	7,710
	Other accrued liabilities	9,015	6,100	6,191	6,213	1,922
	Current maturities of long-term debt	(5,487)	587	16,840	7,464	(1,067)
		58,315	22,300	37,198	39,313	31,335
Decrease in working capital		$(71,105)	$(19,028)	$ (1,810)	$ (7,411)	$(11,549)

The Financial Comments beginning on page 34 are an integral part of the consolidated financial statements.

FIGURE 8-8 (cont.)

McDonald's Corporation and Subsidiaries consolidated statement of retained earnings

	Years ended December 31, 1980	1979	1978	1977	1976
				(In thousands of dollars)	
Balance at beginning of year	$ 871,918	$703,826	$554,106	$423,483	$318,324
Net income	220,893	188,608	162,669	136,696	109,180
	1,092,811	892,434	716,775	560,179	427,504
Cash dividends on common stock	(29,731)	(20,516)	(12,949)	(6,073)	(4,021)
Balance at end of year	$1,063,080	$871,918	$703,826	$554,106	$423,483

The Financial Comments beginning on page 34 are an integral part of the consolidated financial statements.

FIGURE 8-8 (cont.)

Financial Comments

Summary of significant accounting policies
☐ Consolidation policy
The consolidated financial statements include the accounts of the Company and its subsidiaries. Investments in 50% or less owned affiliates, whose operations are not material to the consolidated financial statements, are carried at equity in the companies' net assets.

All significant intercompany transactions are eliminated in consolidation.

☐ Property and equipment
Additions to property for new restaurants include interest, real estate taxes and rents incurred through the development period. Depreciation and amortization are provided on the straight line method over the following estimated useful lives: restaurant buildings—principally 25 years; restaurant equipment and signs—principally 10 years; furniture, fixtures and other equipment—3 to 10 years; leasehold improvements—lesser of useful life of assets or terms of leases (including option periods); and property under capital leases—terms of leases.

☐ Intangible assets
Costs allocated to unlimited term franchise rights reacquired prior to November 1970 are not being amortized. All other costs allocated to reacquired franchise rights are being amortized on the straight line method over periods up to 40 years.

☐ Revenue recognition
Initial location and license fees are recorded as income when the related restaurant is opened. Expenses associated with site assignment and the issuance of franchise agreements are charged to expense as incurred.

Continuing fees from franchised restaurants are recorded as income on the accrual basis as earned.

Gains on sales of Company-owned restaurant businesses are recorded as income when the sales are consummated and other stipulated conditions are met.

☐ Income taxes
United States income taxes have not been accrued on undistributed earnings of certain foreign subsidiaries and affiliates as the Company considers such earnings to be permanently invested in the businesses. Income tax provisions on such earnings, if distributed, would not be material due to the availability of foreign tax credits.

Investment tax credits are accounted for on the flow-through method as a reduction of income tax provisions.

☐ Debt issuance cost
Issuance cost of long-term debt is deferred and amortized over the repayment term.

Restaurant acquisitions, dispositions and number of restaurants in operation
During the five years ended December 31, 1980, the Company acquired restaurant businesses (including related territorial rights) from franchisees in transactions accounted for as purchases, and sold restaurant businesses to franchisees as follows:

	Purchased		Sold
	Number of restaurant businesses	Approximate purchase price	Number of restaurant businesses
		(In thousands of dollars)	
1980	38	$12,800	86
1979	141	52,400	76
1978	29	7,800	82
1977	71	21,900	79
1976	21	6,100	85

The number of restaurant businesses sold includes those resulting from the exercise of purchase options included in the lease agreements as follows: 1980—56; 1979—26; 1978—42; 1977—35; and 1976—63.

Results of operations of restaurant businesses purchased have been included in the consolidated financial statements since dates of acquisition. The results of operations of such businesses for periods prior to purchase and the results of operations of restaurant businesses sold, prior to their sale dates, were not material to the consolidated financial statements. Gains on sales of Company-owned restaurant businesses, included in Other revenues—net, for the last five years are as follows: 1980—$13,188,000; 1979—$14,638,000; 1978—$13,295,000; 1977—$8,778,000; and 1976—$9,393,000.

The table below shows the number of restaurant businesses in operation at the end of each of the last six years.

	1980	1979	1978	1977	1976	1975
Operated by the Company	1,608	1,547	1,406	1,338	1,217	1,123
Franchised to other operators	4,028	3,696	3,466	3,093	2,760	2,390
Leased to other operators	274	231	107	91	81	105
Operated by 50% or less owned affiliates	353	273	206	149	120	88
	6,263	5,747	5,185	4,671	4,178	3,706

Operators of all the restaurants leased to others at December 31, 1980, have options to purchase the businesses.

Segment and geographic information
The Company operates in one industry segment. All significant revenues relate to over-the-counter sales of food products to the general public, whether the restaurants involved are operated by the Company, its affiliates or franchisees.

Restaurants are located in the United States and in foreign markets. Of the 6,263 restaurants in operation at December 31, 1980, 1,050 are operating outside of the United States. Of these restaurants, 366 are located in Canada, and the remaining 684 are located in 25 other international markets.

Financial information for the years 1976 through 1980 applicable to the major geographic areas in which the Company operates and a reconciliation of such information with amounts shown in the consolidated statement of income follow. All areas

FIGURE 8-8 (cont.)

outside of the United States and Canada are combined in the line captioned—Other International.

	1980	1979	1978	1977	1976
					(In thousands of dollars)
Revenues:					
U.S.	$1,763,656	$1,557,938	$1,360,198	$1,160,265	$ 994,800
Canada	245,277	219,363	187,555	162,551	125,982
Other International	206,530	160,634	124,138	83,332	55,654
Total revenues	$2,215,463	$1,937,935	$1,671,891	$1,406,148	$1,176,436
Operating income:					
U.S.	$417,357	$359,520	$327,706	$284,252	$239,360
Canada	43,139	37,200	29,808	27,601	21,202
Other International	32,944	20,380	18,647	10,985	5,014
	493,440	417,100	376,161	322,838	265,576
Interest expense	(90,847)	(72,592)	(63,336)	(56,042)	(50,072)
Income before income taxes	$402,593	$344,508	$312,825	$266,796	$215,504

Canada and Other International revenues and operating income include operations of subsidiaries, fees from franchisees and affiliates and the Company's share of operating results of affiliates—all of which are operating outside of the United States—and all foreign currency exchange gains and losses (including those resulting from hedging activities). Such amounts include fees received in the U.S. (excluding intercompany fees) as follows: 1980—$11,315,000; 1979—$7,782,000; 1978—$5,193,000; 1977—$2,706,000; and 1976—$1,381,000. These fees are included in revenues and operating income of the geographic area from which they are derived. Fees received in the United States which are charged to subsidiaries operating outside of the U.S. are as follows: 1980—$13,292,000; 1979—$11,094,000; 1978—$8,005,000; 1977—$6,165,000; and 1976—$4,253,000. All intercompany fees and expenses are eliminated in computing revenues and operating income. In prior years' reports, fees received in the U.S. and related intercompany expenses were included in U.S. operations. All amounts shown above for years prior to 1980 have been reclassified to conform to the 1980 presentation.

Foreign currency exchange gains (losses), including those resulting from hedging activities, included in Other revenues—net in the consolidated statement of income, are as follows: 1980—$253,000; 1979—$(2,830,000); 1978—$(1,135,000); 1977—$797,000; and 1976—$(42,000).

Identifiable assets applicable to each geographic area at December 31, 1980, 1979 and 1978, respectively, are as follows: United States—$2,112,631,000, $1,907,710,000, and $1,618,799,000; Canada—$220,815,000, $207,338,000, and $176,785,000; and Other International—$309,923,000, $238,958,000, and $157,905,000.

Income taxes

Pretax income and the related provision for income taxes, differentiated by the locale in which the income is generated, consist of the following:

	1980	1979	1978	1977	1976
					(In thousands of dollars)
Pretax income—					
U.S.	$348,792	$304,415	$278,037	$236,808	$195,619
Foreign	53,801	40,093	34,788	29,988	19,885
	$402,593	$344,508	$312,825	$266,796	$215,504
Provision for income taxes—					
U.S.	$159,934	$140,198	$134,666	$117,371	$ 97,593
Foreign	21,766	15,702	15,490	12,729	8,731
	$181,700	$155,900	$150,156	$130,100	$106,324

The foreign provision for income taxes in the preceding table includes U.S. taxes paid on (1) income from fees received in the U.S. which are derived from foreign operations and (2) foreign currency hedging activities, as follows: 1980—$5,271,000; 1979—$744,000; 1978—$3,278,000; 1977—$3,277,000; and 1976—$1,488,000.

The major components of the provision for income taxes, differentiated by the timing and location of payment, consist of the following:

	1980	1979	1978	1977	1976
					(In thousands of dollars)
Current:					
U.S. federal	$113,545	$101,086	$109,790	$ 96,267	$ 76,785
U.S. state	21,596	17,586	17,627	14,987	11,673
Foreign	14,379	11,603	8,993	7,216	5,537
	149,520	130,275	136,410	118,470	93,995
Deferred:					
U.S. federal	26,615	19,073	9,142	8,327	9,575
U.S. state	3,449	3,197	1,385	1,067	1,048
Foreign	2,116	3,355	3,219	2,236	1,706
	32,180	25,625	13,746	11,630	12,329
	$181,700	$155,900	$150,156	$130,100	$106,324

The consolidated income tax provision is reconciled in the following table with amounts computed by applying the statutory United States federal income tax rate (46% for 1980 and 1979 and 48% for other years) to income before income taxes.

	1980	1979	1978	1977	1976
					(In thousands of dollars)
Tax at statutory rate	$185,193	$158,474	$150,156	$128,062	$103,442
State income taxes, net of related federal income tax benefit	13,524	11,223	9,886	8,348	6,615
Investment tax credits	(16,000)	(15,000)	(11,000)	(6,627)	(4,510)
Other	(1,017)	1,203	1,114	317	777
Consolidated tax provision	$181,700	$155,900	$150,156	$130,100	$106,324

Deferred income taxes, computed on the net change method, relate to the tax effect of differences between taxable income and income reported in the financial statements, as follows:

	1980	1979	1978	1977	1976
					(In thousands of dollars)
Additional tax depreciation	$23,575	$16,983	$ 8,517	$ 6,414	$ 6,345
Capitalized costs which are expensed for tax purposes	4,525	4,675	3,951	2,581	1,510
Other	4,080	3,967	1,278	2,635	4,474
Total deferred tax provision	$32,180	$25,625	$13,746	$11,630	$12,329

FIGURE 8-8 (cont.)

Property and equipment

Property and equipment consists of the following at December 31, 1980 and 1979:

	1980	1979
	(In thousands of dollars)	
Land	$ 521,218	$ 472,135
Buildings and improvements on owned land	1,039,758	881,811
Buildings on leased land and leasehold improvements	600,974	493,576
Equipment and signs for restaurants	387,075	323,324
Furniture, fixtures and other equipment	40,102	38,246
Property under capital leases	117,569	122,778
	2,706,696	2,331,870
Less accumulated depreciation and amortization:		
Owned property	429,734	338,496
Property under capital leases	49,814	48,437
	479,548	386,933
Net property and equipment	$2,227,148	$1,944,937

Real estate taxes and rents capitalized for the last five years are as follows: 1980—$2,700,000; 1979—$2,800,000; 1978—$2,500,000; 1977—$2,200,000; and 1976—$1,400,000.

Depreciation and amortization expense, including amortization of property under capital leases, for the last five years is as follows: 1980—$112,660,000; 1979—$91,712,000; 1978—$75,374,000; 1977—$62,124,000; and 1976—$51,429,000.

For additional information related to property under capital leases, refer to the "Lease of properties owned by others" section.

Intangible assets, net

Set forth below is the composition of intangible assets at December 31, 1980 and 1979.

	1980	1979
	(In thousands of dollars)	
Unlimited term franchise rights, not being amortized	$13,599	$13,599
Other franchise rights	55,142	54,520
Other intangible assets	1,951	1,730
Intangible assets, net	$70,692	$69,849

Debt financing and dividend restrictions
☐ Short-term lines of credit

At December 31, 1980, the Company and certain of its subsidiaries have unused bank lines of credit available for short-term borrowings, with interest rates (11% to 22.5% at December 31, 1980) generally tied to local banks' prime rates, in the aggregate amount of $22,000,000. In connection with certain of these lines, the Company has informally agreed to maintain average compensating balances (not material) which are not restricted as to withdrawal.

☐ Long-term debt and dividend restrictions

Long-term debt, other than obligations under capital leases, consists of the following at December 31, 1980 and 1979:

	1980	1979
	(In thousands of dollars)	
Mortgage notes, 5.5% to 10.5%	$164,238	$175,671
Revolving credit notes	125,095	48,000
Short-term notes supported by bank credit agreement, 16.4% to 20.9% (12.5% to 14.4% in 1979)	94,565	127,000
Installment notes, 6.75% to 10.25%	146,704	153,332
Promissory notes	89,555	94,175
Sinking fund notes:		
8⅜ %, due 1988	67,601	79,655
10¼ %, due 1989	50,000	50,000
Serial notes, 9%, due 1985	67,779	70,228
9⅝ % notes, due 1982	59,933	59,895
Other	20,244	17,853
	$885,714	$875,809

Mortgage notes mature at various dates through 1997. At December 31, 1980, land, buildings and improvements with an aggregate net book value of approximately $324,000,000 were mortgaged under these obligations.

The Company has long-term credit consisting of three revolving credit agreements of $75,000,000, $85,000,000 and $100,000,000, a bank credit agreement of $15,000,000, and a term loan commitment of $25,000,000. The $75,000,000, $85,000,000 and $15,000,000 agreements continue indefinitely unless terminated by the participating banks upon advance notice of at least 18 months. Notes issued under these three agreements are repayable in 15 to 18 months. Revolving credit notes outstanding denominated in U.S. dollars amount to $50,000,000 at December 31, 1980 and bear interest at the agent banks' prime rates (20.5% at December 31, 1980 and 15% at December 31, 1979). Revolving credit notes outstanding denominated in German marks amount to $75,095,000 at December 31, 1980 with an interest rate of 11.1%. The $100,000,000 agreement terminates March 31, 1983. Notes issued under this agreement bear interest at the agent bank's prime rate and are payable on March 31, 1983 unless converted into term notes at that date. Upon conversion, the notes are payable in eight equal semiannual installments beginning September 30, 1983, and bear interest at 102% to 104% of the agent bank's prime rate. Short-term notes of $94,565,000 at December 31, 1980, which are supported by this $100,000,000 agreement, have been classified with long-term debt as the Company intends to refinance these short-term obligations on a long-term basis. The $25,000,000 term loan commitment terminates April 1, 1981. Notes issued under this agreement are repayable on April 1, 1987 and bear interest at 104% to 109% of the agent bank's prime rate. All of the agreements provide for a commission of ½ % per annum on the daily unused portion of the total commitment, which commitment may be reduced by the Company at any time. In connection with certain of the agreements, the Company has informally agreed to maintain average compensating balances (not material) which are not restricted as to withdrawal. The agreements restrict the payment of cash dividends and the repurchase of capital stock by the Company. Consolidated retained earnings not restricted total $261,699,000 at December 31, 1980.

FIGURE 8-8 (cont.)

The installment notes mature over various terms through 1998. Notes in the amount of $60,536,000 are subject to an interest rate adjustment of ¾ % in 1986 or 1987 at the option of the note holders. In the event of such adjustment, the Company may, in the following year, redeem all or a portion of these notes at face value.

Promissory notes outstanding at December 31, 1980, include $39,555,000 of industrial revenue bonds due from 1990 to 2000 with interest rates ranging from 6% to 9% (6% in 1979). Other notes in the amount of $50,000,000 are due in 1982, with interest rates ranging from 10.25% to 10.95% (7.9% to 15.25% in 1979).

The 8⅝ % sinking fund notes require annual redemptions of $10,000,000. An additional $10,000,000 may be redeemed each year at the option of the Company. The 10¼ % sinking fund notes have the same provisions as the 8⅝ % notes, except that the mandatory and optional redemptions begin October 1, 1985.

Under the indentures covering certain of the Company's debt, the Company and its subsidiaries are required to maintain stated ratios of net book value of stipulated real property to the principal amount of the outstanding notes, and of net book value of property and equipment to funded debt. If these and certain other conditions are not met, the Company may be required to deliver first mortgages as security for the debt. The indentures also require, for the preceding 12-month period, minimum earnings coverage of interest and rental expense and a minimum ratio of working capital generated from operations to funded debt at the end of the period.

Aggregate maturities of long-term debt for the five years ending after December 31, 1980, are as follows: 1981 — $34,626,000; 1982 — $269,412,000; 1983 — $47,422,000; 1984 — $59,711,000; and 1985 — $141,062,000. Although certain of the Company's long-term credit agreements continue indefinitely, $125,095,000 of related notes are included in the 1982 maturities, as 1982 is the earliest time at which the banks can terminate the agreements. The short term notes of $94,565,000 are included in 1983, 1984 and 1985 maturities in the amounts of $11,821,000, $23,642,000 and $23,642,000, respectively, with the balance payable thereafter. These maturities assume conversion of the short-term notes in 1983 into the term loan available under the $100,000,000 agreement.

Lease of properties owned by others
☐ Description of leasing arrangements
At December 31, 1980, the Company was lessee under ground leases (the Company leases the land and erects and owns the buildings) or improved leases (lessor owns the land and buildings), covering 2,444 restaurant sites. Lease terms are generally for 20 to 25 years and, in many cases, provide for rent escalations and for one or more five-year renewal options. The Company is generally obligated for the cost of property taxes, insurance and maintenance. Other leases are principally for office space and equipment.

☐ Capital leases
The Company was lessee under 1,460 improved leases at December 31, 1980. The building portions of 904 of such leases are capital leases. Future minimum rental payments related to the capitalized portion of improved leases in effect at December 31, 1980, are as follows:

	(In thousands of dollars)
1981	$ 13,032
1982	12,753
1983	12,514
1984	12,215
1985	11,957
Thereafter	122,511
Total minimum payments	184,982
Less imputed interest	96,776
Present value of minimum rental payments	88,206
Less current maturities at December 31, 1980	4,130
Long-term obligations at December 31, 1980	$ 84,076

☐ Operating leases
At December 31, 1980, the Company was lessee under noncancellable operating leases with terms in excess of one year covering (1) land related to 984 ground leases, (2) land related to 904 improved leases in which the building portion is capitalized, (3) land and buildings related to 556 improved leases in which the building portion is not capitalized, (4) land for additional parking, and (5) other property, principally office space and equipment. Future minimum lease payments related to these operating leases at December 31, 1980, are as follows:

	Restaurant	Other	Total
		(In thousands of dollars)	
1981	$ 50,400	$ 8,100	$ 58,500
1982	50,400	6,700	57,100
1983	50,300	4,200	54,500
1984	50,200	2,700	52,900
1985	50,200	2,200	52,400
Thereafter	540,100	15,600	555,700
	$791,600	$ 39,500	$831,100

☐ Rent expense
Rent expense as shown in the consolidated statement of income includes percentage rentals based on sales of the related restaurants in excess of minimum rentals stipulated in certain of the capital and operating lease agreements as follows: 1980 — $3,856,000; 1979 — $3,502,000; 1978 — $2,918,000; 1977 — $2,764,000; and 1976 — $2,177,000.

Total rent expense included in the consolidated statement of income amounted to: $63,883,000 in 1980; $53,216,000 in 1979; $44,058,000 in 1978; $37,397,000 in 1977; and $30,854,000 in 1976.

Franchise arrangements
Franchise arrangements generally provide for location and license fees and continuing payments to the Company based upon a percentage of sales, with a minimum payment. Among other things, the franchisee is provided the use of both land and building, generally for a period of 20 years, and is required to pay property taxes, insurance and maintenance.

As of December 31, 1980, the net book value of assets related to franchised restaurant locations was $1,256,000,000 (including land of $330,000,000) after accumulated depreciation and amortization of $204,000,000.

FIGURE 8-8 (cont.)

Revenues from franchised restaurants for the five years ended December 31, 1980, with minimum payments summarized based upon the Company's real estate interest, consist of:

	1980	1979	1978	1977	1976
				(In thousands of dollars)	
Minimum payments—					
Owned sites	$120,270	$100,596	$ 85,586	$ 68,933	$ 54,831
Leased sites	78,363	68,403	59,418	49,006	40,610
	198,633	168,999	145,004	117,939	95,441
Percentage payments	283,550	243,229	203,188	164,344	133,384
Location and license fees	4,394	4,409	4,736	4,490	4,399
	$486,577	$416,637	$352,928	$286,773	$233,224

Future minimum payments to the Company required after December 31, 1980, under franchise arrangements are as follows:

	Owned sites	Leased sites	Total
		(In thousands of dollars)	
1981	$ 134,100	$ 87,900	$ 222,000
1982	132,400	86,800	219,200
1983	130,200	85,000	215,200
1984	128,400	83,500	211,900
1985	128,200	82,900	211,100
Thereafter	1,386,400	812,200	2,198,600
	$2,039,700	$1,238,300	$3,278,000

Other commitments and security deposits

The Company has guaranteed the payment of loans relating to certain affiliates and others totaling $26,000,000 at December 31, 1980. In addition, the Company is a general partner in two domestic partnerships having total indebtedness of $35,000,000 at December 31, 1980.

Commitments, certain of which are contingent upon future events, and contractual obligations, principally for the acquisition or construction of property, amounted to approximately $40,000,000 at December 31, 1980.

At December 31, 1980, security deposit refunds which will become due for all years through 1985 total $9,900,000. Refunds payable for the individual years 1986 through 2000 range from $1,700,000 to $5,200,000.

Capital stock and additional paid-in capital

A summary of changes in common stock issued and additional paid-in capital during 1980, 1979 and 1978 follows:

	Common stock		Additional paid-in capital
	Shares	Amount	
		(In thousands of dollars)	
Balance at January 1, 1978	40,545,199	$4,509	$90,353
Exercise of stock options	54,106	6	1,930
Other changes			201
Balance at December 31, 1978	40,599,305	4,515	92,484
Exercise of stock options	6,466		238
Other changes			786
Balance at December 31, 1979	40,605,771	4,515	93,508
Exercise of stock options	8,797	1	335
Other changes			180
Balance at December 31, 1980	40,614,568	$4,516	$94,023

At December 31, 1980, a maximum of 2,446,723 shares of common stock were reserved for issuance under stock option plans.

The Company has purchased 550,362 shares of its common stock in connection with the 1975 Stock Option Plan, as follows: 1980—77,362; 1979—320,400; 1978—30,600; 1977—106,000; and 1976—16,000. A total of 74,841 shares were issued in connection with the exercise of stock options under the 1975 Plan as follows: 1980—8,921; 1979—7,353; 1978—56,288; and 1977—2,279.

Series preferred stock authorized for issuance totals 300,000 shares. No shares were issued or outstanding from January 1, 1978 to December 31, 1980.

Stock options and incentive plan

The Company adopted stock option plans in 1973 and 1975. In 1979 the stockholders approved an amendment to the 1975 plan reserving an additional 750,000 shares for issuance under the plan. Options to purchase a total of 2,095,347 shares under the 1975 plan have been reserved for grant to officers and employees at prices not less than the fair market value of the stock at dates of grant.

The terms of the 1975 plan, as first adopted, provided for its termination on May 4, 1980. However, on April 15, 1980, the Company's Board of Directors adopted amendments to the 1975 plan which extended its term to May 4, 1985, and gave the Board authority to extend the plan beyond that date. These amendments are subject to ratification by stockholders; accordingly, 327,655 options granted after May 4, 1980 are contingent upon the stockholders' ratification of the above amendments. The 1973 plan terminated on May 14, 1978, and no further grants can be made thereunder.

Options granted under the 1973 and 1975 plans become exercisable cumulatively in five equal biennial installments commencing one year from date of grant and expire ten years from the date of grant.

The Option Committee has the authority to cancel outstanding options with the consent of the optionee and to grant new options in substitution therefor.

Information as to options at December 31, 1980 and 1979 and for the years then ended follows:

	1980		1979	
	Option price per share	Number of shares	Option price per share	Number of shares
At December 31:				
Options outstanding	$42 to 51	2,345,075	$42 to 54	2,176,680
Options exercisable	42 to 51	763,934	42 to 54	480,425
Shares reserved for future grants		101,648		312,074
Option activity during the year:				
Granted	46	327,655	49	772,045
Forfeited	42 to 54	141,542	42 to 54	91,800
Exercised	42 to 46	17,718	42 to 46	13,819

The Company adopted an incentive plan in 1978 whereby performance units and stock appreciation rights can be granted to recipients of stock options. The values of such performance units and stock appreciation rights are dependent upon the Company's operating results and the market value of its stock, respectively, with stipulated maximum amounts. Generally, the

FIGURE 8-8 (cont.)

performance units and stock appreciation rights are exercisable when the related stock options become exercisable. Subsequent exercise of any one of the above option, unit or right benefits terminates any corresponding benefits. Amounts charged to costs and expenses related to the incentive plan are $744,000 in 1980; $303,000 in 1979; and $814,000 in 1978.

Net income per share
Net income per share is computed based on the average number of common and common equivalent shares (issuable under dilutive stock options) outstanding during each year (40,230,501 in 1980; 40,295,394 in 1979; 40,667,465 in 1978; 40,565,959 in 1977; and 40,518,965 in 1976).

Quarterly results (unaudited)
The following is a summary of selected quarterly financial data for the years ended December 31, 1980 and 1979:

	Quarter ended							
	December 31		September 30		June 30		March 31	
	1980	1979	1980	1979	1980	1979	1980	1979
	(In thousands of dollars, except per share amounts)							
Revenues—								
Sales by Company-owned restaurants	$437,246	$395,690	$450,303	$399,702	$430,981	$378,178	$379,237	$321,646
Revenues from franchised restaurants	128,090	108,468	131,855	113,360	122,392	106,243	104,240	88,566
Other revenues—net	4,697	6,134	6,978	6,545	9,515	5,069	9,929	8,334
Total revenues	570,033	510,292	589,136	519,607	562,888	489,490	493,406	418,546
Costs and expenses—								
Company-owned restaurants	367,735	335,963	374,024	329,065	352,349	308,879	322,912	273,426
Expenses directly applicable to revenues from franchised restaurants	20,206	16,430	19,105	15,137	18,036	13,976	16,954	13,458
General, administrative and selling expenses	62,498	58,248	58,188	56,889	56,387	51,992	53,629	47,372
Interest expense	24,516	20,165	21,750	18,074	22,555	17,104	22,026	17,249
Total costs and expenses	474,955	430,806	473,067	419,165	449,327	391,951	415,521	351,505
Income before provision for income taxes	95,078	79,486	116,069	100,442	113,561	97,539	77,885	67,041
Provision for income taxes	42,703	35,327	52,176	45,354	51,578	44,380	35,243	30,839
Net income	$ 52,375	$ 44,159	$ 63,893	$ 55,088	$ 61,983	$ 53,159	$ 42,642	$ 36,202
Net income per share of common stock	$ 1.30	$ 1.10	$ 1.59	$ 1.37	$ 1.54	$ 1.32	$ 1.06	$ .90

Auditors' report

The Board of Directors and Stockholders
McDonald's Corporation

We have examined the accompanying consolidated balance sheets of McDonald's Corporation and subsidiaries at December 31, 1980 and 1979 and the related consolidated statements of income, retained earnings and changes in financial position for each of the five years in the period ended December 31, 1980. Our examinations were made in accordance with generally accepted auditing standards and, accordingly, included such tests of the accounting records and such other auditing procedures as we considered necessary in the circumstances.

In our opinion, the statements mentioned above present fairly the consolidated financial position of McDonald's Corporation and subsidiaries at December 31, 1980 and 1979 and the consolidated results of operations and changes in financial position for each of the five years in the period ended December 31, 1980, in conformity with generally accepted accounting principles applied on a consistent basis during the period.

ARTHUR YOUNG & COMPANY

Chicago, Illinois
February 5, 1981

FIGURE 8-8 (cont.)

Information on the effects of changing prices—inflation (unaudited)

Basis of presentation

During 1979, the Financial Accounting Standards Board (FASB) adopted experimental disclosure rules requiring the inclusion of supplemental information in annual reports of large publicly owned companies. The FASB Statement intends that these disclosures will provide information useful in assessing the more significant effects of inflation on a business enterprise.

The following condensed financial statements compare the traditional historical cost-based financial statements for 1980 and 1979 with financial statements comprehensively adjusted under two methods: constant dollar, which gives effect to general inflation; and current cost, which gives effect to changes in prices of specific goods and services utilized by the Company.

The FASB Statement requires, under constant dollar adjustment, that the effect of changes in the purchasing power of the dollar (general inflation) be measured by the Consumer Price Index for all Urban Consumers (CPI-U), which is issued by the U.S. Department of Labor. The constant dollar financial statements presented herein are adjusted using the CPI-U index as of December 31, 1980 (constant dollars at December 31, 1980).

The current cost adjusted financial information is also expressed in year-end 1980 constant dollars and gives effect to the changing prices of the specific assets used by the Company in its business, which prices may change at rates different from general inflation. The adjusted data reflects the current cost of actual assets owned (reproduction cost), not the cost of assets that would be incurred to replace existing assets (replacement cost).

These current costs were determined by applying specific price indices for the major components of property, equipment and intangible assets to the applicable historical costs. The land indices were generally developed internally, using actual prices paid by the Company in each year for comparable sites in various geographic areas. For buildings, applicable external indices for each country have generally been used, the integrity of which has been tested internally by accumulating costs related to comparable buildings. The equipment and intangible asset indices were also developed internally based upon actual cost experience. For countries outside the U.S., current costs were determined on a local currency basis and translated at current exchange rates. Although the indices used for these computations appear to be compatible with the changing costs experienced by the Company, the final results could differ significantly from costs that will be incurred in the future.

Depreciation and amortization expense, as adjusted, reflects the same methods and estimated lives used in the historical financial statements. Depreciation and amortization of property, equipment and intangibles included in the adjusted financial data is as follows:

	1980	1979
	(In thousands of dollars)	
Historical cost	$116,409	$ 94,955
Constant dollar	168,955	149,854
Current cost	156,676	142,760

In reporting the adjusted amounts for 1979 financial information, all financial statement items are adjusted to year-end 1980 dollars. For 1980, all monetary balance sheet items are stated at the same amounts as in the historical financial statements. Inventories on both a constant dollar and a current cost basis approximate historical amounts. Other non-monetary assets and stockholders' equity are stated in year-end 1980 dollars or cur-

rent cost expressed in year-end 1980 dollars. All revenues and expenses, except depreciation and amortization and other amounts related to non-monetary items, are adjusted from average to year-end 1980 dollars. The provision for income taxes is also adjusted from average to year-end 1980 dollars. Income taxes have not been adjusted for increased depreciation and amortization expense on either a constant dollar or a current cost basis, as the current tax regulations do not permit a deduction for this increase.

Commentary

The Company believes it has generally dealt effectively with inflationary pressures and rising prices. While the accompanying constant dollar and current cost data is intended to provide information about the more significant effects of inflation on the Company, we believe that there may be limitations as to its meaningfulness in this regard because of the Company's asset composition, its financing activities, and the nature of its operations relative to other companies and the differing effects of inflation on businesses. The following comments are provided to assist in the analysis of the data.

Sales by Company-owned restaurants and Revenues from franchised restaurants principally relate to over-the-counter sales of food products to the public. Menu prices have generally been adjusted to compensate for cost increases. The increases in the Company's systemwide sales for the last five years, as stated in year-end 1980 dollars, better reflect the growth of the Company's operations than do the increases in total revenues for the same period because of the lower percentage growth in the number of Company-owned restaurants as compared to franchised restaurants.

In determining constant dollar and current cost income, the FASB Statement requires that depreciation expense be adjusted for changing prices. For the current year, depreciation and amortization expense is increased by $52,546,000 on a constant dollar basis and $40,267,000 on a current cost basis from the historical cost amount. The effect of inflation on property and equipment is inseparable from its effect on the debt used to finance such assets. The purchasing power gain on the debt is an economic benefit to the Company since, with inflation, the debt is paid back in cheaper dollars. Accordingly, we believe that this gain should be viewed as an adjustment to interest and therefore have included it in arriving at constant dollar net income.

Substantially all existing restaurants conform to the Company's current designs and specifications, and restaurant equipment improvements are made on a continuing basis. Because the related property and equipment expenditures have largely been made in recent years and include substantial amounts for land, the increase in depreciation and amortization for both constant dollar and current cost purposes is not as large as might be expected. At year end 1980 the Company's investment in property and equipment increases from historical cost amounts by $944 million for constant dollar purposes and by $695 million on a current cost basis with corresponding increases in Stockholders' equity.

One objective of the FASB Statement is to permit assessment of a company's ability to replace productive assets which will likely cost more in future years. In making this assessment as it relates to McDonald's, consideration must be given to franchise arrangements covering the majority of restaurants whereby the franchisees repair and maintain restaurant buildings which are

FIGURE 8-8 (cont.)

included in Property and equipment in the accompanying Condensed consolidated balance sheet. Franchisees also spend substantial amounts improving and remodeling the restaurant buildings. In addition, consideration must be given to the fact that land, which represents 23% of historical cost productive assets, is not likely to require significant replacement. Furthermore, during 1980 the Company introduced a new free-standing restaurant building design, the Series 80 building, which is smaller and more standardized and results in lower construction costs than previous free-standing designs. The amounts shown for productive assets in the Company's constant dollar and current cost balance sheet have not been adjusted to reflect this lower cost and therefore should not be considered indicative of the level of future expenditures which the Company will be required to make to maintain the earning power of its productive assets.

The increase in current cost of property and equipment held during the year amounted to $201,435,000 in 1980 and $211,479,000 in 1979. General inflation outpaced these increases by $116,801,000 in 1980 and $103,254,000 in 1979. The specific price increases

for the Company's productive assets have been less than general inflation during the past two years, due primarily to the unusually large increase in the CPI-U, which is not reflective of the actual increases in property costs incurred by the Company during those years.

In summary, the Company feels that its rapid inventory turnover, its menu price adjustments, its substantial property holdings, which are partially financed by debt repayable in cheaper dollars in inflationary times, and its effectiveness in controlling property and equipment costs, have helped to cushion against inflation. Furthermore, as a result of the property holdings, Stockholders' equity per share at December 31, 1980 on a current cost basis is $47.72 and on a constant dollar basis is $53.69, compared to $28.42 on a historical cost basis. However, it should be emphasized that the constant dollar and current cost amounts, which have not been adjusted for any future income tax effects, are based upon procedures prescribed by the FASB Statement and are not based upon appraisal or other traditional methods of valuation.

Condensed consolidated balance sheet *(In thousands of dollars)*

| | December 31, 1980 | | | | December 31, 1979 | | |
| | Historical cost as reported | Year-end 1980 dollars | | | Historical cost as reported | Year-end 1980 dollars | |
		Constant dollars	Current cost			Constant dollars	Current cost
Assets:							
Current assets	$ 233,940	$ 234,754	$ 234,479		$ 246,730	$ 278,069	$ 278,033
Other assets and deferred charges	111,589	143,751	160,247		92,490	125,769	130,919
Property and equipment, at cost	2,706,696	4,005,164	3,698,032		2,331,870	3,647,873	3,478,292
Less accumulated depreciation and amortization	479,548	833,892	776,170		386,933	713,449	698,214
Net property and equipment	2,227,148	3,171,272	2,921,862		1,944,937	2,934,424	2,780,078
Intangible assets, net	70,692	107,574	101,468		69,849	109,365	108,170
Total assets	$2,643,369	$3,657,351	$3,418,056		$2,354,006	$3,447,627	$3,297,200
Liabilities and stockholders' equity:							
Current liabilities	$ 332,622	$ 332,622	$ 332,622		$ 274,307	$ 308,312	$ 308,312
Long-term debt	969,790	969,790	969,790		966,123	1,085,890	1,085,890
Security deposits by franchisees	59,651	59,651	59,651		54,633	61,406	61,406
Deferred income taxes	140,423	140,423	140,423		106,777	120,014	120,014
Stockholders' equity	1,140,883	2,154,865	1,915,570		952,166	1,872,005	1,721,578
Total liabilities and stockholders' equity	$2,643,369	$3,657,351	$3,418,056		$2,354,006	$3,447,627	$3,297,200

FIGURE 8-8 (cont.)

Condensed consolidated statement of income   *(In thousands of dollars, except per share data)*

	Year ended December 31, 1980			Year ended December 31, 1979		
		Year-end 1980 dollars			Year-end 1980 dollars	
	Historical cost as reported	Constant dollars	Current cost	Historical cost as reported	Constant dollars	Current cost
Revenues:						
Sales by Company-owned restaurants	$1,697,767	$1,777,565	$1,777,565	$1,495,216	$1,777,203	$1,777,203
Revenues from franchised restaurants	486,577	509,446	509,446	416,637	495,212	495,212
Other revenues—net	31,119	26,815	27,673	26,082	25,172	26,918
Total revenues	2,215,463	2,313,826	2,314,684	1,937,935	2,297,587	2,299,333
Costs and expenses:						
Company-owned restaurants	1,417,020	1,511,399	1,502,332	1,247,333	1,504,918	1,499,916
Expenses directly applicable to revenues from franchised restaurants	74,301	97,814	94,248	59,001	84,579	82,895
General, administrative and selling expenses	230,702	243,094	242,797	214,501	258,889	257,892
Interest expense	90,847	95,118	95,118	72,592	86,282	86,282
Total costs and expenses	1,812,870	1,947,425	1,934,495	1,593,427	1,934,668	1,926,985
Income before provision for income taxes	402,593	366,401	380,189	344,508	362,919	372,348
Provision for income taxes	181,700	190,240	190,240	155,900	185,302	185,302
Income before holding gain	220,893	176,161	$ 189,949	188,608	177,617	$ 187,046
Purchasing power gain on net amounts owed—holding gain		145,761	$ 145,761		150,334	$ 150,334
Net income	$ 220,893	$ 321,922		$ 188,608	$ 327,951	
Per share:						
Income before holding gain	$5.49	$4.38	$ 4.72	$4.68	$4.41	$ 4.64
Purchasing power gain on net amounts owed—holding gain		3.62	$ 3.62		3.73	$ 3.73
Net income	$5.49	$8.00		$4.68	$8.14	

FIGURE 8-8 (cont.)

Condensed consolidated statement of changes in stockholders' equity			*(In thousands of dollars)*
	Historical cost as reported	Constant dollars	Current cost
Balance at December 31, 1979, historical cost	$ 952,166	$ 952,166	$ 952,166
Cumulative adjustment to year-end 1979 dollars to reflect changing prices		713,369	579,532
Balance at December 31, 1979 in year-end 1979 dollars		1,665,535	1,531,698
Adjustment of December 31, 1979 balance to reflect general inflation in 1980		206,470	189,880
Balance at December 31, 1979 in year-end 1980 dollars		1,872,005	1,721,578
1980 activity:			
Income before holding gain	220,893	176,161	189,949
Purchasing power gain on net amounts owed— holding gain		145,761	145,761
Property and equipment— Increase in current cost Less effect of increase in general prices			201,435 318,236
Excess of increase in general prices over increase in current cost of property and equipment ($103,254 in 1979)			(116,801)
Cash dividends	(29,731)	(31,128)	(31,128)
Other	(2,445)	(7,934)	6,211
Balance at December 31, 1980	$1,140,883	$2,154,865	$1,915,570

Selected additional financial data in year-end 1980 dollars				*(In thousands of dollars, except per share data)*	
	1980	1979	1978	1977	1976
Year ended December 31:					
Systemwide sales	$6,519,000	$6,401,000	$6,050,000	$5,322,000	$4,642,000
Total revenues	$2,313,826	$2,297,587	$2,210,935	$2,001,921	$1,782,939
Cash dividends declared per share	$ .77	$ .61	$ .43	$ .21	$ .15
At December 31:					
Market price per share	$ 48.75	$ 48.76	$ 61.14	$ 71.51	$ 79.13
Stockholders' equity per share					
Constant dollars	$ 53.69	$ 46.57			
Current cost	$ 47.72	$ 42.83			
Consumer price index	258.4	229.9	202.9	186.1	174.3

SOURCE: *McDonald's Corporation Annual Report 1980* (Oak Brook, Ill., 1981).

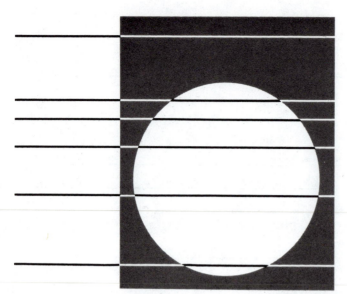

NINE

Company Analysis: Forecasting Earnings

Chapter 8 introduced us to the primary sources of information, internal and external, about firms. We discovered that the principal sources of internal information about a firm were its financial statements. However, the analyst must be aware that there is more to financial statements than meets the eye. More than anything else, it is essential that a good analyst understand the impact of different acceptable methods of accounting for items on the position statement and the statement of income.

The income statement is perhaps used more than any other to assess the future of the firm, and earnings per share has become a key figure on this statement. There is strong evidence that earnings have a direct and powerful effect upon dividends and share prices, so the importance of forecasting earnings cannot be overstated. A study of Niederhoffer and Regan suggests that stock prices are strongly dependent upon earnings changes, both absolute and relative to analysts' estimates. They discovered that the common characteristics of the companies registering the best price changes included a forecast of moderately increased earnings and a realized profit gain far in excess of analysts' expectations. The worst-performing stocks were those characterized by severe earnings declines, combined with unusually optimistic forecasts.[1] The accuracy of earnings forecasts is of enormous value in stock selection.

The present chapter has two aims: First, using financial statements, we will examine the "chemistry" of earnings. The various ingredients in the financial statements can be related in such a way that the analyst is able to visualize the critical aspects of a firm's

[1]Victor Niederhoffer and Patrick J. Regan, "Earnings Changes, Analysts' Forecasts, and Stock Prices," *Financial Analysts Journal,* 28, No. 3 (May-June 1972), 65-71.

operations that dictate the level, trend, and stability of earnings. Second, we shall take a look at traditional methods employed by analysts in assessing the outlook for revenues, expenses, and earnings in the firm over a forward holding period, given the economic and industry outlook. The methods that will be explained are (1) the return-on-investment or ROI approach, (2) the market-share-profit-margin approach, and (3) an independent, subjective approach to the forecast of revenues and expenses.

In Chapter 10 we will examine some newer techniques used in forecasting revenues, expenses, and ultimately earnings; and we will take up the forecasting of dividends and the market price of a share of stock at the end of the holding period.

Let us begin this journey through the next two chapters by taking a look at the ingredients that produce earnings in the firm.

The Chemistry of Earnings

One of the most effective ways of getting "inside" earnings is to explore the financial statements for all possible explanations of a change, or lack of change, in earnings. Changes in reported earnings can result from changes in methods of accounting, as we saw in Chapter 8. Beyond this, they result from changes (1) in the operations of the business, and/or (2) in the financing of the business—that is, changes in productivity or in the resource (asset) base.

The efficiency or profitability with which a firm uses its assets is a key influence on earnings levels and growth. Better-managed companies typically have higher profits (net income) per dollar of assets than do poorly managed firms. The other key to earnings levels and growth lies in how fast a firm increases its asset base and the sources it uses for financing expansion. Debt and equity sources each have a unique effect upon earnings growth.

Our task of earnings analysis will be greatly facilitated by using a simple accounting model to focus on (1) what effect a change in a specific variable will have on earnings, and (2) whether or not each variable can be expected to cause a sustainable influence on earnings over long periods.

Asset Productivity and Earnings

Every firm has an aggregate of invested capital in the form of assets. These assets are utilized by management to generate revenues and net income. The funds necessary to acquire assets come from debt and equity sources of financing. Firms strive to operate in such a way as to provide shareholders the best possible return per dollar invested.

In balance-sheet terms, firms seek to maximize the return on total funds provided (assets). Should all financing be provided from equity money (no debt financing), the return on assets and equity are the same. To the extent that borrowed money is used to provide assets, return to equity will depend upon the relationship between return on total capital and the cost of borrowed funds.

Separation of the investment and financing activities of the firm makes the problem a bit clearer. Shown below are an income statement and a balance sheet in abbreviated form:

Income Statement (millions)		Balance Sheet (millions)		
Sales	$ 100	Assets $50	Liabilities	$25
— Operating Costs	88		Equity	25
= EBIT	12			
— Interest Expense	2			
= EBT	10			
— Taxes	4			
= EAT	6			
÷ No. of shares	5			
= EPS	$1.20			
DPS	.84			

We have used some shorthand to distinguish earnings at various stages:

$$EBIT \ = \ \text{earnings before interest and taxes}$$

$$EBT \ = \ \text{earnings before taxes}$$

$$EAT \ = \ \text{earnings after taxes}$$

$$EPS \ = \ \text{earnings per share}$$

$$DPS \ = \ \text{dividend per share}$$

Let us set aside the effects of taxes and financing for the moment. The productivity of total assets can be seen as

$$\text{Return on assets} \ = \ \frac{\text{EBIT}}{\text{Assets}} \ = \ \frac{12}{50} \ = \ 24\%$$

The $50 million provided the firm (without reference to source of funds—debt or equity) generated a 24 percent return before considering distribution of these earnings to the tax collector, creditors, and shareholders. In general, the greater the return on assets, the higher the market value of the firm, other things being equal.

The return on assets, however, is only the end product of a mixture of events within the firm. If we think of the normal operating cycle of a company as analogous to the functioning of a wheel, we are better able to dissect the forces that contribute to the return on assets. Figure 9-1 shows the ordinary operating cycle for a firm, starting with placing cash into inventories. These inventories are then sold to create revenues. Deducting operating costs from revenues (sales) provides a profit. Thus, each time the operating cycle or wheel goes around, a profit (or loss) results. The key to overall return on funds committed to the enterprise is (1) the number of times per year the wheel spins around and (2) the profits that emerge with each spin. Thus a refinement of the return-on-assets concept is to say that it is the product of the turnover of assets into sales (number of spins of the operating wheel), or intensity of utilization of assets in creating sales, and the margin of profit from each spin, or the profit productivity of sales. In the lexicon of finance, we say that the return on assets is the product of the *turnover* of assets and the *margin* of profit:

FIGURE 9-1
OPERATING CYCLE FOR A FIRM

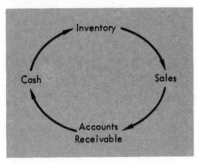

(Turnover) (Margin)

$$\text{Return on assets} = \frac{\text{Sales}}{\text{Assets}} \quad \times \quad \frac{\text{EBIT}}{\text{Sales}}$$

or, as before:

$$\text{Return on assets} = \frac{\text{EBIT}}{\text{Assets}}$$

It is quite possible to find two firms in the same or even different industries earning comparable returns on assets. However, they may have totally different (1) turnover of assets, and/or (2) profit margins on sales. For example, consider the basic character of a jewelry store and a supermarket. They may enjoy similar returns on assets, but jewelry stores turn over their goods very slowly, while supermarkets enjoy an operating cycle that is quite rapid. Yet supermarkets enjoy only modest profit margins, and jewelry-store margins are much higher. So it is conceivable that the following relationship might apply:

	Return on Assets	=	Turnover	X	Margin
Jeweler	.15	=	.5	X	.30
Supermarket	,15	=	15.0	X	.01

Within the same industry, firms with slightly different product mixes and/or operating characteristics might earn competitive returns on assets through skillful compensations for deficiencies in margin or turnover. For example, take two jewelers who differ in the type of merchandise they offer for sale. Jeweler A deals in expensive jewelry, watches, and precious stones; Jeweler B specializes in costume jewelry. Jeweler A might have a higher margin but lower turnover than B, but both may enjoy equal returns on assets. Thus:

	Return on Assets	=	Turnover	X	Margin
Jeweler A	.15	=	.5	X	.30
Jeweler B	.15	=	1.0	X	.15

In sum, the productivity of total funds provided the firm is the product of the management's ability to (1) generate sales and revenues in relation to this package of funds or its intensity of utilization of assets, and (2) increase the profitability that results from each dollar of sales created.

In our hypothetical company, the return on assets is broken down as follows:

$$\text{Return on assets } (R) = \text{Turnover } (T) \qquad \times \qquad \text{Margin } (M) \qquad (9.1)$$

$$R \quad = \quad T \quad \times \quad M$$

$$.24 \quad = \quad \frac{100}{50} \quad \times \quad \frac{12}{100}$$

$$.24 \quad = \quad 2 \quad \times \quad .12$$

So far, so good. But we have sidestepped taxes and distinctions in the sources of financing.

Earnings and the Role of Financing

The sources of funds available to firms are numerous. In the main, they are either borrowed money or equity funds. Some borrowed money is essentially cost-free—for instance, tax and wage accruals, and trade credit paid on time. Other borrowed money, such as bank loans and bond issues, has a readily identifiable dollar interest cost. Equity funds have explicit and implicit costs. The most readily identifiable explicit cost of equity money is the dividend paid. Of course, we know by now that shareholders expect capital gains in addition to dividends when they purchase common shares. However, capital gains must be thought of more as an implicit cost of equity money. For the time being at least, it may help to think of the requirements of those who provide equity money as stated in the form of an earnings return per dollar of equity capital employed by the firm.

DEBT FINANCING AND EARNINGS

Among the many reasons for debt financing, the most important is the leverage provided to common shareholders. In Chapter 5 the notion of financial risk or financial leverage taught us a simple axiom: If you can earn more on borrowed money than you have to pay for it, you come out ahead—provided that you borrow within prudent limits. If you borrow money from your banker at 10 percent and place the funds in another bank to earn 5 percent interest on a savings account, your road to ruin is assured. It would be far better if you had the same deal at a 4 percent cost of borrowing.

The *productivity* of funds was called *return on assets*. The *cost* of borrowed funds is called the *effective interest rate:*

$$\text{Effective interest rate } (I) = \frac{\text{Interest expense}}{\text{Total liabilities}} \qquad (9.2)$$

$$= \frac{2}{25} = 8\%$$

The firm in our example has total liabilities of $25 million. The company may have $5 million in debts with no explicit interest cost and a $20 million bond issue outstanding that bears a rate of interest of 10 percent. The weighted-average or "effective" cost of borrowed money is, thus, 8 percent, since some debt bears no direct cost and the remainder costs 10 percent (0% × $5 million + 10% × $20 million = $2/$25 million = 8%).

Relating the return on assets to the effective cost of funds indicates whether the firm is able to earn more than its direct cost of borrowing funds. Now, let us relate the productivity of borrowed funds to their effective cost:

Benefits of borrowed money = Return on assets − Effective interest rate

or

Benefits of borrowed money = $R - I$

In our example:

$$R - I = .24 - .08 = .16, \text{ or } 16\%$$

The borrowing of money at a fixed cost and the use of these funds to earn a return on assets is known as employing *leverage*. Leverage can also be employed with preferred stock or any form of fixed-cost financing. As long as $R - I$ is a positive difference, leverage is being used to the firm's advantage. The importance of maximizing the difference between R and I is obvious. The necessity to avoid $R < I$ is equally apparent. Less obvious, however, is a reasonable answer to a simple question: If a firm enjoys a positive difference of $R - I$, why not push the mix of total funds acquired to the maximum limit of debt funds and minimize the financing that is done through equity sources? More simply, if you can borrow funds at an effective cost of 8 percent and earn 24 percent on money, why not borrow as much as you possibly can in order to enhance the return on your own funds (equity)?

First, as borrowed funds increase relative to equity funds in the total financing mix, borrowing costs (I) increase, and increase more rapidly than the amounts borrowed. For example, increasing debt funds from $25 million to $30 million (+20 percent) could result in an increase in interest on the additional $5 million to 15 percent from the prior rate of 10 percent (+50 percent). Thus, while $R = 24\%$, the difference $(R - I)$ will shrink. The reason the rate of interest would rise is that creditors are now providing relatively more funds than are owners (equity), and therefore, proportionately more of the risks of the business are being shouldered by the creditors. Creditors will require greater compensation in the form of higher interest rates (and perhaps controls over the business—an indirect cost).

Second, when the cost of debt financing rises—directly and indirectly—so will the cost of equity funds. The employment of leverage causes the *quantity* of earnings available to the owners to increase whenever leverage is employed successfully ($R > I$). However, as more debt is employed relative to equity funds, the *quality* of earnings can deteriorate.

Table 9-1 shows the return on shareholders' equity at book value as the result of differing rates of return on assets and capital structures (L/E). The assumption in the table is that debt costs 5 percent (I), and taxes on income are ignored.

TABLE 9-1
PERCENTAGE RETURNS FOR SHAREHOLDERS UNDER
ALTERNATIVE CAPITAL STRUCTURES*

Percent Rate of Return on Assets (R)	Liability/Equity Ratio (L/E)			
	0	½	1	2
−4	−4	−8	−13	−22
0	0	−2	−5	−10
4	4	3	3	2
5	5	5	5	5
7	7	8	9	11
9	9	11	13	17
10	10	12	15	20

*Assumes 5 percent interest rate (*i*) on debt.

EXAMPLE:

$$\text{Assume } L/E = 2$$
$$\text{Rate of return on equity} = R + (R - I)L/E$$
$$= -4 + [(-4) - (+5)]2$$
$$= -4 + (-9)2$$
$$= -4 + (-18)$$
$$= -22$$

Note that when the return on assets equals the interest rate on borrowed funds (5 percent), the return to shareholders is independent of the degree of financial leverage—that is, L/E. On the other hand, if the rate of return on assets is greater than (less than) the interest rate, the stockholders' percentage return is increased (decreased) by leverage. Furthermore, the increased volatility of shareholder returns increases with the expansion of L/E, or the degree of financial leverage. Note that over the range of return on assets shown, the range of shareholder returns expands from the range (−4% to +10%) to (−22% to +20%) as we move from no leverage to a 2:1 ratio. This increase in variation or range can affect the P/E on the stock downward or increase the cost of equity capital. In addition, equity costs might increase, since the risk of bankruptcy is greater. With no leverage, a series of years of −4 percent returns on assets can injure a firm; however, with L/E of 2, a series of −4 percent returns on assets leads to −22 percent on equity and accelerates the risk of ruin to stockholders markedly.

The greater volatility of earnings (up *and* down) owing to increased leverage can, at certain levels of debt financing, cause the market to pay less per dollar of earnings.

Suppose the quantity of earnings is increased 10 percent owing to expanded leverage, but the market pays 15 percent less for the earnings because of their lower presumed quality or stability. In effect, the result is that a lower price per share of stock is experienced. Thus we might say that the cost of equity capital has increased along with the higher interest cost of debt. In other words, earnings before and after taxes might increase through the expansion of borrowed capital, but the market might pay less for these increased earnings owing to a perceived (real or imagined) deterioration in the stability (quality) of these earnings. Lower stock prices suggest that shareholders are really *worse* off because of additional borrowings!

Finally, while the difference between R and I is decreasing as more debt is raised, and the improved earnings are worth less to stockholders, the likelihood that R will remain constant or increase as funds employed expand is questionable. R itself may become progressively more difficult to maintain (or improve) as a firm gets larger.

If it were not for the relationships noted—(1) higher I, (2) higher cost of equity (lower share prices), and (3) strain on R—we would observe many more firms that we do with debt pushed as close as possible to 100 percent of total funds.

The proportions of debt and equity financing in the total mix of funds can be measured in a variety of ways.[2] We shall simply relate debt to equity as:

$$\text{Debt/Equity} = \frac{\text{Total liabilities}}{\text{Equity}}$$

In our example, total company funds come to $50 million. Debt represents $25 million and equity $25 million. Thus the debt-equity ratio is 25/25, or 1. Translated into words, this means that the firm has $1 of debt for each $1 of equity capital. Suppose the $50 million had been split between $32 million in debt and $18 million in equity. The debt-equity ratio would be 32/18, or 1.77:1—in words, $1.77 in debt for each $1 in equity. The higher the debt-equity ratio, the greater the leverage being employed, and conversely, the lower the equity funds in a relative sense. Thus, larger amounts of debt relative to equity funds leads to increased leverage, or "trading on the equity."

The difference between the return on assets and the effective interest rate on borrowed capital yielded a percentage amount. We were originally concerned with an ultimate explanation of earnings in dollar form. To convert back:

$$
\begin{aligned}
\text{EBT} &= (R)(A) - (I)(L) \\
&= (\text{EBIT/Assets})(\text{Assets}) - (\text{Interest/Liabilities})(\text{Liabilities}) \\
&= \text{EBIT} - \text{Interest}
\end{aligned}
\tag{9.3}
$$

where:

A = assets

L = total liabilities

$$
\begin{aligned}
\text{EBT} &= (.24)(\$50) - (.08)(\$25) \\
&= \$12 - 2 \\
&= \$10
\end{aligned}
$$

[2]Some authors use Debt/Total assets. This measure relates debt to total funds employed.

It is possible to recast Equation 9.3 to enable us to isolate and relate R, I, and L/E in the following manner: Since $A = L + E$ where E = equity, then

$$EBT = (R)(L + E) - (I)(L)$$

and simplifying yields

$$EBT = (RL) + (RE) - (IL)$$

To isolate $(R - I)$ and L/E, further simplification yields

$$EBT = (RE) + (RL) - (IL)$$
$$= (RE) + L(R - I)$$

Dividing each element on the right side of the equation by E while multiplying the entire right side by E maintains the integrity of the equation, so[3]

$$EBT = \left[\frac{RE}{E} + \frac{L(R - I)}{E}\right] E$$

$$= [R + (R - I)L/E]E$$

$$= [.24 + (.24 - .08)\, 25/25]\ \$25$$

$$= (.24 + 16)\ \$25$$

$$= (.40)\ \$25$$

$$= \$10$$

We can now appreciate not only the importance of $R - I$ but the magnification of the difference depending upon L/E. In our example, if total assets ($50) had been divided into debt = $40 and equity = $10, and $(R - I)$ remained unchanged (a questionable assumption), then:

$$EBT = [.24 + (.24 - .08)40/10]\ \$10$$

$$= [.24 + (.16)\, 4]\ \$10$$

$$= (.88)\$10$$

$$= \$8.8$$

With debt $40 and equity $10, EBT is only $8.8. With debt and equity each at $25, EBT was $10. However, if we relate EBT to equity (EBT/Equity), the answers are 8.8/10, or 88 percent, versus 10/25, or 40 percent. Stated in the latter form, we can visualize the point that when the difference $R - I$ is positive, larger values of L/E magnify the difference.

In sum, at this juncture we have been able to define earnings before taxes as follows:

$$EBT = [R + (R - I)L/E]E \tag{9.4}$$

[3]Consider the following: $1 + 2 = 3$. If we divide and multiply by say, 2, we get $(1/2 + 1)$, or $1\ 1/2 \times 2 = 3$.

EQUITY FINANCING AND EARNINGS

Most firms obtain equity financing from (1) the issuance of new shares, and/or (2) retention of earnings.

The issuance of stock occurs through a cash sale or through an exchange for shares in another firm. The effect of issuing new shares depends primarily upon the relationship of the sale price to the asset value of outstanding shares. Asset value is determined in the following manner:

$$\text{Asset value per share} = \frac{\text{Assets}}{\text{Number of common shares}}$$

In our example, 5 million shares are assumed to be outstanding. The value of assets is $50 million. The asset value per share of stock is $10 ($50/5).

To see the earnings effect of new shares, let us assume we sell 1 million new shares at either $15, or $10, or $5 per share:

	New Share Price		
	$15	*$10*	*$5*
(1) Old asset base	$50.00	$50.00	$50.00
(2) Proceeds from sale of new shares	$15.00	$10.00	$ 5.00
(3) New asset base	$65.00	$60.00	$55.00
(4) Rate of return on assets	.24	.24	.24
(5) New EBIT (3 × 4)	$15.60	$14.40	$13.20
(6) EBIT/New shares (new total shares = 6 million)	$ 2.60	$ 2.40	$ 2.20

This exercise suggests that whenever new shares can be sold at a price in excess of asset value per share, earnings can be improved on a per-share basis. Earnings fall only if new shares are sold below asset value and/or if profitability declines. The level of EBIT before the assumed common-stock financing was $12.0 million, and the EBIT per share was $2.40. Notice that EBIT per share remains at $2.40 if new shares are sold at $10, but sales below $10 result in lower earnings per share than before the new financing and new shares sold at prices above $10 bolster earnings per share.

Even though we have been discussing the sale of new shares for cash, the same type of analysis is applicable to a merger in which the book value of assets per share received by the acquiring company exceeds the book value of the assets per share given to the stockholders of the acquired company. Furthermore, asset value per share can also be increased by retiring shares at a discount from existing book value. For example, assume that our hypothetical firm with an asset value per share of $10 is able to repurchase some of its shares in the open market at a price of $8 per share. Suppose sufficient cash is available to repurchase 1 million shares ($8 million). The new asset value per share will be $50 million less $8 million in cash, divided by 4 million remaining shares, or $10.50. This is an increase of 5 percent ($.50/$10). The ability to sustain a rate of return on assets (R) of 24 percent would cause earnings to be $42 million times .24, or $10,080,000. On a per-share basis this is $2.52 ($10,080,000/4 million), or a rise of 5 percent from the previous level of $2.40, corresponding to the percentage increase in asset value per share.

It is vital to remember that these examples of selling or exchanging stock above asset values or redeeming shares below asset values will influence earnings as a function of the ability of the company to maintain the level of the rate of return on assets ($R = 24\%$).

The ability of the firm to maintain $R = 24\%$ is a prerequisite to improved earnings. This can occur under astute management, up to a point. If the ability to sustain (or improve) the return on assets (R) were possible regardless of the size of the firm (total assets), companies whose share prices exceeded asset values would find they could improve earnings per share almost without limit simply by selling more and more and more stock.

Earnings retention provides a basic source of earnings growth. Corporations in general tend to pay out about one-half their earnings. The amounts retained increase the asset base. Our example company had earnings per share of $1.20 and paid a dividend of $0.84 per share. We can say:

$$\text{Dividend payout rate} = \frac{\text{DPS}}{\text{EPS}} = \frac{\$0.84}{\$1.20} = 70\% \tag{9.5}$$

or, alternatively,

$$\text{Retention rate} = 1.00 - \text{Dividend payout (\%)} \tag{9.6}$$
$$= 1.00 - .70$$
$$= .30, \text{ or } 30\%$$

The company's total earnings after taxes of $6 million was split into $4.2 million paid out and $1.8 million retained. The $1.8 million retained adds to the equity base and the total asset base. The maintenance of a return on assets of 24 percent, other things being equal, would add $.432 million to EBIT in the following year:

$$\text{Growth in EBIT} = \text{Retention rate} \times \text{Return on assets}$$
$$= .30 \times .24 = .072 = 7.2\%$$

or

$$g = B \times R \tag{9.7}$$

where:

B = retention rate (%)

g = growth rate of EBIT

R = return on assets

Retention and earnings growth are, once again, dependent upon maintaining the rate of return on assets.

Effects of Taxes

Our discussion so far has been in terms of earnings before taxes. The effects of taxes on income can be accommodated in our model by making the following transformation:

$$EAT = (1 - T) [R + (R - I)L/E] E \qquad (9.8)$$

where:

$$T = \text{Effective tax rate} = \text{Tax expense/EBT}$$

The notion $(1 - T)$ is really indicating what percentage of each $1 of income is available after satisfying Uncle Sam and other taxing authorities. Should $T = 60$ percent, we would say that 40 cents of every dollar of income is available after taxes ($1.00 − $.60). The lower the tax rate, the higher the percentage of income left over, and vice versa. The difference between a tax rate and an "effective" tax rate lies in the fact that not all income to the firm is taxed at the same rate. Hence the effective tax rate is apt to be different from what the rate schedule shows for the level of EBT.

Moreover, as we learned in Chapter 8, the income reported for tax returns may be different from the income shown on the reports to shareholders. For example, a firm may have ordinary operating income of $7 million, subject to a tax rate of 50 percent. Additional income of $3 million may be subject to lower capital gains rates of, say, 25 percent. The effective tax *rate* is the total tax relative to the total income to be taxed, or $4.25/$10, or 42.5 percent. Our example firm has an effective tax rate of

$$T = \text{Tax expense/EBT} = 4/10 = 40\% \qquad (9.9)$$

EAT in the example becomes

$$
\begin{aligned}
EAT &= (1 - T) [R + (R - I)L/E] E \\
&= (1 - .4) (\$10) \\
&= \$6
\end{aligned}
$$

Earnings and Dividends Per Share

To convert EAT to a per-share basis, we need only divide it by the number of common shares outstanding:

$$EPS = \frac{EAT}{\text{Number of shares outstanding}} \qquad (9.10)$$

In general, then, in terms of our total model,[4]

$$EPS = \frac{(1 - T) [R + (R - I) L/E] E}{\text{Number of common shares outstanding}} \qquad (9.11)$$

[4]This model and its enrichment are the result primarily of the work of Lerner and Carleton. See E. Lerner and W. T. Carleton, *A Theory of Financial Analysis* (New York: Harcourt Brace Jovanovich, 1966).

where:

EPS = earnings per share

T = effective tax rate (Tax expense/EBT)

B = retention rate [or $1 - $ (DPS/EPS)]

R = return on assets (EBIT/A)

I = effective interest rate (Interest expense/Liabilities)

L = total liabilities

E = equity

Dividends per share can be calculated as:

$$DPS = (1 - B)(EPS) \qquad\qquad (9.12)$$

The value of the model can now be appreciated in its fullest form. We can see that earnings per share and changes in earnings are a function of:

1. Utilization of asset base (turnover of assets)
2. Profit productivity of sales (margin on sales)
3. Effective cost of borrowed funds (effective interest rate)
4. Debt-equity ratio
5. Equity base
6. Effective tax rate

We have deliberately isolated the critical variables that determine earnings and in turn dividends. The final task we face is to (1) isolate how changes in specific variables affect earnings, and (2) examine the sustainability of each variable as a long-run influence upon earnings.

An Example: The Growth Company

Tables 9-2 and 9-3 show abbreviated financial statements for a company we have chosen to call the Growth Company. Table 9-4 is a summary of values for the key variables in our model for three years of data.[5]

The pattern of earnings over the three-year period indicates that earnings per share have grown 18 percent per year between 19X1 and 19X3. An impressive rate of growth indeed! The big question is, Is the growth rate transitory or is it sustainable? For example, has the growth been achieved through profitability rather than shifts in funds sources? The latter is not sustainable, while the former usually is. Let us take a closer look.

The return on assets has steadily improved, year to year. The primary source is improved profit margins in the face of slower asset turnover and almost stagnant sales. Such a profit-margin improvement is a healthy sign.

[5]The reader is invited to calculate several of the values in Table 9-4 to assure understanding of earlier materials.

TABLE 9-2

THE GROWTH COMPANY: INCOME STATEMENTS FOR THE YEARS
ENDED DEC. 31, 19X1-19X3 (MILLIONS OF DOLLARS)

	19X1	19X2	19X3
Net sales	$117.0	$117.0	$116.0
Other income	1.0		3.2
Cost of sales	105.0	103.0	105.0
Earnings before interest and taxes	13.0	14.0	14.2
Interest expense	.5	.4	1.1
Earnings before taxes	12.5	13.6	13.1
Taxes	6.0	6.0	5.0
Earnings after taxes	6.5	7.6	8.1
Average shares outstanding (millions)	5.6	5.5	5.0
Earnings per share	$1.16	$1.38	$1.63
Dividends per share	.58	.65	.75

TABLE 9-3

THE GROWTH COMPANY: POSITION STATEMENT (ABBREVIATED),
DECEMBER 31, 19X1-19X3 (MILLIONS OF DOLLARS)

	19X1	19X2	19X3
Total assets	$103	$105	$103
Current debt	21	21	21
Long-term debt	9	8	17
Common-stock equity	73	76	65
Total debt and equity	103	105	103

TABLE 9-4

THE GROWTH COMPANY: SUMMARY DATA ON KEY FINANCIAL
VARIABLES, 19X1-19X3

Variable	19X1	19X2	19X3
Dividends per share	.580	.650	.750
Earnings per share	1.160	1.380	1.630
Return on assets:	.126	.133	.138
Margin	.111	.120	.122
Turnover	1.136	1.114	1.126
Effective interest rate	.017	.014	.029
Total liabilities/equity	.410	.380	.580
Equity ($ millions)	73.000	76.000	65.000
Number of shares (millions)	5.600	5.500	5.000
Effective tax rate	.480	.440	.380
Retention rate	.500	.530	.540

Increasing use has been made of debt financing relative to equity (although the retention rate on earnings has moved upward to increase the equity base). The upward movement of the effective rate of interest on borrowed funds shows the following changes in the spread between the return on assets and the effective interest rate $(R - I)$: 19X1, .109; 19X2, .119; 19X3, .109. In effect, increased return on assets between 19X1 and 19X3 (.126 to .138) has been negated by rising debt financing and the associated interest cost. The leverage provided (L/E) has increased. This makes the product $[(R - I)L/E]$ greater in 19X3 than in 19X1. The significance, however, is that earnings are more vulnerable to decline. The relatively fixed nature of I and the possible erosion of R is the key here!

Pre-tax earnings have been taxed at lower effective rates over time. What are the reasons? Is some revenue taxed at capital gains rates? Have differences occurred between reporting to shareholders and to the tax authorities? In general, lower effective rates of taxation, whatever the source, are not sustainable.

Increases in after-tax earnings per share are, in large measure, the result of a dwindling number of outstanding shares. The company could be buying back its own shares. Is it possible that reduced equity is being achieved by increasing debt to take its place?

The possibilities with respect to detailed analysis can be extended. We do not suggest that this company deliberately manipulated earnings. The point is that not all sources of improvement in earnings per share are desirable and/or sustainable. Mere earnings growth should not impress an analyst. The anatomy of earnings growth is the key!

Forecasting via the Earnings Model

Our emphasis thus far in the presentation of the ROI method has been to view it as a device for analyzing the effects of and interaction between the return a firm earns on its assets and the manner in which it is financed. However, this analytical device can be used as a forecasting tool. Once the analyst understands the inner workings of the firm's earnings-formation process, he can forecast the key variables, substitute the values into the model, and forecast EAT for the next period.

For example, assume that a firm's tax bracket is forecast to be 50 percent in 19X4, that 15 percent will be earned on its assets, and that it will pay an effective interest rate of 6 percent. Further assume that the firm will have $100 million of equity and $100 million of debt in its capital structure in 19X4. Then, if we substitute these values into the model, $EAT = (1 - T) [R + (R - I)L/E] E$, its forecast EAT will be as follows:

$$EAT = (1 - .5) [.15 + (.15 - .06)100/100] \$100$$
$$= .5 [.15 + (.09)1] 100$$
$$= .5 [.24] 100$$
$$= \$12$$

We can then subtract any forecast preferred dividends that will be paid, and divide the remainder by the projected number of outstanding common shares to arrive at EPS. This can then be multiplied by the projected P/E ratio to get the projected price. To continue our example, if our firm is expected to have 3 million shares outstanding and a P/E of 15 in 19X4, then EPS will be forecast at $4 ($12 million/3 million) and the price per common share at $60 (15 × $4). This can be translated to HPY by subtracting the beginning per-share price, adding dividends paid in 19X4, and dividing by the beginning price. If the price at the end of 19X3 is $50 and no dividends are expected during 19X4, then the projected HPY for 19X4 is 20 percent $[(60 - 50)/50]$.

Market Share-Profit Margin Approach

The market share/profit margin approach emanates directly from the industry analysis. Once the industry forecast of market shares is completed, the analyst must next decide which firms are likely to be dominant factors, pacesetters, in the industry. If an investor has his choice, he will undoubtedly select a leader rather than a follower. Thus the next logical step for the analyst is to determine what share of the industry's total market the firm under analysis can reasonably be expected to achieve.

If the industry is established and has a track record of performance and stability, the analyst can probably make good use of the historical shares of the market attained by the competing firms. Industries such as autos, steel, oil, and copper have well-entrenched member firms. In a slightly more dynamic industry, such as household appliances, the analyst must translate the ability and aggressiveness of management relative to the competition into a forecast of market share. However, in an evolving and somewhat unstable industry, with new firms entering and leaving the market—such as the fast-food franchising industry—the analyst's job is considerably more difficult, perhaps even impossible, using this approach. He must attempt to start with those firms that have begun to establish their permanence in the industry; then he has at least a point of reference from which to depart. He can then subjectively determine the relative strengths and weaknesses of the firm's most pressing competition. These subjective options can be translated into estimates of the probable share of the market to be attained by both the firm under analysis and the competition.

Assume that the analyst is studying an industry that produces auxiliary swimming-pool equipment—items such as lounge chairs, pads, and beach umbrellas. Industry sales for 19X2 are $10 million, and the Danes Co. captured 10 percent of this market in 19X2, or $1 million in sales. The analyst forecasts a 20 percent increase in 19X3 sales for the industry because of a more favorable economic climate for leisure-time products. If he expects Danes Co. to increase its market share to 12 percent because of an aggressive campaign, what would its projected sales be? Industry sales will be $10 million plus the 19X3 increase of 20 percent ($2 million), for a total of $12 million. Danes Co. share is 12 percent; therefore, its sales will be 12 percent of $12 million, or $1.44 million.

With an estimate of sales for the company for the ensuing year, the analyst must next determine the most likely profit margin this firm can earn, given its manufacturing capacity, its total resources, and its projected level of sales. We define net-income profit margin as net income after taxes, divided by sales.[6]

The analyst must calculate the most likely net-income margin the firm is likely to achieve on each category of sales revenue. In the case of a predominantly one-product firm, the analyst multiplies the sales figure by the net-income margin to get the firm's

[6]Throughout the ensuing discussion and text, we use the terms *net-income margin, net-income profit margin,* and *profit margin* interchangeably.

profit from the predominating product.[7] For a multi-product firm, the analyst multiplies the sales of each division by the appropriate profit margin to obtain the various divisions' earnings, totals these, and arrives at the firm's total earnings. These earnings are then divided by the number of common shares outstanding (after deducting any preferred dividends), to get earnings per share.

EXAMPLE 1.   Danes's sales forecast for 19X3 is $1,440,000. If its net-income margin is forecast to be 5 percent and there are 100,000 shares of common outstanding, what would projected EPS be?[8]

1. Multiply projected sales by the projected margin to get total earnings.
$1,440,000 × 5% = $72,000
2. Divide earnings by common shares outstanding (Danes has no preferred stocks).
$72,000 ÷ 100,000 = $.72/share

Then the EPS is multiplied by the forecast P/E ratio to get the forecast price. The price at the beginning of the period is subtracted from the ending price to calculate the price change for the period. Then the annual dividend is added to the price change, and the sum is divided by the beginning price to calculate the holding-period yield.

EXAMPLE 2.   If the P/E for the end of 19X3 is projected to be 20 and the price at the end of 19X2 was $10, what is the HPY for Danes Co.? Assume that a $.10 annual dividend is paid.

1. Multiply EPS by P/E. $.72 × 20 = $14.40
2. Subtract the beginning price from the ending price. $14.40 − $10.00 = $4.40 price change
3. Add dividend to price change and divide by beginning price.
$$\frac{\$4.40 + \$.10}{\$10} = \frac{\$4.50}{\$10} = 45\% \text{ HPY}$$

This approach involves forecasting only a few key variables, which are easier to get a handle on than the inputs required by the other traditional approaches, and thus it represents a realistic and practical method of forecasting. One last point is perhaps in order before proceeding.

Profit margins are apt to vary little over a very limited range of sales and operating capacity; however, they can vary drastically once the range of possible sales and capacity outcomes is broadened. In order to calculate a useful profit margin (for the relevant range), the analyst must understand the makeup and behavior of prices and costs of the firm in question. We refer, of course, to the relative importance to the firm of *fixed and variable cost.* In other words, we need first to appreciate the degree of operating leverage (the size of the fixed costs) the firm is employing before we can properly relate this

---

[7]The portion of sales arising from the other products of the firm, which are relatively unimportant compared to the predominant product, is often calculated merely by assuming a growth rate in the level of sales arising from these other products. This sales figure is multiplied by the appropriate profit margin, and this profit is added to the profit calculated above to arrive at the firm's total profit.

[8]Usually, estimates of net-income margins are based upon historical performance. If any changes in the mode of operation or market conditions have occurred, the analyst modifies the historical margins to incorporate these changes. The 5 percent figure for Danes reflects this procedure.

information to sales and capacity figures. To facilitate this understanding, analysts frequently employ breakeven analysis and the adjunct breakeven chart.

Breakeven Analysis

A central concept in the breakeven analysis is the breakeven point. The breakeven point is a sales level at which total revenues equal total costs. To state the matter in its simplest form, a firm's total costs are made up of fixed costs plus linear variable costs. Fixed costs—for example, rent—are constant over large ranges of output over a finite time period.[9] Note in Figure 9-2, for example, that when total costs hit the y-axis, variable costs—for example, materials—vary directly in proportion to output. The more items produced, the more variable costs increase. The aspect of breakeven analysis with which we are concerned here is the effect of high fixed costs versus low fixed costs on a company's profit margin, and how the profit margin changes about the breakeven point (level of sales).[10]

Figure 9-2 is a graphical depiction of a high-fixed-cost company; Figure 9-3, of a low-fixed-cost company. Observe that the breakeven point (in units) is higher for the high-fixed-cost company than for the low-fixed-cost company. This is the general case. The high-fixed-cost company might be characterized as more capital-intensive (using larger amounts of equipment and machinery) than the low-fixed company.

FIGURE 9-2
BREAKEVEN POINT OF A HIGH-FIXED-COST COMPANY

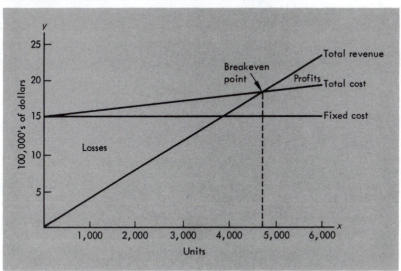

[9]All costs, given some wide dimensions, will be variable. Costs are fixed only over some "relevant" range.

[10]For the mechanics of breakeven analysis as used in an accounting sense, see James C. Van Horne, *Financial Management and Policy* (Englewood Cliffs, N.J.: Prentice-Hall, 1977), pp. 718-25.

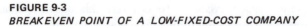

FIGURE 9-3
BREAKEVEN POINT OF A LOW-FIXED-COST COMPANY

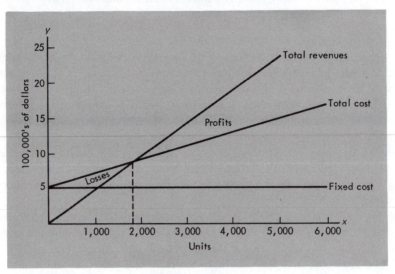

Generally, when a firm has high fixed costs, it also has lower variable costs. The significance of this fact can be seen by examining Figure 9-2. Below the breakeven point, large losses are sustained, and above the breakeven point, large profits are achieved. The losses get larger as the sales volume falls significantly below the breakeven point. Conversely, the profits get larger as sales move further and further above the breakeven point. Graphically, this is depicted by the vertical distance between the total-revenue line and the total-cost line. This situation differs in degree rather than kind when one views the low-fixed-cost company illustrated in Figure 9-3.

Generally, when a firm has lower fixed costs, it has higher variable costs. Thus, while profits increase as sales move above the breakeven point and losses increase as sales fall below the breakeven point, the rate of increased profits and losses is substantially less than the rate for the high-fixed-cost company. In other words, profits and losses "explode" more rapidly in the case of the high-fixed-cost company than in the case of the low-fixed-cost company.

So we can see the importance that an analyst properly perceive (1) the type of firm (high or low fixed costs) he is analyzing, and (2) the level of sales volume the firm is likely to achieve during the forecast period; for these factors will greatly influence the net-income profit margin the firm will achieve. This problem becomes particularly acute as the projected sales volume of the firm approaches its breakeven point. A slight error in estimation in this region can have radical consequences for the success of investing in the firm's shares. This kind of analysis is helpful in determining the return on assets, R, if the analyst is using the earnings model discussed earlier in this chapter.

A breakeven chart for hotels and motels is illustrated in Figure 9-4. A room occupancy of 60.5 percent is required to cover both fixed and variable expenses. Most operating expenses, as well as rent, are semivariable in nature, so the fixed portion of those

FIGURE 9-4
BREAKEVEN ANALYSIS OF ALL HOTELS AND MOTELS

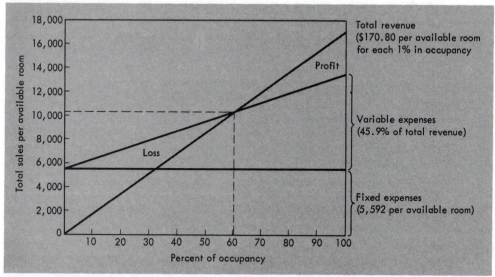

SOURCE: *U.S. Lodging Industry,* 1976 (Philadelphia: Laventhal & Horwith, 1977).

expenses is added to fixed charges which do not vary with changes in occupancy. Thus, at an occupancy level of 60.5 percent, total revenue would be $10,333 per available room ($170.80 × 60.5). Total expenses would include $5,592 in fixed expenses and $4,741 in variable expenses ($10,333 × .459). Thus, revenues of $10,333 and total expenses of $10,333 leaves zero profit at 60.5 percent of occupancy.

Independent Forecasts of Revenue and Expenses

The ROI method skirts the issue of specifically forecasting various categories of income and expenses. The approach we will discuss in this section differs on that score.

The independent forecasting of revenues and expenses, sometimes called the "scientific" method,[11] directly confronts the problem just outlined. The technique generally follows one of two main routes. The first and more specific approach is to forecast each and every revenue and expense item separately. For example, the analyst would separately forecast the sales of each division and each product line of the company, as well as each of the major expense items appearing on the firm's income statement. The advantage of this approach is that it forces the analyst to become intimately familiar with the inner workings of the business—both manufacturing operations and sales and administrative operations. The main disadvantage of this method is that for a company of any size, it is an extremely time-consuming and often tedious procedure; further-

[11] This term is attributed to Benjamin Graham, David L. Dodd, and Sidney Cottle, in *Security Analysis* (New York: McGraw-Hill, 1962), p. 463.

more, there is always the danger that the analyst may become so involved with the detail that he misses some broader, but very fundamental, points of interest.

The second route is to take a broader-brush approach to the forecasting problem. Here the analyst hopes to overcome the pitfalls of the "scientific" method by analyzing the forecasting category totals rather than all the individual components. For example, he would look at the sales of the various divisions as totals, rather than attempting to forecast the sales of all the individual product lines of each division. He would forecast broad categories of expenses, such as administrative and sales expenses, rather than attempting to break these down finely into categories such as salaries, rent, and insurance. The advantage of this approach is that it avoids most of the problems of the scientific approach and is more efficient. Also, it is perhaps more accurate per unit of time spent on the forecast, because generally there are over-and-under estimates of individual components that may be misleading when looked at separately, but that cancel out when they are added together.

When the analyst has completed his forecast of revenues and expenses by using either the specific or the broad approach just outlined, he merely subtracts expenses from the revenues, and he has his forecast of earnings. Then he determines the number of common shares that will be outstanding in the forecast period, and divides it into the forecast earnings (after deducting any preferred dividends) to get earnings per share. Next, the analyst would multiply this earnings-per-share figure by the estimated P/E ratio in order to arrive at his best estimate of price. Then he would subtract the price at the beginning of the period, add dividends, and divide by the beginning price to calculate the HPY.

EXAMPLE.   Kniffen Co. sales consist of two main divisions, one producing lounge chairs and pads, the other beach umbrellas and various other miscellaneous items. Our estimates call for $1.2 million in revenue from the lounge division and $240,000 from the umbrella division. These figures are based on advance orders and projected sales to new resort hotels and motels, as well as anticipated replacement orders. Manufacturing expenses are about 70 percent of total revenues; sales and administrative expenses and taxes are 25 percent of sales revenue. The other pertinent information about Kniffen is as previously noted. What is the projected HPY?

Revenues:	Lounge division	$1,200,000	
	Umbrella division	240,000	
	Total revenue		$1,440,000
Expenses:	Manufacturing	1,008,000	
	S&A	360,000	
	Total expenses		$1,368,000
	Net earnings		$ 72,000

As previously, EPS = $.72, and HPY = 45 percent.

The three approaches we have discussed represent the main lines and methodology traditionally employed by security analysts when performing a company analysis. These main approaches are not mutually exclusive; they are often combined and used to complement each other. Despite the fact that they have been used with much success by many analysts for some time now, it should be pointed out that they all possess some shortcomings. They are based to a large extent on subjective evaluations made at various stages of the analysis by the analyst or investor, and quite frequently involve his estimate of the most likely figure.

In statistics, this type of estimate, which attempts to zero in on *one* number, is called a *point estimate*. For example, a weatherman might estimate that the temperature will reach a high of 72° tomorrow; in this case, 72° is a point estimate. When these point estimates are made in security analysis, there is generally no formal statement about their reliability. That is, the reader of such a report does not know how accurate the analyst himself thinks the forecast may be, or, for that matter, how accurate the analyst thinks will be any of a range of point estimates he may have forecast. In addition, the output generated from such traditional analysis is usually not directly usable in modern portfolio analysis. The approaches to be presented in the next chapter represent newer techniques that have been applied in the field of security analysis in an attempt to overcome these shortcomings.

Earnings-Model Projection for McDonald's

The starting point for the application of the earnings model to any company is to understand the relationships among the key variables for the particular firm. As an example we will look in depth at McDonald's Corporation. McDonald's is the largest food service organization in the world. The company was founded in 1955 by Ray A. Kroc, who bought the rights to franchise the name and operating practices of a limited-menu, quick-service restaurant in San Bernardino, California, owned by two brothers, Richard and Maurice McDonald.

Of the nation's retailing organizations, McDonald's ranks first in profit margins and sixth in return on stockholder's equity. No McDonald's store in the United States has ever been closed because of poor profitability. The name "McDonald's" is among the most widely advertised brand names in the world. The chain has, since its inception, sold nearly 35 billion hamburgers. In a typical month over 50 percent of all Americans eat at a McDonald's restaurant at least once.

McDonald's Corporation usually participates in the operation of the chain's restaurants by operating the units itself or by franchising them to independent operators. In both cases, McDonald's usually controls the land and building in which the store operates, either by leasing the facility from a third party or by owning the property and building outright. For the most part, the company buys the land on which the stores are to be located, except in the case of shopping center locations or those in urban areas where the land is not for sale. The company's ownership of sites has gradually increased as a percentage of the total in recent years.

In addition to selecting the site, McDonald's has responsibility for training the franchisee and members of his management staff and conducts periodic inspections to ensure that the franchisee is fulfilling the operating requirements of the license. Franchising agreements call for the prospective franchisee to pay the company an initial fee ($12,500 plus a refundable security deposit of $15,000) for the right to conduct business for 20 years at a site selected and specified by the company, and in a building which the company has had built. Normally, the franchisee must have access to $280,000 in cash, of which only half may be borrowed. The franchisee then pays McDonald's a royalty fee of 3 percent of sales for the life of the franchising agreement, plus a rental to McDonald's of 8.5 percent of sales. In addition, he is required to contribute 4 1/4 percent of sales to a cooperative advertising fund (3 percent spent locally and 1 1/4 percent for network television).

McDonald's does not sell either supplies or equipment to franchisees. It does, however, exercise the right to approve suppliers to franchisees. In practice, virtually all franchisees and company-operated stores buy supplies and equipment from a very limited number of suppliers. Keystone Foods supplies hamburger meat to 45 percent of the domestic McDonald's stores. In addition, the Coca-Cola Company or its bottlers supply soft-drink syrup to McDonald's stores.

A good starting point for this analysis is to examine historical data. Table 9-5 contains this key financial data for McDonald's (MCD) for the period 1971-80. Table 9-6 contains the key variables for the earnings analysis for the 1977-80 period. The

TABLE 9-5

FINANCIAL DATA, McDONALD'S, 1971-1980

(MILLIONS OF DOLLARS, EXCEPT WHERE NOTED)

	1980	1979	1978	1977	1976	1975	1974	1973	1972	1971
Sales	2,184.3	1,911.9	1,643.5	1,384.2	1,156.4	926.4	715.1	583.5	379.5	274.6
EBIT	505.0	427.4	381.8	326.2	259.6	209.9	161.6	112.1	75.4	56.6
Interest	102.4	82.9	69.0	59.4	42.3	38.0	26.2	10.7	6.1	8.7
EBT	402.6	344.5	312.8	266.8	217.2	171.9	135.3	101.4	69.3	47.9
Taxes	181.7	155.9	150.2	130.1	107.2	85.0	67.9	49.4	33.1	22.1
EAT	220.9	188.6	162.7	136.7	110.0	86.9	67.4	52.0	36.2	25.8
Number of shares	40.1	40.2	40.5	40.4	40.5	40.0	39.7	39.5	38.7	37.5
EPS (dollars)	5.48	4.68	4.00	3.37	2.72	2.17	1.70	1.31	.93	.69
DPS (dollars)	.74	.51	.32	.18	.08	0	0	0	0	0
Assets	2,643	2,654	1,953	1,645	1,284	1,069	853	624	422	319
Liabilities	1,502	1,402	1,157	1,002	759	655	522	363	223	186
Equity	1,141	952	796	643	525	414	331	261	199	133

TABLE 9-6

EARNINGS ANALYSIS, McDONALD'S, 1977-1980

	1977	1978	1979	1980	Average 1977-80
DPS	$.17	$.32	$.51	$.74	
EPS	$3.37	$4.00	$4.68	$5.49	
Payout rate	4.4%	8.0%	10.9%	13.5%	13.5%
Tax rate	48.8%	48.0%	45.3%	45.1%	47.0%
Return on assets	19.8%	19.6%	18.1%	19.1%	19.2%
Profit margin	23.6%	23.2%	22.2%	23.1%	23.0%
Asset turnover	.84	.84	.81	.83	.83
Interest rate	5.92%	5.96%	5.91%	6.82%	6.0%
Debt/equity	1.56	1.45	1.47	1.32	1.45
Equity (millions)	$643	$796	$952	$1141	
Number of shares (millions)	40.4	40.5	40.2	40.1	40.0
Return on equity	21.26%	20.44%	19.81%	19.36%	
Book value per share	$15.91	$19.66	$23.69	$28.42	

extreme right-hand column of Table 9-6 contains the average value for the variables for the 1977-80 period. Since these basic economic relationships are slow to change unless management by specific design takes steps to bring about a change, we will assume, for purposes of illustration, that those average values for 1977-80 persisted in 1981. However, we will use the 1980 value of the dividend payout on the assumption that it seems to be uptrending.[12]

Thus, an estimate for 1981 is

$$EAT = (1 - .47)[.192 + (.192 - .06)1.45]\$1141$$
$$= .53[.192 + (.132)1.45]\$1141$$
$$= .53[427]$$
$$= \$232$$

Using a forecast of 40 million common shares outstanding in 1981 yields a forecast EPS of $5.80. Assuming a P/E of 10, a beginning price of 49, and a forecast dividend of $1.00 yields a return of 20 percent, which is calculated as follows:

$$HPY = \frac{10(\$5.80) - \$49.00 + \$1.00}{\$49.00} = 20\%$$

This represents a point estimate of **HPY**, and based on this the analyst or investor would determine whether an investment in **MCD** is warranted.

The fact that the ROI approach forces the analyst to become very close to the inner workings of the company is a decided disadvantage as well as an advantage, since it involves forecasting a number of key ratios and variables, which is very difficult to do. Thus, although in theory ROI is a very nice, neat approach, in practice it is a difficult one to implement with high degree of accuracy.

Independent Forecast of Revenue and Expenses for McDonald's

Reduced volume growth and eroding operating margins slowed the rate of income gained for McDonald's in recent years. At the same time, however, nonoperating factors eased the negative impact of these trends; therefore, net income advanced more rapidly than revenues. Assumptions underlying near-term estimates for volume growth, operating profitability, and nonoperating factors must be examined in detail.

Revenue Projections

McDonald's revenue growth is expected to slow further in 1981 and 1982, with total volume approximating $2.52 billion and $2.84 billion, respectively, in those years. The primary determinants of near-term volume progress will remain the addition of

[12]For the time being, we ask the reader to go along with our assumption of a P/E of 10 and a dividend of $1.00 for 1981, so that we can illustrate the HPY calculation for a one-year holding period, which is calculated one year forward from the time McDonald's is selling at 49. In Chapter 10 we will discuss procedures for arriving at an estimate of P/E and dividends per share.

units, trends in revenue per outlet, and a continuing shift in the mix of the company's business.

The total number of units in operation moved up at a steadily declining rate during recent years. In 1980 the company added 516 stores; at year-end the number of units in operation was 6,263, 9 percent above the prior-year-end total. The rate of expansion should continue to ebb gradually in 1981 and 1982, with just over 500 outlets constructed in each year and the mix of new stores weighted more heavily toward affiliated and franchised outlets than toward company-operated units.

Total system volume from company-owned stores, franchises, and affiliates reached $6.2 billion in 1980. This 15 percent advance consisted of physical growth of 9 percent and an increase in revenue per store of 6 percent. Increased revenue per outlet was a combination of a 10 percent rise in prices and a 4 percent decline in real volume. Depending on the rate of cost inflation, the pace of price increase may slow somewhat in the near future. Revenue per store, however, may stabilize in 1981 and move up at a more rapid pace in 1982 as a reduced rate of deterioration of real volume per unit results from an improving economic environment. Nevertheless, year-to-year real-volume-per-store comparisons are expected to remain negative in both 1981 and 1982. The growth and structural trends of food-away-from-home demand are projected to remain unfavorable. The total number of fast-food units, including McDonald's outlets in operation, is expected to continue to rise more rapidly than industry receipts excluding inflation. A slowing rate of physical expansion for the McDonald's chain may be about offset by improving per-unit volume gains, permitting estimated total sales to move up at a 15-16 percent annual pace in 1981 and 1982.

The pattern of relative growth anticipated for the different segments of McDonald's business will continue to reduce overall volume progress. Because company-operated units account for about three-fourths of sales, the slower expansion anticipated for this portion of the business is expected to hold corporate revenue gains below the rates of increase achieved by total system sales. Revenues are expected to reach $2.5 billion during 1981 and $2.8 billion in 1982 (about 12 to 13 percent growth per year).

Margin Trends

Since late 1977 operating costs have risen more rapidly than operating revenues for McDonald's. The impact of nonoperating income, operating costs, selling, general and administrative expense, interest outlays, and taxes on net profit margin in recent years shows management's reaction to slowing revenue growth and declining operating profitability.

The following trends have emerged. First, beginning in late 1977, operating cost patterns have had a negative impact on profitability trends. The factor of primary importance in this regard was the decline in the company's operating margin. The reasons operating cost inflation have exceeded revenue gains span the full spectrum of possibilities. These reasons include sharp decreases in real volume per unit; periodic jumps in wage costs, usually precipitated by changes in the minimum-wage law; steep short-term advances in raw material prices; and initiation of costly new marketing programs designed to support declining profitability at the franchise level. The message suggested by this pattern is that a shift in the competitive environment surrounding the domestic fast-food industry has made it impossible in recent years for these companies to fully offset operating cost advances through higher menu prices.

Second, the prevailing trend of decline in operating margins was reversed late in 1980. Franchise profitability continued to decline but overall the system achieved a rise in operating margin. This resulted from a significant decline in the number of units added, which, in turn, led to lower startup costs and reduced the deterioration of real volume per unit. Also, in response to sharply higher feed costs and the destruction of pasture by the summer 1980 drought, cattle were brought to market at younger-than-usual ages during the second half of 1980, pushing 1981 prices below level of a year earlier.

Successful strategy was employed by McDonald's management to offset deterioration of operating profitability and also to advance net income more rapidly than revenues, partly canceling the effect of the slowdown in volume gains. When the operating margin first began to decline in late 1977, interest expense and tax provisions dropped relative to revenues. When this strategy became unsustainable in 1980, substantial advances in nonoperating income early in the year and a significantly lower ratio of marketing expense to sales throughout the 12-month period kept the net income gain in excess of that for operating revenues.

Projected 1981 and 1982 Results

Table 9-7 summarizes a forecast of McDonald's 1981-82 income statement. Earnings-per-share growth is expected to slow from the late-1970 and 1980 rates of gain of 17 to 18 percent. The rate of revenue advance is expected to be lower than in the past, approximating 12 to 13 percent in the near term, with combined revenues reaching $2.5 billion and $2.8 billion in 1981 and 1982, respectively.

Continuing operating-profit pressures may ease somewhat in 1981-82. For the company-owned stores, the combination of (1) more moderate, although continuing, declines in real volume per unit, (2) failure to offset raw material cost inflation through menu price advances as beef quotations begin to move up again late in 1981 or in 1982, and (3) the increasing importance of the less profitable foreign units is expected to reduce full-year operating earnings relative to revenues. For franchised operations, equipment financing programs designed to maintain the expansion rate of the franchise network, and other efforts to provide support for franchises in foreign locations should continue to cut the extremely high operating margin. Not only have the franchised stores been subject to all of the negative pressures that McDonald's results reflected, but also combined service and advertising royalties paid to the parent company have moved up rapidly with revenues during the recent period of accelerated inflation. McDonald's is expected to continue to aid its franchises in order to permit continued growth of the network, perhaps the key determinant of profit progress and stability.

Despite continuing deterioration of operating profitability for both franchised and company-owned stores, combined operating earnings in 1981 and 1982 are expected to move up in line with overall revenues. This projection is based on the forecast differential

TABLE 9-7
McDONALD'S CORPORATION PROJECTED OPERATING RESULTS
(MILLIONS OF DOLLARS, EXCEPT PER SHARE DATA)

	1980*	1981 (est.)	Year-to-Year % Change	1982 (est.)	Year-to-Year % Change
Revenues					
Company-owned restaurants	$1,698	$1,915	12.8	$2,135	11.5
Franchised restaurants	487	569	16.8	662	16.3
Other	31	35	12.9	40	14.3
Total	2,215	2,519	13.7	2,837	12.6
Operating earnings					
Company-owned	281	330	17.4	365	10.6
Franchised	412	478	16.0	553	15.7
Other	31	35	12.9	40	14.3
Total	724	843	16.4	958	13.6
General, administrative, and selling expense	231	262	13.4	289	10.3
Interest expense	91	103	13.2	114	10.7
Pre-tax earnings	403	478	18.6	555	16.1
Taxes	182	218	19.8	153	16.0
Net income	221	260	17.6	302	16.1
Earnings per share	$5.49	$6.47	17.8	$7.52	16.2

*Actual.

in growth rates between the company and the franchised stores, with revenues of the highly profitable franchised operations growing more rapidly than those of the company-owned stores.

General, administrative, and selling expenses moved up on 8 percent in 1980 and declined significantly relative to revenues, primarily because of a cutback in the advertising as a percentage of sales. This reduction could be maintained without damage to traffic only if marketing outlays were decreased by all the major fast-food operators. Domestic media outlays for the five major fast-food companies moved down last year. Thus, margin benefits associated with a reduction in advertising outlays relative to revenues, such as those that substantially benefited 1980 margins, are anticipated once again in both 1981 and 1982.

Reported interest expense should move up at significantly reduced rates of increase during 1981-82 period. McDonald's avoided moving into the permanent debt market during the recent period of extremely high interest rates. As financing costs decline somewhat in the near future, expensive short-term borrowing can be replaced by permanent financing. Furthermore, internally generated funds will exceed fixed-asset spending for the first time in 1981.

The combined impact of volume and operating and nonoperating cost patterns is expected to permit an extension of the favorable pre-tax margin trend noticed initially in 1980. Thus, although per-share earnings are likely to move up at a gradually decreasing rate, growth of net income may continue to exceed that of revenues. Earnings per share in 1981 and 1982 are therefore estimated at $6.47 and $7.52, respectively.

Summary

In this chapter we have shown how company information can be used to calculate holding-period yields. Three traditional techniques for the forecasting of revenues and expenses were examined—the return-on-investment approach, the market-share-net-income-margin approach, and the so-called scientific approach. It was noted that all three yield point estimates, with no statement of their likelihood of occurrence. In the ensuing chapter, newer, more sophisticated techniques will be analyzed.

Questions and Problems

1. What is the relationship between industry analysis and company analysis?

2. Assume that the return on assets of J. G. Company is forecast to be 20 percent. The effective interest rate is forecast at 9 percent, the tax rate at 50 percent, and the capital structure is expected to be $10 million. If J. G. is financed with 70 percent equity and 30 percent debt, what will be your forecast of EAT?

3. What are the advantages and disadvantages of the ROI technique as a forecasting device?

4. What potential uses do you see for the ROI approach other than as a forecasting device?

5. Discuss the market-share-net-income-margin approach to company earnings analysis.

6. Allgent Corp. has two divisions. The A division captures 10 percent of industry sales, forecast to be $50 million. The B division will capture 30 percent of its industry's sales, which are expected to be $20 million. Allgent's A division has traditionally had a 5 percent net-income margin, and the B division has had an 8 percent net-income margin. Allgent has 300,000 shares of common outstanding, which sell at $30. If you require at least a 20 percent, one-year return, and you expect the P/E to be 10 next year, would you purchase Allgent common at this time based on your one-year forecast?

7. How would you go about forecasting a firm's market share and net-income margin a year in advance?

8. How would you go about forecasting the earnings of the local pizza shop via an independent forecast of revenues and expenses?

9. In analyzing any company using each of the three traditional approaches to company analysis, would you expect your forecasts of return to be the same under all the methods? Why, or why not?

10. Determine the sales composition of Textron, Inc., for the year 1981 from sources such as Standard & Poor's, Moody's, the *Value Line,* or the firm's annual report. What would you expect the revenues for the various divisions to be in 1982, based on 1981 figures and your prediction of economic and industry conditions during 1981?

11. Following are data for Patten Products (millions of dollars):

1983		Est. 1984	
Assets	$600	Revenues	$660
Liabilities		Operating exps.	594
Short-term (1989)	25	EBIT	66
8% Debentures	125	Interest	16
10% Bonds (1999)	50	EBT	50
Common stock ($5 par)	100	Taxes	20
Surplus	300	Dividends	5

a. Provide the following information for an analysis of earnings:
  (1) Asset turnover
  (2) Effective interest rate
  (3) Effective tax rate
  (4) Financial leverage (debt/equity)
  (5) Dividend payout rate
b. What growth rate of EBIT can be expected?

12. The following data pertain to the Souergrapes Corp.:

Shares outstanding (millions)	5.0
Effective tax rate	50%
Annual depreciation ($ millions)	$2.0
Total debt ($ millions)*	$60
Total stockholders' equity ($ millions)	$60
Last dividend (per share)	$.72
Rate of return on equity	15%
EBIT/assets	20%
Market price of stock ($)	$20
EAT/sales	12.5%
*Current liabilities	$ 6.0
10%, first-mortgage bonds (1985)	24.0
12%, Subordinated debenture bonds (2000)	30.0

a. What is the firm's implied growth rate of earnings? Do you think this rate is exceptional for firms in general? Why?
b. Suppose that the data above persist into the near future and investors require a rate of return (discount rate) on this stock of 13 percent. Is the stock a "bargain" in theory? Explain.
c. Suppose that $20 million in additional capital is to be raised and is evenly divided between 10 percent bonds and new shares sold at $20 per share. EBIT/assets continues at its present rate. What is the new earnings per share?

13. If a firm enjoys a positive difference between the rate of return on assets and the effective interest rate paid on borrowed funds, why shouldn't it push the mix of total funds acquired to the maximum limit of debt funds and minimize the financing that is done through equity sources?

14. In 1983 Scoville Corp. had assets of $600M, and EBIT of $90M on sales of $750M. In 1983 the company earned $3 per share and paid a dividend of $1.50. What rate of growth in EBIT is implied in these relationships?

15. Selected financial information for Texas Instruments, Inc. is shown below. Trace the sources of the change in earnings between 1979 and 1980.

Years Ended December 31	1980	1979
Millions of Dollars		
Net sales billed	$4,074.7	$3,224.1
Operating costs and expenses	3,656.0	2,904.8
Profit from operations	418.7	319.3
Other income (net)	4.6	8.9
Interest on loans	(44.3)	(19.5)
Income before provision for income taxes	379.0	308.7
Provision for income taxes	166.8	135.8
Net income	212.2	172.9
Earned per common share (average		
outstanding during year)	$9.22	$7.58
Cash dividends declared per common share	2.00	2.00
Common shares (average shares outstanding		
during year, in thousands)	23,021	22,799
Working capital	$ 327.9	$ 200.7
Property, plant and equipment (net)	1,097.4	812.5
Total assets	2,413.7	1,908.2
Long-term debt	211.7	17.6
Stockholders' equity	1,164.5	952.9

16. The following data were reported by Tektronix Corp. for fiscal 1977 and 1981. (All dollar figures in millions.)

	Fiscal 1977	Fiscal 1981
Total Assets	415.3	953.8
Net sales	455.0	1,061.8
Net income after taxes	44.0	80.2
Income taxes	31.8	52.2
Interest charges	4.1	25.3
Dividend payments	4.0	16.6
Total capital	313.9	703.6
Equity capital	274.1	557.5
Common shares (thousands)	17,675	18,574

a. From the data provided what are the sources of sustainable growth in earnings per share. Why are these sources of sustainable growth?

b. In analyzing the fiscal 1977 to fiscal 1981 trend in the data provided comment on your conclusions on possible opportunities and problems which may determine the Company's earnings per share growth during the next several years.

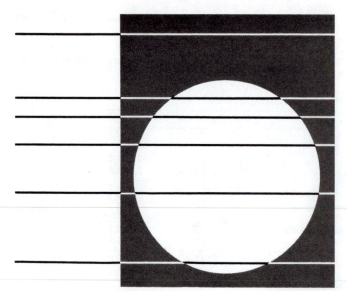

Company Analysis: Newer Approaches to Forecasting Earnings

In the preceding chapter we analyzed three traditional approaches to the fore-casting of company earnings and holding-period yield. We observed that each of these techniques yielded a single estimate of earnings and HPY. In effect, a probability of 100 percent is attached to the outcome.

However, analysts are seldom so certain of the infallibility of their forecasts. Furthermore, modern portfolio analysis requires that we forecast not only the *expected return* but also the *expected risk* of an investment. In this chapter we will present four modern techniques of analysis: regression analysis, trend analysis, decision-tree analysis, and simulation. Collectively, they attempt to overcome the weakness of, while building their conceptual foundations on, the more traditional tools. These techniques are appeal-ing for yet another reason—they are inherently useful, for they can be applied on a limited scale even by the investor who does not have a computer at his disposal.

We shall see that simulation, which can incorporate techniques such as trend and agression analysis, seems to be the superior technique in the areas of security and port-folio analysis. Simulation permits the analyst to uncover a distribution of alternative possible outcomes (returns) and their attendant risks that are associated with a particular investment opportunity. Let us now proceed with a discussion of these newer techniques of company analysis.

Regression and Correlation Analysis in Forecasting Revenues and Expenses

As explained in Chapter 7, regression analysis allows the user to examine the relationship between two variables in the case of simple linear regression, and the relationship of several variables in the case of multiple linear regression. Correlation analysis permits the user to test for the "goodness of fit" between these variables.[1] Many of the usages of regression analysis discussed earlier in conjunction with industry analysis can be translated to the company level. For example, many of the applications of regression analysis for end-use analysis and the regression on industry sales of economic variables such as GNP, disposable income, and indexes of industrial production can be adapted to company analysis by regressing the same variable against items such as company or division sales. Furthermore, experience may have taught the analyst certain relationships not only between external economic variables and company sales but also between internal company variables and external industry variables. Also, relationships may exist among industry, economic, and firm variables and company expenses. These relationships can then be used to build rather sophisticated systems of regression equations.

One advantage of using regression analysis in this way over the methods discussed in the preceding chapter is that the point estimates that are derived by this method are based on a somewhat rigorous statistical and economic foundation. Furthermore, the analyst is forced to think through the various problems of the company and the various complex interrelationships between internal and external variables and company revenues and expenses.[2] Another advantage over more traditional approaches is that correlation analysis permits the analyst to have a very specific measure of the explanatory power of the regression equation; and thus he has a means for assessing the reliability of his point estimates. Correlation analysis tells the analyst how well the independent variable "explains" the dependent variable in the regression equation.

Trend Analysis

In conjunction with regression analysis, the technique of trend analysis can also be very useful. Frequently, trend analysis of time series utilizes regression analysis. For the sake of simplicity, we differentiate the two by referring to regression analysis when we are studying the degree of correspondence between two "real" variables, and we speak of trend analysis when we examine the behavior of an economic series over time (times series). Thus, in the case of trend analysis, we are looking at only one "real" variable (such as earnings), which is being regressed over time—that is, over a period of years. This is how the name *trend analysis* evolved.

---

[1]The reader is urged to review the portions of Chapter 7 in which these techniques were introduced.

[2]In addition, it is possible that more stable, systematic relationships will be found between the company and some macroeconomic variable than will be found between the industry and the same macroeconomic variable.

Figure 10-1 illustrates trend analysis applied to a series of earnings per share of a company. The equation of the "fitted" straight line might then be used to forecast the next year's earnings. For example:

$$\text{Year } x \text{ EPS} = a + bx$$

where a and b have been calculated from the regression analysis and the underlying conditions will remain stable for the forecast period. Therefore, if 1967 = 1, 1968 = 2, 1969 = 3, and so on, the EPS for 1982 would be calculated as:

$$\text{Year } 15 = a + b(15)$$

Frequently analysts employ trend analysis by plotting the data on a special kind of graph paper, semilogarithmic or semilog paper, in order to reveal starkly different growth rates. The advantage of plotting the information on semilog paper as opposed to plotting on arithmetic graph paper can be seen by examining Figures 10-2 and 10-3.

FIGURE 10-1
TREND LINE FITTED TO EARNINGS PER SHARE

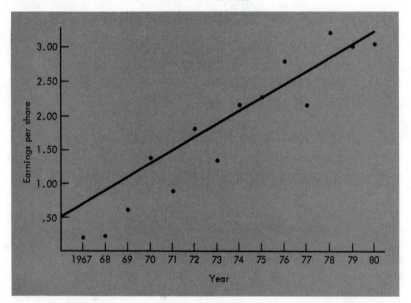

In an arithmetic graph, such as Figure 10-2, equal distances on an axis represent equal absolute quantities. In this example, each demarcation on the y-axis represents $.10 of earnings per share. Because of this construction, Companies A, B, C, and D seem to have achieved identical patterns of growth in earnings per share between 1978 and 1981, since the trend lines are parallel. However, if we examine the data carefully, we see that this is an illusion. Company A's earnings per share have increased from $.10 to $.20, or 100 percent during the period, Company B's earnings have increased from $.30 to $.40, or 33 1/3 percent, Company C's earnings have increased from $.50 to $.60, or 20 percent,

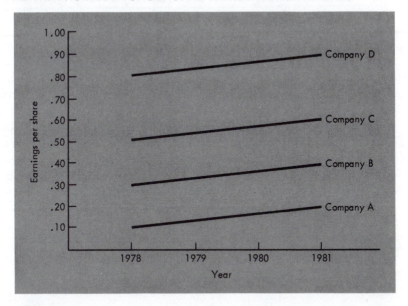

FIGURE 10-2
ARITHMETIC GRAPH FOR DEPICTING TRENDS IN GROWTH RATES

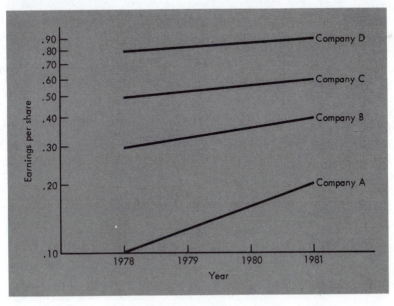

FIGURE 10-3
SEMILOGARITHMIC GRAPH FOR DEPICTING TRENDS IN GROWTH RATES

and Company D's earnings have increased from $.80 to $.90, or 12 1/2 percent. Thus, even though their trend rates are parallel, their performances during the 1978-81 period have in fact been drastically different.

Semilogarithmic graphs attempt to overcome this optical illusion. In a semi-logarithmic chart, one axis, usually the *x*-axis, is drawn as in the arithmetic graph. The difference lies in how the other axis, usually the *y*-axis, is constructed. Here, equal distance between demarcations represents equal percentage changes rather than equal quantities. Figure 10-3 depicts the same information as that in Figure 10-2, but this time on semilog paper. The reader can observe that when this is done, the four companies' trend lines are no longer parallel. In fact, the slopes of the four trend lines are radically different—as they should be. Thus the semilogarithmic graph clearly demonstrates the different growth patterns in Companies A, B, C, and D and does so accurately. Here the different slopes clearly point out the difference in growth patterns of 100, 33 1/3, 20, and 12 1/2 percent. Generally, semilogarithmic graphs are very useful in comparing and visually demonstrating different growth rates among different companies. As a forecasting device, these trend lines can be used by merely extending them for the next period and then reading off the forecast on the *y*-axis. Clearly, this is a crude method that should be used only as an approximation, and only then when the underlying conditions are expected to remain stable during the forecast period.

Let us see how regression analysis and trend analysis can be applied to a forecast for Holiday Inns, a major motel chain in a related industry, for the year 1977.

Regression Analysis and Trend Analysis Applied to Holiday Inns

We know that average hours worked per week, size of the U.S. population between the ages of 20 and 34, and disposable personal income are important variables in determining the revenues of the motel industry in general, and Holiday Inns in particular. In this section we report attempts to investigate the possible validity of these hypotheses by regressing these variables against the sales revenue of the Food and Lodgings Division of Holiday Inns. These tests were carried out to make predictions for the year 1977. The food and lodgings revenue figure is used because it is this figure that is hypothesized to be most influenced by these variables. Table 10-1 contains the values of these variables that were used in the regressions to be discussed below.

TABLE 10-1

VALUES FOR INDEPENDENT VARIABLES IN REGRESSIONS

Year	Holiday Inn F&L Revenue (millions)	Disposable Personal Income (billions)	Auto Registrations (privately owned passenger cars) (millions)	Population Age 20-34 (millions)	Average Hours Worked/Week (private, non-agricultural)
1977	??	$1,312.0	113.7	53.2	36.2
1976	$539.4	1,181.7	109.7	51.7	36.2
1975	525.7	1,080.9	106.7	50.2	36.1
1974	502.3	982.9	104.3	48.5	36.6
1973	467.0	901.7	101.2	47.0	37.1
1972	420.0	801.3	96.6	45.2	37.1
1971	360.4	742.8	92.2	43.9	37.0
1970	301.3	685.9	88.8	42.5	37.0
1969	253.0	603.4	86.4	41.2	37.7
1968	195.5	588.1	83.2	39.8	37.8
1967	159.9	544.5	80.0	38.4	38.0

The procedure used was to collect data on these factors for the past several years, specifically 1967-76, since it was felt that the most relevant data would be the most recent. For if we want to use the coefficients of the fitted line to predict future values of the independent variable—HIA food and lodgings revenues—it is necessary to have (1) high correlation, (2) statistically significant results, (3) economically plausible relationships, and (4) stable underlying conditions. By the last, we mean that the environmental circumstances surrounding the behavior of the variables in the equation will be approximately the same in the forecast period as in the historical period used to calculate the coefficients.

In order to test the hypothesis that shorter workweeks mean more business to Holiday Inns, we regressed the average hours worked per week for private, nonagricultural workers against HIA revenues for food and lodgings. When this was done, we found the correlation coefficient was −.90. This figure is statistically significant,[3] indicating a high degree of negative correlation, since the limits of the values the correlation coefficient can take on are −1 to +1. In other words, the two series moved in opposite directions—exactly what had been hypothesized!

Now the question is: How well can the "hours" figure predict HIA's food and lodgings revenues? It would seem in advance that even though the average workweek is important, it is not the *only* explanatory variable, and therefore, by itself would not be a particularly good predictor despite the high negative correlation. When we substituted into the regression equation resulting from the fitted line, we got

$$1977 \text{ HIA F\&L revenue} = a + b \times (\text{avg. hrs. worked, 1977})$$

Substituting values for *a, b,* and our forecast of average hours worked in 1977 yields

$$\text{HIA F\&L revenue} = 7{,}874.31 - 202.40(36.2)$$

or, simplifying,

$$= \$547.43 \text{ million}$$

The 36.2 figure represents a forecast of the number of hours in the average workweek in the United States during 1977. It should be noted that this forecast is below the figure we arrived at for this division earlier, $580 million, using the revenue-and-expenses approach. This is not surprising, since the importance of the length of the average workweek is not all-pervasive. Let us now look at some other regressions.

To test if the size of the U.S. population between the ages of 20 and 34 was highly correlated with HIA F&L revenues, these variables were regressed against each other. The rationale behind this hypothesis is that this most mobile age group represents a potential market for the motel industry and Holiday Inns. The correlation coefficient of this regression equation was +.99 and, again, highly significant statistically. In other

---

[3]Statistical significance can be determined from a simple test, such as a true-or-false test. The interested reader should consult any basic statistics text. Briefly, these tests tell the analyst if the observed relationship is meaningful in a formal, statistical sense—as it should be before he uses the regression equation as a forecasting tool.

words, these two series moved up together in a very significant fashion during the period 1967-76. Specifically, the regression equation was

$$\text{HIA F \& L revenue} = a + b \times (\text{Population, 20-34})$$

To forecast HIA food and lodgings revenues for 1977, the equation resulting from a fitted least-squares regression line, and substituting the forecast value of the independent variable, yields

$$1977 \text{ HIA F\&L revenue} = -1{,}112.43 + 33.27(53.2)$$
$$= \$657.53 \text{ million}$$

This figure is much higher than earlier forecast based on the length of the workweek. Again, we should point out that although the size of the population between the ages of 20 and 34 is important, it is not the *only* powerful explanatory variable.

Disposable personal income is clearly going to be important to Holiday Inns. Why? Because the more money people have available to spend, the more likely they will travel and require the services of Holiday Inns. When disposable personal income (DPI) was regressed against HIA F&L revenue, a correlation coefficient of +.9741 was obtained. Also, the correlation coefficient was highly significant statistically. Thus it was shown that these two series moved upward together during the sample period in a very close fashion. Since DPI is an economic variable of broad impact, it was felt that it would be a fine predictor. The equation used was

$$\text{HIA F\&L revenue} = a + b(\text{DPI})$$

Substituting into this equation, we obtained

$$1977 \text{ HIA F\&L revenue} = -195.41 + 0.71(1312.0)$$
$$= \$736.1 \text{ million}$$

This is high compared with the $580 million figure forecast in Chapter 9. However, it was still felt that DPI is only one factor, and perhaps combining this variable with another explanatory variable would yield an even better predictive model.

So far we have tested Holiday Inns' food and lodgings revenues against people likely to travel (population, age 20-34), available time (average hours worked), and the discretionary income available to spend for travel (disposable personal income). A fourth variable, privately owned passenger car registrations, was also selected, since this variable is a good proxy for the available means of travel. The correlation coefficient of this regression was +.994 and, again, highly significant statistically. Specifically, the regression equation was

$$\text{HIA F\&L revenue} = a + b \text{ (Auto registrations)}$$

The resulting values for *a* and *b* and the forecast value of auto registration yields

$$1977 \text{ HIA F\&L revenue} = -957.83 + 14.06(113.7)$$
$$= \$640.8$$

When a forecaster uses multiple regression analysis (regression analysis with more than one independent variable), he must strive to select independent variables that are *independent of each other.*[4] To achieve this, we used the following equation:[5]

HIA F&L revenue = $a + b$ (DPI) + c (Auto registrations) + d (Hours worked)

The correlation coefficient of this equation was .9979 and highly statistically significant. Since these factors together are so significant, one might expect them to be good predictors. Substituting values for $a, b, c,$ and d, and forecasts of DPI, auto registrations, and hours worked, we got

$$1977 \text{ HIA F\&L revenue} = -85.63 - .55(1,312) + 22.68(113.7) - 33.67(36.2)$$
$$= \$552.6 \text{ million}$$

This is below the figure in our earlier forecast. The fact is not surprising, because the equation in the multiple regression is a more complete "explanation" than that in the simple regression.

At this point, the analyst could attempt to build models through a similar procedure for the other divisions, or obtain forecasts using one of the other techniques for the other divisions, to get at total 1977 HIA revenue. He would then proceed to obtain expenses, EPS, P/E, and HPY. Again, however, no simple objective measure of risk is directly obtained.

Trend Analysis

Now let us apply trend analysis to HIA. During 1967 a major change took place within Holiday: the acquisition of Continental Trailways and Delta Steamships. Thus, in establishing a base period for calculating our a and b values it is not meaningful to go back further than 1968, because before then HIA was a substantially different company. Thus we express the EPS for 1968 through 1976 over years 1 through 9 to get values for a and b. The reported EPS for 1967 through 1976 are as follows:

EPS FOR HOLIDAY INNS, 1967-1976

Year	EPS	Year	EPS
1967	$ .79	1972	$1.37
1968	1.08	1973	1.33
1969	1.13	1974	.89
1970	1.27	1975	1.37
1971	1.28	1976	1.28

[4]When the independent variables are not independent of each other, complex statistical problems arise, and the results of the regression are suspect and not dependable for forecasting purposes.
[5]The variable, population (20-34), was discarded because it was the poorest predictor in the multiple regression. It did not add significantly to the coefficient of multiple correlation.

The calculated *a* value was 1.018 and the *b* value was .0375. Now, to forecast 1977 EPS for HIA using trend analysis we need merely substitute into the following equation and solve:

$$\text{EPS } 1977 = \$1.018 + (.0375)(10)$$
$$= \$1.018 + .375$$
$$= \$1.39$$

The reader should note that this forecast assumes that the conditions that caused earnings growth in the 1968-76 period will be identical during 1977 and thus cause the same growth trend in 1977. To the extent that this assumption is not valid this forecast will prove inaccurate. Also note that again no simple objective measure of risk is obtained. The next two techniques attempt to overcome this objection by yielding both return and risk estimates.

Decision Trees

The traditional approaches to company analysis were criticized because they lacked an objective measurement of quality. That is, they were based to a large extent on subjective analysis and resulted in a point estimate, which did not carry along with it a formal measure of probability. Even though subjectivity has not been and cannot be removed entirely from the investment process, and the investor's or analyst's judgment will always be required, the newer techniques that have been presented thus far overcome the problem to some extent, because they are based upon formal statistical tools and often economic rationale as well.

Nonetheless, an important disadvantage still remains with these newer techniques: The output of the various regression models still yields a point estimate. Furthermore, this estimate of earnings, dividends, or price still does not carry a statement of the probability of actual occurrence.[6] Techniques are available that attempt to overcome this last shortcoming.

Whenever alternative actions or probabilities exist in an investment environment, there should be some way of assessing the probabilities that the various outcomes will occur.[7] When a sequence of these decisions must be made, and the probability of a particular sequence's occurring is desired, the probabilities of occurrence of the various independent outcomes must be multiplied together. An example of two independent

---

[6]However, the analyst can calculate—or have the program calculate—a standard error of the estimate, which can be used to determine the likelihood that a value within a range of values about the estimate will occur. See a basic statistics text.

[7]There is a special branch of statistics whose purpose is to train the statistician in calculating these probabilities. For example, one such approach, the standard gamble, is explained in Robert Schlaifer, *Probability and Statistics for Business Decisions: An Introduction to Managerial Economics under Uncertainty* (New York: McGraw-Hill, 1959). The application of decision-tree analysis to security analysis is discussed in Jerome H. Buff, G. Gordon Biggar, Jr., and J. Gary Burkhead, "The Application of New Decision Analysis Techniques to Investment Research," *Financial Analysts Journal*, November-December 1968, pp.123-28; and in a monograph prepared by the Research Department of Smith, Barney & Co., entitled *Risk-Adjusted Portfolio Performance: Investment Implications* (New York: Smith, Barney & Co., 1971).

outcomes might be the temperature in Hawaii and the size of trout in a Rocky Mountain stream. Needless to say, the more alternatives that exist, and the more intermediate steps between the original decision and the final solution of a complex problem, the more complex these calculations become. Obviously, the expected value of each of the outcomes will be different, depending on the sequence of events that actually occurs. Decision-tree analysis is a technique aimed at formalizing and simplifying the procedure involved in the solution of such problems.

Perhaps a simple illustration will help clarify this technique. A decision tree contains within its branches *all* possible outcomes at a given stage of the decision-making process. Thus, when one adds up the probabilities of the end points of the branches, the sum will be 1, much as the probability of tossing heads or tails on a flip of a coin is 1. We say that the end points are collectively exhaustive. Since all specific outcomes are specified, we say they represent a discrete distribution—that is, a distribution in which only certain specific values are obtainable. However, even in the discrete case, a decision tree can become very cluttered, for the more discrete possible intermediate steps and outcomes, the more branches there will be.

Generally, when an analyst attempts to use a decision tree in conjunction with security analysis, he begins with a sales forecast. Thus, if sales can be at only one of three levels, such as $10 million, $11 million, or $12 million, there will be three initial branches with their associated probabilities of occurrence specified. However, should the analyst desire to refine his analysis significantly, such as by specifying all possible sales levels at $100,000 intervals between $10 million and $12 million, the number of initial branches, as well as of subsequent branches, will be significantly increased. Just to begin with, there would be twenty initial branches, as opposed to three in the former case.

Figure 10-4 is an example of the application of decision-tree analysis to security analysis. Assume that there are 1 million shares of stock outstanding. There are three key variables with subjectively determined probabilities that have been highlighted by the analyst based on his experience: sales (S), expenses (E), and P/E ratio (P/E). As seen in the partially completed tree, sales can be $12 million, $11 million, or $10 million, with probabilities of .2, .5, and .3 respectively; expenses can be either $4 million or $8 million, with probabilities of .4 and .6 respectively; and finally, the price-earnings ratio can be 30, 20, or 10, with probabilities .2, .6, and .2 respectively. Even in the simplified example, the inherent advantages and disadvantages of this technique can be seen.

We see that a complete set of possible outcomes (prices), together with their probabilities of occurrence, is generated from the analysis. This enables the analyst to set up a frequency distribution of prices for one period in the future. With current price and projected dividend, the analyst can calculate the frequency distribution of expected returns. Recall that the one-year holding-period yield is given by

$$\text{HPY} = \frac{(P_1 - P_0) + D_1}{P_0}$$

where:

P_1 = price one year from now of one share of stock

P_0 = current price of the one share of stock

D_1 = dividends received on one share of stock one year from now

FIGURE 10-4
PARTIAL DECISION TREE APPLIED TO SECURITY ANALYSIS

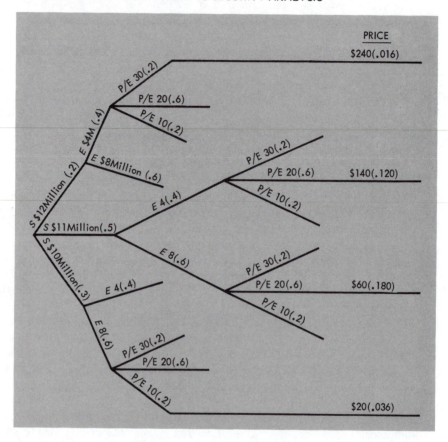

Figure 10-4 reveals that the maximum price of a share of this stock obtainable in one year is $240. The probability of this is about 2 percent. We also see that the minimum possible price will be $20, with a probability of about 4 percent. Two intermediate prices that are considerably more likely to occur are also given.

Let us trace the branches leading to a price of $140 and a probability of 12 percent. We see that sales of $11 million and expenses of $4 million are projected. Since we are assuming 1 million shares outstanding, EPS would be $7 [($11 million − $4 million)/1 million]. The P/E in this series of branches is 20. This leads to a price of $140 (20 × $7). To obtain the likelihood of this event, we must multiply together the probabilities associated with these levels of sales, expenses, and P/E. From the tree we see that these are .5, .4, and .6. When multiplied together, they come to .12, or 12 percent. The other branches can be completed by repeating this process.

When all other sequences of events (branches) are completed and the prices have been converted to HPYs, the analyst can calculate a measure of central tendency, such as the mean, and a measure of dispersion about the mean, such as the standard deviation.

With all the work completed, the analyst and investor are in a much better position to make an informed judgment about the merits of this stock's purchase, since they have *measures of probable returns and risks*, rather than only a *point estimate of return*.

Analysts have also cited additional advantages:

1. Better investment decisions should result from a procedure that demands more intensive analysis. Breaking down investment uncertainties into manageable parts and analyzing them individually should lead to improved decisions when the parts are systematically combined.
2. Communication of investment ideas should be improved by the ability to express degrees of uncertainty more precisely, and by providing those taking investment action a deeper understanding of the thought processes behind the final recommendation.[8]

Let us apply this technique to Holiday Inns.

Decision-Tree Analysis Applied to Holiday Inns

We have seen that if the analyst can determine possible values of key sequential variables with associated probabilities, he can use decision-tree analysis to calculate various terminal prices—that is, prices at the end of some holding period. These prices can then be used to calcuate holding-period yields and their variability. Let us see how this was done for HIA.

First, after careful study of the economy, the lodgings industry, and Holiday Inns in particular, the analyst came up with values for sales, expenses, and P/E that he deemed possible for 1977, and he assigned to them the probabilities he thought most appropriate for each value. These are shown in Table 10-2.

TABLE 10-2
VALUES FOR DECISION TREE AND SIMULATION

Sales (millions)	Probability	Expenses (millions)	Probability	P/E	Probability
$1,025	.2	$ 975	.2	8	.4
1,030	.3	980	.3	9	.4
1,040	.3	990	.3	10	.2
1,050	.2	1,000	.2		

In addition, the analyst determined that there would be 30.6 million common shares outstanding during 1977. To estimate price, the analyst merely deducts an expense figure from a sales figure, divides by 30.6 to get EPS, and multiplies by a P/E to get a forecast of terminal price. Then the beginning price is subtracted from the terminal price, dividends added, and this sum divided by beginning price to arrive at an estimate of HPY. This process is repeated until all branches have been completed. There will be 48 end points in this example. How?

[8]Buff, Biggar, and Burkhead, "Application of New Techniques," p. 123.

TABLE 10-3

PARTIAL DECISION TREE FOR HOLIDAY INNS

Sales	Expenses	P/E	Price	Probability
$1,025	$ 975	8	$13.07	(.016)
		9	$14.71	(.016)
		10	$16.34	(.008)
	$ 980	8	$11.76	(.024)
		9	$13.24	(.024)
		10	$14.71	(.012)
	$ 990	8	$ 9.15	(.024)
		9	$10.29	(.024)
		10	$11.44	(.012)
	$1,000	8	$ 6.54	(.016)
		9	$ 7.35	(.016)
		10	$ 8.19	(.008)

Well, we shall see. Table 10-3 shows a partial decision tree; let us trace out the top branch.

First, subtract expenses of $975 from sales of $1,025 to get income of $50. Divide by 30.6 shares to get EPS of $1.63. Multiply by a P/E of 8 to get $13.07, a forecast of terminal price. The probability is obtained by multiplying .2 X .2 X .4, the probabilites of achieving the given sales, expenses, and P/E figures respectively. The top line of Figure 10-5 shows these same calculations as performed on a computer.

Thus we see twelve end points for this one sales level. Obviously, each of the possible sales values has twelve end points, for a total of 48. Needless to say, it would be extremely time-consuming and tedious to draw out each branch and perform all these calculations manually, even for this simple tree. Two possible solutions to this dilemma are (1) to prepare the data in tabular form, or (2) to let the computer prepare the decision tree. Figure 10-5 shows the tabular output of a computer-projected decision tree. Note that the mean price is $14.38. The HPY of 23.7 percent can in turn be used to calculate a mean HPY and a variance of HPY.

Note that the mean price is $14.38. The yield per share (HPY) in each case is calculated by using a beginning price of $12.00 and an estimated dividend per share of $.47 and whatever ending price per share is shown by the decision tree. For example, the yield per share on line 1 of Figure 10-5 is calculated as:

$$\frac{\$13.07 - \$12.00 + \$.47}{\$12.00} = .128$$

In summary, then, we see that decision-tree analysis is particularly useful when the number of sequential decisions (sales, expense, and P/E, for example) is limited, a manage-

FIGURE 10-5
RESULTS OF COMPUTER-GENERATED DECISION TREE

	EARNING PER SHARE	PRICE PER SHARE	YIELD PER SHARE	PROBABILITY
1	1.63	13.07	0.128	0.016
2	1.63	14.71	0.265	0.016
3	1.63	16.34	0.401	0.008
4	1.47	11.76	0.02	0.024
5	1.47	13.24	0.142	0.024
6	1.47	14.71	0.265	0.012
7	1.14	9.15	−0.198	0.024
8	1.14	10.29	−0.103	0.024
9	1.14	11.44	−0.008	0.012
10	0.82	6.54	−0.416	0.016
11	0.82	7.35	−0.348	0.016
12	0.82	8.17	−0.28	0.008
13	1.8	14.38	0.237	0.024
14	1.8	16.18	0.387	0.024
15	1.8	17.97	0.537	0.012
16	1.63	13.07	0.128	0.036
17	1.63	14.71	0.265	0.036
18	1.63	16.34	0.401	0.018
19	1.31	10.46	−0.089	0.036
20	1.31	11.76	0.02	0.036
21	1.31	13.07	0.128	0.018
22	0.98	7.84	−0.307	0.024
23	0.98	8.82	−0.226	0.024
24	0.98	9.8	−0.144	0.012
25	2.12	16.99	0.455	0.024
26	2.12	19.12	0.632	0.024
27	2.12	21.24	0.809	0.012
28	1.96	15.69	0.346	0.036
29	1.96	17.65	0.51	0.036
30	1.96	19.61	0.673	0.018
31	1.63	13.07	0.128	0.036
32	1.63	14.71	0.265	0.036
33	1.63	16.34	0.401	0.018
34	1.31	10.46	−0.089	0.024
35	1.31	11.76	0.02	0.024
36	1.31	13.07	0.128	0.012
37	2.45	19.61	0.673	0.016
38	2.45	22.06	0.877	0.016
39	2.45	24.51	1.082	0.008
40	2.29	18.3	0.564	0.024
41	2.29	20.59	0.755	0.024
42	2.29	22.88	0.945	0.012
43	1.96	15.69	0.346	0.024
44	1.96	17.65	0.51	0.024
45	1.96	19.61	0.673	0.012
46	1.63	13.07	0.128	0.016
47	1.63	14.71	0.265	0.016
48	1.63	16.34	0.401	0.008

⋈ ⋈

MEAN

PRICE PER SHARE	14.3791
HOLDING PERIOD YIELD	0.237424

⋈ ⋈

able number of alternative outcomes are possible, and the analyst can assess the associated probabilities.

On the surface, decision-tree analysis seems to have done away with most of our objections to the other techniques of company analysis. Unfortunately, we should not celebrate too soon. In a real-world situation, there would be many possible alternatives, and many steps before we arrived at a final solution. Under these circumstances, the number of calculations and the plotting of a decision tree such as that in Figure 10-5 would be all but impossible (even this simplified example has proved somewhat arduous to handle).[9] Therefore, we need another technique that does not require us to specify all the possible branches in our tree. The use of a computer would also help. Such a technique, which has only recently been considered in security analysis, is simulation.

Simulation

Since projecting HPY, even after much rigorous analysis, has been shown to require several key subjective decisions, it would seem to be less than prudent to make only one point estimate of holding-period yield. The judicious use of simulation as a technique allows the seasoned analyst to project a distribution of HPYs with associated probabilities of occurrence.

Simulation is a technique that systematically repeats the application of a rule or formula to a given set of data. Here we will be dealing with a special kind of simulation, Monte Carlo simulation. To use Monte Carlo simulation, all we need do is specify the probability distributions, either discrete or continuous, and the decision rule or formula that should be applied to the selected values of the variables.[10]

Monte Carlo simulation is named after the famous casino because of the procedure of selecting variables by chance (randomly). An example will help illustrate this point. Let us assume that we are attempting to forecast the price of a share of stock one year from now and its probability of occurrence, and that this estimate must be based on forecasts of sales, profit margins, net income, the number of shares outstanding, and P/E ratio.[11] Now that the variables have been enumerated, it is necessary to specify the probability distribution for each variable. This is done in Figure 10-6. For example, we can see that there is a 30 percent probability, in the analyst's judgment, that next year's sales will be $10 million.

[9]Furthermore, this example calculated prices only one year hence. If the analysis were extended to cover additional periods, the calculations would be increased tremendously. Part of the problems created stem from the assessment of additional probabilities several periods in advance.

Payoff matrixes are an alternative that is much easier to construct than the decision tree, but not as useful in sequential problems. For a very readable discussion of payoff matrixes, see Clifford H. Springer, Robert E. Herlihy, Robert T. Mall, and Robert I. Beggs, *Probabilistic Models* (Homewood, Ill.: Richard D. Irwin, 1968), pp. 214-60.

[10]A classic example of the application of simulation to a business problem is seen in David B. Hertz, "Risk Analysis in Capital Investment," *Harvard Business Review*, January-February 1964, pp. 95-106. An interesting application to security analysis is contained in David Whittall, "A Simulation Model for Estimating Earnings," *Financial Analysts Journal*, November-December 1968, pp. 115-18.

[11]This approach, and much of the ensuing discussion, draws from Ronald J. Jordan and Miles Livingston, "Simulation: An Application to Security Analysis," working paper (Storrs, Conn: University of Connecticut, School of Business Administration, 1971).

FIGURE 10-6
PROBABILITY DISTRIBUTIONS OF KEY VARIABLES

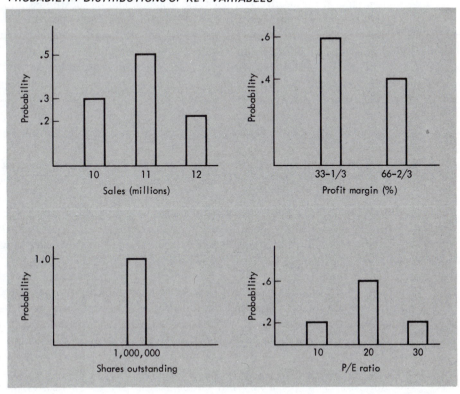

After the probabilities are specified, the next step is to set up the formulas that are to be used. In this example, the formulas are:

$$\frac{\text{Sales} \times \text{Margin (\%)}}{\text{No. of shares outstanding}} = \text{Earnings per share} \qquad (10.1)$$

$$\text{Earnings per share} \times \text{P/E} = \text{Price per share} \qquad (10.2)$$

The computer program that has been written by or for the analyst will then randomly select numbers and match them against the corresponding values in Figure 10-6. One value of each variable will be selected; these variables are the same as in the decision-tree example.[12]

For example, the computer will select four numbers randomly and match each of the four against the distributions of sales, profit margin, shares outstanding (in this case all values will be matched against 1 million shares because it is the only possible value),

---

[12]The expenses have been replaced with approximate net-income profit margins. Simulation can be used whenever decision-tree analysis can be applied; however, simulation is much more practical when there are many alternatives. In fact, if sufficient alternative values are specified, we would represent the data as a continuous distribution.

and P/E ratio. Assume that the random values so selected are $10 million, 33 1/3 percent, 1 million, and 20, respectively. Then these values would be substituted into equations 10.1 and 10.2. This would lead to, first, [$10 million × 33 1/3 percent/1 million], or $3.33 earnings per share. Then EPS of $3.33 times a P/E of 20 yields a price of $66.60. This process is called one iteration.

The process is then repeated as many times as the analyst desires. It is generally repeated at least several hundred times, which takes only a few seconds of computer time. Thus, many prices and returns will have been generated. Next, probability measures can be calculated based on the distribution of these prices and returns.

At this point, the analyst has a calculated distribution of prices with a mean and a standard deviation. This information alone is extremely helpful, for these two statistics are necessary inputs for modern portfolio analysis. (This will be more evident to the reader in Chapter 18.) However, this is not the only information the simulation provides to the analyst. The distribution itself is very important. It can be portrayed graphically in a histogram (a bar graph) when the distrubtion is discrete, in a continuous curve when the distribution is continuous, or in tabular form as a frequency distribution. This allows the analyst to see directly by inspection in which ranges the most likely outcomes will be.[13]

The example just discussed can be made considerably more sophisticated and more accurate.[14] First, the model as it has been set up here implicitly assumes that the various distributions are entirely independent. This implicit assumption is made because we randomly selected values from the various distributions without regard to the other values that have been and will be selected from the other distributions. For example, we draw a value from the profit-margin distribution without regard to the value we have selected from the sales distribution. This can be somewhat unrealistic, because we might select a very low sales figure and a very high profit margin. This event is certainly unlikely to occur in reality, since low sales implies underutilization of facilities, which in turn implies lower profit margins. One way of overcoming this potential problem is to "constrain" the distributions so that the selection of certain values from one distribution is conditional upon the value of a previously selected value from another distribution. For example, if a low sales value has been randomly selected from the sales distributions, only a low profit margin can be selected from the profit-margin distribution. This is accomplished in the simulation program.

Another way of introducing more economic rationale into the simulation model is to generate possible values of key variables in the program itself via regression analysis. That is, generate values from a behavioral model that has been developed from past experience, and then select values randomly from this distribution of outcomes—outcomes that make economic sense. For example, experience may have taught us that obtainable margins are dependent on certain variables. These obtainable margins are generated from the regression that utilizes the "proven" explanatory variables, and then we select randomly from this internal (internal to the simulation) distribution. Thus Monte Carlo

---

[13]If the outcomes are normally distributed (which is very likely), techniques of statistical inference can be used in conjunction with the mean and standard deviation.

[14]In addition, more decision variables (such as input costs, variable sales prices, etc.) can be introduced, and more alternative values of these variables can be hypothesized. These present more of a practical implementation problem than a conceptual problem.

simulation provides much of the information the security analyst requires in terms of price forecasts and overcomes the objections to the other techniques.

At this point it would be helpful to apply simulation to Holiday Inns and observe the transition from theory to practice.

Simulation Applied to Holiday Inns

Fortunately, Monte Carlo simulation is a statistical technique that has considerably more flexibility than does decision-tree analysis. Simulation is able to handle processes that require many decisions and have large numbers of possible outcomes, because the computer has little problem in processing this vast amount of data. All the analyst must provide are the possible outcomes, their associated probabilities, and the formula to be applied repeatedly. In other words, the inputs from the security analyst are the same as in decision-tree analysis, but the situations can be far more complex. You might think of Monte Carlo simulation as a way of handling a huge decision tree.

The formula used in our HIA example is to deduct expenses from sales, divide by the number of shares, and multiply this EPS by a P/E. Values for each of the variables (those contained in Table 10-2) are selected randomly by the computer and substituted into this formula. Thus there is no guarantee that the expected value or mean of the prices generated by the simulation will exactly equal the mean value for price of the decision tree—unless, of course, many hundreds of iterations are performed. However, for a fairly substantial number of iterations, the mean value of the simulation will converge on the "true mean" of the decision tree.[15] This is not necessarily a disadvantage of simulation, however, because (1) it may well be impossible to complete the decision tree because of its complexity, and (2) the values (mean and standard deviation) of the simulation will rapidly converge on the mean and standard deviation of the decision tree as the number of iterations increases.

For those who may not understand how these values are generated randomly, it may be helpful to think of a small wheel of chance with ten numbers—two are 1,025; three are 1,030; three are 1,040; and two are 1,050. This would represent the possible sales distributions for HIA in 1977 as perceived by the security analyst. Similar wheels are set for expenses and P/E's. The wheels are "spun" and one value wins on each wheel. These are combined via the given formula. This yields one price and completes one iteration.

When this process was repeated two hundred times, the distribution shown in Table 10-4 was obtained. The first probability column tells us the probability that a value will fall within a given interval. For example, there is only a 15.7 percent chance that a price between $12.50 and $13.00 will occur, given the input to the simulation, but there is a 33 percent chance that a price between $14.50 and $15.00 will occur. The mean of this distribution is $14.39, with a standard deviation of $1.26.[16]

---

[15]This is because all possible branches (with probabilities) have been traced out in the decision tree.

[16]Note how close the mean of the simulation is to the mean of the decision tree. This is because we have performed 200 iterations. If we continued to increase the number of iterations, the means would eventually be equal.

TABLE 10-4
SIMULATION RESULTS FOR HOLIDAY INNS

	Mean	Standard Deviation
Earning per share	1.63	.02
Price per share	14.39	1.26
Holding period yield	.24	.1

		Frequency Distribution of Values (%)		
Interval	Lower Limit	Prob. of Being within Interval	Prob. of Less Than Value	Prob. of Greater Than Value
1	12	0	0	100
2	12.5	15.7	15.7	84.3
3	13	24.8	40.5	59.5
4	13.5	0	40.5	59.5
5	14	3.7	44.2	55.8
6	14.5	33.0	77.2	22.8
7	15	1.2	78.4	21.6
8	15.5	1.2	79.6	20.4
9	16	15.3	94.9	5.1
10	16.5	5.1	100	0

FIGURE 10-7
HISTOGRAM FROM HIA SIMULATION

```
                   RELATIVE FREQUENCY(%)
   INTERVAL
  LOWER LIMIT   0    5    10   15   20   25   30   35

    12          -
    12.5        -xxxxxxxxxxxxxxx
    13          -xxxxxxxxxxxxxxxxxxxxxxxx
    13.5        -
    14          -xxxx
    14.5        -xxxxxxxxxxxxxxxxxxxxxxxxxxxxxxxxx
    15          -x
    15.5        -x
    16          -xxxxxxxxxxxxxxx
    16.5        -xxxxx
    17          -
```

The information is plotted in Figure 10-7. Again we can add the projected dividend of $.47 to each projected price change and divide by the beginning price of $12.00 to obtain a distribution of projected HPY. This gives us a forecast of risk and return. If we do this using the mean value of the simulation, we get as our estimate of HPY:

$$\frac{\$14.39 - \$12.00 + \$.47}{\$12.00} = .24, \text{ or } 24\%$$

The top of Table 10-4 indicates that the holding-period yield is expected to be 24 percent, with a standard deviation of 10 percent. This would be the forecast of return and risk for Holiday Inns shares for a one-year holding period (in this case for 1977).

Problem Areas in Implementation of Newer Techniques

Thus far in this chapter, we have examined the newer analytical techniques of company analysis. However, we have not addressed some of the problems that face the security analyst or investor when he attempts to implement these tools. In this section we must face up to these difficult issues.

Regression Analysis to Forecast Revenues and Expenses

In order to implement regression analysis for the forecasting of revenues and expenses, it is necessary to develop plausible economic relationships between revenues and expenses of the firm and other economic variables, such as GNP, national income, some index of industrial production, per capita consumption of the firm's output, and so on. Generally, these relationships will be developed after examination of past data, the application of economic rationale to explain logical relationship, and the application and testing of these two items. After the initial testing has been completed, the analyst will undoubtedly find some relation between independent (influencing change) and dependent (affected by the influencing factors) variables that he feels will yield sufficiently good results correlatively. He may be willing to base his stock recommendation upon these relationships. When these relationships have been selected, monitored, and put in final form, the user will apply these various systems of equations to the analysis in order to generate forecasts of revenues and expenses.

Unfortunately for the investor or analyst, isolating key explanatory variables is a time consuming process, and one requiring a thorough understanding of the firm's mode of operation as well as the structure and performance of its industry. But for those able to isolate these key relationships, the payoffs can be great—both in dollars and in personal satisfaction.

Decision Trees

Decision-tree analysis, as we presented it earlier, attempts to enumerate the various possible combinations of events that culminate in the formation of share price and the probabilities of the various events occurring. Specifically, this can involve the forecasting of such things as revenues, expenses, shares outstanding, and P/E ratio, together with their probabilities of occurrence. This process necessitates that the analyst seek out all information he can get concerning these variables, and any others he wishes to add to the analysis, so that a more realistic set of outcomes and associated probabilities can be obtained. In addition to the price outputs that are generated in the specific decision-tree model we have discussed, it is possible with the proper statement of the end points of the branches of a decision tree to construct a cumulative probability distribution. That is, a distribution could take the following form (the values are hypothetical): There is a 30 percent probability that the share price of the firm in question will be at least $60, there is a 45 percent probability that the share price will be at least $50, and there is a 90 percent probability that the share price will be at least $25. In other words, as the combination of events becomes ever more pessimistic, the probability of accuracy of the final outcome increases. This is a very useful output of the technique, for it gives the analyst a "feel" for the underlying price-formation process.

GENERATING THE NECESSARY INPUTS

Up to this point we have said very little about the problems of generating the necessary inputs to decision-tree analysis—or for that matter, simulation. Without going into great detail, let us introduce this required step in the implementation of decision-tree analysis.

First, it is necessary to know enough about the firm so that one can establish the possible outcomes that may occur. This information undoubtedly stems from insight into the workings of the firm in question and, perhaps more likely, insight into the workings of the industry or industries in which the firm is involved. With this understanding of the firm and its industry and a knowledge of historical sales volume, prices, revenues, and costs, the analyst is in an excellent position to estimate the likelihood of the various alternative outcomes. It is not at all unrealistic to expect this knowledge of the analyst. The research organizations of large brokerage firms and large financial institutions have been traditionally organized along industry lines, with a research analyst or group of analysts assigned to a specific industry—such as construction, shoes, and lodgings. This practice, in effect, creates industry experts whose sole job is to become intimately familiar with the inner workings of the industry and the firms comprising it. These industry experts keep on top of all the latest developments within the industry. In addition, they visit the various companies they follow and interview management personnel. The results of their activities, coupled with addresses by company officials at analysts' meetings, round out the analyst's main sources of information.

For those investors who are attempting to reach their own considered judgment, there is opportunity to receive this knowledge in the form of reports from the industry experts at a number of institutions, such as Standard & Poor's, Moody's, the *Value Line*, and a variety of brokerage firms. In addition, the *Wall Street Transcript* regularly publishes these addresses of speakers at the analysts' luncheon meetings, as well as brokerage reports on key corporations. With this variety of expertise assembled by surveying a number of sources, investors can reach a consensus opinion without doing all the legwork themselves. Furthermore, by knowing what constitutes good research (as we hope the readers of this book will be able to do), investors will be in a position to assess the quality of the research before they evaluate its recommendations.

Ultimately, then, analysts or investors using decision-tree analysis arrive at a forecast of a number of possible prices of the shares one period in advance, together with the probabilities of each outcome's occurring. In addition, these analysts or investors can construct a cumulative frequency distribution of price and holding-period yield that gives them an even firmer grasp on the range of the most likely outcomes one period in advance.

Simulation

Simulation can be thought of as a more sophisticated, more efficient approach to handling a sequential decision such as those handled by decision-tree analysis. Thus the problems noted above apply here as well.

The newer analytical techniques of regression analysis, correlation analysis, trend analysis, decision-tree analysis, and simulation are all interconnected in their attempt to get at an accurate forecast of earnings, dividends, P/E, price, and HPY. Simulation is different from the other techniques only in providing more information in the form of probabilities and accompanying frequency distributions. It draws from all the other methods in the process of achieving its goals.

Several key issues, however, still need to be confronted. How does the quality of a firm's management enter the analysis? Where does the all-important P/E come from? And how about the dividend payout ratio? These are the topics of the next several sections.

Management in Company Analysis

Before we can complete our company analysis and make a final decision or an investment action, we need to determine whether management is capable of carrying out its policies so that our expectations are fulfilled.

The future developments that will affect the variables we have discussed in the past several chapters will be in the hands of company management. So it is important that the analyst have faith in the ability of the management of a company he favors. Management should have clear-cut goals in mind, and strategies for achieving them. Obviously, among the key end points that will measure management's success will be the earnings per share, dividends, and share price. In order to assess the likelihood that management will achieve the desired end points of the analysis, the analyst can take a number of steps.

First, the analyst can look at past performance of management to see if his past expectations and management's past hopes have been fulfilled. Second, through interviews with management personnel, he can learn something about their backgrounds, experience, motivations, and outlook on such things as the firm's future research and development expenditures, plans for product improvement, marketing strategy, future competition, sales and profits. In the course of these interviews and his firsthand observations of the firm in operation, he must take note of management's ability to plan, to organize, and to select, motivate, and control personnel.[17]

In the realm of planning, the analyst should ascertain whether clear-cut corporate objectives have been specified. Organization comprises a well-outlined arrangement of duties, including who has what authority and what responsibility. Good personnel selection is management's knowledge of how to recruit, develop, and keep the right people for the right jobs—including the ability to motivate them to do their best in these jobs. Control involves a series of communication devices, such as budgets and reports, that permit management up and down the organization chart to keep tabs on corporate activities.

---

[17]Townsend Hoopes, "Appraising Managements," and Harlow J. Heneman, "The Financial Analyst and Management," in Institute of Chartered Financial Analysts, *Readings in Financial Analysis* (Homewood, Ill.: Richard D. Irwin, 1970).

When this research is coupled with discussions with others who are familiar with the management of the company under analysis, the analyst can get an idea of how much faith he can place in management, and thus how likely it is that his forecast will be fulfilled. He will manifest his conclusion about management abilities in the P/E ratio he assigns to the firm's stock.

Determining a P/E Ratio

Thus far, our analysis has focused on determining a forecast of earnings per share. This was translated into price by applying the "appropriate" P/E ratio as multiplier. The forecast price was then a central figure in the HPY calculation. We now need to zero in on the critical questions, "What is an appropriate P/E ratio?" and "Where does it come from?"

The most commonly used P/E multiplier is defined as the closing price of the stock, divided by the reported earnings of the most recent twelve months. Thus, if the closing price of the stock was $50 and earnings for the last four quarters totaled $2, the P/E multiplier would be 25. Generally, the P/E is based upon the current price—that is, the closing price of the stock on the day the analysis is being conducted. Thus, the P/E can change daily.

The multiplier, or P/E, is primarily determined by the riskiness of the firm and the rate of growth in its earnings. Low P/E's are associated with low earnings growth and high P/E's with high earnings growth. The Dow Jones Industrial Average, which represents a cross section of stocks with average risk and growth prospects, might sell in the range of 8 to 10 P/E. IBM may sell at a P/E of 16 because of its high rate of earnings growth. Standard Oil of California may sell at a P/E of 7 because of below-average growth and above-average risk (that of the ever-present threat of takeover of the company's oil interests in the Mideast).

The analyst seeks various rules of thumb for selecting an appropriate price-earnings ratio that can be applied to a company's earnings to determine his valuation for its shares. The resulting price is compared with current market prices to assess bargains or overpriced stocks—at least, superficially. For example, if IBM is expected to earn $4 per share and normally sells at a P/E of 16, the analyst might conclude that a fair price at present is $64. If the stock is currently selling for $60, some analysts might consider it undervalued. Should the stock sell for $70, it might be judged overpriced (overvalued).

Actual and "Normal" P/E

The determination of the current P/E on a stock must be followed by a standard of comparison, invariably taken from the historical record of the stock. The analyst may ascertain the median or *mean* P/E for a stock, its *range* over time, and the P/E relative to the "market" P/E (e.g., Dow Jones Industrial Average or Standard & Poor's 400 Stock Index). More weight can be given to the recent past. This provides boundaries within which the P/E should fall (assuming nothing has changed drastically) and indicates whether the stock is tending to sell at the upper limits of expectation (high end of P/E range) or lower limits (low end of range). Industry P/E's provide some guidelines; however, different companies in the same industry frequently carry quite different P/E's.

Bing found that several techniques are favored by analysts in determining proper multiples. In the majority of cases, he found that analysts (1) used time horizons from one to three years, and (2) preferred to use several techniques in combination rather than sticking rigidly to one. Seventy-five percent of the analysts surveyed used "normal" multiplier rules of thumb under the following techniques:

1. They compared current actual P/E with what they considered normal for the stock in question.
2. They compared price times estimated future earnings (one to three years out) with what they considered a normal multiplier for the stock in question.
3. They compared the multiplier and the growth of earnings of individual stocks with industry group multiple and earnings growth.[18]

The lingering question is, of course: What is a "proper" or "normal" P/E? The question of a "normal" P/E for the market has been addressed by several sources. Cohen and Zinbarg estimate the P/E for the S&P 425 Industrial Price Index to range from 13 to 23, with a mean value of 17 for the decade 1962-72. The impact of inflation on earnings and the dividend payout ratio in recent years suggests to them a new range closer to 10 to 13 for the market P/E.[19]

The principal determinants of a standard P/E for a stock would be determined by the extent to which the following variables exceed or fall below S&P averages:

1. Expected five-year growth of earnings
2. Dividend payout ratio
3. Sales stability
4. Institutional ownership of stock (e.g., mutual funds, etc.)
5. Financial leverage (use of debt financing)

In practice, analysts frequently attempt to view the price-earnings ratio on a given stock in relation to the price-earnings ratio prevailing on some broad market index. The most common market gauge is Standard & Poor's 425 Stock Index. Once a sense of the relationship is attained, the analyst will attempt to estimate the P/E that will be applicable to the "market" over a forward period and derive a P/E for the stock based thereupon. In other words, how does the multiple (P/E) on the stock behave in relationship to the market?

The annual earnings per share for the stock is related to the high, low, and closing price of the stock for the year. Thus, we get a P/E ratio based on the high, low, and closing price for the year. The resulting P/E in each case is divided by the S&P 425 price-earnings ratio to determine a *price-earnings relative* (i.e., stock P/E relative to the S&P price-earnings ratio). Suppose that the S&P price-earnings ratio was 10 and the calculated P/E for a stock was 15. The price-earnings relative would be

$$\frac{\text{Stock P/E}}{\text{S\&P Index P/E}} = \frac{15}{10} = 1.5$$

[18]R. A. Bing, "Survey of Practitioners' Stock Evaluation Methods," *Financial Analysts Journal,* May-June 1971, p. 56.

[19]J. B. Cohen, E. D. Zinbarg, and A. Zeikel, *Investment Analysis and Portfolio Management* (Homewood, Ill.: Richard D. Irwin, 1977), pp. 245-55.

This in effect says that for the measurement period involved, the stock sold at a P/E that was one and one-half times the "market" P/E.

Statistical Analysis of P/E's

Analysts equate normality with experience conditioned by recent history and intuition. The analyst's job remains essentially unstructured, and analytical approaches are highly individualist and eclectic, and therefore somewhat unstable. In an attempt to bring some scientific evidence to the problem of "normality" in P/E's, several studies have been conducted, using statistical techniques to achieve solutions. Correlation analysis has been prominent among these techniques. When using correlation analysis, the analyst selects factors or variables that he believes are the main influences on the price of stock. The aim of correlation analysis is to determine the nature and extent to which the variables chosen explain stock price.

Whitbeck and Kisor studied a number of stocks over the same time span. They speculated that differences in P/E's between stocks could be explained by (1) projected earnings growth, (2) expected dividend payout, and (3) the variation in the rate of earnings growth, or growth risk.[20] Bower and Bower used a similar approach for a different time period with another sample of firms. They used earnings growth and payout as variables but divided risk into sub-components, including marketability of the stock, its price variability, and its conformity with the market (how it moved with the market).[21]

Whitbeck and Kisor applied their statistical technique to a cross section of 135 stocks in 1962 to explain differences in individual P/E's. They concluded that P/E is an increasing function of growth and payout and inversely related to the variation in the growth rate. In other words, higher P/E's were associated with higher growth and payout and less variation in the growth rate. Bower and Bower showed results similar to Whitbeck and Kisor's for a cross section of stocks over the period 1956-64. They saw the same positive effects of earnings growth and payout. However, their examination of risk was more detailed. They discovered that higher P/E ratios were associated with more rapid earnings growth and higher dividend payout; lower P/E's with less marketability, greater conformity to market price movements, and higher price variability.

Malkiel and Cragg studied the effects of historical growth of earnings, dividend payout ratio, and the stock's rate of return relative to the market in determining P/E. Earnings growth was found to have a positive effect on the P/E. The closer a stock's return followed that of the market, the more negative the P/E effect. The dividend payout effect was not clear; in some years, the higher the payout the higher the P/E, but this was not true for all years.[22]

[20]V. S. Whitbeck and M. Kisor, Jr., "A New Tool in Investment Decision-Making," *Financial Analysts Journal*, May-June 1963, pp. 52-62.

[21]R. S. Bower and D. H. Bower, "Risk and the Valuation of Common Stock," *Journal of Political Economy*, May-June 1969, pp. 349-62.

[22]B. G. Malkiel and J. G. Cragg, "Expectations and the Structure of Share Prices," *American Economic Review*, 60, No. 4 (September 1970), 601-17.

P/E Differences Between Firms and Industries

The main finding of these statistical studies of P/E's was that stable growth in earnings has strong positive effect on a firm's price-earnings ratio. Now let's look at specific firms to see if we can explain in some fashion the P/E's prevailing on these stocks.[23]

It is logical to assume that various industry groups would project an image of growth or lack of growth to the investment community. Therefore it should not surprise us that some groups will sport higher P/E's than others do. Table 10-5 contains data on average P/E's for selected industries for the years 1968-71. Two rather significant facts are apparent.

First is the relative consistency in the average level of price-earnings for these established industries over time—drugs have fluctuated only between 28 and 31, brewing between 22 and 25, and so on. Second, some industry groups have caught the fancy of Wall Street, and some have not. Note the huge difference in P/E level between toiletries and office equipment on the one hand and tobacco on the other. This variance is due in large part to the fact that the projected growth rates in earnings of the former industries are much higher than of the latter group.

TABLE 10-5
SELECTED AVERAGE INDUSTRY PRICE-EARNINGS RATIOS, 1968-1971

	1971	1970	1969	1968
Brewing	22	22	23	25
Toiletries and cosmetics	36	29	28	31
Tobacco	12	11	13	15
Drugs	30	28	31	31
Office equipment and computers	38	35	37	42

But aside from the differences in average levels among industries and the consistency of P/E levels for many industries for a few years, it should be noted that large differences exist between firms in the same industry grouping. For example, Kresge and Woolworth appear to be similar operations, and certainly in the same industry. Yet Kresge's P/E is currently many times that of Woolworth's. The reason seems to be that Kresge's earnings have risen modestly but steadily for a number of years, while Woolworth's earnings have fluctuated erratically. The market appears to favor growth that is *somewhat predictable* as opposed to growth that furnishes recurring surprises. In the auto industry, General Motors usually has a higher P/E than either Ford or Chrysler, probably because of the leadership position GM holds in the industry. In addition, certain stocks, such as IBM, Xerox, Johnson & Johnson, Polaroid, Avon, and Coca-Cola, continue to support high P/E's compared to the market. This seems to be because of their impressive historical growth records, as well as the projected high, stable growth that is forecast to continue for some time into the future.[24] Where does all this leave us?

---

[23]The examples of individual firms in this section come from John C. Perham, "The Riddle of the P/E Ratio," *Dun's Review*, September 1972, pp. 39-42.

[24]See Donald E. Fischer, "Performance of High and Low Price/Earnings Stocks," *Atlanta Economic Review*, 20, No. 6 (June 1970), pp. 11-13.

The business of selecting an appropriate P/E is one requiring *judgment*. The analyst must consider the state of the market and the specific industry group, and scrupulously evaluate *all* aspects of the individual firm. Only then can he make an informed decision.

Projecting Dividends

At this juncture we have gathered all the numbers we need to compute the projected HPY, except for the dividend. We already have the projected price, beginning price, and necessary tax and commission information. The starting point for the dividend calculation is the earnings projection, since dividends ultimately stem from earnings. The projected figure for earnings per share available to common is multiplied by the *payout ratio* (the percentage of EPS that is paid out as a dividend) to arrive at projected dividends.

This seems relatively simple; all we need is the payout ratio. Empirical studies have produced several interesting findings: (1) companies appear to have a predetermined payout ratio that they attempt to adhere to over the long run; (2) dividends are raised only if corporate management feels that a new, higher level of earnings can be supported in the future; and (3) managements are extremely reluctant to cut the absolute dollar amount of cash dividends.[25] We might apply these findings to the problem at hand—namely, projecting dividends.

First, we must keep in mind the evidence that firms have a long-run payout ratio. This means, for example, that on balance over time, a firm with a target payout of 50 percent is likely to pay out $1 in dividends if the EPS is $2; however, the *long-run average* need not be the figure decided upon in any one year.[26] The analyst must look at any trend in earnings, as well as at the absolute level of recent cash dividends. For example, suppose that our firm with the 50 percent target payout had earnings of $.90 in 1974, $1.00 in 1975, $1.10 in 1976, $1.20 in 1977, and $1.40 in 1978, and had paid $.45, $.45, $.50, and $.50 in cash dividends during the first four of these years, respectively. We must decide if management feels strongly enough about the growth rate in earnings [note that it rose between 1977 and 1978, from 9 percent ($.10/$1.10) to 17 percent ($.20/$1.20)] to raise the absolute dollar dividend from $.50 to, say, $.65 or $.70. It appears that management will at least raise the dividend; the question is, How much? Will the payout again approach the 50 percent long-run target? (It has not been at that level since 1974.) If management is optimistic about future prospects, the $.70 dividend may well come about. Projecting dividends, much like projecting a P/E ratio, requires experience, insight, and sound judgment.

---

[25]See John Lintner, "Distribution of Income of Corporations," *American Economic Review*, May 1956, pp. 97-113; John A. Brittain, *Corporate Dividend Policy* (Washington, D.C.: The Brookings Institution, 1966); and Eugene F. Fama and Harvey Babiak, "Dividend Policy: An Empirical Analysis," *Journal of the American Statistical Association*, December 1968, pp. 1132-61.

[26]The analyst can zero in on a target-payout ratio by computing the average payout over a number of recent fiscal years.

Now that we have discussed the theory behind the formulation of P/E ratio, dividend payouts, and dividends, it remains for us to arrive at a justification for the P/E and dividend for McDonald's (MCD) in our example in Chapters 9 and 10.

Table 10-6 contains dividend data on MCD for 1976 through 1980. Prior to 1976 the company had not paid a cash dividend. This policy prevailed since during these days of vigorous expansion McDonald's was also depending upon much needed internal financing to support additions to unit capacity. Pressure has come to bear upon McDonald's for dividends as the investing public has shifted interest toward requiring some of total expected return on the "front end." That is, many investors have expressed the sentiment that a "bird-in-the-hand" (dividend) is worth more than something-in-the-bush (price appreciation). Since 1977 a combination of a slightly lower share price and improved dividends has raised the yield above the 1.3 percent level, on average.

Based upon the recent trend of quarterly dividends, it is realistic to assume that the annual dividend per share in 1981 will approach $1.00. This amount is also in line with what we perceive to be a rising growth in dividends of about 30 percent per annum.

TABLE 10-6

McDONALD'S CORP.: HISTORICAL DIVIDEND INFORMATION

Year	Dividends per Share	Dividend Payout Ratio (%)	Average Dividend Yield* (%)
1980	$.74	13	1.6
1979	.51	11	1.3
1978	.32	8	.8
1977	.18	5	.4
1976	.08	3	.2

*Dividend/price using average of high and low price.

SOURCE: Company Annual Reports.

In Table 10-7 we see the P/E range for McDonald's during the 1974-80 period.

The slowdown in McDonald's earnings growth rate commencing in 1975 is reflected in Table 10-7. The P/E applied to McDonald's shares eroded relative to what investors were willing to pay for a dollar of market earnings. The average P/E (average of high and

TABLE 10-7

McDONALD'S P/E RATIO: ABSOLUTE AND RELATIVE TO THE MARKET, 1974-1980

	1974	1975	1976	1977	1978	1979	1980
P/E ratio range	37-13	28-12	24-18	16-11	15-11	11-8	9-7
P/E relative to S&P 400							
Highest monthly	4.2	3.1	2.4	1.9	1.8	1.5	1.3
Lowest monthly	1.6	1.8	1.6	1.3	1.4	1.2	.8
Average monthly	3.1	2.3	2.0	1.6	1.6	1.3	1.1

SOURCE: Standard & Poor's *Stock Reports.*

low) for McDonald's had the following pattern from 1974 through 1980: 25, 20, 21, 14, 13, 10, 8. It would appear from the P/E relatives that the P/E for McDonald's using the year-end closing price will be in the range of 110 to 130 percent of the S&P 400 price-earnings ratio. Based upon our earlier examination of the economic outlook for 1981, we would predict that the S&P 400 Index price-earnings ratio for the year would be in the vicinity of 7 to 8. Thus a reasonable estimate for the P/E to use with our earnings forecast for McDonald's might be in the 9 to 10 range.

Summary

In this chapter we have discussed several newer techniques of company analysis—regression analysis and the related tools of trend and correlation analysis, decision-tree analysis, and simulation. We have noted the strengths of these approaches as well as potential troublespots; however, on balance, we have concluded that they are superior to the more traditional techniques. In short, the newer methods have the strengths of the traditional methods while attempting to overcome their shortcomings.

Questions and Problems

1. What is the primary shortcoming of the traditional approaches to company analysis?

2. How should an analyst go about selecting variables to use in a regression during the company-analysis phase of his security evaluation procedures?

3. What variables do you think might "explain" the sales of a steel manufacturer? Why?

4. Differentiate between trend analysis and regression analysis.

5. Why are semilog graphs useful in plotting growth rates?

6. What are the pros and cons of using decision trees?

7. Prepare a decision tree for U.S. Steel, with no more than three branches at each stage of the tree.

8. What is simulation? Do you think it might be a useful technique in security analysis? Why? How would you simulate the data in your answer to Question 3? Would you expect the means of the end points of the decision tree and the mean value of the result of simulation to be equal?

9. If you were a junior security analyst in a conservative research department, how might you try to convince management to experiment with more modern techniques of company analysis?

10. What determines an appropriate P/E for the analyst to use? Why is this important?

11. What variables have been found to be useful in "explaining" P/E's?

12. Would you expect firms in the same industry to have approximately the same P/E's? Explain.

13. How might you forecast a firm's dividend for the next year? Forecast U.S. Steel's dividend for next year using this approach.

14. Based on your analysis of U.S. Steel performed above, what is your forecast of a one-year holding-period yield for U.S. Steel, beginning with yesterday's price?

part four
BOND ANALYSIS

Because of their fascination and preoccupation with the potential rewards associated with investing in common stocks, investors often lack an interest in or an understanding of fixed-income securities as an investment vehicle. The reasons behind the "second-string" role of fixed-income securities are not too difficult to sort out.

First, recent returns from investing in long-term bonds have not been impressive. For example, from the early 1960s to the early 1980s, long-term interest rates moved higher and higher—from 4 1/2 to 16 percent—causing bond prices to undergo steady declines. The second reason is the nature of the beast. Bonds pay a fixed and unchanging income with the expectation that their price will not be subject to wide fluctuations. The rather straightforward type of analysis of bonds that centers on quality and safety certainly lacks the sex appeal of discovering the wonder stock of the future.

Notwithstanding the record of returns on bonds and the somewhat unglamorous nature of bond analysis, several factors make bond analysis a very challenging topic. First, stabilization, or even a moderate downward trend, in interest rates over the next decade would contribute to renewed enthusiasm for bonds as an investment medium. Second, regardless of the future trend of interest rates, trading in bonds has always been a path to more glamour and returns. Trading involves taking advantage of technical, seasonal, and cyclical factors in the bond markets. Third, in recent years the relative odds in the stock and bond markets have shifted noticeably. Whereas the long-term return on common stocks has averaged about 9 percent, long-term interest rates moved from the 4 1/2 percent level in 1960 to near 15 percent in the early 1980s. This very tendency toward more equalization could contribute to a surge in participation in the bond markets.

With an eye to the validity of bonds as an investment medium, the next three chapters of the text discuss bond analysis. Preferred stocks are also discussed throughout, since their fixed-income nature provides close similarities to bonds.

Chapter 11 explores the nature and sources of systematic risk affecting bonds and preferred stocks. The impact of purchasing-power and interest-rate risk are noted. A substantial portion of the chapter is devoted to the underlying causes of changes in the overall level of interest rates and the structure of yields according to time.

Chapter 12 analyzes unsystematic risk in bonds and preferred stocks by examining and measuring business and financial risk bearing upon them. In addition, we note how changes in financial and business risk contribute to alterations in the risk premiums demanded by investors. Certain key nonrisk factors that influence yields are also probed.

The final chapter in this section, Chapter 13, examines active and passive bond management strategies.

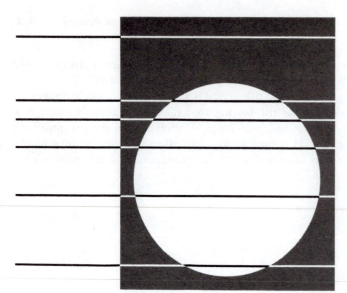

ELEVEN

Bond Analysis: Returns and Systematic Risk

The Strategic Role of Bonds

Portfolio management can be viewed as a two-level process. It includes the macro decision regarding the proportion of the portfolio to hold of the available asset classes (e.g., stocks and bonds) and the micro decision of which individual securities to hold which will make up the respective components. Our initial interest in this chapter will be in the role that bonds can play in the macro analysis. For most of recent history, investors looked to bonds for certainty of income. Bonds served as a kind of anchor to the winds of adversity. For those who find less volatility more emotionally acceptable or for those who realize their investment needs are more modest than those promised by an all-equity portfolio (over the long term), bonds tend to represent an important investment alternative in the portfolio asset allocation decision. If minimizing risk is the only objective, then investment in Treasury instruments will achieve a return which is accepted as being "risk-free." If maximizing return is the only objective, then investment in the highest expected return asset is the answer. Given the usual range of alternatives, this choice is common stock. The real problem is when a trade-off is desired between return and risk.

For the long sweep of time, bond returns are less than stock returns; however, bonds also experience less risk. The implication is that, although stocks might be expected to outperform bonds over sufficiently long periods of time, the associated risk may also be greater. Whether the risk preference of the investor can tolerate the associated intraperiod risk is a significant issue.

The total risk of a portfolio may be thought of as the individual risk of each investment and their correlation or tendency to move relative to each other. For example, if one had two assets of the same return and individual risk, there would be benefits to holding both assets if there was a tendency for one asset to counteract the volatility of the other.

There has been a historical positive, albeit low, correlation between stocks and corporate bonds. Between stocks and Treasury securities, there has been a negative relationship. The implications of these relationships is that combining stocks and bonds in a portfolio can help to reduce the portfolio's risk, perhaps more than proportionate to the reduction in overall return. Thus, bonds not only possess lower risk than stocks, they also can be useful when combined with stocks in a portfolio.

Finally, bonds have a place for an ever-increasing number of investors who do not wish to buy-and-hold. For those investors interested in capitalizing on bond price movements, bond trading can offer every bit of the excitement normally associated with trading in stocks.

Listed Bond Tables

CORPORATE BONDS

Basic information on bond trading appears regularly in the newspaper. The format appears in Figure 11-1. A key difference from the stock tables is that bond prices are shown as a percentage figure of $1,000, par value, whereas stock prices are listed in actual dollars and fractions thereof. For example, a bond price shown as 106 means 106 percent of $1,000 per bond or $1,060. A stock listed at 106 means $106 per share.

To examine the reading of these tables, look at the Exxon Corporation bond listed in the following table.

Bonds	1	2 Cur Yld	3 Vol	4 High	5 Low	6 Close	7 Net Chg.
Exxon	6s97	12.0	55	50 7/8	50	50/78	+5/8

1. The bond description sets forth the abbreviated name of the issuer, the interest rate, and the year of maturity. In this illustration the issuer of the bond is the Exxon Corporation, the interest rate is 6 percent of the bond's $1,000 face value, and the bond must be redeemed in the year 1997. The "s" after the "6" is simply pluralization, or the "6's." The specific month and day of maturation cannot be determined from these tables. Interested investors must refer to a research service that provides such information.

2. The current yield is a function of the investor's annual interest dollars and the latest value of the bond. The analytical formula is the annual interest divided by the current market value shown in column 6. Therefore, the current yield for this debenture is

$$\frac{60.00 \ (6\% \ of \ \$1,000)}{\$508.75 \ (50 \ 7/8\% \ of \ \$1,000)} = .12, \ or \ 12\%$$

The current yield of a convertible bond is not calculated in this bond table. It is identified by the letters "cv" appearing in this column. Investors do not normally buy convertible bonds just for their yield. They also look for a movement in the underlying stock to provide them with capital gains. Interest income is of secondary importance.

FIGURE 11-1

CORPORATION BONDS
Volume $21,930,000

Bonds	Cur Yld	Vol	High	Low	Close	Net Chg.
AMF 10s85	12.	3	82	82	82	+2
AMInt 9⅜95	18.	22	52	51	52	.....
AbbtL 9.2s99	14.	10	68	68	68	.....
AlaP 9s2000	16.	1	58	58	58	+1
AlaP 8½s01	15.	1	55⅜	55⅜	55⅜	+ ⅜
AlaP 7¾s02	15.	15	51¼	51¼	51¼	+ ¾
AlaP 8⅞s03	16.	29	55½	55	55	+ ⅛
AlaP 8¼s03	16.	5	52	52	52	−4⅞
AlaP 9¾s04	16.	1	61½	61½	61½	.....
AlaP 10⅞05	16.	5	67½	67½	67½	+1½
AlaP 8⅞06	16.	4	56½	56½	56½	.....
AlaP 8¾07	16.	15	54	53½	53½	−1½
AlaP 9¼07	17.	18	55	54	55	−1
AlaP 9½08	16.	7	59	59	59	−1½
AlaP 9⅝08	15.	2	62⅜	62⅜	62⅜	+2⅜
AlaP 15¼10	17.	66	88⅜	87½	88⅜	+ ⅜
AlaP 17⅜11	18.	176	97¼	95½	96⅞	+ ⅛
Alskin 12¾99	17.	10	73	73	73	.....
AlskH 16¼94	16.	5	98¾	98¾	98¾	.....
Alexn 5½96	cv	10	54	54	54	−3½
Allgl 4s81	cv	6	116	116	116	−7½
Allgl 9s89	13.	8	68	68	68	.....
AlsCha 12s90	15.	8	79	79	79	−3⅜
AllstF 8⅛87	12.	5	68	66	66	−8
AluCa 9½95	15.	9	64⅝	64⅝	64⅝	+ ¼
AMAX 8s86	10.	29	78	78	78	.....
Amerce 5s92	cv	22	70	70	70	.....
AFoP 4.8s87r	8.3	5	58	58	58	.....
AForP 5s30	13.	3	38¾	38¾	38¾	+ ¾
AAirl 4¼92	9.7	5	44	44	44	+ ½
AAirl 11s88	14.	2	79½	79½	79½	−1½
ABrnd 4⅝90	6.5	5	71	71	71	.....
ACyan 7⅜01	14.	1	52	52	52	− ¾
AExC 8½s86	11.	14	75	72¾	75	+ ¼
AmMed 8s00	cv	10	138	138	138	−6
AmMot 6s88	cv	2	58	58	58	.....
ASug 5.3s93	9.9	3	53¾	53¾	53¾	− ¾
ASu 5.3s93r	9.3	1	57	57	57	.....
ATT 2¾s82	3.0	141	92½	92¼	92⅜	.....
ATT 3¼s84	4.3	66	76⅜	75¾	75¾	.....
ATT 4⅜s85	5.7	26	76½	75⅜	76½	+2¼
ATT 2⅝s86	4.1	5	64¼	64¼	64¼	.....
ATT 3⅞s90	7.5	29	52	51½	51⅞	− ⅜
ATT 8¾00	13.	267	66	65¼	65¼	− ¼
ATT 7s01	14.	424	51⅛	50½	50¾	.....
ATT 7⅛s03	14.	788	50⅞	50⅝	50¾	.....
ATT 8.80s05	14.	186	61⅞	61⅛	61⅛	− ¾
ATT 7¾s82	8.1	73	96	95 21-32	96	.....
ATT 8⅝s07	14.	226	59¾	58⅝	59⅝	+ ½
ATT 10⅜90	14.	85	76⅞	76½	76¾	+ ⅜
ATT 13¼91	15.	331	90¾	88¾	88⅞	+ ⅛
Amfac 5¼94	cv	51	62	58½	59	−2½
Ampx 5½94	cv	30	81	81	81	.....
Anhr 9s05	cv	15	106½	106½	106½	− ½
AppP 10½84	12.	3	85	85	85	+ ½
AppP 11s87	14.	5	80	80	80	−5
Arco 8.70s81	8.9	20	98 5-32	98 3-32	98 5-32	+ ⅛
Arco 8⅜s83	9.8	5	85⅜	85⅜	85⅜	−1⅞
Arco 7½82	8.3	5	90¾	90	90	−1
Arco 7¾86	11.	10	72⅛	70¼	70¼	−2¾
ArizP 9½s82	9.9	52	96	96	96	+ ⅛
ArizP 10⅝00	15.	5	72⅜	72⅜	72⅜	− ⅝
Armr 5s84	5.6	12	90	90	90	.....
AshO 4¾93	cv	1	113	113	113	+3
AsCp 9¼90	13.	3	71¾	71¾	71¾	.....
AsCp 8.2s87	12.	5	70⅜	70⅜	70⅜	+1⅝
AsInv 7⅜88	12.	7	62⅞	62⅞	62⅞	− ⅛
Atchsn 4s95	7.9	1	50⅜	50⅜	50⅜	+6⅜
ARich 8⅝00	14.	40	63¼	63	63	− ¼
ARich 7.7s00	14.	29	57⅜	56½	56½	− ⅞
ARich 7¾03	14.	4	55	55	55	.....
Augat 8¼05	cv	9	104½	104½	104½	−3

New York Exchange Bonds

Wednesday, August 26, 1981

Total Volume $22,130,000

SALES SINCE JANUARY 1

1981	1980	1979
$3,232,496,000	$3,201,476,000	$2,293,980,000

	Domestic Wed	Domestic Tues	All Issues Wed	All Issues Tues
Issues traded	950	989	961	1001
Advances	283	187	286	192
Declines	445	612	450	614
Unchanged ..	222	190	225	195
New highs ...	4	3	4	3
New lows	193	256	195	258

Dow Jones Bond Averages

−1979− High	−1979− Low	−1980− High	−1980− Low	−1981− High	−1981− Low		−−−WEDNESDAY−−− −1981−	−1980−	−1979−
86.10	73.35	76.61	60.96	65.78	57.83	20 Bonds	57.83 − .59	68.87 − .23	85.44 − .03
88.60	72.40	78.63	59.40	66.18	56.11	10 Utilities	56.11 − .71	68.50 − .11	87.51 + .04
84.28	74.25	74.92	61.55	66.15	59.33	10 Industrial	59.55 − .48	69.25 − .35	83.37 − .10

Bonds	Cur Yld	Vol	High	Low	Close	Net Chg.
Dow 8⅞2000	14.	5	63½	63½	63½	+2⅛
Dow 8.92000	15.	9	61⅜	61⅜	61⅜	−1⅝
Dow 7⅝s03	14.	1	54⅜	54⅜	54⅜	−1⅞
Dow 8½s05	15.	8	57	57	57	+3
Dow 7⅞07	15.	21	52	52	52	−6
Dow 8⅝08	15.	5	58	58	58	−2
duPnt 8s81	8.2	12	97 19-32	97 9-16	97 19-32	+ ¼
duPnt 8.45s04	14.	80	59½	57⅞	59½	+1½
duPnt 8s86	10.	23	77	77	77	+1
duPnt 8½06	15.	36	58½	58½	58½	+ ¾
DukeP 7⅜02	15.	30	50½	50½	50½	.....
DukeP 7¾03	15.	10	52½	51½	52½	.....
DukeP 8⅛03	15.	20	54½	54½	54½	−1½
DukeP 9¾04	15.	13	64⅜	64	64⅜	− ⅛
DukeP 9⅜08	15.	15	61⅝	61¼	61¼	− ¼
DukeP 10⅞09	15.	10	70¼	70¼	70¼	− ¼
DukeP 14⅜87	15.	5	94½	94½	94½	− ½
DuqL 4¼89	8.4	5	50½	50½	50½	−2½
DuqL 8¾00	16.	15	56⅛	55¾	55¾	− ¾
DuqL 10⅛09	16.	25	63¾	63	63	.....
DuqL 12¼10	16.	13	76⅝	74½	74½	−3½
DuqL 14¼10	17.	10	86	86	86	−1
EasAir 5s92	cv	4	41⅞	41¾	41¾	− ⅛
EasAir 4¾93	cv	20	43½	43¼	43¼	− ¼
EasAir 11½99	cv	82	74⅛	73½	74	−1
EasAir 11¾05	cv	11	85⅛	85⅛	85⅛	− ⅜
EasAir 17½97	18.	5	95½	95½	95½	− ½
ElPas 6s93A	cv	1	145	145	145	−11
Empir 9s05	cv	21	67¼	67¼	67¼	− ¼
Esmk 8.4s82	8.8	5	95 11-32	95 11-32	95 11-32	+1-32
Estrl 12½95	16.	10	79⅛	79⅛	79⅛	.....
Exxon 6s97	12.	55	50⅞	50	50⅞	+ ⅝
Exxon 6½98	13.	45	53	52	52	+ ½
ExxP 9s04	15.	55	62¼	61½	62	− ½
ExxP 8⅞00	14.	15	62¾	62¾	62¾	− ¼
ExxP 7.65s83	8.7	12	88¼	88	88¼	+ ¼
ExxP 8¼01	14.	9	58⅞	57¼	58⅞	+1⅝
FMC 4¼92	cv	12	69	69	69	−2
FMC 7½01	14.	5	53¼	53¼	53¼	−3

Bonds	Cur Yld	Vol	High	Low	Close	Net Chg.
JoneL 6¾94	14.	10	48	47⅝	47⅝	− ⅜
JoneL 9⅞95	16.	15	64	62¼	63⅛	− ⅞
K mart 6s99	cv	13	68½	68¼	68¼	.....
K Mart 9⅞85	12.	50	83¼	82½	83	+ ⅜
Kaisr 9s05	cv	10	89½	89½	89½	−1½
KaufB 12¼99	17.	10	73	73	73	+ ½
Kenn 7⅞01	14.	11	56⅝	56½	56½	− ½
Kystn 8½05	cv	12	103	103	103	.....
KeyStl 7¼93	13.	10	55¼	55¼	55¼	−2¼
Kraft 6⅞96	13.	5	54	54	54	.....
Krogr 8.7s98	14.	10	62⅛	61⅝	61⅝	− ⅝
Krogr 9⅞83	11.	51	91¼	91	91	− ⅛
Krogr 10¼06	cv	5	96½	96½	96½	+ ½
LTV 5s88	8.9	30	56	55	55⅞	+ ⅞
LTV 9¼97	16.	52	58¾	57¾	57¾	− ¼
LTV 11s07	17.	68	66½	66	66	+1
LearS 10s04	15.	10	66⅜	66⅜	66⅜	.....
Leucd 13¾99	19.	2	73½	73½	73½	.....
Lockh 4¼92	cv	10	60	60	60	−2
Loew 6⅞93	13.	68	51¼	51	51	+ ½
Lorilld 6⅝93	13.	10	50¼	50¼	50¼	.....
LouN 7⅜93	13.	3	59	59	59	+1½
LouGs 9¼00	15.	4	60¼	60	60	−2
Lykes 7½94N	16.	16	48½	46⅝	48⅜	+1⅞
Lykes 7½94	16.	55	47¾	47	47¼	− ½
Lykes 11s00	17.	38	65½	64¼	64¼	.....
Lynch 8½99	cv	5	78⅛	78⅛	78⅛	.....
MACOM 9¼06	cv	10	93¾	93¾	93¾	− ½
MCI 15s00	18.	56	83	82⅝	82⅞	− ⅛
MCI 14⅛01	18.	3	78	78	78	− ⅜
MGM 10s93	15.	2	67½	67½	67½	−1
MGM 10s94	16.	12	62	62	62	.....
MGM 10½s96	16.	12	66⅛	66	66	− ⅝
McyCr 8s82	8.4	2	95 17-32	95 17-32	95 17-32	+1-32
MeYk 8½02	15.	30	56⅞	56¾	56⅞	+1⅞
MfrH 8⅛04	15.	15	53⅜	53⅜	53⅜	−1⅝
MfrH 8⅛07	15.	15	56	55⅞	55⅞	+1⅞
MfrH 14.9s87	16.	13	90½	90	90½	+ ½
MfrHT 8½85	11.	30	79½	79½	79½	−2
Mapco 10s05	cv	46	94½	93	93	−1¼

EXPLANATORY NOTES
(For New York and American Bonds)

Yield is current yield. cv-Convertible bond. ct-Certificates. f-Dealt in flat. m-Matured bonds, negotiability impaired by maturity. r-Registered. st-Stamped. wd-When distributed. ww-With Warrants. x-Ex-interest. xw-Without warrants.

vi-In bankruptcy or receivership or being reorganized under the Bankruptcy Act, or securities assumed by such companies.

SOURCE: *The Wall Street Journal,* August 26, 1981.

3. Volume figures are expressed in the number of $1,000 face-value bonds traded today. Simply add three zeros to the number in this column to find that $55,000 worth of face-value Exxon bonds changed hands on the NYSE.

4. High indicates the highest value at which these bonds traded today (50 7/8 percent of $1,000 = $508.75). You cannot determine from this information how many bonds traded at that price. It could have been a single bond, 10 bonds, or maybe even more.

5. Low is the minimum value at which the Exxon bonds traded on the NYSE. It is not apparent here, either, how many of these debentures changed hands at this price.

6. The Close is the last price at which a transaction took place on August 26, 1981, in the Exxon 6 percent bonds on the NYSE.

7. Net Chg., representing net change in value between day-to-day closing prices, is expressed as a percentage of a bond's $1,000 typical face value. Thus, a change of +5/8 means an increase in value of 5/8 percent of $1,000 ($6.25 per bond) over the previous closing price of that issue. The Exxon debentures due 1997 obviously closed yesterday at 50 1/4 (50 7/8 − 5/8).

GOVERNMENT BONDS

A portion of the business section in the daily newspaper is often used to present price information for most U.S. government, government agency, and quasi-government debt securities (see Figure 11-2). Some local papers may publish such information weekly only, although the major ones print daily quotations solicited from market-makers in those issues. The listings are categorized by issuer. In the case of U.S. government securities, they are categorized by type (such as bills, notes, bonds) and arranged in order of maturity. The earliest maturation dates are first, without regard to interest rate or yield. As with securities traded over the counter, only bid and asked prices are shown, defined in increments as small as 1/32 percent of the issue's par value. 1/32 percent amounts to $.3125 per $1,000. The figure in the column labeled "Yld." is a yield to maturity, not a current yield. Yield to maturity will be examined shortly.

In analyzing Figure 11-2, let us focus upon the 4 1/4s of May 1975-85 outlined in the section headed "Treasury Bonds and Notes."

1	2	3	4	5 Bid	6
Rate	Mat. Date	Bid	Asked	Chg.	Yld.
4 1/4s	1975-85 May	78.28	79.28	. . .	10.99

1. These bonds pay 4 1/4 percent interest. The small letter "s" following the interest rate is the traditional way these securities are identified; that is, in the plural form. It means that there is more than one debt instrument outstanding in this series to represent the obligation characterized by this issue. The absence of an "n" after the maturation month informs us that this is a bond and not a government note.

2. What appears to be a double maturation date (1975-85) is, in reality, advice that this issue is a term bond. The earlier year signifies that anytime after May 1975 until the time the bond must be redeemed in May 1985, the government can retire it at par by exercising its option to call this issue pursuant to such privilege stated in the indenture. It seems unlikely to do so because it cannot borrow medium-term funds at better than

FIGURE 11-2

Treasury Issues
* * *
Bonds, Notes & Bills

Wednesday, August 26, 1981
Mid-afternoon Over-the-Counter quotations; sources on request.

Decimals in bid-and-asked and bid changes represent 32nds; 101.1 means 101 1/32. a-Plus 1/64. b-Yield to call date. d-Minus 1/64. n-Treasury notes.

Treasury Bonds and Notes

Rate	Mat. Date		Bid	Asked	Bid Chg.	Yld.
9⅝s,	1981	Aug n.............	99.28	100	+ .1	9.19
6¾s,	1981	Sep n.............	99.1	99.5	+ .1	15.80
10⅛s,	1981	Sep n.............	99.10	99.14	+ .2	15.80
12⅝s,	1981	Oct n.............	99.4	99.8	+ .1	16.39
7s,	1981	Nov n.............	97.24	97.28	+ .1	16.92
7¾s,	1981	Nov n.............	97.28	98	.....	17.03
12⅛s,	1981	Nov n.............	98.20	98.24	− .1	16.71
7¼s,	1981	Dec n.............	96.26	96.30	.....	16.58
11⅜s,	1981	Dec n.............	98.3	98.7	.....	16.61
11½s,	1982	Jan n.............	97.17	97.21	.....	17.28
6⅛s,	1982	Feb n.............	95.4	95.8	.....	17.12
6⅜s,	1982	Feb.............	95.6	95.10	.....	17.23
13⅞s,	1982	Feb n.............	98.13	98.17	.....	17.01
7⅞s,	1982	Mar n.............	94.28	95	.....	17.09
15s,	1982	Mar n.............	98.24	98.28	.....	17.07
11⅜s,	1982	Apr n.............	96.10	96.14	.....	17.16
7s,	1982	May n.............	93.10	93.18	− .2	16.87
8s,	1982	May n.............	94	94.8	.....	16.81
9¼s,	1982	May n.............	94.22	94.26	.....	17.22
9⅜s,	1982	May n.............	94.12	94.16	.....	17.39
8¼s,	1982	Jun n.............	93.14	93.18	.....	16.74
8⅜s,	1982	Jun n.............	93.19	93.23	.....	16.92
8⅞s,	1982	Jul n.............	93.6	93.10	.....	16.98
8⅛s,	1982	Aug n.............	92.22	92.30	.....	16.32
9s,	1982	Aug n.............	93.10	93.14	− .3	16.63
11⅛s,	1982	Aug n.............	94.30	95.2	+ .2	16.64
8⅜s,	1982	Sep n.............	92.2	92.6	+ .1	16.48
11⅞s,	1982	Sep n.............	95.8	95.12	.....	16.68
12⅛s,	1982	Oct n.............	95.10	95.14	+ .2	16.54
7⅛s,	1982	Nov n.............	90.6	90.10	+ .6	16.20
7⅞s,	1982	Nov n.............	90.20	90.28	.....	16.43
13⅞s,	1982	Nov n.............	96.20	96.24	− .6	16.84
9⅜s,	1982	Dec n.............	91.16	91.24	− .2	16.47
15⅛s,	1982	Dec n.............	97.26	97.30	.....	16.90
13⅜s,	1983	Jan n.............	95.22	95.26	− .3	17.06
8s,	1983	Feb n.............	89.15	89.23	− .1	16.16
13⅞s,	1983	Feb n.............	95.28	96	− .1	16.99
9¼s,	1983	Mar n.............	90.2	90.10	+ .7	16.40
12⅝s,	1983	Mar n.............	93.26	93.30	− .3	17.13
14½s,	1983	Apr n.............	96.8	96.12	+ .1	17.07
7⅞s,	1983	May n.............	87.11	87.19	− .1	16.44
11⅜s,	1983	May n.............	92.30	93.2	.....	16.41
15⅝s,	1983	May n.............	98.1	98.5	+ .4	16.88
3¼s,	1978-83	Jun.............	82.24	83.24	.....	13.74
8⅞s,	1983	Jun n.............	88.4	88.12	+ .2	16.43
14⅞s,	1983	Jun n.............	96.10	96.14	.....	16.95
15⅞s,	1983	Jul n.............	98.14	98.18	+ .2	16.78
9¼s,	1983	Aug n.............	88.7	88.15	− .7	16.34
11⅞s,	1983	Aug n.............	92.20	92.28	− .5	16.25
16¼s,	1983	Aug n.............	99.9	99.13	− .1	16.61
9¾s,	1983	Sep n.............	88.20	88.28	+ .4	16.23
7s,	1983	Nov n.............	83.30	84.6	+ .6	15.71
9⅞s,	1983	Nov n.............	88.16	88.24	+ .3	16.10
10½s,	1983	Dec n.............	89.20	89.28	+ .9	15.84
7¼s,	1984	Feb n.............	82.26	83.2	.....	15.81
14¼s,	1984	Mar n.............	96.28	97.4	+ .3	15.64
9¼s,	1984	May n.............	85.18	85.26	− .4	15.88
13¼s,	1984	May n.............	93.19	93.27	− .1	16.14
15¾s,	1984	May n.............	98.28	99	+ .2	16.22
8⅞s,	1984	Jun n.............	84.6	84.14	+ .1	15.89
6⅜s,	1984	Aug.............	79.17	80.17	.....	14.71
7¼s,	1984	Aug n.............	80.18	80.26	− .2	15.57
13¼s,	1984	Aug n.............	92.30	93.6	+ .2	16.24
12⅛s,	1984	Sep n.............	90	90.8	− .6	16.26
16s,	1984	Nov n.............	98.30	99.2	+ .2	16.39
14s,	1984	Dec n.............	94.2	94.10	+ .2	16.27
8s,	1985	Feb n.............	80	80.16	− .1	15.49
13⅜s,	1985	Mar n.............	92	92.8	− .3	16.30
3¼s,	1985	May.............	78.30	79.30	+ .3	9.60
4¼s,	1975-85	May.............	78.28	79.28	.....	10.99
10⅜s,	1985	May n.............	85.8	85.16	+ .16	15.68
14⅜s,	1985	May n.............	96	96.8	+ .4	15.75
14s,	1985	Jun n.............	93.23	93.27	+ .4	16.22
8¼s,	1985	Aug n.............	78.25	79.1	+ .7	15.53

10⅜s,	2004-09	Nov.........	72.19	72.27	+ .7	14.35
11¾s,	2005-10	Feb.........	81.13	81.21	− .1	14.45
10s,	2005-10	May.........	70.16	70.24	+ .10	14.25
12¾s,	2005-10	Nov.........	87.26	88.2	− .2	14.41
13⅞s,	2006-11	May.........	95.4	95.12	+ .2	14.57

U.S. Treas. Bills

Mat. date	Bid	Asked	Yield Discount	Mat. date	Bid	Asked	Yield Discount
-1981-				-1981-			
9- 3	15.25	14.83	15.07	12-24	15.72	15.52	16.58
9-10	15.31	14.95	15.24	12-31	15.75	15.55	16.67
9-17	15.24	14.90	15.23	-1982-			
9-24	13.66	13.40	13.72	1- 7	15.49	15.37	16.52
10- 1	15.23	15.01		1-14	15.47	15.33	16.52
5.44				1-21	15.78	15.58	16.86
10- 8	15.32	15.06	15.54	1-28	15.83	15.63	16.98
10-15	15.45	15.21	15.74	2- 4	15.93	15.73	17.15
10-22	15.45	15.19	15.77	2-11	15.93	15.73	17.20
10-29	15.51	15.25	15.88	2-18	15.90	15.76	17.36
11- 5	15.74	15.52	16.22	2-25	15.88	15.72	17.37
11-12	15.85	15.67	16.43	3-25	15.47	15.33	16.88
11-19	15.83	15.69	16.51	4-22	15.47	15.31	16.93
11-27	15.83	15.77	16.65	5-20	15.45	15.31	17.04
12- 3	15.83	15.63	16.54	6-17	15.24	15.08	16.89
12-10	15.77	15.57	16.53	7-15	15.20	15.04	16.99
12-17	15.61	15.41	16.40	8-12	15.02	14.76	17.05

SOURCE: *The Wall Street Journal*, August 26, 1981.

the 4 1/4 percent it is paying on this bond now. This is also why the Treasury Department has not called the bond since 1975 either.

   3. A holder anxious to sell this bond must accept the bid price of 78.28, which is 78 28/32 percent of $1,000 or $788.75 per bond.

   4. An investor interested in buying the bond must pay the offering price of 79.28, which is 79 28/32 percent of $1,000 or $798.75 per bond.

   5. This issue was unchanged from yesterday's bid. Net changes are always measured from day to day based upon the bid price.

   6. The $798.75 offering price per bond is equivalent to a yield to maturity of 10.99 percent when one takes into account the appreciation if held until 1985, plus the interest coupon of $42.50 ($1,000 X 4 1/4 percent) per year.

   Treasury bills, which range in duration up to 1 year from date of issuance, are listed in order of maturity month and day. There is no column for yield because bill prices are already discounted and expressed in terms of that security's yield-to-maturity. Hence, the bid price is always numerically higher than its offering price. The higher percentage discount from par value always means a lower dollar price.

   For example, look at the November 27 bill noted in the tables. Its remaining lifetime is just 93 days from August 26, 1981. This bill is offered at a dollar value, discounted from its face amount. If purchased on August 26, 1981, the average rate of return for that investor, on an annualized basis, would be 15.77%. Because it is purchased for less than face amount and redeemed at maturity for its face amount, the difference in dollars, based upon the money actually invested, equals 15.77 percent.

Bond Returns and Prices

   Bond returns can be calculated in the standard way introduced in Chapter 4 as holding period yield. It is also common practice to determine bond returns by adjusting for the timing of the ingredients of the return. We will examine these methods of calculating bond returns in the sections just ahead.

Holding-Period Yield

   Bonds and preferred stocks are commonly referred to as fixed-income or fixed-dollar securities, since the annual interest or dividend income received from them is fixed by contract. The holding-period yield on preferred stocks is calculated in the same manner as that on common stocks. The basic difference is evident in the fixed nature of preferred dividends. Common-stock dividends are variable and may trend upward, whereas preferred dividends are generally set at a maximum but are relatively more certain.

   The dividends paid on preferred stocks are frequently stated in dollar or percentage-of-par terms. A "$2 preferred stock" indicates the annual dollar dividend. Alternatively, a "4 percent preferred" with a $50 par value would also pay a $2 dividend, since the dollar value is the product of the dividend rate (percentage) multiplied by the par value.

   The holding-period yield on bonds is defined much like that on stocks, except that interest payments rather than dividends are received. Interest is customarily paid semi-annually, whereas dividends on stocks are paid quarterly as a rule. The nature of debt contracts is such that the interest payments on a bond issue are fixed and are more certain than dividends, either common or preferred. The holding-period-yield formula for bonds is:

$$HPY = \frac{(P_1 - P_0) + I}{P_0}$$

(11.1)

where:

HPY = holding-period yield

I = interest payments

P_0 = beginning price

P_1 = ending price

The single most important fact to observe about HPYs on fixed-income securities is that, since the annual income received is fixed in dollar terms, any shifts in required HPY must come from changes in price. This is not so in the case of common stocks, where dividends can fluctuate up and down and, it is hoped, will grow larger over time.

Time-Adjusted Yield on Bonds

As long as a bond is not expected to go into default, the expected return is made up of annual interest payments plus the price to be recovered at maturity or sooner. Take an example of a three-year bond with a principal value of $1,000, bearing a nominal rate of interest (coupon) of 6 percent. Assume that an investor wishes to purchase this bond for a rate of 6 percent. Since bond interest is normally paid twice a year, $60 of interest per annum would be paid in two semiannual installments of $30 each ($60/2). The 6 percent annual rate is thus 3 percent per six-month period (6/2). What should he be willing to pay for a series of ten $30 interest payments and a lump sum of $1,000 at the end of the fifth year?

In general, what a bond is worth can be determined thus:

$$V = \sum_{n=1}^{2N} \frac{I_n/2}{(1 + i/2)^n} + \frac{P_N}{(1 + i/2)^{2N}}$$

(11.2)

where:

V = value of bond

I = annual interest (dollars)

i = required rate of interest (percent)

P = principal value of maturity

N = life of bond

It is easy to see that although bonds carry a promise to maintain a constant-dollar interest payment to maturity, I, and pay a fixed principal at maturity, P, the number of years to maturity, N, and the required rate of interest, i, can vary.

The present value of the interest-payment stream of $60 per year for three years is as follows:

$$V = \frac{\$30}{1 + .03} + \frac{\$30}{(1 + .03)^2} + \frac{\$30}{(1 + .06)^3}$$

$$+ \frac{\$30}{(1 + .06)^4} + \frac{\$30}{(1 + .06)^5} + \frac{\$30}{(1 + .06)^6} = \$163$$

The present value of the principal at maturity (end of year 3) is $\$1,000/(1+.03)^6 = \$837$. The total value of the bond is thus $163 + $837, or $1,000. In other words, a $1,000 bond is worth $1,000 today if the nominal rate and the required rate of interest are equal. The $1,000 value is a composite of $163 of interest payments and $837 of principal.

Suppose new three-year bonds are offered at 8 percent. Outstanding 6 percent bonds will continue to pay $60 per $1,000 by contract. The advance in interest rates will cause the price of the outstanding bond to fall:

$$V = \frac{\$30}{1 + .04} + \frac{\$30}{(1 + .04)^2} + \frac{\$30}{(1 + .04)^3}$$

$$+ \frac{\$30}{(1 + .04)^4} + \frac{\$30}{(1 + .04)^5} + \frac{\$30}{(1 + .04)^6}$$

$$+ \frac{\$1,000}{(1 + .04)^6}$$

$$= \$948$$

Had new three-year bonds been offered at 4 percent, or less than the outstanding 6 percent bonds, the price of the 6 percent bonds would have risen to $1056. A basic principal concerning bonds is that *prices move inversely to interest rates.*

Most people now use calculators or computers to get bond prices and yields. Hand held calculators can perform necessary price and/or yield calculations very quickly.

Yield-to-Call

When a bond is subject to redemption prior to maturity, the cash flow implicit in the yield-to-maturity figure is subject to possible early alteration. Most corporate bonds sold today are callable by the issuer, but with a certain period of protection before the call option can be exercised. At the expiration of this period the bond may be called in at a specified call price which usually involves some premium over par.

To provide some measure of the return in the event that the issuer were to exercise his call option at some future point, the yield-to-call is often computed and compared with the yield-to-maturity. This computation is based on the assumption that the bond's cash flow is terminated at the "first call date" with redemption of principal at the specified call price. For a given rate, the present value of this assumed "cash flow to call" can be determined and the yield-to-call is then defined as that discount rate which makes this present-value figure equal to the bond's market value.

For example, suppose one has a 30-year 8 3/4 percent bond priced at 107 3/4 which is callable at 107 starting in 5 years. The cash flow to maturity consists of 60 semiannual coupon payments of $43.75 each followed by a redemption payment of $1,000. The yield-to-maturity turns out to be 8.15 percent. The cash flow to an assumed call in 5 years consists of 10 coupon payments followed by a redemption payment of $1,070. Using a discount rate of 8 percent the present value of the cash flow to call is $1,077.70, that is, close to the bond's market price:

Coupon payment (semiannual)	$43.75 × 8.1109 =	$ 354.85
Redemption payment	$1,070.00 × .6756 =	722.89
		$1,077.74

The investor would have to choose between the higher yield to maturity (8.15 percent) and the lower yield-to-call (8 percent) for investment purposes. With the bond selling above par, if interest rates were expected to fall below 8 percent over the next five years, it would be both prudent and conservative to use the lower yield.

Yield-to-call can be calculated by the following general formual:

$$P_M = \sum_{n=1}^{2NC} \frac{I_n/2}{(1 + i/2)^n} + \frac{P_C}{(1 + i/2)^{2NC}} \qquad (11.3)$$

where:

NC = number of years to first call date

P_C = call price

P_M = market price

Systematic Risk in Holding Fixed-Income Securities

The same general categories of risk that influence common stocks also influence fixed-income securities, but there are differences in the degree of their impact. The primary sources of *systematic* risk in holding fixed-income securities are interest-rate and purchasing-power risk.

Purchasing-Power Risk

Over very broad lapses of time no single economic or financial variable appears to be strongly positively correlated with the level of interest rates than does the commodity price trend. Either historically, in periods as long as 1900 to the present, or in less encompassing periods, such as the postwar era, the positive relationship seems unambiguous. The problem with this relationship lies in predicting interest rates over much shorter intervals using inflation forecasts as the major explanatory variable.

Theoretically, when commodity prices are perceived to rise, lenders require higher rates of interest to protect depreciating purchasing power of the debt payments, while borrowers are willing to repay in cheaper dollars at higher nominal rates. It is also theorized that rising commodity prices raise the level of interest rates, since rising commodity prices increase nominal credit demands, thereby boosting interest rates.

To a great extent, the return expected on U.S. government securities at any point in time will reflect the rate of inflation in the economy, since the rate on USGs embodies a riskless rate plus some compensation for purchasing-power risk. Governments are devoid of business and financial risk, owing to a monopoly status and taxing powers available to ensure that debt-servicing obligations are met.

Extensive studies of interest rates by the Federal Reserve Bank of St. Louis tend to indicate that the riskless rate of interest fluctuates around 3 percent. If this is true, adding to this an allowance for the rate of price change (purchasing-power risk) might produce a fair approximation of the rate of interest on long-term government bonds.

The rate of price change is the annual percentage change in prices; we often refer to it as the change in the cost of living. If a price index begins the year at 100 and ends at 103, we say the rate of increase (inflation) is 3 percent [(103 − 100)/100]. If, from the second to third year, the index changes from 103 to 109, the rate of price change is said to be about 5.8 percent [(109 − 103)/103]. The rate of change in prices can also be downward (deflation).

The necessity to adjust the rate of interest for price changes can be seen in a simple example. Suppose you lend $100 today for a promise to be repaid $105 at the end of a year. The rate of interest is 5 percent. However, assume that prices over the next year are expected to advance 6 percent. Because of inflation, the $105 received at the end of the year has a purchasing power of only 94 percent of $105, or $98.70. You must charge 5 percent plus an inflation premium of 6 percent, or a total of 11 percent, to allow for inflation.

The rate of inflation experienced in the United States over long time periods prior to 1969 was on the order of 2-3 percent. The rate was 8.5 percent compounded per annum between 1973 and 1979.

The tricky part of the whole process is that long-term interest rates reflect both *expected* inflation and *uncertainty* about inflation. Rates of expected future inflation will not necessarily be the same as those experienced in the past, even the most recent past.

Interest-Rate Risk

Interest-rate risk can be identified as the truly overwhelming systematic risk associated with holding fixed-income securities. Interest rate risk refers to the possibility that income and/or capital loss will result because of an increase in the level of interest rates; this is the major risk element for most high-quality, investment-grade debt securities. This risk can be illustrated by observing the impact of a change in interest rates on bonds with different coupon rates and maturities.

PRICE RISK

High-grade bond prices react to a given change in yield as a function of maturity, the coupon rate, and the general level of yields from which the change occurs. All other things being equal, with the same percentage change in yield, the *volatility* of the price of a bond *increases*

1. As the maturity lengthens (the longer the maturity, the greater the bond price volatility), but at a diminishing rate as maturity is lengthened

2. As the coupon rate declines (the lower the coupon, the greater the price volatility)

3. As the yields rise (the higher the yield level from which a yield fluctuation starts, the greater the price volatility)

Before attempting to explore the structural forces that create these three determinants of volatility, let us look at Table 11-1 which illustrates the volatility effect of these three variables: maturity, coupon, and the starting level of yields.

TABLE 11-1
VOLATILITY OF BOND PRICES

1. Price Changes and Maturity

Face = $100   Coupon = 6%

Required Yield (%)	Years to Maturity			
	1	10	20	30
4	102*	116	127	135
5	101	108	112	115
6	100	100	100	100
7	99	93	89	88
8	98	86	80	77

2. Price Changes and Coupon (20-year maturity)

Coupon Value (%)	Interest Rates Rise			Interest Rates Fall		
	7%	8%	% Change	7%	5%	% Change
4	68*	60	−11.3	68	87	+28.7
5	78	70	−10.5	78	100	+27.1
6	89	80	−10.0	89	112	+25.8
7	100	90	−9.8	100	125	+25.1
8	110	100	−9.5	110	137	+24.4

3. Price Changes and Level of Rates

6%, 20-year bond. Basis point change of 10% from original yield in each case.

Original Yield (%)	Interest Rates Rise				Interest Rates Fall			
	Price	New Yield	New Price	% Change	Price	New Yield	New Price	% Change
4	127*	4.4	121	−4.9	127	3.6	134	+5.3
5	112	5.5	106	−5.8	113	4.5	120	+6.3
6	100	6.6	93	−7.0	100	5.4	107	+7.3
7	89	7.7	83	−7.3	89	6.3	96	+8.1
8	80	8.8	74	−8.0	80	7.2	87	+9.0

*All prices are rounded for simplification. Thus, percentages will not correspond exactly.

The first section of Table 11-1 illustrates the relationship between price changes and maturity. The example being used assumes a 6 percent coupon bond with a face value of $100. Notice that when the required yield is 6 percent, the bond price is 100 regardless of the number of years to maturity. As the required yield moves away from the coupon rate, notice that prices move in an inverse direction. For example, for a bond with a one-year maturity and a 6 percent coupon, if the required yield is 4 percent, the suggested bond price is 102. Similarly, if the required yield is 8 percent, the suggested bond price is 98. Note, however, that the volatility of a bond's price will increase, but at a diminishing rate, as the maturity is lengthened. Table 11-2 illustrates this point. This table ultilizes the data appearing in part 1 of Table 11-1.

TABLE 11-2
BOND PRICE VOLATILITY RELATIVE TO MATURITY
PERCENTAGE CHANGE IN BOND PRICE
AS MATURITY CHANGES FROM:

Required Yield	1-10	10-20	20-30
4%	+13.7	+9.5	+6.3
8%	−13.2	−7.0	−3.7

Two coupon rates were selected and the percentage change in the price of a bond was calculated as maturity was lengthened. From Table 11-1 we saw that a 6 percent bond with a ten-year maturity would sell for 116 if the investor's required yield was 4 percent. Using the same required yield, the price at twenty years would be 127 and for thirty years it is 135. Table 11-2 suggests that the price change moving from ten to twenty years maturity is +9.5 percent [(127 − 116)/116]; moving from twenty to thirty years the percentage price change is only +6.3 percent [(135 − 127)/127]. Note that volatility changes are not linear relative to maturity.

For a given difference between the coupon rate and required yield, the longer the term to maturity, the greater the accompanying price change. For example, if rates move from 6 percent to 7 percent, the price of the bond will move to 99 if the maturity is one year; at the forty year maturity the price would fall to 87. Note that the *percentage* decline in price is 1 percent at one year [(99 − 100)/100] and 13 percent at forty years [(87 − 100)/100].

The relationship between price changes and the coupon rate is illustrated in the second section of Table 11-1. All the examples in this table assume a constant 20-year maturity bond. A 20-year bond with a 4 percent coupon will sell at 68 if the required yield is 7 percent. If interest rates rise to 8 percent, the bond will fall to 60. The same 4 percent coupon bond would rise to 87 if interest rates fell to 5 percent. Looking at the entire second section of Table 11-1, it is obvious that the greatest price volatility occurs in the lowest coupon bonds.

The relationship between price changes and the level of rates is illustrated in the third section of Table 11-1. Using a 6 percent, 20-year bond throughout this table illustrates the price effects of a 10 percent change from the original yield level in each case. If the original yield is 7 percent, the suggested price for a 6 percent, 20-year bond is 89. If interest rates rise 10 percent to 7.7 percent, the new bond price is 83. This represents a 7.3 percent decline in the bond price. Looking at the entire third section of Table 11-1, it becomes apparent that price volatility is greatest when interest rates change from a high level of yields versus a lower level of yields.

REINVESTMENT RISK

There is a second dimension to interest rate risk. This aspect is referred to as reinvestment risk. If after you purchase a bond, interest rates decline (rise), it will not be possible to reinvest interest payments at the proposed yield to maturity, but they will be reinvested at lower (higher) rates and the ending sum would be below (above) what you expected. For example, suppose you purchase a one-year, 8 percent bond at $1,000 today in order to pay a debt of $1,081.60 one year from now. Because coupon payments are semiannual, your plan is sound enough if you can reinvest the semiannual $40 coupon at 8 percent.

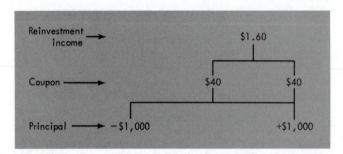

However, if interest rates drop by the semiannual payment time to, say, 6 percent, your reinvestment income will not be $1.60 ($40 × .04) but rather $1.20 ($40 × .03). Thus, a drop in interest rates causes a decline in the expected income from investing interim coupon payments. Table 11-3 shows the total realized compound yield over the life of an 8 percent bond due in twenty years and purchased for $1,000 under varying assumptions relative to coupon reinvestment rates. Note that the yield to maturity of 8 percent (bond purchased at par with an 8 percent coupon) is a valid measure of the return on the bond *only* if coupons are reinvested at the calculated yield to maturity. For example, reinvesting coupons at 10 percent provides a lifetime yield of 9.01 percent.

TABLE 11-3
REALIZED COMPOUND YIELD
(8 PERCENT BOND DUE IN 20 YEARS
PURCHASED AT PAR)

Reinvestment Rate (%)	Total Realized Compound Yield (%)
0	4.84
6	6.64
8	8.00
10	9.01

Note that the price risk and the reinvestment risk resulting from a change in interest rates have opposite effects on an investor's ending wealth position. Specifically, an increase in the level of interest rates will cause an ending price that is below expectations, but the reinvestment of interim cash flow (coupons) will be at a rate above expectations.

The reverse is true for declining interest rates. In Chapter 13 we will look more closely at aggressive and defensive tactics designed to capitalize on or immunize against these effects.

Forecasting Interest-Rate Trends

Varied socioeconomic and political forces have an impact upon the level and direction of interest rates.[1] These forces tend to push rates up or down in harmony over a broad spectrum of fixed-income securities. In the process, however, two significant developments are watched closely by an investor. First, for securities in the same class, rates move in harmony but to differing degrees, depending upon term to maturity. Second, securities of different default-risk classes with similar terms to maturity also move in differing degrees.

Bonds and preferred stocks are often traded by speculators and money managers to take advantage of the very short-term, day-to-day or seasonal (month-to-month) fluctuations in yields. The skills required include keen insight into both random and predictable supply-demand relationships, courage, and, of course, impeccable timing. Our main concern is with forecasting interest rates over the medium term or business cycle.

The forecaster must be both a psychoanalyst and a value analyst. Interest rates are determined not only by what is currently happening but by what people think will happen. Let us turn our attention first, however, to the information that can be brought to bear upon value analysis.

Assuming an Economic Model

The analyst must first develop an economic model for the year ahead that takes into account recent economic trends and known government policies. In Chapter 6 we examined tools and techniques for assessing the economic outlook in terms of short-run forecasting. GNP model-building, indicators, and econometric models were seen to be powerful allies in assessing the level and direction of various measures of economic activity. The key is to determine what stage of the cycle the economy is in, where it is moving, and how fast.

The movement of the economy and of interest rates is of overriding importance in the purchase of fixed-income securities generally. An article of faith among most financial persons is the proposition that business recessions bring low interest rates (rising bond prices) and business booms bring high interest rates (falling bond prices). Therefore an outlook for an extended upward trend in interest rates would tend to augur against a commitment to bonds. However, an opportunity for capital gains lies in the possibility of a decline in interest rates subsequent to a bond or preferred-stock purchase.

Interest rates have typically turned at about the same time as industrial production. To the extent that this relationship prevails, interest rates could be classified as a coinci-

---

[1]This section draws heavily upon Sidney Homer, "Techniques for Forecasting Interest-Rate Trends," an address before the Chicago chapter of the American Statistical Association on June 14, 1966; and W.C. Freund and E.D. Zinbarg, "Sources and Uses of Funds," in *Financial Institutions and Markets*, ed. M.E. Polakoff (Boston: Houghton Mifflin, 1970), pp. 463-84.

dent economic indicator. However, these relationships are not always consistent, and the determination of economic turning points is difficult (see Chapter 6). If the time to buy bonds was at the peak of economic activity, not before, and an analyst was good at picking these turning points, then bond investing would indeed be easy![2] Aside from the difficulties in forecasting economic (interest-rate) turns, another problem exists. Do fluctuations in business activity of less importance than booms or recessions promise correspondingly (if milder) increases or decreases in interest rates?

Sidney Homer, long recognized as the bard of the bond business, suggests an answer to this question. His work indicates that the correlation between bond yields and the business cycle

> can only be relied upon in periods when cyclical forces are powerful, such as peaks of booms or recessions, and that at other times the bond market is capable of a wide variety of patterns which do not correlate with business trends and are influenced no doubt partly by long-term secular fundamentals and partly by transitory political or economic events. . . .[3]

C.C. Abbott found two long cycles in bond prices since 1874, each lasting about forty-six years. Within these cycles, he noted that periods of falling rates (rising prices) lasted about twenty-six years; periods of rising rates (falling prices) lasted about twenty years. This would suggest long cycles within which short undulations (seasonal, cyclical influences) take shape.[4]

The existence of short cycles and transitory effects on the way to a peak or toward a recession provides opportunities for respectable returns in fixed-income securities by gearing investment and speculative strategies to cyclical and transitory events. Obviously, if the long-term trend in interest rates is downward, long-term investing in bonds is desirable.

Prices and Employment

Business activity and interest rates are closely tied; however, there is divergence between their relative cycles. The early stages of economic recoveries sometimes bring bear bond markets, but often the bond market is little affected until late boom stages. Since interest rates really reflect the price of money, it helps to examine other relative prices, such as those for materials and labor—the latter from the viewpoint of employment.

The trend of prices and employment affects government policies in the areas of fiscal and monetary policy. Stable or soft prices accompanied by high unemployment enable monetary and fiscal policy to promote economic expansion without fear of inflation. Rapid economic growth under such conditions could mean stable or even declining bond yields. Conversely, low unemployment and rising prices would imply that any economic outlook predicting growth could bring rising bond yields.

---

[2] It was long believed that business recessions meant falling interest rates and stock prices. But in the 1981-82 period, the recession brought the stock market down, and interest rates rose.

[3] Homer, "Techniques for Forecasting Interest-Rate Trends."

[4] C.C. Abbott, "Yes, But Rates Can't Act That Way," in Institute of Chartered Financial Analysts, *1972 Supplementary Readings in Financial Analyses* (Homewood, Ill: Richard D. Irwin, 1972). pp. 67-79. Abbott thought the softening of rates in 1968 signaled the end of a long cycle. He was in error—at least temporarily.

Supply and Demand for Credit

Given the outlook for the economy and its components, it is necessary to look into where the money will come from. This stage of forecasting requires a systematic look at all the factors making up the supply of and demand for funds. The Federal Reserve has developed a system that accounts for this supply and demand, using the flow of funds through the varied sectors of the economy similar to that of the national income accounts. For those seeking a summary of these flows, as well as a one-year forecast, Salomon Bros., a large bond house in New York, publishes its *Prospects for the Financial Markets* each February.

The aim of flow-of-funds accounts and the Salomon Bros. research is to quantify the forces of supply and demand for funds in the economy, and to see (1) whether the balance of force lies in the direction of higher or lower interest rates, and (2) which segments (short and/or long term) will face more or less pressure. Imbalances detected between supply and demand indicate interest-rate effects: Unsatisfied demands place upward pressures on interest rates; excess supply tends to force rates down.

Table 11-4 is taken from 1981 *Prospects for the Financial Markets*. This is a summary table of supply and demand for credit. Similarly, the tables referred to inside Table 11-4 provide detail on specific aspects of the markets.

"Net Demand" represents demand for funds, both historically and forecast into the future one year. In this case, the years 1975-79 represent historical data (1980 is estimated, since refined data were not available at press time). The estimate of demand is shown for 1981. The numbers for each year show the net annual increase in demand in each important department of the capital market. "Net Supply" shows net annual acquisitions of various instruments by investor groups.

We can see which types of credit demand are dynamic or stable. In addition, we can see the appetites of particular investor groups over time. Large or small increases in total credit do not, in themselves, indicate tendencies toward higher or lower interest rates, because supply and demand will balance by definition. A small expansion in total demand can be the result of a shortage of funds (tight money = high rates) or insufficient demand (easy money = lower rates). Surplus supply (lower rates) or excessive demand (higher rates) can cause large total expansion.

Freund and Zinbarg find that the clues to the level of interest rates to be found in forecasts of sources and uses of funds lie in two key areas. First, as these forecasts are being built, source by source and use by use, the first approximation ends with an imbalance between the two. Balance will ultimately be achieved between supply and demand as the analyst assumes, say, contracting demand through tightening in the markets for funds (higher interest rates). This iterative process of closing the gap provides insight into the probable direction of interest rates.[5] Salomon Bros. analysts reach the conclusions found in the verbal analysis of their tables through much of this kind of iterative process of getting supply and demand to balance.

Second, Homer suggests that the "Residual" category in Table 11-4 can help indicate the direction of rates.[6] This category includes individuals and miscellaneous

---

[5]W.C. Freund and E.D. Zinbarg, "Application of Flow of Funds to Interest Rate Forecasting," *Journal of Finance*, May 1963, p. 237.

[6]Homer, "Techniques for Forecasting Interest-Rate Trends."

TABLE 11-4

SUMMARY OF SUPPLY AND DEMAND FOR CREDIT ($ Billions)

	1975	1976	1977	1978	1979	1980	1981	Amt. Out. 31Dec80	Table Refer
	Annual Net Increases in Amounts Outstanding								
Net Demand									
Privately Held Mortgages	40.0	70.0	109.6	118.1	109.7	69.1	100.5	*1,163.12*	2
Corporate & Foreign Bonds	40.2	41.4	37.2	32.7	27.1	4.15	39.0	*524.2*	3
Subtotal Long-Term Private	80.2	111.4	146.8	150.8	136.8	110.6	139.5	*1,687.3*	
Short-Term Business Borrowing	−14.8	10.6	45.8	71.7	89.9	53.3	84.5	*600.3*	8
Short-Term Other Borrowing	15.0	40.7	50.8	66.6	51.5	5.4	47.0	*496.3*	8
Subtotal Short-Term Private	0.2	51.3	96.6	138.3	141.4	58.7	131.5	*1,096.6*	
Privately Held Federal Debt	82.6	71.7	74.6	78.4	72.2	111.3	107.9	*902.4*	6
Tax-Exempt Notes and Bonds	14.3	15.0	31.3	32.9	27.5	30.0	33.0	*359.6*	4
Subtotal Government Debt	96.9	86.7	105.9	111.3	99.7	141.3	140.9	*1,262.2*	
Total Net Demand for Credit	177.3	249.4	349.3	400.4	377.9	310.6	411.9	*4,045.9*	
Net Supply[1]									
Thrift Institutions	53.5	70.7	82.2	76.7	56.2	40.0	62.3	*778.1*	9
Insurance, Pensions, Endowments	39.6	49.3	67.2	71.7	67.9	69.1	71.9	*727.3*	9
Investment Companies	3.7	4.9	6.8	6.3	24.8	29.9	42.0	*86.6*	9
Other Nonbank Finance	−3.0	8.0	18.6	16.6	28.6	7.9	26.8	*202.7*	9
Subtotal Nonbank Finance	93.8	132.9	174.8	171.3	177.5	146.9	203.0	*1,794.7*	9
Commercial Banks[2]	30.1	60.8	84.1	105.9	103.9	57.6	106.0	*1,149.2*	10
Business Corporations	11.6	8.2	3.4	4.4	10.8	6.7	7.5	*116.2*	11
State & Local Government	−1.7	4.2	15.5	15.1	10.9	0.5	5.5	*65.6*	11
Foreign[3]	6.1	19.6	47.0	58.5	7.4	31.1	23.0	*268.4*	11
Subtotal	139.9	225.7	324.8	355.2	310.5	242.8	345.0	*3.394.1*	
Residual (mostly household direct)	37.4	23.7	24.5	45.2	67.4	67.8	66.9	*651.8*	12
Total Net Supply of Credit	177.3	249.4	349.3	400.4	377.9	310.6	411.9	*4,045.9*	
Percentage Growth in Outstandings									
Total Credit	8.1	10.6	13.4	13.5	11.3	8.3	10.2		
Government	15.6	12.1	13.2	12.2	9.8	12.6	11.2		
Household	7.1	11.8	15.3	15.5	13.2	6.7	10.4		
Corporate	3.9	7.7	11.4	12.9	12.8	9.2	11.0		
Long-Term	8.2	10.1	12.9	11.8	9.4	7.4	8.4		
Short-Term	8.1	11.1	13.9	15.5	13.2	9.3	12.0		
Held by Nonbank Finance	10.5	13.4	15.5	13.2	12.1	8.9	11.3		
Commercial Banks	4.3	8.3	10.5	12.0	10.5	5.3	9.2		
Foreign	6.2	18.7	37.8	34.1	3.2	13.1	8.6		
Household Direct	9.7	5.6	5.5	9.6	13.0	11.6	10.3		

[1] Excludes funds for equities, cash and miscellaneous demands not tabulated above.
[2] Domestically chartered banks and their domestic affiliates.
[3] Includes US branches of foreign banks.

SOURCE: Salomon Brothers, *1981 Prospects for Financial Markets* (New York: Salomon Brothers, 1981).

investors, a group that appears to be sensitive to interest rates and is a marginal provider of funds. When demand exceeds supply, one way to induce this group to bring about a balance is for rates to rise sufficiently. Particularly good examples of periods of rising rates in tune with rising "residuals" is the period 1979-81.

The sources of supply expand and contract to different degrees over time. Commercial banks play a key but volatile role. The major swings in funds supplied by thrift institutions such as savings and loan associations directly affect the mortgage markets, their principal outlet for funds. Note, for example, the surge in real estate mortgages and the increase in funds in thrift institutions in 1976 and 1977. By contrast, note the small decrease in funds supplied by thrift institutions in 1978, while mortgages rose.

The details of the analysis could go on and on, but the point seems clear. Information on sources and uses of funds from the Federal Reserve accounts or in summary and forecast form from Salomon Bros. provide useful insight into the level of interest rates. It must all be considered, of course, against a backdrop of the outlook for the economy, and prices and employment in particular.[7]

Monetary and Fiscal Policy

Monetary policy, as used here, refers to government activities with respect to the cost and availabilty of credit. *Fiscal policy* refers to government taxing and spending activities.

The major goals of monetary policy are to help smooth out business cycles and promote economic growth, maintain price stability and full employment, and maintain external equilibrium in terms of balance of payments and the value of the dollar. These goals are fostered by the control of spending and investment, through influencing the cost and availability of funds through the banks. Fiscal policy influences credit markets through the manner in which government debt is managed, whether deficits or surplus are forecast for the year ahead, and how they will be handled. Without joining the heated debate over the role and effectiveness of monetary versus fiscal policy, let us trace the general effects of policy on interest rates.

Prospects of price inflation, balance-of-payments deficit, and pressure on the dollar would probably lead to restraint in monetary policy. Decelerated economic growth, business recession, and high unemployment could call for monetary ease and lower interest rates.

To tighten or loosen credit, the Federal Reserve System has generally influenced short-term rates of interest. These changes are gradually transmitted to longer-term rates. The Federal Reserve System (the "Fed") influences rates largely by buying and selling U.S. government securities in the market, an activity referred to as *open-market operations.* Buying and selling activity influences bank reserves and lending power. For example, monetary ease is achieved through buying governments and expanding bank reserves. Monetary restraint is achieved through sale of governments. To a lesser extent, the Fed can affect interest rates by adjusting the level of reserves required to back bank deposits (*reserve requirements*) and adjusting the rate at which it will lend money to banks (*discount rate*).

Of course, the goals of monetary policy are often conflicting. The balance between full employment and stable prices is delicate indeed. Low interest rates help promote economic growth by encouraging borrowing and spending. However, these same low interest rates place pressure on the dollar when balance-of-payments deficits exist for this country. That is, to settle accounts and make up the deficit, the United States would normally pay in either gold or IOUs. The nation to whom we owe money might prefer

[7]The reader is particularly encouraged to examine the analysis and many interesting tables of the latest *Prospects for the Financial Markets.*

interest-bearing IOUs (for instance, Treasury securities) rather than non-interest-bearing gold. But if low interest rates prevail on U.S. obligations, then gold might be taken instead and converted to higher-interest IOUs in other countries. The balance-of-payments problem may suggest a level of interest rates somewhat above the one produced by the "real" influences in an analysis of supply and demand for credit. Also, the late 1970s showed us the paradox of inflation along with high unemployment. These simultaneous problems would seem to indicate contrasting monetary policy; higher interest rates to restrain inflation, but low rates to encourage economic growth and full employment.

Fiscal policy makes its mark on the credit markets and interest rates. Budget deficits or surpluses mean that additional borrowing is added to pressures in the markets for funds, or that additional funds are supplied through debt retirement. Moreover, government securities are maturing every day, and the manner in which they are replaced has an effect upon the credit markets. Of course, deficits need not be met by added borrowing; they can be reduced or eliminated by increased taxes. The consequences of this strategy may have reverse effects upon interest rates, depending upon whose taxes are raised and how taxpayers adjust to meet the payments.

These cross currents and conflicting effects of monetary and fiscal policy on the level and direction of interest rates are significant. For the domestic economy as a whole, we might think of monetary and fiscal policy as reacting to and influenced by (1) the economic outlook, (2) price and employment prospects, and (3) the natural forces of supply and demand in financing this outlook. When we expand the sphere of concern to include the international situation, political and economic (for example, balance of payments and the dollar), the influence of monetary and fiscal policy can move against the thrust of the other three forces. The investor must, therefore, look carefully at the probable effect of monetary and fiscal policy on the outlook for interest rates.

If projections suggest that interest rates are expected to move to a certain level, the question is whether all maturities and classes of securities will move in unison and to the same degree.

The Term Structure of Interest Rates

Interest-rate levels, direction, and patterns can be analyzed in three categories: short term, medium term, and long term. Short-term fluctuations often last from a few weeks to a few months.[8] Long-term movements or secular trends can last from several business cycles to several decades. Medium-term or cyclical trends roughly coincide with trends of the business cycle.[9] Our discussion has concerned itself mainly with the last.

For a given bond issuer, such as the U.S. government, the structure of yields that is observed for bonds with different terms to maturity (but no other differences) is called

[8]Studies of seasonal factors suggest that they have a strong influence upon short-term rates and negligible effects on long-term rates. Between 1951 and 1960, Conrad found tendencies for highs in December and lows in June or July. See J.W. Conrad, *The Behavior of Interest Rates* (New York: National Bureau of Economic Research, 1966), pp. 53-54.

[9]Homer, "Techniques for Forecasting Interest-Rate Trends," p. 23.

the *term structure of interest rates.* In more everyday financial parlance, a diagram of the rates prevailing on a class of securities that are alike in every respect except term to maturity provides us with a *yield curve.* The most common portrait of yields plotted against time, or yield curve, is for marketable U.S. government securities.

The record of interest rates, when viewed according to term to maturity, suggests that at times short rates are above long rates, and vice versa. We want to explain the possible determinants of such changes in the term structure of interest rates. Figure 11-3 shows interest rates on governments by term to maturity at two different points in time. The first, May 15, 1967, is identified as a period of recessed business activity and interest rates. The other is a period of business boom and high interest rates. Why do these disparate configurations exist?

FIGURE 11-3
YIELD CURVE FOR U.S. GOVERNMENT SECURITIES

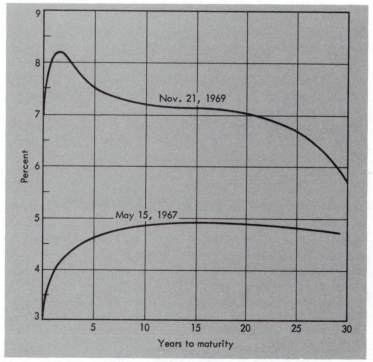

SOURCE: Donald P. Jacobs, Loring C. Farwell, and Edwin Neave, *Financial Institutions*, 5th Ed. (Homewood, Ill.: Richard D. Irwin, 1972), p. 204.

One of the most frequently noted behavior patterns concerning the term structure is the observation that, over the business cycle, short-term rates have a greater magnitude of variation than long-term rates have. Over the course of a complete cycle from recession to peak and back to recession, the level of rates will move upward and downward; however, the shorts will move more frequently and to a greater extent than the longs.

The lower curve (at May 15, 1967) is a classic upward-sloping configuration when interest rate levels were relatively low. In eighteen months, rates had tightened up considerably, as evidenced by the yield curve on November 21, 1969. The *level* of rates rose sharply and the *shape* of the yield curve turned downward (long rates below short rates). Notice the relative movements in short and long rates between the two dates. For example, very short-term rates (one year or less) moved up from around 3 percent to 7 percent. Very long rates (25 years) rose from just under 5 percent to around 6 1/2 percent.

From an operational point of view, it is necessary for an investor to recognize that (1) short-term *rates* do fluctuate more violently than long-term rates over a business cycle, (2) long-term *prices* are apt to fluctuate more than short-term prices, (3) the shape of the curve at recession, recovery, and boom phases moves from upward to horizontal to downward sloping; the short end becomes progressively more shallow (differences between very short and three years' rates become narrow); and the long end tends to remain level as it rises or falls. Figure 11-4 shows the yield curve for governments over successive stages of a business cycle. Figure 11-5 shows a large number of positive and

FIGURE 11-4

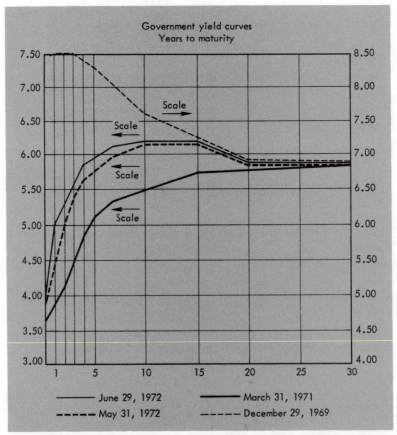

SOURCE: Henry Kaufman et al., eds., *Bond Market Monthly Review* (New York: Salomon Brothers, June 1972), p. 5.

FIGURE 11-5

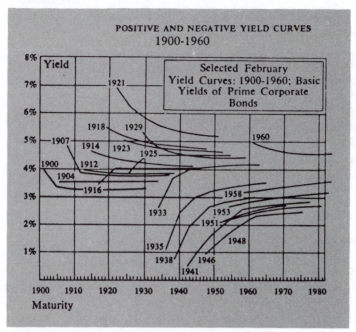

SOURCE: Sidney Homer, *A History of Interest Rates* (New Brunswick, N.J.: Rutgers University Press, 1963).

negative government yield curves through history. Note the negative (declining) curves of the early 1900s and the positively sloped curves of the 1940s and 1950s.

Causes of Term Structure

The underlying cause of differing shapes and overall level in the yield curve seems to be investor expectations of the future course of interest rates. Controversy arises as to whether there are other important factors.

The *expectations theory* provides a very simple explanation of the term structure of interest rates. If expected future short-term rates are above the current short rate, then the yield curve will slope upward. That is, the rate on a bond with a two-year maturity will be above the rate on a one-year bond. Similarly, if expected short rates are below the current short rate, the yield curve will slope downward. The yield curve will be flat (horizontal) if future short rates are expected to be the same as the current short rate. Hence the rate of interest on any long-term security will equal the average of the current short rate and intervening expected short rates.[10] Other theories can be viewed as alternatives to the expectations hypothesis, based upon criticisms lodged against it.

The *liquidity-premium theory* argues that although expectations are important, the existence of risk aversion among investors (and speculators) will result in a preference

[10]Actually, it will equal the *geometric* or compound average.

for shorts over longs, since the principal value of shorts is more certain than that of longs. More will be paid for shorts as a liquidity premium. This inherent aversion to risk requires that longs yield more than shorts. Liquidity premiums thus may modify the steepness of the slope of the yield curve caused by basic expectations.

The existence of downward-sloping yield curves might appear to negate the liquidity-premium idea. The implication is that the aversion to longs cannot cause long rates to be below shorts. The fairest explanation seems to be that downward-sloping curves are still explained by basic expectation of lower short rates; liquidity premiums may modify the steepness of the downward slope.

The *segmentation hypothesis* recognizes that risk aversion can lead to a preference for shorts *or* longs. Long-term securities have the risk of principal uncertainty, but shorts have the risk of income uncertainty. Some investors want to ensure a certain income return over time. Buying a succession of shorts subjects them to the uncertainty of short rates.

The segmentation theory recognizes that the supply and demand for funds is segmented in submarkets for those individuals and institutions that prefer to lend or borrow on one end of the time spectrum or the other. For example, institutions with long liabilities, such as pension funds and insurance companies, prefer long-term securities. Banks, with primarily short-term liabilities, prefer short-term investments. If the markets had just these two segments, the relative supply and demand for funds in each would, in the aggregate, explain the shape of the overall yield curve. But observed behavior suggests that investors often leave preferred maturities temporarily to take advantage of favorable yields in other maturity ranges. So it seems that, in practice, maturity leeway exists and is taken advantage of. This suggestion does not invalidate the segmentation hypothesis; it points up the possibility that premiums are needed to induce such shifting.

The *eclectic theory* of the yield curve suggests that investors have an expectation of a "normal" range of interest rates. They lack a precise way, or an inclination, to predict short rates well into the future. "Normal" ranges are perhaps determined by experience. If rates have varied in the recent past between 10 and 12 percent, investors might expect them to remain in that band. This "normal" range expectation can explain upward- and downward-sloping yield curves.

When short rates are high in the band, the yield curve will slope downward. When short rates are low, there is likely to be an upward-sloping curve. Suppose that rates have ranged between 10 and 12 percent. Now they are 11 percent. The highest they might go is 12 percent, but they may fall much of the way (although not all the way) down to 10 percent. The capital gains possibilities outweigh the loss possibilities. There is more to gain than to lose from buying long bonds. Prices on longs will be bid up and their yields will fall relative to shorts. With rates at the lower end of the band, there is more to lose with longs. Hence a preference for shorts will bid their prices up and their yields down relative to longs. The eclectic theory is an expectations theory; however, it does not require the heroic assumptions on the ability and willingness of investors to make precise forecasts of short rates well into the future.

Most empirical studies highlight the important role of expectations in explaining yield curves. A bias in recent years toward upward-sloping yield curves lends some support to the liquidity-premium hypothesis. Studies give some indication that liquidity premiums vary inversely with the level of interest rates, in keeping with the changing risk of capital loss. Tests of the segmentation theory are largely inconclusive.

Summary

The contractually fixed nature of interest on bonds and dividends on preferred stocks is such that any changes in required holding-period yields occur through market-price changes, which result from changes in systematic and unsystematic risk factors. Perceived increases (decreases) in risk lead to lower (higher) market prices.

Changes in interest rates are the most powerful forces affecting prices of fixed-income securities. This systematic risk factor is really two-dimensional: First, the level of interest rates may move up or down. Second, as the level of rates changes, securities that differ in maturity dates may not move up or down to the same extent; short-term rates may move above long-term rates, or vice versa.

Forecasting the level of interest rates requires insight into business activity, prices, and employment for the period ahead. Along with predicting the economic outlook and price and employment prospects, the analyst needs to gauge the natural forces of supply and demand in financing this outlook. Monetary and fiscal policy must be predicted as a force that will augment or upset projections of business activity, prices, and employment.

As the level of interest rates is forecast to move up or down (or remain relatively stable), the shape of the yield curve may change. The underlying cause of differing shapes in the yield curve seems to be investor expectations of the future course of interest rates. Even though there are other factors involved, it appears that if expected future short-term rates are above current short-term rates, then the yield curve will slope upward. Similarly, if expected short rates are below current short rates, the yield curve will slope downward. Alternative explanations serve to modify somewhat this rather simple explanation.

Questions and Problems

1. Assume that you loan a friend $200 at 6 percent interest. The loan plus interest is to be repaid at the end of one year. The level of consumer prices is expected to advance 4 percent during the year.

    a. How much money will you receive at the end of one year?

    b. What is the true purchasing power of the money you receive?

2. The current interest rate on quality corporate bonds is 7 1/2 percent on a $1,000 instrument due in one year. Suppose that one-year rates drop to 7 percent because of shifts in supply and demand. What should the price of the 7 1/2 percent bond be to adjust to a 7 percent market?

3. Using the present value method for determining yield to maturity, what is the yield to maturity on a 10 percent, 20-year bond, selling for 110?

4. Using present-value tables and Equation 11.2 determine:

    a. The present worth of a bond where $P = \$1,000$, $I = \$80$, $N = 40$, and $i = .10$.

    b. Assume the same data as above, except that $N = 5$. Determine the present worth of the bond.

    c. How do you account for the effect of merely reducing the life of the bond in part (b)?

5. a. Set up the equation for determining the rate of interest (*i*) implied by a 4 percent, ten-year bond selling at $790 (principal at maturity is $1,000).

   b. Solve the equation for the implied rate of interest. Can you see any advantages to yield tables such as Table 4-5?

6. Prove the entry in Table 4-5 that states that the return on a 6 percent bond due in three years and selling at 90 is about 10 percent.

7. A bond is available at a price of 102. The bond has a coupon of 15 percent and matures in twenty years. The bond is callable in five years at 111. Interest rates are expected to trend downward over the foreseeable future.

   a. What is the yield to maturity on this bond?

   b. What is the yield-to-call on the bond?

   c. Which yield calculation should an investor regard as the most important for decision making purposes? Why?

8. Under what specific circumstances would continuous reinvestment in one-year bonds yield superior total income relative to a one-time purchase of a 25-year bond?

9. You are interested in buying some bonds. The *Wall Street Journal* lists two bonds for a company you are very much interested in:

   UVM, Inc. 4s90 70

   UVM, Inc. 10s90 110

   What would you be willing to pay for the "4s90" if you required a return of 10 percent on bonds of this quality/maturity;

10. a. Discuss what is meant by the term *reinvestment risk.*

    b. Discuss whether reinvestment risk is greater when the current market rate is 6 percent or 11 percent.

    c. Discuss the differences in the reinvestment risk between a 5 percent coupon bond selling at 65 to yield 8.5 percent and a 9 percent coupon bond selling at 103 to yield 8.8 percent.

    d. Discuss whether the reinvestment risk is different between two 10 percent bonds, one due in 1990 and the other due in 2006.

11. Refer to Table 11-4. What specific sources or uses of funds can you identify as exhibiting (a) dynamic and (b) stable influences since 1975?

12. In analysis of sources and uses of funds, what is the pivotal role that has been attributed to the so-called residual category?

13. If the Federal Reserve wanted to ease credit and exert a downward influence on interest rates, in what ways might it act?

14. How can the goals of economic growth and equilibrium in the balance of payments suggest both lower and higher levels of short-term interest rates at the same time?

15. In what way(s) do fiscal and monetary policy (a) conflict and (b) complement each other in the credit markets?

16. What is the significance to an investor of a downward-sloping yield curve (long rates below short rates)?

17. Compare and contrast the expectations theory and the eclectic theory of the yield curve.

18. Is the existence of downward-sloping yield curves proof that the liquidity-preference idea is invalid? Why?

TWELVE

Bond Analysis: Unsystematic Risk

In forecasting purchasing-power and interest-rate risk, what we are really talking about are expectations concerning the outlook for the price of commodities and of money. These major sources of risk in fixed-income securities explain why it is that the level and time shape of interest rates shift.

There are also influences that create risk and explain why certain classes of fixed-income securities, such as governments and corporates, or different subgroups of corporates, may move in general harmony with interest rates, but not in a parallel or synchronous fashion.

Investors must learn to react not to a single yield curve but to a whole family of them. The yield curve for corporates might have the same shape as that for governments on any given day, but it could be at a different level and less stable. There are different yield curves for each type of bond, and they change every day!

The analytical thrust of high-grade bond selection differs markedly from common-stock selection, although earning power is the fundamental basis of value for both. High-grade bond selection emphasizes continuity of income and protection against loss of principal, whereas common-stock selection emphasizes earnings and dividend growth and capital appreciation potential.

Losses in high-grade bonds arise from either of two factors: changes in the level of interest rates or impairment in quality. Market fluctuations due to interest-rate changes may be short run or long run, but in any event the original principal is recovered at maturity and the only loss is an opportunity cost in maximizing income.

An impairment in quality causes a greater loss in market value, which may become permanent in case of default. Quality impairment arises principally from a decline in earning power relative to the level of debt and fixed charges (or an increase in debt and fixed charges relative to earning power), which may portend future financial difficulties. Normally, a decline increases sensitivity to interest-rate changes, so that market price fluctuation is typically greater for lesser-quality bonds than for the highest-quality issues.

Secondary-quality bonds may improve in quality over time due to increased earnings and asset protection, or they may be paid at maturity despite underlying uncertainties. Such bonds will provide an extra return in capital appreciation in addition to interest. The task of analysis is to weigh the risk of uncertainty of payment relative to the potential return, just as for common stocks.

Business and Financial Risk

Corporate bonds sell at higher yields than governments do, mainly because of business and financial risk. Within the generic group called corporate bonds, yield differentials or "spreads" will exist. Business and financial risk are absent from government bonds because of the monopoly status of the government and its ability to meet debt-servicing requirements through taxation. For corporates, the concepts of business and financial risk are generally combined in a single term, *default risk*.

Default in a legal sense is the failure of the issuer to meet the terms of the debt contract. In investment terms, default refers to the probability that the return realized will be less than promised, rather than to total loss. For example, if you buy an 8 percent bond for $1,000 to hold ten years to maturity, you expect $80 in interest each year and the return of principal at the end of ten years. Assume—an unlikely event—that interest payments are delayed ten years, at which time accumulated interest and principal are paid in full. You *realize* less than 8 percent because of the time value of money. The $1,800 ($800 interest plus $1,000 principal) you receive at the end of the tenth year provides a realized return of only about 6 percent.[1]

Default is a matter of degree, from the simple *extension* of time to make an interest payment, to legal *liquidation* of the debtor to settle accumulated interest and principal. An extension occurs when creditors voluntarily allow extension of maturity and/or postponement of interest payments. Liquidation may occur when a number of successive interest payments are missed owing to underlying problems of management. When it appears that the borrower has no hope of turning the situation around, liquidation proceedings are instituted. Creditors hope to recover some portion of the original principal advanced, plus back interest.

Between extension and liquidation, we have the practice called *reorganization*. A financial reorganization involves the issuance of new securities of the reorganized company for defaulted bonds. In such a case, the nature of interest and/or sinking-fund payments is such that the company cannot generate sufficient cash from operations to meet these requirements. So new securities with revised payment schedules, in amount and/or timing. replace the defaulted securities in the hope that the cash strain is relieved.

[1]$1,000 \times (1 + r)^{10} = \$1,800$
$r = 6\%$

These varied degrees of default stem largely from inadequate liquidity and/or earnings. The former case is a manifestation of weak cash-flow management. The earnings problem results from some combination of (1) an inadequate revenue-operating cost relationship (business risk), and (2) too much borrowed capital (financial risk).

Default Ratings by Independent Agencies

Bond-investment agencies evaluate the quality of bonds and rank them in categories according to relative probability of default. For the typical investor, this evaluation some-what simplifies the task of assessing default risk. The principal rating agencies are Moody's Investors Service and Standard & Poor's Corporation.[2]

The bond categories are assigned letter grades. The highest-grade bonds, whose risk of default is felt to be negligible, are rated triple A (Aaa or AAA). The rating agencies assign pluses or minuses (e.g., Aa+, A−) when appropriate to show the relative standing within the major rating categories. Table 12-1 shows the ratings used by the two leading rating agencies, with brief descriptions of each. Table 12-2 shows more-detailed descriptions for the ratings of Standard & Poor's Corporation.

TABLE 12-1
RATINGS BY INVESTMENT AGENCIES

Moody's	
Aaa	Best quality
Aa	High quality
A	Higher medium grade
Baa	Lower medium grade
Ba	Possess speculative elements
B	Generally lack characteristics of desirable investment
Caa	Poor standing; may be in default
Ca	Speculative in a high degree; often in default
C	Lowest grade

Standard & Poor's	
AAA	Highest grade
AA	High grade
A	Upper medium grade
BBB	Medium grade
BB	Lower medium grade
B	Speculative
CCC-CC	Outright speculation
C	Reserved for income bonds
DDD-D	In default, with rating indicating relative salvage value

[2]Preferred stocks are also rated by the agencies, but not on a basis consistent with bond ratings. For example, Standard & Poor's preferred-stock ratings are not necessarily graduated downward according to the issuer's debt. Preferred ratings refer to relative security of dividends and prospective stability of yield.

TABLE 12-2
STANDARD & POOR'S CORPORATE BOND RATINGS

AAA	Bonds rated AAA are *highest grade* obligations. They possess the ultimate degree of protection as to principal and interest. Marketwise they move with interest rates, and hence provide the maximum safety on all accounts.
AA	Bonds rated AA also qualify as *high grade* obligations, and in the majority of instances differ from AAA issues only in small degree. Here, too, prices move with the long term money market.
A	Bonds rated A are regarded as *upper medium grade.* They have considerable investment strength but are not entirely free from adverse effects of changes in economic and trade conditions. Interest and principal are regarded as safe. They predominantly reflect money rates in their market behavior, but to some extent, also economic conditions.
BBB	The BBB, or *medium grade* category is borderline between definitely sound obligations and those where the speculative element begins to predominate. These bonds have adequate asset coverage and normally are protected by satisfactory earnings. Their susceptibility to changing conditions, particularly to depressions, necessitates constant watching. Marketwise, the bonds are more responsive to business and trade conditions than to interest rates. This group is the lowest which qualifies for commercial bank investment.
BB	Bonds given a BB rating are regarded as *lower medium grade.* They have only minor investment characteristics. In the case of utilities, interest is earned consistently but by narrow margins. In the cases of other types of obligors, charges are earned on average by a fair margin, but in poor periods deficit operations are possible.
B	Bonds rated as low as B are *speculative.* Payment of interest cannot be assured under difficult economic conditions.
CCC-CC	Bonds rated CCC and CC are *outright speculations*, with the lower rating denoting the more speculative. Interest is paid, but continuation is questionable in periods of poor trade conditions. In the case of CC ratings the bonds may be on an income basis and the payment may be small.
C	The rating of C is reserved for *income bonds* on which no interest is being paid.
DDD-D	All bonds rated DDD, DD and D are *in default*, with the rating indicating the relative salvage value.

SOURCE: Standard & Poor's *Bond Guide* (New York: Standard & Poor's Corporation, June 1977), p. 6.

Not all bonds are rated by the agencies. Small issues and those placed privately are generally not rated. For those bonds that are rated, the competing services generally rank the same bond in the same rating category; seldom do they disagree by more than one grade.[3] Overall, the evidence indicates a close correspondence between rating category and subsequent default experience.[4]

Ratings, however, do not totally solve the investor's problem of default-risk discrimination between bonds. First, fully 90 percent of all rated bonds fall into the top four rating categories—not a very detailed distinction for making choices. Second, although the agencies seldom differ widely in their evaluation and classification, they do occasionally differ. Third, and of considerable importance, ratings are changed (up or down) slowly. Under constant review, they are altered only when the agencies deem that

[3]Louis Brand, former head of Standard & Poor's bond department, estimated that S&P and Moody's disagreed on ratings of about one in twenty utility bonds and one in ten industrial bonds. See H.C. Sherwood, "How They'll Rate Your Company's Bonds," *Business Management*, 29 (March 1966), 38-42ff.

[4]See W.B. Hickman, *Corporate Bond Quality and Investment Performance* (New York: National Bureau of Economic Research, 1958). Hickman concluded that the record of rating agencies between 1900 and 1943 was remarkably good.

sufficient changes have occurred. Thus, letter grades assigned by rating agencies serve only as a general, somewhat coarse form of discrimination.

In the sections that follow, we will consider key factors that an analyst examines to verify and refine default ratings. The major factors include earnings power, cash flow, financial leverage, and liquidity.[5]

Earnings Coverage

Heavy burdens of fixed-interest and preferred-dividend payments have led many companies into default and eventual bankruptcy. The degree of default risk is measured in two ways by analysts: (1) earnings-coverage ratios and (2) capitalization ratios. Each of these will be explored in turn.

Earnings coverage rests on income relative to charges on debt and preferred stock. The higher the income relative to charges, the lower the risk of default, other things being equal. This income-charges relationship is normally cast in ratio terms, Income/ Charges.

EARNINGS AND CHARGES—BONDS

The income referred to is generally EBIT (earnings before interest and taxes). Since interest is a tax-deductible expense, it is logical to compare it with earnings before taxes.[6]

The *level of income* used in the computation of earnings-coverage ratios deserves serious consideration. The most important consideration here is: What level of income will be most representative of the amount that will actually be available in the *future* for the payment of debt-related fixed charges? An average earnings figure encompassing the entire range of the business cycle, and adjusted for any known factors that may change it in the future, is most likely to be the best approximation of the average source of funds from future operations which can be expected to become available for the payment of fixed charges. Moreover, if the objective of the earnings-coverage ratio is to measure the creditor's maximum exposure to risk, then the proper earnings figure to use is that achieved at the low point of the enterprise's business cycle.

The *total charges* on bonds usually amount to the sum of the annual interest charges on all debts. Although a company may have several bonds outstanding with different priorities to income (and assets), such as mortgage bonds and debentures, we generally do not calculate a separate mortgage-bond coverage and debenture-bond coverage. Ability to meet interest payments on mortgage bonds but not debentures can put the company into bankruptcy. Then the mortgage bondholders are in jeopardy as well. The chain of bond priorities is only as strong as the weakest link.

---

[5]Fisher found that risk premiums on bonds were related to (1) earnings variability of the firm, (2) the length of time it was solvent, (3) the equity/debt ratio, and (4) the market value or marketability of its debt issue. In effect, companies of long standing, with relatively stable earnings, whose bonds are highly marketable and covered by a large equity cushion, sell at lower default-risk premiums than their counterparts with opposite traits. See L. Fisher, "Determinants of Risk Premiums on Corporate Bonds," *Journal of Political Economy*, 67 (June 1959), 217-37.

[6]It is customary to exclude extraordinary and/or nonrecurring income from earnings. Such extraordinary items cannot be assumed to occur regularly or predictably.

Let us illustrate our *coverage-ratio* idea. The income statement of ABC, Inc., shows its EBIT to be $25 million. The company has outstanding a 6 percent, first-mortgage bond issue in the amount of $50 million. In addition, an 8 percent debenture-bond issue is outstanding in the amount of $25 million. Total interest payments would be $5 million (6 percent of $50 million, plus 8 percent of $25 million). Earnings coverage would be calculated as follows:

$$\text{Interest coverage on all bonds} = \frac{\text{EBIT}}{\text{Interest charges on all bonds}} \quad (12.1)$$

$$= \frac{\$25 \text{ million}}{\$5 \text{ million}} = 5$$

The earnings coverage is said to be five times. The larger this ratio, the better. We must recognize, however, that the significance of this coverage is enhanced by gauging it (1) over a period of years, future as well as past, and (2) against some standard to ascertain whether it is high or low, good or bad.

The adequacy of the ratio must be related to the volatility and other characteristics of earning power. Coverage ratios in cyclically sensitive businesses such as autos, machinery, or chemicals should average higher than for more stable businesses such as food or drugs. If a company is to enjoy a high credit rating, it should show sufficient coverage so that even under the worst of foreseeable conditions, there is a cushion against unexpected adversity. Companies in this position will continue to enjoy adequate credit standing and have access to financial markets under even the most adverse conditions.

Debt-Service Analysis. The use of borrowed capital also typically requires cash outlays to discharge part or all of the principal of the debt in future years. Serial maturities or sinking funds are the typical contractual covenants that indicate cash requirements for this purpose. Although payments on debt principal may represent a regular flow of cash out of the company, they are not reflected on the income statement. Investor protection can be impaired by the inability of the issuer to meet sinking-fund or amortization requirements, since these are also legal obligations, just like regular interest. Therefore the analyst should make some determination of the issuer's capacity to cover total requirements, including both interest payments and annual debt reduction. Coverage of both is essential.

In this light, it is customary to determine *debt-service coverage* by the following:

$$\frac{\text{EBIT}}{\text{Interest charges on bonds} + [\text{Sinking-fund payments}/(1 - \text{Tax rate})]} \quad (12.2)$$

Since sinking-fund payments are not expenses but return of principal, they are not reported on the income statement. Hence they must be paid out of after-tax dollars. This is the reason for the mathematical setup in the denominator of the fraction. Thus, for a company in the 40 percent tax bracket to cover $300,000 for sinking-fund payments, $500,000 must be earned before taxes ($500,000 less $200,000 in taxes is $300,000). Hence, for ABC, Inc., let us assume that a 40 percent tax rate applies, and that the $25 million in 8 percent debentures calls for an annual sinking-fund payment of $300,000. Debt-service coverage could be calculated as

$$\frac{\$25}{\$5 + [\$0.3/(1 - .4)]} = \frac{\$25}{\$5 + \$.5} = \frac{\$25}{\$5.5} = 4.5$$

EARNINGS AND CHARGES—PREFERRED STOCK

Preferred-stock dividends are paid after interest. Recognition of this fact means that preferred dividend coverage must include in the total charges all prior interest. Preferred dividend requirements could be added to interest charges, if any, and this sum could be divided into earnings. However, complications arise.

Preferred dividends are paid after taxes, whereas bond interest is paid before taxes. Adding both together is like mixing apples and oranges. Either preferred dividends must be adjusted to a before-tax basis or interest payments must be adjusted to an after-tax basis. The former is preferable. At a tax rate of 50 percent, a corporation needs $2 in EBIT to pay $1 in preferred dividends; only $1 of EBIT is needed to pay $1 in interest, since interest is a pre-tax expense. In general, to adjust preferred dividends to a before-tax basis:

$$\text{Pre-tax preferred dividend requirement} = \frac{\text{Preferred dividends}}{1 - \text{Tax rate}}$$

In other words, at a 40 percent tax rate, a company has to earn $5 million before taxes to pay $3 million in preferred dividends [$3 million/(1 − .4) = $5 million].

After adjustment for the tax factor, earnings coverage on preferred dividends becomes

$$\text{Preferred dividend coverage} = \frac{\text{EBIT}}{\text{Interest} + [\text{Preferred dividend}/(1 - \text{Tax rate})]} \quad (12.3)$$

Assume that ABC, Inc., has EBIT of $25 million and the balance sheet shows (in millions):

Current assets	$ 90	Current liabilities	$ 30
		6% first-mortgage bonds	$ 50
		8% debentures	25
Fixed assets	$140	8% preferred stock	25
		Common equity	100

Total interest was determined earlier to be $5 million. Preferred dividends are determined in dollars as 8 percent of $25 million, or $2 million. Assuming a tax rate of 40 percent, total charges are covered:

$$\text{Preferred dividend coverage} = \frac{\text{EBIT}}{\text{Interest} + [\text{Preferred dividends}/(1 - \text{Tax rate})]}$$

$$= \frac{\$25}{\$5 + (\$2/.6)} = \frac{\$25}{\$5 + \$3.33} = \frac{\$25}{\$8.33} = 3 \text{ times}$$

Note that where a company has both bond and preferred-stock financing, the coverage of the preferred is always lower than the coverage on the bonds.[7]

Capitalization

Financial leverage or risk can also be measured on the balance sheet. Capital from each of varied sources—debt, preferred stock, and common stock—can be related in percentage form to total funds. To the bondholder or preferred stockholder, the greater the percentage of total funds that common stockholders provide, the better. Extending our ABC, Inc., example (reported in millions of dollars):

6% first-mortgage bonds	$ 50
8% debentures	25
8% preferred stock	25
Common equity	100
Total long-term capital	$200

Capitalization ratios, at book value, can be stated as:

Long-term bonds	37.5%	(75/200)
Preferred stock	12.5	(25/200)
Common equity	50.0	(100/200)
Total	100.0%	

If the ABC bonds were being analyzed, the relevant capitalization ratio would consider preferred and common stock as junior in standing to bonds. In this case, a bondholder would note that his equity "cushion" is 62.5 percent (125/200) of total long-term funds. For preferred stockholders, the cushion is 50 percent (common equity). Bondholders and preferred stockholders desire a strong common-equity base to cushion their position.[8]

Analysts often deduct intangible assets from common equity in calculating capitalization ratios. The result is a lower common-equity percentage of total capital. The reason lies in the fact that many intangible assets (patents, goodwill, franchises and so on) are placed on balance sheets at doubtful values. The removal of these amounts from the asset side of the balance sheet necessitates similar elimination from common equity. The resulting figure is called *tangible net worth*, or tangible common equity.

The rating services and analysts look at capitalization in alternative ways to the percentage breakdown of long-term capital shown above. The possibilities seem almost

[7]The reader can see the fallacy in subtracting interest from EBIT and dividing the result by adjusted preferred dividends. The result is $20/$3.33 = 6 times. Recall that bond interest coverage was 5 times. Preferred dividends cannot be better protected than bond interest.

[8]At times, preferred stock has no par value or has a nominal value, such as $1 per share. Preferred stockholders would be entitled to more on liquidation of the company—say $50 maximum per share. To compute capitalization ratios, it is appropriate to show preferred stock at liquidation value. Any difference between nominal value and liquidating value would come from a reduction of surplus accounts. The result is to lower the common-equity percentage of total funds.

unending if we look again at the components and how they might be related:

Total assets	$100	Liabilities (debt)	$20
		Equity	80
		Total debt and equity	$100

Financial risk can be measured on the balance sheet by Total debt/Equity (20/80 = .25). This is interpreted as 25 cents of debt for every $1 of equity. The percentage breakdown, or capitalization ratios, would be Debt = .2, and Equity = .8. Debt is 20 percent of total long-term funds. A kind of asset-coverage relationship similar to the earnings-coverage idea is derived by relating assets to debt (Assets/Debt), or 100/20 = 5. Debt is covered five times by assets in the event that assets are liquidated now at book value.

Leases

An analytical complication arises when a company leases some or all of its fixed assets. Instead of borrowing long-term funds to buy buildings and equipment, many companies lease them.[9] Financial analysts call this "off-balance-sheet" financing, referring to the fact that since leased facilities are not owned, their cost is typically not carried as an asset. More important, at most only current lease installments appear as a liability. In effect, two companies may be utilizing the same amount of fixed assets, one leasing and the other owning. They may generate identical profits, but they will show different debt outstanding and interest charges, as well as different earnings coverage and capitalization ratios.

Payments under a lease are designed to cover three basic ingredients required by the lessor or the landlord: (1) depreciation on the property, (2) interest expense on the borrowing, and (3) a profit margin. Only interest expense plus profit margin is analogous to bond interest.

Analysts attempt to make financial statements of companies comparable. When companies lease property, fixed charges and long-term debt must be adjusted upward. How? A rule of thumb is to assume that about one-third of a lease payment represents interest payments.[10] Dividing this amount by prevailing rates available to the company on long-term debt at the time the lease was arranged in effect "capitalizes" the lease.

[9]For analytical purposes, use of the alternative of borrowing rather than selling stock stems from the debt-like nature of most lease contracts.

[10]The inclusion of a portion of lease (rental) expense (deemed to be an interest factor representative of leases) is typically performed only for "financing leases." These are defined by the SEC as non-cancelable leases that (1) cover 75 percent or more of the economic life of the property, or (2) assure the lessor a full recovery of his intial investment plus a reasonable return. For years prior to 1973 it was necessary to rely on conventions such as capitalizing total lease rentals. Since 1973 the SEC has required that notes to the financial statements of annual reports show how these leases are capitalized. Generally these leases are capitalized at the present value of gross minimum rentals based on the interest rate implicit in the terms of the lease. The use of the one-third total net rental payments is an inexact method, but it is the best available for years prior to 1973 and is preferable to omitting rentals.

The interested reader should refer to the footnotes to the financial statements of McDonald's Inc. (Chapter 8) to see how lease commitments are reported. FASB *No. 13* goes into great detail on the subject of how leases are to be disclosed in financial statements.

This capitalization provides us a debt-value equivalent represented by the lease.[11]

Suppose ABC, Inc., makes lease payments of $4.5 million on a building. At the time of the lease arrangment, the company could have borrowed at 6 percent (the rate on its mortgage bonds). With the suggested rule of thumb:

$$\frac{1/3 \times \$4.5 \text{ million}}{.06} = \frac{\$1.5 \text{ million}}{.06} = \$25 \text{ million}$$

The $25 million is the equivalent amount of debt presented by the lease. When the building was built, if ABC had borrowed money at 6 percent rather than signing a lease agreement, annual interest expense would be $1.5 million higher than shown in the income statement, and long-term debt on the balance sheet would be greater by $25 million.

Revised coverage and capitalization ratios for ABC would be determined by adding back one-third of the lease payments to EBIT on the income statement. This has the effect of raising EBIT. Interest expense is then raised by $1.5 million. Thus:

$$\frac{\text{EBIT} + 1/3 \text{ lease payment}}{\text{Interest} + 1/3 \text{ lease payment}}$$

$$\frac{\text{EBIT (revised)}}{\text{Interest on bonds (revised)}} = \frac{\$25 + \$1.5}{\$5 + \$1.5} = \frac{\$26.5}{\$6.5} = 4.1$$

Our earlier bond coverage of five times has been reduced. Since defaults on lease payments have legal consequences, the revised coverage of 4.1 times adds meaning to our default-risk measurement using earnings coverage. Preferred-dividend coverage would have to be adjusted accordingly.

Lease (rental) payments would have to be reflected in a revised *debt-service coverage ratio*. The interest coverage computation included only that portion of leases (rentals) that is attributable to the interest factor. As a long-term obligation, from a contractual point of view, the interest portion is indistinguishable from the principal portion (the remaining two-thirds, as it were). Consequently, debt-service coverage should account for the entire amount of leases (rentals), rather than only the interest portion. Thus:

$$\frac{\text{EBIT} + \text{Lease payments}}{\text{Interest} + \text{Lease payments} + [\text{Sinking-fund payments}/(1 - \text{Tax rate})]}$$

$$= \frac{\$25.0 + \$4.5}{\$5 + \$4.5 + \$.5} = \frac{\$29.5}{10.0} = 2.95$$

Preferred dividend coverage would be revised as follows:

$$\frac{\text{EBIT} + 1/3 \text{ Lease payment}}{\text{Interest} + [\text{Preferred dividends}/(1 - \text{Tax rate})] + 1/3 \text{ Lease payment}}$$

$$= \frac{\$25 + \$1.5}{\$5 + \$3.33 + \$1.5} = \frac{\$26.50}{9.83} = 2.7$$

[11]It would be best to use present-value calculations using the term to maturity of the lease. However, most financial data available to the investor do not include all the terms of lease contracts to make this refined calculation possible.

Similarly, revised capitalization ratios would recognize the added $25 million debt equivalent:

Long-term debt	$ 75.0	33.3%	(75/225)
Debt equivalent	25.0	11.1	(25/225)
Preferred stock	25.0	11.1	(25/225)
Common equity	100.0	44.5	(100/225)
	$225.0	100%	

The common-equity cushion was calculated earlier to be 50 percent.

The methods employed to adjust for leases are admittedly somewhat crude. Security analysts and accountants have grappled with the problem of wide-spread, adequate lease-disclosure standards for many years. More and more companies are providing some information on leases in footnotes to financial statements. We are still some way from having the kind of detail necessary to sound analysis, but at least the methods presented here are significantly better than making no adjustment for leases at all.

Liquidity

Adequate earnings coverage does not mean that adequate cash will be on hand to make actual payments required on bonds and preferred stock. Companies rich with earnings can be cash-poor.

The amount of cash and working capital (current assets minus current liabilities) a company has will provide a good indication of its ability to ride out a general recession or a temporary decline in its particular industry, and still make interest, dividend, and sinking-fund payments. The size of its cash and working capital will also indicate its ability to finance improvements or expand sales volume without resorting to further borrowing.

The analyst is interested in (1) the size and (2) the character of a company's liquid position. Levels of cash and sources of cash should be examined. Stable or increasing cash positions are desired, generated mainly internally, rather than from outside sources such as bank borrowing. Analysts want to be certain that the company's dividend policy is in line with the industry. Over-liberal dividends weaken defenses against business downturns and benefit only common shareholders.

Liquidity connotes the ability to meet obligations as they mature and to sustain current operations. The liquidity position of a company may be thought of as a reservoir into which cash is deposited from revenues and cash flows out to pay obligations incurred for expenses and expansion. When the reservoir gets too low, it may be replenished in the first instance from liquidation of short-term financial assets or by borrowing in the capital market or from banks or by sales of equity. If these avenues are not available, a financial crisis develops. Often a weakness in one type of cash resource is quickly followed by weakness in the others. The bondholder's interest in the company's liquidity is directed toward the overall financial position and ability to meet debt maturities without recourse to a refunding operation in the capital market, which might happen to be congested at the time.

There are several key funds items of interest to the analyst as measures of basic cash flow in the business on a long-run basis. *Internal funds* are defined as retained earnings plus depreciation, the change in deferred taxes, and, where material, minority interest. Also where material, we remove undistributed earnings of unconsolidated subsidiaries accounted for by the equity method. In an extreme situation, dividends could be stopped to increase cash flow as defined, but usually the capacity to pay dividends is one evidence of financial strength and hence we use retained earnings. This is a conservative measure because it excludes other sources of funds; importantly, any increase in payables and accruals. *Funds used* are capital expenditures plus the change in receivables and inventories. There are other uses of funds, of course, but these are the principal expenditures necessary for the operation and growth of the business.

Companies that keep these two totals in balance seldom need to raise new capital. An occasional imbalance may be financed by temporary bank credit. Often the excess of funds used over internal cash flow may be funded steadily into debt while holding the debt ratio constant. However, sustained excesses of funds used over internal cash flow and a rising debt ratio can be a danger signal.

The bondholder is interested in appraising the company's ability to repay debt out of internal cash flow, in comparison with other uses of funds. This has been shown to be an important measure of credit quality and liquidity and is briefly defined as follows:

$$\frac{\text{Total debt}}{\text{Internal funds}}$$

It indicates the number of years required to retire all debt out of internal cash flow. Excluded from this calculation are other fixed obligations (leases), since these are retired via direct charges to expense or revenues.

While actual appropriation of all internal cash flow to debt reduction for several years would hamper the future growth of the business and be tantamount to liquidation, a high ratio of cash flow to debt—or a low number of years to pay—gives a company considerable flexibility in financing its business internally and/or externally and therefore is an indicator of credit quality.

The actual maturity schedule is also important to the bondholder. One possible measure of the ability to handle maturities would be the ratio of present internal cash flow to annual debt maturities, including sinking-fund requirements, for the next five to ten years. However, maturity schedules generally are highly variable from year to year, so that it is not useful to compute such a ratio. But a simple comparison of the maturity schedule with internal funds generation could indicate potential problems over the next few years. For a long-term measure, the ratio of debt to internal funds described above is useful here also. In effect, this ratio is another way of indicating that the level of earning power, as expressed in various ways, is the wellspring of credit standing and liquidity, and hence of bond safety.

Among the conventional tests of the adequacy of liquid resources are the current ratio (current assets/current liabilities), the cash ratio (cash/current liabilities), and working-capital adequacy (current assets minus current liabilities/long-term debt).

Expanding our data on ABC, Inc., will help to illustrate these tests of liquidity (reported in millions of dollars):

Cash	$ 6.0	Current liabilities	$ 30.0
Total current assets	90.0	Long-term debt	75.0
Fixed assets	140.0	Preferred stock	25.0
		Common equity	100.0

Cash ratio   =   6/30   =   .2
Current ratio   = 90/30   = 3.0
Working capital/long-term debt   = 60/75   =   .8
Working capital/long-term debt (including lease equivalent) = 60/100 = .6

It is difficult to generalize about what constitutes high or low cash and working-capital ratios. A standard of 2 to 1 is often set for the current ratio. However, liquidity requirements are largely dependent upon the industry in question.

Net income is generally not a reliable measure of funds provided by operations that are available to meet fixed charges. The reason is, of course, that fixed charges are paid with cash or, from the longer-term point of view, with funds (working capital), while net income includes items of revenue that do not generate funds as well as expense items that do not require the current use of funds. Thus a better measure of fixed-charges coverage may be obtained by using as numerator funds obtained by operations rather than net income. This figure can be obtained from the statement of changes in financial position, which is now a required financial statement and should, consequently, be generally available.

Under this concept the coverage ratio could be computed by dividing funds provided by operations by fixed charges (i.e., interest, sinking-fund, and lease payments).

The Security Contract

Bond indentures and preferred-stock contracts spell out the legal rights of holders and the restrictions under which a company must operate once it has issued bonds and/or preferred stocks.[12] The many covenants of these lengthy and complex legal documents are designed to insure against the kind of bad housekeeping that may lead to default. These various thou-shalts and thou-shalt-nots specify what a company may do while it is among the living as well as what happens if it dies. *Analysts and investors should look to see that contracts contain certain protective covenants.*

Security contracts do not ensure rising sales and profit margins. However, they can attempt to (1) control the total amount of debt and preferred-stock financing relative to common equity—a prime source of default—and (2) protect priorities to interest or dividends and principal payments in the event of default.

Controls that attempt to minimize default risk and maximize recovery in bond issues are generally stated in the areas of sinking funds, collateral, additional funded

[12]For other details on features found in bond indentures and preferred-stock contracts, the reader may wish to review Chapter 1.

debt, and divided restrictions. Comfort seems to lie in knowing that principal will be recaptured on a regular payments schedule (sinking fund) and/or that certain assets are pledged to support principal (collateral). Further, current bondholders want to exercise a degree of control over the amount of debt permitted over future time periods (additional funded debt). Dissipation results when too many creditors vie for limited earnings and/or assets. Dividend restrictions protect future ability to generate interest payments.

Periodic repayment of principal between date of issuance and the final due date has several advantages to investors. First, it provides greater assurance that the company will not default than does the promise of payment of the total issue in one lump sum at a distant due date. Second, with preferreds, this buy-back method lends price support to a security that, unlike bonds, has no nominal maturity. Third, if earnings are steady, piecemeal retirement enhances earnings and asset coverage on the remaining principal. On the other hand, however, as interest rates fall, a sinking-fund buy-back can take from an investor a security with an attractive yield.

An annual sinking-fund payment is usually made on corporate bonds to provide funds to buy them back through the marketplace or random call. Less frequently, the funds are placed in an escrow account (at interest) to retire the entire issue at once. Municipal bonds are normally divided into parts, each part having a different maturity date. This is a serial-maturity arrangement. The holder knows exactly when his bond is due (avoiding the chance aspects of sinking funds). Sinking-fund arrangements are designed to cope with investor fears of default risk. Serial bond issues are designed to match the repayment ability of the issuer.

Indentures normally provide for additional debt financing if certain tests are met. Added debt is given no more than an equal, and often junior, security position to debt previously issued. A common test to be met before new debt financing can occur is to relate net tangible assets to total old and new debt.[13] A rule might be that new debt can be issued only if, after the issue, net tangible assets amount to at least two and one-half times as much as current and proposed debt. Suppose a company has $100 million in net tangible assets and $25 million in long-term debt. Its ratio of net tangible assets to debt is 4:1. A proposed new long-term debt issue of $25 million would bring the ratio to 2 1/2:1 (125/50).[14]

If additional debt is to be backed by collateral, it is common to provide equal or lesser standing to other lienholders. This feature is important when debentures (unsecured bonds) are used. Should mortgage bonds be sold subsequent to a debenture issue, it is common for debentures to be given equal and proportionate secured standing.

Dividend restrictions attempt to avoid excessive payout, which weakens the equity base and liquidity. In some instances, dividends may be limited to retained earnings subsequent to the issuance of a particular bond issue, or subsequent earnings plus some stipulated amount of accumulated earnings.

Owners of preferred stocks normally enjoy equal claim to assets and dividends behind bondholders. Rarely, a "prior" preferred receives first claim to income and assets; this might be called a "first" preferred. Preferred issues protect against issuance of subsequent debt and preferred stock of equal or greater rank by veto rights. In such a case,

[13]Net tangible assets are net assets less intangibles, such as patents, copyrights, and goodwill.
[14]The reader may note that an asset-to-debt ratio is a sort of asset-coverage counterpart to the earnings-coverage ratio.

the votes of, say, two-thirds of the preferred holders are required to approve prior or parity securities *unless* total debt and preferred-stock charges are covered to a specified extent (maybe two and one-half times fixed charges), and/or common-stock equity is not less than preferred-stock equity after new preferred is sold (that is, common equity ⩾ preferred equity).

It is standard for preferred-stock contracts to provide for cumulation of dividends. In other words, if dividends are missed, they must be made up before any dividends can be paid on common shares. Moreover, when a certain number of dividends are missed, preferred stockholders can elect a number of directors to prevent further difficulties. This voting right is contingent upon missing dividends and is relinquished when arrears are cleared up.

Tests of Corporate-Bond Risk: A Review Example

Table 12-3 shows single-year data for Husky Industries. Table 12-4 is a summary of key tests of default risk bearing on the bonds and preferred stock of the company if they were being analyzed on the statement dates. This example is included to assist the reader

TABLE 12-3
HUSKY INDUSTRIES, FINANCIAL STATEMENTS FOR THE YEAR 198X

Income Statement for the Year Ended 12/31/8X (millions of dollars)	
Net revenues*	$101.2
Cost of sales	78.0
Depreciation	10.0
Lease payments†	1.0
EBIT	12.2
Interest expense	2.2
EBT	10.0
Income taxes‡	4.7
EAT	5.3
Preferred dividends	1.2
Earnings available to common	4.1
Common dividend	2.1

Position Statement 12/31/8X (millions of dollars)			
Cash	$ 2.0	Current debt	$ 10.0
Other current assets (net)	60.0	4% 1st-mortgage bonds	10.0
Intangible fixed assets (net)	5.6	4½% debenture bonds§	40.0
Tangible fixed assets (net)	83.0	6% cumulative preferred	20.0
		Common stock ($1 par)	.6
		Surplus accounts	70.0
Total assets	$150.6	Total debt and equity	$150.6

*Includes pre-tax long-term capital gains on sale of land, $1.2 million.
†Financial lease. Borrowing equivalent cost = 8%.
‡Tax rates on income: ordinary income = 50%; capital gains = 25%.
§Annual sinking fund of $2.4 million.

TABLE 12-4

KEY MEASURES OF RISK IN FIXED-INCOME SECURITIES

Ratio	Calculation	Result
Coverage ratios:		
Interest coverage	[(11.0) + (.3)]/[(2.2) + (.33)]	4.47
Preferred-dividend coverage	[(11.0) + (.3)]/[(2.53) + (2.4)]	3.87
Debt-service coverage	[(11.0) + (1.0)]/[(2.2) + (1.0)]	3.75
Cash flow coverage	[(11.0) + (1.0) + (10.0)]/[(11.0) + (1.0) + (2.4)]	1.53
Capitalization ratios:		
Long-term debt	$50.00	.36
Debt equivalent for lease	$ 4.17	.03
Preferred stock	$20.00	.14
Tangible common equity	$65.00	.47
Liquidity ratios:		
Cash ratio	2/10	.20
Current ratio	62/10	6.20
Working capital: funded debt	52/54.17	.96

in pulling together the many strands of analysis introduced so far.[15]

Key items to note are:

1. Extraordinary income (land sale) is included in revenues. Exclude $1.2 from EBIT as nonrecurring, leaving EBIT = $11. (Note: Income taxes of $4.7 include $.3 from 25 percent tax on land sale of $1.2.)
2. Regarding lease payments, a net lease might assume that one-third the payment is equivalent to interest. Capitalized at a borrowing cost of 8 percent (.33/.08), this gives a long-term debt equivalent of $4.17. Add one-third of the lease payment to previously adjusted EBIT, and the interest portion to interest expense. EBIT = $11.33; Long-term debt = $54.17; Interest and lease payment = $2.53.
3. Pre-tax preferred dividend adjustments should use a tax rate of 50 percent, not the effective rate on the income statement (Income tax/EBT = 4.7/10.0 = 47%). (See item 1, above.) Pre-tax preferred dividend is $1.2/.5, or $2.4.
4. Total tangible assets equal $145 ($150.6 minus $5.6). Tangible common equity is $65.0 ($70.6 minus net intangible fixed assets of $5.6).

Municipal-Bond Analysis

There are two principal types of municipal securities: general-credit obligations and revenue bonds. General-obligation bonds are backed by the full taxing power of the municipality. Revenue bonds, however, are backed only by the revenue of the specific project for which they were issued. A toll-road bond issue is an example of a revenue bond. Because of the greater risk of revenue bonds, they must provide higher yields to maturity.

Municipal securities, like corporates, are subject to default risk and are rated by Moody's and Standard & Poor's as to their probability of default.

---

[15]To illustrate certain points, some statement items have been placed and/or combined in a manner contrary to good accounting practices.

GENERAL-OBLIGATION BONDS

The general factors that must be considered in assessing default risk on municipals are the taxing base, existing debt in relation to this base, and the variability of tax revenues. Several common ratios can be used to judge the relative risk of default.

First, what is the amount of tax-dependent debt relative to the assessed valuation of taxable real estate? The wealth and income of a community can be measured roughly in terms of property values. The resulting ratio is a debt-to-property-value measure. Care must be taken in making comparisons, to ensure that assessment methods are standardized. Communities normally take market values of property and reduce them to assessed value by some percentage multiplier. One may assess property at 60 percent of market value, and another at 80 percent. High-quality bonds would normally fall in a range of 8 to 10 percent for debt to assessed value. In a sense, this measure is a rough equivalent of a debt-to-asset ratio for corporates. The reciprocal is an asset-coverage ratio.

Second, debt per capita is also measured. The number of residents of a community does not necessarily represent the number of taxpayers, so care must be taken not to use this ratio in isolation.

Third, debt service as a percentage of the community's budgeted operating expenses can be measured. Debt service refers to the sum of annual interest plus debt retirement. This ratio is a roundabout equivalent of interest-coverage ratios on corporates. Instead of using earnings or revenues as with corporates, however, it measures the community's burden in paying for debt service relative to other operating costs out of tax receipts.

REVENUE BONDS

Revenue bonds bear risks similar to those of corporate bonds. Interest and principal must be paid from earnings, so earnings-coverage ratios become vitally important. The investor must assess the future revenue-generating ability of the project (toll road, sports stadium, or whatever).

Default Risk and Market Yields

Figure 12-1 indicates the pattern of the structure of yields on governments, municipals, and corporates over time. The general correspondence of governments and various grades of corporates is in line with basic differences in underlying default risk and premiums.

The reader should be warned that default risk alone does not explain the differentials or spreads in yields. Identical agency ratings of quality can disguise differentials among industrial, finance, and electric and gas utility bonds, and even among issues within these categories.

Differences in taxation can be seen in the low levels of yields on municipals. Certain situations that exist with corporates provide different tax situations in the same rating category. Call features and differences in degree of marketability are other factors that are hidden in Figure 12-1.

CHANGES IN YIELD DIFFERENTIALS

Yields on different instruments do not move in lockstep. Differentials, or spreads, are altered when circumstances that caused them in the first place change. Figure 12-2 depicts the historical pattern and variability of yield spreads. Average levels of AAA

FIGURE 12-1
PATTERN AND STRUCTURE OF YIELDS ON GOVERNMENTS, MUNICI-
PALS, AND CORPORATES OVER TIME

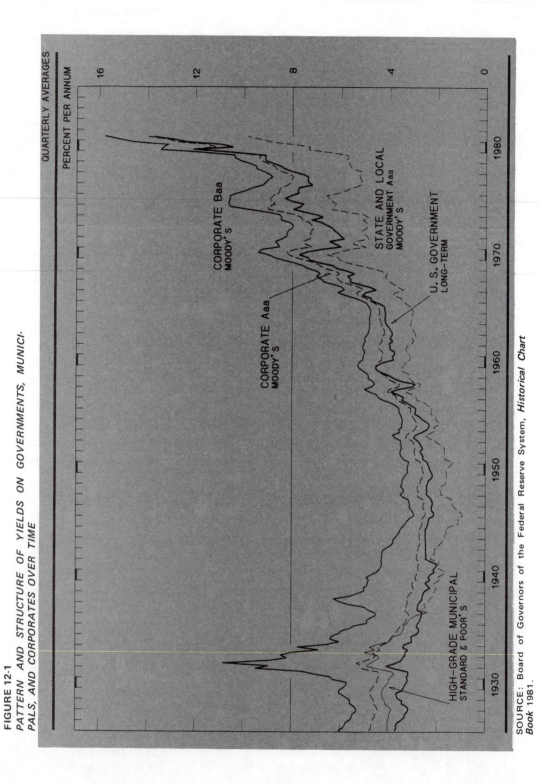

SOURCE: Board of Governors of the Federal Reserve System, *Historical Chart Book* 1981.

FIGURE 12-2
YIELD DIFFERENTIALS

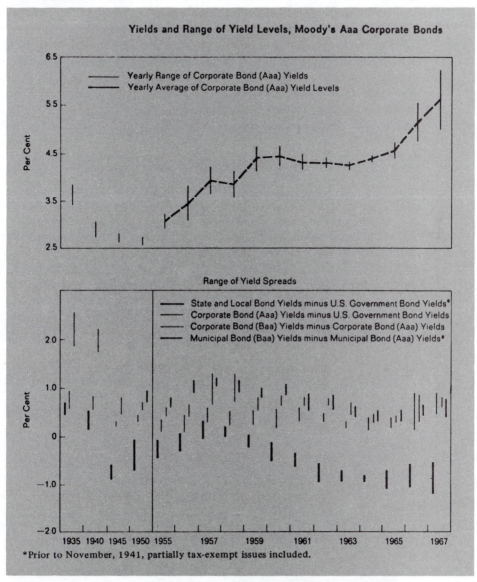

Yields and Range of Yield Levels, Moody's Aaa Corporate Bonds

— Yearly Range of Corporate Bond (Aaa) Yields
— Yearly Average of Corporate Bond (Aaa) Yield Levels

Range of Yield Spreads

— State and Local Bond Yields minus U.S. Government Bond Yields[a]
— Corporate Bond (Aaa) Yields minus U.S. Government Bond Yields
— Corporate Bond (Baa) Yields minus Corporate Bond (Aaa) Yields
— Municipal Bond (Baa) Yields minus Municipal Bond (Aaa) Yields[a]

*Prior to November, 1941, partially tax-exempt issues included.

SOURCE: Board of Governors of the Federal Reserve System, *Banking and Monetary Statistics*, 1943; Board of Governors of the Federal Reserve System, *Supplement to Banking and Monetary Statistics*, Section 12, 1966; Board of Governors of the Federal Reserve System, *Federal Reserve Bulletin*, reprinted in A. M. Wojnilower, "Yield Differentials," in M. E. Polakoff, ed., *Financial Institutions and Markets* (Boston: Houghton Mifflin, 1970), p. 453.

corporates over time are shown in the upper panel. The vertical lines show yield ranges during each year. Fluctuations of yields within given years are large relative to year-to-year changes in the average level of yield. The lower panel shows spreads between four different types of bonds. The size of the spreads has fluctuated greatly over the years. The variability of the differentials within many years is as large as or larger than the range of the level of rates shown in the upper panel. The shrinkage in the Aaa-Baa differential from about 2 percent in pre-World War II years to almost nothing in 1964 and 1965 is striking. This is the result of diminished worries about default or another depression. The Aaa-U.S. government spread shrank in the postwar period until after 1965, when it widened again. During these years, no hard evidence suggested that Aaa corporates had become more default-prone. There is some reason to believe that the spread resulted from dramatic increases in corporate-bond financing and diminished long-term-debt financing by the government.[16]

In general, although change and fluctuations are the rule in yield spreads, the basic cyclical behavior of these spreads can be characterized as follows: Risk premiums in the market for bonds fluctuate in a systematic way with the business cycle. During upturns, the premium for risk is expected to narrow; during downturns, the premium is expected to widen. In recessions, bondholders are mostly concerned with safety. Prices of higher-grade bonds are bid up relative to those of lower-grade bonds (high-grade yields fall relatively). During prosperity, less concern may be shown for safety and more willingness to bear a greater risk of default. The seeking out of higher-yielding securities will tend to drive down risk premiums relative to lower-yielding, higher-grade bonds.

FORCES BEHIND CHANGING SPREADS

Among the long-run factors influencing the size of yield spreads are (1) the breaking down of market imperfections, and (2) growing confidence that serious depressions can and will be avoided. Yield spreads have tended to narrow among the markets as borrowers and lenders have been willing to take advantage of various opportunities offering better rates. Strict segmentation of markets in which some investors participate and others do not has gradually been breaking down. Money is becoming more mobile. The result has perhaps been to narrow spreads but make levels more volatile. The effect of reduced fear of depressions is narrower-yield spreads. No doubt government commitments to economic stability and a long period of low default rates contribute to this greater sense of safety among leaders.

In the shorter run, the forces at work on yield spreads necessitate looking behind forecasts of sources and uses of funds such as those provided by Salomon Bros. and the more detailed Federal Reserve Flow of Funds Accounts.

Nonrisk Factors Influencing Yields

Certain qualities inherent in bonds, common stocks, and preferred stocks have nothing in particular to do with risk in its traditional definition. Some of these factors result from *laws*, some from *terms in security contracts* and others from the way *securities markets* function.

---

[16]A.M. Wojnilower, "Yield Differentials," in *Financial Institutions and Markets*, ed. M.C. Polakoff (Boston: Houghton Mifflin, 1970), pp.425-54.

Each of these factors might make a security desirable to some investors and not to others. The more desirable a particular factor or factors might be to an investor, the more he will pay for a security that bears it, other things being equal. Conversely, if an investor is neutral or can get along without a particular feature, he will not pay more to obtain it. Investors who are averse to a given quality in a security will be willing to buy it only at a lower price. In all cases, the change that results from a willingness or unwillingness to pay for a particular quality has an effect on a security's yield or return.

Three principal ownership qualities are of interest to us: marketability, call features, and taxation of returns.

Marketability

Differences in yield for various securities may result from differences in marketability. *Marketability* refers to the ability of the owner to convert to cash. This conversion process relies upon price realized and time required to sell the security. Price and time are interrelated, since it is often possible to sell a security quickly if enough price concession is given. For securities, marketability is the ability of the seller to sell a significant volume of the securities in a short period of time without significant price concessions (which include the matter of transaction costs). The more marketable a security, the greater the investor's ability to execute a large transaction near the quoted price.

Usually, marketability of a security is judged by the difference between the quoted bid and asked prices in relation to the level of prices, since the percentage difference depends upon the price level. For example, if we express bid-asked differentials as a percentage of the bid price, a $1 spread on a bid of $10 is 10 percent. The same $1 spread on a bid of $100 is only 1 percent. The bid price is the price the dealer stands ready to buy a security for; the asked price is the price he is willing to sell the security for. The smaller the spread, expressed as a percentage of the bid price, the more marketable the security.

Dealer spreads are like a retailer's markup: They must cover expenses, risk of loss, and a profit. In general, like any fast-moving merchandise, securities with a large volume of transactions carry narrower markups or spreads. Competition keeps dealers from taking larger markups than required by expense, risk, and a reasonable profit.

Investors find advantages in more marketable securities because the cost of buying and selling them is less. A highly marketable preferred stock might be quoted as 50 bid, 50 1/2 asked. The 1/2-point spread is the markup. If you bought 100 shares for $5,050 and sold them again for $5,000, the service charge would be $50. (Of course, it is unlikely that the quotes would stay constant.) The cost of buying and selling the security is 1 percent of the bid price ($50/$5,000). Consider another case where a preferred is quoted as 100 bid, 102 asked. If you purchased 50 shares at $5,100 and resold at the bid price for $5,000, you would pay a service fee of $100. This is double the dollar and percentage cost in the first example.

It is quite common for investors to refer to a stock or a bond as having a "thin" market. The connotation is that there is not much of the security for sale at the asked price, and not much sought at the bid price. If you place an order to buy or sell a relatively large block, it may be executed at a price materially different from the price of the last transaction. The converse is thought of as a "broad" market, in which one can sell large amounts at once with little or no effect upon the quoted price. Poorly marketable securities have thin markets. Buying or selling small blocks in a market dominated by large trades can lead to similar marketability problems.

The marketability of a security can be judged by observing the bid-asked spread over several different time periods. It is commonplace to assume that securities of small, unseasoned companies listed on the over-the-counter market have less marketability than those of large, seasoned companies listed on the New York Stock Exchange. This is only a generalization. Each case must be considered individually. Frequently, "thin" markets are referred to in regard to stocks that have small numbers of shares in active supply. Large percentages of shares might be held by family trusts, or the companies may be small and have few shares issued and outstanding.

Small investors who purchase bonds must assess marketability very closely. The bond markets are dominated by large institutional holders who tend to buy and sell in blocks in the millions of dollars. The bid-asked prices appearing in the financial press will most probably be for transaction sizes (in dollars) that reflect institutional supply and demand. For example, the latest quote on a corporate bond is 100 bid and 100 1/4 asked. Should you wish to buy or sell $2,000 worth, the dealer might quote you 99 1/2 bid and 101 asked, because the published quotes reflect a market of transactions many times greater than yours. Yours is, in a sense, an odd-lot order.

One final comment is in order relative to the marketability of an issue. Certain liquidity problems or trading difficulties can be encountered as the bond gets older, that is, as it approaches maturity. These bonds typically begin to move into the portfolios of permanent investor types who tend to hold them to maturity.

Thus, differences in return (yield) between different securities are caused not only by differences in default risk but also by differences in marketability. The lower the marketability, the greater the yield an investor would demand, and vice versa.

SEASONED VERSUS NEW ISSUES

Bonds that have been outstanding for some time are generally referred to in the bond trade as "seasoned." The yields on older, "seasoned" issues will typically be below those on "new" issues, with the difference depending upon the level of interest rates. The yields on new issues frequently exceed those on seasoned issues of the same quality and maturity when interest rates are high. The reason for these higher yields is that underwriters do not want to hold the new issues in inventory because of the associated carrying costs and the danger of a further rise in the level of interest rates. Their behavior is such that they mark down the prices on new issues (higher yields) vis-à-vis seasoned issues. In addition, older, lower-coupon bonds tend to sell at a discount. Their inherent tax advantages and call protection cause their prices to be bid up (lowering yields). These tax and call advantages will be discussed shortly.

Overall, the spread between seasoned and new issues is a function of the level of interest rates and can vary anywhere from 0 to 50 basis points (seasoned issues are below new issues by this amount). The higher the level of interest rates, the larger will be the spread.

A study by Martin and Richards suggests that the yield differential between new and seasoned corporate bond issues exists but does not decline with the passage of time.[17] They suggest that coupon and call differences explain virtually all of the observed differences in yields. The implication of this research is that there is no seasoning process and, more importantly, buying new rather than seasoned bonds is unlikely to result in above average returns.

The Call Feature

Many issuers put terms in the contract giving them the right to redeem or *call* the entire outstanding amount before maturity, subject to certain conditions. Most corporate bonds and preferred-stock issues provide for a call feature, and some Treasury securities (governments) are callable. Generally, municipal securities are not callable; they are serial.

In the case of corporate bonds and preferred stocks, the call price is usually above the face or par value of the security and decreases over time. For example, an 8 percent, 25-year bond issue may be callable initially at 108 (108 percent of par). The call price might decline by 1/4 percent per year (108, 107.75, 107.50, and so on). It is common for the initial call price to be the equivalent of one year's interest plus the par value of the bond.

The call feature modifies maturity and thereby affects a security's relative yield. The call feature is exercisable immediately or it is deferred for some time. The most widely used deferred-call periods are five years for public utility bonds and ten years for industrial bonds. During the deferment period, the investor is protected from a call by the issuer.

The issuer pays a premium for the option of calling the bonds before their nominal maturity. The option to call provides the issuer with flexibility. Should interest rates decline significantly, the issuer does not have to wait until maturity to refinance but can call the bonds and reissue others at a lower interest cost. The call may also be exercised to eliminate any protective covenants in the bond contracts that have become unduly restrictive.

The call feature does not come free. When interest rates are high and expected to fall, the call feature is likely to have significant value. Investors will be unwilling to invest in callable bonds unless yields are more than those of bonds that are noncallable or unless call is deferred, other things being equal. Borrowers are willing to pay a premium in yield for some sort of call privilege. When rates are expected to rise, the call feature has negligible value to the issuer. The spread between immediately callable and deferred call bonds may narrow close to zero.

Yield differentials are available for newly issued corporate bonds having similar ratings but immediate and five-year-deferred call. These are shown in Figure 12-3. The spread widens in periods of high interest rates, narrows in periods of low interest rates. High-interest periods in 1959 and 1966-68 show a differential of about 1/2 percent (or 50 basis points, in the jargon of the bond analyst). During the 1963-65 period, no premium was evident. Overall, the evidence would suggest that the call privilege has the most value and cost to issuers when interest rates are high and expected to fall.

[17]J.D. Martin and R.M. Richards, "The Seasoning Process for Corporate Bonds", *Financial Management* (Summer 1981), pp. 41-48.

FIGURE 12-3
YIELD DIFFERENTIAL BETWEEN IMMEDIATELY CALLABLE AND DEFERRED CALLABLE Aa PUBLIC UTILITY BONDS, 1958-1968

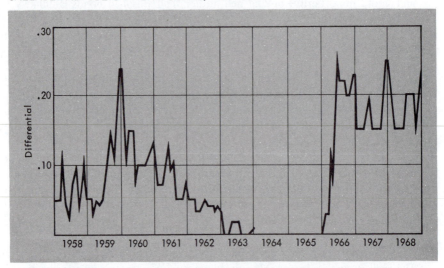

SOURCE: James C. Van Horne, *Function and Analysis of Capital Market Rates* (Englewood Cliffs, N.J.: Prentice-Hall, 1970), p. 125. As reprinted from *An Analytical Record of Yields and Yield Spreads* (New York: Salomon Brothers).

About one-third of all governments have a call feature. The primary purpose is to obtain flexibility in new financing near the maturity date of an outstanding obligation. This contrasts sharply with the principal purpose of savings in interest cost attributable to corporate issues. The Treasury constantly replaces its debts as they mature, instead of paying them off. The market may or may not be "right" at maturity; so the Treasury places optional maturity dates on some bonds to provide flexibility in refinancing. For example, the terms of the 4 1/4 percent bonds of 1987-92 state that the call privilege may be exercised any time between 1987 and the final maturity in 1992. The bonds' life may be shortened no more than five years from the original maturity. In a thirty-year corporate with a ten-year-deferred call, the maturity could be shortened by twenty years.

Thus the threat of a call feature to an investor is dependent upon his expectations that interest rates will fall significantly during the life of the bond or preferred-stock issue. Accepting securities with immediate call privileges will tend to provide more return (yield) than accepting some deferral period. In periods of high interest rates, this can mean a difference of 1/4 percent in yield. Whether the risk of call is worth the extra 1/4 percent is principally a function of the outlook for interest rates and whether the issuer feels he will be able to refund the bonds at a profit (savings).

Another strategy for approaching the call-risk problem is to buy deep-discount bonds—bonds that sell well below par or face value.[18] The principal reason for this condition is that they bear coupon rates far below prevailing rates required in the market. Using bond-yield tables, it is possible to show that in a market where the returns on

[18]It is important to recognize the fact that a bond selling far below its face value is not necessarily in trouble.

ten-year AAA bonds are 8 percent, a newly issued ten-year-AAA bond with an 8 percent coupon would sell for 100, whereas an older bond with a 4 percent coupon, due in ten years, would sell at 73. The 4 percent bond provides most of its required return of 8 percent through appreciation in price at maturity.

If market rates fall to 6 percent, the 8 percent bond will move to 115, and the 4 percent bond to 85. But the 8 percent bonds are in danger of call, whereas the 4 percent bonds are still far below their probable call price. It is important to realize, however, that the deep discount aspects of bonds are really attractive on two counts: call protection and tax advantages. Since ordinary interest income is taxed at regular tax rates and long-term capital gains (increases in principal values) are taxed at lower capital gains rates, deep discount bonds possess tax-savings appeal.

SINKING FUNDS

Sinking funds have been designed to provide for the retirement of a certain portion of a bond issue through purchases by the issuing corporation at predetermined regular intervals. Nearly all industrial bonds have sinking funds. Although less frequently used by electric utilities in the past (less than 50 percent), investor pressure has built recently to force the increasing inclusion of a sinking fund in new utility issues.

The sinking fund provides two broadly defined benefits to an investor. The orderly retirement of debt by the corporation should provide the bond investor increasing credit safety, since the amount of debt outstanding is reduced and the pressure on the company to refinance a large amount of debt at maturity is moderated. A second important benefit is that the sinking fund provides an additional element of liquidity to the issue through regular purchase activity to meet sinking-fund requirements.

As a result, investors have traditionally held the notion that the existence of a sinking fund provided some extra value over and above what would be the bond's market value at any given point in time. Within the context of rising interest rates over the last twenty-five years, the sinking fund has indeed provided extra value to the bondholder. The mere fact that a sinking fund shortens the average life of the bond and therefore provides the investor an opportunity to reinvest at a higher yield earlier has provided substantial incremental value.

However, when interest rates reach high levels, the existence of the sinking fund may actually reduce the relative value of the bonds, since the potential exists for bonds to be retired at par if rates subsequently fall and prices rise.

Since the sinking fund is placed in a bond issue largely for the benefit of the investor, the typical sinking-fund price is a *maximum* of par value plus any accumulated interest. Thus, if interest rates rise subsequent to the issuance of a bond, the bond will tend to fall below par. Since issuers are obliged to pay no more than the par value of the bond for sinking-fund purposes, they will generally satisfy the sinking-fund requirement by purchasing bonds in the open market. This injects demand into the market for the bonds and, depending upon the size of the sinking fund, provides support for the bond price. Should interest rates fall subsequent to the issuance of a bond, the bond will rise in price above par value. Again, since the maximum price to be paid for the bond for sinking-fund purposes is the par value, the question remains: What is the most equitable way to repurchase bonds if the required sinking-fund price is below the market price? Typically, bonds will be redeemed by random lot. That is, bonds are selected randomly by bond number, and a sufficient number are repurchased to satisfy the sinking-fund requirement. Thus, in a period of declining interest rates, the operation of a sinking fund injects a lottery risk into the holding of such bonds. You may have purchased a bond at, say, 102 only to see it called at 100.

Therefore the presence of a sinking fund in a bond issue is a mixed blessing. It may provide the bondholder with some peace of mind that there is a regular redemption schedule in place and provide some price support for the bond in a period of rising interest rates. However, if interest rates decline subsequent to the issuance of a bond, an investor may have his bond called away for sinking-fund purposes and be faced with a knotty problem of reinvestment at lower rates.

Tax Factors

Chapter 3 dealt with the broad question of taxes. Our present discussion will concern the tax effects primarily related to bonds and preferred stocks. In particular, we will explore the tax impact of (1) discount bonds, (2) municipal and government bonds, and (3) preferred stocks.

DISCOUNT BONDS

As we have noted, discount bonds are bonds selling below their par or face value. These bonds provide not only a large measure of call protection but also certain tax advantages. The most important tax we shall consider is, of course, the federal income tax. The differential impact upon yields arises because interest and dividends are taxed at ordinary rates, whereas gains on securities held more than twelve months receive the more favorable capital gains treatment in which only 40 percent of the gain is taxable.

The greater the discount on a bond, the greater its capital gains attraction and the lower its yield relative to what it would be if the coupon rate were such that the bond sold at par. A simple example will illustrate the tax implications.

Consider the alternatives of buying two bonds of similar quality. The first can be bought for par with an 8 percent coupon to yield 8 percent to maturity. The second has a 4 percent coupon and sells at a discount sufficient to provide an added 4 percent in capital gains yield, so the total yield to maturity is also 8 percent. An investor in the 50 percent tax bracket would realize 4 percent after taxes on the par bond and 5.2 percent on the discount bond. This is because the entire return from the 8 percent bond is subject to ordinary tax rates (50 percent in this case); the other bond is subject to a 50 percent rate on the 4 percent coupon, but only .4 of the capital gain of 4 percent is taxed. In other words, the tax on the 4 percent capital gain is .8 percent (.5 × 2/5 × 4%). After taxes, the investor is left with 3.2 percent plus the 2 percent from coupons.

The result of this example suggests that, in order for the high-coupon and the deep-discount bond to sell on an identical yield-to-maturity basis (after taxes), the 4 percent bond would have to be priced to yield 6.50 percent to maturity.[19] This rate, of course, is hypothetical, since other factors are involved. Par and deep-discount bonds of the same quality are purchased by people in various tax brackets that achieve different net yields. Also, the value of call protection in discount bonds bears on the issue.

---

[19]The mathematics of these arguments will be developed in Chapter 13.

GOVERNMENTS AND MUNICIPALS

Unlike the case with all other categories of securities, interest income (but *not* capital gains) from state and local government securities is exempt from federal income taxes. This unique tax status accounts for the fact that municipal-bond yields are lower than those of other securities. Most states do not tax income from their own bonds, or income from bonds of their political subdivisions. Thus, from an overall tax standpoint, there are advantages to buying municipals issued in the state of residence of an investor.

Typically, municipal bonds will yield less than taxable bonds, depending on the level of interest rates. Since the tax exemption on municipal bonds applies only to the interest, discount and premium municipal bonds are less attractive than municipal bonds selling at par. Therefore, discount and premium municipal bonds will not sell at the same yield to maturity as municipal bonds selling at par.

Commercial banks are among the largest holders of municipal bonds, particularly at times when the demand for loans is soft. Investment in municipal bonds serves as a substitute when the demand for consumer and business loans is weak. When the level of interest rates is high, banks generally sell municipal bonds to meet loan demand. This has a tendency to force down the prices on municipal bonds and therefore raises the level of rates. Thus, yields on municipal bonds during such periods will tend to rise faster than yields on taxables. That is, the spread between municipals and taxable bonds narrows. Conversely, when the demand for consumer and business loans falls, the reverse occurs. That is, banks tend to purchase municipal bonds, and this demand raises the price of municipal bonds and lowers their yields. The spread between municipal yields and taxable bonds widens.

In addition to the federal income tax, the federal tax on estates has an impact upon Treasury securities. The estate tax is levied on assets upon the death of the owner. Certain Treasury bonds, if owned by the deceased, are redeemable at par if the proceeds are used to pay federal estate taxes. These are referred to as "flower bonds." A $1,000-par government bond purchased at $800 would be worth $1,000 in settlement of estate taxes. For this reason, qualifying government bonds selling at discounts have a special attraction above and beyond the capital gains implications.

Figure 12-4 shows the yield distinction between high-grade governments and high-grade municipals over time. The spread in yields, or differential, has ranged from 100 to 150 basis points (1 to 1 1/2 percent), owing almost entirely to the difference in taxation of these two categories of bonds under the federal income tax law.[20]

PREFERRED STOCKS

Federal tax laws provide that intercorporate dividends shall not be excessively taxed. One corporation receiving dividends from another and, in turn, paying dividends to its own shareholders could be faced with double taxation. Taxing the dividend to the ultimate shareholder would amount to triple taxation. To alleviate this chain of taxation, intercorporate dividends are taxed at very low rates.

[20]For a detailed historical perspective on the use of preferred stock, see Donald E. Fischer and Glenn A. Wilt, Jr., "Non-Convertible Preferred Stock as a Financing Instrument, 1950-1965," *Journal of Finance*, 33 (September, 1968), 611-24.

FIGURE 12-4
YIELD DIFFERENTIAL BETWEEN LONG-TERM TREASURY BONDS AND PRIME MUNICIPAL BONDS AFTER TAXES, 1950-1968, ANNUAL AVERAGES

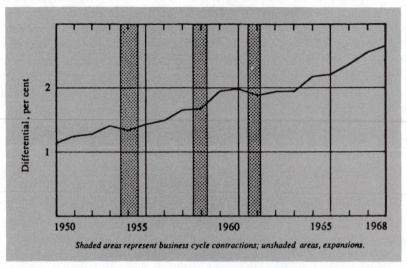

Shaded areas represent business cycle contractions; unshaded areas, expansions.

SOURCE: James C. Van Horne, *Function and Analysis of Capital Market Rates* (Englewood Cliffs, N.J.: Prentice-Hall, 1970), p. 113.

A substantial portion of dividends received on preferred or common stocks held by corporations may be deducted when they compute their taxable income. Under existing federal income tax law, such investors (including, in certain cases, life insurance companies and mutual savings banks) are entitled to a deduction equivalent to 85 percent of dividends received on certain preferred-stock holdings. This deduction applies to income from all preferred issues other than issues of public utility operating companies; income from these is entitled to the 85 percent deduction only if such preferred stocks were issued for "new-money" purposes on or after October 1, 1942. New-money issues are those sold to raise funds for the first time, rather than to redeem existing financing. For corporations in the 46 percent tax bracket, with only 15 percent of such dividend income taxable, 6.9 percent of the dividends on such issues will be paid in taxes (.46 × .15), thus providing an after-tax return equal to 93.1 percent of the dividend.

For financial institutions that have an effective tax rate of 25 percent, slightly more than 96 percent of the dividend on industrial or "new-money" utility preferred stocks is retained after tax (see Table 12-5).

Table 12-5 shows how these calculations are made. To make similar calculations for effective tax rates other than 46 percent or 25 percent, substitute the appropriate effective tax rate in the first column and compute as shown.

Table 12-6 indicates pre-tax yields and enables corporations to determine yield needed on interest-bearing obligations to equal the after-tax yield on 85 percent tax-exempt preferreds. For example, using the 46 percent tax-rate section, if a taxpaying institution were to purchase a preferred stock yielding 9.00 percent (see left-hand column), it would have to receive a 15.52 percent yield on a government or corporate

TABLE 12-5

EXAMPLES: 9.00 PERCENT DIVIDEND (OR YIELD)

Effective Tax Rate		Percent Dividend Subject		Percent of Dividend (or Yield) Paid in Tax		Percent Remaining After Tax		Dividend Rate (or Yield) (%)	After-Tax Dividend (or Yield) (%)
46%	X	15	=	6.90	thus	93.10	X	9.00	8.38
25%	X	15	=	3.75	thus	96.25	X	9.00	8.66

SOURCE: *Preferred Stock Guide*, 1976 Edition (New York: Salomon Brothers, 1976), p. 4.

TABLE 12-6

PREFERRED STOCK EQUIVALENT YIELD TABLE (46% TAX RATE)

Yield on Preferred Entitled to 85% Exemption	Yield Needed to Equal After-Tax Return on 85% Exempt Preferred on:	
	*Bonds, Mortgages** *(100% Taxable)*	*Tax-Exempt Obligations*[†]
8.00	13.79	7.45
9.00	15.52	8.38
10.00	17.24	9.31
12.00	20.68	11.17

*Yield X .931
.54

[†]Yield X .931

bond or on a mortgage, or an 8.38 percent yield on a tax-exempt issue, in order to obtain the same after-tax yield as is received on the preferred issue on a 9.00 percent basis.

Investing in Preferred Stocks. The small investor has been effectively priced out of the market for preferred stocks, because of the advantage taxable institutions have of excluding 85 percent of dividends received from income. Bond interest, other than that on municipals, is fully taxed. For institutional investors, the relative after-tax yields on high-quality corporate bonds and high-grade preferred stocks is obvious. A tax rate of 50 percent applied to an 8 percent bond and an 8 percent preferred stock gives an after-tax yield of 4 percent on the bond and 7.4 percent on the preferred stock. This is more than enough difference to overcome any perceived differences in risk.

Table 12-7 shows the yields on high-quality corporate bonds and preferred stocks over time. Preferreds generally yield *less* than bonds, with the average differential being about 35 basis points. The underlying causes are the tax anomaly and the diminishing supply of available preferred stocks. *For the small investor without the income tax exclusion on preferreds, it hardly seems worth taking more risk and getting a lower return than on bonds.*

From time to time, there is talk of a speculative strategy involving noncallable preferreds. There are about a dozen of these outstanding, mostly issues by industrial firms. The record shows that many noncallable preferreds have been retired at sizable premiums over market price. The small number still outstanding makes this type of speculation one with very long-shot possibilities.

TABLE 12-7

YIELDS ON HIGH-GRADE BONDS AND PREFERRED
STOCKS, 1965-1980

Year	(1) Aaa Corporate Bonds	(2) Preferred Stocks	(3) Spread (2) − (1)
1965	4.49%	4.33%	−0.16
1966	5.13	4.97	−0.16
1967	5.51	5.34	−0.17
1968	6.18	5.78	−0.40
1969	7.03	6.41	−0.62
1970	8.04	7.22	−0.82
1971	7.39	6.75	−0.64
1972	7.21	7.27	+0.06
1973	7.44	7.23	−0.21
1974	8.57	8.23	−0.34
1975	8.83	8.38	−0.45
1976	8.43	7.97	−0.46
1977	8.04	7.65	−0.39
1978	8.73	8.25	−0.48
1979	9.63	9.07	−0.56
1980	11.94	10.57	−1.37

SOURCE: *Federal Reserve Bulletin.*

Default Risk in Holiday Inns Long-Term Debt and Preferred Stock

Table 12-8 contains, in summary form, financial data and certain ratios applying to Holiday Inns. The information was gleaned from various sources, including the annual statements of the company.

Interest coverage dropped significantly from 1972 through 1974 and then improved noticeably subsequent to 1974. The significance of the erratic nature of this coverage is that Holiday Inns faced rising borrowing costs during a period of eroding

TABLE 12-8

FINANCIAL DATA AND RATIOS RELATIVE TO DEFAULT
RISK BEARING UPON DEBT AND PREFERRED STOCK OF
HOLIDAY INNS, INC. (MILLIONS OF DOLLARS)

	1972	1973	1974	1975	1976
EBIT	$100.40	$102.20	$ 87.60	$ 95.20	$ 90.00
Interest	22.30	27.30	30.20	27.10	25.00
Interest coverage	4.50	3.70	2.90	3.50	3.60
Preferred dividends	.40	.30	.20	.00	.00
Preferred dividend coverage	4.50	3.70	2.90	3.50	3.60
Depreciation and amortization	40.40	46.40	57.00	59.40	57.80
Cash flow (per share)	2.71	3.00	2.92	3.31	3.18
Cash	47.00	33.30	46.40	61.10	61.60
Current assets	155.00	152.90	178.10	177.70	180.60
Current liabilities	102.70	109.30	135.20	128.30	137.30
Cash ratio	.46	.30	.34	.48	.45
Current ratio	1.60	1.40	1.30	1.40	1.30
Working capital adequacy	.16	.12	.13	.16	.16

earnings (1972-74). The company was able to reverse the decline in interest coverage as interest rates eased and total debt was reduced (1975-76). The mortgage bonds of HIA (9 1/2 percent bonds due in 1995) are rated Bbb. Since it is difficult to determine directly the standard for giving certain coverage relationships specific ratings, two things can be done in this regard. First, we shall examine some of the thoughts of Standard & Poor's on the Bbb rating. Second, in Figure 12-5 we will examine the yield at which HIA's 9 1/2 percent bonds have traded in the recent past, relative to other Bbb-rated bonds.

Standard & Poor's suggests two specific tests that an issue of debt must pass in order to get a rating of Bbb or higher: a minimum cash flow/debt ratio of 25 percent, and a net tangible assets/debt ratio of over 200 percent. (Neither of these tests shows on our tabulation in Table 12-6, but these figures for HIA have been calculated separately.) The HIA 9 1/2 percent mortgage bonds were offered in 1970. At the end of 1969, the cash flow/debt ratio for HIA was 26 percent and the net tangible assets/debt ratio was 256 percent. It is easy to see that HIA's bonds are close to the lower limit of the Bbb rating on these two measures. Of course, there are other tests that serve as the basis of the Bbb rating, many of them derived from the data in Table 12-6. The ratios calculated in the table are also utilized.

Figure 12-5 shows the yield to maturity each quarter between March 1973 and March 1977 for HIA 9 1/2 percent bonds and S&P's index of Bbb-rated bonds. Notice that the HIA bonds sold at a higher yield than the class of bonds of which they are a part during 1972-74, suggesting that the HIA bonds, for any number of reasons, traded closer to the next lower rating (Bb), although they do tend to move in conjunction with Bbb bonds in general. Since 1974, Holiday Inns' 9 1/2 percent bonds have yielded a return

FIGURE 12-5
HOLIDAY INNS, INC., 9 1/2 PERCENT DEBENTURE BONDS' YIELD TO MATURITY, VARIOUS DATES

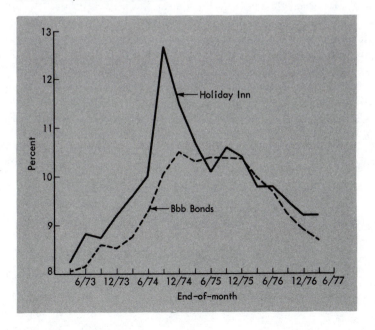

much closer to the Bbb average. This is due in large part to the improved coverage ratio noted earlier. Over the entire period, the Holiday Inns' bonds yielded about 50 basis points more, on average, than the rating class of which they were a part. One possible explanation of the higher yield than Bbb bonds in general is no doubt the small size of the issue ($30 million), which somewhat inhibits marketability and produces borderline ratios from a rating standpoint. Also, the yield on the HIA 9 1/2 percent bonds is affected by a deferred-call option, which prohibits call prior to June 15, 1980, from money borrowed at an interest-rate cost less than 9.50 percent. The high coupon (9 1/2 percent), with Bbb bonds moving down toward the 9 percent level, will no doubt serve as a damper or lid on price rises, owing to the possibility of call in 1980 at a call price at that time of 105. This bond issue also contains a sinking fund that began in 1976. At that time and through 1994, the company is required to redeem $2.25 million in bonds each year, with the option to retire more in a given year.

Preferred-dividend coverage has improved over time, mainly as the result of regular retirement of preferred shares for sinking-fund purposes. Preferred dividends have fallen from about $800,000 in 1967 to almost nil in 1977.

Summary

Yields differ on various kinds of bonds and preferred stocks. A rational way to view these differences is to isolate differences in risk associated with each. Market yields on U.S. government securities reflect compensation for the pure cost of lending or borrowing money without risk, plus compensation for purchasing-power risk. The structure of yields on corporates and municipals can be examined by differences in default risk and certain nonrisk variables influencing yield.

Investors are aided in assessing relative risks of default by established, independent rating agencies. However, the investor is well advised that these broad default ratings are only guides and provide, at best, a rough discrimination between bonds. Detailed analysis of the factors likely to contribute to default can pay handsome rewards. These factors mainly relate to asset and earnings coverage on bonds and preferreds.

Nonrisk factors influence yields as the result of tax laws, various features of security contracts, and the way in which securities markets function. Not all returns from securities are taxed in a similar manner. Municipal bonds and discount bonds possess unique tax appeal. Sinking-fund and call features represent advantages and disadvantages to investors. The cost and benefits of these contractural features must be weighed in an investment decision. Not all securities have active, broad markets. As a result, conversion back to cash may result in price concessions that detract from realized yield.

Questions and Problems

1. Refer to the ABC, Inc., example on page 344. What would interest coverage be if the first-mortgage and debenture bonds were considered separately—in other words, in order of risk priority?

2. Of what significance to investors are bonds that sell below par value?

3. Can you think of any advantages to the issuer of making periodic repayments of principal via a sinking fund? Are there disadvantages to the investor?

4. How would you go about analyzing an opportunity to purchase a few bonds of an issue that is currently in default? Locate a bonds issue quoted in the *Wall Street Journal* that is in default and analyze the prospects.

5. It has been argued that the loss to the federal government in income taxes because of the tax-exempt status of municipal bonds is greater than the savings in interest realized by issuing municipalities.
   a. How could this be so?
   b. What would be the overall effects of abolition of tax exemption on munici-
      pal-bond interest after a specified date in time?

6. The table on page 367 indicates relative yields required by corporate holders of bonds and preferreds to achieve levels of indifference between them with respect to after-tax return. Prove that an 8 percent preferred entitled to 85 percent exemption provides the same after-tax yield as a taxable bond yielding 13.79 percent and a tax-exempt obligation yielding 7.45 percent.

7. What has been the historical behavior of bond-yield spreads in terms of cycles and trends? What investment strategies are suggested if these historical relationships hold in the future?

8. Mortgages are really bonds backed by real property that are retired monthly via sinking fund. Determine the present relationship between yields on 25 to 30-year Aaa corporate bonds and 25 to 30-year conventional home mortgages. How do you explain the differences?

9. The following data are for Salt Lake Industries (tax rate = 50 percent):

Year	EBIT (thousands)
1983	$4,750
1982	4,500
1981	4,500
1980	4,250
1979	4,000

DEBT AND PREFERRED CAPITALIZATION (12/31/83)
(THOUSANDS OF DOLLARS)

Long-term debt:	
8% first-mortgage bonds (due 1991)	$25,000
6½% debentures (due 2000)	10,000
Preferred stock:	
$1.40 cumulative first preferred	
(par value $20/share)	2,000
7% noncumulative preferred	14,000

Analyze the default risk bearing upon the bonds and preferred stock in the greatest detail possible.

10. Obtain a recent edition of *Moody's Industrial Manual*. Examine the major contractual features of the following Aaa bonds: Texaco 5.75 percent (due 1997), and Exxon 6 percent (due 1997). How do you account for the fact that these two bonds of identical rating and maturity sell at differing prices over time?

11. Dairee, Inc., earned $50 million after interest, taxes, and preferred dividends in 1983. The company had an effective tax rate of 40 percent. Its capital structure consists in part of $12.5 million in 8 percent debentures and $5 million in 9 percent cumulative preferred stock. Calculate pre-tax coverage of interest and preferred dividends for 1983.

12. What kinds of protective covenants should a prospective bondholder look for in a bond contract?

13. The following information applies to Noll Products, Inc. (millions of dollars):

Revenues	$125
Operating expenses:	
Variable	25
Fixed	82*

*Includes depreciation of $10.5 million; tax rate = .4.

6% first-mortgage bonds (1990)	$ 50†
10% subordinated debentures (1998)	60†
$6 preferred stock ($50 par)	50
Common equity	600

†Combined sinking-fund payments of $6 million.

        a. What is the *debt-service* coverage for this firm?
        b. How safe are the preferred-stock holders' dividends (ignore sinking-fund payments on the debt)? Explain.

14. What two strategies might bond investors utilize in attempting to guard against the threat of a call feature?

15. A 7 percent preferred, entitled to 85 percent exemption, provides the same after-tax yield as a taxable bond yielding _____ and a tax-exempt obligation yielding _____ for a corporation in the 25 percent bracket.

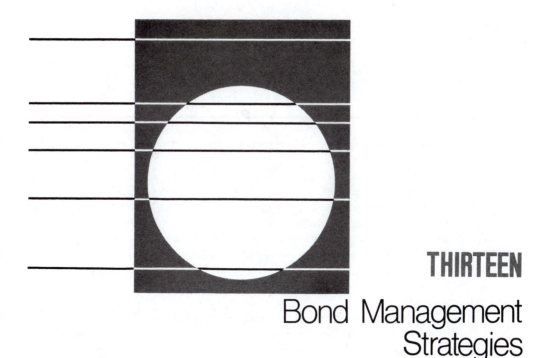

THIRTEEN

Bond Management Strategies

Bond investors may adopt passive or active approaches to the management of their portfolios. The passive approach is usually identified with a buy-and-hold strategy. Active bond portfolio management involves switching and swapping bonds as circumstances change in the markets for fixed-income securities. This chapter is concerned primarily with the necessary ingredients in a successful approach to passive and active bond management.

Passive Portfolio Management Strategies

The distinguishing feature of passive versus active bond management strategies is the minimal expectational inputs required in the process. Forecasts of the level and time shape of interest rates or yield spreads in different sectors of the bond market are not crucial. The investor's objectives are primarily broad diversification, predictable returns, and low management costs.

A *buy-and-hold* strategy is the simplest strategy for bond management. As the term implies, securities are bought and held to maturity. The main considerations are to be assured that there will be no default and to achieve a reasonable yield to maturity.

Implementation of a passive strategy would involve placing equal amounts in each bond, evenly spacing maturities with the most distant maturity one that the investor is comfortable with. This maturity spacing is referred to as "laddering" the portfolio. Proceeds from cash flows (interest, maturing bonds) are reinvested to maintain the balanced distribution of maturities. There is a certain built-in liquidity since a relatively constant number of bonds mature each year. The returns to a ladder portfolio will average the average rates on the bonds held. Principal risks will be price fluctuations which depend upon rates trends and maturities. In the face of fluctuating or rising interest rates, a buy-and-hold approach has a potentially severe disadvantage since there will be a tendency to miss opportunities from anticipated changes in interest rates as well as being subject to a lag in yield to maturity as rates rise.

Another type of passive strategy is the *index fund* approach. The objective is to replicate the performance of the overall bond market using a designated index. Typically, either the Salomon Brothers Bond Index or the Lehman Kuhn Loeb Bond Index is used. Presumably, it would be very difficult to outperform the index through expectational inputs and by combining securities in a portfolio with characteristics similar to the market, the efficiency of the market would be captured. (For the stock market the S&P 500 has been designated the favored index. It is not representative of the entire market of equities but does reflect the performance of the usual universe of stocks held by institutional investors.)

A fundamental issue is the identification of the appropriate index. The characteristics desired include being representative of the overall market and having a well-defined and stable composition. The broader the representation, the closer the replication of the market and consequently the greater the opportunity for efficiency. At the extreme, holding every security outstanding in the portfolio would be ideal, but in deference to the number of issues necessary, a sampling technique is sensible. This may take the form of a statistical selection which will provide a representative cross section of securities or perhaps based upon defined market characteristics which are to be achieved in the portfolio.

Bond Strategies: Immunizing Against Interest-Rate Risk

A major problem encountered in managing a bond portfolio is assuring a given rate of return to satisfy an ending funds requirement at a future specific date. If the term structure of interest rates was flat and the level of market rates never changed between the time of purchase and the future specific date when the funds were required, it would be possible to acquire a bond with a maturity equal to a desired investment horizon and the ending wealth from the bond purchase would equal the promised wealth position implied by the promised yield to maturity. Unfortunately, in the real world the term structure of interest rates is not typically flat and the level of interest rates is constantly changing. Because of changes in the shape of the term structure and changes in the level of interest rates, the bond investor faces interest-rate risk between the time of investment and a future holding period. Interest-rate risk is composed of two risks: Price risk and coupon reinvestment risk. The price risk occurs because if interest rates change prior to the end of the holding point and the bond is sold prior to maturity, the market price for the bond will differ from the expected price assuming that there had been no change in rates. If rates increased (decreased) since the time of purchase, the price received for the bond in the market would be below (above) expectations.

The coupon reinvestment risk arises because the yield to maturity computation implicitly assumes that all coupon flows will be reinvested at the promised yield to maturity. If after you purchase a bond, interest rates decline (rise), it will not be possible to reinvest interest payments at the proposed yield to maturity, but they will be reinvested at lower (higher) rates and the ending sum would be below (above) what you expected.

Note that the price risk and the reinvestment risk derived from a change in interest rates have an opposite effect on the investor's ending wealth position. Specifically, an increase in the level of market interest rates will cause an ending price that is below expectations, but the reinvestment of interim cash flow will be at a rate above expectations, so this flow will be above expectations. In contrast, a decline in market interest rates will provide a higher than expected ending price, but lower than expected ending wealth from the reinvestment of interim cash flows. It is clearly important to a bond investor with a known holding period to attempt to eliminate these two risks derived from changing interest rates. The elimination of these risks from a bond portfolio is referred to as immunization. A portfolio of investments in bonds is immunized for a holding period if its value at the end of the holding period, regardless of the course of interest rates during the holding period, is as large as it would have been had the interest-rate function been constant throughout the holding period. If the realized return on an investment in bonds is sure to be at least as large as the appropriately computed yield to the horizon, then that investment is immunized.

Duration

Most bonds provide coupon (interest) payments in addition to a final (par) payment at maturity. Depending upon the relative magnitudes of these payments, a bond may be more or less like others with the same maturity date. A measure of the average time prior to receipt of payment is duration.[1]

Duration is the weighted-average measure of a bond's life, where the various time periods in which the bond generates cash flows are weighted according to the relative sizes of the present value of those flows. Specifically, duration (D) is equal to

$$D = \frac{\sum_{n=1}^{N} \frac{C_n(n)}{(1+i)^n}}{\sum_{n=1}^{N} \frac{C_n}{(1+i)^n}} \qquad (13.1)$$

where N is the life of the bond in years, C is the cash receipt at the end of year n—equal to the annual coupon except for the last year, when it is equal to the annual coupon plus the maturity value—and i is the yield to maturity. The numerator of the expression is the weighted present value of cash receipts; the denominator is the sum of all these present values, which is equal to the total present value or price of the bond. The n in

[1] An excellent discussion of duration and its uses may be found in R. W. McEnally, "Duration as a Practical Tool for Bond Management," *The Journal of Portfolio Management*, Summer, 1977, pp. 53-56.

parentheses in the numerator is simply the number of years from the present when the cash is received $(1, 2, 3,$ and so on).

TABLE 13-1
DURATION OF A 7 PERCENT COUPON
THREE-YEAR BOND PRICED AT 100

(1)	(2)	(3) P.V. of $1 at 7%	(4) = (2) × (3) P.V. of Flow	(5) = (4)/Σ(4) P.V.'s Price	(6) = (1) × (5)
Year	Cash Flow				
1	$ 70	.9346	$ 65.42	.065	.065
2	70	.8734	61.14	.061	.122
3	1070	.8163	873.44	.873	2.619
Sum			$1,000.00	1.000	2.806
Price			$1,000.00		
Duration					2.81 years

$$D = \frac{(1)\,\dfrac{70}{1.07} + (2)\,\dfrac{70}{(1.07)^2} + (3)\,\dfrac{1070}{(1.07)^3}}{\dfrac{70}{1.07} + \dfrac{70}{(1.07)^2} + \dfrac{1070}{(1.07)^3}} = 2.81 \text{ years}$$

Table 13-1 contains an example that should make this measure considerably more comprehensible. It shows the computation of the duration of a 7 percent coupon bond with three years to maturity that is priced at par. Here the operation of the weighting scheme is fairly evident. For instance, at maturity after three years this bond is expected to pay off $1,800, which accounts for about 87.3% of its current value. Multiplying the three years by 0.873 we find that this receipt contributes approximately 2.62 years to the duration of this bond of 2.81 years.

In contrast, single-payment bonds, which sell at a discount and do not pay coupon interest, have durations that are exactly equal to their terms to maturity. For example, if the three-year bond in the illustration above did not carry coupons but promised to pay $1,000 three years from now and currently sold for $816, it would have a duration of three years, that is,

$$D = \frac{(3)\,\dfrac{1000}{(1.07)^3}}{\dfrac{1000}{(1.07)^3}} = 3 \text{ years}$$

Examine calculated duration in Table 13-2 for a bond yielding 8 percent with varying coupons and years to maturity. Generally, duration is shorter than term to maturity and increases as time to maturity increases and the coupon on the bond or market yields decrease. The duration of a bond is bounded by $(r + p)/rp$, where $r =$ yield to maturity (in decimal form, e.g. 6% = .06) and $p =$ the number of times per year interest is paid (compounded, usually twice). Thus, a 6 percent bond which pays interest twice each year has a duration boundary of 17 years, regardless of its maturity. This is calculated as:

$$\frac{.06 + 2.00}{(.06)(2)} = \frac{2.06}{.12} = 17 \text{ years}$$

Further, take an extreme example of a long, long bond with a low coupon (which should have a long duration). A 3 1/2 percent bond due in 100 years priced to yield 6 percent to maturity has a duration of only 19.5 years. Given the general presence of high coupon bonds (due to recent levels of inflation) and a tendency for shorter maturities (due to the same underlying reason) it is easy to see how difficult it is to find long-duration bonds in the public market today.

TABLE 13-2
DURATION (YEARS) FOR BONDS YIELDING 8 PERCENT
(SEMIANNUAL COUPONS)

Years to Maturity	Coupon Rate			
	2%	4%	6%	8%
1	.995	.990	.985	.981
5	5.742	5.533	4.361	4.218
10	8.762	7.986	7.454	7.067
20	14.026	11.966	10.922	10.292
50	14.832	13.466	12.987	12.743

Now that we know how to calculate a bond's duration, we know how much its price will change as its yield changes without needing to resort to trial-and-error experiments. Algebraically, an approximate direct relationship between the duration of a bond and its price volatility for a change in market interest rates is:

$$\% \text{ Change price} = -D(\text{Change in interest rate}) \tag{13.2}$$

or

$$\%\Delta \text{ Price} = -D(\Delta r)$$

where

$\%\Delta$ Price = percent change in price for the bond

D = duration of the bond in years

Δr = change in the market yield in basis points divided by 100 (e.g., for a 50 basis point decline, Δr would be $-.5$)

As an example, assume that a bond has a duration of 10 years and interest rates go from 8 percent to 9 percent. Then:

$$\%\Delta \text{Price} = -10(100/100)$$
$$= -10(1)$$
$$= -10\%$$

In this example, the price of the bond should decline (rise) by 10 percent for every 1 percent (100 basis point) increase (decrease) in market rates. The important point is:

the longer the duration of a bond, the greater the price volatility of the bond for a given change in interest rates; i.e., there is a very direct relationship between duration and interest-rate risk.

This direct relationship between duration and interest-rate sensitivity is important in actively managing a bond portfolio because it is crucial to construct a bond portfolio with maximum interest-rate sensitivity during a period when the manager expects a decline in interest rates and vice versa during a period of rising interest rates. The point is that the portfolio should be constructed with the maximum or minimum duration rather than considering only term to maturity. Duration is a superior measure of the time structure of bond returns because of the direct relationship between duration and interest-rate sensitivity.

It is possible to immunize a bond portfolio against interest-rate risk if you can make one assumption. The required assumption is that if the yield curve shifts, the shift is parallel (all rates change by the same amount) or a shape-preserving shift.[2]

Given this assumption *a portfolio of bonds is immunized from the interest-rate risk if the duration of the portfolio is equal to the desired holding period.* As an example, if the desired holding period of a bond portfolio is eight years, in order to immunize the portfolio, the duration of the bond portfolio should be set equal to eight years. In order to have a portfolio with a given duration, the weighted-average duration (with weights equal to the proportion of value) is set at the desired length following an interest payment and then all subsequent cash flows are invested in securities with a duration equal to the remaining horizon value.

The two risks discussed (price risk and reinvestment rate risk) are affected differently by a change in market rates—i.e., when the price change is positive, the reinvestment change will be negative, and vice versa. Duration is the time period at which the price risk and the coupon reinvestment risk of a bond portfolio are of equal magnitude but opposite in direction.

Example of Immunization

An example of the effect of attempting to immunize by matching the holding period and the duration of a bond is contained in Table 13-3. It is assumed that the holding period is eight years and the current yield to maturity for eight year bonds is 8 percent. Therefore, the ending wealth ratio the investor requires should be 1.8509 $[(1.08)^8]$. For example, assume that the parents of a 10-year-old daughter plan to enroll her in a public college in eight years. Given the rate of inflation in college costs they expect they will need to accumulate $18,500 at the end of eight years. Assume that they have $10,000 to invest now. They must earn 8 percent per annum to have $10,000 grow to $18,500 in eight years $[\$10,000(1.08)^8]$. The ratio of initial to ending wealth is 1.8509. This should be the ending wealth ratio for an immunized portfolio. The example considers two portfolio strategies. The first is a maturity strategy where the term to maturity is set at eight years. The other is a duration strategy where the duration is set

[2]Given a five-year horizon, the initial portfolio duration will be five years; after one year, the duration should be four years; and so on, until at the end of four years it will be one year. By insuring that the portfolio duration is rebalanced to the appropriate remaining time to the horizon, the effects of non-parallel shifts in the yield curve can be mitigated.

TABLE 13-3
MATURITY STRATEGY VERSUS DURATION STRATEGY

Year	Maturity Strategy			Duration Strategy		
	Cash Flow	Reinv. Rate	End Value	Cash Flow	Reinv. Rate	End Value
1	$ 80	.08	$ 80.00	$ 80	.08	$ 80.00
2	80	.08	166.40	80	.08	166.40
3	80	.08	259.71	80	.08	259.71
4	80	.08	360.49	80	.08	360.49
5	80	.06	462.12	80	.06	462.12
6	80	.06	596.85	80	.06	596.85
7	80	.06	684.04	80	.06	684.04
8	1,080	.06	1,805.08	80	.06	1,845.72
				1,040.64*		

Expected wealth ratio = 1.8509

*The bond could be sold for a market value of $1,040.64. This is the value of an 8 percent bond with two years to maturity priced to yield 6 percent.

at eight years. For the maturity strategy it is assumed that the portfolio manager acquires an eight-year 8 percent bond. In contrast, for the duration strategy it is assumed the portfolio manager acquires a ten-year, 8 percent bond which has approximately an eight-year duration (actually 8.12 years) assuming an 8 percent yield to maturity. For purposes of the example it is assumed that there is a single change in the interest-rate structure at the end of year 4 and the market yield goes from 8 percent to 6 percent and remains at 6 percent through year 8.

As shown in the example, because of the interest-rate change, the wealth ratio for the maturity strategy bond is below the desired wealth ratio because of the shortfall in the reinvestment cash flow after year 4 (i.e., the interim coupon cash flow is reinvested at 6 percent rather than 8 percent). Note that the maturity strategy eliminated the price risk because the bond matured at the end of year 8. Alternatively, the duration portfolio likewise suffered a shortfall in reinvestment cash flow because of the change in market rates. Notably, this shortfall due to the reinvestment risk is offset by an increase in ending value for the bond due to the decline in market rates (i.e., the bond is sold at 104.06 because it is an 8 percent coupon bond with two years to maturity selling to yield 6 percent).

Note that if market interest rates increased during this period that the maturity strategy portfolio would have experienced an excess of reinvestment income compared to the expected cash flow, and the wealth ratio would have been above expectations. In contrast, in the duration portfolio any reinvestment cash flow excess would have been offset by a decline in the ending price for the bond. While under the latter assumptions the maturity strategy would have provided a higher than expected ending value, the whole purpose of immunization was to eliminate uncertainty, which is what is accomplished with the duration strategy.

It is possible to use duration as a passive or an active strategy. That is, passively it is useful in neutralizing interest rate risk. Actively, it can be employed to capitalize on interest-rate risk. The latter use would mean that as interest rates are expected to change, an investor would seek out bonds with long durations or short durations depending upon whether the forecast is for falling or rising interest rates. Let us turn our attention to the many facets of active bond portfolio management.

Pressures for Active Bond Management

There is now a growing trend toward active, or decision-oriented management of fixed-income securities. Bond investors have made these investments a viable alternative to equities. For the passive, buy-and-hold bond investor the investment horizon is long-term and the emphasis is upon assurance of income. In contrast, actively managed portfolios typically have a shorter time horizon, varying from a few days to a year or so. Major emphasis is focused upon price appreciation.

There are three primary reasons for an emphasis on active bond management, the first and most important of which is the impact of inflation on real fixed-income investment returns. In the early 1960s the inflation rate averaged 2 to 3 percent a year, an only mildly discomfiting level from the standpoint of the fixed-income investor. But in the late 1960s and early 1970s, inflation began to accelerate, touching 12 percent and becoming a matter of serious concern for owners of fixed-income securities.

The trend of inflation-adjusted *real* rates of return for five-year governments, 10-year governments, and 30-year AA utilities from 1960 to 1975 shows how severely inflation has eroded the real return on fixed-income investments. Over the 15-year period real compound annual returns average out to 4.8 percent for five-year governments, 4.1 percent for 10-year governments, and 3.2 percent for 30-year AA utilities. The compound annual rate of inflation (Consumer Price Index) for the period was 4.1 percent. Historical evidence would seem to suggest that passive ownership of fixed-income securities has not produced significant real rates of return.

The second reason for the growing interest in active bond management is the increased volatility of interest rates. Beyond the effects of inflation, volatility has also resulted from worldwide political instability, the fleeing of small investors from bonds (a historical source of steadiness to the market), and the alarmingly "thin" markets—dealer reluctance to carry inventories of bonds in the face of high carrying costs. Between the years 1961 and 1966, interest rates as reflected in the AA utility yield series fluctuated between 4.2 and 5.7 percent—a range of only 150 basis points. But from 1971 to 1976, they fluctuated between 7.25 and 10.50 percent—a range of 325 basis points. What this means, of course, is that there are today both greater risks and greater opportunities in fixed-income securities than there were a decade ago.

Finally, the generally disappointing performance of the equity markets in recent years, and the resulting perceived need for a stabilizing influence in portfolios constitutes a third motivation for active management of fixed-income portfolios.

Ingredients in Active Bond Management

Incremental returns to bond portfolio management derive essentially from correctly positioning the portfolio's maturity structure, coupon, and quality to benefit from changes in the general level of interest rates. This positioning calls for major strategy decisions or judgments regarding market rates and the shape of the yield curve.

A second source of incremental return results from weighing the bond portfolio in the more favorably situated bond sectors (Treasuries, corporates, utilities, municipals). The third source involves substitutions where similar bonds are substituted for one another when their yields get out of line. Sector and substitution switching or swapping are more tactical in nature since they may be made independent of interest-rate forecast strategies and depend upon opportunities available only briefly.

Active Strategies: Rate Anticipation

Switching bonds based upon rate forecasting can be the most productive bond portfolio action. It is also the riskiest. The types of portfolio decisions required fall roughly into four categories: maturity, quality, coupon, and sector. Of these, maturity is probably most important.

MATURITY

As a broad guideline, interest-rate expectations are an important guideline for maturity selection. Maturities should be lengthened when interest rates are expected to fall and prices to rise, and maturities should be shortened when interest rates are expected to rise.

This general rule is, however, an oversimplification, because portfolio moves must be made with a view to total return, including coupon income, reinvestment rates, and price and volatility. Assumptions about the length and amplitude of bond price cycles are important. For example, if only a modest and gradual increase in interest rates were expected, accompanied by a flattening of the yield curve, a higher total return might be derived from holding longer-term bonds. As another example, in the higher-yield ranges, price volatility of bonds with maturities of more than one or two years is very large and relatively larger for medium-maturity bonds. Consequently, an investor sensitive to cyclical fluctuations in bond prices might be better off shifting from long bonds to cash equivalents or very short bonds rather than shifting to medium maturities if one expects interest rates to rise.

The maturity structure of a bond portfolio depends heavily upon cyclical forecasts of interest rates if an investor is going to engage in active bond portfolio management. Such forecasts should consider expected interest rates for various maturities and also the expected slope of the yield curve. Moreover, such forecasts should be reviewed frequently, as expected interest rates may change significantly due to changing economic expectations, Federal Reserve policy, and international considerations.

SECTOR

Sector transactions attempt to increase total return by anticipating changes in yield differentials between different categories of bonds, such as governments, industrials, utilities, and the like. These relationships change because of factors such as the relative supply of new issues and the outlook for specific areas of the economy. For example, the economic effects of inflation have caused general widening of yield differentials between utility bonds and many other sectors in the past several years. However, improvement in utilities' ability to cope with inflation through a more understanding regulatory environment and reduced requirements for new construction may affect their outlook favorably and cause yield differentials to narrow.

Assume that the yield spread was 25 basis points between AAA industrials versus governments; if this spread were expected to widen, the trader would swap from the industrials to the governments now, and then back to the industrials when the wider spread had occurred. During the widening of the spread, the prices of the industrials would decline relative to the governments, thereby providing a price gain via the swapping. How does one forecast such changes in the spreads? The most common forecasting method is to observe historical yield spreads at various points in the interest-rate cycle, and then to adjust for current supply-and-demand effects. However, this is difficult. For example, during the 1977-78 period of extremely narrow spreads between AAA's and U.S. government issues, many managers bought government issues early in 1977 expecting the spread to widen, only to have to take a second look.

QUALITY

Quality diversification is another important consideration in constructing a bond portfolio. Ratings by Moody's and Standard & Poor's help the investor to differentiate between the quality of bonds, based on the ability of the borrower to pay interest and principal promptly when due. Uncritical acceptance of bond ratings is not advisable, however; these ratings have a tendency to lag behind changes in the financial characteristics of a company. Therefore, good bond research into the economic forces affecting an industry or a company as well as its financial position often can anticipate changes in credit quality and bond ratings and thereby provide investment opportunities. Even though a rating may not be changed, identifying companies near the upper or lower limits of a particular quality range can prove rewarding.

As a general statement, as the quality of a bond lessens, the interest rate that the issuing company must pay to its lenders increases. Because yield spreads between different-quality bonds generally narrow during an economic recovery and widen during an economic contraction, high-quality bonds should be purchased when the economy is expected to contract and lower-quality bonds acquired when an economic expansion is expected.

However, high-grade bonds have tended to lead market turns. As prices of high-grade bonds begin to decline, investors who have an income requirement continue to purchase and thus support the prices of medium-grade issues. As a result, the peak in prices of medium-grade issues often is later in the market cycle than is the peak for high-grade issues. When investors do perceive a drop in bond prices of some duration and magnitude, prices of medium-grade bonds decline rapidly. At the trough of the bond price cycle, an upturn in prices of high-grade bonds precedes an increase in the prices of medium-grade bonds. Knowledge of these characteristics, coupled with good interest-rate forecasts, can enhance the profitability of quality diversification as a bond management technique.

COUPON

Because of the downtrend and the wide fluctuations in bond prices during the past decade or so and the heavy volume of new issues, investors now have a wide selection of bonds with varying coupons. The investor may select from high-coupon bonds, ordinarily selling at a premium above par, current coupon issues at or about par, and low-coupon issues selling at discounts. High-coupon bonds trading at or above their redemption price are often called *cushion* bonds. Although their potential for further price appreciation is restricted regardless of further declines in long-term interest rates, in a subsequent period of rising interest rates the high coupon provides a cushion against significant price declines. Yield and price relationships between bonds of different coupons change because of factors such as the supply of new issues, sinking-fund activity, calls features, dealer carrying costs, and the general level and expected trend of interest rates.

Selecting the appropriate coupon for an investor can be a somewhat complex matter, depending upon the investment objectives previously established. The tax status of the investor is important; the investment return of a discount bond is higher for a taxpayer because of the lower capital gain tax incurred when the bond is paid at par at maturity. For a nontaxpayer (e.g., a corporate pension fund) the total return is a more important consideration. Consequently, selection of the appropriate issue would be influenced by the need for current income, the sensitivity to interim price fluctuations, and interest-rate expectations. For example, an investor seeking maximum income who is indifferent to price fluctuations ordinarily would select the high coupon bond. The investor seeking maximum total return would be influenced by expectations for future interest rates. If an investor expects interest rates to rise, but prefers to maintain a position in long-term bonds, high-coupon issues would be his first choice; if one expects interest rates to fall, the discount bonds would be preferable. Again the significance of interest-rate expectations in portfolio adjustments should be emphasized. These expectations involve not only identifying peaks and troughs but also the magnitude of the expected changes. The latter factor is important in selecting the appropriate coupon issue. For example, an interest-rate decline to a level below the trough of the previous interest-rate cycle can produce greater total returns from discount bonds than from high-coupon bonds, because price appreciation of the high-coupon bond would be limited by its redemption characteristics.

QUALITY-SECTOR PREMIUMS

The performance of a bond portfolio can also be improved through identification of yield spreads that are out of line with historical spreads in comparable market conditions. But historical perspective indicates very strongly that yield spreads between bonds of comparable maturity are nothing more than risk premiums primarily reflecting the consensus view of future economic activity, inflation, and the general level of interest rates. Interest-rate judgments thus necessarily affect construction of the portfolio's invested position.

Figure 13-1 traces the movement of four examples of risk premiums in the fixed-income market during the 1971-76 cycle. The issuer spread between utilities and industrials demonstrates the fact that as we entered the recession of 1973 and 1974, with its high levels of inflation and high interest rates, the yield spread widened sharply. Investors were becoming risk-averse and demanding more compensation for owning utilities. This same phenomenon occurred for A-rated debt versus AAA-rated debt and private versus public debt. During 1975 and 1976, as the pace of economic activity increased, inflation expectations decreased, interest rates declined, and risk premiums narrowed substantially.

FIGURE 13-1

RISK PREMIUMS—THE FIXED INCOME MARKET

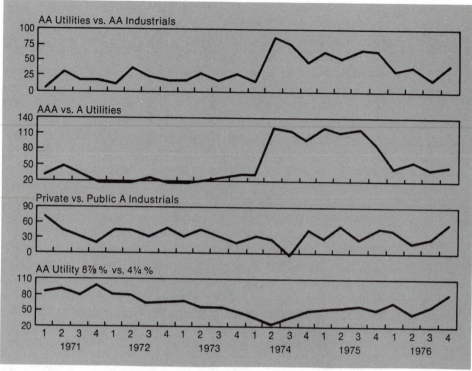

SOURCE: Harris Bank; FIPS; Salomon Brothers. Reprinted from K.R. Meyer, "Forecasting Interest Rates: Key to Active Bond Management," *Financial Analysts Journal,* November 1978, p. 61.

Sector swapping involves continually studying yield spread relationships among different sectors in the market. When one detects what appears to be a transient aberration, he can dig deeper into the fundamental sources of this aberration. Market experience, widespread daily contacts, knowledge, and insights into market forces are critical. This can put one in a position to make the key judgments as to whether the existing sector relationship is, in fact, a transient aberration which will revert to more normal levels over time, or whether it is the first signal of a new trend and a new market structure.

In 1971 and 1973, there were a number of examples of sector swap situations. One of the situations occurred in the fall of 1973 when the yield on a new instrument, Government National Mortgage Association (GNMA) Certificates, rose to unprecedented levels relative to both corporate and other issues. Searching behind the statistics, the underlying cause could easily be traced to a drying up of new investable funds among thrift institutions. These had been the primary buyers of the then relatively new instrument. Because of their apparent complexity relative to straight bonds, the certificates had not yet established a wide following among pension fund managers. However, at the extraordinarily attractive yields that then prevailed (and the even more attractive probable cash flow yields), it was fairly likely that some major pension fund managers would soon overcome their initial problems with analysis and accounting for the new certificates. In fact, this is what occurred. The investor who moved quickly into GNMA certificates reaped considerable rewards as the spread relative to corporates narrowed by over 75 basis points in the course of the next six months. The GNMA example illustrates a "new vehicle" type of sector swap. If an investor recognizes the value in a newly introduced sector, he may then reap sizable rewards as the sector becomes increasingly accepted by the marketplace at large.

Active Strategies: Yield-Curve Anticipation

The preceding discussion placed the primary emphasis on effective rate anticipation. Figure 13-2 shows the Treasury yield curve on September 1, 1974, and March 1, 1975. Over this six-month period, rates not only declined, but the yield curve moved down from an inverted shape to a mildly positive shape. This effect resulted in intermediate maturities undergoing a much greater downward movement in yield than the longs. For example, the five-year maturity declined by 170 basis points, almost two and one-half times greater than the 68-basis-point improvement at 30 years. Moreover, an investment in the five-year maturity on September 1, 1974, would have moved to a 4 1/2-year maturity over the six-month holding period, thus adding some further yield improvement. The combination of these factors shows the total return performance of the five-year investment came very close to that of the long end over this particular period.

FIGURE 13-2
HISTORICAL YIELD CURVES

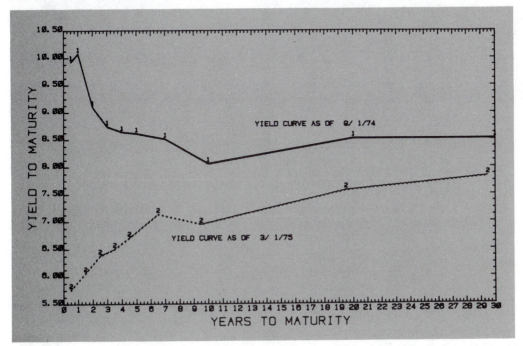

This example indicates that the downward movement from a peaking inverted curve can lead to attractive returns from intermediate maturities. It should also be pointed out that in deteriorating markets, there can also be an upward movement effect, with the result that intermediates perform worse than longs. This can hurt investors who believe that intermediates offer reduced price volatility relative to longs. On average, the intermediates probably do have less price volatility than longs. However, strongly inverted or strongly positive yield-curve shapes are not reflective of average conditions.

FIGURE 13-3
YIELD CURVES AT BEGINNING AND END OF 1978

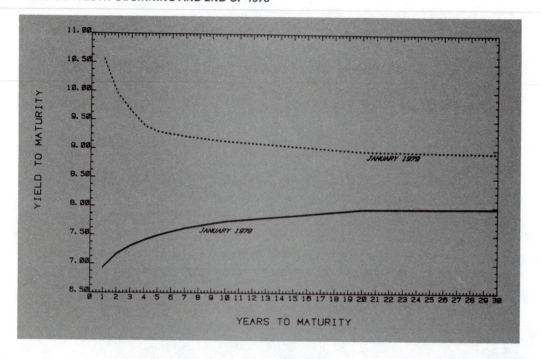

A good example of the upward movement occurred in the course of 1978, when the Treasury yield curve changed significantly in both level and shape (see Figure 13-3). The change in the level of rates over 1978 ranged from approximately +100 basis points in 30-year maturities to over +350 basis points at the one-year point. These yield changes reshaped the yield curve.

The moderately positive shape at the beginning of 1978 turned into a strongly inverted shape at the end of the year. One measure of this shape change is the spread of 30-year over one-year rates. This spread began the year at about +100 basis points and ended at over −150 basis points.

The prospects of yield-curve reshaping can add an important refinement and balance to the rate anticipation process. For example, suppose an investor with a defensive short-term posture anticipates that the long market rates are approaching a peak. He must then determine the correct time to begin deploying at least a portion of his short-term reserves. This action may be based either on the definite belief that the peak level of rates is actually at hand or simply as a counterbalance to his uncertainty as to when and how that peak will occur. In any case, once the decision has been made to commit some reserves, then the second decision must be to select the most appropriate maturity sector. If the investor believes that there is a good prospect for lower rates to be accompanied by a drop in the yield curve, then intermediate maturities should be explored as an interesting reentry vehicle on a risk-reward basis. On the one hand, if rates improve and yield curve does move down to a more positive shape, then the right intermediate maturities can provide returns that are comparable to the long-term market. On the other hand, should long rates continue to rise (without a significant increase in the degree of inversion), then the shorter maturity of the intermediates will provide a certain protection against the full deterioration that would be experienced in the long market.

Finding the best distribution of maturities to take advantage of yield-curve reshaping is no simple matter. In many instances, the proper balance of return may be available only with a rather narrow range of maturities.

Active Strategies: Mapping Expected Returns

If today's yields reflect all information about supply and demand, then an investor who buys a bond would expect his or her total return to reflect today's yield curve. Thus total return would be equal to: coupon income (C), amortization of premium or discount (A) and repricing because of a higher or lower yield to maturity on the yield curve as the bond ages (roll or R). Because coupon income (C) and amortization (A) are the components of yield to maturity (YTM), then

$$\text{Total return} = \text{YTM} + \text{roll} = C + A + R$$

For example, from Figure 13-4(a) assume that a 30-year bond has a yield to maturity of 8.5 percent at the beginning of the period with 8.4 percent expected three months later. If the bond had an 8 percent coupon, then over a horizon of one quarter:

Beginning price at 8.5% for 30 years   = 94.60%

Ending price at 8.5% for 29.75 years = 94.59%

Ending price at 8.4% for 29.75 years = 95.63%

8% coupon payment accrued   = 2.00%

Thus,

$$C = \frac{\text{Coupon earned}}{\text{Beginning price}} = \frac{2.00}{94.60} = .0211$$

$$A = \frac{\text{Price change on level yield curve}}{\text{Beginning price}} = \frac{-.01}{94.60} = -.0001$$

$$R = \frac{\text{Price change due to slope}}{\text{Beginning price}} = \frac{1.04}{94.60} = .0110$$

so that the total return is

$$\text{Total return} = .0211 - .0001 + .0110 = 3.20\%$$

We know from our earlier discussions of bond price volatility that long-maturity, low coupon bonds are the most volatile. Knowledge of these facts plus a forecast of interest rates (I) is the basis for a strategy of interest-rate anticipation. Assume that you forecast a rise in interest rates, as shown in the top two curves of Figure 13-4(b). Further, let us assume that you make a comparison between the previously considered 30-year 8 percent bond versus a three-year 8 percent bond.

Thus, the total return of each bond can now be viewed as

$$\text{Total return} = C + A + \overbrace{R}^{\text{Expected}} + \overbrace{I}^{\text{Forecast}}$$

	3-Year	30-Year
Beginning yield (maturity 3, 30)	7.0	8.5
Beginning yield (maturity, 2 3/4, 29 3/4)	6.8	8.4
Ending yield (maturity 2 3/4, 29 3/4)	8.8	8.7
Beginning prices	102.66	94.60
Ending prices (7.0%, 8.5%)	102.45	94.59
Ending prices (6.8%, 9.4%)	102.95	95.63
Ending prices (8.8%, 8.7%)	98.06	92.57
8% coupon payment accrued	2.00	2.00

Then,

		3-Year	30-Year
$C = \dfrac{\text{Coupon earned}}{\text{Beginning price}} =$		.0195	.0211
$A = \dfrac{\text{Price change on level curve}}{\text{Beginning price}} =$		$-.0020$	$-.0001$
$R = \dfrac{\text{Price change due to slope}}{\text{Beginning price}} =$		.0048	.0110
$I = \dfrac{\text{Price change due to interest shift}}{\text{Beginning price}} =$		$-.0476$	$-.0323$
$\text{Total return} = \dfrac{\text{Price change and coupon}}{\text{Beginning price}} =$		$-.0253$	$-.0003$

where "I" for the 3-year bond, for example, was calculated as (98.06-102.95) ÷ 102.66.

Using the above forecast, it would be preferable to stick with the 30-year relative to the three-year bond. This is because, although you are forecasting a rise in interest rates, the shape of the curve is forecasted to change such that intermediate maturities will be hurt more than longer-term bonds. How much you shift toward the 30-year maturity range would depend upon your confidence about your forecast, as well as the degree or risk aversion you have for incorrect forecasts.

In our discussion of rate anticipation and appropriate responses, it is important to remember that an analysts' anticipations may be already built into bond prices. For example, there is evidence that in large interest rate declines low coupon bonds do not experience the largest price gains. Perhaps this is accounted for by the fact that such

FIGURE 13-4
YIELD CURVE

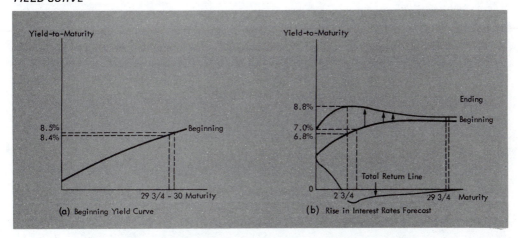

(a) Beginning Yield Curve

(b) Rise in Interest Rates Forecast

moves are anticipated by the market generally, and that the prices of the deep discount bonds are bid up in advance of the move. Ideally, the analyst should make forecasts of future rates and then see how the returns from specific coupon-maturity combinations behave under these anticipations *given current prices.*

Applying Interest-Rate Analysis

Interest rates have historically followed a reasonably cyclical and repetitive pattern. Figure 13-5 shows the quarterly plots for long-term AA utilities over six defined interest-rate cycles between 1950 and the end of 1976. The beginning yield level for each cycle has been equated to 100, with the ensuing interest-rate changes plotted as percentage changes, allowing for more convenient comparisons.

The figure reveals two interesting patterns, the first being the time duration of the cycles. The trough-to-peak legs of cycles (i.e., the upward movement of interest rates) have historically extended 13 to 14 quarters (over three years). The peak to trough, or downside, leg is historically much shorter, usually occurring within three or four quarters (the 1958-63 and the 1971-76 cycles look like aberrations).

The second pattern revealed in Figure 13-5 is the consistency of the magnitude of change in the level of interest rates. The movement from trough to peak is generally in the range 40 to 50 percent. The movement from peak to trough is almost uniformly within the range 20 to 25 percent. For example, rates may start a cycle at 8 percent, move up to 12 percent at peak, and fall back to 9 percent as the cycle is completed.

The cyclical behavior described does not suggest that one can forecast the precise timing, or even the levels, of interest rate peaks and troughs. Furthermore, aberrations in the overall pattern strongly suggest that investors must be alert to the differences and exceptions from one cycle to another. For example, if an investor had slavishly followed the pattern and sold long-term bonds in the fourth quarter of the downward leg of the 1971-76 cycle, he would simply have been wrong: The downward leg of that cycle lasted nine quarters.

FIGURE 13-5
HISTORICAL INTEREST-RATE CYCLES, 1950-1976
(All Rate Levels on Base of 100)

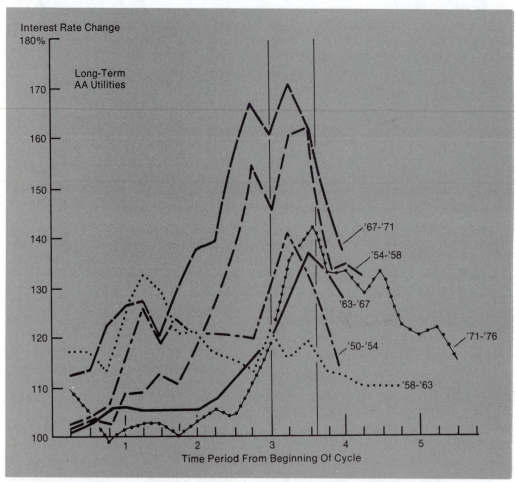

SOURCE: Bond Management Seminar, Harris Bank, Chicago, May 1977. Reprinted from K.R. Meyer, "Forecasting Interest Rates: Key to Active Bond Management," *Financial Analysts Journal,* November 1978, pp. 58-63.

Kept in perspective, however, interest-rate cycles can prove a useful tool for bond management. Using the cycle 1971-1976, Table 13-4 compares potential returns to an investor using near-perfect analysis of interest-rate cycles with returns to an investor who completely misreads interest-rate movements. By owning all short-term investments (90-day commercial paper) in the upward leg of the cycle, selling them at the peak, and buying long-term bonds (here represented by Salomon Brothers' High Grade Corporate Bond Index), the perfect decision maker would have produced a rate of return of approximately 11.6 percent compounded annually. The worst decision maker would have held long bonds throughout the upward leg of the cycle, sold them at the peak, and invested in short-term cash equivalents, for a rate of return of 2.9 percent annually.

TABLE 13-4

TOTAL RATE OF RETURN COMPARISON (PERCENT)
(APRIL 1971-DECEMBER 1976)

	4/1/71 to 9/30/74 (3.5 Years)	10/1/74 to 12/31/76 (2.25 Years)	5 3/4 Years Compound (per Annum)
Perfect decision making	26.5	48.7	11.6
Wrong decision making	2.7	15.0	2.9
Salomon Brothers Index	2.7	48.7	7.6

SOURCE: K. R. Meyer, "Forecasting Interest Rates: Key to Active Bond Management," *Financial Analysts Journal,* November 1978, pp. 58-63.

The perfect decision maker would have ended up outperforming a passive fixed-income portfolio—represented in Table 13-4 by the Salomon Brothers Index—by 4 percent. The worst decision maker would have underperformed the unmanaged portfolio by 4.7 percent. Clustering a series of decisions to shorten maturities around interest-rate troughs and to lengthen maturities around interest-rate peaks can achieve an edge in return one or two percentage points above the index. This type of activity does not depend on the investor's ability to forecast precise turning points, but on his ability to discern merely the direction of interest-rate movements and to start building momentum in that direction by shortening or lengthening maturities.

A thorough acquaintance with the interest-rate cycle can help ensure successful forecasting. But translating a successful forecast into an effective portfolio policy is the real challenge. The investor has to make the policy decision regarding the extent to which he will modify his interest-rate exposure as his forecast changes or as the level of interest rates changes. Specific decisions at any point in time within an extremely aggressive position or an extremely defensive position should reflect the relative confidence level of his forecast and the current level of rates relative to that forecast.

Active Tactics: Swapping

Bond substitution (swapping) is done to take advantage of temporary aberrations in the bond market due to supply and demand factors, such as long or short dealer positions and purchases to satisfy sinking-fund requirements. Such swaps may result in exchanging bonds of similar quality, sector, coupon, and maturity at relatively favorable levels. These changes are made independent of interest-rate forecasts and depend upon opportunities ordinarily available only briefly.

It is important to realize that the expected return from any swap is usually based upon several motives, not just one—thus, swaps are really just sources of return.

YIELD PICKUP SWAP

This type of swap involves the replacement of one security by another offering a higher yield but similar in all other aspects such as quality and maturity. As the name implies, the objective is to increase the total return over the life of the security.

One of the simplest and most fundamental types of swaps involves the sale of a fixed-income security and the purchase of a lower-priced security of the same or a very similar issuer that is equivalent in coupon, quality, and maturity. Often these swaps are carried out between similar securities of the various operating subsidiaries of the Bell Telephone System, or between various government agencies having similar degrees of safety. For example, the investor might execute the following transaction:

	Price		Yield to Maturity
Sell: 25-year maturity, 8% bond A at	100	=	8.00
Buy: 25-year maturity, 8% bond B at	99	=	8.10
Gain in yield to maturity			0.10

The swap from A bonds to B bonds generates a gain of 10 points in yield to maturity and enables the investor to free up $10 per $1000 bond for any desired use. An additional benefit of this type of swap comes about if the newly purchased security begins to trade on a basis similar to that of the security that was originally owned. If, after six months, interest rates have fallen to 7 3/4 percent for securities such as the ones above, and if both the A bonds and the B bonds trade in line with these new yield levels and with each other, the original bond would have gained about three points in price (from 100 to 103), while the newly purchased bonds would have experienced a larger price gain, of four points (from 99 to 103). If the two bonds begin to trade on an equivalent basis while general yield levels remain the same or trend upward, the newly purchased bonds will still perform better.

A number of swap opportunities of this type arise when a new issue, even though it is the equivalent of seasoned issues already outstanding, declines in price after the underwriting syndicate has disbanded. In this case the investor could sell his existing holding and purchase the equivalent security at a lower price (higher yield to maturity). Table 13-5 shows another, somewhat more complex example of a yield pickup swap. The amount of the trade is large in order that the dollar gain offset trading costs. Moreover, since these bonds might require only 10 percent margin, the out-of-pocket cash is less than the million dollars face.

THE SUBSTITUTION SWAP

The next type of swap, the substitution swap, attempts to profit from a change in the yield spread between two nearly identical bonds. The trade is based upon a forecast change in the yield spread between the two nearly identical bonds. The bonds could be issued by the same company, but with slightly different maturities and similar coupons; or the bonds could be between two different companies in the same sector-quality-coupon category. The forecast is generally based upon the past history of the yield spread relationship between the two bonds, with the assumption that any aberration from the past relationship is temporary, thereby allowing profit by buying the bond with the lower (higher) yield if the spread is to widen (narrow); this trade is later reversed, leaving you in the original position, but with a trading profit from the relative changes in price.

In a substitution or replacement swap, the portfolio manager continuously analyzes the spread relationship among groups of similar types of securities. A swap is made whenever the yield spread between two highly similar bonds reaches some extreme limit

TABLE 13-5

EXAMPLE OF TYPICAL YIELD PICKUP SWAP

Sell: $1,000,000 (par value) U.S. Treasury 5 7/8 percent due August 31, 1976, at 98.375 to yield 7.70 percent

Buy: $1,060,000 (par value) Treasury bills due August 24, 1976, at 7.32 percent (discount yield) to yield 7.82 percent (coupon equivalent)
Assumption: settlement date of trade is September 16, 1975

1. If the 5 7/8 percent Treasury notes are held to maturity, then the holder would receive $1,000,000 in principal plus $58,750 in interest for a total on August 31, 1976, of $1,058,750.

2. If the 5 7/8 percent Treasury notes are sold and the proceeds are reinvested in $1,060,000 par value of Treasury bills due August 24, 1976, then the results would be as follows:

Sale price of 5 7/8 percent notes (98 3/8)	$ 983,750
Accrued interest	2,582
Total proceeds of sale	$ 986,332
Purchase price of bills	986,072
Remaining funds	$ 260
Maturity proceeds of bills to be received on August 24, 1976	$1,060,000

3. The two advantages of making this swap are as follows:
First advantage:

Maturity proceeds of bills	$1,060,000
Maturity date of notes	1,058,750
Advantage of swap	$ 1,250

Second advantage:

Maturity date of bills	8/24/76
Maturity date of notes	8/31/76
Advantage of swap	7 days*

---

*That is, we are able to obtain our proceeds seven days earlier and thus can reinvest these proceeds for this period of time, and thereby obtain an added advantage.

(as a result of temporary market imbalances). The portfolio manager hopes to obtain a profitable "reversal" of this swap at a later date when the spread returns to a more normal historical level. This technique usually is referred to as an arbitrage.

The major obstacle to the substitution swap is the absolute necessity to give up yield to maturity when required. However, this yield give-up is only temporary. A substitution swap may require giving up nominal yield for a short while with the intention of eventually being able to increase the total real return. An example is shown in Table 13-6.

Newer Innovations in Bonds

High and volatile interest rates have driven borrowers to become increasingly innovative in structuring their debt issues. The principal objective of the issuers is to lower the interest rate they must pay. Some also want to borrow money for the long term (15 to 30 years) in an era when most investors, burned by inflation, want to lend only for much shorter periods. To achieve these objectives, issuers have offered various

TABLE 13-6
EXAMPLE OF TYPICAL SUBSTITUTION SWAP*

Sell: U.S. Treasury 6 3/4 percent due May 31, 1977, at 98.03125 to yield 7.97 percent.

Buy: U.S. Treasury 6 7/8 percent due May 15, 1977, at 98.3125 to yield 7.95 percent.

1. Above trade results in a small yield give-up.

2. However, this trade is made on the basis of past yield spread relationships between these two issues.

3. Past records indicate that the widest spread between these two issues occurred when the 6 3/4s yielded 15 basis points more than the 6 7/8s, while the narrowest spread resulted in the 6 7/8s yielding 3 basis points more than the 6 3/4s.

4. Thus, on the basis of past history, a portfolio manager should sell the 6 3/4s and buy the 6 7/8s whenever the spread relationship narrows, with the intention of reversing the swap when the hoped-for spread widening occurs at some later date.

5. In our example, this is precisely what occurs. In 30 days, the following swap was made:

Sell: U.S. Treasury 6 7/8 percent due May 15, 1977, at 98.28125 yield 7.97 percent.

Buy: U.S. Treasury 6 3/4 percent due May 31, 1977, at 97.84375 to yield 8.10 percent.

Result: Although a 1/32 loss (.03125) was sustained on the 6 7/8s, the 6 3/4s were purchased at a price 6/32s lower (.1875) than they were originally sold at, thereby resulting in a net profit of 5/32s (.15625) or $1,562.50 per million par value.

---

*This swap was based upon actual market prices which existed during August and September 1975.

inducements not available from conventional bonds. These inducements are often described as "kickers" or "sweeteners."

All of the issues with kickers that have appeared on the market thus far fall into one of five categories that will be described. One category—the commodity-backed bond—is somewhat different from the rest. While like them in that it serves to reduce the interest paid by the issuing company, it is unique in that it is designed to appeal to individuals who are of an entirely different stripe than traditional bond buyers.

It should be emphasized that the bonds are a two-way street. Whenever investors receive a privilege, they must give up something in exchange. The purchase of any issue with a kicker means that an investor will be penalized in at least one way; the investor will receive lower coupon interest than can be obtained from a conventional issue of comparable quality and maturity.

Put Privileges

Option tender bonds—for convenience, referred to as issues with put options—give holders the right to sell back their bonds to the issuers, normally at par. Issues with puts are aimed both at investors who are pessimistic about the ability of interest rates to decline over the long term and at those who simply prefer to take a cautious approach to their bond buying.

In addition to being able to get out of their positions, investors derive a collateral benefit from owning bonds with puts. In the period before the put becomes effective, these issues should tend to hold their value to a greater degree than straight bonds of comparable maturity if interest rates should rise. The reason, of course, is that the put privilege acts as a floor under the market price of the bonds.

The Brevard County Housing Finance Authority of Florida sold almost $150 million of 9.00 percent tax-exempt bonds due February 1, 2013, that give holders the right to sell the bonds back to the Authority on February 1, 1986, and each succeeding February 1. The bonds were sold at par and would be bought back at par, if tendered.

Investors purchasing the Brevard bonds give up a substantial amount of interest in return for the put feature. The issue's 9.00 percent coupon interest compared to coupons of more than 11 percent available on straight municipal bonds with a three-year maturity at the time of issuance.

But the put privilege also means that the issue is currently trading as though it were to mature in 1986, the first year in which the bonds can be "put" back to the issuer. After February 1, 1986, the issue will trade as though it were a one-year note paying 9.00 percent interest.

Floating Rates

Whether they are named floating-, adjustable-, or variable- rate, these issues have the same underlying concept. The interest rate paid to holders changes periodically, sometimes as often as once a month, but usually once or twice a year. In most instances, the rate has been based on formulas that involve the discount on three- or six-month U.S. Treasury bills.

But when the interest rate of an intermediate- or long-term issue is based on the yield of a three- or six-month money-market instrument, many institutional bond buyers shun the issue. The reason is that short-term rates fluctuate to a far greater degree than long-term, and these investors do not want to gamble that today's high short-term yields will remain a part of the economic scene for the next five or ten years.

One solution devised by issuers has been to tie the interest on floating-rate bonds to a combination of short- and long-term yields on stipulated securities. General Motors Acceptance Corporation (GMAC) offered investors a 10-year $250 million adjustable-rate issue whose interest is tied to the yield of U.S. Treasury notes maturing in 10 years.

Until mid-November 1982, the GMAC notes paid 13.45 percent interest, but on each November 15 starting with 1982, the annual rate is established at 107.2 percent of the two most recent weekly average yields on 10-year T-notes. If, for example, on November 15, 1982, that average was 10.00 percent, the GMAC notes would pay 10.72 percent for the following 12 months. The rate is adjusted again on November 15, 1983, and so on.

The advantage of owning these GMACs is that in periods when intermediate-term rates rise, the annual refixing of the interest will act as a floor under the market price, especially since GMAC has put no ceiling on the rate it will pay.

But if intermediate-term rates experience a lengthy decline, the notes have several disadvantages: (1) just as the interest rate has no ceiling, it has no floor, so your yield could fall to a low single-digit number; (2) the annual rate adjustment will act as a lid on the market price of the notes; (3) GMAC might redeem the issue prior to maturity and sell a new issue at the then-prevailing lower rates.

Original Issue Discount Bonds

One of the new debt species—the long-term original-issue deep-discount bond— is designed to appeal more to tax-exempt institutional investors such as pension funds than to the average individual.[3] That is so because the difference between the discounted price at which the bonds are sold and the $1,000 paid at maturity is not viewed as a cap- ital gain by the Internal Revenue Service. Instead, the tax rules require that the discount be taxed as ordinary income spread over the life of the bond. Individual investors can only realize capital gains at maturity if the discount is not an original-issue discount.

The advantage to institutions is that the deep-discount price virtually guarantees that they have locked in a high yield for the life of the bond—usually 30 years—since it is most unlikely that any issuer would retire an original-issue deep-discount bond prior to maturity. Issuers of such bonds benefit by succeeding in borrowing for the long term when they might otherwise have difficulty in doing so and by paying substantially less coupon interest than they would otherwise have to pay.

Martin-Marietta Corp. sold a deep-discount issue maturing in 2011 at a price of 53.835 percent of par and paying coupon interest of 7.00 percent. Original purchasers of the bonds obtained a respectable 13.00 percent current yield and a yield to maturity of 13.25 percent.

The $175 million of Martin-Marietta bonds were so well received that the sale was quickly followed by other issues. Northwest Industries offered $125 million of 30-year 7.00 percent bonds at a price of 52.75 and Trans-America Financial sold a $200 million 6.5 percent 30-issue whose price was only about 48 percent of par. In addition, GMAC offered $400 million of 6.00 percent 30-year bonds at a price of 44.51 percent of par.

Commodity-Backed Bonds

Most of the new types of bonds have been structured to appeal essentially to fixed- income investors seeking either to profit from an interest-rate decline or to protect themselves from the possibility of escalating inflation and interest rates. But one type of issue—referred to as commodity-backed—has been designed to appeal to investors of a quite different category, those who seek protection from inflation through direct or indirect ownership of commodities.

Bonds backed by gold made their debut in Europe some years ago, but nothing similar appeared in the United States until Sunshine Mining Company offered a $25 million issue of silver-backed bonds. Investors snapped it up and Sunshine offered a second issue, identical to the first except for its maturity and interest payment dates.

However, the recent Sunshine issue serves to demonstrate the principle behind commodity-backed—or asset-linked—issues, more of which are widely anticipated to appear on the market in the future.

Sunshine's second issue of silver-indexed bonds carries an 8.5 percent coupon interest rate and matures December 15, 1995. The lure to buyers was that upon maturity

---

[3]Certain "zero" coupon bonds have successfully found their way into IRA accounts.

they will receive either the $1,000 face value of each bond or the market value of 50 ounces of silver, whichever is higher.

One of the provisions that Sunshine makes in its agreement with the bondholders is that it reserves the right to redeem the issue on or after December 15, 1985, if the 50 ounces of silver have a market value equal to or exceeding $2,000 for 30 consecutive days. Another provision is for a sinking fund which will retire a portion of the bonds annually beginning in 1982, but holders will be entitled to refuse redemption by the fund.

When the bonds reached the market the price of silver was roughly $15 an ounce. Thus, the value of each bond in silver was about $750. Nevertheless, investors purchased the bonds at their $1,000 face value, thereby paying a premium of 33 percent over silver's market value. Other commodity-backed issues are expected on the market. These might be secured by assets such as oil, coal, or timber. Their holders would have the choice of being paid off at maturity either at the bonds' face value or at the market value of a stipulated amount of the asset to which the bonds are linked.

Summary

The management of bond portfolios historically was mostly a passive exercise. A passive strategy generally involves a buy-and-hold philosophy wherein the investors objectives are to achieve broad diversification, predictable returns, and low management costs.

In recent years active bond management has taken center stage. Accelerating inflation, volatility in interest rates, and disappointing stock market returns have converged as forces encouraging a search for incremental returns in the bond market. Investors have begun to focus on correctly positioning their portfolio's maturity structure, coupons, and quality to benefit from changes in the general level of interest rates. Such strategies require decisions or judgments regarding market rates and the shape of the yield curve. Such judgments are not an integral part of a passive approach to bond management. Other active judgments are made in weighing the portfolio in the more favorably situated sectors of the bond market (Treasuries, utilities, and so on).

High levels of interest rates and their underlying volatility have led to some interesting new innovations in the types of bonds available for purchase. Among the more prominent additions to the bond arena are bonds with put options, floating-rate instruments, original issue discount bonds, and bonds whose principal is backed by a commodity.

Questions and Problems

1. Describe the critical decision variables required to establish and maintain a passive bond portfolio management strategy. What are the risks of such a strategy?

2. A bond can be acquired with a four-year maturity. The bond has a coupon rate of 12 percent and is priced in the market at 100.
   a. What is the duration of this bond?
   b. What should the percentage change in the price of the bond be if interest rates rose to 13 percent?

3. A portfolio manager for an insurance company has a known liability that will occur at the end of eight years. She can either purchase an 8 percent bond due in eight years or a 4 percent bond due in ten years that would be sold at the end of eight years. Suppose interest rates make a single downward change at the end of year six when the market yield falls to 7 percent and remains there through year eight. Show how the purchase of the 4 percent bond is superior to the purchase of the 8 percent bond if the goal is to immunize against interest-rate risk.

4. Mr. Sly Codger is a retired bond investor. When asked what the ideal trading strategy should be when the level of interest rates is expected to decline he responds, "buy long, low and strong." He really means buy long maturities with low coupons of the strongest quality ratings.

    a. Why would this strategy tend to lead to superior performance?

    b. How would you amend his wisdom in light of your knowledge of the concept of duration?

5. A twenty-year bond has a yield to maturity of 10 percent now. It is expected to have a yield to maturity of 8 percent one year from now. The bond has a coupon of 9 percent. Map the expected return in terms of coupon, appreciation (depreciation), and roll.

6. It appears that the economic cycle is beginning to mature, inflation is expected to accelerate, and in an effort to contain the economic expansion Federal Reserve policy is moving toward constraint. In each of the situations below, assuming that you had to own one of the two bonds listed, which would you prefer? Why? It is now 1981.

    (1) U.S. Treasury 11 7/8 due in 1983 and priced at 100
                     or
        U.S. Treasury 11 3/4 due in 2010 priced at 96.06 to yield 12.25 percent to maturity

    (2) Texas Power and Light Co. 7 1/2 due in 2002, rated AAA and priced at 62 to yield 12.75 percent to maturity
                     or
        Arizona Public Service Co. 7.45 due in 2002, rated A- and priced at 56 to yield 13.98 percent to maturity

    (3) Commonwealth Edison 2 3/4 due in 1999, rated BAA and priced at 25 to yield 14.25 percent to maturity
                     or
        Commonwealth Edison 15 3/8 due in 2000, rated BAA and priced at 102.75 to yield 14.93 percent to maturity

    (4) Shell Oil Co 8 1/2 sinking fund debentures due in 2000 (rated AAA, sinking fund begins 9/80 at par) priced at 69 to yield 12.91 percent to maturity
                     or
        Warner-Lambert 8 7/8 sinking fund debentures due in 2000 (rated AAA, sinking fund begins 4/86 at par) priced to 75 to yield 12.31 percent to maturity

7. An investor has engaged in the following transactions:

    (1) Sell: 8 percent, 20-year, A-rated, Gas Co. bond. Price = 95 1/4.
        Buy: 8 percent, 20-year, AAA-rated, Electric Utility bond. Price = 100.

    (2) Sell: 7 1/2 percent, 20-year, AAA-rated, Food Co. bond. Price = 95.
        Buy: Treasury bills, 90-day maturity. Price = 98 1/2.

    (3) Sell: 8.10 percent, 10-year, AA-rated, Drug Co. bond. Price = 100 1/4.
        Buy: 8.90 percent, 8-year, AA-rated, Chemical Co. bond. Price = 100.

(a) For each of these "swaps," what are the apparent underlying motivations and the associated risks?

(b) Did each one work out?

8. You are the portfolio manager for Citizens Property-Casualty Insurance Company. You are currently examining the fixed-income securities listed below in an environment of business contraction, declining inflation, and monetary ease. The company is in an effective tax bracket of 30 percent. It is now August 1981.

Security	Price	Yield to Maturity (%)
City of Kent, 5% general obligations (2001)	57	10.00
U.S. Treasury, 8% notes (August 1982)	98 1/2	
PetroChem Inc., 10 1/2% preferred stock ($25 par)*	26	
Midland Drug Co., 0% debentures (1991)	38 1/2	10.00
Midland Drug Co., 11% debentures (2006)†	100	
Burger Queen, 7% debentures (2006)‡	66	11.00

*Currently callable at par plus one year's dividend.
†Callable beginning in 1982 at 108; no sinking fund.
‡Callable beginning in 1982 at 106; sinking fund of 4% of issue starts 1980.

a. Which security provides the best after-tax yield to maturity, Kent or PetroChem? Explain.

b. The Midland 11s and the Burger Queen bonds are both rated Aa. List reasons why these bonds are or are not efficiently priced relative to one another.

c. Suppose that Citizens had a ten-year insurance policy it wished to match with an appropriate security: Does it matter whether the Midland 0 percent or the 11 percent bonds are acquired? Explain.

d. Rank these securities from most to least desirable for holding, given the economic outlook. Explain your rationale.

9. Three bonds are being examined by an investor with a holding period of ten years. Each bond is highest in quality. It is now 1980.

	Bond A	Bond B	Bond C
Coupon rate	0%	4%	4%
Maturity	1990	2000	1985
Yield to maturity	6%	6%	6%
Duration	10	13	4 1/2

a. Does it matter whether bond A or B is purchased? Explain.

b. Should s(he) be indifferent between buying bond B and selling it at the end of ten years or buying bond C and replacing it at its maturity? Explain.

c. Assume that bond B is acquired at a price of 80 to yield 6 percent to maturity. Shortly thereafter, yields on similar bonds fall to 5 1/2 percent. What should the new price be on these bonds?

10. You are given the following data on U.S. Treasury securities:

	1/15/79 Price	Yield to Maturity (%)	Time to Maturity (years)	Adjusted Duration
U.S. Treasury 7.875% notes 5/15/83	95.19	9.25	4.33	2.95
U.S. Treasury 3.250% bonds 6/15/83	81.56	8.34	4.42	3.34

a. Explain why a difference exists in the duration between the two U.S. Treasury securities.

b. Using the duration, calculate the expected total returns that will be realized on *each* of the two securities if held for one year under each of the following interest-rate conditions:

(1) No change in interest rates.

(2) One percentage point (100 basis points) drop in interest rates.

11. Georgia-Pacific Corporation has outstanding the following intermediate-term debt issues:

	10.10% Notes	Floating Rate Notes
Rating	Aa	Aa
Maturity	1990	1987
Issued:	6/12/90	9/27/79
At par to yield	10.10%	12.00%
Amt. Outs. (Mils)	$150.0	$150.0
Callable:	6/15/86	10/1/84
At	$100.00	$100.00
Sinking fund	None	None
Current Coupon:	10.10%	16.90%
Changes	Fixed	Every 6 months
Rate adjusts to	—	0.75% above 6 months Treasury bill rate
Range since issue	—	16.90-12.00%
Price (10/31/81)	73 3/8	97
Current yield	13.77%	17.42%
Yield to maturity	15.87%	—

a. What are two reasons why the Floating Rate Notes (FRN's) do not sell at par (offering price)?

b. Which issue would be most appropriate for an actively managed bond portfolio where total return is the primary objective? Why?

c. Why is the yield to maturity not shown for the Floating Rate Notes?

d. Which issue is most attractive for purchase if the yield curve tends to slope downward, i.e., is inverted? Why?

part five
OPTIONS

We have looked at stocks and bonds in some detail. Our primary goal in this section is to convey an understanding of the rapidly emerging area of *options*. Options are rights to buy and sell bonds or stocks.

Chapter 14 is concerned with *warrants, calls,* and *puts.* These instruments enable the owner to buy or sell shares of common stock at a specified price for a stipulated period of time. Call options are rights to buy; a put option is an option to sell. Call options are similar to warrants in many respects. Warrants, however, are the liability of the issuing corporation, while call options are the liability of the options' writer. The writer in the latter case is often an individual. Chapter 14 will consider the use of warrants, calls, and puts both for speculative and risk management, or hedging, purposes.

Chapter 15 deals with *convertible securities* and *interest rate futures.* Convertible bonds and preferred stock give the owner the right to exchange the security for a given number of shares of common stock of the issuer during a specified period of time. The owner has a right to put the convertible to the issuer for common shares. Chapter 15 concludes with an examination of the rapidly rising use of interest rate futures. These contracts can provide inexpensive speculation or hedging in underlying debt securities.

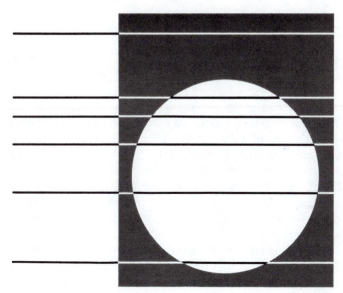

FOURTEEN

Warrants, Calls, and Puts

So far we have discussed risk and return on common stocks from the view-point of a direct commitment. But it is also possible to buy, sell, and even issue rights to a stock with price and time stipulations. These rights to buy and sell underlying securities are called *options*. Options are in reality "derivative" assets. Their value flows directly from the underlying common stock to which they are related. The right to buy a security is referred to as a *call* option; the right to sell is a *put* option.

Corporations issue call options against their own securities. Individual and institutional investors issue (write) and purchase put and call options in order to speculate in securities they do not own at the time or to hedge a position already established in a security. These speculative and hedging ingredients in options will be examined as our discussion unfolds.

Warrants

A *warrant* is a call option to buy a stated number of shares of stock at a specified price. The typical warrant has a period of a number of years during which it is exercisable.

Warrants often originate in company reorganizations or are offered as inducements to potential investors to purchase bonds or preferred stocks offering terms less favorable than those the investors would otherwise require. But in return for accepting less favorable terms on the senior securities, such as a lower interest rate, the investor acquires an option on the possible appreciation of the common stock of the firm. He may then sell the warrants if he desires, since warrants are normally detachable from the senior security and may be traded separately.

As a warrant holder, the investor has no equity rights in the firm, does not receive dividends, and does not have voting rights. The terms of the warrant are specified on the certificate. Provisions are made for the number of shares that can be purchased for each warrant, the *exercise* (purchase) price per share, and the *expiration date* of the warrant. Most warrants entitle the holder to purchase stock on a 1:1 ratio; that is, one share may be purchased per warrant. In the event of a stock split or a stock dividend, warrants are generally adjusted accordingly; investors should review these provisions carefully and should relate them to the observed behavior of the firm with respect to splits and stock dividends. The exercise price is always greater than current market price at the time the warrant is issued. This price may be fixed for the entire life of the warrant or (less commonly) it may be increased periodically. Expiration may be set for any date and, in a very few cases, warrants are perpetual; most warrants expire from five to ten years after they are issued. Warrants are usually traded as over-the-counter securities but a modest number are traded on the NYSE and AMEX.

The Range of Warrant Values

Prices of warrants are subject to minimum and maximum limits. The minimum value of a warrant may be identified as:

Condition	Minimum Value
$P_s > P_e$	$(P_s - P_e) \times N$
$P_s \leqslant P_e$	0

where:

P_s = current market price of the common stock

P_e = exercise price of the warrant

N = number of common shares per warrant (generally, $N = 1$)

A warrant will be worth at least the difference between the stock's market price and the warrant's exercise price; this will be the minimum value provided that the market price exceeds the exercise price. Arbitrage assures this minimum value because at any lower warrant price an investor could purchase and immediately exercise the warrant, realizing an instantaneous risk-free profit. For market prices equal to or lower than the exercise price, the minimum warrant value is zero. Generally, the actual market value of the warrant will be greater than the minimum value.

The maximum value of a warrant is

$$P_s \times N$$

Maximum value is the value of the associated common stock; it will not be greater because the warrant offers no income potential beyond that provided by the growth of the common stock. Since warrant holders are not entitled to dividends, and because most warrants have finite lives, a warrant price at or near the maximum value is rare. Figure

14-1 describes these limits and it traces the price of a typical warrant over a wide range of common stock values, with all other factors held constant. The difference between the actual price of a warrant and its minimum value is the premium over minimum value.

FIGURE 14-1
RELATION AMONG MAXIMUM, MINIMUM, AND ACTUAL WARRANT VALUE

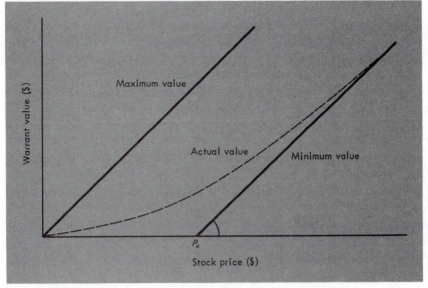

Slope depends on number of shares exchanged per warrant; if 1:1, slope = 45°.

As the price of common stock rises above the exercise price of its associated warrant, the warrant approaches its minimum value. Thus the premium over minimum value decreases and it ultimately vanishes as the price of the stock increases. This vanishing point tends to occur when stock price levels are about four times the exercise price of the warrant ($P_s/P_e = 4$). When the current stock price equals the exercise price, the warrant typically sells in the range 25 to 50 percent of the price of the stock. The magnitude of the premium over minimum value for any given differential between stock price and exercise price depends on a number of interrelated factors. All these factors are inputs to the valuation process which determines the investor's expected rate of return. Time remaining to expiration, stock price volatility, and leverage provided by the warrant are the factors of primary importance. The following paragraphs will examine these elements more closely.

Warrant Premiums

The existence of premiums on warrants is partly due to the attractive leverage features that they offer. The lower price of warrants, which usually enjoy the same absolute change in value as the underlying common stock, enables them to return much higher profits as a percentage of investment. Suppose that warrants entitling their holder to purchase one share of AT&T at $52 are selling at $12, and that the AT&T common is selling at $48. The warrants have a theoretical value of zero (48 − 52). As the AT&T common moves to $52, assume that the price of the warrant moves to $16. The holder of the common stock receives a holding-period yield of about 8 percent [(52 − 48)/48]. The holder of a warrant receives a 33 percent holding-period yield [(16 − 12)/12]. However, this leverage can also work against the warrant holder if the common moves downward.

If a stock has any potential for rising above the option price during the life of the warrant, then the warrant will become a valuable instrument, with its ability to generate high-percentage returns on investment. Thus, warrants on more volatile stocks, or stocks with higher probabilities of obtaining prices above the option price, will have higher premiums. Likewise, the longer the remaining period of the warrant, the higher the probability that the price of the common will exceed the option price, and thus the higher the premium.

The leverage effect leads one to expect a higher premium on a warrant whose associated common stock has a value that is a high multiple of the value of the warrant. Consider a warrant providing the holder the option to buy one share of stock at $10. Assume that the warrant and the stock trade on parity over time; that is, the warrant sells at its theoretical value, or a zero premium. The price relationships below are intended to depict behavior over six years:

	Period					
	1	2	3	4	5	6
Stock price	$12	$15	$30	$45	$90	$99
Warrant price	$ 2	$ 5	$20	$35	$80	$89
Stock warrant ratio	6	3	1.5	1.29	1.13	1.11

From period 1 to 2, the stock advanced 25 percent (12 to 15) while the warrant jumped 150 percent (2 to 5); from period 2 to 3, the stock advanced 100 percent (15 to 30) and the warrant climbed 300 percent (5 to 20); and so on. Notice how leverage is operating—and how it is gradually dwindling. In the first case, the warrant moved six times as much as the stock (150/25). From period 2 to 3, the warrant moved only three times as much as the stock (300/100). The stock-warrant ratio is a kind of leverage or magnification index. As it becomes smaller, the leverage effect is diminishing.

Potential warrant holders should note that as times goes on, the remaining option period decreases (if the warrant has an expiration date), and as the price moves upward significantly, the leverage effects are lessened. These changes, as well as changing expectations for the associated stock, can result in changes in the premium a warrant commands.

The existence of a positive premium on a warrant means that it will always be more beneficial for the warrant owner to sell his warrant, thus realizing its theoretical value plus its premium, than to exercise it. The reason is that in exercising it he would receive only the theoretical value. This also, however, shows that the premium associated with a warrant will shrink as its expiration date approaches, other factors remaining constant. On the expiration date, the actual value of the warrant will equal its theoretical value.

Warrant holders receive no dividends. The dividend on the common can affect the value of the warrant because this current income is forgone by the investor who chooses to hold a warrant rather than the common stock. A high dividend payout may also have an adverse effect on the price of a warrant, because if the dividends were not paid out but were retained, their reinvestment could cause the market price of the stock to rise.

These are some of the factors that are thought to determine the premiums on warrants. The most important is obviously the outlook for the underlying common stock. An investor's expectations in this regard should be the prime consideration in whether or not he purchases a warrant. The leverage effects mentioned are a two-edged sword, with the effects on the downside being severe. After the investor determines his expectations concerning the common stock, he must then look at the warrant, determine its premium, and consider what changes in the premium, if any, might take place. The change in the value of the warrant will be made up of changes in the value of the underlying common and in the premium that the market places on the warrant.

Table 14-1 gives examples of three warrants with different life spans. The U.S. Air warrants afford high leverage due to the fact that they have no theoretical value and sell at an infinite premium over underlying value.[1] The stock must rise to $24 or almost double before the purchaser of a warrant at $6 would begin to make money. The Mattel warrants, on the other hand, have some intrinsic or theoretical value and a hefty premium. The Textron warrants are selling at just about their theoretical value.

TABLE 14-1
EXAMPLES OF WARRANTS

	U.S. Air Corp.	Mattel Corp.	Textron Corp.
Expiration date	1987	1986	1984
No. shares per warrant	1	1	1
Exercise price (per share)	$18.00	$4.00	$11.25§
Market prices: (9/81)			
Common	$12.75	$7.75	$28.50
Warrant	$ 6.00	$5.00	$17.50
Theoretical value of warrant*	($5.25)	$3.75	$17.25
Warrant % premium†	‡	33.3%	2.9%
Stock price/warrant price	2.13	1.55	1.01

* [(Market price common − Exercise price) X Number of shares per warrant].
† (Market price − Theoretical value)/Theoretical value.
‡ Infinite.
§ To 5/84.

[1]For a discussion of speculating in warrants that are away from their theoretical value, see Donald E. Fischer, "Shorting Expiring Warrants," *Mississippi Valley Journal of Business and Economics*, 10, No. 2 (Winter 1974-75), 73-83.

Table 14-2 displays a sample of warrants in different industries with varying expiration dates.

TABLE 14-2
EXAMPLES OF WARRANTS

Company	Expiration Date	Common Shares per Warrant	Exercise Price
Alleghany Corp.	Perpetual	1.00	$ 3.75
Applied Solar Energy	8/6/85	1.00	10.00
Atlas Corp.	Perpetual	1.00	31.25
Braniff International	2/1/86	3.18	73.00
Charter Co.	9/1/88	1.00	10.00
Chrysler	6/15/85	1.00	13.00
Commonwealth Edison	Perpetual	1.00	30.00
Eastern Air Lines	6/1/87	1.00	10.00
Frontier Airlines	3/1/87	1.06	10.60
Mattel	4/5/86	1.00	4.00
Rapid-American	5/15/94	1.00	35.00
Reliance Group	7/1/87	1.00	15.86
Trans World Corp.	10/1/86	1.00	31.00
U.S. Air	4/1/87	1.00	18.00

Put And Call Options

Options Terminology

To ensure a proper understanding of the following discussion of put and call options, it is imperative that certain terms be made clear at the outset. A standard option *contract* allows the buyer to buy *100 shares* of stock at a specific price during a specific period of time, regardless of the market price of that stock. A *call* is an option contract giving the buyer the right to purchase the stock. A *put* is an option contract giving the buyer the right to sell the stock. The *expiration date* is the date on which the option contract expires—the last day on which an option can be exercised. The *exercise (or striking) price* is the price at which the buyer of a call can purchase the stock during the life of the option, and the price at which the buyer of a put can sell the stock during the life of the option. Finally, the *premium* is the price the buyer pays the writer for an option contract. The term premium is often synonymous with the word price. The terms buyer and holder are synonymous as often are the expressions seller and writer. In the latter case, however, a seller of an existing option is not necessarily the writer. He or she might have purchased the option from a writer.

Let us review the transaction reporting techniques of the listed options market place. To date only call options have traded on exchanges in significant volume and numbers and consequently references to items shown in Figure 14-2 refer to calls exclusively. The put options that trade are identifiable in the tables by the letter "p" between the option name and exercise price. For example "Avon ... Oct 30p. ..." The presentation is organized first by expiration month, and then exercise prices available for those issues.

FIGURE 14-2

OPTIONS TRADING

Chicago Board

Options Exchange

Option		Sales (100s)	Open Int.	High	Low	Last	Net Chg.	N.Y. Close
Alcoa	Oct25	15	119	2½	1⅞	2½	– ⅛	26⅞
Alcoa	Oct25 p	21	501	⅞	⅝	⅝	– ⅜	26⅞
Alcoa	Oct30	119	1600	⅜	5-16	5-16	......	26⅞
Alcoa	Oct30 p	84	142	4	3¼	3¼	– ¼	26⅞
Alcoa	Oct35	55	1057	1-16	1-16	1-16	– 1-16	26⅞
Alcoa	Jan25	24	89	3¼	2⅝	3¼	+ ¾	26⅞
Alcoa	Jan25 p	28	234	1½	1¼	1 7-16	– 1-16	26⅞
Alcoa	Jan30	71	1847	1 9-16	1⅛	1⅛	– 3-16	26⅞
Alcoa	Jan30 p	17	160	4⅛	3⅞	3⅞	+ ⅜	26⅞
Alcoa	Jan35	83	368	½	⅜	½	+ 1-16	26⅞
Alcoa	Apr25	4	7	4¼	4	4	– 1	26⅞
Alcoa	Apr25 p	30	44	2	1 9-16	1 9-16	+ 1-16	26⅞
Alcoa	Apr30	10	82	2 5-16	2	2	– ⅜	26⅞
Amdahl	Nov25	82	374	6½	4	6½	+ 1⅛	29½
Amdahl	Nov25 p	401	441	1⅝	⅞	⅞	– ½	29½
Amdahl	Nov30	575	955	3⅛	1¾	3	+ ⅝	29½
Amdahl	Nov30 p	513	1087	4⅛	2½	2½	– ½	29½
Amdahl	Nov35	409	800	1¼	11-16	1¼	+ ⅛	29½
Amdahl	Nov35 p	148	185	8	5⅞	6¼	– ½	29½
Amdahl	Nov40	91	768	⅝	⅜	½	+ 1-16	29½
Amdahl	Feb25	46	48	7½	5⅞	7½	– 2	29½
Amdahl	Feb25 p	92	62	1⅞	1⅛	1⅜	– ⅛	29½
Amdahl	Feb30	106	105	5	3	4½	+ ⅝	29½
Amdahl	Feb30 p	58	124	4⅛	2¾	2¾	– ½	29½
Amdahl	Feb35	159	415	2⅞	1 11-16	2¾	+ ½	29½
Amdahl	Feb35 p	9	69	8¼	5⅝	5⅝	– ⅞	29½
Amdahl	Feb40	23	215	1⅝	1⅛	1⅝	+ 5-16	29½
Amdahl	May25 p	13	508	2¼	1⅝	1¾	– ¼	29½
Amdahl	May30	49	556	6	4½	5¾	– 2	29½
Amdahl	May30 p	11	503	4	3⅛	3⅛	+ ⅛	29½
Amdahl	May35	17	23	4½	3⅛	4½	+ ¼	29½
Amdahl	May35 p	5	.....	6	6	6	......	29½
A E P	Nov15	127	4020	1¾	1⅜	1¾	+ ¼	16½
A E P	Nov20	80	9645	1-16	1-16	1-16	......	16½
A E P	Feb15	17	2703	2⅜	2	2⅜	+ ⅛	16½
A E P	Feb20	204	6248	3-16	1-16	1-16	– 1-16	16½
A E P	May15	34	89	2½	2¼	2½	......	16½
A E P	May20	310	797	⅜	¼	5-16	+ 1-16	16½
Am Exp	Oct40	220	1352	3½	3	3½	– ⅛	43
Am Exp	Oct40 p	202	784	1½	¾	¾	– ⅛	43
Am Exp	Oct50	4	2921	⅛	⅛	⅛	– ⅛	43
Am Exp	Jan40	10	1113	3¾	3¾	3¾	– 1½	43
Am Exp	Jan50	6	1162	½	½	½	– ⅞	43
Am Hos	Nov35	143	1377	3	2½	2⅝	+ ⅛	35⅞
Am Hos	Nov40	38	1038	15-16	⅝	⅝	– 3-16	35⅞
Am Hos	Nov45	5	501	3-16	3-16	3-16	......	35⅞
Am Hos	Nov50	3	999	1-16	1-16	1-16	......	35⅞
Am Hos	Feb35	75	137	4¼	4	4	+ ¼	35⅞
Am Hos	Feb40	20	1031	1 15-16	1⅝	1⅝	– 5-16	35⅞
Am Hos	May35	4	1	5¼	5¼	5¼	+ ½	35⅞
Am Hos	May40	1	5	2¼	2¼	2¼	– ¼	35⅞
Am Tel	Oct50	18	1119	7	5½	7	+ 1⅛	56½
Am Tel	Oct50 p	843	2378	3-16	1-16	1-16	– 1-16	56½
Am Tel	Oct55	994	7963	2⅝	1 7-16	2⅜	+ 7-16	56½
Am Tel	Oct55 p	679	3060	1⅜	9-16	9-16	– 9-16	56½
Am Tel	Oct60	1750	16138	⅜	3-16	⅜	+ 3-16	56½
Am Tel	Oct60 p	13	44	5	4¾	4¾	– ¼	56½
Am Tel	Oct65	25	470	1-16	1-16	1-16	......	56½
Am Tel	Jan50	56	1583	8¼	6	8¼	+ 1¼	56½
Am Tel	Jan50 p	91	693	¾	½	½	– 1-16	56½
Am Tel	Jan55	376	4640	3⅞	2⅝	3⅞	+ ¾	56½
Am Tel	Jan55 p	193	847	2¼	1⅜	1⅜	– ⅝	56½
Am Tel	Jan60	1754	10622	1½	15-16	1½	+ ⅜	56½
Am Tel	Jan60 p	9	127	5½	4¼	4⅜	– ⅞	56½
Am Tel	Jan65	121	245	⅜	¼	⅜	+ ⅛	56½
Am Tel	Apr50	1	48	8	8	8	......	56½
Am Tel	Apr50 p	2	168	15-16	9-16	9-16	– 7-16	56½
Am Tel	Apr55	102	591	5	3½	5	+ 1½	56½
Am Tel	Apr55 p	23	93	2¾	2	2¼	......	56½
Am Tel	Apr60	1277	2876	2½	1¾	2½	+ ¾	56½
Am Tel	Apr60 p	1	25	4¾	4¾	4¾	– ⅝	56½
Am Tel	Apr65	7	151	¾	9-16	¾	+ 1-16	56½
A M P	Nov45	26	8	4¼	4	4¼	– 3⅜	47¼
A M P	Nov50	96	387	1¾	1	1¼	– 2¼	47¼
A M P	Nov55	1	.....	½	½	½	......	47¼
A M P	Nov60	5	839	¼	¼	¼	– ⅜	47¼
A M P	Feb45	2	1	6½	6¼	6¼	– 2⅛	47¼
A M P	Feb50	1	1251	3½	3½	3½	– 2	47¼
Atl R	Oct60	1050	6802	⅛	1-16	1-16	– 1-16	44⅛
Atl R	Oct60 p	32	11	15½	15½	15½	+ 3¼	44⅛
Atl R	Oct70	11	2504	1-16	1-16	1-16	......	44⅛
Atl R	Jan40	368	649	8	6½	7⅛	– 1⅜	44⅛
Atl R	Jan40 p	429	658	1¾	15-16	1½	+ ¾	44⅛
Atl R	Jan45	710	1406	4½	3½	4	– 1	44⅛
Atl R	Jan45 p	308	906	3½	2⅜	3¼	+ ⅝	44⅛
Atl R	Jan50	705	2584	2¾	2	2⅜	– ¾	44⅛
Atl R	Jan50 p	121	377	6½	5½	6	+ 1⅛	44⅛
Atl R	Jan55	2362	1465	1¼	⅞	1	– ⅜	44⅛
Atl R	Jan55 p	1	54	10	10	10	+ 2½	44⅛
Atl R	Jan60	2993	3899	⅞	7-16	7-16	– 3-16	44⅛
Atl R	Apr40	1	.....	8⅛	8⅛	8⅛	......	44⅛
Atl R	Apr45	172	118	7	4½	5⅞	– ⅛	44⅛
Atl R	Apr50	143	316	4⅜	3⅛	3⅜	– ⅝	44⅛
Atl R	Apr50 p	13	19	7	5½	6¼	+ 2¼	44⅛
Atl R	Apr55	557	218	2½	2	2⅜	– ⅜	44⅛
Atl R	Apr60	609	741	1¾	1⅛	1⅛	– ⅞	44⅛
Avon	Oct30	12	173	4¾	4¾	4¾	– 1¼	35
Avon	Oct30 p	645	1627	3-16	1-16	1-16	......	35
Avon	Oct35	1028	1394	2⅛	⅞	1⅜	– ¾	35
Avon	Oct35 p	1242	2002	1⅝	⅞	1¼	+ ⅜	35
Avon	Oct40	1969	4811	3-16	1-16	⅛	– 1-16	35
Avon	Oct40 p	817	294	6⅜	4¾	5⅞	+ 1⅜	35
Avon	Oct45	112	2527	1-16	1-16	1-16	......	35
Avon	Oct45 p	390	5	10⅝	10⅝	10⅝	+ 3⅛	35
Avon	Jan35	131	998	3⅛	2¼	2½	– ⅝	35
Avon	Jan35 p	147	664	2	1 9-16	1 9-16	– 1-16	35
Avon	Jan40	786	1842	1⅛	⅝	⅞	– ⅛	35
Avon	Jan40 p	76	50	6⅛	5¼	6⅛	+ 1⅝	35
Avon	Jan45	13	1152	¼	⅛	¼	......	35
Avon	Apr35	181	55	3½	2½	3¼	– ¾	35
Avon	Apr35 p	38	166	2¼	1⅝	1¾	– ¼	35
Avon	Apr40	22	275	1½	1¼	1 7-16	– 7-16	35
Bally	Nov20 p	5	3198	5-16	5-16	5-16	– ⅛	24⅜
Bally	Nov25	13	14362	1 9-16	1	1 9-16	+ 11-16	24⅜
Bally	Nov25 p	5	3554	2½	2½	2½	+ ⅛	24⅜
Bally	Nov30	13	12422	⅜	⅜	⅜	+ ⅛	24⅜
Bally	Feb25	23	5551	2 15-16	2⅛	2 15-16	+ 3-16	24⅜
Bally	Feb30	6	5659	1	1	1	+ ¼	24⅜
BankAm	Oct20	199	460	3	2¼	3	+ ¾	22½
BankAm	Oct25	688	5374	⅜	¼	⅜	+ 1-16	22½
BankAm	Oct30	147	4215	1-16	1-16	1-16	......	22½
BankAm	Jan20	116	284	3½	3⅛	3½	+ ½	22½
BankAm	Jan25	347	1825	1 5-16	13-16	1 5-16	+ 5-16	22½
BankAm	Jan30	4	1830	5-16	5-16	5-16	+ 1-16	22½
BankAm	Apr20	6	112	4	4	4	– ⅛	22½
BankAm	Apr25	32	379	2	1⅝	2	+ ⅛	22½
BankAm	Apr30	2	397	11-16	11-16	11-16	+ 1-16	22½
Baxter	Nov45	20	25	5¾	5½	5⅝	– ⅝	50½
Baxter	Nov45 p	5	20	⅝	½	½	– ⅛	50½
Baxter	Nov50	178	1250	3	2⅛	3	+ ½	50½
Baxter	Nov50 p	64	109	2⅜	1¾	2⅛	+ ⅞	50½
Baxter	Nov55	12	1028	¾	¾	¾	– 3-16	50½
Baxter	Nov55 p	42	155	6¼	5⅝	5¾	......	50½
Baxter	Nov60	25	1538	⅜	⅛	⅛	– ⅛	50½
Baxter	Nov60 p	5	11	10	10	10	– ¼	50½
Baxter	Feb50 p	10	47	3¼	2¾	2¾	+ ⅛	50½
Baxter	Feb55	90	25	2	2	2	– 1½	50½
Baxter	Feb60	7	1846	1	¾	¾	+ 1-16	50½
Baxter	Feb60 p	2	13	11½	11½	11½	+ ½	50½
Baxter	May60	5	5	1½	1½	1½	......	50½
Beth S	Oct20	41	637	3⅛	2¼	2¾	– ½	22
Beth S	Oct25	77	3015	7-16	¼	5-16	– 3-16	22
Beth S	Oct25 p	18	51	3	2⅞	2 15-16	+ 11-16	22
Beth S	Oct30	3	2830	1-16	1-16	1-16	......	22
Beth S	Jan20	55	196	4	3⅜	3½	......	22
Beth S	Jan20 p	17	73	15-16	⅝	⅝	......	22
Beth S	Jan25	38	1462	1⅛	¾	1	......	22
Beth S	Jan25 p	19	219	3¼	3⅛	3⅛	+ 11-16	22
Beth S	Apr20 p	4	1	1	1	1	......	22
Beth S	Apr25	31	394	1⅝	1½	1½	– ¼	22
Beth S	Apr25 p	1	44	3⅜	3⅜	3⅜	+ ½	22
Blk Dk	Nov15	34	399	1⅞	1¾	1⅞	+ ⅛	16¼
Blk Dk	Nov20	334	3740	3-16	1-16	1-16	– ⅛	16¼
Blk Dk	Feb15	14	117	2¼	2¼	2¼	– ⅛	16¼
Blk Dk	Feb20	118	1224	9-16	7-16	9-16	+ 1-16	16¼
Blk Dk	May15	25	73	3⅛	2⅞	3⅛	+ ⅛	16¼

SOURCE: *Barron's*, September 14, 1981.

To explain how to read these tables, let us analyze the activity that took place in January 40 call options of Atlantic Richfield Corporation (as highlighted in Figure 14-2).

1. Atlantic Richfield Corporation is abbreviated in the table as "Atl R." Each option gives you as holder a right to buy 100 shares of the underlying stock at $40 per share anytime up to the expiration date.

2. The closing price of the underlying stock on the New York Stock Exchange is given in the last column to allow you to compare prices of the option and the stock. On this day Atlantic Richfield closed at 44 1/8 on the NYSE. The call privilege there-fore has a *conversion value* of $4.125. (The conversion value is the difference between $44 1/8 for the underlying stock and 40, the exercise price of the option.) The actual value of this call option is determined by the forces of supply and demand as reflected in the prices listed for the call options. If you exercise a January 40 call option for Atlantic Richfield, you do not automatically make a profit of $4.125 per share. Your profit, if any, is the amount you paid for the option privilege plus the aggregate exercise price ($40 × 100 shares = $4,000) subtracted from the net proceeds from the sale of the stock itself. Another way to profit from this option transaction is to sell the option privilege for more money than your original cost to acquire it.

3. The *expiration month* appears to the right of the company name for an option series. Although listed options have fixed quarterly expiration dates, only the next nearest three dates are made available for trading at one time. Therefore, on September 14, 1981, only options set to expire in October and January 1982 and April 1982 are available. When the October options expire, the exchanges will list the July series.

4. The *sales figure* indicates the total number of contracts traded today in that particular series. On the CBOE, 368 contracts for the January 40 call options were traded. Because each contract usually commands at least 100 shares of underlying stock, options on the CBOE equals 36,800 shares of stock.

5. The *open interest* is the aggregate number of exercisable contracts existing on the record from cumulative activities. Any opening writing transaction would increase the figure of 649 contracts, whereas a closing writing transaction would reduce it.

6. The *high, low,* and *last* columns indicate that the January 40 options sold as high as 8, as low as 6 1/2, and closed at 7 1/8 for that day's trading. The closing (last) trade of 7 1/8 was 1 3/8 below the prior day's last trade.

Mechanics of Options Trading (CBOE)

Options may be purchased or sold by placing an order with a broker, as for other types of securities. Orders specify whether the order is for puts or calls, the underlying security, expiration month and exercise price, the number of contracts to be purchased or sold, and whether the purchase or sale is an "opening" or "closing" transaction (the former being intended to result in a new position as a holder and the latter to close out a preexisting writer's position). The types of orders found generally in securities markets (that is, market orders, limit orders, etc.) are also used with puts and calls.

An innovative development in listed options is the elimination of a physical instru-ment to evidence ownership of an option. Ordinarily, no certificate is issued, transferred, or canceled in connection with a purchase or sale of any exchange-traded option. This facilitates prompt settlements of transactions and thus improves the listed option's liquidity.

Lack of a certificate means that each transaction and associated money activity must be handled as a bookkeeping entry. Additions and subtractions of option positions and related monies are inscribed on the records of participating brokers and on those of a central agency. This agency, the Options Clearing Corporation (OCC), was created to coordinate and complete operations functions for member organizations.

The success of certificateless trading results from placing the OCC between purchasing and selling brokers on each transaction. The OCC becomes holder and obligor of each option contract on behalf of the members to that transaction. It is also the only issuer of listed options, creating long and short (writing) positions in response to agreements arranged on the trading floors of the participating exchanges.

Book entry record keeping means that the OCC maintains a running total record of option positions and related monies in behalf of each clearing member's customer accounts. Options may be exercised immediately after purchase until the day before expiration. The owner of a listed option can exercise the privilege, requiring performance from the contra party to the agreement. Exercise proceedings are initiated when the clearing member organization, whose ledger at the OCC shows it long on a particular option series, delivers to the OCC an Exercise Notice form regarding that series.

Although the OCC is the obligor for listed option contracts, it does not own the underlying stock to deliver pursuant to exercise of a call. Nor will it pay money if an investor exercises a put option. It is only an intermediary for buyers and sellers of listed option contracts. It promptly assigns any exercise notification to one of many writers of that option series whose open positions are recorded and maintained on its records. The assignment is made by computer on a random selection basis. Consequently, this procedure can result in assignment of an exercise notice to a member who initiated a writing transaction that very day.

Each member firm carrying customer accounts must also establish an equitable procedure for processing assignments made to it by the OCC. Exercise notices from the OCC must be reassigned among the firm's specific customer accounts with a writing position in that options series. Fair play dictates that an equitable internal allocation process be used that is consistent and based upon a random selection or first-in, first-out method.

The OCC does not automatically pair off and eliminate long positions with each sale of the same option series. Nor does it reduce or eliminate standing short positions with each purchase of the same option series. This means that in addition to basic order and execution information, each ticket must signify whether it is

1. *An opening purchase transaction*: a purchase to establish or add to a long position; the buyer is known as an option holder;
2. *An opening sale transaction*: a sale to establish or add to a short position; the seller is known as a writer;
3. *A closing purchase transaction*: a purchase to reduce or cancel a short position by the writer of that series; or
4. *A closing sale transaction*: a sale to reduce or cancel a long position by an option holder of that series.

From the foregoing list of possibilities, it is clear that a purchase of an option does not necessarily establish a position. Nor does the sale of an option necessarily close a position. An investor may purchase an option to offset an option written. Thus with this purchase the investor actually eliminates a short position. Similarly, an investor may write or sell an option as a way of establishing a position.

Table 14-3 shows quotations of call options for the Jinx Company. Jinx options are quoted at four different option or exercise prices ($40-$45-$50-$60) for each of three standard expiration dates (January-April-July). The exercise price of an option is set by the exchange when trading first begins in that option. For example, suppose today is February 1. All January options have just matured, and trading will start in October options. If Jinx is currently $46 per share on the NYSE, the exercise price for its October call option will likely be set at $45. This will be the only call option for Jinx for October unless Jinx stock makes a big move. If Jinx stock dropped down to $42, for example, an additional class of Jinx October options—such as Jinx/40—could be established by the exchange. This new option would trade in addition to the Jinx/45.

TABLE 14-3
HYPOTHETICAL OPTION QUOTATIONS

Options and Exercise Price	Closing Prices for Options Expiring End of:			Stock Price
	January	April	July	
JINX 60	1/16	1/2	3/4	46 1/2
JINX 50	1/8	1 1/2	2 5/8	46 1/2
JINX 45	*	3 1/4	4 1/4	46 1/2
JINX 40	*	6 3/4	7 5/8	46 1/2

*Unavailable.

Examine Table 14-3. At the time the quotations were available, the price of Jinx common stock was $46.50 per share. Those exercise prices quoted at the left that are below the prevailing price of the common stock are referred to as being "in-the-money." This means that the options have some "intrinsic" value represented by the difference between the stock price and the exercise price. Therefore we know that the "intrinsic" value of the Jinx/40 is $6.50, and for the Jinx/45 it is $1.50 (regardless of the expiration date). Any difference between these "intrinsic" values and the price of the option is what is being paid for an expected rise in the price of the common that *may* lie ahead. This could be referred to as the "time" value of the option contract.

Those option contracts with an exercise price that exceeds the current market price of the stock are referred to as being "out-of-the-money." In effect, these options have no "intrinsic" value. The prices quoted for these options are what is being paid for any perceived "time" value.

Option Premiums

The option premium at any given moment is a reflection of existing supply and demand, a consensus judgment of the option's current value. This delicate equilibrium can be rapidly tilted either higher or lower by any of a number of events or combinations of them.

In times of rising stock prices, there is generally increased interest in owning options to purchase stock but less interest in writing options. Other things equal, more would-be buyers and fewer would-be writers usually leads to an increase in option premiums. When stock prices are declining or weak, there is more interest in writing options but less incentive to buy them. Premiums thus tend to decline.

The current market price of the stock in relation to the exercise price of the option is a major factor affecting the option premium. For example, if a stock is currently selling at $40 a share, an option with an exercise price of $30 is obviously more valuable—and will command a higher premium—than an otherwise identical option with an exercise price of $50. In general, option premiums tend to move point for point with the price of the underlying stock only when the option is at parity, that is, when the exercise price plus the premium equals the market price of the stock. Prior to reaching parity, premiums tend to increase *less* than point for point with stock prices. There are two major reasons: first, because a point-for-point increase in the option premium would result in sharply *reduced leverage* for option buyers (the ratio between the premium and the price of the stock). Reduced leverage means reduced demand for the option. Second, a higher option premium entails increased capital outlay and increased risk—again reducing demand for the option. Declining stock prices also do not normally result in a point-for-point decrease in the option premium. This is because even a steep decline in the stock price in the span of a few days has only a slight effect on one major component of the option's total value, its time value.

As a wasting asset, if an option cannot be exercised at a profit by its expiration, it becomes valueless. Thus, as the expiration is approached, its time value decreases. All else being equal, the more time remaining until the expiration date, the higher the premium will be. The volatility of the underlying security is still another factor influencing an option premium. The option for a stock that traditionally fluctuates a good deal is likely to demand a higher premium than the option for a stock that normally trades in a narrow price range.

Option premiums must be sufficiently high to encourage investors to write options, rather than seek alternative investments that may involve less or no risk. Rising interest rates therefore tend to put upward pressure on option premiums, and declining interest rates normally lead to lower option premiums.

Looking at the various Jinx options in Table 14-3, notice that for any standard exercise price (e.g., Jinx/50), the market price of the option increases as the contract gets longer. For example, the Jinx/50 due in April can be purchased for $1.50. This means $1.50 per share in the standard contract of 100 shares, or a total of $150. This $1.50 plus the exercise price of $50 brings the total to $51.50, or about a $5 premium above the current market price of Jinx stock of $46.50. The premium of $5 is about 11 percent above the prevailing price of the stock ($5/$46.50). In effect, the dollar premium is calculated by adding the exercise price and the option price together and subtracting the market price of the stock. The premium for the Jinx/50 for July is about $6.125, or 13 percent ($6.125/$46.50).

The percentage premium rises as the contract grows longer and also as the amount of cash the buyer must put up gets smaller. For example, look at the July Jinx/40 and Jinx/45. The Jinx/40 sells at a 2 1/2 percent premium and requires the buyer to put up $762.50 (7 5/8 × 100 shares). The Jinx/45 sells at a premium of 6 percent but requires the buyer to put up only $425 (4 1/4 × 100 shares). The cash required in the latter case is about half that of the Jinx/40 option. Most option prices are between 5 percent and 20 percent of the price of the stock, depending upon the stock's volatility as well as the particular terms of the option.

CBOE option contracts carry commissions based upon the option price, not the stock price, in accordance with regular NYSE commission schedules. There is a minimum commission of $25 each way (buy or sell), and option buyers are limited to owning no more than 1,000 calls (100,000 shares) on a single stock to prevent the use of call options to gain control of a firm.

A model for estimating the prices of call options is presented in some detail in the appendix to this chapter.

Why Buy Options?

The basic reasons underlying the motivation for buying call options can be illustrated quite clearly. Following are some hypothetical quotes for listed options available for shares of the GTX Corp.:

Expiration/Exercise Price	Price of Option (Premium)	Stock Price
Apr./15	7	21 1/2
Apr./20	2	21 1/2
Apr./25	1/2	21 1/2

The first reason may be too obvious—speculators get a hot tip on a stock but do not have the money to buy it. A call is cheaper in actual dollars. To buy an April/20 call option on GTX stock costs $200 (excluding commissions) versus $2,150 required to own 100 shares of the stock outright. The second reason is that an investor who wants to buy the stock might be afraid that it will decline in value. Buying a call rather than the stock will reduce his profit by the amount of the premium if the stock advances, but it will limit his loss to the amount of the premium if it declines sharply. In the case of GTX, if the stock were purchased outright at $21.50 and the shares declined to $18, the investor would lose $350 on the purchase of 100 shares. The maximum that could be lost on the purchase of an April/20 option is $200. While the judicious use of a stop order might reduce the loss potential through the outright purchase of common shares, one is never certain at what price a stop order will be executed.

Other investors want to take profits in a stock that they have held for a long time—either for tax purposes or simple profit-taking desires—but cannot separate themselves from their love affair with the stock that has made them so much money. A call can be bought with a percentage of the profits, although this is emotional, not intelligent, investing. A call can be bought for protection: A speculator has sold his stock short but wants to limit his loss should the stock advance. He could enter a stop order, but he then runs the risk of being whip-sawed. A call would prevent that at least until expiration or the maximum loss can easily be identified. There are other more esoteric reasons for buying calls, but these are the basic ones, and the others are merely variations of these.

In summary, investors buy listed calls with the hope of selling the option at a higher price. This use is a speculation, and the buyer risks losing 100 percent of the price paid for the call. For his capital, the buyer gets an impressive array of risk opportunities. First, leverage is obtained. A small investment of hundreds of dollars in a call controls underlying stock valued in the thousands. Second, profit potential is relatively unlimited. Many times call-option prices double or triple in a week. These "quantrum jump" potentials attract speculators. A third benefit is the fixed risk. The option buyer has peace of mind in knowing the limit of his loss and the knowledge that his loss can never exceed his total capital commitment. This is the speculative side of option buying.

In its simplest form, the put is used by the buyer as a safer way of betting on a decline in the stock than going short. The put increases in value as the underlying stock declines. If the buyer of the put was right about the prospects of the stock, he will get a much higher return on investment than if he had gone short. If he is wrong, he loses the entire price of the option. And if his timing was merely off, the limited loss may give him the courage to wait for the reversal to come. Of course, on the buy side, not all purchasers of puts are going to be speculating on a decline in the underlying stock. Some will be long-term investors who want to buy some insurance against a short-term or intermediate setback in appreciated stock they already hold.

Why Sell Options?

Most calls are sold by conservative investors who want additional income. An investor may own a stock for which he paid $30 and is now $40. He does not want to sell it at this level, but if he could get five points more he would be willing to part with it. He can get these five points by selling a call, but his gain is limited to those five points. On the other hand, if the stock price declines, he has the $500 premium and still owns the stock which he would have kept anyway (although if the stock rises quickly to $45, the buyer might not exercise, waiting for higher prices, and then watch the price decline; this would prevent the seller from taking his profits). If a writer is particularly bullish on the stock, he can sell a straddle, thereby getting additional premium money for the put side which he does not expect to be exercised. However, he is committing himself to buy stock only if that stock is declining in price, a practice that can be quite dangerous. Of course, it is also possible to write puts on short positions. Many writers of options write them naked (i.e., without either owning or being short the underlying stock). This is dangerous if done for one or two stocks, but if an investor utilizes substantial amounts of capital and writes puts and calls on a largely diversified group of securities, the percentage gains work out well, since, as we have already seen, most short-term options are significantly overvalued. It should be pointed out that writing naked options well requires nerves of steel and substantial capital.

Writing puts is a sensible strategy for an individual who wants to accumulate a particular stock but believes a better buying opportunity will arise at a later date. With XYZ selling at $50, the investor writes a put at 50 for which he receives a premium of $500, or $5 a share. If the stock drops to 40, and the put is exercised, he must buy the stock at 50, which is offset by the premium received, so the effective purchase price is 45. This is better than 50, at which the decision was made, but worse than the 40 that could have been received if he had waited longer.

On the other hand, if the investor is wrong and the stock climbed immediately, the missed opportunity to buy at 50 is compensated by the income from the premium received.

Another investor, though, may believe the stock is going to rise. He writes the put hoping that the put will expire without being exercised and he will have made a profit from the premium without significantly encumbering any capital.

Option Positions and Strategies

Option strategies can be for speculative, hedging, or spreading purposes. Speculation in options involves the purchase or the sale of an option without any position in the underlying stock. Such speculation can be magnified by buying or selling options in multiples or by packaging various combinations of put and call options. Hedging involves attempts to manage or control risk. Such hedging frequently involves the purchase or sale of an option in conjunction with a long or short position in the stock. Hedging can be done strictly within the options market, that is, by the simultaneous purchase of one option and the sale of another. This is called spreading.

This section deals with the analysis of option positions using graphs, which allows us to examine the risk-reward characteristics of any holding. These graphs facilitate a profit-loss analysis of any position. A specific set of stock and option terms and prices has been selected to make the examples comparable and permit the reader to combine two or more strategies. To simplify our analysis, the following basic assumptions have been adopted:

1. A call option is available with six months remaining until expiration. It has a striking price of $100. The current price of this call is $10.
2. It is possible to buy or sell a put analogous to the call with a striking price of $100. These puts are selling at $11.
3. The common stock the investor purchases or sells short or which underlies any options he may buy or write is selling at $95 a share.

Each investment position or strategy is depicted on a standardized graph. The profit-loss line on the graph shows the dollar profit or loss the investor will experience at each possible stock price approximately six months after the position is initiated. In the case of strategies involving options, one assumes that the options will expire in six months, so the price six months out is also the price of the stock when the option expires. Any two strategies can be compared at any stock price by transferring the profit-loss line from one graph to the other or by preparing a new graph and imposing both strategies on that graph.

The discussion of various strategies and their outcomes which follows use cases that are, in effect, "pure" strategies. It is possible to adopt intermediate strategies. For example, it is possible to purchase stock and write a lesser amount of call options. The lines in our graphs can be made to assume any slope, not merely those illustrated.

BUY SHORT-TERM DEBT SECURITIES

Our first graph (Figure 14-3) helps explain the use of the graphic technique. The vertical axis on the chart measures the dollar profit that the investor will realize by following this strategy. The horizontal axis lists possible prices for the hypothetical stock six months from the day the investment is initiated.

In the example illustrated here, the investor buys a short-term debt instrument paying 6 percent annually, or 3 percent over the six-month period. On a $95 investment, the interest income for six months is 3% × $95, or $2.85. As indicated by the horizontal profit-loss line, income is totally independent of the price of the security.

FIGURE 14-3
PURCHASE SHORT-TERM DEBT SECURITIES

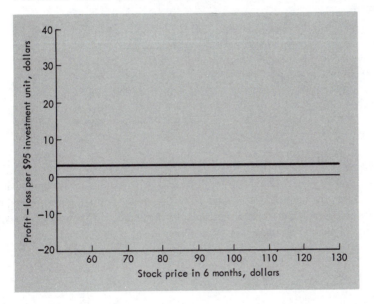

BUY STOCK

In Figure 14-4, assume that the investor purchases 100 shares of common stock at a price of $95 per share. The profit or loss is exclusively a function of the price of the stock six months in the future. If the price of the stock falls to $75, the investor suffers a loss of $20 per share over the six-month period. If the price of the stock rises to $120, there is a profit of $25. The key feature of this strategy is that the investor's profit or loss bears a direct linear relationship to the price of the stock on the date the determination of return is made. If an investor is optimistic about the probable course of stock prices in general and the price of this stock in particular, this position would be favored. If the investor is not overly optimistic, a strict long position in the stock would probably be avoided.

FIGURE 14-4
PURCHASE STOCK

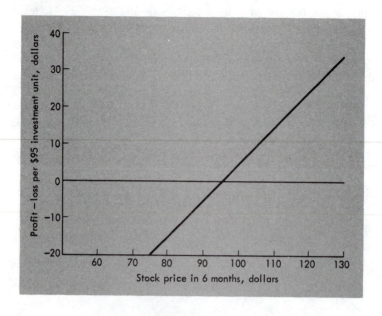

SELL STOCK SHORT

The graph (Figure 14-5) depicting the short seller's position is the converse of the stock buyer's graph illustrated in Figure 14-4. For every point the stock rises, the buyer gains $1 per share and the short seller loses $1 per share. If the stock declines, the short seller profits to exactly the extent that the buyer loses.

PURCHASE A PUT

Unless the put buyer is able to sell or exercise his put at a time when the price of the stock is below the striking price, he can lose his entire investment. To the extent that the price of the stock drops, the buyer of a put participates point for point in any decline below the striking price. In the example in Figure 14-6, the put is profitable at any price below $89 (the striking price minus the option premium, or $100 − $11), neglecting the effect of commissions.

The purchase of a put option is an alternative to short selling. A short sale of stock at $100 which subsequently falls to $89 would represent an $11 profit to the short seller (excluding commissions). For the put buyer his profit would not begin until the stock reached $89. However, the put buyer invests less cash ($110 vs. $10,000), is not responsible for the dividend (which the short seller is), does not have to borrow stock, and pays a smaller commission. Above all, however, the most the put buyer can lose is the premium. The loss exposure for the short seller is not so finite if the stock moves up. Table 14-4 illustrates the relative positions of a put buyer and short seller at varying closing stock prices.

Put options can also be used for downside protection of existing stock positions. For example, an investor who bought stock at $80 that has risen to $100 may be willing to pay an option premium of several points to be assured of the right to sell the stock later for at least $100.

FIGURE 14-5
SELL STOCK SHORT

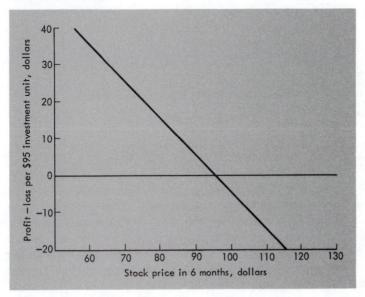

FIGURE 14-6
PURCHASE A PUT

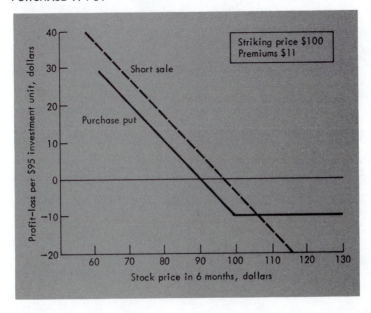

TABLE 14-4

RELATIVE POSITIONS OF A SHORT SELLER
AND PUT BUYER AT VARIOUS CLOSING
STOCK PRICES*

| | Gain (+) or Loss (−) | |
Stock at:	Short Sale ($100)	Purchase Put (100/11)
80	+20	+9
90	+10	−9
100	0	−11
110	−10	−11
120	−20	−11

*At $80 you make $20 ($100 − $80) on the short sale.
You "put" the stock to the buyer at $100, making $20,
less the $11 put premium, to net $9. At $120, the short
position loses $20 ($100 − 120). The put option is not
exercised and the $11 premium is lost.

BUY A CALL

With the purchase of a call (see Figure 14-7), the profit-loss line is no longer a
straight line passing through the price of the stock on the day the purchase was made.
The purchase of a call with a striking price of $100 at a premium of $10 would result
in the loss of the entire investment if the call expired with the stock selling below the
striking price of $100 per share. In addition, the investor does not even begin to make
money until the price of the stock exceeds the striking price plus the option premium
paid for the call. In this case, $100 (striking price) plus $10 (option premium) equals

FIGURE 14-7
PURCHASE A CALL

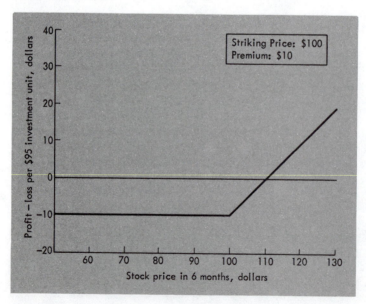

$110 (breakeven point). However, if, for example, the price of the stock rises to $130 per share, the call buyer will have at least tripled his investment, since the call option is worth at least $30 ($130 − $100).

The key advantages and disadvantages of owning a call option should be evident. Although the buyer loses his entire investment if the stock sells below the striking price when the option expires, his maximum risk exposure is limited to the amount of the option premium. This is true regardless of how low the price of the stock may fall. On the other hand, the call buyer participates in any advance in the price of the stock above the striking price. Profit increases point for point, no matter how high the price of the stock may rise over the life of the option.

SELL OR WRITE A CALL

The graph in Figure 14-8 illustrates the position of the writer of a call option who does not own the underlying stock. Such a position is referred to as uncovered, or "*naked*." The uncovered writer gets to keep all of the call premium if the buyer of the option does not exercise it. The naked writing position will be profitable as long as the price of the stock does not rise above the writer's breakeven point: $100 (striking price) plus $10 (call premium) equals $110 (breakeven point).

The premium received by the option writer is available to him to invest in Treasury bills, reduce the debit balance in his margin account, or whatever.

The risk position of the naked call writer is such that he can never gain more than the amount of the call premium, yet his possible loss in the event of a runaway stock is substantial. The loss could easily be many times the amount of the option premium. In spite of this risk, naked writing can be an effective strategy when used intelligently.

FIGURE 14-8
SELL OR WRITE A CALL

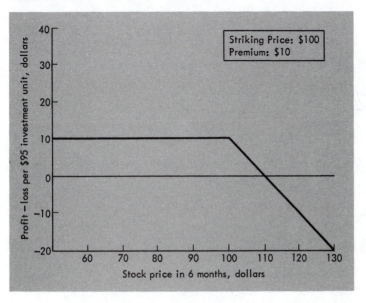

If an investor feels strongly that a particular stock is going to decline but does not anticipate that the decline will be of such magnitude that a short sale will be highly profitable, he may elect to write naked calls. As long as his commitment in this case is not substantial relative to his resources, the profitability can be excellent, and the naked writing position can actually reduce the overall level of risk in the portfolio. The way in which this apparently high-risk strategy can reduce risk will be clear when we discuss option hedging shortly.

PURCHASE THE STOCK AND SELL A CALL

This strategy is illustrated by the solid line in the graph (Figure 14-9) and is the classic posture of the covered call writer. The covered call writer buys 100 shares of the underlying stock and writes one call contract using the stock position as collateral. The call premium provides a degree of protection should the underlying stock decline during the life of the option. In return for this downside protection, the covered writer's profit is limited, in this case to $15 per share over six months, no matter how high the stock price rises. At any stock price in excess of $110 per share, the writer would have been better off not to have written the call, as indicated in owning the stock without writing a call.

The reasons for writing covered options are diverse. An investor may have a long-term position in the underlying stock which, for tax reasons, he is reluctant to sell even though he is not optimistic about the near-term price action of the stock. Rather than

FIGURE 14-9
PURCHASE THE STOCK AND SELL A CALL

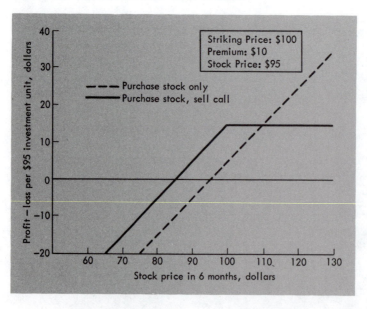

incur a large tax liability, he writes options to partially insulate himself from what he feels is a significant downside risk. In the event that this investor's appraisal of the stock proves incorrect and it rises over the life of the option, he does not have to deliver his long-term low-cost stock. He can repurchase the option, terminating his writer's obligation and realizing an ordinary loss on the option.

Some writers write calls only on stocks they feel positive about and are willing to hold. This tactic may seem odd, for by writing the option, these investors are precluded from obtaining more than limited profit if the stock rises as they anticipate. If the stock rises above the striking price, these writers are sure to earn the option premium. When earned consistently, option premiums can provide a highly satisfactory return. The major risk in adopting this strategy is that the premium may limit the return when the stock rises by substantially more than it reduces the loss when the stock declines.

Others will write covered options only when they feel the option premium is high relative to the fair value of the option. Such persons are usually relatively neutral toward the stock but can have a strong opinion that the option is overpriced.

SELL A PUT

Just as the writer of naked calls receives 100 percent of the premium if the stock is selling below the striking price when the call expires, the seller of naked puts receives 100 percent of the put premium if the stock is selling above the striking price when the put expires. The naked put seller's reward declines as the price of the stock falls below

FIGURE 14-10
SELL OR WRITE A PUT

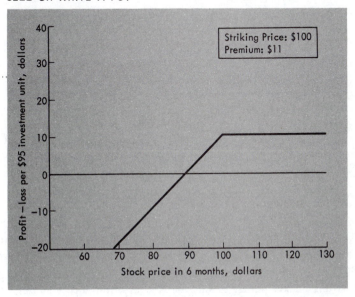

the striking price. In the example illustrated in Figure 14-10, the seller of the naked put actually begins to lose money when the stock price falls below 89.

Writing a put can be an attractive alternative to placing a limit order to buy for an investor who basically likes a stock but expects near-term weakness. With a limit order, he may miss getting the stock by just a fraction and lose all his profit. By writing a put instead at a price below the market, he will earn the premium even if the stock goes up without first dipping down. And if his expectations turn out to be correct, he will also end up owning the stock at the lower price.

A put writer places himself in virtually the same position as a covered call writer. Assume that the covered call writer's shares are selling at a price exactly equal to the call's exercise price. Like the covered call writer, the put writer (at the same striking price) takes in a premium and loses point for point on a stock decline—although in his case the loss is not in the stock but in buying back the put. And if the stock rises, he, too, will profit by an amount limited to the option premium. The put will expire worthless, and he won't have to buy it back.

The major difference is that the covered call writer has a larger sum invested in the market, and receives dividends on his investment. The put writer, on the other hand, holds his money in cash, earning interest on it all the while—and also keeping it available to buy stock in the event it is later put to him. Another difference is that the put and call premiums may not be exactly the same. Then, too, the put writer hopes never to have to pay the commissions to buy the stock.

The essential equivalence of a naked put writer and a covered call writer can easily be seen in the example illustrated below. The example assumes the stock is at $50 and put and call options with exercise prices of 50 are available at 5. The writer of a covered

With Stock at:	Buying 100 Shares at 50 and Writing One $50 Call at 5 Will Show at Expiration			Writing One Naked $50 Put Will Show at Expiration This Change in Value of Put:
	Stock Change	+ Net Change	= Call Change	
0	−5,000	+500	−4,500	−4,500
25	−2,500	+500	−2,000	−2,000
35	−1,500	+500	−1,000	−1,000
40	−1,000	+500	−500	−500
45	−500	+500	0	0
50	0	+500	+500	+500
55	+500	0	+500	+500
100	+5,000	−4,500	+500	+500

call earns $500 if the stock stands still; if it falls, he will lose the amount of the decline, less $500. The naked put seller makes $500 if the stock stands still or rises. If the stock falls, he will lose the amount of the decline, less $500. Thus, the economic opportunity and risk of writing a naked put are exactly the same as writing a covered call.

COMBINATIONS OF PUT AND CALL OPTIONS

The simultaneous availability of puts and calls makes for some interesting combinations. Four basic kinds of options are a combination of puts and calls. A *straddle* is a put and a call on the same security at the same exercise price and for the same time period. A *strip* is two puts and one call at the same exercise price for the same period. A *spread* consists of a put and a call option on the same security for the same time period at different exercise prices. A *strap* is two calls and one put at the same contracted exercise price and for the same period.

The buyer of a straddle is betting the premium paid that the price of the option security will deviate (either up or down) from the exercise price. The writer of a straddle accepts this bet and implicitly asserts confidence that the security's price will not vary significantly before the option expires. The buyer of a strip is betting the price of some security will change from the exercise price, but the buyer believes that the security's price is more likely to fall than it is to rise. Since a strip is two puts and a call, the buyer evidently believes a decrease in the price of the option security is more probable than an increase. A strap is like a strip that is skewed in the opposite direction. The buyer of a strap evidently foresees bullish and bearish possibilities for the optioned security, with a price rise being more likely.

Call Spreads.   A "*spread*" is a trade involving the purchase of one option and the sale of another, both on the same stock. The person doing the "spreading" is hedging. Although spreads often become complicated, all are based on either of two patterns. If both options have the same exercise price, but one expires later than the other, we refer to this as a "*time*" *spread*. If both expire in the same month, but one exercise price is higher than the other, we have a "*price*" *spread*.

To illustrate the price spread, let us suppose that we have three options on the same stock, expiring in the same month: one at an exercise price of 50, another at 60, and a third at 70. If these options have about three months to run, and the stock is now selling at 60, we might see these prices:

Option at 70	2
Option at 60	4
Option at 50	11

"*Bullish*" *spreads* involve buying the more expensive option (lower exercise price) and selling the cheaper option (higher exercise price). The spread will show a profit if prices rise. For example, let us assume the 60's are selling for 4 points and the 70's for 2. If you were bullish on the stock, you might but the 60's. Or you might prefer the bullish spread, buying the 60's and selling the 70's. You would pay out $400 and take in $200, so your net cost would be $200. If the stock is selling above 70 at the expiration date, the option at 70 that you sold will then be exercised. In turn, you may exercise the option at 60 that you bought. But your profit can never be more than $1,000, less the net cost of $200 you paid at the outset. This is an attractive ratio of risk to reward; you stand to lose $200 or make $800.

Let us examine some results of this bull spread under varying assumptions regarding the stock price:

Stock Price at:	Bull Spread — Gain (Loss) from:		
	Buy Side 60 at 4	Sell Side 70 at 2	Net
55	(400)	200	(200)
60	(400)	200	(200)
62	(200)	200	0
65	100	200	300
70	600	200	800
75	1100	(300)	800

Breakeven: Stock price = Buy exercise price + difference in premiums (62)

Maximum profit: Stock price $\geq$ Sell option exercise price (70) and dollar profit equal to difference in exercise prices less difference in premiums:
$(70 - 60) - (4 - 2) = 8 \times 100 = \$800$

Maximum loss: Stock price $\leq$ Buy option exercise price (60) and dollar loss equal to difference in premiums:
$4 - 2 = 2 \times 100 = \$200$

Suppose the stock closes at 75. The option you purchased with an exercise price of 60 will be exercised. You must pay 60 per share, and can sell these shares for 75, for a net of 15 less the original premium paid of 4 for a final net of 11 ($1,100). Netted together, the buy and sell sides give an $800 gain (excluding commissions). Notice that had you simply bought the 60 option at 4, the range of outcomes if the stock closed between 55 and 75 would have been between ($400) and +$1,100. Hedging your bet with the sale of a 70 at 2 (creating a spread) narrows the outcomes from ($200) to +$800. The spread is less risky than the simple purchase of a call. Beneath the table are some general rules for determining maximum profits and losses for bullish spreads as well as the breakeven point.

Suppose the stock closes at 60. The person purchasing the contract with a 70 exercise price will let it expire. You gain the premium paid of 2 ($200) excluding commissions. As the buyer of a contract with an exercise price of 60, you will let it expire. Your loss of $400 is offset by the premium collected from the option you sold for $200. Net loss to you is $200. At a closing price of 75 the following occurs: The person buying the 70 from you at 2 will exercise the option, paying 70 for the stock (per share). You will have to pay 75 to buy the stock. The difference between your cost of 75 and his payment of 70 is dampened by the original premium received of 2. The net result is a loss of 3 ($300).

If you were bearish on the stock, you might find it attractive to sell the option at 50 and buy the option at 60. You would thus take in $1,100 from your sale, and pay out $400 on your purchase. The difference would be $700, which would be credited to your account. To make the trade, you must put up margin equal to the difference in the exercise prices. In this instance, it would be 10 points, or $1,000. But you need supply only $300 of your own funds, since the spread itself would give you a credit of $700. We speak of this as a *"bearish" spread*, since it becomes profitable as the price of the stock goes down. The best outcome would be if the stock declined to 50 or lower and both options expired worthless. Then you would keep the $700 as your profit. The worst outcome would be if the stock rose to 60 and if the option at 50, which you sold, were then exercised. In turn, you could exercise the option at 60, which you bought. The purchase and sale of the stock would show a loss of $1,000, since you would buy at 60 but sell at 50. However, you would still have the $700 you took in at the outset. So your net loss would be reduced to $300.

This bearish spread, where a profit is anticipated if the stock declines, generally involves buying the lowest-priced option (highest exercise price) and selling the most expensive option (lowest exercise price). In this case we are dealing with options with the same expiration date.

Of course, it is also possible to enter into time spreads. These are trades involving the purchase of one option and the sale of another, both on the same stock at the same exercise price. The purchase and sale, however, involve different expiration dates. In using time spreads it is generally useful to sell the option with the smallest premium (closest expiration date) and to buy the option with the larger premium (later expiration date).

A bearish price spread is illustrated graphically in Figure 14-11. Specifically, this spread assumes that the investor buys the $10 option with the $100 striking price used in the previous graphs. To set up the spread, the investor writes an option having the same expiration date, but a striking price of $90, that is selling for $16, that is, $1,600 per 100-share contract. The unadjusted profit-loss line shows a fair profit if the stock declines and a loss if the stock rises.

FIGURE 14-11
CALL SPREAD

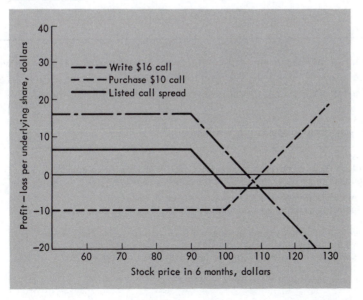

Taxes. and Margin Requirements.   The tax problem with options can be summarized rather briefly. The buyer of an option realizes a short-term or long-term gain or loss just as with stocks if he sells the option or lets it expire. If a call is exercised, the price he paid for it is added to the exercise price to determine the cost of the stock he acquires. His holding period on the stock begins on the day he exercises, and the holding period of the call is not added to the holding period of the stock.

The writer of an option receives a premium. This premium is "held in suspense" until the option transaction is consummated. The termination of the option, by expiration, causes the premium to be subject to treatment as a short-term capital gain. Termination by repurchase results in a short-term gain or loss. Exercise of the option results in a short-term or long-term gain or loss depending upon how long the writer has held the stock. If the option position is terminated with a closing purchase, the profit or loss realized is the difference between the premium of the option sold and the price paid for the closing option. Such profit or loss is reported as a short-term capital gain or loss. This rule does not apply to options written by broker-dealers in the ordinary course of their trade or business. Gain or loss from such transactions is to be treated as ordinary gain or loss.

The minimum margin that must be maintained on a daily basis in the margin account of an uncovered writer of an option is the greater of 100 percent of the current market value of the option or $250. Margin is not required with respect to a covered writing position in an option. However, margin must be maintained with respect to the underlying stock position in the account in an amount equal to 25 percent of the current market price of the underlying stock or of the exercise price of the option, whichever is less. The New York Stock Exchange's rules require an uncovered writing transaction to be margined as if the option has been exercised. This means that 30 percent of the market value of the underlying stock must be maintained in the margin account. Many brokers impose more stringent requirements upon their option-writing customers.

Option Commissions

Commissions on put and call contracts are negotiable, just as they are with stocks. To provide a sense of the order of magnitude of these commissions, Table 14-5 gives the formula for calculating commissions utilized by a leading brokerage house.

TABLE 14-5
CALCULATION OF BROKERAGE COMMISSIONS

Base Commission:	($14 + 1.6% of option execution price × 100) × Number of contracts — Subject to a maximum of 17% of the principal value
Less:	3% of base commission × Number of contracts in the order — Subject to a maximum reduction of 48% for 16 or more contracts

Notes:	There is a minimum charge applicable if the commission calculated is less than $30.00:
	    $30.00 on orders of principal value of $187.50 or greater.
	    16% of principal value on orders of less than $187.50.
	The maximum charge per contract will be $92.00.

There are thus three steps in calculating an option commission:

Step 1 :   Multiply 1.6% × Market price × Number of underlying shares.
Add $14.00 to the result.
Multiply sum by number of contracts.
Note: Subject to a maximum of 17% of principal value per contract.

Step 2 :   Subtract from result, 3% of commission for each contract.
Answer is the computed commission.
Note: Subject to a maximum of 48% for 16 or more contracts.

Step 3 :   Test for maximum/minimum charge:
Maximum charge = $92.00 per contract.
Minimum charge = If computed charge is less than $30.00, use the following table:

MINIMUM CHARGE TABLE

Condition	Actual Charge
If principal value is less than $187.50	16% of principal value
If principal value is $187.50 or greater	$30.00

Let us look at a few examples.

EXAMPLE 1.   Buy one contract at $15/16. (Total of 15/16 × 100 = $93.75.)

Step 1 :   (1.6% × $.9375) × 100 = $1.50.
$14.00 + $1.50 = $15.50.
$15.50 × 1 = $15.50.

Step 2 :   (1 contract × 3%) × $15.50 = $.47
$15.50 − $.47 = $15.03 is the computed commission.

Step 3 :   The charge is 16% of principal value if principal value is less than $187.50 and computed commission is less than $30.00. Computed commission from step 2 is less than the $30.00 minimum, so the minimum charge applies (16% × $93.75 = $15.00).
Actual charge is $15.00.
Percentage commission (one-way) = $15.00/$93.75 = 16% (Ouch!)

EXAMPLE 2.   Buy three contracts at $2. (Total of $2 × 100 × 3 = $600.)

Step 1 :   (1.6% × $2.00) × 100 = $3.20.
$14.00 + $3.20 = $17.20.
$17.20 × 3 = $51.60.

Step 2 :   (3 contracts × 3%) × $51.60 = $4.64.
$51.60 − $4.64 = $46.96 is the computed commission.

Step 3 :   Computed commission is greater than $30.00; use the computed charge.
Actual charge is $46.96.
Percentage commission (one-way) = $46.96/600 = 7.8%

EXAMPLE 3.   Buy 10 contracts at $5. (Total of 10 × 100 × $5 = $5,000.)

Step 1:   (1.6% × $5) × 100 = $8.00.
          $14.00 + $8.00 = $22.00.
          $22.00 × 10 = $220.00.
Step 2:   (10 contracts × 3%) × $220.00 = $66.00.
          $220.00 − $66.00 = $154.00 is the computed commission.
Step 3:   Computed commission does not exceed $92.00 per contract; use computed
          commission $154.00.
          Actual charge = $154.00.
          Percentage commission (one-way) = $154.00/5,000 = 3.1%.

The lesson: Purchasing low premium options and/or a small number of contracts is
mighty expensive! It is better to purchase more than one or two contracts on an option.
In any event, option commissions are often high and can detract significantly from
potential returns.

This commission schedule would be applied to the purchase, sale, or writing of an
option. Should you exercise an option or have an option exercised against you, the
commission would be calculated by the broker using separate commission schedules for
stocks. Thus, if you exercise a contract for 100 shares of stock at an exercise price of
$40, the commission would be calculated based on a $4,000 transaction ($40 × 100).

McDonald's Call Options

Call options on McDonald's (MCD) stock are traded. In early October 1981 the
following quotes were available:

Exercise Price	December	March	June	Stock Price
	Expiration Month			
55	9 3/8	*	12 1/4	62 1/2
60	6 1/4	8 1/2	10 1/4	62 1/2
65	3	5	*	62 1/2

*Not traded.

The MCD/55 contracts are already "in-the-money" 7 1/2 points. That is, these
options have an intrinsic value of $7.50. Any difference between the $7.50 value and the
actual quote was what buyers were willing to pay for the time value of the option. For
example, the MCD/55 option sells for 12 1/4 with a June 1982 expiration date. Its
intrinsic value is 7 1/2 and the time value is $4.75 (12 1/4 − 7 1/2). The MCD/65 con-
tracts were "out-of-the-money" since the striking price was above the market price of
the stock. Any amount paid for the MCD/65 options was pure time value perceived by
traders.

The Dec/65 was clearly the most speculative purchase in the set and the June/55
was the safest buy. The purchase of one June/55 contract would involve a commission
of $32.59 ($14 + $19.60 − $1.01). For each 100-share contract this means that the
round-trip cost per share is $0.65 [($32.59 × 2)/100]. The stock would have to rise to
almost $68 for you to break even. Further, during the period between October and
June, McDonald's would pay three dividends (October 27, February 24, and May 13).

At rates prevailing at the time this would be a total of $.75 per share ($.25 per quarter). This dividend goes to the option writer (seller) under option exchange rules. If McDonald's rose above 68 1/2 before late June 1982 the option buyer would begin to make money and see price leverage operating beyond that point. Would you buy or would you sell a McDonald's call option? Which striking price is best? Which expiration date is optimal? What do you think?

Summary

This discussion of the various options on common stocks has shown how they are similar and dissimilar. They are all dependent on the price movement, or expectations of price movement, of the associated common stock. They all vary in the length of time during which they are in effect—an important difference, since, in buying an option, the investor must predict not only a price movement but also the period within which the movement will take place.

The options discussed here give the investor varying amounts of leverage that are unobtainable by owning the common stock. They also offer somewhat more safety than the common, in that the investor need not put as much capital at risk to obtain the same reward. These features cause the options to sell at a premium, as a general rule. Thus it is important to know *why* the particular option sells at a premium, in order to tell if the premium is so high that it overshadows these attributes of the option. This trade-off between the premium demanded and the advantages gained by the option, along with the outlook for the associated common stock, determines whether an option is an attractive buy.

Questions and Problems

1. Consult Moody's manuals or Standard & Poor's *Stock Guide*. Determine data similar to those shown in Table 14-1 for the stock and warrants of Alleghany Corp. and Charter Co.

2. Assume that Xerox (XRX) stock is currently at $100. It is now July 1. Three call options are quoted: XRX/Nov/110... $1; XRX/Nov/100... $10; XRX/Jan/90... $20. Ignoring commissions:

    a. List two reasons why the premium on the Jan/90 call is so much higher than the premium on the Nov/100 call.

    b. Suppose that you purchased 100 shares of Xerox on June 1 at a cost of $95/share. You wrote (sold) one XRX/Jan/90 on July 1. Suppose that on January 15 Xerox stock was at $105.

        (1) Would the holder of the XRX/Jan/90 benefit from exercising the call? Why?

        (2) If the call were exercised on January 15, what is your tax status?

    c. Suppose that you do not own Xerox shares. You simultaneously write one XRX/Nov/110 and buy one XRX/Nov/100. What is your annualized rate of return if Xerox stock closes in November at 115? (Ignore commissions and dividends.)

3.   Assume that Texas Instruments stock is currently at $100. Two call options are quoted: TI/Nov/110... $1 and TI/Jan/90... $20. Ignoring commissions:

    a. Why is the premium on the January call so much higher than the premium on the November call?

    b. Suppose you owned 100 shares of TI at a cost of $95/share. At what price would you begin to lose money if you wrote a call on the TI/Jan/90?

    c. If you were short TI, would there be any advantage in buying a call? How so?

4.   You wrote a call for Holiday Inns/Oct/10 for a premium of $1 in January. The option was written against stock held long at a cost of $12/share. Ignoring commissions, and assuming the call was exercised in early October, what is your tax status on HIA at the end of October?

5.   Trace carefully the ramifications of purchasing a call on a warrant.

6.   You are interested in buying some low-priced call options. You have located an option trading at $1.50. You ask your broker to acquire fifty contracts (100 shares each). What is the commission to purchase these contracts?

7.   Measuronics Corp. (MRX) is a manufacturer of memory components for high-speed computers. The company has call options listed on the Pacific Stock Exchange. Recent quotes on call options are:

	June	September	December
MRX/260	17	24	30
MRX/280	6	13	19
MRX/300	1	6	11

The current price of the common shares is $270. No dividends are paid.

    a. Assume that you engage in a bullish spread involving the Sept./280 and Sept./300 call options. What is your expected rate of return (nonannualized, excluding commissions) if Measuronics closes at $270 in late September?

    b. How might one go about creating a "homemade" put if there was a desire to purchase a put on Measuronics but none were quoted or available? Would such a strategy be superior to a short sale? Explain.

APPENDIX

The Option Pricing Model of Black and Scholes

Black and Scholes[2] reached the conclusion that the estimated prices of calls could be calculated with the following equation:

$$P_C = [P_S N(d_1) - P_E e^{-R_f T} N(d_2)]$$ (14.1)

[2]Fischer Black and Myron Scholes, "The Pricing of Options and Corporate Securities," *Journal of Political Economy*, 81, No. 3 (May-June 1973) 637-54.

where:

$$P_c \quad = \text{ price of the call option}$$

$$P_s \quad = \text{ price of the stock}$$

$$P_E \quad = \text{ striking price of the option}$$

$$R_f \quad = \text{ continuously compounded interest rate per time period}$$

$$e \quad = 2.71828\ldots$$

$$T \quad = \text{ number of time periods to expiration}$$

$N(d_1) \text{ and } N(d_2) \quad = \text{ values of the cumulative normal distribution, defined by the following expressions:}$

$$d_1 = \frac{\ln(P_s/P_E) + (R_f - \sigma^2/2)T}{\sigma\sqrt{T}} \tag{14.2}$$

$$d_2 = \frac{\ln(P_s/P_E) + (R_f - \sigma^2/2)T}{\sigma\sqrt{T}} \tag{14.3}$$

and σ^2 is the variance of continuously compounded rate of return on the stock per time period.

The definitions of d_1 and d_2 are somewhat difficult to understand. They result from solving very complex mathematical equations and are admittedly not quickly grasped by the reader. Nonetheless, the basic properties of the Black and Scholes model are easy to envision. Estimated option prices vary directly with an option's term to maturity and with the difference between the stock's market price and the option's striking price. In addition, Equations 14.2 and 14.3 reveal that they increase with the variance of the rate of return on the stock price, reflecting the logic that greater volatility increases the chance that the option will become more valuable.

The way that option premiums fluctuate as a stock price moves below or above the exercise price is important to understand. Generally, it is rare for option premiums to move point per point with the price of the underlying stock. This happens only at parity (when the exercise price plus the premium equals the market price of the stock). Prior to reaching parity, premiums tend to increase less than point for point with stock prices. The two major reasons for this are (1) because point for point increase in the option premium would result in sharply reduced leverage for option buyers (reduced leverage means a reduced demand for the option), and (2) a higher option premium entails increased capital outlay and increased risk, again reducing demand.

Declining stock prices also do not normally result in a point-for-point decrease in the option premium. This is because even a steep decline in the stock price in the span of a few days has only a slight effect on one major component of an option's total value, its time value. This term-to-maturity effect exists because an option is a wasting asset. Simply, all else equal, the more time remaining until expiration, the higher the premium will be. An "out-of-the-money" option will approach zero as expiration nears. An "in-the-money" option will be left only with its tangible value.

Volatility is the big unknown in the option formula. It is the only input that must be estimated. Part of the problem it causes is due to the fact that it changes over time. The problem may be minimized by using historical data for estimation purposes. A very rough way to get a beginning estimate is

$$\text{Volatility} = \frac{\text{high} - \text{low}}{1/2(\text{high} + \text{low})}$$

where high and low reflect prices of the underlying stock over a recent period of time. The length of time used affects the volatility and may change all results and the decision made. Some people use the annual standard deviation of the rate of return for the stock as its input for volatility. The original models use the variance of the rate of return for the stock, also annualized.

Option premiums must be sufficiently high to encourage investors to write options rather than to seek alternative investments which may involve less risk. Rising interest rates therefore tend to put upward pressure on option premiums, and declining interest rates increase the present price of the exercise price; since the exercise price is a potential liability for the holder of the option, this reduces the option price. An increase in interest rate will most affect the options that have a longer time to maturity. It usually takes more than a one-percentage-point change in interest rate to cause a major change in option price. Usually, changes in other major variables such as stock price occur when interest rates change. Thus it is many times ha ler to pinpoint the individual factor that caused a premium price change.

The option formula uses a low-risk security rate, such as that of certificates of deposit or prime commercial paper, of an instrument which matures at the time the option expires. This means that there is normally a different interest rate for each different option maturity. Note that the value of an option for a given stock does not depend on what the stock is expected to do. An option on a stock that is expected to go up has the same value in terms of the stock as an option expected to go down. An investor who thinks the stock will go up will think that both the stock and the option are underpriced. An investor who thinks the stock will go down will not buy either the stock or the option.

To illustrate the application of the Black and Scholes model, let us suppose that a stock is selling at \$52 per share, that its variance of continuously compounded monthly rates of return is .0422, and that the continuously compounded interest rate is 0.5 percent per month. With these assumptions we can calculate the value of a call option with a striking price of \$45 and expiration date six months hence as follows:

$$d_1 = \frac{\ln(52/45) + (.005 + .0422/2)6}{.205\sqrt{6}} = .60$$

$$d_2 = \frac{\ln(52/45) + (.005 - .422/2)6}{.205\sqrt{6}} = .09$$

The values of $N(.60)$ and $N(.09)$ are obtained from tables of cumulative normal distribution and are approximately .7257 and .5359, respectively[3] (see Table 14-6). Thus,

$$P_c = [52(.7257) - (45)e^{-.005(6)}(.5359)] = \$14.33$$

TABLE 14-6
VALUES OF THE CUMULATIVE STANDARD NORMAL DISTRIBUTION,
$N(d)$, FOR VALUES OF d FROM .0 to −3.99

−d	0.00	0.01	0.02	0.03	0.04	0.05	0.06	0.07	0.08	0.09
0.0	0.5000	0.4960	0.4920	0.4880	0.4840	0.4801	0.4761	0.4721	0.4681	0.4641
0.1	0.4602	0.4562	0.4522	0.4483	0.4443	0.4404	0.4364	0.4325	0.4286	0.4246
0.2	0.4207	0.4168	0.4129	0.4090	0.4052	0.4013	0.3974	0.3936	0.3897	0.3859
0.3	0.3821	0.3783	0.3745	0.3707	0.3669	0.3632	0.3594	0.3557	0.3520	0.3483
0.4	0.3446	0.3409	0.3372	0.3336	0.3300	0.3264	0.3228	0.3192	0.3156	0.3121
0.5	0.3085	0.3050	0.3015	0.2981	0.2946	0.2912	0.2877	0.2843	0.2810	0.2776
0.6	0.2742	0.2709	0.2676	0.2644	0.2611	0.2578	0.2546	0.2514	0.2482	0.2451
0.7	0.2420	0.2388	0.2358	0.2327	0.2297	0.2266	0.2236	0.2206	0.2177	0.2148
0.8	0.2119	0.2090	0.2061	0.2033	0.2004	0.1977	0.1949	0.1922	0.1894	0.1867
0.9	0.1841	0.1814	0.1788	0.1762	0.1736	0.1711	0.1685	0.1660	0.1635	0.1611
1.0	0.1587	0.1562	0.1539	0.1515	0.1492	0.1469	0.1446	0.1423	0.1401	0.1379
1.1	0.1357	0.1335	0.1314	0.1292	0.1271	0.1251	0.1330	0.1210	0.1190	0.1170
1.2	0.1151	0.1131	0.1112	0.1094	0.1075	0.1056	0.1038	0.1020	0.1003	0.0985
1.3	0.0968	0.0951	0.0934	0.0918	0.0901	0.0885	0.0869	0.0853	0.0838	0.0823
1.4	0.0808	0.0793	0.0778	0.0764	0.0749	0.0735	0.0721	0.0708	0.0694	0.0681
1.5	0.0668	0.0655	0.0643	0.0630	0.0618	0.0606	0.0594	0.0582	0.0570	0.0559
1.6	0.0548	0.0537	0.0526	0.0516	0.0505	0.0495	0.0485	0.0475	0.0465	0.0455
1.7	0.0446	0.0436	0.0427	0.0418	0.0409	0.0401	0.0392	0.0384	0.0375	0.0367
1.8	0.0359	0.0352	0.0344	0.0336	0.0329	0.0322	0.0314	0.0307	0.0300	0.0294
1.9	0.0287	0.0281	0.0274	0.0268	0.0262	0.0256	0.0250	0.0244	0.0238	0.0233
2.0	0.0228	0.0222	0.0217	0.0212	0.0207	0.0202	0.0197	0.0192	0.0188	0.0183
2.1	0.0179	0.0174	0.0170	0.0166	0.0162	0.0158	0.0154	0.0150	0.0146	0.0143
2.2	0.0139	0.0136	0.0132	0.0129	0.0126	0.0122	0.0119	0.0116	0.0133	0.0110
2.3	0.0107	0.0104	0.0102	0.0099	0.0096	0.0094	0.0091	0.0089	0.0087	0.0084
2.4	0.0082	0.0080	0.0078	0.0076	0.0073	0.0071	0.0070	0.0068	0.0066	0.0064
2.5	0.0062	0.0060	0.0059	0.0057	0.0055	0.0054	0.0052	0.0051	0.0049	0.0048
2.6	0.0047	0.0045	0.0044	0.0043	0.0042	0.0040	0.0039	0.0038	0.0037	0.0036
2.7	0.0035	0.0034	0.0033	0.0032	0.0031	0.0030	0.0029	0.0028	0.0027	0.0026
2.8	0.0026	0.0025	0.0024	0.0023	0.0023	0.0022	0.0021	0.0020	0.0020	0.0019
2.9	0.0019	0.0018	0.0018	0.0017	0.0016	0.0016	0.0015	0.0015	0.0014	0.0014
3.0	0.0014	0.0013	0.0013	0.0012	0.0012	0.0011	0.0011	0.0011	0.0010	0.0010
3.1	0.0010	0.0009	0.0009	0.0009	0.0008	0.0008	0.0008	0.0008	0.0007	0.0007
3.2	0.007	0.0007	0.0006	0.0006	0.0006	0.0006	0.0006	0.0005	0.0005	0.0005
3.3	0.0005	0.0005	0.0004	0.0004	0.0004	0.0004	0.0004	0.0004	0.0004	0.0004
3.4	0.0003	0.0003	0.0003	0.0003	0.0003	0.0003	0.0003	0.0003	0.0002	0.0002
3.5	0.0002	0.0002	0.0002	0.0002	0.0002	0.0002	0.0002	0.0002	0.0002	0.0002
3.6	0.0002	0.0002	0.0002	0.0001	0.0001	0.0001	0.0001	0.0001	0.0001	0.0001
3.7	0.0001	0.0001	0.0001	0.0001	0.0001	0.0001	0.0001	0.0001	0.0001	0.0001
3.8	0.0001	0.0001	0.0001	0.0001	0.0001	0.0001	0.0001	0.0000	0.0000	0.0000
3.9	0.0000	0.0000	0.0000	0.0000	0.0000	0.0000	0.0000	0.0000	0.0000	0.0000

Note: $N(d) = 1.0 - N(-d)$.

[3]$N(d_1)$ is also called the hedge ratio. It shows the number of round lots of common stock required to balance one option contract in creating a risk-free hedge. In this example, $N(d_1) = .6$, which means that a long position in one option contract will require taking a short position of .6 round lot of common stock to create a riskless hedge.

Option Valuation Nomograms

A method exists for valuing options by using nomograms. Nomograms allow one to obtain the value of any option without undertaking any mathematical calculations. With only a pencil and ruler, anyone can obtain accurate values for any traded option.

The nomogram user requires only four items of information: the maturity of the option, the share price expressed as a percentage of the exercise price, the volatility of the share (i.e., the standard deviation of the continuously compounded annual returns on the share), and the annual rate of interest. The nomogram provides the *value* of a call option, *expressed as a percentage of the current share price*.

Each nomogram consists of four quadrants separated by four axes. The investor must draw four lines, one for each item of data, parallel to the axes. Table 14-7 summarizes the general approach, which is the same regardless of the nomogram being used.

Figure 14-12 illustrates the valuation of an eight-month call option on a stock that has an annual standard deviation of 60 percent. Since the exercise price is $40.00, the current share price of $52.00 is 130 percent of the exercise price. The annual interest rate is 10 percent. First, a vertical line has been drawn through the eight-month maturity, then a horizontal line through the 10 percent interest rate. Next, a vertical line was drawn through the share price as a percentage of the exercise price (130 percent). Finally, a horizontal line was passed through the 60 percent standard deviation. The intersection of this line with the previous vertical line indicates a call option value of 34 percent of the share price, or $17.68.

The nomograms have two characteristics that greatly enhance their value. First, they allow the reader to examine the sensitivity of the results to changes in the input variables. For example, it is very easy to see the effect on the option value of a change in the volatility of the underlying share. Second, the nomograms can be operated in reverse. If the user knows the price of an option, he can, by reversing step 4, estimate the implied standard deviation of the underlying share—information that he can use to appraise other options written on the same stock.

The nomogram presented here provides as much accuracy as a single-page, general-purpose nomogram will allow. Specialized nomograms can, of course, be produced to almost any desired degree of accuracy.

TABLE 14-7
HOW TO USE A NOMOGRAM

Step	Procedure
1. Maturity	Draw a vertical line through the *maturity*.
2. Interest rate	Draw a horizontal line from the point of intersection with the *interest rate* through the lower right-hand quadrant of the nomogram.
3. Share price	Draw a vertical line from the point of intersection with the share price as a percentage of the exercise price, through the upper right-hand quadrant.
4. Standard deviation	Draw a horizontal line from the point of intersection with the *standard deviation*, through the upper right-hand quadrant.
5. Result	Interpolate the result from the intersecting lines in the upper right-hand quadrant of the nomogram.

FIGURE 14-12
VALUING A CALL OPTION

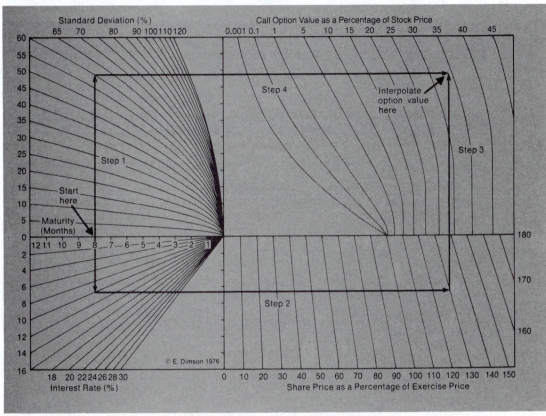

SOURCE: E. Dimson, "Option Valuation Nomograms," *Financial Analysts Journal*,
November-December 1977.

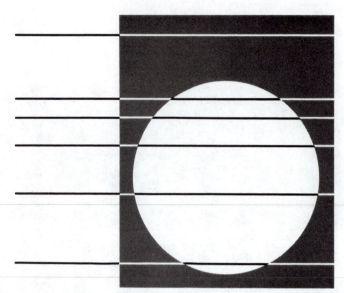

FIFTEEN

Convertibles and Interest-Rate Futures

This chapter considers two additional areas where options are available. Both these areas involve the use of options with fixed-income securities. The first is of long standing and essentially involves securities with an option to put a preferred stock or a bond to the issuer in exchange for common shares. These hybrids are called *convertible securities*. The second area is very new. It embraces rapidly emerging *interest-rate futures*.

Convertible Securities

Convertible bonds and convertible preferred stocks combine the basic attributes of common stocks and corporate bonds or preferred stocks in a single security. Because they may be exchanged for common shares, convertibles participate in the growth and appreciation potential of the underlying equities. Equally significant, their status as senior securities with the obligation to pay fixed interest or dividends gives convertibles those qualities of nonconvertible senior securities that reduce risk. All convertibles possess such dual stock/bond characteristics; the extent to which one or the other attribute is more influential varies from issue to issue, and even for a single issue over a period of time. Therefore, convertibles may satisfy a wide range of investment objectives.

Basic Features

The discussion that follows deals with convertible bonds. Analysis and selection of convertible preferred stock parallels the examination of convertible bonds with slightly less complication along certain lines.

The number of common shares for which a bond may be exchanged (converted) is established when the bond is issued, but this number is usually subject to adjustment in the event of stock splits or stock dividends of given amounts. The number of shares of stock per bond is referred to as the *conversion rate*. The stock value of the bond at any given point in time can simply be derived by multiplying the stock price by the conversion rate. For example, suppose a convertible bond can be exchanged for 20 shares of common stock. If the current market price of the common is $45, then the *conversion value* is $900 (20 × $45). The conversion value will change as the stock price changes.

The convertible bond will also have what is called an *investment* or *straight value*. This is its theoretical value based upon the yield to maturity of similar issues having no conversion feature. For example, suppose a 6 percent convertible bond due in twenty-five years is convertible into 20 shares of common stock. The common is currently at $55. Thus the conversion value is $1,100 (55 × 20). However, suppose similar-quality bonds due in twenty-five years but without a conversion option are yielding 6 percent to maturity. This suggests an investment value for our 6 percent convertible bond of $1,000. This investment value is often regarded as a support level for the convertible bond in a declining stock market. However, the investment value also declines if interest rates rise during this period, as they usually do.

The investment value of a convertible preferred stock can be found in a similar manner. Since the preferred stock is a form of ownership, its life is assumed to be infinite and therefore the present-value factor used to find its value is not readily available. The investment value of a convertible preferred stock is assumed to equal the present value of preferred dividends over an infinite life discounted at the yield on a straight preferred stock. The present-value factor for an infinite-lived annuity is given by

$$V = \frac{D}{r}$$

where:

D = dividend on the preferred

r = appropriate discount rate or current yield on nonconvertible preferreds

An example will clarify the calculations required to find the value of preferred stock. The Strong Company has just issued a 9 percent convertible preferred stock with a $100 par value. If the firm had issued a nonconvertible preferred stock, the annual dividend would probably have been 11 percent. Dividends are paid annually at the end of each year. Dividing the annual dividend of $9 (9 percent of $100) by the yields on nonconvertible preferreds, or 11 percent, yields an investment value for the preferred stock of $89 (9/.11). In other words, the straight value of the preferred stock continues.

Market Values

The *market value* of a convertible is likely to be greater than either its investment value or its conversion value. The amount by which the market price exceeds the straight or conversion value is often designated as the market *premium*. The market premium is larger the closer the straight value is to the conversion value. Even when the conversion value is below the straight value, a premium based on expected stock price movements exists. The same type of premium exists when the conversion value is above the straight value; this premium is attributed to the convertible security purchaser's expectations also. The general relationship among the straight value, the conversion value, the market value, and the market premium of a convertible bond, described in the preceding examples, is shown in Figure 15-1. As Figure 15-1 shows, the straight bond value acts as a floor for the security's value and when the market price of the stock exceeds a certain value the conversion value of the bond exceeds the straight bond value. Also, due to the expectations of investors about movements in the price of the firm's common stock, the market value of the convertible often exceeds both the straight and the conversion value of the security, resulting in a market premium on the security.

FIGURE 15-1

THE VALUES AND MARKET PREMIUM FOR A CONVERTIBLE BOND

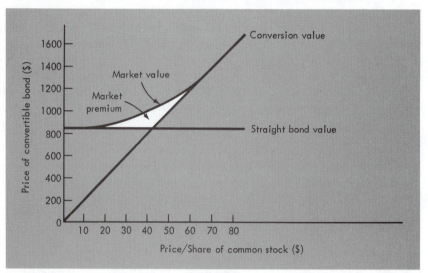

The reader should take particular note now of the parallel of convertibles with the call options discussed in Chapter 14. Take a moment to compare Figure 14-1 with Figure 15-1. They look alike in many respects. *Convertibles are like bonds with options attached where the bond must be used to pay for the stock.*

The notion of conversion and investment values (or the stock value of the bond and the bond value of the bond, as it were) must be compared with the actual market price of the bond to determine the extent to which the market price exceeds these levels. Consider the following for our 6 percent convertible bond that can be exchanged for 20 shares of common stock:

```
Market Prices:
    Stock       $55
    Bond        $1,200
Conversion value:   $1,100 ($55 × 20 shares)
Investment value:   $1,000 (to yield 6%)
```

In absolute terms the bond sells $100 above its conversion value and $200 above its investment value. In relative terms we have

$$\text{Premium over conversion value} = \frac{\text{Bond price} - \text{Conversion value}}{\text{Conversion value}} \quad \textbf{(15.1)}$$

$$\text{Premium over investment value} = \frac{\text{Bond price} - \text{Investment value}}{\text{Bond price}} \quad \textbf{(15.2)}$$

$$\text{Conversion parity price of stock} = \frac{\text{Bond price}}{\text{No. shares upon conversion}} \quad \textbf{(15.3)}$$

The *premium over conversion value* is 9.09 percent [($1,200 − $1,100)/$1,100], suggesting that the stock must rise about 9.09 percent for the breakeven point to be reached, or: ($55) + (.0909)($55) = $60. The *conversion parity* of the stock tells us the same thing: $1,200/20 = $60. The bond will generally sell some distance above its conversion value, since investors know the leverage potential in holding the convertible bond and are looking ahead at the future price potential of the common.

The market price of a convertible bond will normally equal or exceed the conversion value of the bond. That is, negative conversion premiums are unlikely. This will be guaranteed by arbitrageurs. Let us see why. Suppose a bond is convertible into 20 shares of common stock. If the common stock was selling for $55 and the bond was selling for $1,000, the bond would be selling for $100 less than its conversion value ($55 × 20 = $1,100). Traders would see a profit opportunity in the *simultaneous* placement of orders to buy a bond and short sell 20 shares of stock (or multiples of this arrangement). They would pay $1,000 for each bond and receive $1,100 by delivering 20 shares of common stock to cover the short position—a nice $100 profit for each bond purchased. A lot of simultaneous trades of this sort will have the effect of raising the price of the bond and lowering the price of the common until an equilibrium relationship exists where the bond's conversion value is at least equal to or less than its market value.

The *premium over investment value* is 16.67 percent [($1,200 − $1,000)/$1,200], suggesting that the bond could fall 16.67 percent if the stock declined significantly before it reached a kind of price "floor."[1] Presumably, if the stock declined from $55 to, say, $40, the bond might cease falling at $1,000 even though its conversion value would be $800 ($40 × 20 shares). However, it is likely that the deterioration in the stock price implies certain fundamental changes in risk surrounding the company, which will also reflect upon the quality of the bond. Increased risk in the bond might alter the required straight yield from 6 percent to a higher level, suggesting a lower investment value. Thus the bond floor (investment value) is not necessarily a rigid value.

It is also important to contrast the *current yield* on the bond and the stock to determine the relative income advantage (disadvantage) of holding one or the other. Suppose the underlying stock, selling currently at $55, pays an annual indicated dividend of $1.65 per share. Thus:

$$\text{Current yield on stock} = \frac{\text{Dividend}}{\text{Price}} = \frac{\$1.65}{\$55.00} = 3\%$$

$$\text{Current yield on bond} = \frac{\text{Interest}}{\text{Price}} = \frac{\$60}{\$1,200} = 5\%$$

[1] The premium over investment value is calculated using the bond price in the denominator. Some people would place the investment value in the denominator instead.

In this instance the current yield on the stock is 3 percent and the current yield on the bond is 5 percent. In effect, the outright holding of the bond provides a higher relative income yield than the outright purchase of the common stock. Alternatively, a $1,200 investment yields $60 per year in interest or $36 in dividends [($1,200/$55) × $1.65].

Convertibles Are a Compromise

Let us see where we are at this point:

Market Prices:
Stock	$55
Bond	$1,200

Conversion Rate: 20 shares per $1,000 (par) bond

Values:
Conversion	$1,100
Investment	$1,000
Parity	$ 60

Premiums:
Conversion	9.09%
Investment	16.67%

Current Yields
Stock:	3.00%
Bond:	5.00%

The central question is: Why wouldn't someone interested in capital gain (with some risk) buy the common outright at $55 and why wouldn't someone desiring current income and safety of principal buy a nonconvertible bond yielding 6 percent? Why buy this "hybrid"?

The general answer seems to be, in this case, that the buyer of the convertible would be looking for some compromise vehicle that provides a blend of current income, safety of principal, and capital gain potential. How much of each an investor wants and where he will compromise on each can only be determined by assessing (1) the bond's conversion premium, (2) the bond's investment premium, and (3) the relative current yields on the stock and the bond.

At current prices, purchase of the convertible bond provides a current yield that is higher than holding the common (5 percent vs. 3 percent) but less than owning a nonconvertible issue (6 percent). Purchase of the common at $55 and a subsequent rise to, say, $66 would represent a 20 percent capital gain. Purchase of the bond at $1,200 would suggest a price of at least $1,320 (maybe slightly higher). This represents a capital gain of only 10 percent. Thus, from a capital appreciation standpoint, there is less potential with the bond than with the common (10 percent vs. 20 percent). Another compromise. From a safety-of-principal viewpoint, a 20 percent decline in the common from $55 to, say, $44 would suggest that the bond should fall to a level of only $1,000, or 16.7 percent (to its investment value). There is relatively more "downside" protection on the bond than on the stock.

Different mixes of yield, investment, and conversion premiums will thus appeal to different investment objectives. The extent to which one or another of these attributes is more influential varies from issue to issue, and even for a single issue over a period of time.

Risk of Call

The possibility of call must be considered when investing in convertible bonds. That risk increases as the price of the common stock moves above the conversion price. A corporation that calls a convertible security expects most holders to exchange their bond for common stock instead of accepting cash (the call price). Therefore, convertible bonds are unlikely to be called until the bond is selling well above the call price and probably at little or no premium above conversion value. To continue our example, suppose the 6 percent convertible bond is callable at $1,050 and that the common sells for $60. The conversion value of $1,200 ($60 × 20 shares) is above the call price. What would most bondholders do if a call were made: accept $1,050 in cash or $1,200 worth of common stock? The answer is obvious.

As the price of the common passes $52.50 (conversion value = call price = $1,050), it will be difficult to justify paying any premium over conversion value for the bond. This is true since any premium paid will be lost in a call. Suppose that the common is at $60 and the bond is at $1,300. If a call is exercised at $1,050, $100 is lost, since the common stock you receive is only worth $1,200.

Examples of the Convertible Spectrum

Table 15-1 shows pertinent data for three convertible bonds. They are each quite different in technical characteristics that make them compatible with specific portfolio goals. Let us try to sort out the complicated set of parameters to judge the compatibility of each of these bonds to specific investment goals.

Union Pacific's 4.75 percent bonds due in 1999 are selling at 146, which is very far above par. The price has been pulled up by the common, which has advanced sharply. The bond sells right on its conversion value and far above its investment value. Buying this bond at 146 is essentially a quasi-equity commitment, since the bond is vulnerable to call (at 103.60). Moreover, there is probably a lot of conversion taking place, since the stock provides better current income than the bond (3.35 percent versus 3.25 percent). The risk of price decline is similar to that of the common stock. In sum, the Union Pacific bonds are an example of a convertible that has just about "run its course."

The Heublein, 4 1/2 percent bonds due in 1997 are diametrically opposite to the Union Pacific bonds. These bonds exemplify a convertible bond that has "fallen out of bed." It has an option of only remote value. The price of the stock has fallen drastically and taken the bond to a point just above its investment value. At the current level of the bond price, the stock would have to advance from $24 to $44 to reach conversion parity (hence the sizable premium over conversion value). This bond offers a holder relative safety of principal (vis-à-vis the stock), and better current income (7.1 percent versus 5.5 percent). Appreciation potential is strictly a long shot!

The Greyhound 6 1/2 percent bonds due in 1990 represent what many would call a true convertible bond. This bond has an interesting mix of current income, safety of

TABLE 15-1

	Union Pacific Corp.	Greyhound Corp.	Heublein Corp.
1. Rating	A	Baa	Baa
2. Coupon/maturity	4.75%, '99	6 1/2%, '90	4 1/2%, '97
3. Bond price (% of par)	146.00	86.75	63.00
4. Yield to maturity	6.52%	8.20%	8.33%
5. Current yield on bond	3.25%	7.49%	7.14%
6. Dividend yield	3.35%	4.50%	5.5%
7. Stock price	$83.50	$14.00	$24.00
8. Conversion rate (shares)	17.50	54.42	14.39
9. Conversion value (% of par)	146.00	76.19	34.54
10. Call price (% of par)	103.60	103.88	103.15
11. Premium over conversion value	0.0%	13.9%	82.4%
12. Investment value (% of par)	62.38	83.00	61.50
13. Premium over investment value	57.3%	4.3%	2.4%

Notes:

(3) = % of par (i.e., 146.00 = $1,460/$1,000 par bond)

(5) = (2)/(3)

(6) = Indicated common dividend/(7)

(9) = (7) X (8)

(11) = [(3) − (9)]/(9)

(12) = Price required to give equivalent yield to maturity on similar "nonconvertible"
      bonds

(13) = [(3) − (12)]/(3)

principal, and appreciation potential versus the common. The Greyhound bond is clearly superior to the stock in the production of current income (7.5 percent versus 4.5 percent). The bond sells at only about 14 percent above its stock value (conversion value) and at just about 4 percent above its worth as a nonconvertible bond (investment value). Clearly, there is better downside safety of principal than on the common and upside appreciation potential, though it is less than for an outright purchase of the common. Some would say that this is equivalent to "having one's cake and eating it too."

In the real world of investment opportunities, convertible bonds will take on shades of the income, safety of principal, and price appreciation potential exemplified by the three bonds above. The potential convertible bond investor must always assess the trade-offs and compromises in current income, safety of principal, and price appreciation that are inherent in a given bond. The outright purchase of straight (nonconvertible) bonds or common stock is a viable alternative.

XEROX CONVERTIBLES

Figure 15-2 represents a list of convertible bonds from Moody's *Bond Survey*. The bonds listed represent investment-grade types with ratings at or above Baa. Let's look at the Xerox bonds in detail.

Xerox Corporation has a subordinated debenture outstanding due in 1995. The bonds are convertible and bear a coupon rate of 6 percent. The bonds are callable at 102.70 and the conversion price is $92.00. The indicated dividend on the common stock of Xerox at the time was $3.00 per share (not shown in the table). Listed on page 446 are the parameters relevant to an evaluation of the convertible subordinated debenture.

FIGURE 15-2

1370 • *Moody's Bond Survey* September 21, 1981

Convertible Bonds with Estimated Investment Values

Below is a listing of convertible bonds, rated in the investment-grade categories, for which we have estimated straight debt values. An extensive list of convertible bonds (more than 600) appears in Moody's BOND RECORD.

Rating	Amount Outst. ($ Mill.)	Issue	*Call Price	Conversion Price	Recent Price Com.	Recent Price Debs.	Maturity Yield (%)	Debs'. Conv. Values Based on Com.	††Com. Values Based on Debs.	‡Approx. Straight Debt Values Price	‡Approx. Straight Debt Values Yield (%)
Baa	100.0	†Anheuser-Busch 9s, 10/1/2005	109.00	35.94	35⅝	107	8.32	99	38½	55	16.70
Baa	100.0	†Baxter Labs, 4¾s, 1/1/2001	103.25	[1]46.88	50½	108½	4.11	107¾	51	33½	16.00
Baa	36.5	†Becton Dickinson 5s, 12/1/89	102.00	64.90	39½	75	9.44	60¾	48¾	50	16.25
Baa	100.0	†Big Three Industries, 8½s, 4/15/2006	108.50	43.50	29¼	88⅞	9.69	67¼	38¾	52	16.70
A	250.0	†Boeing 8⅞s, 6/15/2006	106.51	42.25	25⅝	76	11.90	60½	32⅛	56½	16.00
Baa	32.0	†Burlington Ind. 5s, 9/15/91	101.25	39.00	23⅛	67	10.38	59⅜	26⅛	45½	16.25
A	200.0	†Caterpillar Tract. 5½s, 6/30/2000	103.85	50.50	56	111¾	4.56	111¾	56⅜	39½	15.50
Baa	28.0	†Celanese 9¾s, 6/15/2006	109.75	71.00	57⅞	90	10.92	81½	64	60	16.50
Baa	20.0	Cincinnati Financial 9⅜s, 11/15/2005	109.37	41.00	44¾	113	8.14	109¼	46⅜	57	16.70
A	73.8	Dana Corp. 5⅞s, 6/15/2006	100.0	[11]75.64	25⅛	45¾	13.49	33¼	34⅝	38½	15.80
A	60.0	†Dart Indus. 4¼s, 7/15/97	102.34	[2]93.02	49¾	62	8.72	53⅜	57¾	33	16.00
A	100.0	†Deere & Company 5½s, 1/15/2001	104.13	32.75	37½	114½	4.38	114½	37½	39	15.50
Baa	50.0	†Equitable Gas 9½s, 1/15/2006	109.50	37.33	28¼	95	10.05	75½	35½	55½	17.30
Baa	83.6	†FMC Corp. 4¼s, 7/15/92	101.28	41.50	27¼	66¼	9.24	65⅜	27½	40½	16.00
Aa	50.0	†First Bank System 6¼s, 6/30/2000	105.32	48.50	36	74	9.18	74	36	43	15.75
A	100.0	†First Int'l Bancshares 7¾s, 8/15/2005	107.75	25.75	29	112	6.73	112	29	50½	15.80
A	100.0	†First Interstate Bancorp 7¼s, 8/1/2004	107.25	36.75	36	102	7.07	98	37½	47	16.00
A	40.0	†First Security 9½s, 6/15/2006	106.97	28.55	20⅞	99	9.60	73	28⅜	58½	16.50
Baa	87.4	†Ford Motor Cr. 4⅞s, 7/15/98	103.8	[3]55.43	20	44	13.27	36	24⅜	33½	16.90
Baa	80.0	†Foremost-McKesson 9¾s, 3/15/2006	109.75	43.75	34	94	10.43	77¾	41⅛	59	16.70
Baa	50.0	†Gen. Amer. Transport. 5¾s, 3/1/99	103.50	[4]60.00	32¾	59½	11.02	54½	35¾	38½	16.70
A	125.0	†Georgia-Pacific 5¼s, 4/1/96	102.63	30.87	22	76	8.08	71¼	23½	40	16.00
Baa	29.9	†Granite City Steel 4⅝s, 12/1/94	101.48	[5]66.02	24¾	54⅜	11.38	37½	36	36½	16.60
Baa	35.4	†Greyhound Corp. 6½s, 1/15/90	102.75	18.38	15⅜	84	9.30	83¾	15⅜	53½	17.20
Baa	48.4	Gulf States Utilities 7¼s, 9/1/92	105.35	14.85	11	78	10.70	74	11½	50½	17.55
Baa	100.0	†Gulf United 9¼s, 9/1/2005	109.25	24.00	18	84½	11.11	75	20½	55½	17.00
Baa	30.0	†Hammermill Paper 5s, 5/15/94	102.00	40.00	26⅜	66	9.72	66	26⅜	39½	16.60
Baa	100.0	†Heublein 4½s, 5/15/97	102.48	69.50	27⅞	50¼	11.37	40	35	33½	16.50
Baa	125.0	†Hospital Corp. of Amer. 8¾s, 2/15/2001	108.75	41.17	38¾	100	8.75	94	41¼	55	16.50
Baa	40.0	Houston L. & P. 5½s, 2/1/85	101.08	[6]35.98	19	80⅛	12.93	52¾	28¾	71½	17.00
Baa	150.0	†Intel 7s, 8/15/2005	107.00	60.50	30¼	68	10.74	50	41⅛	43	16.70
A	53.3	†Int'l Paper Co. 4¼s, 11/1/96	N.C.	[7]38.00	25¼	72	7.34	66	27⅜	33½	16.10
Baa	61.0	†Int'l Tel. & Tel. 8⅝s, 6/1/2000	106.04	25.38	27	106	8.00	106	27	54½	16.50
A	200.0	†K mart Corp. 6s, 7/15/99	103.90	35.50⅛9		68	9.84	53½	24⅛	43½	15.40
Baa	50.0	†Kroger 10¼s, 6/15/2006	110.25	29.24	21¾	94	10.95	74⅜	27½	62	16.70
Baa	30.0	†Mallinckrodt 5¾s, 11/1/2000	104.03	33.50	38¾	116	4.49	116	38¾	38½	16.25
A	100.0	†Merrill Lynch 9¼s, 12/15/2005	109.25	40.00	33¾	98½	9.41	84	39⅜	57	16.50
Aaa	150.0	J.P. Morgan 4¾s, 11/1/98	103.80	80.00	55	69	8.13	69	55	37	15.10
Baa	31.6	†North Amer. Philips 4s, 6/1/92	101.20	[8]46.61	39⅛	96	4.47	84	44¾	39½	16.00
Aa	50.0	†Northwest Bancorp, 6¾s, 7/1/2003	106.75	30.00	26⅛	92	7.50	87	27⅛	45	15.75
Baa	60.0	†Norton 9½s, 11/1/2005	109.50	56.00	43¼	99	9.60	77	55⅜	58	16.60
Baa	41.5	†Owens-Illinois 4½s, 11/1/92	101.35	29.50	28	95	5.09	95	28	41	16.00
A	150.0	†Pfizer Inc. 8¾s, 2/15/2006	108.75	56.50	42¾	92	9.60	75¾	52	55½	16.00
A	27.8	†Pittston 9.20s, 7/1/2004	108.28	50.00	26½	80¾	11.62	53	40⅜	59½	15.85
Baa	32.6	†Purex Corp. 4⅞s, 1/15/94	101.88	34.83	21	75	8.12	60	26⅛	39½	16.40
A	100.0	†Ralston Purina 5¾s, 4/1/2000	104.03	15.33	12½	82	7.57	81½	12⅝	41½	15.40
Baa	146.0	†RCA 4½s, 8/1/92	102.20	59.00	20	49⅛	13.58	34	29	41½	16.00
Baa	50.0	†Rexnord 9¼s, 10/1/2005	109.25	21.25	15⅝	89	10.51	73½	19	56½	16.70
A	100.0	†Security Pacific 9¾s, 5/15/2006	109.75	40.50	35¾	99¼	9.83	88⅜	40¼	66	16.50
A	389.1	†Sun Company 10¾s, 4/1/2006	110.75	[9] 60.00	39½	89	12.16	65¾	53⅜	67	16.25
Baa	85.4	†Textron 7¾s, 6/15/2005	106.00	[10] 59.00	45⅜	85	9.33	77	50¼	49	16.20
Baa	50.0	†Toys "R" Us 9¼s, 1/15/2007	109.25	35.25	25¼	94	9.90	71¼	33⅛	56	16.80
A	150.0	†Union Carbide 10s, 3/15/2006	110.00	65.88	49¼	88½	11.40	74¾	58½	62½	16.20
Baa	385.0	†U.S. Steel 5¾s, 7/1/2001	104.32	62.75	29¼	55½	11.49	46¾	34¾	38	16.40
Baa	50.0	†Virginia El. & Pr. 3⅝s, 5/1/86	101.53	24.38	11¾	63½	14.79	48¼	15½	58	17.10
Baa	25.0	†West Point-Pep. 7¾s, 10/15/2000	105.43	38.38	20½	104	7.36	53½	40	50	16.35
A	129.0	†Xerox 6s, 11/1/95	102.70	92.00	48¼	63	11.30	52½	58	44½	16.00

* Lowest in effect over next 12 months. †Denotes subordinate debentures. †† Approximate price at which common would have to sell to equal indicated market for the debentures. ‡ Moody's estimates based on prevailing yields of non-convertible bonds of comparable quality and maturity, but giving weight to call price considerations where applicable. [1] Convertible into Baxter Travenol Laboratories common. [2] Exchangeable into Minnesota Mining & Manufacturing common. [3] Convertible into Ford Motor Co. common. [4] Convertible into GATX Corp. common. [5] Convertible into National Steel Corp. common. [6] Convertible into Houston Industries common. [7] Exchangeable into C.R. Bard Common. [8] Until 6/1/82. [9] Exchangeable into Becton, Dickinson common. [10] Exchangeable into Allied Corp. common. [11] Until 12/15/93.

SOURCE: *Moody's Bond Survey*, September 21, 1981.

Note that the premiums over conversion and investment values are about 20 and 29 percent, respectively. These are a bit high relative to what we might consider appropriate boundaries in an aggregate sense. This would be the case if, say, rules of thumb of a 25 percent limit on the conversion premium and a 15 percent limit on the investment premium were adhered to. The stock was as high as $60 only four months prior to the September 1981 data in the table. Thus the 20 percent conversion premium could be overcome fairly quickly if the stock begins to move. We note that it would be advisable to have a current yield on the bond at least one and one-half times that of the stock. The ratio here is actually 2.53. This just barely meets an income advantage test. The bond is selling well below the call price of 102.70, so the call risk is rather remote.

Xerox 6s, 11/1/95	
Market Prices:	
Stock	$48 1/4
Bond	63 ($630 per $1,000 par)
Conversion rate:	10.87 shares per $1,000 par bond ($1,000/$92.00)
Values:	
Conversion	52.44 ($48 1/4 times 10.87 shares)
Investment	44 1/2 (to yield 16.00% to maturity)
Parity	57.96 ($630/10.87 shares)
Premiums:	
Conversion	20.1% (63/52.44 − 1.0)
Investment	29.3% (63 − 44 1/2)/(63)
Current Yields:	
Stock	6.2% ($3/$48 1/4)
Bond	9.5% ($60/630)
Bond/stock	1.53 (9.5%/6.2%)

Interest Rate Futures

Rising interest rates are scarcely a new phenomenon, but the swings are getting wider and wilder. For example, three-month Treasury bills in 1978 traded 375 basis points higher than the level at which they sold in 1975. In the mid-1960s, 3.75 percent or 375 basis points represented the entire yield of a T-bill!

What is happening in Treasury bills, bonds, notes, and other credit instruments, in fact, bears a striking resemblance to the fluctuations that have long been part of the world of commodities, where prices traditionally gyrate in reaction to severe changes in the weather, the outbreak of war in a commodity-producing country, or the like. The answer there, of course, was the creation of the *futures contract,* an instrument that enables farmers, grain dealers, investors, and speculators to hedge their bets by buying or selling contracts for future delivery of the commodities in which they are involved.

Once interest rates began to acquire the volatility of commodity prices, it was inevitable that someone would come up with the idea of selling options on fixed-income securities. These options are referred to as *interest-rate futures.* That someone turned out to be the Chicago Board of Trade, which in 1975 began trading Ginnie Mae (*G*overnment

*N*ational *M*ortgage *A*ssociation) futures (the underlying certificate itself represents a pool of government-insured home mortgages).

Futures contracts have been developed for Treasury securities (bills, notes, and bonds) and commercial paper as well. Trading volume has grown rapidly. By year-end 1979, interest-rate futures were being traded at four organized exchanges in the United States and the New York Stock Exchange opened its own futures floor in 1980.

Mechanics of Trading Interest-Rate Futures

Now, five different exchanges deal in many kinds of interest-rate contracts. Five types of contracts along with their main features are shown in Table 15-2.

The basic rules of interest-rate futures are fairly easy to understand. The first step is to open a commodities account with a broker. This must be done even if you already have a securities account because additional agreements are required. The second step is to deposit money into the account. Amounts may vary from broker to broker, and according to the type of trading you'll be doing, but a $5,000 minimum is typical.

TABLE 15-2
FEATURES OF INTEREST-RATE FUTURES

Contract	Trading Unit	Price Increments	Typical Margin
90-day Treasury bills	$1 million	1/100 of 1% or $25 per contract*	$800-$1,500
One-year Treasury bills	$250,000	1/100 of 1% or $25 per contract	$600
90-day Commercial paper	$1 million	1/100 of 1% or $25 per contract	$1,500
4- to 6-year Treasury notes	$100,000	1/32s or $31.25 per contract**	$500-$900
Long-term Treasury bonds	$100,000	1/32s or $31.25 per contract	$2,000

*($1,000,999 X .0001) ÷ (4) (to equate to 90-days or 3 months)
**$100,000 (.01/32)

Let's assume you believe interest rates are going to fall sharply over the next several months. This means that the price of Treasury bills (and all other fixed-income securities) will rise accordingly. Suppose you decide to act on that belief. You buy (or go long on) a standard-sized $1 million contract in 90-day T-bills at today's price and yield for settlement in June. You don't put up $1 million, of course. What you must do is set aside, say, $1,000 in margin from the $5,000 in your trading account. This margin represents your equity in the contract; the amount may vary from firm to firm.

What happens next? Treasury bill contracts, as well as commercial paper contracts, are quoted in so-called basis points, or in increments of 1/100 of 1 percent. If the current T-bill yield is 11.25 percent, the price of a contract is quoted as 88.75 percent, or 100 percent less 11.25 percent. This means that on a $1 million contract for 90-day T-bills, each rise or fall of one basis point in price figures out to $25—or 1/100 of 1 percent times $1 million divided by 4 (to account for the 90-day, or one-fourth of a year maturity of the bills).

As a safety precaution, the exchanges do not permit you to accumulate losses, if any, from day-to-day. Say, on the day after you bought your contract, the yield on T-bills rises 10 basis points to 11.35 percent. This means that the price of your contract falls correspondingly from 88.75 percent to 88.65 percent. The loss on your contract is $250, or 10 basis points times $25 per point. Immediately, under the rules, $250 must be added to your margin to make up for the loss.

Here is how you would stand at the end of the second day. You had deposited $5,000 and used $1,000 of it for margin on one T-bill contract. This left $4,000 in funds available for additional margin. Since your contract fell by $250 the next day, your margin was reduced to $750. Your broker would restore the margin to $1,000 by adding $250 from your $4,000 in available funds. Now your margin is back up to $1,000 and your available funds are reduced to $3,750. On T-bills, or any other instrument, your contract will be revalued, or marked-to-market, in this manner at the end of every trading day. Profits are added to available funds, losses are subtracted and the margin remains at a constant level.

Suppose it turns out that you were right about the direction of interest rates, and along about April the yield on T-bills has dropped by a full 2 percent, or 200 basis points. As a result, the price of your contract has risen by the same amount, or from the original 88.75 percent to 90.75 percent. Since every basis point move equals $25 on a $1 million T-bill contract, you are now ahead of the game by $5,000—or 200 basis points times $25.

You don't have to wait until June to cash in your gain. You could cash in the gain right now, at the higher April price by "offsetting" your contract by selling (or going short on) a second June contract at the April price. This would cancel out your obligation to take delivery under the first contract and put you out of the market with a $5,000 gain.

At that point, the $5,000 that had been added to your account as it was marked-to-market, along with your original deposit, could be withdrawn. Of course, a commission would be deducted.

If, on the other hand, you were wrong about the market, and interest rates rose, you would obviously lose money. As your paper losses accumulated, additional margin would be deducted from your available funds until they became exhausted. If still more margin was then required, you would get a margin call, requiring you either to pony up more money or have your position sold out. If rates rose by 200 basis points, your loss would amount to $5,000 or your entire initial deposit. You would have gotten a margin call, and selling out would have left your account at zero—although you would still owe the broker his commission, of course.

HEDGING

The example we have just seen illustrates the simplest, most straightforward kind of commodity futures transaction: a pure speculation. You bear the risk of unexpected changes in interest rates. You make a profit if you guess correctly about rate movements;

but you can lose if you guess wrong. But the fundamental economic purpose of futures markets is hedging—by shifting the time risks involved in ownership of a commodity from the producers and users to speculators.

In other commodities, such as grains, this kind of defensive transaction or "hedge" is standard practice. A farmer, for example, expects an excessively large corn crop to reduce prices this summer. That is, he believes that he can make a better profit at today's futures price. So he might elect to sell his corn for future delivery at today's price. If the price of corn falls between now and harvest-time, he'll get less money for his crop but make an equivalent profit on his hedge. The farmer's transaction goes like this:

Believing that the cash price will fall months hence, he sells a July corn contract at $2.50 per bushel. By June the price has indeed dropped to $2.25 a bushel. So he offsets—this time buying a July contract at $2.25 to cash in his $.25 less a bushel gain on the hedge, which makes up for the $.25 less a bushel he receives for his crop. His cost: a commission plus the use of capital for margin.

With interest-rate futures, hedging is necessarily even more indirect. A mortgage lender may seek protection against changes in mortgage rates by using futures in Ginnie Maes, which are participations in pools of mortgages guaranteed by the Government National Mortgage Association (GNMA). He needs that protection because he has agreed to grant mortgages to a builder's customers at the rate prevailing at the time of closing some months hence.

As a hedge, the banker buys Ginnie Maes for future delivery at a price that reflects present interest levels. If rates fall, he will be forced to grant mortgages at the lower rate because of his commitment to the builder. But the value of his Ginnie Mae contract will rise, making up the opportunity loss.

The bank gives the builder a commitment for $200,000 of mortgages at market rates. The current rate is 12 percent. As a hedge, the bank buys two standard-sized $100,000 Ginnie Mae contracts. If the mortgage rate has fallen to 10 percent when the builder begins to sell houses, the bank must lend money two percentage points lower, thereby incurring an opportunity loss of about $4,000. But it makes a profit of $4,000 (2 percent of $200,000 in Ginnie Maes) by closing out the futures contracts it bought as a hedge.

Chances are that the Ginnie Mae contract won't change by exactly the same number of points as the bank's mortgage rates, and it is unlikely that the profit or loss will exactly equal the increase or reduction of earnings income from the mortgages. But it will usually be close enough to spare the bank a large loss.

If mortgage rates rose, of course, the bank would lose on its hedge, but earn more on its loans.

SPREADING

For speculators, the number of tools available is even more abundant than for the hedger. One of the basic strategies is the spread. This involves buying one contract month and simultaneously selling another contract month of the same interest-rate instrument. The speculator does this when he spots an abnormal relationship between the yields and prices of the two contracts. He hopes to profit when a normal relationship is restored.

Like Treasury note and Ginnie Mae contracts, Treasury bond futures move in increments of 1/32s of 1 percent of the principal amount of the instrument, with each

1/32 increment equaling $31.25 on a standard $100,000 contract. The speculator notices that Treasury bonds for June delivery are selling for 80-11, or a discounted price of 80 and 11/32s, while the September T-bond contract is at 81-05. (For uniformity, pricing of T-bond contracts is adjusted to the basis on an 8 percent coupon and a 15-year maturity.)

After doing some careful homework, the speculator decides that the difference of 26/32 between the two is much too large. Of course, the difference could be corrected when the higher price of the more "distant" September contract falls, when the lower price of the more "nearby" June contract rises, or some combination of both. So he sells the September contract and buys the June contract. After a few weeks, the September contract has moved up slightly, to 81-08, instead of falling, but the June contract has climbed all the way to 80-24.

The result: Since each 1/32 is worth $31.25 on a $100,000 T-bond contract, he has lost 3/32, or $93.75 on the September contract. On the June contract, he has a gain of 13/32, or $406.25. If he chooses to close out his contracts at this point, he has a profit of $312.50 minus commissions.

More elaborate spreading techniques are also available. A plausible one might be an intersector spread in which long-term rates are played against short-term rates. For example, a speculator may be convinced that today's inverted, downward-sloping yield curve—with short-term rates above long-term rates—will return to its normal upward slope in the near future. In other words, he agrees with many experts that short-term rates will soon be lower than long-term rates.

The speculator who wants to back this opinion with cold cash can buy contracts in short-term T-bills and sell contracts in long-term Treasury bonds. Then, if short-term rates fall sharply while long-term rates stay about the same, the price of his T-bill would climb, giving the speculator a profit while he breaks even on his Treasury bond contract.

What spreading boils down to is a balancing act along the yield curve. If short-term rates are lower than long-term rates, which is normally the case, the yield curve will slope upward from left to right. There are two main variations to this balancing act, depending on whether you expect the slope of the yield curve to become flatter or steeper.

In a bear spread, you would sell nearby contracts and buy distant ones when you think that the upward slope of the yield curve is too steep and is likely to become flatter. Of course, if the yield curve happens to be inverted, with short-term rates running higher than longer-term rates, you would do just the opposite if you expected the curve to become flatter: buy nearby and sell distant contracts.

In a bull spread, where you expected a normal-shaped yield curve to develop a sharper upward slope from shorter maturities to longer ones, you would buy nearby contracts and sell distant ones.

Importance of Interest-Rate Futures Markets

The new financial futures markets permit investors to obtain flexibility in ownership of securities at a very low cost. By transferring the interest-rate risk to those willing to assume it, interest-rate futures may increase the commitment of funds for some future time intervals. This could reduce the premium attached to funds committed for that future interval relative to funds committed for the nearer term. For example, the yield on 52-week and nine-month bills might fall. The resulting greater liquidity represents a gain to investors, while the lower interest rate on Government debt reduces the taxes needed to service the debt.

This new, inexpensive way to hedge risk also generates information on expected prices. While one can obtain information on future interest rates by comparing yields on outstanding securities which have different maturities, the interest-rate futures markets also provide this information in a more convenient form.

Summary

Based on our discussion of convertibles it is easy to see that buyers are really obtaining an option to put a preferred stock or a bond to the issuer for a predetermined number of underlying common shares. The convertible security possesses a value related to its basic character as a preferred stock or bond and a value related to the conversion property.

Interest-rate futures markets have generated much activity within a very short time. These futures provide inexpensive hedging facilities and flexibility in investment. They also provide a mechanism for participants to speculate on interest-rate movements on low margins. Whether these markets will be used primarily for managing interest-rate risk or just for speculation will become clearer as they mature.

Questions and Problems

1. A convertible bond has the following characteristics: market price = 106, call price = 109, conversion price = 25, stock price = 28, bond investment value = 100. What is your assessment of this situation?

2. A convertible preferred stock has the following characteristics: dividend = $4.50, par value = $100, call price = $106, conversion rate = 4 shares, market price = $126. Equivalent straight preferreds are selling to yield 9 percent. The underlying common stock pays an annual dividend of $1.00 and sells for $28. Would you buy the convertible? Why?

3. KWIK Corp. has a 6 percent ($50 par) preferred stock outstanding that is callable at $53 and convertible into two shares of common stock. The preferred is selling for $60. The common is selling for $25 (and paying a $2 dividend). Straight preferreds are currently selling to yield 8 percent.

    a. Calculate the investment and conversion values of the 6 percent preferred stock.

    b. Assume that the preferred sold at $47. How might a speculator capitalize on this fact, other things equal?

    c. If the preferreds were called at this time, what would most holders likely do? Why?

4. Archway Corp. has a $10 ($100 par) convertible preferred stock selling for $108. The preferred are convertible into two shares of common stock. The common stock is currently selling for $53. Nonconvertible preferred stocks of a similar quality are currently selling to yield 10 percent. If the common stock were to fall from $53 to $45, a decline of about 15 percent, about how much would the preferred decline? Why?

5. The Ford Motor Credit Corp. has a 4 1/2 percent debenture (Bbb) (1996) outstanding that is convertible into Ford Motor stock at a price of $78 1/8. The bonds are callable at 103.55 and have an investment value of 8.60 percent. Ford common currently sells for $55.50, with an indicated dividend of $4.00. The current price on the bonds is $750 ($1,000 par). Provide a systematic analysis of this bond. Indicate whether you would buy it *today* in light of the economic outlook and normal tests of attractiveness.

6. Shale Industries is a small to medium-sized company actively engaged in the oil services industry. The company provides replacement parts for drilling rigs and has just begun to test a device that measures oil shale content in certain rock formations. The company has a $4 convertible preferred stock outstanding ($100 par). There are 120,000 shares outstanding (47,500 owned by institutions). The preferred stock is callable at $102 with a conversion price of $47.17. Shale common is currently paying an indicated dividend of $1.40 on earnings per share of $2.80. Consensus opinion on the "Street" is that long-term interest rates will be flat to down over the next year. The common stock is currently selling for $14 and the preferred is at $32. Nonconvertible preferreds of companies in this industry which have similar quality ratings (Bbb) are yielding 14 percent at this time.

    a. Provide a systematic analysis of the convertible preferred.

    b. Assess the attractiveness of purchase of the convertible preferred at this time.

7. Albert Cane is seeking to trade 90-day Treasury bill futures. A bill future has been located which sells for a yield of 13.00 percent. A single contract is purchased. Three days after the transaction, contract yields have risen to 14.00 percent. The broker required an initial $4,000 in the trading account.

    a. What is the status of Cane's trading account balance at the end of the third day?

    b. What is Cane's dollar return if interest rates on 90-day bills drop to 12.00 percent?

8. Suppose that the Federal Reserve Board has just raised the discount rate from 12 to 13 percent. You expect Treasury securities to experience rising interest rates with longer-term Treasuries rising less than shorter-term instruments. A six-month Treasury bill futures contract is quoted at 87.27 and an eighteen-month contract is at 88.25. Given your expectations, what action should you take if you wanted to engage in an interest-rate futures spreading transaction?

9. It is February 1. You expect a large U.S. Treasury sale of securities for refunding purposes. You also feel that Government National Mortgage Association (GNMA) securities will maintain stable rates for awhile. The following transactions are consumated: Sell one GNMA future due June 1 at 70 1/32 and buy one U.S. Treasury future due June 1 at 68 26/32 (1/32 = $31.25). On February 28 you reverse these transactions: Buy GNMA at 69 6/32 and sell U.S. Treasury at 69. No margin is used. Exclude commissions.

    a. Why sell the GNMA's in addition to buying the Treasuries?

    b. Was your forecast correct?

    c. What is your net profit on these transactions?

part six
TECHNICAL ANALYSIS AND THE EFFICIENT MARKET THEORY

The approach to security analysis presented thus far is generally called *fundamental analysis*. The technique is based on the premise that the analyst needs to consider the major factors affecting the economy, the industry, and the company in order to determine an appropriate investment decision. In this section, we will discuss two different approaches to investment decision making.

Chapter 16 contains a discussion of a number of rather mechanical indicators of the stock market, individual security prices, and price behavior. Technical analysis in its truest form examines historical price and volume information.

Among the market indicators we will discuss are the Dow Theory, advances and declines, and the list of most-active stocks. Among the volume indicators we will review are short-selling statistics, odd-lot trading statistics, and odd-lot short sales. We will also look at mutual-fund activity, confidence indicators, the credit balance theory, and several charting approaches including point-and-figure and bar charting.

The theory of efficient markets, the subject of Chapter 17, in essence refutes technical analysis. The efficient market hypothesis, sometimes called the theory of random walk, states that historical price and volume information is of no use in predicting future price movements of either individual securities or groups of securities.

More specifically, we will discuss three main forms of the efficient market hypothesis. The weak form of the efficient market hypothesis says that the current prices of stocks already fully reflect *all* the information contained in the historical sequence of prices. The semi-strong form of the hypothesis goes still further. It states that the current prices of stocks not only reflect all informational value of historical prices, but also reflect all *publicly available information* about the corporation being studied. The strong form goes the farthest by saying that all information is useless to the investor for purposes of earning consistently superior investment returns. Empirical tests and results of tests of various forms of the efficient market hypothesis will be presented.

The chapter ends with a reconciliation of the theory of random walk and fundamental analysis, as well as a discussion of the investment implications of this theory, in both the selection of individual stocks and the construction of portfolios.

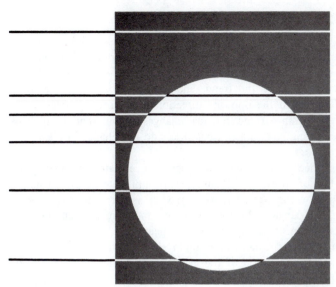

SIXTEEN
Technical Analysis

Fundamentalists forecast stock prices on the basis of economic, industry, and company statistics. The principal decision variables ultimately take the form of earnings and dividends. The fundamentalist makes a judgment of the stock's value with a risk-return framework based upon earning power and the economic environment.

In this chapter we will examine an alternative approach to predicting stock price behavior. This approach is called *technical analysis*. Technical analysis is frequently used as a supplement to fundamental analysis rather than as a substitute for it. Thus, technical analysis can, and frequently does, confirm findings based on fundamental analysis.

The technician does not consider value in the sense in which the fundamentalist uses it. The technician believes the forces of supply and demand are reflected in patterns of *price* and *volume* of trading. By examination of these patterns, he predicts whether prices are moving higher or lower, and even by how much. In the narrowest sense, the technician believes that price fluctuations reflect logical and emotional forces. He further believes that price movements, whatever their cause, once in force persist for some period of time and can be detected.

Thus, technical analysis may be used for more than a supplement to fundamental analysis. Fundamental analysis allows the analyst to forecast holding-period yield and the riskiness of achieving that yield, but these figures alone do not necessarily prompt a buy or sell action. Technical analysis, however, may be useful in *timing* a buy or sell order—an order that may be implied by the forecasts of return and risk. For example, the technical analysis may reveal that a drop in price is warranted. Postponement of a purchase, then, if the technical analysis is correct, will raise the forecast HPY. Conversely, a sell order might be postponed because the charts reveal a rise in the price of the security in question.

The technician must (1) identify the trend, and (2) recognize when one trend comes to an end and prices start in the opposite direction. His central problem is to distinguish between reversals within a trend and real changes in the trend itself. This problem of sorting out price changes is critical, since prices do not change in a smooth, uninterrupted fashion.

The technician views price changes and their significance mainly through price and volume statistics. His bag of tools, or indicators, helps him measure price-volume, supply-demand relationships for the overall market as well as for individual stocks. Technicians seldom rely upon a single indicator, as no one indicator is infallible; they place reliance upon reinforcement provided by groups of indicators.

The remainder of this chapter concentrates upon some of the major technical indicators employed to assess the direction of the general market and the direction of individual stocks.[1]

Market Indicators

The use of technical "indicators" to measure the direction of the overall market should precede any technical analysis of individual stocks, because of the systematic influence of the general market on stock prices. In addition, some technicians feel that forecasting aggregates is more reliable, since individual errors can be filtered out.

First, we will examine the seminal theory from which much of the substance of technical analysis has been developed—the Dow Theory—after which, other key indicators of market activity will be examined in turn.

Dow Theory

Around the turn of the century, Charles H. Dow formulated a hypothesis that the stock market does not perform on a random basis but is influenced by three distinct cyclical trends that guide its general direction. By following these trends, he said, the general market direction can be predicted. Dow classified these cycles as primary, secondary, and minor trends. The primary trend is the long-range cycle that carries the entire market up or down. The secondary trend acts as a restraining force on the primary trend, tending to correct deviations from its general boundaries. Secondary trends usually last from several weeks to several months in length. The minor trends are the day-to-day fluctuations in the market. These have little analytic value, because of their short duration and variations in amplitude. Primary and secondary trends are depicted in Figure 16-1.

The basic proposition in the Dow Theory is relatively simple. A bull market is in process when successive highs are reached after secondary corrections, and when secondary upswings advance beyond previous secondary downswings. Such a process is illustrated in Figure 16-1. The theory also requires that the secondary downswing

---

[1]An excellent source of much of the raw data for various indicators is found in the "Market Laboratory" section of *Barron's*, a weekly publication of Dow Jones, Inc.

corrections will be of shorter duration than the secondary upswings. The reverse of these propositions would be true of a bear market.

The classical Dow Theory utilizes both the industrial average and the transportation average in determining the market position. When both averages are moving in the same direction, valid indicators of a continuing bull or bear market are implied.

FIGURE 16-1
REPRESENTATION OF DOW THEORY

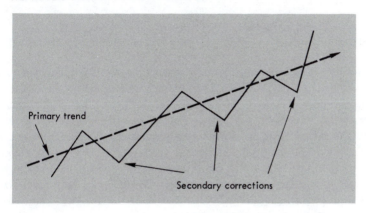

Price Indicators

The two variables concerning groups of stocks or individual stocks that technicians watch with the most interest are the behavior of prices and the volume of trading contributing to and influenced by changing prices.

It was amply noted earlier that the change in a security's price is probably *the* most important component in the total rate of return resulting from holding a security. This fact has not escaped the technician any more than it has the fundamentalist. In examining the influence of the market on stock prices in general, technicians particularly note certain signals, or price indicators: price advances versus declines, new highs versus new lows, and the price patterns of the "most active" stocks.

ADVANCES AND DECLINES

Looking only at the popular stock averages such as the Dow Jones Industrial Average (DJIA) can often be misleading. A relatively few stocks may be moving ahead while the majority of stocks either are making no progress or are actually moving down. The average may be behaving contrary to the larger population of stocks.

The basic idea behind the measurement of advances and declines is to determine what the main body of stocks is really doing. Comparison of advances and declines is a means of measuring the dispersion, or breadth, of a general price rise or decline. The phrase often used is "breadth of the market."

Many measures could be used. The most common is to calculate the daily net difference between the number of New York Stock Exchange stocks that advance and the number of those that decline. This net difference is added to the next day's difference, and so on, to form a continuous cumulative index. The index is plotted in line form and compared with the DJIA. For example:

	Advances	Declines	Breadth (Cumulative Advances Less Declines)
Monday	1000	400	+600
Tuesday	650	800	+450
Wednesday	500	1100	−150
Thursday	900	700	+ 50
Friday	1200	400	−850

The technician is more interested in change in breadth than in absolute level. Further, breadth is compared with a stock-market index, such as the DJIA. Normally, breadth and the DJIA will move in unison. The key signals occur when there is divergence between the two. When they diverge, the advance-decline line will show the truer direction of the market. The DJIA cannot move contrary to the market as a whole—at least, not for long. The longer the resistance, the greater the expected reversal. During a bull market, if breadth declines to new lows while the DJIA makes new highs, a peak in the averages is suggested. This peak will be followed by a major downturn in stock prices generally. Breadth can also be used to detect recovery. The advance-decline line will begin rising as the DJIA is reaching new lows.

Figure 16-2 is a monthly plot of cumulative net advances and the DJIA. The important feature to note is cycle-to-cycle breadth versus DJIA, and not the trend. Like other indicators, this one has been useful as a leading indicator at times. At other times, such as the early 1970s, this method was of little value.

NEW HIGHS AND NEW LOWS

A supplementary measure to accompany breadth of the market is the high-low differential or index. The theory is that a rising market will generally be accompanied by an expanding number of stocks attaining new highs and a dwindling number of new lows. The reverse holds true for a declining market.

The number of New York Stock Exchange stocks making new highs for the year minus the number making new lows is averaged for a five-day period. A moving average smooths out erratic daily fluctuations and exposes the trend. Such a high-low index would normally move with the market. Again, divergence from the market trend is a clue to future price movements.

THE MOST-ACTIVE LIST

Most major weekly market newspapers in the United States publish the twenty most active stocks for the week. By itself, this segment of the market is at first glance relatively useless, since the makeup of the list changes from week to week. However, these issues taken as a whole represent only 1 percent of the total issues traded but account for almost 15 percent of the total volume. Viewed in this way, the list tends to have a recognizable pattern if certain dimensions are assigned.

FIGURE 16-2

NET ADVANCES VERSUS DJIA

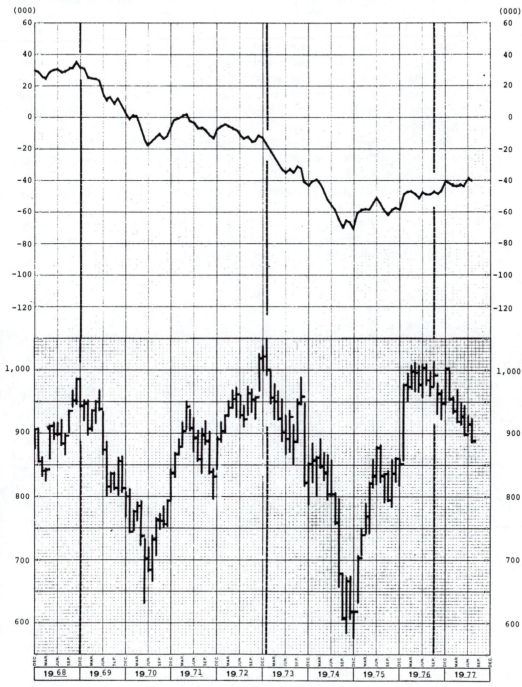

SOURCE: *Long-Term Technical Trends* (Boston: Stone & Mead, 1977).

The number of issues each week showing a net gain cannot exceed twenty, nor can they exceed twenty for a net loss. Since random variations often occur in the stock market, an additional time dimension of several weeks will tend to smooth an otherwise erratic curve. If three weeks of activity are added together to act as a stabilizer, then the upper and lower limits of the most-active list become +60 and −60.

When plotted on a three-week basis, the twenty most active stocks oscillate within a certain range. The maximum three-week upside plurality during the period 1962-69 was +51. The lowest net weekly plurality has been −52. One low point occurred on June 20, 1961, and was followed by a 350-point gain in the Dow Jones Industrial Average over a 190-week period.

Figure 16-3 provides some interesting insights. On February 11, 1966, the Dow closed at 989.03, with the most-active indicator at +15. During the following thirty-four weeks, the DJIA lost 245 points. On October 7, 1966, the Dow closed at 744.32, with the most-active indicator at −47. This condition was reminiscent of the indicator's position just before the 1962 upturn. The Dow climbed over 200 points, to 960, during the next fifty weeks. Perhaps one of the most interesting things about the twenty-six-week decline from 934 was the way in which the bear market terminated: The most-active list showed signs of bullishness as the market drew closer to its bottom.

FIGURE 16-3
MOST ACTIVE STOCKS VERSUS DJIA

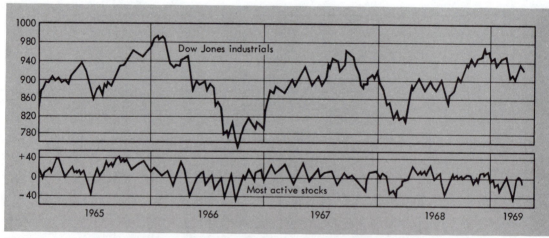

SOURCE: F. R. West, "New Market Tool, "*Barron's*, 49, No. 17 (April 28, 1969), 5.

The experience of the past decade has shown that the most-active indicator should approach −50 following a long and continuous decline that results in a selling climax, but in the case of an eroding decline, the indicator should move toward zero while the market continues to decline. In a bull market, the conditions are reversed, and oscillations around +35 are indications of strength in a rising market. A warning signal is flashed when the market continues to rise in the face of subsequent declines in the indicator.

Volume changes are believed by most technicians to be prerequisite to any change in price. Volume is a function of the demand for and supply of stocks and can signal turning points for the market as well as for individual stocks.

A Dow Theory tenet is that during bull markets, volume increases with price advances and decreases with price declines. In a major downward price trend, the reverse will hold true; volume will generally increase as prices decline and dwindle on price rallies. Further, volume generally falls in advance of major declines in the stock price averages and rises sharply during market bottoms. Thus, forecasting price changes requires examination of the trend of price changes as well as fluctuations in volume of transactions.

The financial press publishes daily data on upside and downside volume, and the technician can look closely at volume generated when the market was rising or falling during a given trading day. These data provide insight that is not available when net figures are utilized.

NEW YORK AND AMERICAN EXCHANGE VOLUME

The American Stock Exchange has long been identified as listing smaller, more fledgling companies than those listed on the New York Stock Exchange. It is estimated that three-fourths of the shares traded on the ASE are accounted for by the public, and three-fourths of the trading volume on the NYSE is institutional. Therefore, the American Exchange is, rightly or not, viewed as a market for more speculative securities. Many technicians regard the relative volume on the New York Stock Exchange and the American Stock Exchange as a measure or index of changes in the trend of prices.

Daily volume on each exchange is compared most often by dividing ASE volume by NYSE volume. ASE volume in excess of NYSE volume is rare, so the index would assume values between zero and 1.00. Values closer to 1.00 indicate that activity is high on the American (more speculative stocks) relative to the New York (more investment-grade stocks). High percentage values in excess of .60 are thought to represent a zone of high speculation and an eventual change in trend from bullish to bearish as speculative excesses bring about a collapse. Percentage values below .30 are considered healthy and representative of buying opportunities. Historically, when the index has gone above 60 percent, the market top was generally reached several months later.

SHORT SELLING

Around the twentieth of each month, the ASE and NYSE make public the number of shares of key stocks that have been sold short. Recall that short selling refers to selling shares that are not owned. The seller has behaved in this way because he feels the stock will fall in price. He hopes to purchase the shares at a later date (cover his short position) below the selling price and reap a profit.

As a technical indicator, short selling is called *short interest*. The theory is that short sellers must eventually cover their positions. This buying activity increases the potential demand for stock. In effect, short interest has significance for the market as a whole, as well as for individual stocks.

Monthly short interest for the market can be related to average daily volume for the preceding month. Thus, monthly short interest divided by average daily volume gives a ratio. The ratio indicates how many days of trading it would take to use up total short interest. Historically, the ratio has varied between one-third of a day and four days.

In general, when the ratio is less than 1.0, the market is considered weak or weakening. It is common to say that the market is "overbought." A decline should follow sooner or later. The zone between 1.0 and 1.5 is considered a neutral indicator. Values above 1.5 indicate bullish territory, with 2.0 and above highly favorable. This market is said to be "oversold." The most bullish effect would occur when the market is turning up and the short-interest ratio is high.

Figure 16-4 shows the short-interest ratio over a period of years in conjunction with the DJIA. It does not seem to be too revealing at market highs, but does give good clues of important lows when it reaches the 1.7-2.0 range.

Data are now being made public regarding short selling by stock specialists. Specialists are permitted to use short selling as one of their tools to promote orderly markets in the stocks they specialize in. Increasing and high levels of specialist short selling tend to signal important market tops. Conversely, low levels of specialist short selling tend to signal market bottoms.

ODD-LOT TRADING

The small investor more often than not buys fewer than 100 shares of a given stock—an odd lot—and such buyers and sellers are called *odd lotters*. Many find reason to watch the buying and selling activities of the odd lotters very closely.

Odd lotters try to do the right thing most of the time; that is, they tend to buy stocks as the market retreats and sell stocks as the market advances. However, technicians feel that the odd lotter is inclined to do the wrong thing at critical turns in the market.

If we relate odd-lot purchases to odd-lot sales (purchase ÷ sales), we get an odd-lot index. An increase in the index suggests relatively more buying; a decrease indicates relatively more selling. During most of the market cycle, odd lotters are selling the advances and buying the declines. During advances, the odd-lot index is falling. However, at or near the market peak, the index begins to rise as odd lotters sell proportionately less. The volume of odd-lot purchases increases noticeably just before a decline in the market. Similarly, during declines, the index is rising. Just before a rise in the market, the volume of odd-lot sales increases greatly and the index begins to fall.

Figure 16-5 shows the ratio of odd-lot purchases to sales as compared with the DJIA. A declining trend in the purchases-to-sales line is a sign of technical deterioration. A rising trend is a sign of improvement.

Odd-Lot Short Sales. The presumed lack of sophistication on the part of odd lotters is often further verified by looking at their activities in short selling. A ratio can be calculated by dividing odd-lot short sales by total odd-lot sales. This short sales/sales ratio is gauging the speculative activities of the man on the street, who, as a speculator, is presumed to be more wrong than the average odd lotter. Odd-lot short sellers tend to increase their short sales sharply near the bottom of a declining market. As soon as the market turns around, they tend to lose faith and reduce their short sales noticeably.

FIGURE 16-4
SHORT INTEREST VERSUS DJIA

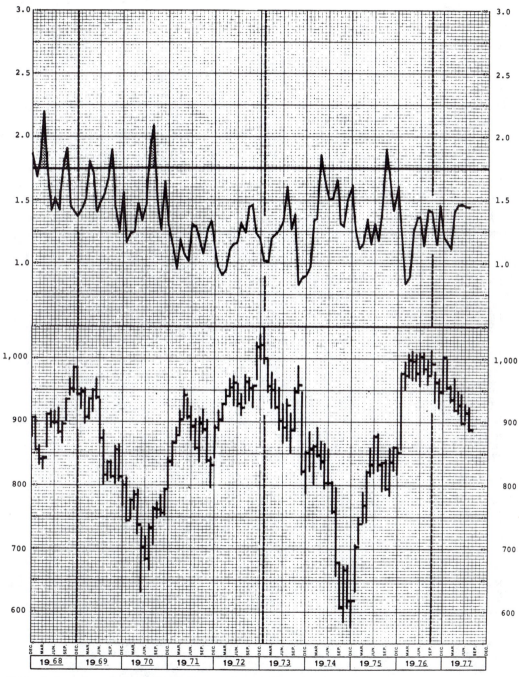

SOURCE: *Long-Term Technical Trends* (Boston: Stone & Mead, 1977).

FIGURE 16-5

ODD-LOT INDEX VERSUS DJIA

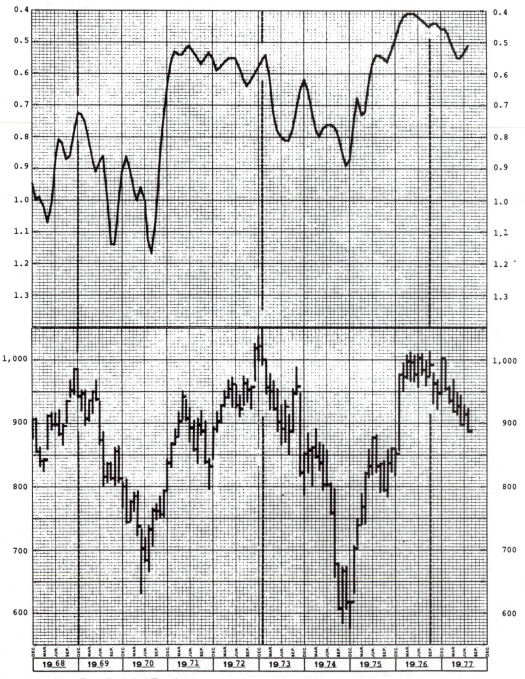

SOURCE: *Long-Term Technical Trends* (Boston: Stone & Mead, 1977).

An increasing ratio of short sales to sales suggests increasing bearishness; a falling ratio indicates decreasing bearishness.

Normally, a short-sale ratio of .5 percent suggests high optimism. A ratio over 3 percent suggests high pessimism.

Other Market Indicators

The number of indicators technicians use to predict changes in the trend of the overall market is almost limitless.[2] In the following paragraphs we will try to capture the essence of some other popular market indicators.

MUTUAL-FUND ACTIVITY

Mutual funds represent one of the most potent institutional forces in the market, and they are a source of abundant data that are readily available. The cash position of funds and their net subscriptions are followed closely by technicians.

Mutual funds keep cash to take advantage of favorable market opportunities and/or to provide for redemption of shares by holders. It is convenient to express mutual-fund cash as a percentage of net assets on a daily, monthly, or annual basis. In theory, a low cash ratio would indicate a reasonably fully invested position, with the implication that not much reserve buying power remains in the hands of funds as a group. Low ratios (on the order of 5-5 1/2 percent) are frequently equated with market highs. At market bottoms, the cash ratio would be high to reflect heavy redemptions, among other things. Such a buildup of the cash ratio at market lows is an indication of potential purchasing power that can be injected into the market to propel it upward.

Another mutual-fund indicator that is monitored quite closely is net subscriptions (subscriptions to new shares, less redemptions of existing shares). Like the odd-lot statistics, this indicator measures public sentiment and the outlook for the stock market. The trend to more or less buying moves in tandem with the odd-lot purchase-to-sale ratio. The sales-redemption differential narrows considerably prior to market advances. In effect, market advances are preceded by a relative shift toward redemptions. Shifts toward relative buying (sales of new shares) tend to precede market declines.

CREDIT BALANCE THEORY

Typically, investors receive credit balances in their accounts at their brokerage houses when they sell stock. At this point the investor has two choices: He can either have the credit balance forwarded to him or leave the credit balance in the account. However, these balances frequently earn no interest. Thus the only reason for maintaining the credit balances in the account would be for purposes of reinvestment of these funds in the very near future.

Figures on these credit balances at brokerage houses are published regularly in the financial press and in such publications as the *Federal Reserve Bulletin*. It is thought that

---

[2]Many who are cynical about technical analysis cite elaborate efforts to tie market movements to sunspot activity (lunacy and speculation) or the length of women's skirts (hemline theory), and the use of various aspects of the occult, including tarot-card reading, palmistry, and so on.

a build-up in these cash balances represents large reservoirs of potential buying power. In effect, investors are leaving the credit balances in their brokerage firm accounts because they anticipate a drop in prices and thus a buying opportunity. Conversely, a drop in credit balance suggests that prices will go up. Because an increase in prices was expected, investors have already used up their credit balances. However, technicians feel that investors in general as their actions get reflected in credit balances are usually wrong. That is, the investors are buying stocks when they should be selling them and selling stocks when they should be buying. As such, the credit balance theory is a contrary opinion theory.

In other words, technicians suggest that a wise investor will buy stocks as credit balances are rising and sell stocks as credit balances are dropping. In short, technicians say the wise investor should do the opposite of what the credit balances are doing.

CONFIDENCE INDICATORS

Two indicators of confidence have been popular with market analysts. One is based upon *Barron's* ratio of higher- to lower-grade bond yields. The other compares Standard & Poor's low-priced and high-grade common stocks.

The *Barron's* indicator divides high-grade bond yields by the relatively higher yields of low-grade bonds. A rise in the index indicates a narrowing of the spread between high- and low-grade bonds. In a previous chapter we saw that narrowing yield spreads were indicative of boom times or rising stock markets; so a fall in the index would imply widening yield spreads and recessed conditions in the economy and markets. The assumption behind the value of the index is that "smart" money moves from high to low quality, or vice versa, in anticipation of major market shifts, and such a move causes yield spreads to change. To the extent that this is true, *Barron's* confidence index is a leading indicator of the economy and the stock market.

The S&P confidence indicator measures low-priced common stocks and high-grade common stocks. Speculative stocks are assumed to be closely identified with low-priced shares. Thus we have a low- and high-grade stock indicator much like *Barron's* low- and high-grade bond indicator. When the market is advancing, investors are willing to take greater risks and buy speculative (low-priced) stocks. During market declines, quality (in high-grade stocks) is sought. The index (low-priced/high-grade) would fall prior to a market peak as confidence wanes and speculative stocks are changed for high-quality shares. A rise in the index would signal revival from a market bottom.

Forecasting Individual Stock Performance

After the technical analyst has forecast the probable future performance of the general market, he can turn his attention to individual stocks. Let us examine a few of the tools used for the technical analysis of individual common stocks.

As in forecasting the market, the technician believes that understanding historical price-volume information of individual securities is the key for determining their probable future performance. Technical analysts believe that history repeats itself, and thus, historical trends and patterns will be repeated through time. They seek to detect an evolving key trend or pattern in supply and demand conditions of the stock in question. The techniques that have evolved are aimed at detecting shifts in underlying supply and demand conditions as reflected in changes in volume and, consequently, prices. In this section we will discuss representative approaches in two broad categories of tools—those looking only at price, and those looking at price-volume relationships.

Price Analysis Approaches

POINT-AND-FIGURE CHARTING

Charting represents a key activity for the technical analyst. It provides visual assistance to him in detecting evolving and changing patterns of price behavior. The two oldest and most widely used charting procedures are point-and-figure charting and bar charting. These lie at the core of many technical schemes for individual stock analysis.

Perhaps the most baffling form of stock analysis, in the mind of the average investor, is the technique of point-and-figure charting.[3] The major features of this method of charting a security are that (1) it has no time dimension, (2) it disregards "small" changes in the stock price, and (3) it requires a stock to reverse direction a predetermined number of points before a change in direction is recorded on the chart.

A simple illustration will demonstrate the plotting technique quite easily. For stocks priced above 50 and below 100, the plotting increments are often one point, although the user may elect any increment he desires. All fractions are then discarded, so that 51 7/8 becomes 51. On a sheet of graph paper, the closing price of the stock being charted is recorded with an X. If the price at the close of the next trading day is within the plotting increment, no additional X can be entered. (We are assuming that the chart only records closing-price information, to the exclusion of intraday activity.) Only when the stock price moves into another plotting increment are changes recorded. Therefore a stock may move upward several points over a fairly long period with only a small amount of plotting. For example, if a stock moved from a price of 50 in small increments to a price of 53 over a three-month period, only four X's will have been made on the chart, as in Figure 16-6(a).

Obviously, if no additional parameters were assigned, only one vertical line of X's would develop. A *reversal spread* is used to prevent this. A reversal spread is the number of points (dollars) an issue must fall from its immediately previous high, or rise from its immediately previous low, to develop a new vertical column. When this occurs, a new column is started to the right. These reversal spreads are assigned according to the volatility of the issue. In the example, if the reversal spread were three points, and if the stock had gone from 50 to 60 without ever closing three points below the high for the column, the chart would look like Figure 16-6(b). However, if the stock developed a downtrend after reaching 60 and hit 56 1/2 on a close, a new column would be started, and all the points from 60 to 56 would be filled in, as in Figure 16-6(c). The stock is now in a downward cycle and will remain classified as such until a three-point reversal occurs, as in Figure 16-6(d), which shows that the stock moved from 40 to 43.

[3]One reason for this is the great number of variations on the basic point-and-figure approach. We present only one representative approach.

FIGURE 16-6
SAMPLE POINT-AND-FIGURE CHARTS

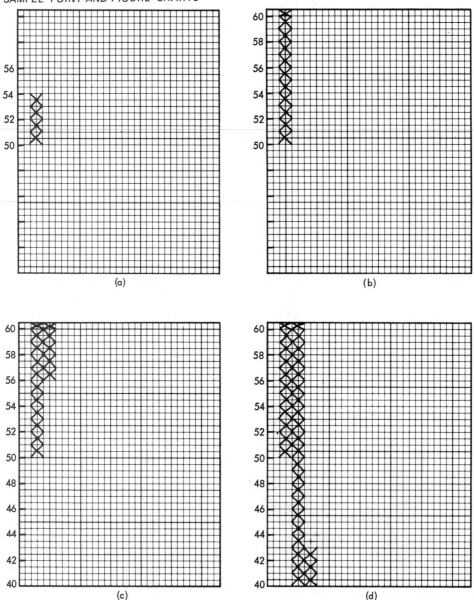

By ignoring the time element, we can see the forces of supply and demand at work in Figure 16-7(a), where the equilibrium price of the issue seems to be between 45 and 50. At any price above 50, the sellers move in, and at any price below 45, the buyers move in and clear the market. If the stock suddenly moves to 55, we are aware that this is outside the realm of the stock's normal trading range and some form of unusual activity is taking place.

FIGURE 16-7
SAMPLE POINT-AND-FIGURE CHARTS

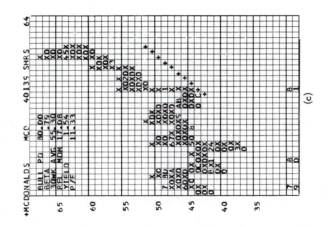

(c)

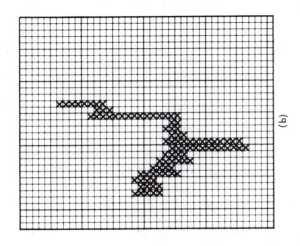

(b)

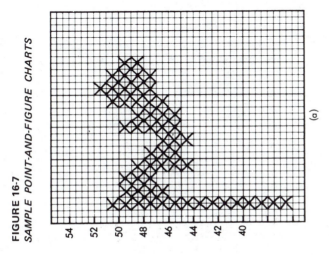

(a)

Over the years, point-and-figure adherents have observed various formations that occur before major price movements. One such formation, for example, is the *triple top*, as illustrated in Figure 16-7(b). A triple top occurs when a stock reaches its third consecutive high at the same price level. A buy signal is given when the stock surpasses the third high. A time element should be noted somewhere on the chart for each high, since the shorter the period from the first to the third high, the greater the underlying strength.[4]

Another key formation to point-and-figure chartists is the *congestion area*. A congestion area is formed on the chart by the lateral movement of X's. This comes about by a series of brief rallies and reversals, such as in Figure 16-7(a), that preclude the establishment of lengthy vertical columns. The width of the congestion area gives the technician some insight into the probable size and direction of a move by the stock to a "price target." Unfortunately, it is difficult to pinpoint when this target will be hit.[5]

A substantial number of patterns and corresponding rules have been developed by point-and-figure proponents over the years. These patterns can take considerable periods of time to evolve on the chart, particularly when large plotting increments (several points) and reversal spreads are used. To the extent that large numbers of investors adhere to the basic tenets of point-and-figure charting, the prophesies of the charts may very well be self-fulfilling. Figure 16-7(c) contains a chart of McDonald's Corp. from the Chartcraft service.

BAR CHARTING

Point-and-figure charts have a measure scale only on the vertical axis (no time dimension). Bar charts contain measures on both axes—price on the vertical axis, and time on the horizontal axis. The horizontal axis can be marked off in any dimension the analyst wishes—days, weeks, or months. On bar charts, rather than just plotting a point on the graph at a point in time, the analyst plots a vertical line to represent the range of prices of the stock during the period. That is, if the analyst were plotting daily data, the top of the vertical line would represent the high price of the stock during the day, and the bottom of the line would represent the low price of the stock during the same day. A small horizontal line is drawn across the bar to denote the closing price at the end of the time period. Generally, bar charts contain, at the bottom, volume information for the same period that the price information covers. The *Wall Street Journal* publishes bar charts of the three Dow Jones Averages—industrials, transportation, and utilities—each day.

Bar chartists, like point-and-figure chartists, have found key patterns to look for in determining the most probable price action of a stock. Typical patterns are illustrated in Figures 16-8 and 16-9. Figure 16-9 (p. 472) contains interpretations of certain of these patterns.

Figure 16-10(a) presents a bar chart for McDonald's from the Mansfield Stock Service. This service also provides bar charts of industry grouping. Figure 16-10(b) contains an explanation of the vast amount of information contained in the charts of this service. These figures are on page 473.

---

[4]See Ernest J. Staby, *Stock Market Trading* (New York: Cornerstone Library, 1970), pp. 28-30.

[5]Daniel Seligman, "The Mystique of Point-and-Figure," *Fortune*, 65, No. 3 (March 1962), 113-15 ff. See also Robert A. Levy, "The Predictive Significance of Five Point Chart Patterns," *Journal of Business*, July 1971.

FIGURE 16-8
TYPICAL GRAPHIC PATTERNS USED IN TECHNICAL MARKET ANALYSIS

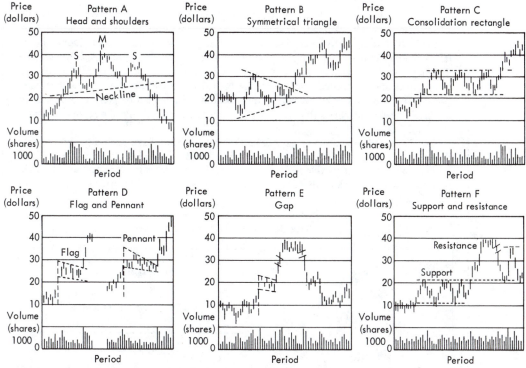

SOURCE: Sidney M. Robbins, *Managing Securities* (Boston: Houghton Mifflin, 1954), p. 502.

THE 200-DAY MOVING AVERAGE

One of the most reliable and easily read technical indicators available to investors is the 200-day moving average of a security. The technique for computing the average is simple. The closing prices of the stock market observation are added up for the most recent 200 days it has been traded. This sum is divided by 200. The objective is to obtain a relatively simple and smooth curve for the issue. Random variations and erratic price changes tend to cancel out, and a general underlying trend becomes visible. For those who see this as a maze of adding-machine tape, the entire process for 744 major issues can be obtained each week from the Trendline Market Service.

In his book, Joseph E. Granville listed eight basic rules for using the 200-day moving average, in a chapter on "The Grand Strategy of Stock Trading":

1. If the 200-day average line flattens out following a previous decline, or is advancing, and the price of the stock penetrates that average line on the upside, this comprises a major buying signal.

2. If the price of the stock falls below the 200-day moving average price while the average line is still rising, this is also considered to be a buying opportunity.

FIGURE 16-9
FIVE STANDARD CHART PATTERNS

MARKET EQUAL TO SUM OF ITS PARTS

In the fall of 1969, Alan R. Shaw, Harris, Upham & Company vice president, took on a herculean task. He wanted to examine the price behavior of all the stocks on the New York Stock Exchange to determine the technical position of each stock. Doing so, he felt, would enable him to get a picture of where the market stood. Accordingly, he designed five typical chart patterns which could best describe the price behavior of most stocks and proceeded to place all the N Y S E stocks into one of these five categories. Over a period of six weeks, all the stocks were arranged by pattern and listed in the firm's weekly market letter. (At the time, more stocks fell into the second category than in the others.)

The five patterns are shown and described below. They have been arranged so that the most vulnerable pattern with the least upside potential appears first. Then, progressing to more favorable patterns, the one most favorable is at the bottom. It should be noted that all stocks will usually fit one of these patterns no matter what kind of market we are in.

Five Standard Chart Patterns

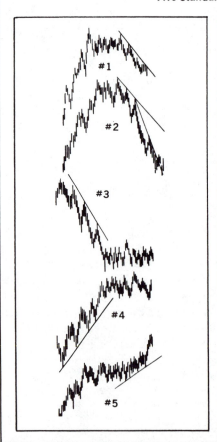

Chart Pattern #1

Stocks with vulnerable trends and/or possible downside potential.

Chart Pattern #2

Stocks with less vulnerability that appear to have reached possible lows, but need consolidation.

Chart Pattern #3

Stocks that have declined and experienced consolidation, and could do well in a favorable market.

Chart Pattern #4

Stocks that have performed relatively well but are currently in "neutral" trends.

Chart Pattern #5

Stocks in established uptrends and/or with possible upside potential.

SOURCE: Yale Hirsch, *The 1971 Stock Trader's Almanac* (Old Tappan, N.J.: The Hirsch Organization, 1970), p. 37.

FIGURE 16-10(a)
BAR CHART OF McDONALD'S CORPORATION STOCK

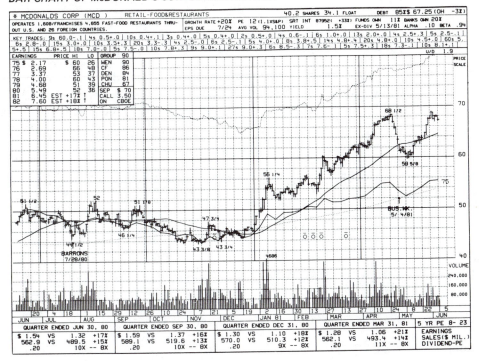

FIGURE 16-10(b)
INFORMATION CONTAINED IN MANSFIELD STOCK SERVICE CHARTS

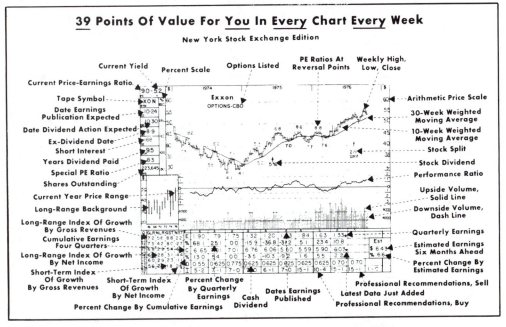

SOURCE: Mansfield Stock Chart Service, 26 Journal Square, Jersey City, NJ 07306.

3. If the stock price is above the 200-day line and is declining toward that line, fails to go through and starts to turn up again, this is a buying signal.
4. If the stock price falls too fast under the declining 200-day average line, it is entitled to an advance back toward the average line and the stock can be bought for this short-term technical rise.
5. If the 200-day average line flattens out following a previous rise, or is declining, and the price of the stock penetrates that line on the downside, this comprises a major sell signal.
6. If the price of the stock rises above the 200-day moving average price line while the average line is still falling, this also is considered to be a selling opportunity.
7. If the stock price is below the 200-day line and is advancing toward that line, fails to go through and starts to turn down again, this is a selling signal.
8. If the stock price advances too fast above the advancing 200-day average line, it is entitled to a reaction back toward the average line and the stock can be sold for this short-term technical reaction.[6]

Obviously, these rules are only a guideline to assist the analyst in using the 200-day moving average as an indicator for individual securities. For the person who is trading in speculative issues, the technique gives signals based on trends or changing trends in the price of the security in question. See Figure 16-11 for an example of this type of chart. Here the smooth line represents the 200-day moving average.

RELATIVE STRENGTH

A more recent approach to technical analysis of price has been proposed by Robert Levy.[7] His method is called *relative-strength analysis*. A basic tenet of this technique is that certain securities perform better than other securities in a given market environment and that this behavior will remain relatively constant over time. Generally, this technique is used in conjunction with either (1) the stocks of individual companies or industries or (2) portfolios consisting of stocks and bonds.

When the stock application is used, the analyst calculates ratios for the returns (over time) of the stock to those of its industry group, returns of the stock to those of the general market, and returns of the industry group to those of the general market.[8] These ratios are then plotted over time to see the relative strengths. Technicians using the relative-strength approach have observed that those firms and industries displaying greatest relative strength in good markets (bull) also show the greatest weakness in bad markets (bear). These "relatively strong" firms could well have high betas.

When the stock-bond approach is used, the analyst opts for a higher proportion of stocks in the portfolio (relative to bonds) as the market moves upward, and a higher proportion of bonds (relative to stocks) as the market moves downward. In other words, he selects the security type with the most relative strength in the prevailing market. Levy has tested this procedure of switching between stocks and bonds and has con-

[6]Joseph E. Granville, *A Strategy of Daily Stock Market Timing for Maximum Profit* (Englewood Cliffs, N.J.: Prentice-Hall, 1969), pp. 237-38.
[7]Robert A. Levy, "Relative Strength as a Criterion for Investment Selection," *Journal of Finance*, December 1967, pp. 595-610.
[8]Both Moody's and Standard & Poor's services provide industry averages that can be used to calculate industry performance.

FIGURE 16-11

SAMPLE 30-WEEK MOVING-AVERAGE STOCK CHART

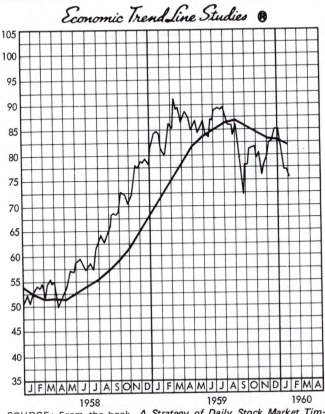

Economic TrendLine Studies ®

SOURCE: From the book, *A Strategy of Daily Stock Market Timing for Maximum Profit*, by Joseph E. Granville, © 1960 by Prentice-Hall, Inc. Published by Prentice-Hall, Inc., Englewood Cliffs, New Jersey.

cluded that the returns earned by a portfolio utilizing this technique outperform portfolios managed in a more naive manner—that is, by the "buy-and-hold strategy" of purchasing securities and then merely holding them regardless of any changes in the economic environment.[9]

Price-Volume Analysis Approaches

RESISTANCE-SUPPORT CHARTS

Earlier we discussed two well-known types of charts—point-and-figure and bar charts. There is a much newer variety of chart, whose avowed purpose is to detect resistance (areas of supply) as a stock's price goes up, and support (areas of demand) as a stock goes down. The chart is constructed to show, in a series of horizontal lines,

[9]Robert A Levy, "Random Walks: Reality or Myth," *Financial Analysts Journal*, November-December 1967, pp. 69-77.

the levels at which the stock in question has traded in the past. The levels are determined regardless of the volume at which the stock traded, but rather at those levels at which the stock traded most often—the more often, the longer the horizontal line. The hypothesis is that popular levels (longer lines) encountered by the stock in an upward move present resistance; and conversely, popular levels (longer lines) encountered by the stock in a downward move provide support. A specimen of this chart form is shown in Figure 16-12.

PRICE-VOLUME BAR CHARTING

When we discussed the role of bar charting, we saw that the emphasis of technicians using this chart form was generally on price behavior; however, we noted that volume information is often included on bar charts. Chartists, following the seminal Dow Theory, believe that volume goes with the price trend—that a volume increase with an upward move in prices is good, and a volume increase with a downward move in prices is bad. Furthermore, if volume decreases during a price drop, this is good (a drying up of supply), and if volume decreases during a price rise, this is bad (a drying up of demand). These statements represent traditional technical folklore. It would be interesting to test the statistical validity of these views.

Ying has conducted an empirical study of price-volume relationships. His results were:

1. A small volume is usually accompanied by a fall in price.
2. A large volume is usually accompanied by a rise in price.
3. A large increase in volume is usually accompanied by either a large rise in price or a large fall in price.
4. A large volume is usually followed by a rise in price.
5. If the volume has been decreasing consecutively for a period of five trading days, then there will be a tendency for the price to fall over the next four trading days.
6. If the volume has been increasing consecutively for a period of five trading days, then there will be a tendency for the price to rise over the next four trading days.[10]

Ying's conclusions seem to provide support for the traditionally held view, with one notable exception—number 5. That is, declining volume seems to be associated with price declines and thus would not be a bullish indicator.[11]

Other Tests, Conclusions, and Summary

A number of tests have been conducted to obtain statistically reliable estimates of the worth of various technical trading strategies. Many of these tests fall into a body of literature called the random-walk theory. These will be discussed in some detail in Chapter 17.

[10]Charles C. Ying, "Stock Market Prices and Volumes of Sales," *Econometrica*, July 1966, p. 676.

[11]We are aware of at least one trading system that refines the analysis even further. It looks at *each* transaction in the stock and weights the direction of price changes (upticks and downticks) between transactions by the number of round lots associated with the price change (trade).

FIGURE 16-12
SAMPLE RESISTANCE-SUPPORT CHARTS

NEW INVENTION: RESISTANCE & SUPPORT CHARTS

Basically, there are two kinds of stock charts in use today: the *bar chart* and the *point-and-figure chart*. The more widely known bar chart is a graphic representation on a grid, of a stock's past price action on either a daily, weekly or monthly basis. Vertical bars show a stock's high, low and closing prices. (Some charts may show closing prices only). The volume of shares traded also appears as vertical lines at the bottom of the chart. Chart services such as *Trendline* and *Mansfield* fall into this category.

P & F charts came into being about 75 years ago. Adherents to this system of charting ignore the elements of time and volume and concentrate solely on price action. These are the charts that show strange-looking columns of X's moving to the right, corresponding to prices marked along the side of the chart. A stock moving in price from $40 to $50 without changing directions would appear as a column of ten X's. On a subsequent decline to $45, five corresponding X's would be entered in the next column on the right, and so on. Two well known P & F chart services are *Paflibe* and *Chartcraft*.

Early in 1970, a new kind of chart was introduced by Chart Service Institute (450 New England Bldg., Winter Park, Florida 32789) headed by Samuel F. Sipe, creator of the new chart. Its name, *Resistance & Support Charts*, implies just what it attempts to do—show where a stock moving upward may meet resistance (supply) and where a declining stock may find support (demand). Here are several samples:

Sample Resistance & Support Charts

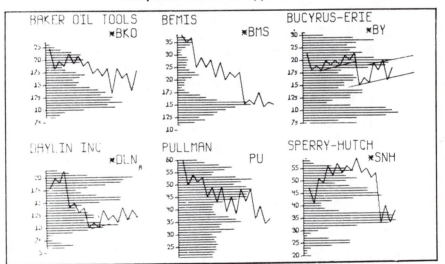

Many years of each stock's price movements were fed into a computer. The resulting horizontal lines drawn by the computer show at what levels in the past the stock has traded most often—irrespective of time and the volume of shares traded. Short lines, little activity; longer lines, greater activity. Superimposed over the horizontal lines is a graph of the stock's most recent action with little wiggles eliminated.

In theory, a stock might decline more swiftly through the shorter lines—where few investment decisions were made in the past—and find support at a cluster of long lines —where many investment decisions were made and may be made again. Conversely, a rising stock might move up through an area of short lines quite handily till it bumped into a "ceiling" of resistance at a group of long lines.

The charts appear to be useful by themselves. They could also serve as an adjunct to the other two kinds of charts. They are worth investigating.

SOURCE: Yale Hirsch, *The 1971 Stock Traders Almanac* (Old Tappan, N.J.: The Hirsch Organization, 1970), p. 25.

Here we will report in a general fashion their key conclusions.[12] First, with respect to tests of mechanical trading rules (procedures that are strictly followed regardless of economic circumstances) and price-volume relationships, the results have been inconclusive because of different findings of different researchers using different procedures and different samples. Attempts to reconcile these differences have been difficult. Tests of possible relationships between price and short interests have been more conclusive. Generally, no significant relationship between stock prices and short interests were found. Finally, tests of odd-lot and advance-decline theories have detected very tentative and unconvincing results regarding their validity. Thus, in summary, these tests have given less than overwhelming support to the various technical theories examined to date, while at the same time not supporting random walk unequivocally.[13] There are several reasons for this.

First, some have questioned whether the tests have been performed on technical theories as they are actually used in practice.[14] To the extent that the tests accurately reflect the practice, the results may have some meaning. To the extent that they do not, the results and their implications are of dubious value. Second, only selected phases of technical analysis have been rigorously tested, and then only one at a time. It is possible that yet untested technical procedures will prove to have greater usefulness than those already examined. Furthermore, technicians very infrequently use only one indicator at a time, but rather use several in conjunction with one another.[15] Thus it is possible that tools found lacking when tested one at a time are useful when combined. This has not yet been empirically investigated. Random-walk theorists, however, feel that they have gathered sufficient evidence to relegate technical analysis to a position comparable to reading a crystal ball.

Questions and Problems

1. Explain the relationship of a basic law of economics and an underlying premise of technical analysis.

2. Dr. Knowitall of the Psychology Department at a large midwestern university claims he has a sound theoretical argument in favor of technical analysis. What do you think that argument is?

3. Assume that you are a statistician. Like every good statistician, you are extremely concerned with good sampling techniques. Comment on technical analysis from this point of view.

---

[12]This section draws heavily from a fine, nonmathematical review of tests of technical analysis by George E. Pinches, "The Random Walk Hypothesis and Technical Analysis," *Financial Analysts Journal*, March-April, 1970, pp. 104-10.

[13]Technical analysis should be thought of as an adjunct to fundamental analysis, not as its replacement.

[14]It should be pointed out that the same technical theories are often applied differently by different technical analysts. Therefore the success of the strategy is often dependent on the man rather than the method alone.

[15]Commercial investment services exist which combine numerous technical indicators into a composite index or diffusion index. There are problems, however, such as which indicators to select, how to combine them, and then how to weight them in the index. Finally, the validity of the index needs to be tested.

4. Since you are the top technical analyst in your firm, your boss has turned to you for an answer to a difficult question. He wants to know which one single indicator you think is the best, and why you think so. What is your answer?

5. What is the alleged purpose of technical market indicators? Why is this important?

6. What is meant by "breadth of the market"? How is it measured?

7. Explain (a) the logic behind, and (b) the method of measuring, either Barron's confidence indicator or odd-lot trading.

8. If short selling indicates that the investor expects the price of the shorted security to decline, why does the technician become optimistic as the short interest goes up?

9. What is the basic premise of analysts who use the odd-lot trading index?

10. If a stock sells for 60 and moves in the following pattern over a ten-day period—60, 60 1/4, 60 3/4, 60 1/2, 61, 61 1/2, 63, 62 1/4, 61 3/4, 60 1/2—how many X's would be plotted if the investor used point-and-figure charting with a one-point chart and a three-point reversal spread?

11. If the investor used bar charting and the data in Question 10, how many bars would there be in his chart? Why is this different from the number of X's in Question 10?

12. Compare and contrast bar charting and point-and-figure charting.

13. What general price-volume relationships do researchers use to predict the trend of the market?

14. What implications, if any, do Levy's findings using the relative-strength criterion have for a buy-and-hold strategy?

15. Suppose that the stock market has been declining. A technician is looking for signs of an upturn in the market. What sorts of reading should he or she be expecting from (a) breadth of the market, (b) volume of trading, (c) odd-lot trading, (d) short selling?

16. Why do technicians feel that past price movements are useful in predicting future price movements?

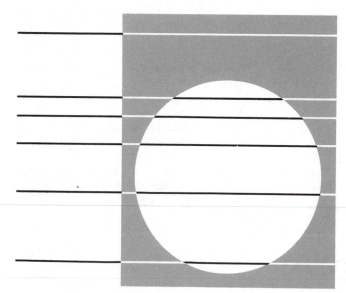

SEVENTEEN

Efficient
Market Theory

The primary aim of the text thus far has been to systematize the vast amount of publicly available information, both objective fact and subjective feeling, into a valuation framework so that one can reach a buy, sell, or hold decision. The methodology employed up until the preceding chapter is generally categorized as fundamental analysis, or fundamentalism. The more mystical approach discussed in Chapter 16 is called technical analysis. Our objective in this chapter is to review briefly these two approaches and then present yet a third theory to stock price behavior, one that had its origin in a voluminous body of literature generally lumped together under the label of the theory of random walk. In the process, we will explore this theory and explain the various statistical measures that have been employed to test its appropriateness or inappropriateness. Finally, we will discuss implications of random walk for both fundamental and technical analysis.

Fundamental and Technical Analysis

The reader will recall that in the fundamental approach, the security analyst or prospective investor is primarily interested in analyzing factors such as economic influences, industry factors, and pertinent company information such as product demand, earnings, dividends, and management, in order to calculate an intrinsic value for the firm's securities. He reaches an investment decision by comparing this value with the current market price of the security.

Technical analysts, or chartists, as they are commonly called, believe that they can discern patterns in price or volume movements, and that by observing and studying the past behavior patterns of given stocks, they can use this accumulated historical information to predict the future price movements in the security. Technical analysis, as we observed in the preceding chapter, comprises many different subjective approaches, but all have one thing in common—a belief that these past movements are very useful in predicting future movements.[1]

In essence, the technician says that it is somewhat an exercise in futility to evaluate accurately a myriad of detailed information as the fundamentalist attempts to do. He chooses not to engage in this type of activity, but rather to allow others to do it for him. Thus, after numerous analysts and investors evaluate this mountain of knowledge, their undoubtedly diverse opinions will be manifested in the price and volume activity of the shares in question. As this occurs, the technician acts solely on the basis of that price and volume activity, without cluttering his mind with all the detail that he feels is super-fluous to his analysis. He also believes that his price and volume analysis incorporates one factor that is not explicitly incorporated in the fundamentalist approach—namely, the psychology of the market.

Random Walk

Can a series of historical stock prices or rates of return be an aid in predicting future stock prices or rates of return? This, in effect, is the question posed by the random-walk theory.

The empirical evidence in the random-walk literature existed before the theory was established. That is to say, empirical results were discovered first, and then an attempt was made to develop a theory that could possibly explain the results. After these initial occurrences, more results and more theory were uncovered. This has led then to a diversity of theories, which are generically called the theory of random walk.

A good deal of confusion resulted from the diversity of the literature; and only recently has there been some clarification of the proliferation of empirical results and theories.[2] Our purpose here is to discuss briefly the substantive differences among these theories; however, in the rest of this chapter, we will not be concerned with these distinc-tions, but rather we will deal with an impressionistic stereotype that will represent the substance if not the detail of this random walk model, perhaps more properly called the efficient market model.

[1] The reader is encouraged to read, for an excellent treatment of the bar-chart and the point-and-figure approaches to technical analysis, Daniel Seligman's two excellent and somewhat cynical articles, "Playing the Market with Charts," *Fortune*, 65, No. 2 (February 1962), 118, and "The Mys-tique of Point-and-Figure," *Fortune*, 65, No. 3 (March 1962), 113.

[2] Much of the material in this section was adapted from Eugene F. Fama, "Efficient Capital Mar-kets: A Review of Theory and Empirical Work," *Journal of Finance*, 25, No. 2 (May 1970), 383-417; and Eugene F. Fama, "Random Walks in Stock Market Prices," *Financial Analysts Journal*, 21, No. 5 (September-October 1965), 55-59.

It is advantageous to view the random-walk model or hypothesis as a special case of the more general efficient market model or hypothesis. In fact, one might more readily understand the distinctions and variations of the various forms of the more general efficient market hypothesis by viewing this hypothesis and its variations as lying on a continuum, with the so-called random-walk model at one end. In the following paragraphs we will briefly consider the three generally discussed forms of the efficient market hypothesis—namely, the weak form of the efficient market hypothesis, the semistrong form, and the strong form.

Weak Form

The weak form says that the current prices of stocks already fully reflect all the information that is contained in the historical sequence of prices. Therefore, there is no benefit—as far as forecasting the future is concerned—in examining the historical sequence of prices. This weak form of the efficient market hypothesis is popularly known as the random-walk theory. Clearly, if this weak form of the efficient market hypothesis is true, it is a *direct* repudiation of technical analysis. If there is no value in studying past prices and past price changes, there is no value in technical analysis. As we saw in the preceding chapter, however, technicians place considerable reliance on the charts of historical prices that they maintain even though the efficient market hypothesis refutes this practice.

In later sections of this chapter we will analyze statistical investigations of this weak form of the efficient market hypothesis.

Semistrong Form

The semistrong form of the efficient market hypothesis says that current prices of stocks not only reflect all informational content of historical prices but also reflect all *publicly available knowledge* about the corporations being studied. Furthermore, the semistrong form says that efforts by analysts and investors to acquire and analyze public information will not yield consistently superior returns to the analyst. Examples of the type of public information that will not be of value on a consistent basis to the analyst are corporate reports, corporate announcements, information relating to corporate dividend policy, forthcoming stock splits, and so forth.

In effect, the semistrong form of the efficient market hypothesis maintains that as soon as information becomes publicly available, it is absorbed and reflected in stock prices. Even if this adjustment is not the correct one immediately, it will in a very short time be properly analyzed by the market. Thus, the analyst would have great difficulty trying to profit using fundamental analysis. Furthermore, even while the correct adjustment is taking place, it will not be possible for the analyst to obtain superior returns on a consistent basis. Why? Because the incorrect adjustments will not take place in a consistent manner. That is, sometimes the adjustments will be overadjustments and sometimes they will be underadjustments. Therefore, an analyst will not be able to develop a trading strategy based on these quick adjustments to new publicly available information.

Tests of the semistrong form of the efficient market hypothesis have tended (but not unanimously) to provide support for the hypothesis.[3] More on these tests will be discussed in a later section of the chapter.

Strong Form

To review briefly, we have seen that the weak form of the efficient market hypothesis maintains that past prices and past price changes cannot be used to forecast future price changes and future prices. In the paragraphs that follow we will review many of the tests that have been conducted to test the *weak* form of the efficient market hypothesis, more commonly known as the random-walk theory. We have examined the semistrong form of the efficient market hypothesis, which says that publicly available information cannot be used consistently to earn superior investment returns. Several studies that tend to support the semistrong theory of the efficient market hypothesis were cited. Finally, the strong form of the efficient market hypothesis maintains that not only is publicly available information useless to the investor or analyst but *all information* is useless. Specifically, no information that is available, be it public or "inside," can be used to consistently earn superior investment returns.

The semistrong form of the efficient market hypothesis could only be tested indirectly—namely, by testing what happened to prices on days surrounding announcements, of various types, such as earnings announcement, dividend announcements, and stock split announcements. To test the strong form of efficient market hypothesis, even more indirect methods must be used. For the strong form, as has already been mentioned, says that no type of information is useful. This implies that not even security analysts and portfolio managers who have access to information more quickly than the general investing public are able to use this information to earn superior returns. Therefore, many of the tests of the *strong* form of the efficient market hypothesis deal with tests of *mutual-fund performance*. Shortly, we will review some of the findings of these tests of mutual-fund performance and in Chapter 21 we will examine them in greater depth.

Tests of the trading of specialists on the floor of the stock exchanges and tests of the profitability of insider trading suggest that the possibility of excess profits exists for these two very special groups of investors who can use their special information to earn profits in excess of normal returns.[4]

The strict form of the efficient market hypothesis states that two conditions are met: first, that successive price changes or changes in return are independent; and second,

---

[3]See, for example, Eugene F. Fama et al., "The Adjustment of Stock Prices to New Information," *International Economic Review,* 10, No. 1 (February 1969), 1-21. Also see Myron S. Scholes, "The Market for Securities: Substitution vs. Price Pressure and the Effects of Information on Share Prices," *Journal of Business,* 45, No. 2 (April 1972), 179-211; Ray Ball and Phillip Brown, "An Empirical Evaluation of Accounting Income Numbers," *Journal of Accounting Research,* 6 (Autumn 1968), 159-78; and Ronald J. Jordan, "An Empirical Investigation of the Adjustment of Stock Prices to New Quarterly Earnings Information," *Journal of Financial and Quantitative Analysis,* 7, No. 4 (September 1973), 609-20.

[4]See James H. Lorie and Victor Niederhoffer, "Predictive and Statistical Properties of Insider Trading," *Journal of Law and Economics,* 11 (1968), 35-53; and Scholes, "Market for Securities." It should be emphasized that these two examples of market inefficiencies represent very minor inefficiencies when compared with the market as a whole.

that these successive price changes or return changes are identically distributed—that is, these distributions will repeat themselves over time. In a practical sense, this seems to imply that in a random-walk world, stock prices will at any time fully reflect all publicly available information, and furthermore, that when new information becomes available, stock prices will instantaneously adjust to reflect it. The reader will note that the random-walk theorist is not interested in price or return levels, but rather in the changes between successive levels.[5]

The more general efficient market model, when interpreted loosely, acknowledges that the markets may have some imperfections, such as transactions costs, information costs, and delays in getting pertinent information to all market participants; but it states that these potential sources of market inefficiency do not exist to such a degree that it is possible to develop trading systems whose expected profits or returns will be in excess of expected normal, equilibrium returns or profits. Generally, we define *equilibrium profits* as those that can be earned by following a simple buy-and-hold strategy rather than a more complex, mechanical system.[6] Thus, we see that the random-walk model represents a special, restrictive case of the efficient market model.

The Efficient Market Hypothesis and Mutual-Fund Performance

It has often been said that large investors such as mutual funds perform better in the market than the small investor does because they have access to better information. Therefore, it would be interesting to observe if mutual funds earned above-average returns, where these are defined as returns in excess of those that can be earned by a simple buy-and-hold strategy. The results of such an investigation would have interesting implications for the efficient market hypothesis.

As we shall see in Chapter 21, researchers have found that mutual funds do not seem to be able to earn greater net returns (after sales expenses) than those that can be earned by investing randomly in a large group of securities and holding them. Furthermore, these studies indicate, mutual funds are not even able to earn *gross* returns (before sales expenses) superior to those of the naive buy-and-hold strategy. These results occur not only because of the difficulty in applying fundamental analysis in a consistently superior manner to a large number of securities in an efficient market but also because of portfolio overdiversification and its attendant problems—two of which are high bookkeeping and administrative costs to monitor the investments, and purchase of securities with less favorable risk-return characteristics. Therefore, it would seem that the mutual fund studies lend some credence to the efficient market hypothesis.

Empirical Tests of the Weak Form

Over the years an impressive literature has been developed describing empirical tests of random walk.[7] This research has been aimed at testing whether successive or lagged price changes are independent. In this section we will review briefly some of the

---

[5]Often one will read in the random-walk literature of percentage changes in the prices or returns themselves.

[6]We will defer our discussion of such mechanical systems to a later section of this chapter.

[7]For an excellent collection of many of the early random-walk studies, see Paul H. Cootner, ed., *The Random Character of Stock Market Prices* (Cambridge, Mass.: MIT Press, 1967).

major categories of statistical techniques that have been employed in this research, and we will summarize their major conclusions. These techniques generally fall into two categories: those that test for trends in stock prices and thus infer whether profitable trading systems could be developed, and those that test such mechanical systems directly.

SIMULATION TESTS

Note Figures 17-1 and 17-2. These graphs were produced a few years ago as part of an interesting experiment performed by Harry Roberts. The essence of this experiment was to examine the appearance of the actual level of the Dow Jones index expressed both in levels and in terms of weekly changes, and to compare these graphs with a simulated set of graphs.[8] A series of price changes was generated from random-number tables and then these changes were converted to graphs (on pages 486, 487, and 488) depicting levels of the simulated Dow Jones index.

The reader will note the similarity between panels (a) and (b) of Figure 17-1, and also the similarity between panels (a) and (b) of Figure 17-2. Both figures reveal the "head-and-shoulders" pattern that is often referred to in the chartist literature. Since these very similar patterns were observed, between the actual and the simulated series, the inference is that the actual results may well be the result of random stock price movements.

SERIAL-CORRELATION TESTS

Since the random-walk theory is interested in testing for independence between successive price changes, correlation tests are particularly appropriate. These tests check to determine if price changes or proportionate price changes in some future period are related. For example, we are interested in seeing if price changes in a period $t + 1$ are correlated to price changes in the preceding period, period t. If in fact price changes are correlated, points plotted on a graph will tend to lie along a straight line. Figure 17-3(a) and (b) depict such a relationship. Figure 17-3(a) implies that, on average, a price rise in period t is followed by a price rise in period $t + 1$; Figure 17-3(b) implies that, on average, a price decline in period $t + 1$ follows a price rise in period t; the former, then, implies a correlation coefficient of close to +1, the latter a correlation coefficient of close to −1. Figure 17-3(c), which does not appear to demonstrate any linear relationship in the scatter diagram, implies close to a zero correlation coefficient. In other words, the correlation coefficient can take on a value ranging from −1 to +1; a positive number indicates a direct correlation, a negative value implies an inverse relationship, and a value close to zero implies no relationship. Figure 17-3 is on page 490.

[8]Harry Roberts, "Stock Market Patterns and Financial Analysis: Methodological Suggestions," *Journal of Finance*, March 1959, pp. 1-10.

FIGURE 17-1

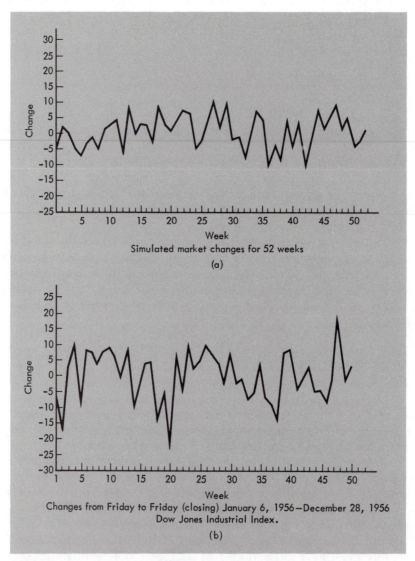

Simulated market changes for 52 weeks

(a)

Changes from Friday to Friday (closing) January 6, 1956—December 28, 1956
Dow Jones Industrial Index.

(b)

SOURCE: Harry Roberts, "Stock Market Patterns and Financial Analysis: Methodological Suggestions," *Journal of Finance*, March 1959. Reprinted from *An Introduction to Risk and Return from Common Stocks* by Richard A. Brealey by
permission of the MIT Press, Cambridge, Massachusetts. Copyright 1969 by the
Massachusetts Institute of Technology.

Table 17-1 reports the findings of one such test of serial correlation. As can be seen
in this table, no large departure from zero was found in these particular serial and lagged
serial correlation coefficients in daily prices of the Dow Jones stocks. Similar results
have been found using series of commodity prices, other individual stocks' prices, and
price indexes.

FIGURE 17-2(a)
SIMULATED AND ACTUAL MARKET LEVELS

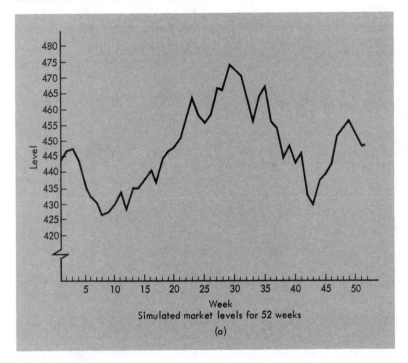

Simulated market levels for 52 weeks

(a)

RUNS TESTS

There is a potential problem, however, when one uses a correlation coefficient to evaluate the possibility of independence in a particular series. This problem arises because correlation coefficients can be dominated by extreme values. That is, an extremely large or extremely low value or two in the series can unduly influence the results of the calculation used to determine the correlation coefficient. To overcome this possible shortcoming, some researchers have employed the runs test.

Runs tests ignore the absolute values of the numbers in the series and observe only their sign. The researchers then merely count the number of runs—consecutive sequences of signs—in the same direction. For example, the sequence ———+0+ has four runs. Next, the actual number of runs observed is compared with the number that are to be expected from a series of randomly generated price changes. It has been found that when this is done, no significant differences are observed. These results further strengthen the random-walk hypothesis.

FILTER TESTS

The empirical tests of random walk we have examined thus far have been aimed at testing directly whether successive price or return changes are in fact independent— or in statistical terms, that their serial-correlation coefficients are not statistically signifi-

FIGURE 17-2 (b)
SIMULATED AND ACTUAL MARKET LEVELS

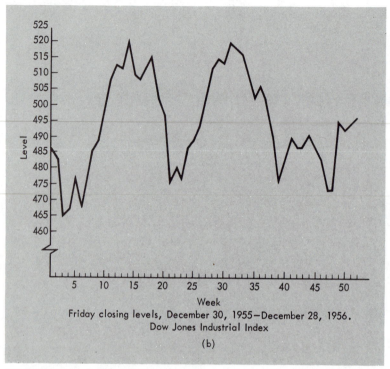

Friday closing levels, December 30, 1955–December 28, 1956.
Dow Jones Industrial Index

(b)

SOURCE: Harry Roberts, "Stock Market Patterns and Financial Analysis: Methodological Suggestions," *Journal of Finance*, March 1959. Reprinted from *An Introduction to Risk and Return from Common Stocks* by Richard A. Brealey by
permission of the MIT Press, Cambridge, Massachusetts. Copyright 1969 by the
Massachusetts Institute of Technology.

cantly different from zero. If this is so, then an inference can be made that stock price
changes appear to be random, and therefore it would be extremely difficult to develop
successful mechanical trading systems. Now we will discuss briefly another set of tests
that examine the random-walk hypothesis from a different, but more direct, approach.
Categorized as filter tests, they have been developed as direct tests of specific mechanical
trading strategies. In other words, no inferences about such strategies need be made, for
the approach is to examine directly the validity of specific systems.

One such test is based on the premise that once a movement in price has surpassed
a given percentage movement, the security's price will continue to move in the same
direction. Thus the following rule, which is similar to the famous Dow Theory:

If the daily closing price of a security moves up at least X%, buy the security
until its price moves down at least X% from a subsequent high, at which time
simultaneously sell and go short. The short position should be maintained

FIGURE 17-3
SCATTER DIAGRAMS TO "OBSERVE" CORRELATION

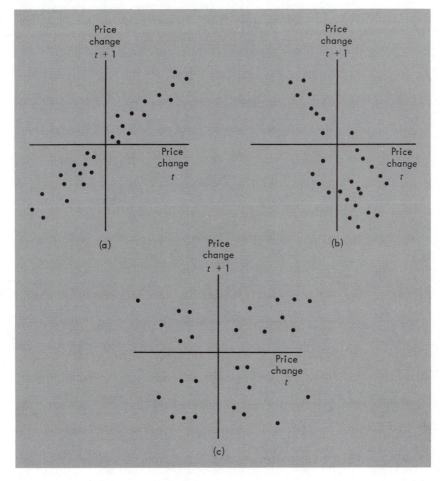

until the price rises at least X% above a subsequent low, at which time cover and buy.[9]

As the reader has undoubtedly observed, the selection of a high filter will cut down his number of transactions and will lead to fewer false starts or signals, but it will also decrease his potential profit because he would have missed the initial portion of the move. Conversely, the selection of a smaller filter will ensure his sharing in the great bulk of the security's price movement, but he will have the disadvantage of performing many

[9]R.A. Brealey, *An Introduction to Risk and Return from Common Stocks* (Cambridge, Mass.: MIT Press, 1969), p. 25. Adapted from Eugene F. Fama and Marshal E. Blume, "Filter Rules and Stock Market Trading," *Journal of Business,* 39 (January 1966), 226-41.

TABLE 17-1

CORRELATION COEFFICIENTS BETWEEN DAILY PRICE CHANGES
AND LAGGED PRICE CHANGES FOR EACH OF THE DOW JONES STOCKS

Stocks	Lag (days)									
	1	2	3	4	5	6	7	8	9	10
Allied Ch	.02	−.04	.01	−.00	.03	.00	−.02	−.03	−.02	−.01
Alcoa	.12	.04	−.01	.02	−.02	.01	.02	.01	−.00	−.03
Am Can	−.09	−.02	.03	−.07	−.02	−.01	.02	.03	−.05	−.04
Am T&T	−.04	−.10	.00	.03	.01	−.01	.00	.03	−.01	.01
Am Tob	.11	−.11	−.06	−.07	.01	−.01	.01	.05	.04	.04
Anacond	.07	−.06	−.05	−.00	.00	−.04	.01	.02	−.01	−.06
Beth Stl	.01	−.07	.01	.02	−.05	−.10	−.01	.00	−.00	−.02
Chrysler	.01	−.07	−.02	−.01	−.02	.01	.04	.06	−.04	.02
duPont	.01	−.03	.06	.03	−.00	−.05	.02	.01	−.03	.00
E Kodak	.03	.01	−.03	.01	−.02	.01	.01	.01	.01	.00
Gen Elec	.01	−.04	−.02	.03	−.00	.00	−.01	.01	−.00	.01
Gen Fds	.06	−.00	.05	.00	−.02	−.05	−.01	−.01	−.02	−.02
Gen Mot	−.00	−.06	−.04	−.01	−.04	.01	.02	.01	−.02	.01
Goodyr	−.12	.02	−.04	.04	−.00	−.00	.04	.01	−.02	.01
Int Harv	−.02	−.03	−.03	.04	−.05	−.02	−.00	.00	−.05	−.02
Int Nick	.10	−.03	−.02	.02	.03	.06	−.04	−.01	−.02	.03
Int Pap	.05	−.01	−.06	.05	.05	−.00	−.03	−.02	−.00	−.02
Johns Man	.01	−.04	−.03	−.02	−.03	−.08	.04	.02	−.04	.03
Owens Ill	−.02	−.08	−.05	.07	.09	−.04	.01	−.04	.07	−.04
Proct G	.10	−.01	−.01	.01	−.02	.02	.01	−.01	−.02	−.02
Sears Ro	.10	.03	.03	.03	.01	−.05	−.01	−.01	−.01	−.01
St Oil Cal	.03	−.03	−.05	−.03	−.05	−.03	−.01	.07	−.05	−.04
St Oil NJ	.01	−.12	.02	.01	−.05	−.02	−.02	−.03	−.07	.08
Swift Co	−.00	−.02	−.01	.01	.06	.01	−.04	.01	.01	.00
Texaco	.09	−.05	−.02	−.02	−.02	−.01	.03	.03	−.01	.01
Un Carbide	.11	−.01	.04	.05	−.04	−.03	.00	−.01	−.05	−.04
Unit Aire	.01	−.03	−.02	−.05	−.07	−.05	.05	.04	.02	−.02
US Steel	.04	−.07	.01	.01	−.01	−.02	.04	.04	−.02	−.04
Westg El	−.03	−.02	−.04	−.00	.00	−.05	−.02	.01	−.01	.01
Woolworth	.03	−.02	.02	.01	.01	−.04	−.01	.00	−.09	−.01
Averages	.03	−.04	−.01	.01	−.01	−.02	.00	.01	−.02	−.01

SOURCE: R. Brealey, *An Introduction to Risk and Return from Common Stock*
(Cambridge, Mass.: MIT Press, 1969), p. 13, from Eugene F. Fama, "The Behavior of
Stock Market Prices," *Journal of Business*, January 1965, pp. 34-105.

transactions, with their accompanying high costs, as well as often operating on false signals.

As Table 17-2 shows, only when the filter was at its smallest did this mechanical procedure outperform a simple buy-and-hold strategy, and even then, only before transactions costs were considered. Similar tests of various other trading systems have yielded similar results, thus giving additional validity to the random-walk hypothesis.

DISTRIBUTION PATTERNS

It is a rule of statistics that the sum or the distribution of random occurrences will conform to a normal distribution. Thus, if proportionate price changes are randomly generated events, then their distribution should be approximately normal. When such a

TABLE 17-2

AVERAGE ANNUAL RATES OF RETURN PER STOCK

Value of x (%)	Return with Trading Strategy (%)	Return with Buy-and-Hold Strategy (%)	Total Transactions with Trading Strategy	Return with Trading Strategy, After Commissions (%)
0.5	11.5	10.4	12,514	−103.6
1.0	5.5	10.3	8,660	−74.9
2.0	0.2	10.3	4,784	−45.2
3.0	−1.7	10.3	2,994	−30.5
4.0	0.1	10.1	2,013	−19.5
5.0	−1.9	10.0	1,484	−16.6
6.0	1.3	9.7	1,071	−9.4
7.0	0.8	9.6	828	−7.4
8.0	1.7	9.6	653	−5.0
9.0	1.9	9.6	539	−3.6
10.0	3.0	9.3	435	−1.4
12.0	5.3	9.4	289	2.3
14.0	3.9	10.3	224	1.4
16.0	4.2	10.3	172	2.3
18.0	3.6	10.0	139	2.0
20.0	4.3	9.8	110	3.0

SOURCE: R.A. Brealey, *An Introduction to Risk and Return from Common Stocks* (Cambridge, Mass.: MIT Press, 1969). From Eugene F. Fama and Marshal E. Blume, "Filter Rules and Stock Market Trading," *Journal of Business*, January 1966, pp. 226-41.

test was conducted, only very slight deviations from normality were noted.[10] See Figure 17-4 for verification of this point. The differences, as can be seen, are, first, the appearance of a greater than normal number of extremely large and extremely small values; and second; a more peaked distribution—that is, a deficiency of medium-sized changes. This type of distribution is a member of the stable Paretian family. Generally, the small differences between these two distributions are overlooked in empirical work.

Empirical Tests of the Semistrong Form

As has already been stated, the semistrong form says that current stock prices will instantaneously reflect all publicly available information. The tests that will be summarized briefly in this section test whether in fact all publicly available information and news announcements, such as quarterly earnings reports, changes in accounting information, stocks splits, stock dividends, and the like, are quickly and adequately reflected in stock prices. Furthermore, these tests attempt to analyze if an analyst using such data when they become available to him can successfully use this information to obtain superior investment results. Fama, Fisher, Jensen, and Roll made a major contribution with their study of the semistrong-form hypothesis.[11] They tested the speed of the

[10]Eugene F. Fama, "The Behavior of Stock Market Prices," *Journal of Business*, 38 (January 1965), 34-105.

[11]Eugene F. Fama *et al.*, "The Adjustment of Stock Prices to New Information," *International Economic Review*, 10, No. 1 (February 1969), 1-21.

FIGURE 17-4
*DISTRUBUTIONS OF DAILY PRICE CHANGES OF SIX STOCKS,
SUPERIMPOSED ON A NORMAL DISTRIBUTION*

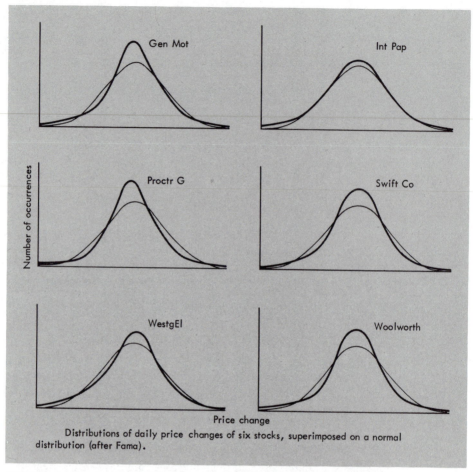

Distributions of daily price changes of six stocks, superimposed on a normal distribution (after Fama).

SOURCE: Eugene F. Fama, "The Behavior of Stock Market Prices," *Journal of Business*, January 1965, pp. 34-105. Reprinted from *An Introduction to Risk and Return from Common Stocks* by Richard A. Brealey by permission of the MIT Press, Cambridge, Massachusetts. Copyright 1969 by the Massachusetts Institute of Technology.

market's reaction to a firm's announcement of a stock split and the accompanying information with respect to a change in dividend policy. The authors concluded that the market was efficient with respect to its reaction to information on the stock split and also was efficient with respect to reacting to the informational content of stock splits vis-à-vis changes in dividend policy.

Ball and Brown conducted another test in this area by analyzing the stock market's ability to absorb the informational content of reported annual earnings per share information. In their study the authors examined stock price movements of companies that experienced "good" earnings reports as opposed to the stock price movements of companies that experienced "bad" earnings reports. A "good" earnings report was a reported earnings per share figure which was higher than the previously forecast earnings per share, and conversely a "bad" earnings report was a report which reported lower earnings per share than had been forecast previously. They found that those companies with "good" earnings reports experienced price increases in their stock and those with "bad" earnings reports experienced stock price declines. The interesting result was that about 85 percent of the informational content of the annual earnings announcement was reflected in stock price movements prior to the release of the actual annual earnings figure.[12]

Joy, Litzenberger, and McEnally conducted another stock price-earnings report test in this area. In their study the authors tested the impact of quarterly earnings announcements on the stock price adjustment mechanism. Some of their results somewhat contradicted the semistrong form of the efficient market hypothesis. In some of their subtests, the authors found that favorable information contained in published quarterly earnings reports was not instantaneously reflected in stock prices.[13]

A final test which we will review of the semistrong form was a study conducted by Basu.[14] In his study, Basu tested for the informational content of the price-earnings multiple. He tested to see whether low P/E stocks tended to outperform stocks with high P/E ratios. If historical P/E ratios provided useful information to investors in obtaining superior stock market returns, this would be a refutation of the semistrong form of the efficient market hypothesis. Because if historical publicly available P/E information led an investor to buy a particular type of stock and this in turn led to abnormal returns, this would be a direct contradiction of the semistrong form. His results indicated that the low P/E portfolios experienced superior returns relative to the market and high P/E portfolios performed in an inferior manner relative to the overall market.

By way of summary, then, of the semistrong efficient tests which we have reviewed here, the great majority provide strong empirical support for the hypothesis; however, there have been some notable exceptions to this support. Most of the reported results demonstrate that stock prices do adjust rapidly to announcements of new information about stocks. Some of the studies indicate further that investors are typically unable to utilize this information to earn consistently above-average returns.

What the Random-Walk Model Says

Our generalization of the random-walk model, then, says that previous price changes or changes in return are useless in predicting future price or return changes. That is, if we attempt to predict future prices in absolute terms using only historical price-change information, we will not be successful.

Note that random walk says nothing more than that successive price changes are independent. This independence implies that prices at any time will on the average

[12]Ray Ball and Philip Brown, "An Empirical Evaluation of Accounting Income Numbers," *Journal of Accounting Research*, 6 (Autumn 1968), 159-78.

[13]O. Maurice Joy *et al.,* "The Adjustment of Stock Prices to Announcements of Unanticipated Changes in Quarterly Earnings," *Journal of Accounting Research*, 15 (Autumn 1977), 207-25.

[14]S. Basu, "The Investment Performance of Common Stocks in Relation to their Price-Earnings Ratios: A Test of the Efficient Market Hypothesis," *Journal of Finance*, 32 (June 1977), 663-82.

reflect the intrinsic value of the security. (Often the reader will find this intrinsic worth referred to as the present value of the stock's price, or its equilibrium value.) Furthermore, should a stock's price deviate from its intrinsic value because, among other things, different investors evaluate the available information differently or have different insights into future prospects of the firm, professional investors and astute nonprofessionals will seize upon the short-term or random deviations from the intrinsic value, and through their active buying-and-selling of the stock in question will force the price back to its equilibrium position.

What the Random-Walk Model Does Not Say

It is unfortunate that so many misconceptions of the random-walk model exist. It is, in point of fact, a very simple statement.[15]

The random-walk model says nothing about relative price movements—that is, about selecting securities that may or may not perform better than other securities. It says nothing about decomposing price movements into such factors as *market*, *industry*, or *firm* factors. Certainly, it is entirely possible to detect trends in stock prices after one has removed the general market influences or other influences; however, this in no way would refute the random-walk model, for after these influences have been removed, we will in fact be dealing with relative prices and not with absolute prices, which lie at the heart of the random-walk hypothesis. Furthermore, these "trends" provide no basis for forecasting the future.

In addition, it should be reemphasized that the empirical results came first, to be followed by theory to explain the results; therefore, discussions about a competitive market, or instantaneous adjustments to new information, or knowledgeable market participants, or easy access to markets, are all in reality not part of the random-walk model, but rather possible explanations of the results we find when performing our empirical investigations.

Also, there seems to be a misunderstanding by many to the effect that believing in random walk means that one must also believe that analyzing stocks, and consequently stock prices, is a useless exercise, for if indeed stock prices are random, there is no reason for them to go up or down over any period of time. This is very wrong. The random-walk hypothesis is entirely consistent with an upward or downward movement in price, for as we shall see, the hypothesis supports fundamental analysis and certainly does not attack it.

Implications of Random Walk for Technical and Fundamental Analysis

The random-walk theory is inconsistent with technical analysis, or chartism.[16] Whereas random walk states that successive price changes are independent, the chartists claim that they are dependent—that is, that the historical price behavior of the stock

[15]Material in this section is in part adapted from C. W. J. Granger, "What the Random Walk Model Does NOT Say," *Financial Analysts Journal*, May-June 1970, pp. 91-93.
[16]Specifically, random walk denies that a technical approach can be consistently successful over a long period of time.

will repeat itself into the future, and that by studying this past behavior the chartist can in fact predict the future. Random walk, through the statistical testing discussed earlier in this chapter, directly opposes this line of reasoning and relegates technical analysis to a curious position of mysticism, seemingly completely unfounded on any substantive facts. The technicians, however, deny the findings of researchers in this area by saying that the statistical procedures employed in the literature of the past were too simple to detect complex, historical price relationships.

The relationship between random walk and fundamental analysis is a bit more complex. First, random walk implies that short-run price changes are random about the true intrinsic value of the security. Thus we can see that it is the day-to-day or week-to-week price changes, and consequently return changes, that are random, and not the price levels themselves. Consequently, it is entirely possible while believing in random walk to believe also in the existence of an upward or downward drift in prices of individual securities over a longer period. In other words, random walk says nothing about trends in the long run or how price levels are determined; it speaks only of the phenomenon of short-run price-change independence.

As a result, what the random-walk theory (particularly, the semistrong form) really says to the fundamentalist operating in a random-walk world is that his fundamental analysis must be truly *exceptional* so that he can seize upon opportunities when security prices differ somewhat significantly from their intrinsic value. This means that the fundamentalist can be successful only in those instances when he either *possesses superior insight into the company's future prospects or possesses inside information*. It is clear even under random walk that such superior fundamental analysis will lead to superior profits for the astute security analyst or investor who projects his own data and does not merely rely on already publicly available historical data.

FUNCTIONS OF ASTUTE INVESTORS AND ANALYSTS IN A RANDOM-WALK MARKET

In a random-walk market, then, the functions of the analyst are (1) to determine the risk-return characteristics of stocks in the hope of occasionally coming across situations where his expectations differ markedly from those of the market as a whole, and (2) to make these risk-return combinations available to investors and investment counselors so they can construct portfolios with appropriate risk-return characteristics for their needs. The implications for the investor are (1) to plan on buying and holding the selected securities until he sees adequate reason for revising his portfolio, and (2) under normal conditions, to buy a well-diversified portfolio whose returns are likely to parallel those of the market. The former implication arises because of the empirical findings discussed already, and the latter because of the difficulty of outperforming the market portfolio in an efficient market.

EMPIRICAL RESULTS OF TECHNICAL ANALYSIS

To date, little empirical work has been conducted in the area of technical analysis—certainly not nearly as much as has been done on random walk. What little has been done is not conclusive, nor are the results as consistent as those found in the random-walk literature. Most, if not all, chartist theories tested to date have yielded results that are not very reassuring to the chartist.

These negative chartist results can perhaps be defended. It is argued that the tests of various trading strategies that have been carried out thus far do not adequately simulate the behavior of the technical analysts that we meet in actual practice. The tests have been too simple, because they have been of one trading system or technical tool at a time, rather than testing various methods concurrently and then somehow weighing the results of the various tools and reaching a consensus decision.[17]

As for the empirical results of random walk, the chartists are not as concerned, for they state that either the tests employed are too simple or they are inappropriate. This latter reason refers to the point that most of the statistical methods employed in the random-walk literature assume that a linear relationship exists. If that assumption is inappropriate, then the methods and thus the results are also inappropriate.

Summary

There are three broad theories concerning stock price movements. The fundamentalists believe that by analyzing key economic and financial variables, they can estimate the intrinsic worth of the security and then determine what investment action to take. The technical or chartist school maintains that fundamental analysis is unnecessary; all that has to be done is to study historical price patterns and then decide how current price behavior fits into these. Since the technician believes that history repeats itself, he can then predict future movements in price based on the study of historical patterns. The random-walk school has demonstrated to its own satisfaction through empirical tests that successive price changes over short periods, such as a day, a week, or a month, are independent. To the extent that this independence exists, the random-walk theory directly contradicts technical analysis; and furthermore, to the extent that the stock markets are efficient in the dissemination of information and that they have informed market participants and the proper institutional setting, the random-walk school poses an important challenge to the fundamentalist camp as well.

If the markets are truly efficient, then the fundamentalist will be successful only when (1) he has inside information, or (2) he has *superior ability* to analyze publicly available information and gain insight into the *future* of the firm, and (3) he uses (1) and/or (2) to reach long-term buy-and-hold investment decisions.

The empirical evidence in support of the random-walk hypothesis rests primarily on statistical tests, such as runs tests, correlation analysis, and filter tests. The results have been almost unanimously in support of the random-walk hypothesis, the weak form of the efficient-market hypothesis. The results of semistrong-form tests have been mixed.

The technician has done very little if anything to defend any of the chartist theories against the onslaught of random walk. All chartists have done is to claim that their various systems work. In the future, if their theories are to have widespread acceptance

---

[17]An excellent summary and review of the literature in this area can be found in George E. Pinches, "The Random Walk Hypothesis and Technical Analysis," *Financial Analysts Journal, 26*, No. 2 (March-April 1970), 104-10.

in the academic community, it will be necessary for them to test and demonstrate that their methods can consistently outperform a simple buy-and-hold strategy. The fundamentalist needs also to show that his efforts in analyzing securities are successful enough—that is, earn enough more profit than does a simplified strategy—to justify his expenditure of time and effort.

Questions and Problems

1. Discuss in abbreviated fashion the essence of fundamental and of technical analysis.

2. How do technicians and random-walk advocates differ in their view of the stock market?

3. What connection is there between the efficient market hypothesis and the studies of mutual-fund performance?

4. Explain the implications of the serial-correlation tests for (a) the random-walk theory, (b) technical analysis, and (c) fundamental analysis.

5. What are the implications of filter tests for (a) the random-walk theory, (b) technical analysis, and (c) fundamental analysis?

6. What sequence of events might bring about an "efficient market"?

7. Does the random-walk theory suggest that security price levels are random? Explain.

8. How is technical analysis generally regarded in the academic literature? Why? What do technical analysts have to say about this?

9. According to random-walk theorists, what does a chartist (technician) need to succeed in the stock market? A fundamentalist?

10. Mr. Elf Gnome is a well-known technical analyst (and authority on tarot). He shares an office with Randy Wok, MBA, who has recently joined the firm from Farout U. The market has been bearish for some time. Elf is keenly watching his charts for a signal of a rally on the upside.

   a. Which *three* of the more *reliable* technical indicators might Elf be watching closely? What *signal* would he expect to see from each that would suggest a reversal?

   b. Wok, amused by Gnome's antics, cried "Rubbish!" Why might he not trust Gnome's indicators? What might Gnome offer as a logical retort?

11. How can an investor identify an analyst with "superior" abilities?

part seven
PORTFOLIO ANALYSIS, SELECTION, AND MANAGEMENT

Thus far we have dealt with the investment environment and the valuation of individual securities. The final section of the book deals with portfolio management.

The observed behavior of most investors suggests that they prefer to hold groups of securities rather than a single security that seems to offer the greatest expected return. The implication is that return is not the only feature of securities that concerns investors; they also seek to avoid risk.

The expected return on a portfolio is directly related to the returns on its component securities; however, it is not possible to know portfolio risk merely through knowing the riskiness of individual securities. Risk is not only individual but also interactive between securities.

The risk-return output of security analysis is the raw material for portfolio management. The remaining four chapters of this book deal systematically with problems of analyzing and selecting portfolios, revising them over time, and evaluating their performance in line with stated goals. Chapter 18 deals with modern methods for *analyzing* portfolios and packaging securities in such a way as to achieve diversification of risk. In Chapter 19 we examine both traditional and newer methods available to assist investors in *selecting* the best portfolio from those available, given the way in which they trade off risk and return. Chapter 20 deals with the question of how securities would be *priced* if investors constructed portfolios along the lines suggested in Chapters 18 and 19. Chapter 21 provides an in-depth treatment of some well-known techniques for *revising* portfolios over time, as economic conditions alter and the prospects for individual securities change. The primary techniques discussed include the varied forms of formula planning.

The concluding chapter in the text, Chapter 22, explores the ways in which the performance of a portfolio might be *evaluated* over time. Performance evaluation in an empirical sense has reached its widest application in the area of investment companies. We take this opportunity to examine investment companies as an alternative to do-it-yourself portfolio management by looking at the performance results of these managed-money alternatives.

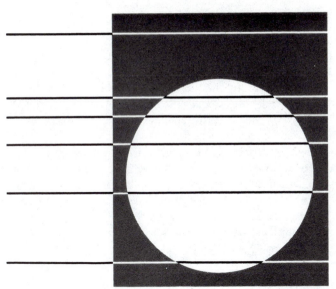

EIGHTEEN

Portfolio Analysis

Individual securities, as we have seen, have return-risk characteristics of their own. Portfolios, which are combinations of securities, may or may not take on the aggregate characteristics of their individual parts.

Portfolio analysis considers the determination of future risk and return in holding various blends of individual securities. In this chapter we shall analyze the range of possible portfolios that can be constituted from a given set of securities. We will show how the "efficiency" of each such combination can be evaluated.

Traditional Portfolio Analysis

Traditional security analysis recognizes the key importance of risk and return to the investor. However, direct recognition of risk and return in portfolio analysis seems very much a "seat-of-the-pants" process in the traditional approaches, which rely heavily upon intuition and insight. The results of these rather subjective approaches to portfolio analysis have, no doubt, been highly successful in many instances. The problem is that the methods employed do not readily lend themselves to analysis by others.

Most traditional methods recognize return as some dividend receipt and price appreciation over a forward period. But the return for individual securities is not always over the same common holding period, nor are the rates of return necessarily time-adjusted. An analyst may well estimate future earnings and a P/E to derive future price.

He will surely estimate the dividend. But he may not discount the values to determine the acceptability of the return in relation to the investor's requirements.

In any case, given an estimate of return, the analyst is likely to think of and express risk as the probable downside price expectation (either by itself or relative to upside appreciation possibilities). Each security ends up with some rough measure of likely return and potential downside risk for the future.

Portfolios, or combinations of securities, are thought of as helping to spread risk over many securities. This is good. However, the interrelationship between securities may be specified only broadly or nebulously. Auto stocks are, for example, recognized as risk-interrelated with rubber stocks; utility stocks display defensive price movement relative to the market and cyclical stocks like steel; and so on.

This is not to say that traditional portfolio analysis is unsuccessful. It is to say that much of it might be more objectively specified in explicit terms.

Why Portfolios?

You will recall that expected return from individual securities carries some degree of risk. *Risk* was defined as the standard deviation around the expected return.[1] In effect, we equated a security's risk with the variability of its return. More dispersion or variability about a security's expected return meant the security was riskier than one with less dispersion.

The simple fact that securities carry differing degrees of expected risk leads most investors to the notion of holding more than one security at a time, in an attempt to spread risks by not putting all their eggs into one basket.[2] Diversification of one's holdings is intended to reduce risk in an economy in which every asset's returns are subject to some degree of uncertainty. Even the value of cash suffers from the inroads of inflation. Most investors hope that if they hold several assets, even if one goes bad, the others will provide some protection from an extreme loss.

Diversification

Efforts to spread and minimize risk take the form of diversification. The more traditional forms of diversification have concentrated upon holding a number of security types (stock, bonds) across industry lines (utility, mining, manufacturing groups). The reasons are related to inherent differences in bond and equity contracts, coupled with the notion that an investment in firms in dissimilar industries would most likely do better than in firms within the same industry. Holding one stock each from mining, utility, and manufacturing groups is superior to holding three mining stocks. Carried to its extreme, this approach leads to the conclusion that the best diversification comes through holding large numbers of securities scattered across industries. Many would feel that

[1] Standard deviation is a risk surrogate, not a synonym for risk. For a review of some aspects of risk, see Fred D. Arditti, "Risk and the Required Return on Equity," *Journal of Finance*, March 1967, pp. 19-36.

[2] The reader should note that some advocate a concentration philosophy. This point of view stresses "putting all your eggs into one basket and keeping a sharp eye on the basket." See, for example, Gerald M. Loeb, *The Battle for Investment Survival* (New York: Simon and Schuster, 1965).

holding fifty such scattered stocks is five times more diversified than holding ten scattered stocks.

Most people would agree that a portfolio consisting of two stocks is probably less risky than one holding either stock alone. However, there is disagreement over the "right" kind of diversification and the "right" reason. The discussion that follows introduces and explores a formal, advanced notion of diversification conceived by the genius of Harry Markowitz.[3] Markowitz's approach to coming up with good portfolio possibilities has its roots in risk-return relationships. This is not at odds with traditional approaches in concept. The key differences lie in Markowitz's assumption that investor attitudes toward portfolios depend exclusively upon (1) expected return and risk, and (2) quantification of risk. And risk is, by proxy, the statistical notion of variance, or standard deviation of return. These simple assumptions are strong, and they are disputed by many traditionalists.[4]

Effects of Combining Securities

Although holding two securities is probably less risky than holding either security alone, *is it possible to reduce the risk of a portfolio by incorporating into it a security whose risk is greater than that of any of the investments held initially?* For example, given two stocks, X and Y, with Y considerably more risky than X, a portfolio composed of some of X and some of Y may be less risky than a portfolio composed exclusively of the less risky asset, X.

Assume the following about stocks X and Y:

	Stock X	Stock Y
Return (%)	7 or 11	13 or 5
Probability	.5 each return	.5 each return
Expected return (%)	9*	9†
Variance (%)	4	16
Standard deviation (%)	2	4

*Expected return = (.5)(7) + (.5)(11) = 9
†Expected return = (.5)(13) + (.5)(5) = 9

It is clear that although X and Y have the same expected return, 9 percent, Y is riskier than X (standard deviation of 4 versus 2). Suppose that when X's return is high, Y's return is low, and vice versa. In other words, when the return on X is 11 percent, the return on Y is 5 percent; similarly, when the return on X is 7 percent, the return on Y is 13 percent. Question: Is a portfolio of some X and some Y in any way superior to an exclusive holding of X alone (has it less risk)?

[3]Harry M. Markowitz, *Portfolio Selection: Efficient Diversification of Investments* (New York: John Wiley, 1959). Competing portfolio models are found in Henry A. Latané, "Investment Criteria—A Three-Asset Portfolio Balance Model," *Review of Economics and Statistics,* 45 (November 1963), 427-30; and Jack Hirschleifer, "Investment Decision under Uncertainty: Application of the State-Preference Approach," *Quarterly Journal of Economics,* 80 (May 1966), 252-77.

[4]Many other assumptions underlying portfolio analysis and the math to carry it off are still in dispute. For a look at how practitioners view some aspects of the Markowitz approach, see Frank E. Block, "Elements of Portfolio Construction," *Financial Analysts Journal,* May-June 1969, pp. 123-29.

Let us construct a portfolio consisting of two-thirds stock X and one-third stock Y. The average return of this portfolio can be thought of as the weighted-average return of each security in the portfolio; that is;

$$R_p = \sum_{i=1}^{N} X_i R_i \qquad (18.1)$$

where:

R_p = expected return to portfolio

X_i = proportion of total portfolio invested in security i

R_i = expected return to security i

N = total number of securities in portfolio

Therefore,

$$R_p = (2/3)(9) + (1/3)(9) = 9$$

But what will be the range of fluctuation of the portfolio? In periods when X is better as an investment, we have $R_p = (2/3)(11) + (1/3)(5) = 9$; and similarly, when Y turns out to be more remunerative, $R_p = (2/3)(7) + (1/3)(13) = 9$. Thus, by putting part of the money into the riskier stock, Y, we are able to *reduce* risk considerably from what it would have been if we had confined our purchases to the less risky stock, X. If we held only stock X, our expected return would be 9 percent, which could in reality be as low as 7 percent in bad periods or as much as 11 percent in good periods. The standard deviation is equal to 2 percent. Holding a mixture of two-thirds X and one-third Y, our expected and experienced return will always be 9 percent, with a standard deviation of zero. We can hardly quarrel with achieving the same expected return for less risk. In this case we have been able to eliminate risk altogether.

The reduction of risk of a portfolio by blending into it a security whose risk is *greater than* that of any of the securities held initially suggests that it is not possible to deduce the riskiness of a portfolio simply by knowing the riskiness of individual securities. It is vital that we also know the *interactive risk* between securities!

The crucial point of how to achieve the proper proportions of X and Y in reducing the risk to zero will be taken up later. However, the general notion is clear. The risk of the portfolio is reduced by playing off one set of variations against another. Finding two securities each of which tends to perform well whenever the other does poorly makes more certain a reasonable return for the portfolio as a whole, even if one of its components happens to be quite risky.

This sort of hedging is possible whenever one can find two securities whose behavior is inversely related in the way stocks X and Y were in the illustration. Now we need to take a closer look at the matter of how securities may be correlated in terms of rate of return.

A Closer Look at Portfolio Risk

The risk involved in individual securities can be measured by standard deviation or variance. When two securities are combined, we need to consider their interactive risk, or *covariance*. If the rates of return of two securities move together, we say their interactive risk or covariance is positive. If rates of return are independent, covariance is zero. Inverse movement results in covariance that is negative. Mathematically, covariance is defined:

$$\text{cov}_{xy} = \frac{1}{N} \sum^{N} [R_x - \bar{R}_x][R_y - \bar{R}_y] \qquad (18.2)$$

where the probabilities are equal and:

cov_{xy} = covariance between x and y

R_x = return on security x

R_y = return on security y

$\bar{R}_x$ = expected return to security x

$\bar{R}_y$ = expected return to security y

N = number of observations

Using our earlier example of stocks X and Y:

	Return	Expected Return	Difference
Stock X	7	9	−2
Stock Y	13	9	4
			Product −8
Stock X	11	9	2
Stock Y	5	9	−4
			Product −8

Covariance $= \frac{1}{2}[(7-9)(13-9) + (11-9)(5-9)] = \frac{1}{2}[(-8) + (-8)] = \frac{-16}{2} = -8$

Instead of squaring the deviations of a single variable from its mean, we take two corresponding observations of the two stocks in question at the *same point in time*, determine the variation of each from its expected value, and multiply the two deviations together. If whenever x is below its average, so is y, then for those periods each deviation will be negative, and their product consequently will be positive. Hence, we will end up with a covariance made up of an average of positive values, and its value will be large. Similarly, if one of the variables is relatively large whenever the other is small, one of the deviations will be positive and the other negative, and the covariance will be negative. This is true with our example above.

The *coefficient of correlation* is another measure designed to indicate the similarity or dissimilarity in the behavior of two variables. We define

$$r_{xy} = \frac{\text{cov}_{xy}}{\sigma_x \sigma_y}$$

where:

r_{xy} = coefficient of correlation of x and y

cov_{xy} = covariance between x and y

σ_x = standard deviation of x

σ_y = standard deviation of y

The coefficient of correlation is, essentially, the covariance taken not as an absolute value but relative to the standard deviations of the individual securities (variables). It indicates, in effect, how much x and y vary together as a proportion of their combined individual variations, measured by $\sigma_x \sigma_y$. In our example, the coefficient of correlation is

$$r_{xy} = -8/[(2)(4)] = -8/8 = -1.0$$

If the coefficient of correlation between two securities is -1.0, then a perfect negative correlation exists (r_{xy} cannot be less than -1.0). If the correlation coefficient is zero, then returns are said to be independent of one another. If the returns on two securities are perfectly correlated, the correlation coefficient will be $+1.0$, and perfect positive correlation is said to exist (r_{xy} cannot exceed $+1.0$).

Thus, correlation between two securities depends upon (1) the covariance between the two securities, and (2) the standard deviation of each security.

Portfolio Effect in the Two-Security Case

We have shown the effect of diversification on reducing risk. The key was not that two stocks provided twice as much diversification as one, but that by investing in securities with negative or low covariance among themselves, we could reduce the risk.[5] Markowitz's efficient diversification involves combining securities with less than positive correlation in order to reduce risk in the portfolio without sacrificing any of the portfolio's return. In general, the lower the correlation of securities in the portfolio, the less risky the portfolio will be. This is true regardless of how risky the stocks of the portfolio are when analyzed in isolation. It is not enough to invest in *many* securities; it is necessary to have the *right* securities.

Let us conclude our two-security example in order to make some valid generalizations. Then we can see what three-security and larger portfolios might be like.

In considering a two-security portfolio, portfolio risk can be defined more formally now as:

$$\sigma_p = \sqrt{X_x^2 \sigma_x^2 + X_y^2 \sigma_y^2 + 2 X_x X_y (r_{xy} \sigma_x \sigma_y)} \qquad (18.3)$$

[5]The approach adopted in this section was suggested in Fred Weston and Eugene Brigham, *Managerial Finance*, 6th ed. (New York: Holt, Rinehart and Winston, 1978), pp. 355-56.

where:

σ_p = portfolio standard deviation

X_x = percentage of total portfolio value in stock X

X_y = percentage of total portfolio value in stock Y

σ_x = standard deviation of stock X

σ_y = standard deviation of stock Y

r_{xy} = correlation coefficient of X and Y

Note: $r_{xy}\sigma_x\sigma_y = \text{cov}_{xy}$

Thus we now have the standard deviation of a portfolio of two securities. We are able to see that portfolio risk (σ_p) is sensitive to (1) the proportions of funds devoted to each stock, (2) the standard deviation of each stock, and (3) the covariance between the two stocks. If the stocks are independent of each other, the correlation coefficient is zero $(r_{xy} = 0)$. In this case, the last term in Equation 18.3 is zero. Second, if r_{xy} is greater than zero, the standard deviation of the portfolio is greater than if $r_{xy} = 0$. Third, if r_{xy} is less than zero, the covariance term is negative, and portfolio standard deviation is less than it would be if r_{xy} were greater than or equal to zero. Risk can be totally eliminated only if the third term is equal to the sum of the first two terms. This occurs only if (1) $r_{xy} = -1.0$, and (2) the percentage of the portfolio in stock X is set equal to $X_x = \sigma_y/(\sigma_x + \sigma_y)$.

To clarify these general statements, let us return to our earlier example of stocks X and Y. In our example, remember that

	Stock X	Stock Y
Expected return (%)	9	9
Standard deviation (%)	2	4

We calculated the covariance between the two stocks and found it to be −8. The coefficient of correlation was −1.0. The two securities were perfectly negatively correlated.

CHANGING PROPORTIONS OF X AND Y

What happens to portfolio risk as we change the total portfolio value invested in X and Y? Using Equation 18.3, we get:

Stock X (%)	Stock Y (%)	Portfolio Standard Deviation
100	0	2.0
80	20	0.8
66	34	0.0
20	80	2.8
0	100	4.0

Notice that portfolio risk can be brought down to zero by the skillful balancing of the proportions of the portfolio devoted to each security. The preconditions were $r_{xy} = -1.0$ and $X_x = \sigma_y/(\sigma_x + \sigma_y)$, or $4/(2 + 4) = .666$.

CHANGING THE COEFFICIENT OF CORRELATION

What effect would there be using $x = 2/3$ and $y = 1/3$ if the correlation coefficient between stocks X and Y had been other than -1.0? Using Equation 18.3 and various values for r_{xy}, we have

r_{xy}	Portfolio Standard Deviation
−0.5	1.34*
0.0	1.9
+0.5	2.3
+1.0	2.658

$$*\sigma_p = \sqrt{(.666)^2 (2)^2 + (.334)^2 (4)^2 + (2)(.666)(.334)(-.5)(2)(4)}$$
$$= \sqrt{1.777 + 1.777 - (.444)(4)} = \sqrt{1.777} = 1.34$$

If no diversification effect had occurred, then the total risk of the two securities would have been the weighted sum of their individual standard deviations:

$$\text{Total undiversified risk} = (.666)(2) + (.334)(4) = 2.658$$

Since the undiversified risk is equal to the portfolio risk of perfectly positively correlated securities ($r_{xy} = +1.0$), we can see that favorable portfolio effects occur only when securities are not perfectly positively correlated. The risk in a portfolio is less than the sum of the risks of the individual securities taken separately whenever the returns of the individual securities are not perfectly positively correlated; also, the smaller the correlation between the securities, the greater the benefits of diversification.

In general, some combination of two stocks (portfolios) will provide a smaller standard deviation of return than either security taken alone, so long as the correlation coefficient is less than the ratio of the smaller standard deviation to the larger standard deviation:

$$r_{xy} < \frac{\sigma_a}{\sigma_b}$$

Using the two stocks in our example:

$$-1.00 < \frac{2}{4}$$

$$-1.00 < +.50$$

If the two stocks had the same standard deviations as above but a coefficient of correlation of, for example, $+.70$, there would have been no portfolio effect, since $+.70$ is not less than $+.50$.

GRAPHIC ILLUSTRATION OF PORTFOLIO EFFECTS

The various cases where the correlation between two securities ranges from −1.0 to +1.0 are shown in Figure 18-1. Return is shown on the vertical axis and risk is measured on the horizontal axis. Points A and B represent pure holdings (100 percent) of securities A and B. The intermediate points along the line segment AB represent portfolios containing various combinations of the two securities. The line segment identified as $r_{ab} = +1.0$ is a straight line. This line shows the inability of a portfolio of perfectly positively correlated securities to serve as a means to reduce variability or risk. Point A along this line segment has no points to its left. That is, there is no portfolio composed of a mix of our perfectly correlated securities A and B that has a lower standard deviation than the standard deviation of A. Neither A nor B can help offset the risk of the other. The wise investor who wished to minimize risk would put all his eggs into the safer basket, stock A.

The segment labeled $r_{ab} = 0$ is a hyperbola. Its leftmost point will not reach the vertical axis. There is no portfolio where $\sigma_p = 0$. There is, however, an inflection just above point A that we shall explain in a moment.

The line segment labeled $r_{ab} = -1.0$ is compatible with the numerical example we have been using. This line shows that with perfect inverse correlation, it is possible to reduce portfolio risk to zero. Notice points L and M along the line segment AGB,

FIGURE 18-1
*PORTFOLIOS OF TWO SECURITIES WITH DIFFERING
CORRELATION OF RETURNS*

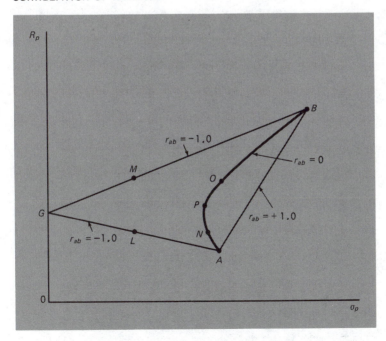

or $r_{ab} = -1.0$. Point M provides a higher return than point L, while both have equal risk. Portfolio L is clearly inferior to portfolio M. All portfolios along the segment GLA are clearly inferior to portfolios along the segment GMB. Similarly, along the line segment APB, or $r_{ab} = 0$, segment BOP contains portfolios that are superior to those along segment PNA. Markowitz would say that all portfolios along all line segments are *"feasible,"* but some are more *"efficient"* than others.

The Three-Security Case

Figure 18-2 depicts the graphics surrounding a three-security portfolio problem. Points A, B, and C each represent 100 percent invested in each of the stocks A, B, and C. The locus AB represents all portfolios composed of some proportions of A and B, the locus AC represents all portfolios composed of A and C, and so on. The general shape of the lines AB, AC, and BC suggests that these security pairs have correlation coefficients less than +1.0.

What about portfolios containing some proportions of all three securities? Point G can be considered some combination of A and B. The locus CG is then a three-security line. The number of such line segments representing three-security mixtures can be seen from Figure 18-3, where any point inside the shaded area will represent some three-security portfolio. Whereas the two-security locus is generally a curve, a three-security locus will normally be an entire region in the R_p, σ_p diagram.

FIGURE 18-2
THREE-SECURITY PORTFOLIOS

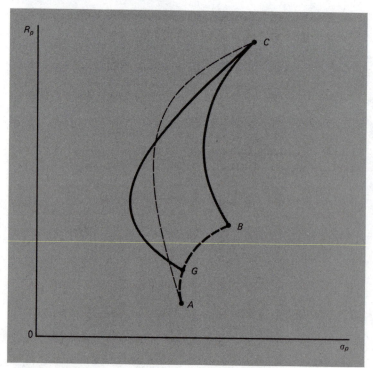

FIGURE 18-3
REGION OF PORTFOLIO POINTS WITH THREE SECURITIES

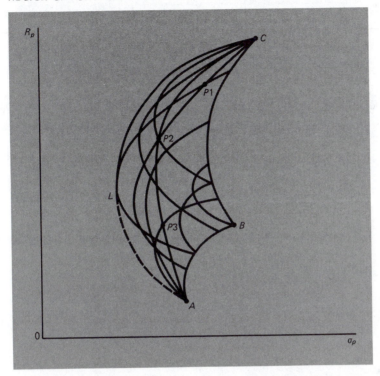

Consider for a moment three portfolio points within the R_p, σ_p diagram in Figure 18-3. Call the portfolios $P1$, $P2$, and $P3$. If we stop to think for a moment, the number of three-security portfolios is enormous—much larger than the number of two-security portfolios. Faced with the order of magnitude of portfolio possibilities, we need some shortcut to cull out the bulk of possibilities that are clearly nonoptimal. Looking at portfolios $P1$ and $P2$, we might observe the fact that since $P2$ lies to the left of and below $P1$, $P2$ is probably more appealing to the conservative investor, and $P1$ appeals to those willing to gamble a bit more. Would a rational investor select $P3$? We think not, since it involves a lower return than $P2$ but has the same risk. Thus we say that a portfolio is "inefficient" or dominated if some other portfolio lies directly above it in the risk-return space.

In general, an efficient portfolio has either (1) more return than any other portfolio with the same risk or (2) less risk than any other portfolio with the same return. In Figure 18-3 the boundary of the region identified as the curve LC dominates all other portfolios in the region. Portfolios along the segment AL represent inefficient portfolios, since they show increased risk for lower return. Each point on the segment AL is dominated by a more efficient portfolio directly above it on segment LC.

The actual determination of risk and return on various three-security portfolios such as $P1$, $P2$, and $P3$ requires that we extend our earlier formulas for two-asset portfolios.

RISK-RETURN IN A THREE-SECURITY PORTFOLIO

The three-security case uses the same formulation for expected portfolio return indicated earlier in Equation 18.1:

$$R_p = \sum_{i=1}^{N} X_i R_i$$

The portfolio standard deviation depends as before upon the standard deviations of return for its components, their correlation coefficients, and the proportions invested.

$$\sigma_p^2 = \sum_{i=1}^{N} \sum_{j=1}^{N} X_i X_j r_{ij} \sigma_i \sigma_j \qquad (18.4)$$

where:

σ_p^2 = expected portfolio variance; $\sqrt{\sigma_p^2}$ = portfolio standard deviation

X_i = proportion of total portfolio invested in security i

X_j = proportion of total portfolio invested in security j

r_{ij} = coefficient of correlation between securities i and j

σ_i = standard deviation of security i

σ_j = standard deviation of security j

N = total number of securities in the portfolio

$\sum_{i=1}^{N} \sum_{j=1}^{N}$ = double summation sign means N^2 numbers are to be added together. Each number is obtained by substituting one of the possible pairs of values for i and j into the expression.

For $N = 2$:

$$\sigma_p^2 = X_1 X_1 r_{1 \cdot 1} \sigma_1 \sigma_1 + X_1 X_2 r_{1 \cdot 2} \sigma_1 \sigma_2 + X_2 X_1 r_{2 \cdot 1} \sigma_2 \sigma_1 + X_2 X_2 r_{2 \cdot 2} \sigma_2 \sigma_2$$

The first and last terms can be simplified. Clearly, the return on a security is perfectly (positively) correlated with itself. Thus, $r_{1 \cdot 1} = 1$, as does $r_{2 \cdot 2} = 1$. Since $r_{2 \cdot 1} = r_{1 \cdot 2}$, the second and third terms can be combined. The result is

$$\sigma_p^2 = X_1^2 \sigma_1^2 + X_2^2 \sigma_2^2 + 2 X_1 X_2 r_{1 \cdot 2} \sigma_1 \sigma_2$$

Since $r_{ij} \sigma_i \sigma_j = \text{cov}_{ij}$, we can simplify further to

$$\sigma_p^2 = \sum_{i=1}^{N} \sum_{j=1}^{N} X_i X_j \text{cov}_{ij} \qquad (18.41)$$

EXAMPLE: Consider the following three securities and the relevant data on each:

	Stock 1	Stock 2	Stock 3
Expected return	10	12	8
Standard deviation	10	15	5
Correlation coefficients:			
Stocks 1,2 = .3			
2,3 = .4			
1,3 = .5			

Question: What are portfolio risk and return if the following proportions are assigned to each stock? Stock 1 = .2, stock 2 = .4, and stock 3 = .4.

The portfolio return would be as per Equation 18.1:

$$R_p = \sum_{i=1}^{N} X_i R_i$$

or

$$R_p = (.2)(10) + (.4)(12) + (.4)(8) = 10$$

Using the formula for portfolio risk (Equation 18.41) and expanding it for $N = 3$, we get:

$$\sigma_p^2 = X_1^2\sigma_1^2 + X_2^2\sigma_2^2 + X_3^2\sigma_3^2 + 2X_1X_2r_{1\cdot2}\sigma_1\sigma_2 + 2X_2X_3r_{2\cdot3}\sigma_2\sigma_3 + 2X_1X_3r_{1\cdot3}\sigma_1\sigma_3$$

Substituting the appropriate values, we have

$$\sigma_p^2 = (.2)^2(10)^2 + (.4)^2(15)^2 + (.4)^2(5)^2 + (2)(.2)(.4)(.3)(10)(15) +$$
$$(2)(.4)(.4)(.4)(15)(5) + (2)(.2)(.4)(.5)(10)(5)$$

$$= 4 + 36 + 4 + 7.20 + 9.6 + 4$$

$$= 64.8$$

$$\sigma_p^2 = 8.0$$

What we have just done, through a process that is somewhat arduous (particularly without a calculating machine), is to calculate return and risk on a portfolio consisting of certain proportions of stocks 1, 2, and 3. This portfolio is simply one of many three-security combinations that would make up our risk-return space or diagram. Although we found that a portfolio consisting of 20 percent of stock 1 and 40 percent each of stocks 2 and 3 had an expected return of 10 percent and a variance of return of 8.0, is it possible that a portfolio of different weights lies (1) directly above or (2) directly to the left of our example portfolio? Remember, if another portfolio met conditions (1) or (2) relative to our example portfolio, it would dominate, or be more efficient.

Tracing Out the Efficiency Locus

Figure 18-4 is intended to enunciate the dilemma of determining efficient portfolios. Our example three-security portfolio is identified among a mass of feasible portfolios in the risk-return diagram. We can see that it is inefficient, since there are other portfolios that (1) exceed its return at the same level of risk (e.g., portfolio A), and (2) have lower risk for the same level of return (e.g., portfolio D).

FIGURE 18-4
FEASIBLE PORTFOLIOS IN A RISK-RETURN SPACE

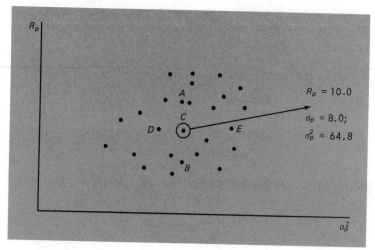

Harry Markowitz devised an ingenious computational model designed to trace out the efficiency locus and to identify the portfolios that make it up. In other words, he produced a scheme whereby large numbers of feasible portfolios could be ignored completely where they were dominated by more efficient portfolios.

In the calculations, Markowitz used the techniques of quadratic programming.[6] He assumed that one could deal with N securities or fewer. Using the expected return and risk for each security under consideration, and covariance estimates for each pair of securities, he is able to calculate risk and return for any portfolio made up of some or all of these securities. In particular, for any specific value of expected return, using the programming calculation he determines the least-risk portfolio. With another value of expected return, a similar procedure again yields the minimum-risk combination.

Figure 18-5 depicts the process. For return level R_i, the programming calculation indicates that point L_i is the least-risk portfolio at that level of return. Since no portfolio points lie to the left of L_i, it is the most efficient portfolio at that level of return. The locus of points from A to B is the end result of tracing process. We have our effi-

---

[6]For the interested reader, a graphic approach to the solution of the efficient frontier can be found in J. F. Weston and W. Beranek, "Programming Investment Portfolio Construction," *Analysts Journal*, May 1955, pp. 51-55.

ciency locus, or so-called *efficient frontier*. The line *AB* divides the space between port-folios that are "possible" and those that cannot be attained ("impossible").

FIGURE 18-5
SCHEMATIC SHOWING MARKOWITZ EFFICIENCY CALCULATION

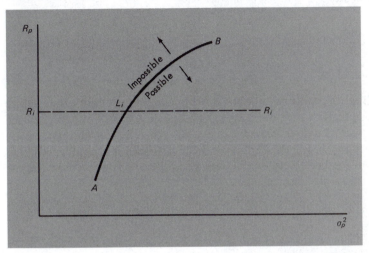

The N-Security Case

Most real-world portfolio-analysis problems involve portfolios larger than three stocks, chosen from a universe of securities that itself is quite large. In dealing with two-stock portfolios drawn from a modest universe of three-stock candidates, the number of possible portfolio combinations is not overwhelming. Neglecting the proportions devoted to each security, the possible two-stock combinations from stocks D, E, and F are DE, DF, and EF. Now let us gauge the changes brought about by attempting to draw two-stock portfolios from an expanded universe of five candidates, D, E, F, G, and H. The possible combinations are DE, DF, DG, DH, EF, EG, EH, FG, FH, and GH. The mere addition of two new stock candidates causes the number of possible portfolios to rise from three to ten. In general, the number of possibilities increases far more rapidly than does the number of stocks to be considered. Mathematical analysis and the computer go a long way toward culling out the bulk of possible portfolios on the ground that they are clearly nonoptimal. The time required to calculate and discriminate by hand ten-stock portfolios, with varying percentages devoted to each security, taken from the almost two thousand stocks on the New York Stock Exchange alone boggles the mind!

The movement from three- to *N*-security portfolios not only highlights the enormousness of the calculation problem and the assistance provided by the Markowitz algorithm, it also points up the expansion of the data bits required for fundamental analysis. The inputs to the portfolio analysis of a set of *N* securities are (1) *N* expected returns, (2) *N* variances of return, and (3) $(N^2 - N)/2$ covariances. Thus the Markowitz calculation requires a total of $[N(N + 3)/2]$ separate pieces of information before efficient portfolios can be calculated and identified. To use the Markowitz technique for portfolios of the following size, we need the corresponding pieces of information (estimates):

Number of Securities	Bits of Information
10	65
50	1,325
100*	5,150
1,000	501,500

*[100(100 + 3)/2]

It is easy to see that the Markowitz model is extremely demanding in its data needs and computational requirements. The intractable nature of these demands upon estimating time as well as computer time (and their related dollar costs) has perhaps limited the extent to which the Markowitz technique has been used directly for portfolios of any size. Further efficiencies in programming and computer technology will no doubt lower some of the impediments.

The Sharpe Index Model

William Sharpe, who among others has tried to simplify the process of data inputs, data tabulation, and reaching a solution, has developed a simplified variant of the Markowitz model that reduces substantially its data and computational requirements.[7]

First, simplified models assume that fluctuations in the value of a stock relative to that of another do not depend primarily upon the characteristics of those two securities alone. The two securities are more apt to reflect a broader influence that might be described as general business conditions. Relationships between securities occur only through their individual relationships with some index or indexes of business activity. The reduction in the number of covariance estimates needed eases considerably the job of security-analysis and portfolio-analysis computation. Thus the covariance data requirement reduces from $(N^2 - N)/2$ under the Markowitz technique to only N measures of each security as it relates to the index. In other words:

Number of Securities	Markowitz Covariances	Sharpe Index Coefficients
10	45	10
50	1,225	50
100	4,950	100
1,000	499,500	1,000
2,000	1,999,000	2,000

However, some additional inputs are required using Sharpe's technique, too. Estimates are required of the expected return and variance of one or more indexes of economic activity. The indexes to which the returns of each security are correlated are

[7]W. F. Sharpe, "A Simplified Model for Portfolio Analysis," *Management Science*, 9 (January 1963), 277-93.

likely to be some securities-market proxy, such as the Dow Jones Industrial Average or the Standard & Poor's 500 Stock Index. The use of economic indexes such as gross national product and the consumer price index was found by Smith to lead to poor estimates of covariances between securities.[8] Overall, then, the Sharpe technique requires $3N + 2$ separate bits of information, as opposed to the Markowitz requirement of $[N(N+3)]/2$.

Sharpe's single-index model has been compared with multiple-index models for reliability in approximating the full covariance efficient frontier of Markowitz. The more indexes that are used, the closer one gets to the Markowitz model (where every security is, in effect, an index). The result of multiple-index models can be loss of simplicity and computational savings inherent in these shortcut procedures. The research evidence suggests that index models using stock price indexes are preferable to those using economic indexes in approximating the full covariance frontier. However, the relative superiority of single versus multiple-index models is not clearly resolved in the literature.[9]

RISK-RETURN AND THE SHARPE MODEL

Sharpe suggested that a satisfactory simplification would be to abandon the covariances of each security with each other security and to substitute information on the relationship of each security to the market. In his terms, it is possible to consider the return for each security to be represented by the following equation:

$$R_i = \alpha + \beta_i I + e_i \qquad (18.5)$$

where:

R_i = expected return on security i

α_i = intercept of a straight line or alpha coefficient

β_i = slope of straight line or beta coefficient

I = level of index (market)

e_i = error term with a mean of zero and a standard deviation which is a constant.

In other words, the return on any stock depends upon some constant (α), plus some coefficient (β), times the value of a stock index (I), plus a random component (e). Let us look at a hypothetical stock and examine the historical relationship between the stock's return and the returns of the market (index).

Figure 18-6 shows the historical relationship between the return on a hypothetical security and the return on the Dow Jones Industrial Stock Average (DJIA). If we mathematically "fit" a line to the small number of observations, we get an equation for the

---

[8]Keith V. Smith, "Stock Price and Economic Indexes for Generating Efficient Portfolios," *Journal of Business,* 42 (July 1969), 326-36.

[9]See K. J. Cohen and J. A. Pogue, "An Empirical Evaluation of Alternative Selection Models," *Journal of Business,* 40, No. 2 (April 1967), 166-93; and B. A. Wallingford, "A Survey and Comparison of Portfolio Selection Models," *Journal of Finance and Quantitative Analysis,* June 1967, pp. 85-106.

line of the form $y = \alpha + \beta x$. In this case the equation turns out to be $y = 8.5 - .05x$.

FIGURE 18-6
SECURITY RETURNS CORRELATED WITH DJIA

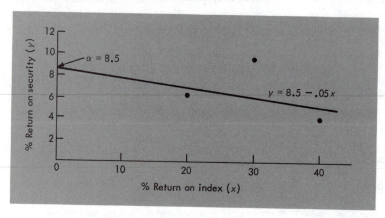

The equation $y = \alpha + \beta x$ has two terms or coefficients that have become common-place in the modern jargon of investment management. The "α" or intercept term is called by its Greek name "alpha." The "β" or slope term is referred to as the "beta" coefficient. The alpha value is really the value of y in the equation when the value of x is zero. Thus for our hypothetical stock when the return on the DJIA is zero the stock has an expected return of 8.5 percent $[y = 8.5 - .05(0)]$. The beta coefficient is the slope of the regression line and as such it is a measure of the sensitivity of the stock's return to movements in the market's return. A beta of +1.0 suggests that, ignoring the alpha coefficient, a 1 percent return on the DJIA is matched by a 1 percent return on the stock. A beta of 2.5 would suggest great responsiveness on the part of the stock to changes in the DJIA. A 5 percent return on the index, ignoring the alpha coefficient, leads to an expected return on the stock of 12.5 percent (2.5 times 5 percent). While the alpha term is not to be ignored, we shall see a bit later the important role played by the beta term or beta coefficient.

The Sharpe index method permits us to *estimate* a security's return then by utilizing the values of α and β for the security and an estimate of the value of the index. Assume the return on the index (I) for the year ahead is expected to be 25 percent. Using our calculated values of $\alpha = 8.5$ and $\beta = -.05$ and the estimate of the index of $I = 25$, the return for the stock is estimated as:

$$R_i = 8.5 - .05 \ (25)$$

$$R_i = 8.5 - 1.25$$

$$R_i = 7.25$$

The expected return on the security in question will be 7.25 percent if the return on the index is 25 percent, and if α and β are stable coefficients.

For portfolios, we need merely take the weighted average of the estimated returns for each security in the portfolio. The weights will be the proportions of the portfolio devoted to each security. For each security, we will require α and β estimates. One estimate of the index (I) is needed. Thus:

$$R_P = \sum_{i=1}^{N} X_i(\alpha_i + \beta_i I) \tag{18.6}$$

where all terms are as explained earlier, except that R_p is the expected portfolio return, X_i is the proportion of the portfolio devoted to stock i, and N is the total number of stocks.

The notion of security and portfolio *risk* in the Sharpe model is a bit less clear on the surface than are return calculations. The plotted returns and some key statistical relationships are shown below.[10]

Year	Security Return (%)	Index Return (%)
1	6	20
2	5	40
3	10	30
Average	= 7	30
Variance from average	= 4.7	66.7
Correlation coefficient	= −.189	
Coefficient of determination	= .0357	

Notice that when the index return goes up (down), the security's return generally goes down (up). Note changes in return from years 1 to 2 and 2 to 3. This reverse behavior accounts for our negative correlation coefficient (r).

The *coefficient of determination* (r^2) tells us the percentage of the variance of the security's return that is explained by the index (or market). Only about 3.5 percent of the variance of the security's return is explained by the index; some 96.5 percent is not. In other words, of the total variance in the return on the security (4.7), the following is true:

$$\text{Explained by index} = 4.7 \times .0357 = .17$$

$$\text{Not explained by index} = 4.7 \times .9643 = 4.53$$

Sharpe noted that the variance explained by the index could be referred to as the *systematic risk*. The unexplained variance is called the residual variance, or *unsystematic risk*.

[10]It should be noted that such a small number of observations makes results prone to considerable error. The modest number of observations is simply an illustrative convenience. The negative beta coefficient is not typical for stocks in general.

Sharpe suggests that systematic risk for an individual security can be seen as:

$$\text{Systematic risk} = \beta^2 \times (\text{Variance of index})$$

$$= \beta^2 \sigma_I^2$$

$$= (-.05)^2 (66.7) \qquad (18.7)$$

$$= (.0025)(66.7)$$

$$= .17$$

Unsystematic risk = (Total variance of security return) − (Systematic risk)

$$= e^2$$

$$= 4.7 - .17 \qquad (18.8)$$

$$= 4.53$$

Then:

$$\text{Total risk} = \beta \sigma_I^2 + e^2$$

$$= .17 + 4.53 \qquad (18.9)$$

$$= 4.7$$

And portfolio variance:

$$\sigma_p^2 = \left[\left(\sum_{i=1}^{N} X_i \beta_i \right)^2 \sigma_I^2 \right] + \left[\sum_{i=1}^{N} X_i^2 e_i^2 \right] \qquad (18.10)$$

where all symbols are as above, plus:

σ_p^2 = variance of portfolio return

σ_I^2 = expected variance of index

e_i^2 = variation in security's return not caused by its relationship to the index

Table 18-1 demonstrates the calculation of the key statistics we have discussed in the preceding paragraphs.

Portfolio Analysis: An Expanded Example

We shall use an example to show how efficient portfolios might be constructed using the ideas of Markowitz and Sharpe. What follows is concerned with generating the efficient frontier. In Chapters 19 and 22 we will extend the example to include selection of a "best" portfolio and the monitoring of performance over subsequent time periods.

TABLE 18-1
CALCULATION OF ALPHA, BETA, AND RESIDUAL VARIANCE,
THE PALMER COMPANY

X = S&P 500 annual rate of return n = number of observations

Y = Palmer Co. annual rate of return

Year	X	Y	XY	X^2	Y^2
1	.123	.1564	.0192	.0151	.0244
2	−.100	.1161	−.0116	.0100	.0135
3	.237	.5300	.1256	.0561	.2809
4	.108	.2944	.0318	.0116	.0867
5	−.083	.1277	−.0106	.0069	.0163
6	.028	.3103	.0087	.0008	.0963
7	.142	.5355	.0760	.0202	.2867
8	.173	.6008	.1039	.0299	.3610
9	−.130	.2736	−.0356	.0169	.0748
	ΣX = .498	ΣY = 2.9448	ΣXY = .3074	ΣX^2 = .1676	ΣY^2 = 1.2406
	$\overline{X}$ = .0553	$\overline{Y}$ = .3272			

Formulas:

Beta (the slope of the line):

$$\beta = \frac{n\Sigma XY - (\Sigma X)(\Sigma Y)}{n\Sigma X^2 - (\Sigma X)^2} = \frac{(9)(.3074) - (.498)(2.9448)}{(9)(.1676) - (.248)} = \underline{\underline{+1.03}}$$

Alpha (the intercept of the line):

$$\alpha = \overline{Y} - \beta\overline{X} = .3272 - [(1.03)(.0553)] = \underline{\underline{+.27}}$$

Residual variance (unsystematic risk):

$$e^2 = \frac{\Sigma Y^2 - \alpha\Sigma Y - \beta\Sigma XY}{n} = \frac{(1.2406) - (.27)(2.9448) - (1.0315)(.3074)}{9} = \underline{\underline{.0142}}$$

Correlation coefficient (an estimate of the extent to which the rate of return on the stock is correlated to the rate of return on the market):

$$r = \frac{n\Sigma XY - (\Sigma X)(\Sigma Y)}{\sqrt{n\Sigma X^2 - (\Sigma X)^2}\sqrt{n\Sigma Y^2 - (\Sigma Y)^2}} = \frac{(9)(.3074) - [(.498)(2.9448)]}{\sqrt{[(9)(.1676)] - (.248)}\sqrt{[(9)(1.2407)] - (8.672)}}$$

$$= \underline{\underline{+.73}}$$

Coefficient of determination (the percentage of variation in the stock's rate of return explained by the variation in the market's rate of return). It is the square of the correlation coefficient:

$$r^2 = (.73)^2 = \underline{\underline{.53}}$$

Listed in Table 18-2 are seventeen common stocks. Let us assume that these stocks have emerged from the security-analysis stage as candidates for portfolios. A uniform holding period was used in estimating risk and return for each stock. Specifically, each stock was examined as a possible holding for a one-year period. Our task here is to discover the efficient combinations of these stocks.

TABLE 18-2
STOCK SELECTION CANDIDATES

Company	Description
Aetna Life and Casualty	Largest all-line insurance company in the United States.
Citicorp	Owns Citibank, the second largest commercial bank in the United States.
High Voltage Engineering Company	Manufactures plastic insulation products, electrical connectors and switches, builders' instruments, electron processing systems, and scientific equipment.
K-Mart	The second largest retail store chain in the United States.
McDermott	Provides the oil industry with offshore oil development and production facilities.
McDonald's Corporation	World's largest chain of fast food restaurants.
Nucor Corporation	Steel fabricator.
Pargas	One of the largest distributors of liquified petroleum gas on the east and west coasts.
Pitney-Bowes, Inc.	World's largest manufacturer of postage meters and related mailing equipment.
Quaker Oats	Major world-wide producer of brand-name packaged foods.
Raytheon Company	Produces a wide range of electronic and computer equipment.
Southwest Forest Products Company	Produces news print.
Texaco	One of the largest integrated oil companies in the United States.
Transworld Corporation	A holding company that owns Transworld Airlines.
United States Shoe	Manufactures, imports, wholesales, and retails footwear for men.
United States Steel	Steel manufacturer and producer of cement, chemicals, and oilfield equipment.
Wisconsin Gas Company	The largest distributor of natural gas in Wisconsin.

Data Needed for Each Stock

Under the Markowitz system of portfolio analysis, we need three bits of information for each stock: (1) expected return for the holding period, (2) expected risk for the holding period, and (3) expected covariance for each pair of stocks. The Sharpe simplification would require (1) and (2), and for (3), covariance estimates for each stock relative to the market (index).[11] In addition, for the Sharpe model we need to estimate the return and variance on the index for the holding period.

For each of the stocks listed in Table 18-2, the regression coefficients (α, β) and the residual variance (e^2) were calculated from historical data. Monthly rates of return on each stock were regressed against the Standard and Poor's 500 Stock Index monthly rates of return for a five year period.[12] Results are shown in Table 18-3.

The most crucial input before beginning to generate efficient portfolios was an estimate of the return and risk on the S&P index for the holding period (one year ahead). The return on the S&P was estimated by projecting an estimated level of the index one year ahead plus expected dividends on the index. The return was estimated at 11 percent, with a risk (variance) of 26 percent.

[11]Markowitz data requirements for seventeen stocks would be 170, and Sharpe 53.

[12]It is customary to calculate alpha and beta using monthly data for the most recent five year period. Some analysts use quarterly data.

TABLE 18-3

TABLE 18-3
ALPHA, BETA, AND RESIDUAL VARIANCE FOR 17 STOCKS
(VERSUS S&P 500 INDEX)

	Alpha (%)	Beta	Expected Return (%)*	Residual Variance (%)
Aetna Life & Casualty	0.17	0.93	10.4	45.15
Citicorp	−0.59	1.26	13.3	29.48
High Voltage Engineering Co.	1.27	1.50	17.8	150.30
K-Mart	−0.28	1.17	12.6	45.42
McDermott	1.02	1.05	12.5	114.06
McDonald's Corp.	0.85	1.36	15.8	43.29
Nucor Corporation	2.48	1.37	17.5	132.25
Pargas	0.47	0.86	9.9	82.08
Pitney-Bowes, Inc.	1.55	1.07	13.3	66.58
Quaker Oats	−0.16	0.97	10.5	86.49
Raytheon Co.	2.52	1.17	15.4	51.98
Southwest Forest Products Co.	0.76	0.87	10.3	59.28
Texaco	−0.28	0.91	9.7	22.27
Transworld Corp.	1.47	1.73	20.5	196.28
United States Shoe	1.63	1.09	13.6	94.09
United States Steel	0.64	0.98	11.4	48.86
Wisconsin Gas Co.	0.28	0.87	9.8	17.64

*Assuming a return on the index (market) of 11%

These two estimates, return and risk on the S&P, serve as the focal point for estimating return and risk for each stock and, therefore, portfolios of stocks. Recall that, using the Sharpe method, return and risk estimates for portfolios are built by using the α, β, and e^2 estimates for portfolios for individual stocks applied to the projected return-risk variables for the index. Let us examine what the return-risk values would be for a one-stock portfolio, using Transworld Corp. (TWA) data and Equations 18.6 and 18.7 for portfolio return and portfolio risk:

$$R_p = \sum_{i=1}^{N} X_i (\alpha_i + \beta_i I)$$

$$= 1.00 \left[1.47 + (1.73)(11) \right]$$

$$R_p = 20.5$$

$$\sigma_p^2 = \left(\sum_{i=1}^{N} X_i \beta_i \right)^2 \sigma_I^2 + \sum_{i=1}^{N} (X_i^2 e_i^2)$$

$$= \beta_i^2 \sigma_I^2 + e_i^2 \quad \text{(since } X_i = 1.00\text{)}$$

$$= (2.99)(26.37) + (196.28)$$

$$= 78.84 + 196.28$$

$$= 275.12$$

$$\sigma_p = 16.6$$

Generating the Efficient Frontier

Using the required inputs, the Sharpe model and a computer, a series of "corner" portfolios was generated rather than an infinite number of points along the efficient frontier. The traceout of the efficient frontier connecting corner portfolios is shown in Figure 18-7. Table 18-4 shows the stocks and relative proportions invested at several corner portfolios.

Corner portfolios are portfolios calculated where a security either enters or leaves the portfolio. Corner portfolio 1 is a one-stock portfolio. It contains the stock with the greatest return (and risk) from the set—in this case, TWA. Notice in Table 18-4 that the return of 20.5 percent (.205) and the standard deviation or risk of 16.6 percent (.1659) for corner portfolio 1 (TWA) correspond to the earlier calculations shown to arrive at these figures.[13] The computer program proceeds down the efficient frontier finding the corner portfolios. Corner portfolio 2 is introduced with the appearance of a second stock, High Voltage Engineering. Typically, the number of stocks increases as we move down the frontier until we reach the last corner portfolio—the one that provides the minimum attainable risk (variance) and the lowest return. To better understand what is happening between any two successive corner portfolios, examine numbers 8 and 9. Between these two, Pitney Bowes stock makes its initial appearance.

FIGURE 18-7
EFFICIENT FRONTIER CONNECTING "CORNER" PORTFOLIOS

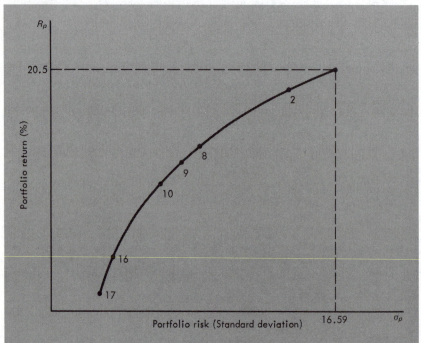

[13]The reader is invited to prove the expected return and standard deviation for corner portfolio 2, using Equations 18.6 and 18.7.

TABLE 18-4
SELECTED CORNER PORTFOLIOS

Security	Corner Portfolio Number					
	1	2	8	9	13	17
Aetna Life & Casualty						.055
Citicorp					.018	
High Voltage Engineering Co.		.060	.139	.113	.074	.026
K-Mart					.015	.020
McDermott					.040	.037
McDonald's Corp.			.228	.221	.178	.074
Nucor Corporation			.180	.153	.110	.053
Pargas						.041
Pitney-Bowes, Inc.				.061	.106	.082
Quaker Oats						.019
Raytheon Co.			.257	.262	.236	.146
Texaco						.065
Transworld Corporation	1.00	.940	.178	.134	.075	.020
Southwest Forest Products Co.					.022	.068
United States Shoe			.018	.056	.081	.060
United States Steel					.044	.072
Wisconsin Gas Co.						.163
Expected Return (%)	20.5	18.9	16.47	16.54	15.4	12.8
Expected Standard Deviation (%)	16.6	11.2	8.38	7.90	7.2	5.9

The actual number of stocks entering into any given efficient portfolio is largely determined by boundaries, if any, set on the maximum and/or minimum percentage that can be devoted to any one security from the total portfolio. If these percentages (weights) are free to take on any values, the efficient frontier may contain one- or two-security portfolios at the low or high extremes. Setting maximum (upper-bound) constraints assures a certain minimum number of stocks held. The efficient frontier in Figure 18-7 had no constraints placed upon weights.

A method for constructing optimum portfolios using simple ranking devices will be illustrated in Chapter 19.

"Adequate" Diversification

Many traditional approaches to diversification stress that the more securities one holds in a portfolio, the better. Markowitz-type diversification stresses not the number of securities but the right kinds; the right kinds of securities are those that exhibit less than perfect positive correlation.

An unfortunate fact is that nearly all securities are positively correlated with each other and the market. King noted that about half the variance in a typical stock results from elements that affect the whole market (systematic risk).[14] The upshot of this is that risk cannot be reduced to zero in portfolios of any size. The one-half of total risk that is not related to market forces (unsystematic) can be reduced by proper diver-

[14]B. F. King, "Market and Industry Factors in Stock Price Behavior," *Journal of Business*, 39, No. 1 (January 1966), 139-90.

sification, but once unsystematic risk is reduced or eliminated, we are left with systematic risk, which no one can escape (other than by not buying securities).

Thus, beyond some finite number of securities, adding more is expensive in time and money spent to search them out and monitor their performance; and this cost is not balanced by any benefits in the form of additional reduction of risk! Evans and Archer's work suggest that unsystematic risk can be reduced naively by holding as few as ten to fifteen stocks.[15] (In fact, risk can be increased by duplicating within industries.) This results from simply allowing unsystematic risk on these stocks to average out to near zero. With Markowitz-type diversification, risk can technically be reduced below the systematic level if securities can be found whose rates of return have low enough correlations. Negative correlations are ideal.

Summary

Investors are concerned not only with expected return on their investments but also their riskiness. However, knowing the riskiness of individual securities does not make it possible to deduce the riskiness of a portfolio of those securities. Using the ideas of Markowitz and others, we learned that portfolios are packages of securities that are constructed by knowing the return and risk on individual securities and also the *interactive* risk that exists *between* securities.

Our discussion in this chapter proceeded logically from the construction of feasible portfolios of two securities to bigger portfolios from a large universe of securities. We noted that some portfolios dominate others in that they provide either (1) the same return but lower risk, or (2) the same risk but higher return. These criteria distinguish portfolios that are feasible (possible) from those that are more "efficient."

The growing complexities of considering interactive risk in large populations of security candidates call for shortcuts in method. The ideas of Sharpe in simplifying the portfolio-analysis process were introduced. Finally, seventeen candidate stocks for analysis were packaged into feasible and efficient portfolios, using the Sharpe methodology and a large, highly efficient computer.

Questions and Problems

1. Can you think of any reasons for portfolios other than to minimize risk?

2. Stocks R and S display the following returns over the past two years:

Year	Stock	Return (%)
19X3	R	10
19X3	S	12
19X4	R	16
19X4	S	18

[15]John L. Evans and S. H. Archer, "Diversification and the Reduction of Dispersion: An Empirical Analysis," *Journal of Finance*, December 1968, pp. 761-69.

a. What is the expected return on a portfolio made up of 40 percent R and 60 percent S?

b. What is the standard deviation of each stock?

c. What is the covariance of stocks R and S?

d. Determine the correlation coefficient of stocks R and S.

e. What is the portfolio risk of a portfolio made up of 40 percent R and 60 percent S?

3. Consider a third security, T, along with stocks R and S in question 2. Its return over the past two years was: 19X3, 16%; 19X4, 10%. Would this security provide any advantages in combination with stock R? with stock S? with stocks R and S together?

4. Stocks Y and Z display the following parameters:

	Stock Y	Stock Z
Expected return	15	20
Expected variance	9	16
Covariance$_{yz}$ = +8		

Is there any advantage in holding some of Y and some of Z? Why?

5. Write out the expressions for expected return and standard deviation for the case of four securities.

6. Distinguish between a "feasible" and an "efficient" portfolio in the Markowitz-sense.

7. How many inputs are needed for a portfolio analysis involving sixty securities if covariances are computed using (a) the Markowitz technique, or (b) the Sharpe index method?

8. Shown below are the returns on Xerox and the Standard & Poor's 500 Stock Index for a five year period.

Year	Return on Xerox	Return on S&P 500
1	.29	(.10)
2	.31	.24
3	.10	.11
4	.06	(.08)
5	(.07)	.03

a. Plot the returns on Xerox vs. the S&P 500.

b. Calculate the regression equation for the returns you have plotted (i.e. alpha, beta, and residual variance) and draw the line on your graph.

c. Indicate (1) total variance for Xerox, and (2) the proportions that are explained and not explained by the S&P 500.

9. The return on Xerox for year 6 was .177. The S&P return was .14. Would the return on Xerox for year 6 be suggested by your regression equation in 8b above? Why or why not?

10. Refer to the stock example in Table 18-3.

a. Which stock would most likely be selected by an agressive investor wishing to hold a single security and expecting the S&P 500 return next year to be (1) .10; (2) −.10?

b. The last column in Table 18-3 shows the unexplained variance (risk) for each of the seventeen candidate stocks. What significance, if any, is there to stocks with the largest unexplained variances (e^2).

c. Which stock would a defensive investor place all his money in if he wanted to minimize his risk when the S&P 500 was expected to decline 10 percent?

11. Show that the portfolio return and variance for corner portfolio 2 in Table 18-4 are 18.9 and 11.2, respectively.

12. Stock L has a standard deviation of 5 and stock M has a standard deviation of 15. The coefficient of correlation of the returns of stocks L and M is +.40. Is it possible to produce a portfolio of these two stocks that has a smaller standard deviation of return than either security taken alone? Why or why not?

13. Following are data for several stocks. The data result from correlating returns on these stocks versus returns on a market index:

Stock	α	β	e^2
MNO	−.05	+1.6	.04
PQR	+.08	−.3	.00
LUV	.00	+1.1	.10

a. Which *single* stock would you prefer to own from a risk-return viewpoint if the market index were expected to have a return of +.10?

b. What does the e^2 value for PQR imply? The α value for LUV?

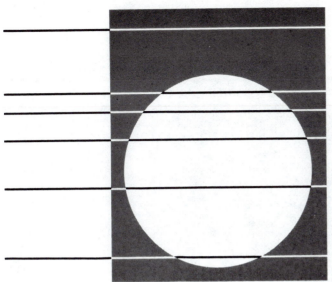

NINETEEN

Portfolio Selection

This chapter is concerned with the question, How should an investor go about selecting the one best portfolio to meet his needs? Or, more explicitly, how should an investor go about selecting which securities to purchase and how many dollars to invest in each?

First, we will examine newer selection techniques suggested by the work of Markowitz and others. Next, we shall explore the more traditional means employed to provide investment counsel and portfolio selection, such as is preeminent among portfolio managers at the present time.

Risk and Investor Preferences

Our examination of the theory behind Markowitz-type diversification revealed the substance behind the determination of an efficient frontier, or locus of portfolio opportunities. The issue now is, How should investors (analysts) choose a "best" option on the efficient frontier?

Our central vehicle for attacking this problem is the satisfaction an investor receives from investment opportunities. Our assumption has been that risk-return measures on portfolios are the main determinants of an investor's attitude toward them. We need to look closely at the manner in which risk affects preference.

Utility functions, or indifference curves, are normally used to represent someone's preferences. Let us invent a set of preferences or indifference curves for a hypothetical investor, as displayed in Figure 19-1. For the moment, we will make no pretense that

FIGURE 19-1

INDIFFERENCE MAP FOR HYPOTHETICAL INVESTOR

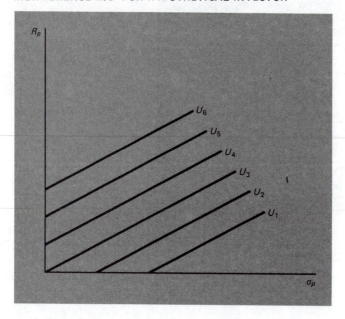

this indifference "map" depicts any real investor any of us may know. This investor (call him M) has indifference curves that are parallel to one another and linear. The higher a curve, the more desirable the situations lying along it. Each curve carries equal satisfaction along its length. We have labeled the indifference (utility) curves from 1 to 6 in order of increasing desirability. M's problem is to find the feasible portfolio tangent to the best attainable (highest) indifference curve (line). If we combine the efficient frontier with the family of indifference curves, as in Figure 19-2, we can see how M might solve his problem. Point B is his "best" portfolio, since (1) it is efficient, and (2) at that point, the frontier will be tangent to the indifference curve (line).

Since most investors would be expected to seek more return for additional risk assumed, utility or indifference curves (lines) are positively sloped. Figure 19-3 depicts a set of indifference curves (lines) for a risk lover. His indifference curves are negative sloping and convex toward the origin. With the risk averter, the lower the σ_p of his portfolio, the happier he is; the risk lover is happier the higher the level of σ_p.[1]

The degree of slope associated with indifference curves will indicate the degree of risk aversion for the investor in question. A sort of aggressive versus conservative risk preference is shown in Figures 19-4 and 19-5. The conservative investor (Figure 19-4) requires large increases in return for assuming small increases in risk; the more aggressive investor will accept smaller increases in return for large increases in risk. Both dislike risk, but they trade off risk and return in different degrees.

[1]It might be noted that if an efficient frontier were drawn on Figure 19-3, the only point of tangency with the risk lover's indifference curves would be at the upper-right point of the frontier. This point contains one security and follows the risk lover's maxim of putting all one's eggs into a single basket.

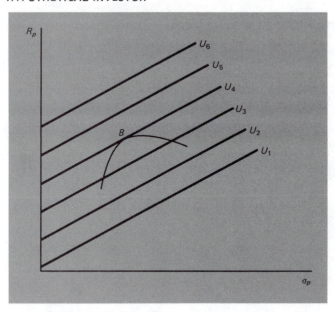

FIGURE 19-3
RISK-LOVER INDIFFERENCE CURVES

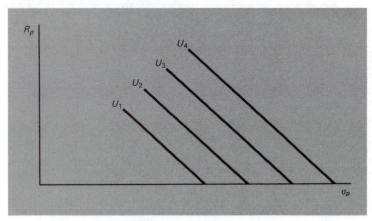

Although differences may occur in the slope of indifference curves, they are assumed to be positive sloping for most rational investors. A more important question is whether indifference curves are curves and not straight lines as depicted so far.

Does different utility accrue to given increments of return? For example, the utility received from $100,000 may or may not be worth twice that received from $50,000. In

FIGURE 19-4
RISK-FEARING INVESTOR'S INDIFFERENCE CURVES

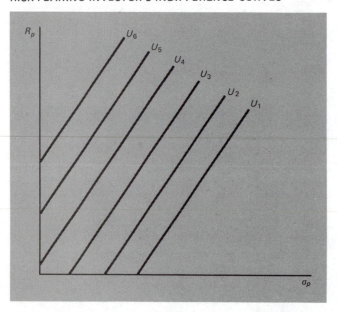

FIGURE 19-5
*LESS-RISK-FEARING INVESTOR'S
INDIFFERENCE CURVES*

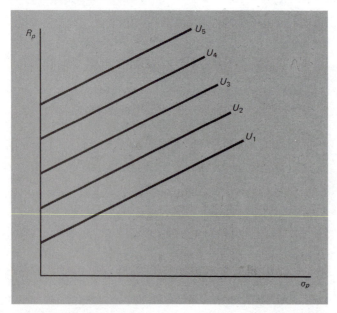

effect, in Figure 19-6 we can see three different slopes to an indifference or utility curve (line). Curve *A* depicts increasing marginal utility, curve *B* constant utility, and curve *C* diminishing marginal utility. While constant marginal utility (straight line) would suggest that, say, doubling return doubles utility (satisfaction), increasing marginal utility means that increasingly larger satisfaction is to be found from the same increase in return. Increasing marginal utility would suggest the case of the inveterate gambler who is, in fact, a risk lover. Curve *C*, diminishing marginal utility, is probably identified with the way most investors behave. In sum, constant marginal utility of return means that an investor is risk-neutral; decreasing marginal utility means that he is risk-averse; increasing marginal utility suggests that he likes risk.

FIGURE 19-6
VARIOUS MARGINAL-UTILITY CURVES

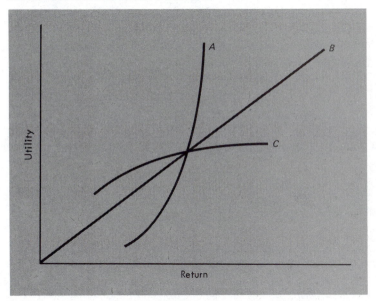

Constructing the "Best" Portfolio

The construction of an optimal portfolio[2] is simplified if there is a single number that measures the desirability of including a stock in the optimal portfolio. If we accept the single index model (Sharpe), such a number exists. In this case, the desirability of any stock is directly related to its *excess return to beta ratio*:

$$\frac{R_i - R_F}{\beta_i}$$

[2]This analysis draws upon E. J. Elton, M. J. Gruber, and M. W. Padberg, "Optimum Portfolios from Simple Ranking Devices," *Journal of Portfolio Management*, Spring 1978, pp. 15-19.

where:

R_i = expected return on stock i

R_F = return on a riskless asset

β_i = expected change in the rate of return on stock i associated with a 1 percent change in the market return

If stocks are ranked by excess return to beta (from highest to lowest), the ranking represents the desirability of any stock's inclusion in a portfolio. The number of stocks selected depends on a unique cutoff rate such that all stocks with higher ratios of $(R_i - R_F)/\beta_i$ will be included and all stocks with lower ratios excluded.

To determine which stocks are included in the optimum portfolio, the following steps are necessary:

1. Calculate the "excess return to beta" ratio for each stock under review and and rank from highest to lowest.
2. The optimum portfolio consists of investing in all stocks for which $(R_i - R_F)/\beta_i$ is greater than a particular cutoff point C^*.

Ranking Securities

Tables 19-1 and 19-2 represent an example of this procedure. Table 19-1 contains the data necessary to determine an optimal portfolio. It is the normal output generated from a single index model, plus the ratio of excess return to beta. There are ten securities in the tables. They are already ranked. Selecting the optimal portfolio involves the comparison of $(R_i - R_F)/\beta_i$ with C^*. For the moment, assume that $C^* = 5.45$. Examining Table 19-1 shows that for securities 1 to 5, $(R_i - R_F)/\beta_i$ is greater than C^*, while for security 6 it is less than C^*. Hence an optimal portfolio consists of securities 1 to 5.

Establishing a Cutoff Rate

All securities whose excess return-to-risk ratio are above the cutoff rate are selected and all whose ratios are below are rejected. The value of C^* is computed from the characteristics of all of the securities that belong in the optimum portfolio. To determine C^* it is necessary to calculate its value as if there were different numbers of securities in the optimum portfolio. Suppose C_i is a candidate for C^*. The value of C_i is calculated when i securities are assumed to belong to the optimal portfolio.

Since securities are ranked from highest excess return to beta to lowest, we know that if a particular security belongs in the optimal portfolio, all higher-ranked securities also belong in the optimal portfolio. We proceed to calculate values of a variable C_i as if the first-ranked security was in the optimal portfolio ($i = 1$), then the first- and second-ranked securities were in the optimal portfolio ($i = 2$), and so on. These C_i are candidates for C^*. We have found the optimum C_i, that is, C^*, when all securities used in the calculation of C_i have excess returns to beta above C_i and all securities not used to calculate C_i have excess return to betas below C_i. For example, column (7) of Table 19-2 shows the C_i for which all securities used in the calculation i [columns (1) through (5) in the table] have a ratio of excess return to beta above C_i and all securities not used in the calculation of C_i [columns (6) through (10) in the table] have an excess return to beta ratio below

TABLE 19-1

DATA NEEDED TO FIND OPTIMAL PORTFOLIO ($R_F = 5\%$)

(1)	(2)	(3)	(4)	(5)	(6)
Security No., i	Mean Return, R_i	Excess Return, $R_i - R_F$	Beta, β_i	Unsystematic Risk, σ_{ei}^2	Excess Return over Beta, $(R_i - R_F)/\beta_i$
1	15.0	10.0	1.0	50	10.0
2	17.0	12.0	1.5	40	8.0
3	12.0	7.0	1.0	20	7.0
4	17.0	12.0	2.0	10	6.0
5	11.0	6.0	1.0	40	6.0
6	11.0	6.0	1.5	30	4.0
7	11.0	6.0	2.0	40	3.0
8	7.0	2.0	.8	16	2.5
9	7.0	2.0	1.0	20	2.0
10	5.6	.6	.6	6	1.0

TABLE 19-2

CALCULATIONS FOR DETERMINING CUTOFF RATE WITH $\sigma_m^2 = 10$

(1)	(2)	(3)	(4)	(5)	(6)	(7)
Security No.	$\dfrac{(R_i - R_F)}{\beta_i}$	$\dfrac{(R_i - R_F)\beta_i}{\sigma_{ei}^2}$	$\dfrac{\beta_i^2}{\sigma_{ei}^2}$	$\displaystyle\sum_{j=1}^{1}\dfrac{(R_j - R_F)\beta_j}{\sigma_{ei}^2}$	$\displaystyle\sum_{j=1}^{1}\dfrac{\beta_j^2}{\sigma_{ei}^2}$	C
1	10	2/10	2/100	2/10	2/100	1.67
2	8	4.5/10	5.625/100	6.5/10	7.625/100	3.69
3	7	3.5/10	5/100	10/10	12.625/100	4.42
4	6	24/10	40/100	34/10	52.625/100	5.43
5	6	1.5/10	2.5/100	35.5/10	55.125/100	5.45
6	4	3/10	7.5/100	38.5/10	62.625/100	5.30
7	3	3/10	10/100	41.5/10	72.625/100	5.02
8	2.5	1/10	4/100	42.5/10	76.625/100	4.91
9	2.0	1/10	5/100	43.5/10	81.625/100	4.75
10	1.0	.6/10	6/100	44.1/10	87.625/100	4.52

C_i. C_5 serves the role of a cutoff rate in the way a cutoff rate was defined earlier. In particular, C_5 is the only C_i that when used as a cutoff rate selects only the stocks used to construct it. There will always be one and only one C_i with this property and it is C^*.

Finding the Cutoff Rate C^*

For a portfolio of i stocks, C_i is given by

$$C_i = \frac{\sigma_m^2 \displaystyle\sum_{j=1}^{i} \frac{(R_j - R_F)\beta_j}{\sigma_{ej}^2}}{1 + \sigma_m^2 \displaystyle\sum_{j=1}^{i} \frac{\beta_j^2}{\sigma_{ej}^2}}$$

where

$$\sigma_m^2 = \text{variance in the market index}$$

$$\sigma_{ej}^2 = \text{variance of a stock's movement that is not associated with the movement of the market index; this is the stock's unsystematic risk}$$

The value of C_i for the first security in our list is thus:

Expression	Calculation	Data Location Table
$\dfrac{(R_j - R_F)/\beta_i}{\sigma_{ej}^2}$	$\dfrac{(15-5)1}{50} = \dfrac{2}{10}$	Column (3)
$\displaystyle\sum_{j=1}^{1} \dfrac{(R_j - R_F)/\beta_i}{\sigma_{ej}^2}$	Same as above (since $i = 1$)	Column (5)
$\dfrac{\beta_j^2}{\sigma_{ej}^2}$	$\dfrac{(1)^2}{50} = \dfrac{2}{100}$	Column (4) [cumulated in column (6)]

Putting all this information together yields

$$C_i = \frac{10\left(\dfrac{2}{10}\right)}{1 + 10\left(\dfrac{2}{100}\right)} = 1.67$$

For security 2 ($i = 2$) column (3) is

$$\frac{(17-5)1.5}{40} = \frac{4.5}{10}$$

Now column (5) is the sum of column (3) for security 1 and security 2 or

$$\frac{2}{10} + \frac{4.5}{10} = \frac{6.5}{10}$$

Column (4) is

$$\frac{(1.5)^2}{40} = \frac{5.625}{100}$$

Column (6) is the sum of column (4) for security 1 and 2, or

$$\frac{2}{100} + \frac{5.625}{100} = \frac{7.625}{100}$$

and C_2 is

$$C_2 = \frac{\sigma_m^2 \, [\text{column (5)}]}{1 + \sigma_m^2 \, [\text{column (6)}]} = \frac{10\left(\dfrac{6.5}{10}\right)}{1 + 10\left(\dfrac{7.625}{100}\right)} = 3.69$$

Proceeding in the same fashion, we can find all the C_i's.

Arriving at the Optimal Portfolio

Once we know securities that are to be included in the optimum portfolio, we must calculate the percent invested in each security. The percentage invested in each security is

$$X_i^0 = \frac{Z_i}{\sum\limits_{j=1}^{N} Z_j}$$

where

$$Z_i = \frac{\beta_i}{\sigma_{ei}^2}\left(\frac{R_i - R_F}{\beta_i} - C^*\right)$$

The second expression determines the relative investment in each security, and the first expression simply scales the weights on each security so that they sum to 1 (ensure full investment). The residual variance on each security σ_{ei}^2 plays an important role in determining how much to invest in each security. Applying this formula to our example, we have

$$Z_1 = \frac{2}{100}(10 - 5.45) = .091$$

$$Z_2 = \frac{3.75}{100}(8 - 5.45) = .095625$$

$$Z_3 = \frac{5}{100}(7 - 5.45) = .0775$$

$$Z_4 = \frac{20}{100}(6 - 5.45) = .110$$

$$Z_5 = \frac{2.5}{100}(6 - 5.45) = .01375$$

$$\sum_{i=1}^{5} Z_i = .387875$$

Dividing each Z_i by the sum of the Z_i, we would invest 23.5 percent of our funds in security 1, 24.6 percent in security 2, 20 percent in security 3, 28.4 percent in security 4, and 3.5 percent in security 5.

The characteristics of a stock that make it desirable can be determined before the calculations of an optimal portfolio is begun. The desirability of any stock is solely a function of its excess return to beta ratio.

Consideration of New Securities

The techniques discussed also simplify the problem of revising portfolios as new securities enter the decision universe.

In our example, C^* was equal to 5.45; thus, if a new security is suggested that has an excess return-to-risk ratio of less than C^* (5.45), we would know that it could not enter into the optimum portfolio. The existence of a cutoff rate is extremely useful since most new securities candidates that have an excess return-to-beta ratio above 5.45 would have to be included in the optimal portfolio.

The impact of a new security on which securities are included in the optimal portfolio is easy to figure. For example, consider a security with a excess return of 9, a beta of 1, and a residual risk of 10. Then, initially assuming that this security should be added to the previously optimum portfolio, we obtain a cutoff rate of 5.37. Since this is larger than the excess return to beta ratio for any security previously excluded from the portfolio, the optimum portfolio consists of the old portfolio with the addition of the new security. It is possible that the old portfolio will not remain optimal. The change may involve a change in one or two of the securities whose excess return-to-beta ratio is near the cutoff rate.

Portfolio Selection Example

Our example in Chapter 18 is extended here. Figure 18-7 was a traceout of the efficient frontier. Figure 19-7 introduces a risk-free borrowing and lending rate (R_F) which makes the efficient frontier a straight line. The borrowing and lending rate of 7 percent is the one-year rate on Treasury securities.[3]

The optimal stock portfolio is corner portfolio 9.[4] Corner portfolios to the left of 9 (10 to 17) can be made more "efficient" by choosing 9 plus partial lending. Portfolios to the right of 9 (1 to 8) are similarly dominated by 9 plus some amount of borrowing. Corner portfolio 9 maximizes the ratio: $[(R_p - R_F)/\beta_p]$.[5] The translation of security proportions for corner portfolio 9 is shown in Table 19-3.

Significance of Beta in the Portfolio

Sharpe notes that proper diversification and the holding of a sufficient number of securities can reduce the unsystematic component of portfolio risk to zero by averaging out the unsystematic risk of individual stocks. What is left is systematic risk which, because it is determined by the market (index), cannot be eliminated through portfolio balancing. Thus the Sharpe model attaches considerable significance to systematic risk and its most important measure, the beta coefficient (β).

According to the model the risk contribution to a portfolio of an individual stock can be measured by the stock's beta coefficient. The market index will have a beta coefficient of +1.0. A stock with a beta of, for example, +2.0 indicates that it contributes far more risk to a portfolio than a stock with, say, a beta of +.05. Stocks with negative betas are to be coveted, since they help reduce risk beyond the unsystematic level.

---

[3]Many would use the higher rate on high-grade commercial paper.

[4]The "best" portfolio is probably the market itself from the notions introduced in our discussion of capital market theory and the CAPM. However, transaction costs may effectively prevent its use (see Chapter 20).

[5]Some proportions were modestly altered to enable purchase of round lots as nearly as possible. The savings in transaction costs (brokerage fees) and resulting increased return should be weighed against any added risk.

FIGURE 19-7
EFFICIENT FRONTIER WITH BORROWING-LENDING LINE

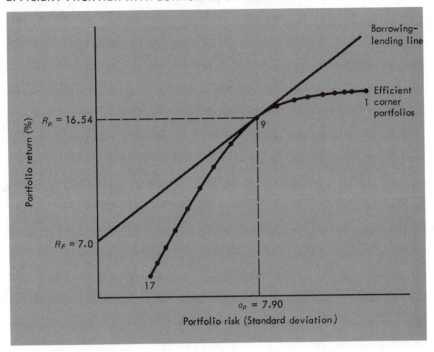

TABLE 19-3
STOCK PORTFOLIO FOR ONE-YEAR HOLDING PERIOD

Company	(1) Beta	(2) Portfolio Proportion (%)	(1) × (2) Weighted Beta
High Voltage Engineering Co.	1.50	11.3	.169
McDonald's Corp.	1.36	22.1	.300
Nucor Corporation	1.37	15.3	.223
Pitney-Bowes, Inc.	1.07	6.1	.065
Raytheon Co.	1.17	26.2	.305
Transworld Corporation	1.73	13.4	.232
United States Shoe	1.09	5.6	.061
		100.0	1.355

Since efficient portfolios eliminate unsystematic risk, the riskiness of such port-folios is determined exclusively by market movements. Risk in an efficient portfolio is measured by the portfolio beta. Table 19-3 indicates the beta coefficients of each stock in the portfolio that was chosen from the efficient frontier. The beta for the portfolio is simply the weighted average of the betas of the component securities. Corner portfolio 9 has a beta of 1.36 which suggests that it has a sensitivity above the +1.0 attributed to the market. If this portfolio is properly diversified (proper number of stocks and elimination of unsystematic risk), it should move up or down about one-third more than the market. Such a high beta suggests an aggressive portfolio. Should the market move up over the holding period, corner portfolio 9 will be expected to advance substantially. However, a market decline should find this portfolio falling considerably in value.

Beta in Stock Selection

It is easy to see the central role played by the beta coefficient in the determination of expected return and risk for stocks as well as portfolios.

Some analysts have proposed using beta coefficients to approach the problem of stock selection. In this approach, the outlook for the market is assessed. Portfolios are constructed by optimizing beta coefficients in line with the market outlook. For example, if the market is expected to advance in the future, portfolios would be constructed containing stocks with beta coefficients that give maximum return. Such stocks would also carry high risks when the beta coefficients are large. A beta of +1.0 would indicate a stock with "average" volatility relative to the market. A beta of +2.0 would mean that if the market return was forecast as 10 percent, the stock would have an estimated return of 20 percent (excluding the value of alpha).

Should the outlook suggest a market decline, stocks with large positive beta coefficients might be sold short. Stocks with negative betas would provide resistance to the market downtrend. Suppose the forecast is for a 10 percent decline in the market. A stock with a beta of +2.0 would provide a negative return of 20 percent if held long. If the stock is sold short, a gain of 20 percent is suggested. Should the 10 percent market decline be forecast, a stock with a beta of −1.0 would provide a return of +10 percent [−1.0 x −.10]. Unfortunately, stocks with negative betas are scarce.

These approaches to stock selection are valid under two key assumptions. First, it is necessary to forecast the timing and direction of market moves with reasonable accuracy. Second, the historical measure of beta must persist at roughly similar levels during the forecast period.

Under the first assumption, the continuous tailoring of portfolio volatility in order to capitalize on anticipated market moves can operate *against* the investment-return objectives of the portfolio. This is especially the case if the timing and direction of the forecast market moves are not consistently correct.

The second assumption is equally important. Whereas the variability of market returns is able to explain roughly 75-95 percent of the variability of the returns of most portfolios, owing to the averaging effects that are achieved by diversification, the market is able to explain only 15-65 percent of the volatility of most individual securities. As a result, the statistical significance of the estimated coefficients is suspect in the cases of some common stocks. Moreover, questions have been raised on the stability of these coefficients during short-to-intermediate-term periods, and this is the time horizon of interest to most portfolio managers.

Table 19-4 contains a volatility analysis of several securities taken from a group of fifty-six examined in a study by Smith, Barney & Co. The beta coefficients are computed for two adjacent time periods, January 2, 1968-November 3, 1969, and November 3, 1969-October 1, 1971. Both periods encompassed rising and falling stock markets.

TABLE 19-4
MARKET VOLATILITY ANALYSIS OF SELECTED COMMON STOCKS

Security	11/03/69-10/01/71		01/02/68-11/03/69	
	Beta	% Variation Explained by S&P 500	Beta	% Variation Explained by S&P 500
Allegheny Power System	1.10	43.9	.54	12.3
Allied Stores	2.01	68.3	1.16	31.3
American Airlines	2.49	55.0	1.63	31.6
American Cyanamid	.47	12.1	1.26	65.1
American Investment	2.51	55.3	1.01	21.3
American Tel. & Tel.	.77	47.8	.46	25.2
Atlantic Richfield	1.64	54.5	1.87	34.1
Bausch & Lomb	2.38	35.0	2.22	54.9
CMI Investment	1.63	35.0	2.23	25.2
Coastal States Gas	.68	29.4	1.19	28.5

SOURCE: G. Gordon Biggar, Jr., *Risk-Adjusted Portfolio Performance: Its Investment Implications* (New York: Smith, Barney, & Co., 1971), p. 37.

For example, in reviewing the volatility performance of the first security, Allegheny Power System, we note that its beta coefficient increased significantly from one time period to the next. However, the market was able to explain only 12 percent of the stock's volatility during the initial time span. An increase in the stock's responsiveness to market moves accompanied the increase in its volatility, as evidenced by the ability of the market to explain nearly 44 percent of the stock's variability during the latter period.

One noteworthy observation from the Smith, Barney analysis of fifty-six stocks is the number of sizable shifts in the values of the volatility coefficients between the two time periods. Coefficients for twelve of the issues remained reasonably stable, twenty-eight significantly, and sixteen declined notably. The sampling of securities is by no means large enough to draw any firm conclusions concerning the stability of beta factors. However, the Smith, Barney study tends to suggest caution in the use of beta coefficients in stock selection.

This stationariness or lack thereof of betas is of significant concern to the investor who wishes to make predictive decisions using beta coefficients. Levy has written on this matter and concluded that beta coefficients are fairly unpredictable for individual securities. In the same study, however, Levy suggested that portfolio betas were somewhat stationary for small portfolios and very stable over time for large portfolios.

PREDICTING BETA

Care must be exercised in interpreting a historical beta. It cannot be assumed that beta is fixed over time. Quite the contrary, there is reason to expect that beta does change. Historical betas should not obscure the fact that although they are useful when interpreting past performance, prediction requires betas that are forward-looking estimates.

Much of the mystery surrounding beta can be avoided by remembering that beta does not describe a causal relationship. A certain level of market return does not result in a certain level of security return. Instead, both market and security returns depend on a third variable—the economy. Economic events cause systematic changes in both security and market prices.

Properly viewed, beta reflects the fact that both market and security returns depend on common events. Thus, the most logical way to forecast beta is to quantify the relationship between market and security returns and these factors. What, for example, is the relationship between changes in the expected rate of inflation and the returns of both individual securities and the market? Compared to the market, which securities are sensitive to inflation and which are not?

Most of the risk and return in a portfolio are linked to the market. In turn, the market component of risk and return for a security is derived from the economic events that affect many stocks. It follows that there are considerable benefits to be derived from an extension of fundamental security analysis that is concerned with the relationship between a security's return and economywide events—so-called *fundamental betas*.

Barr Rosenberg has developed a way of predicting fundamental betas through *relative response coefficients*. Basically, a relative response coefficient is the ratio of the expected response of a security to the expected response of the market if both the security and the market are affected by the same event. For example, if the event is inflation, those stocks that react to inflation in the same way as the market will have a high relative response coefficient for this event. Similarly, stocks that are not as sensitive to inflation as the market will have a low relative response coefficient for inflation.

Assume that we wish to study the impact of future energy and inflation developments on the market and on two stocks. There is an equal likelihood that future events in each of these areas will turn out to have favorable, unchanged, or unfavorable implications. This situation, plus the relative response that each event-outcome combination is expected to elicit, are depicted in Table 19-5. Stock T is expected to respond two-thirds as much as the market to an energy-related event, whereas stock U is anticipated to react twice as strongly as the market. To an inflation event, stock T is expected to respond twice as much as the market, whereas stock U is not expected to show any reaction to inflation events.

TABLE 19-5
CONTRIBUTIONS TO RETURN FOR HYPOTHETICAL
EVENT-OUTCOME SEQUENCES

Event	Outcome	Percentage Contribution to Return		
		Market	*Stock T*	*Stock U*
Energy	Favorable	+3	+2	+6
	Unchanged	0	0	0
	Unfavorable	−3	−2	−6
Inflation	Favorable	+2	+4	0
	Unchanged	0	0	0
	Unfavorable	−2	−4	0

The relationships portrayed in Table 19-5 can be used to contrast the expected values and variances of returns on securities with those of the market when both are affected by the same macroeconomic events. In this illustration, the expected (average) impact of these two events on market return is zero, and the variance is 30 percent.[6] The variance of future market returns can be separated into the variances generated by each of the two events. In this illustration, energy uncertainties cause 24 percentage points of the variance in market returns. Similarly, the variance caused by inflation uncertainty amounts to 6 percent.

In general terms, a security's beta is determined by:

1. The proportional contributions of various categories of economic events to market variance
2. The relative response of security returns to these same events—the relative response coefficients

More specifically, the beta for any security is the weighted average of its relative response coefficients, each weighted by the proportion of total variance in market returns due to that event.

In the example in Table 19-5, energy is the greatest source of uncertainty (variance). Thus, in the calculation of beta, energy uncertainty receives proportionately more emphasis. In terms of response to the two economic events, stock B is expected to be volatile in a changing energy situation. It is not surprising, therefore, that the betas for stocks A and B are 0.9 and 1.1, respectively.

The importance of the foregoing discussion of the composition of beta is that a security's beta will change when:

1. The variance contributed by the various categories of economic events changes
2. The response coefficients change

Also, to the degree that these changes can be predicted or explained, beta can be predicted or explained.

An accurate prediction of beta is the most important element in predicting the future behavior of a portfolio. That is, in the portfolio context, the relevant risk of a security lies in its impact on the risk of a portfolio. Further, the risk of a well-diversified portfolio is almost exclusively linked to the sensitivity of its component securities to future market moves. For this purpose, backward-looking betas are inappropriate.

Instead, it is necessary to (1) consider the sources of such future moves, (2) project the security's reaction to such sources, and (3) assign probabilities to the likelihood of each possible occurrence. This process, in turn, requires a thorough understanding of (1) the economics of the relevant industry, (2) both operating leverage and financial leverage of the company, and (3) other fundamental factors with meaningful relative response coefficients.

---

[6]To assist the reader who wishes to pursue this subject in more detail, the numerical example used here is identical to that used by Rosenberg. The interested reader can find the procedure used to calculate this variance (as well as other information) in B. Rosenberg, and J. Guy,"Prediction of Systematic Risk from Investment Fundamentals," *Financial Analysts Journal,* 32, No. 3 (May-June 1976), 60-72, and No.4 (July-August 1976), 62-70.

Rosenberg's fundamentally derived betas have been shown to be more accurate than historically derived estimates. Six risk indexes are based on current fundamental characteristics of each company and are measures of the following: (1) market variability, (2) earnings variability, (3) low valuation and unsuccess, (4) immaturity and smallness, (5) growth orientation, and (6) financial risk. Rosenberg has found that, in the past, stock returns have tended to be related to these factors, and forecasts of beta are improved by adjusting them through appropriate weightings of these factors. To calculate fundamentally based predictions of beta and residual risk, Rosenberg uses the following six indexes of risk:

1. *Market variability.* Measures the impact of certain factors on the relationship between the market variability of returns and security returns.
2. *Earnings variability.* Measures the variability of earnings. Earnings variability contributes to risk.
3. *Low valuation and "unsuccess."* Designed to measure the variability of returns (risk) inherent in consistently low-market-valuation stocks with dismal operating records.
4. *Immaturity and smallness.* Differentiates between the older and larger firms—which have accumulated substantial fixed assets and have a more secure economic position and a lower degree of risk—and the small, younger, and riskier firms.
5. *Growth orientation.* Measures the risk associated with the so-called high-multiple (P/E) stocks.
6. *Financial structure.* Measures financial risk by incorporating leverage (long-term debt and equity as a percentage of book value), coverage of fixed charges, the ratio of debt to total assets, liquidity, and net monetary debt. In general, the more highly leveraged a financial structure, the greater is the risk to the common stockholders.

Since stock returns are now specified relative to this more detailed multifactor model, the system can provide a more precise measurement of the risk characteristics of a portfolio. Instead of simply separating systematic risk from unsystematic or residual risk, we can now split residual risk into what is called specific risk and extramarket covariance.

Specific risk is the uncertainty in the return that arises from events that are specific to the firm. Specific risk is unrelated to events that affect other firms and is sometimes referred to as the "unique" or "independent" risk of the company.

Extramarket covariance is the remaining component of residual risk. It is manifested as a tendency of related assets to move together in a way that is independent of the market as a whole. The term "covariance" refers to the tendency of stock prices to move together, or "covary." The term "extramarket" means that these comovements are not related to the movements of the market as a whole. Extramarket covariance can be thought of as the middle ground between systematic and specific risk. Systematic risk affects all firms. Specific risk affects only one firm. Extramarket covariance impacts a homogeneous group of firms, such as those belonging to a certain industry or those with large capitalizations.

For individual stocks specific risk is most important, accounting for about 50 percent of the total risk, with the remainder about equally divided between systematic risk and extramarket covariance. For a well-diversified portfolio, systematic risk is likely to be 80 to 90 percent of the total risk.

For portfolios with concentrations of stocks in certain industry groups, or classes of stocks such as interest-sensitive stocks, extramarket covariance is very important. Thus, the construction of prudent, well-reasoned portfolios requires the prediction of all three aspects of risk: systematic, specific, and extramarket. It is noteworthy in this regard that the Rosenberg prediction scheme derives estimates of both market returns and extramarket covariances from a single underlying model.

Traditional Portfolio Selection

Traditionally, portfolio selection has been viewed as an art form, perhaps even a craft. Portfolio men are builders. Much of their work has its roots in a kind of life-cycle, interior-decorator approach.

Security-portfolio selection must be preceded by attention to financial planning. Needs must be analyzed and provision made for such things as emergency savings, adequate insurance, and home ownership. For many people, basic living expenses, savings, insurance, and shelter costs absorb most, if not all, income and resources. For these people, direct securities investing may never be a practical reality. Others frequently plunge into the securities markets before paying proper attention to financial planning prerequisites. The question of appropriate portfolio selection would presume that an investor had his financial house in order first.

A step-by-step traditional approach to portfolio building recognizes several basic tenets.[7] First, investors prefer larger to smaller returns from securities. Second, the way to achieve this goal is to take more risk. Third, the ability to achieve higher returns is dependent upon (1) the investor's judgment of risk, and (2) his ability to assume specific risks. Spreading money among many securities can reduce risk.

As components of risk, the theory recognizes specific types of risk and nonrisk factors bearing upon return—namely, interest-rate risk, purchasing-power risk, financial risks (including business, financial, and market risk), and nonrisk variables such as taxation and marketability. Portfolios are presumably constructed by employing securities associated with varying degrees of risk and nonrisk factors.

The financial interior-decorator approach would follow a general sequence of steps. First, it is necessary to establish the minimum income an investor must have to avoid hardship under the most adverse economic conditions. Family and economic factors are the principal ingredients in the projection of nonsecurity income and expenses. Economic factors take into account the family balance sheet (assets and debts) and income statement (income and expenses). Family factors affect income and expenses through such variables as the number of dependents and their ages and health. Income-expense differentials establish the minimum income required from investments.

Second, the larger the principal in relation to the minimum investment income required, the greater the risk of loss of income that can be tolerated. Of course, one must plan for changes in principal available, changes in income from other sources, and changes

[7]Harry Sauvain, *Investment Management* (Englewood Cliffs, N.J.: Prentice-Hall, 1973).

in minimum expenses. Take two contrasting situations. In both, the principal amount is $100,000 and future expenses are forecast at $20,000 per year. Salary income is $18,000 in one case and only $8,000 in the other. In the former situation, the income "gap" is $2,000; the latter case has a gap of $12,000. A portfolio of $100,000 would have to yield 2 percent in the first case ($2,000/$100,000), and 12 percent ($12,000/$100,000) in the second. If good-quality bonds yield 8 percent, in the first example only $25,000 of principal is needed to provide the required income. This means that $75,000 can be invested at greater risk. The latter case requires (1) increasing outside income, and/or (2) reducing expenses, and/or (3) using some of the principal (assuming that additional principal is not forthcoming). Thus the future budgeting of nonsecurity income and expenses tells us the *degree of risk of principal or income the portfolio can tolerate.* Quality bonds and common stocks with generous, stable yields provide income with minimum risk to principal. The greater price volatility associated with stocks in general over bonds can be tolerated when required portfolio income is not substantial relative to principal available.

Third, the more nearly investment income generated at current rates of yield on high-grade bonds meets the minimum investment-income requirements projected on an inflation basis, the greater is the ability to risk loss of purchasing power of investment income. It is necessary to see that nonsecurity income (such as salary) and expenses may rise at different rates as price-level changes occur. Should expenses rise more rapidly than nonsecurity income, income from fixed-income securities will make the investor vulnerable to rises in the price level. This would suggest a need for some defense against inflation, in the form of securities that provide larger dollar income at a higher price level. More relative emphasis might be placed upon convertible securities that can be purchased at modest premiums over investment and conversion value. The greater the need for inflation protection, the more the emphasis moves to straight common-stock commitments.

Overall, in this decision-making process, an investor would be assessing the kinds of risk and degree of each type that he can tolerate. In addition, the importance of nonrisk factors such as marketability and taxation would be assessed after the risk factors. The fundamental risk factors bear upon income and principal in constant (price-level-adjusted) dollars. Financial risk can be minimized by commitments to top-quality bonds. These securities, however, offer poor resistance to inflation. Stocks provide better inflation protection than bonds but are more vulnerable to financial risk. Good-quality convertibles may bridge the financial-risk-purchasing-power-risk dilemma. The problems associated with interest-rate risk suggest that maturity is of major concern. Short-term fixed-income securities offer greatest risk to income; long-term fixed-income securities offer greatest risk to principal.

What we emerge with from this approach is a series of *compromises* on risk and nonrisk factors after an investor has assessed the major risk categories he or she is trying to minimize. The final answer will be in terms of relative portfolio weights assigned to classes of securities—that is, bonds (quality, maturity), stocks (income, cyclical, growth), and hybrids (convertibles). The specific securities chosen will be the more attractive in each class as judged by security analysis. Not uncommonly, the dollar amounts devoted to each security or class of securities will be a simple equal allotment.

Defining Investment Objectives[8]

Establishing portfolios for individuals is the most diverse of investment situations. There is literally a different set of circumstances, needs, and opportunities for every individual investor. Considerations that shape and modify investment strategies and objectives are extremely wide.[9]

Portfolios differ widely in their requirements, time horizons, risk thresholds, and cash flows. The objective of portfolio management is to reconcile these variables in such a manner as to minimize risk and maximize return, but the goal and the process of reconciling the variables is the same regardless of who owns the assets in question.

All portfolios share one objective: to provide the largest pool of assets from which the owner can finance expenditures now or at some future date. Since the future is uncertain, however, we can never know precisely what the value of assets will be over time, and we know even less about what their purchasing power will be. The degree of risk that we take should, therefore, vary in each case, based upon the *time horizon* within which we have to work and the likelihood that the portfolio will enjoy a net cash inflow or will be subject to cash withdrawals. The latter is a matter of *liquidity*. The art of portfolio management consists of nothing more than selecting securities that fit within the time and cash flow constraints of the investor; the application of this process to differing portfolios is only a variation on a constant theme.

Traditionally investors differentiate among three goals: maximum income, capital appreciation, and preservation of capital. If viewed rationally, however, all investors should want to achieve all three of these goals; obviously, no one wants to lose money, while everyone wants to have as much as possible. The problem is that most of the time circumstances deny us the opportunity to achieve all three goals simultaneously. The search for capital gains inevitably involves risk of loss of capital; assured income is seldom available with opportunities for capital gains—high income is frequently associated with high risk. Therefore, when the time horizon is short or when investors have to face cash withdrawals from the portfolio, they lean towards assets with the greatest certainty of income and capital value. As the time horizon stretches out into the future, and when investors are adding to rather than withdrawing principal, they can live more comfortably with uncertainty.

LIFE CYCLE APPROACH

The return and risk possibilities are virtually unconstrained for individuals, a unique investing situation. Why? Because, assuming a minimum wealth or income position, essentially all possible asset categories and all investment strategies are open to the individual investing directly for his own account.

---

[8]Donald L. Tuttle and John Maginn. *Determinants of Portfolio Policy* (Charlottesville, VA.: The Institute of Chartered Financial Analysts, 1982).

[9]Our discussion emphasizes personal portfolio selection. Institutional portfolios are addressed along similar lines. Basic security types are dictated very much by laws and regulations in addition to the debt-equity ratios and the term structure of debts.

That is, the individual has available the entire risk spectrum of investable assets ranging from essentially risk-free assets such as short term government fixed income securities to the riskiest assets such as common stock option contracts and commodities futures contracts.

In addition, the individual can choose from among the entire spectrum of investment strategies. Unlike other investors, he can establish either long or short positions in securities. And he can opt for a variety of different leverage positions. That is, the individual can invest all of his net worth in a portfolio of risky assets or part of net worth in risky assets and part in safe assets, or all in risky assets plus borrowing on margin and investing that borrowed money in risky assets.

Individuals' risk and return preferences are often portrayed in terms of stages of their "life cycle." That is, individuals are described by the stage of their lifetime or career where they are currently located.

The first stage is the early career situation. Assets are typically much less than liabilities, especially when the latter include a large house mortgage and other debts from credit purchases. The individual's assets are typically nondiversified, with house equity the largest asset held, and inaccessible, in the form of employer pension contributions. Priorities include savings for liquidity purposes, life insurance for death protection and, only third, investments. But because the individual has a very long time horizon with a potentially growing stream of discretionary income, he can undertake high return-high risk capital gain-oriented investments.

The middle stage is the mid-career individual. Assets equal or exceed liabilities, savings and life insurance programs are well under way, a basic investment program has been established and home equity and potential pension benefits are substantial. At the same time, while the time horizon is still relatively long, it is not so long that capital preservation is unimportant. The investor can continue to undertake high-risk, high-return investments and reap the growth and capital gain benefits therefrom, but may wish to reduce the overall risk exposure involved.

The final phase is late career or brink-of-retirement where the individual's time horizon has diminished and income needs—in terms of size and stability—have risen. Assets significantly exceed liabilities, savings, pension, and life insurance programs are complete and the house mortgage has been repaid. Income is reduced to investment returns, Social Security, and other pension payments. The investor's portfolio is typically shifted to significantly lower-return, lower-risk assets with large dividend or interest payment components and relatively secure asset values, since inflationary economic conditions may require the sale of assets to make up income shortfall.

Investment Constraints

LIQUIDITY

Just as was true of investment objectives, the constraints imposed on individual investors are subject to wide variance. That is true of liquidity needs which are highly individualistic, and hence, highly variable across individuals.

Some individuals use their investment accounts as combinations of checking and savings accounts. For these individuals, an adequate amount of funds should be kept in a liquidity reserve as large as the largest cash drain net of cash inflows that is budgeted.

This reserve is usually easy to program. It should be invested in exceptionally high quality, short maturity debt issues such as a money market fund or the types of issues—Treasury bills, commercial paper, certificates of deposit and bankers acceptances—in which these funds are invested.

Furthermore, if the assets held have poor marketability, such as residential real estate or stock in a closely held business, liquidity needs should be estimated especially carefully and funded generously.

TIME HORIZON

Almost as important as risk and return in investment decision making is time horizon. This is the investment planning period for individuals. It is highly variable from individual to individual.

As indicated in the discussion of life cycles, individuals who are early in their life cycle have a long horizon, one which can absorb and smooth out the ups and downs of risky combinations of assets like common stock portfolios. These individuals can build portfolios of riskier assets and can use more risky investment strategies.

Other individuals who are later in their lifetimes have a much shorter horizon and should therefore tend toward less volatile portfolios, typically consisting of more bonds than stocks, with the former of higher quality and shorter duration (maturity/coupon combination) and the latter of higher quality and lower volatility.

TAX CONSIDERATIONS

Individuals are subject to a wide range of marginal tax rates. Our discussion in Chapter 3 noted that taxes were an important modifier of portfolio strategy. High bracket investors should consider investing the fixed income portion of their portfolio in a diversified group of municipal bonds if their taxable equivalent expected return exceeds that of taxable issues of equal risk. These same investors no doubt will look to investing the equity portion of their portfolios in a diversified group of stocks with large capital gains components relative to dividend income for a given level of risk.

CONSIDERING RISK

Our discussions of risk have emphasized the fact that, for most investment decisions, the major uncertainty is the probable volatility in the price of the asset and, in particular, its volatility relative to the prices of all similar types of assets.

Since everyone obviously wants to make as much money as possible, the determining question in structuring a portfolio is the consequences of loss. This seems far more important than the chance of loss. Even if the chance of loss is small (such as the probability of dying at age 30), the consequences can be so serious that the individual must either avoid the risk altogether or must insure against it if he is unable to avoid it.

This is why the widow is conventionally viewed as an investor unable to take much risk. Because she typically has neither the life expectancy nor the earning power outside her portfolio to provide the opportunity to recoup losses, any diminuition in her capital or income may immediately impact upon her standard of living. Her opposite, the aggressive businessman, on the other hand, has sufficient earning power to sustain his living standard and also many years to recoup his losses. At an even further extreme, the consequences would be virtually minimal for a young man who will inherit millions from aging parents.

We might ask the same questions about the consequences of gain. To what extent would an increase in capital or income significantly improve the living standard of the investor? A widow with less than $100,000 to invest might lead an entirely different life if it were $200,000, while a multimillionaire (and his heirs) might live precisely the same whether his assets never changed in value or whether they doubled.

The consequences of loss or gain seldom fit in such a way that the risk exposure of the portfolio is easy to determine. This is often a subjective decision; some people never feel rich enough, while others would rather take a chance of going broke next year. The authors know of a 75-year-old man who asked his broker to place most of his wealth in the options market. He was tired of being beseiged by inflation. Here is a classic case of presumed risk aversion gone awry. Additionally, we know a millionaire whose broker tried to get him into the options market. This august gentleman reminded his broker, "Remember, you don't have to make me rich—I am rich!" This presumed risk seeker also did not fit the mold.

An Example of Traditional Portfolio Selection [10]

Shown below is an illustration of traditional portfolio construction. The case illustrated has many different ingredients that provide some interesting challenges.

K.J. Smith, recently deceased president of Interstate Cartage Company, left a net estate of $400,000. Under his will, trusts of $300,000 and $100,000 were created for his surviving spouse and adult daughter, Jan, respectively, with Second Trust Company named sole trustee. Jan is the beneficiary of her mother's trust. The widow's trust is comprised of the following assets:

	Amount at Market	Current Yield	Yield to Maturity
Money market fund	$ 75,000	14.7%	
Tax exempt municipal bonds	105,000	8.0	12.0%
Interstate Cartage Co., common stock	120,000	7.9	
	$300,000		

Mrs. Smith is 65 and in good health (mortality tables indicate an expected life span of 18 years). As a retirement benefit, she is eligible for life for Interstate's generous group medical insurance plan. Her estimated household and other expenses last year, adjusted to allow for inflation this year, indicate a need for at least $28,000 in pretax income. In the absence of her husband's salary, her tax bracket will decline from 50% to 30%. Next week she will be eligible to receive Social Security payments of $600 per month. Mrs. Smith plans to purchase a $60,000 condominium as a vacation residence within the next six months, using $15,000 in deferred compensation (after taxes) due her husband as the down payment. Conventional mortgage financing is available for 75 percent of the

---

[10]This example is adapted from Chartered Financial Analysts Examination I: 1982 with permission of the Institute of Chartered Financial Analysts (ICFA).

cost at 17.5 percent for 30 years. She anticipates that any tax savings from the credit for mortgage interest payments will be consumed by maintenance fees charged to owner residents. She also intends to join an adjacent country club where monthly dues are $125 per month. She wishes to retain all of the Interstate common stock because it is the only stock her husband ever owned and he had great confidence in the company's future. Also, the yield is very generous, despite the dividend reduction last year when the economy declined. Her daughter, Jan, 40, is single and is a harpist with the symphony orchestra of a medium-size city in the Midwest. She suffers from arthritis and has expressed concern to her mother regarding the financial status of the orchestra which relies upon private donations as well as ticket sales. Her marginal tax bracket is 30 percent. Mrs. Smith has requested that the assets in her trust be left intact if possible.

MRS. SMITH'S INVESTMENT OBJECTIVES AND CONSTRAINTS

The sources of annualized income for Mrs. Smith can be summarized as follows:

Trust assets:	
Money market mutual fund ($75,000 × 14.7%)	$11,025
Tax exempt municipals ($105,000 × 8.0%)	8,400
Interstate Cartage common ($120,000 × 7.9%)	9,480
	$28,905
Social Security ($600 × 12)	7,200
Total Annualized Income	$36,105

Her annualized expenses are:

Household and other last year	$28,000
Mortgage on new second home ($45,000 × 17.5%)	7,875
Country club dues ($125 × 12)	1,500
Total Annualized Expenses	$37,375

Thus, her income needs *cannot* be met by the existing portfolio ($37,375 − $36,105 = $1,270 shortfall).

Investment objectives for Mrs. Smith should be defined in terms of risk/return relationships. To maintain her desired standard of living, the current income component of return must approximate 10 percent before taxes, a modest increase from the present level. Total return, including a capital change component, must be larger to assume maintenance of "real" income for an extended period (18 years) and preservation of as much principal as possible for the ultimate benefit of her daughter. Mrs. Smith should not risk permanent loss of principal by investment in risky categories of assets or assets having high unsystematic risk. Since the trust must provide the majority (81 percent) of her living expenses, current income volatility must also be avoided. Because the trust appears sufficient to meet current needs without downgrading quality or sacrificing diversification, market volatility can be tolerated. In summary, a realistic objective for Mrs. Smith is to increase return to at least 10 percent and maintain or decrease portfolio risk through improved diversification by asset category. Some key investment constraints must be considered. First, her need for liquidity is low since she has anticipated her largest discretionary capital and routine expenses. Moreover, the usual risk of large and unpredictable medical expenses for the elderly is not material because of full medical insurance coverage. Second, Mrs. Smith's time horizon is long enough to make inflation a significant risk factor. Therefore, attention to asset value preservation is important to the income to her as well as her daughter. Last, she has a nondiversified equity portfolio. The emotional request of Mrs. Smith to retain all the Interstate Cartage common may limit portfolio construction options.

REVISING THE EXISTING PORTFOLIO

Recommended changes in Mrs. Smith's portfolio no doubt should include actions to improve diversification, increase current income, and reduce unsystematic risk within the equity segment of the portfolio. Capital market and economic data at the time of the portfolio review appear in Table 19-6. Specifically, changes might include:

1. A decrease in liquidity (the money market fund) from 25 percent to 5 to 10 percent of assets because money market rates tend to fluctuate widely from year-to-year which is in conflict with the assured minimum level of income objective. Also, the in-

TABLE 19-6
CAPITAL MARKET
AND ECONOMIC DATA

Fixed Income Securities			Common Stocks			
Category	Current Market Yield		Category	Current Yield	Implied Total Return	Beta Coef.
Money market funds	14.7%		Industrials	5.2%	17.0%	1.0
Government bonds:			Truckers	4.0	14.8	1.1
Intermediate-term	14.4		Interstate			
Long-term	14.0		Cartage Co.	7.9	14.8	1.3
Corporate bonds (A-rated)						
Intermediate-term	15.1					
Long-term	16.0					
Tax exempt municipals						
Intermediate-term	10.2					
Long-term	11.1					

Consumer Price Index			
(Avg. Annual Increase)			
		Projected	
		Next Five Years	
Current Year	Next Year	Range	Most Probable
8.9%	8.0%	5-15%	7-10%

flation outlook in Table 19-6 indicates the possibility for lower yields over the near and long term which implies the possibility of an extended reduction in short-term yields.

2. Sale of the tax exempt municipal bonds (35 percent of assets) and purchase of intermediate-term government and/or corporate bonds is advisable. In addition, it seems prudent to add 5 to 15 percent of assets to this category with proceeds from the money market fund. This allows after-tax income to be increased and stabilized. Current yield is more important than yield to maturity since cash income is needed. Because of her change from a 50 to 30 percent tax bracket, taxable issues are more attractive on a net yield basis. In addition, both near- and long-term projected inflation rates indicate a "real" rate of return is available from intermediate bonds and principal volatility caused by interest rate fluctuations prior to maturity is not a major risk factor. Long-term bonds are not attractive because the incremental yield over intermediates is small and inflation remains a risk as per Table 19-6.

3. Sell the Interstate Cartage common stock (40 percent of assets) and buy a diversified portfolio of industrial common stocks (40 to 50 percent of assets). This is advisable because the stock portfolio should be diversified rather than concentrated in one company in one industry. Also, Interstate's recent dividend cut suggests that elimination of the dividend is possible and that serious company and/or industry problems exist. The emotional request of Mrs. Smith must be evaluated in conjunction with Table 19-6 which indicates the risk-adjusted return of this issue is inferior to trucking company stocks and other industrial stocks. Interstate is probably not appropriate even as a small percentage of the total portfolio. A diversified portfolio of industrial common stocks should provide superior returns over the long term relative to other investment options offered. While she is a defensive investor, Mrs. Smith needs inflation protection and assurance of a "real" return over many years. The reduction in current income yield from 7.9 to 5.2 percent will not jeopardize current income needs.

In summary, the following asset mix should satisfy Mrs. Smith's objectives:

	Amount	Percentage of Portfolio	Current Yield	Annual Income
Money market fund	$ 30,000	10%	14.7%	$ 4,410
Government/corporate bonds (Intermediate-term)	120-150,000	40-50	14.5	19,575
Common stocks	120-150,000	40-50	5.2	7,020
	$ 300,000	100%		$31,005

Summary

This chapter considered both modern and traditional approaches to portfolio selection. A simple technique was introduced for constructing optimal portfolios based upon the basic ideas of Markowitz and others. In addition, this chapter expanded on the significance of beta in stock and portfolio selection.

The chapter concluded with an examination of the basic principles of traditional portfolio selection applicable to the portfolios of individuals. An extensive example showed how these principles could be utilized to construct a hypothetical portfolio.

Questions and Problems

1. Using the notion of corner points and the efficient frontier developed earlier, show on a risk-return diagram that the "best" portfolio (corner point) for a risk lover would be corner point 1 in Figure 18-7.

2. Refer to the diagram below.
   a. Which portfolios shown are "feasible" (possible)?
   b. Which portfolio would a risk-lover choose? Why?
   c. Which portfolio would an irrational investor choose? Why?
   d. Which portfolios shown are "efficient"? Why?

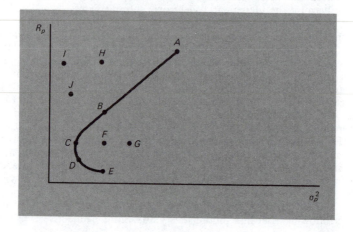

3. What is the optimum portfolio in choosing among the following securities and assuming $R_F = 5\%$.

Security	Expected Return	Beta	σ^2_{ei}
A	15	1.0	30
B	12	1.5	20
C	11	2.0	40
D	8	.8	10
E	9	1.0	20
F	14	1.5	10

4. How is the cut-off point determined in the portfolio ranking system introduced in this chapter? What is the interpretation of this cut-off point in economic terms?

5. Describe the manner in which raising the return on a riskless asset (R_F) would alter the selection of the optimal portfolio in Question 3 above. (No calculations are required).

6. The "best" stock portfolio can be discovered as that corner portfolio that maximizes $\theta = (R_p - R_F)/\sigma_p$ where R_p = expected return on the portfolio; σ_p is the expected standard deviation on the portfolio, and R_F = risk-free rate.
   a. Show that corner point 9 provides a higher value for θ than corner point 8 in Table 18-4.
   b. Determine the riskless rate at which θ is the same for corner points 8 and 9.

7. The candidate stocks in the sample problem in the chapter led to a "best" portfolio shown in Table 19.3.

    a. Why do you suppose that McDonald's and Raytheon account for almost half the total portfolio?

    b. How would we go about assessing the trade-off between transaction-cost savings and changes in portfolio return and risk by making Pitney-Bowes and United States Shoe Co. an even 6% each of the portfolio?

8. In what ways is corner portfolio 17 better for a risk-averse person than the placement of all funds in the least-risk stock, Wisconsin Gas Co. (see Table 18-4)?

9. As an investment adviser, describe an appropriate investment program for the following:

    a. An associate's parents, ages seventy-three and seventy-five, have $60,000 to invest. They have pension income in the amount of $6,000 annually, although they have been accustomed to an income of $14,000. This sum and their home, owned free and clear, are their only assets.

    b. An unmarried career woman is approaching forty, has no dependents, and has a secure and well-paying job as an advertising art director which is supplemented by an attractive retirement program. She saves $2,000 to $2,500 every year but is bored with talk about investments and the stock market. She has just inherited $100,000.

10. A widow in her seventies and in good health comes to you for advice about her investments. Her husband left her a portfolio that consists mostly of low-yielding "growth" stocks that are now at prices that approximate their adjusted cost. She has found that the income available is not nearly enough to help her maintain a comfortable standard of living. She needs $25,000 income before taxes from her investments. The current market value of the portfolio is $400,000, and its current yield is 2.3 percent.

    Since she will need this higher income for perhaps the next ten years, you have suggested that she place at least half of the portfolio in high-yielding straight corporate bonds.

    a. List the assumptions you made regarding the investment environment and the widow's situation in order to consider the immediate investment of one-half of the portfolio in bonds is a *prudent* decision.

    b. Describe the types of investments you would select for the remainder of the portfolio that is not invested in high-yielding straight corporate bonds.

11. A detailed portfolio analysis was provided in the chapter for Mrs. Smith. Select the portfolio below which appears most appropriate for her daughter Jan who is mentioned in the analysis. Provide reasons for your selection by reference to investment objectives and constraints.

	"A"	"B"	"C"
	Percentage of Portfolio Assets		
Money market fund	10%	15%	30%
Government/corporate bonds:			
Intermediate-term	—	10	20
Long-term	30	40	5
Tax-exempt municipals:			
Long-term	20	10	10
Common stocks:			
Industrials	40	25	35
	100%	100%	100%
After-Tax Annual Income	$8,000	$8,600	$8,100

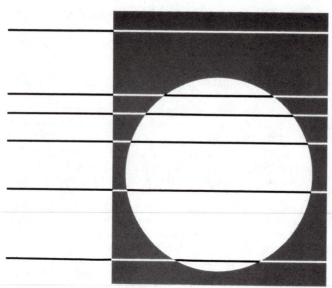

Capital Market Theory
and International
Diversification

Chapter 18 presented the fundamental principles of portfolio management. Here we use these principles to discuss capital market theory and the capital asset pricing model and to extend the concept of diversification to include international securities.

In a few words, capital market theory is concerned with how asset pricing should occur if investors behaved as Markowitz suggested. The capital asset pricing model uses the results of capital market theory to derive the relationship between the expected returns and systematic risk of individual securities and portfolios. The search for assets that have low covariance with the market has increased attention towards portfolios more widely diversified among wide asset types. The area of international securities is considered here as one of these asset types.

Capital Market Theory

Assumptions Underlying Capital Market Theory

Capital market theory is a major extension of the portfolio theory of Markowitz.[1] *Portfolio theory* is really a description of how rational investors should build efficient portfolios. *Capital market theory* tells us how assets should be priced in the capital markets if, indeed, everyone behaved in the way portfolio theory suggests. The *capital*

---

[1] The development of capital market theory is traceable largely to William Sharpe, "Capital Asset Prices: A Theory of Market Equilibrium under Conditions of Risk," *Journal of Finance*, September 1964, pp. 425-42.

asset pricing model (CAPM) is a relationship explaining how assets should be priced in the capital markets.

The real world is complex to be sure. To understand it and build models of how it works, we need to sweep away those complexities we think have only a minor effect on its behavior. Most of the complexities that have to be removed in the stock market concern institutional frictions. These include such things as commissions, taxation, short-selling rules, and margin requirements, to name a few.

The specific assumptions underlying capital market theory are:

1. Investors make decisions based solely upon risk-and-return assessments. These judgments take the form of expected values and standard deviation measures.
2. The purchase or sale of a security can be undertaken in infinitely divisible units. We can buy one dollar's worth of McDonald's stock.
3. Investors can short sell any amount of shares without limit.
4. Purchases and sales by a single investor cannot affect prices. This means that there is perfect competition where investors in total determine prices by their actions. Otherwise, monopoly power could influence prices (returns).
5. There are no transaction costs. Where there are transaction costs returns would be sensitive to whether or not the investor owned a security before the decision period.
6. The purchase or sale of securities is done in the absence of personal income taxes. This means that we are indifferent to the form in which the return is received (divided or capital gains).
7. The investor can borrow or lend any amount of funds desired at an identical riskless rate (e.g., the Treasury bill rate).
8. Investors share identical expectations with regard to the relevant decision period, the necessary decision inputs, their form and size. Thus, investors are presumed to have identical planning horizons, and to have identical expectations regarding expected returns, variances of expected returns, and covariances of all pairs of securities. Otherwise, there would be a family of efficient frontiers because of differences in expectations.

This might seem to many as creating a kind of "toy world" fabricated to satisfy the whims of eccentric academics. Many of the assumptions no doubt seem objectionable. However, despite the strict assumptions, the model we will view does a very good job of describing prices in the capital markets. Reality is not materially distorted by making these assumptions.

The Capital Asset Pricing Model

Recall that portfolio theory implied that each investor faced an efficient frontier. In general, the efficient frontier will differ among investors because of differences in expectations. When we introduce riskless borrowing and lending there are some significant changes involved. Lending is best thought of as an investment in a riskless security. This security might be a savings account, Treasury bills, or even high-grade commercial paper. Borrowing can be thought of as the use of margin. Borrowing and lending options transform the efficient frontier into a straight line. Figure 20-1 shows the standard efficient frontier *ABCD*. Assume that an investor can lend at the rate of $R_F = .05$, which represents the rate on U.S. Treasury bills. Hence the point R_F represents a risk-free

FIGURE 20-1
EFFICIENT FRONTIER WITH INTRODUCTION OF LENDING

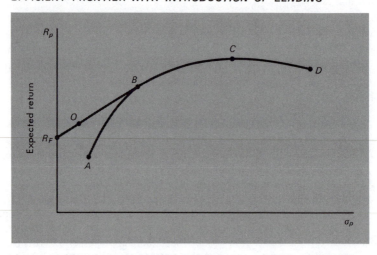

investment (R_F = .05; σ_p = 0). The investor could place all or part of his funds in this riskless asset. If he placed part of his funds in the risk-free asset and part in one of the portfolios of risky securities along the efficient frontier, what would happen? He could generate portfolios along the straight-line segment R_FB.

Let us examine the properties of a given portfolio along the straight-line segment R_FB. Consider point B on the original efficient frontier $ABCD$ where, say, R_p = .10 and σ_p = .06. If we placed one-half of available funds in the riskless asset and one-half in the risky portfolio, B, the resulting combined risk-return measures for the mixed portfolio, O, can be found from Equations 20.1 and 20.2:

$$R_p = XR_M + (1 - X)R_F \qquad (20.1)$$

where:

R_p = expected return on portfolio

X = percentage of funds invested in risky portfolio

$(1 - X)$ = percentage of funds invested in riskless asset

R_M = expected return on risky portfolio

R_F = expected return on riskless asset

and:

$$\sigma_p = X\sigma_M \qquad (20.2)$$

where:

σ_p = expected standard deviation of the portfolio

X = percentage of funds invested in risky portfolio

σ_M = expected standard deviation on risky portfolio

For our example, the risk-return measures for portfolio M are:

$$R_p = (\tfrac{1}{2})(.10) + (\tfrac{1}{2})(.05) = .075$$

$$\sigma_p = (\tfrac{1}{2})(.06) + (\tfrac{1}{2})(.00) = .03$$

The result indicates that our return and risk have been reduced. All points between R_F and B can be similarly determined using Equations 20.1 and 20.2. As stated, the locus of these points will be a straight line.

Introduction of the possibility of borrowing funds will change the shape of our efficient frontier in 20.1 to the right of point B. In borrowing, we consider the possibilities associated with total funds invested being enlarged through trading on the equity.

Consider three cases. If we assume that X is the percentage of investment wealth or equity placed in the risky portfolio, then where $X = 1$, investment wealth is totally committed to the risky portfolio. Where $X < 1$, only a fraction of X is placed in the risky portfolio, and the remainder is lent at the rate R_F. The third case, $X > 1$, signifies that the investor is borrowing rather than lending. It may be easier to visualize this by rewriting Equation 20.1 as follows:

$$R_p = XR_M - (X-1)R_F \tag{20.3}$$

where all terms are as in Equation 20.1 and the term R_F is the borrowing rate. For simplicity, the borrowing rate and lending rate are assumed to be equal or 5 percent. The first component of Equation 20.3 is the gross return made possible because the borrowed funds, as well as the original wealth or equity, are invested in the risky portfolio. The second term refers to the cost of borrowing on a percentage basis. For example, $X = 1.25$ would indicate that the investor borrows an amount equal to 25 percent of his investment wealth. This is equivalent to a margin requirement of 80 percent ($X = 1/\text{Margin requirement}$). His *net* return on his investment wealth would become:

$$R_p = (1.25)(.10) - (0.25)(.05) = .1125$$

The associated risk would become:

$$\sigma_p = X\sigma_p = (1.25)(.06) = .075$$

Hence the levered portfolio provides increased return with increased risk.

The introduction of borrowing and lending has given us an efficient frontier that is a straight line throughout. Figure 20-2 shows the new efficient frontier. Point M now represents the optimal combination of risky securities. The existence of this combination simplifies our problem of portfolio selection. The investor need only decide how much to borrow or lend. No other investments or combination of investments available is as efficient as point M. The decision to purchase M is the investment decision. The decision to buy some riskless asset (lend) or to borrow (leverage the portfolio) is the financing decision.

These conditions give rise to what has been referred to as the *separation theorem*. The theorem implies that all investors, conservative or aggressive, should hold the same mix of stocks from the efficient set. They should use borrowing or lending to attain their preferred risk class.[2] This conclusion flies in the face of more traditional notions of selec-

---

[2]W. F. Sharpe, *Portfolio Theory and Capital Markets* (New York: McGraw-Hill, 1970), p. 70.

FIGURE 20-2
EFFICIENT FRONTIER WITH BORROWING AND LENDING

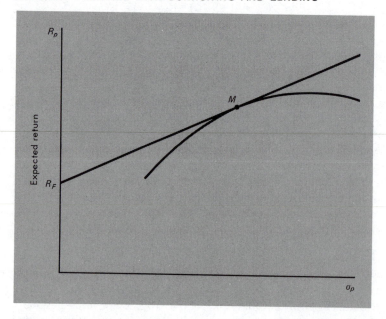

tion of portfolios. Traditional portfolio-building rules would construct certain types of portfolios for conservative clients and others for investors who are more daring. *This analysis suggests that both types of investors should hold identically risky portfolios. Desired risk levels are then achieved through combining portfolio M with lending and borrowing.*

If all investors face similar expectations and the same lending and borrowing rate, they will face a diagram such as that in Figure 20-2 and, furthermore, all of the diagrams will be identical. The portfolio of assets held by any investor will be identical to the portfolio of risky assets held by any other investor. If all investors hold the same risky portfolio, then, in equilibrium, it must be the market portfolio (*M*). The market portfolio is a portfolio comprised of all risky assets. Each asset will be held in the proportion which the market value of the asset represents to the total market value of all risky assets. For example, if Exxon represents 2 percent of all risky assets, then the market portfolio contains 2 percent Exxon stock and each investor will take 2 percent of the money that will be invested in risky assets and place it in Exxon stock. This is the key: All investors will hold combinations of only two portfolios, the market portfolio and a riskless security.

The straight line depicted in Figure 20-2 is referred to as the *capital market line.* All investors will end up with portfolios somewhere along the capital market line and all efficient portfolios would lie along the capital market line. However, not all securities or portfolios lie along the capital market line. From the derivation of the efficient frontier we know that all portfolios, except those that are efficient, lie below the capital market line.

Observing the capital market line tells us something about the market price of risk. The equation of the capital market line (connecting the riskless asset with a risky portfolio) is

$$R_e = R_F + \frac{R_M - R_F}{\sigma_M} \sigma_e$$

where the subscript e denotes an efficient portfolio.

The term $(R_M - R_F)/\sigma_M$ can be thought of as the extra return that can be gained by increasing the level of risk (standard deviation) on an efficent portfolio by one unit. The entire second term on the right side of the equation is thus the market price of risk times the amount of risk in the portfolio. The expression R_F is the price of time. That is, it is the price paid for delaying consumption for one period. The expected return on an efficient portfolio is

(Price of time) + (Price of risk)(Amount of risk)

Although this equation sets the return on an efficient portfolio, we need to go beyond to deal with returns on nonefficient portfolios or on individual securities.

Security Market Line

For well-diversified portfolios, nonsystematic risk tends to go to zero and the only relevant risk is systematic risk measured by beta. Since we assume that investors are concerned only with expected return and risk, the only dimensions of a security that need be of concern are expected return and beta.

We have seen that all investments and all portfolios of investments lie along a straight line in the return-to-beta space. To determine this line we need only connect the intercept (beta of zero, or riskless security) and the market portfolio (beta of one and return of R_M). These two points identify the straight line shown in Figure 20-3. The equation of a straight line is

$$R_i = \alpha + b\,\beta_i$$

The first point on the line is the riskless asset with a beta of zero, so

$$R_F = \alpha + b(0)$$

$$R_F = \alpha$$

The second point on the line is the market portfolio with a beta of 1. Thus,

$$R_M = \alpha + b(1)$$

$$R_M - \alpha = b$$

$$(R_M - R_F) = b$$

Combining the two results gives us

$$R_i = R_F + \beta_i (R_M - R_F)$$

This is a key relationship. It is called the *security market line*. It describes the expected return for all assets and portfolios of assets, efficient or not. The difference between the expected return on any two assets can be related simply to their difference in beta. The higher beta is for any security, the higher must be its expected return. The relationship between beta and expected return is linear.

FIGURE 20-3
THE SECURITY MARKET LINE

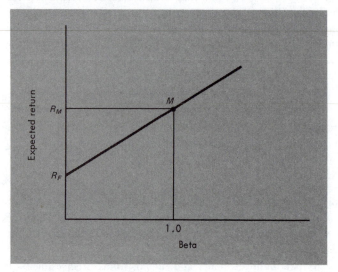

Recall that in Chapter 5 we said that the risk of any stock could be divided into systematic and unsystematic risk. Beta is an index of systematic risk. This equation suggests that systematic risk is the only important ingredient in determining expected returns. Unsystematic risk is of no consequence. It is not total variance of returns that affects returns, only that part of the variance in returns that cannot be eliminated by diversification.

International Diversification

We have noted the importance of diversification for reducing the risk of the portfolio and pointed out that the important factor when selecting an asset for diversification purposes is the covariance of the asset with all other assets in the portfolio. Further, with the CAPM it is shown that the relevant covariance is that between the asset and the market portfolio of all risky assets in the economy. In the search for investment assets that have low covariance with the market portfolio, increasing attention has been paid to international capital markets because of the expectation that the covariance between international securities and United States securities should be very low. Hence, one should consider adding such investments to a portfolio composed of domestic stocks. International investment is a good example of a more general trend towards portfolios more widely diversified among wide asset types. Investment in real estate, for example, has gained in popularity among large investors for much the same reason.

Expanding securities holdings beyond domestic borders has been gaining interest among investors. The potential advantages lie in a better ratio of reward to risk than is obtainable from a purely domestic portfolio. This advantage might be gained by consistently investing in specific foreign companies, industries, or areas. Some macroeconomic swings might provide specific opportunities in areas or countries. For example, one might consider China trade, or development of Mexican or North Sea oil. Other major changes can bring high risks (e.g., the sweeping of the Socialists to power in France). Some industries are better positioned outside the United States and may even be unique. One could point to autos, to gold, and to diamonds. Some companies are unique or do better than their U.S. counterparts. Companies such as Perrier, Sotheby's, Rossignol, and Kirin Beer are among many possible examples.

The true benefits from international diversification, however, are more likely to follow from the fact that risk-return combinations available within an internationally diversified portfolio are likely to be superior to those of the individual stock markets.

A careful analysis of the available evidence indicates that a properly conceived and executed program of international equity investing offers U.S. investors an important means of increasing the probability of attaining superior long-term results. The increased diversification possible through an international investment strategy provides an opportunity for improving the fundamental risk-return trade-offs U.S. investors face. The essence of the argument for international investing is simple yet powerful. Not all world equity markets move together in a highly synchronized fashion. In varying degrees, each market has its own performance cycle because different national economies are subject to varying socio-economic and political forces. Since the returns on common stocks in different markets do not move in lock-step, the opportunity exists to *reduce the uncertainty of portfolio returns* materially by diversifying across stock markets as well as within them.

The desirability of an international investment strategy is obviously dependent upon expected returns in foreign equity markets as well as the risk reduction potential from additional diversification. Both financial history and fundamental economic factors suggest that for countries of practical investment interest, future rates of return (translated into U.S. dollars) should be at least competitive with the U.S. equity market. Indeed, if history is at all suggestive of the future, returns from an international investing strategy are likely to enhance the performance of a U.S. portfolio.

Potential Advantages of International Portfolios

Within the United States the degree of correlation between returns on shares of individual firms and the broad-based market index is typically around .5 (systematic risk is one-half the total risk). Correlations between U.S. industry groups and the U.S. market averages about .6. However, correlations between foreign markets and the U.S. market are lower than U.S. market-industry correlations. Thus, *international diversification is more powerful than industry diversification domestically.*

Properly implemented, international diversification virtually assures lower risk for the U.S. investor but the magnitude of these benefits depends on the degree of correlation existing between markets. In examining the interrelationships among world markets, an "inner core" of international markets consisting of the United States, Canada, Netherlands, Switzerland, West Germany and, to a lesser extent, Belgium, have discernible comovement similarities. These results are similar to a consistently strong relationship among the United States, Canada, Switzerland, and the Netherlands. This suggests that diversification among such "inner core" countries should logically provide lesser amounts of risk reduction than diversification among a broader universe of countries where correlations are likely to be lower. This is particularly true when investments are restricted to the U.S. market, Canada, and the six major industrially developed western European countries. Risk under these constraints is reduced only one-third, which nonetheless is still quite significant. However, when the potential investment universe is expanded to include Japan, Australia, and South Africa, countries more economically and geographically distinct from the original eight North Atlantic national markets, risk declined half again as much or by 50 percent in total.

Table 20-1 indicates correlation coefficients between the Standard & Poor's 500 Stock Index and similar indexes in foreign countries. Since the average for fifteen countries is about .43 compared to the U.S. interindustry correlation of about .6 *the international "cut" may be the most important in achieving diversification.*

When diversification is extended across national boundaries, a substantial proportion of risk which is systematic within each country can be eliminated. The reason is that many factors affecting share values are essentially domestic in nature. Differences among nations in tax laws, monetary policies, and general economic climate are illustrative. Even factors that influence the world economy, such as the sudden increase of oil prices in 1973, can affect individual economies differently.

The low correlation between foreign and domestic stock markets will provide risk reduction. Further, the returns from various foreign markets over the recent past suggest what we all dream of—lower risk and higher returns. Table 20-2 shows total rates of return per year for a number of countries for the period 1959-1979. The ability to sustain this performance in the future lies in the economic outlook for individual nations. The sources of growth in nations will be the quantity of inputs necessary for growth (capital, labor), and the output per unit of input (productivity) in the main. The Japanese example of high savings rates, extensive capital formation, economies of scale, and high labor productivity is particularly noteworthy. The ability to discriminate among countries

TABLE 20-1

CORRELATIONS BETWEEN U.S. MARKET
AND VARIOUS FOREIGN STOCK
MARKETS, 1974-1978

Canada	.70
Switzerland	.54
United Kingdom	.52
France	.46
Japan	.28
West Germany	.24
Spain	.17
Average (15 countries)	.43

TABLE 20-2
REWARD-TO-VARIABILITY RATIOS, 1959-1979

Country	Reward*	Variability†	Ratio‡
Japan	17.0	18	.94
West Germany	11.5	18	.64
Switzerland	12.4	21	.59
Netherlands	8.5	21	.40
Canada	6.5	18	.36
United States	6.5	18	.36
Australia	8.3	25	.33
United Kingdom	9.3	39	.24
France	5.8	28	.21

*Annualized rates of return for the 20 years ending 1979.
†Standard deviation of annual returns.
‡Reward/Variability

regarding future GNP is important in predicting future relative rankings of equity returns therein.

Risks to International Investment

CURRENCY EFFECTS

Since international investing implies returns in a variety of currencies whose relative values may fluctuate, it involves taking foreign exchange risks. It is possible, for example, to invest in Japanese securities which experience excellent price increases denominated in yen only to see such returns completely overwhelmed by the currency factor. That is, the dollar could be extremely weak relative to the yen. Such currency risks may be borne across enough countries in an attempt to diversify the foreign exchange risk.

A number of careful analyses of the effect of currency factors on international equity portfolios have been conducted. During the 1966-1971 period, currency factors were of very minor importance as they only slightly increased the variability of international portfolios. This period, of course, was characterized by "pegged" or fixed exchange rates among most major currencies.

In the present floating rate currency environment, the important question about exchange rates which must be addressed relates to the size of exchange rate fluctuations. If exchange rate fluctuations are sufficiently small relative to equity market fluctuations, then clearly little consideration of their effects would be necessary. Examinations of data from the "floating" exchange rate period (post 1971) indicate that while the magnitude and, therefore, the importance to investors of exchange rate fluctuations has increased in recent years, they are still, in general, considerably smaller than stock market fluctuations. They are, however, large enough to be a meaningful consideration in designing international investment strategies. During the April 1973 to March 1975 period, for example, the world economy was buffeted by the worst recession since World War II, sharply increased inflation rates, an enormous escalation in energy costs, and rapid shifts of financial reserves between countries. While extraordinary stresses were placed on foreign exchange markets, the variability (measured by annual standard deviations) of the U.S. dollar versus the Canadian dollar, the British pound, and the German mark was 2.4 percent, 6.6 percent, and 13.9 percent, respectively. During this same unusually volatile interval, the comparable variability of U.S. equities was 30.1 percent and the variability of U.S. Treasury bill returns was 3.1 percent. Thus, currency fluctuations were about half the magnitude or less of fluctuations in the U.S. stock market, suggesting that while they are of significance they are not nearly as important as fluctuations in the underlying equity markets.

The most direct way to assess the importance of currency fluctuations to internationally diversified portfolios is simply to measure the aggregate variability of typical international portfolios including both currency and equity market changes. From March 1971 through June 1975, internationally diversified equity portfolios supervised by the Putnam Management Company had about 30 percent less variability or risk than the New York Stock Exchange Index. From October 1974 through July 1978, the Ford Foundation's international investment program (which included some foreign fixed income securities) experienced about 50 percent less risk than the S&P 500 index, while achieving returns approximately equal to the index. Therefore, even with currency fluctuations the total risk of these international portfolios has been significantly less than U.S. stock market indices.

POLITICAL RISKS

Political or "sovereign" risks, including the possibilities of capital withdrawal restrictions, expropriation, or punitive taxation, are important issues in international investing. Political factors do have a major influence on securities prices.

There is considerable evidence that suggests that most major world markets are generally efficient in rapidly reflecting new information. If this is true, the consequence is that when political risks increase, local and foreign investors alike will sell securities, and prices will adjust to a new equilibrium level where other investors are satisfied to hold them. Thus, individual markets generally can be presumed to reflect most political uncertainties at any given time; foreign investors therefore are unlikely to pay too high an entry price because of political risks only the "locals" understand. Indeed, the domestic investor is more likely to be guilty of "overkill" selling in reacting to potential political risks simply because he has so much more at stake.

There are still questions about unanticipated political risks that may develop in a country once an investment position has been taken. Stimulated by this problem, several services which attempt to regularly codify the magnitude of investment risk presented by political, social and legal developments within foreign nations have sprung forth. The extent to which their efforts can protect against unanticipated political risks is not well established. Nonetheless, this emerging discipline offers the potential to establish a useful political prudence screen.

LIQUIDITY OF MARKETS

Many foreign markets are regarded as small and less liquid than those of the United States. The United States alone accounts for nearly 50 percent of world capitalizations. Eight countries account for about 90 percent of total world stock capitalizations outside the United States (Japan, Switzerland, West Germany, United Kingdom, Canada, France, Netherlands, Australia). Table 20-3 shows the relative size of various countries in the

TABLE 20-3
STOCK MARKET CAPITALIZATION FOR 1978

Country	Capitalization (in billions of U.S. dollars)	Percentage of Non-U.S. Capitalization	Percentage of Total World Capitalization
Japan	$ 327	40	20
United Kingdom	118	14	7
West Germany	83	10	5
Canada	67	8	4
France	45	6	3
Switzerland	41	6	3
Australia	27	4	2
Netherlands	22	2	1
All others	78	10	5
Non-U.S. Subtotal	808	100	50
Total	$1,625		100

"world" stock market. Some large investors are concerned about being able to accumulate meaningful holdings in foreign markets. Table 20-4 lists the top ten companies ranked by market capitalization in key international markets and each company's market capitalization relative to market totals. For example, in the Netherlands and Switzerland the top 10 companies account for 65 to 75 percent of total market capitalization. This means there are many, many smaller companies as a rule. However, on the other hand, the turnover of shares in foreign markets has been increasing substantially over time. This speaks to the issue of liquidity and depth. (By contrast notice the breadth of the U.S. and Japanese markets.) The growth of share turnover in foreign markets has increased from 24 percent of the world total in 1966 to 53 percent in 1978. These size and liquidity problems suggest, at the very least, a certain amount of patience when buying and selling in foreign markets.

OTHER OBSTACLES

There are other obstacles that make foreign investing difficult or even impossible. These include barriers to international transactions such as the outright banning or limiting of foreign holding of shares (fixed pool or by nationality), difficulty in obtaining information about a market, differences in accounting and reporting practices, and higher transaction costs.

Thus, there are significant diversification advantages to broadening a portfolio to include foreign securities. These advantages, in turn, need to be weighed against specific risks related to the currency factor, political differences, size and liquidity problems, and barriers to holdings and information flows experienced by investors.

The Mechanics of Foreign Securities Investment

The principal markets for the individual foreign securities is generally in their home countries. Exceptions do occur. For example, London has been an active market for South African gold mining stocks and a number of Australian securities, just as New York has been a market for specific foreign stocks (e.g. Rank Organisation, KLM Royal Dutch

TABLE 20-4

THE 10 LARGEST COMPANIES IN SPECIFIC COUNTRIES
AND THEIR SHARE OF NATIONAL STOCK MARKETS (1978)

United States	% of Total	Japan	% of Total	Germany	% of Total
American Tel & Tel	4.7	Toyota Motor	2.5	Siemens	6.5
IBM	4.6	Tokyo Electric Power	2.0	Daimler-Benz	5.9
Exxon Corp.	2.5	Nissan Motor	2.0	R W E	4.9
General Motors	2.1	Matsushita El Ind	1.4	Bayer	4.3
General Electric	1.5	Nippon Steel	1.4	Deutsche Bank	4.0
Eastman Kodak	1.1	Kansai Electric Power	1.2	B A S F	3.8
Sears Roebuck	1.0	Hitachi	1.1	Hoechst	3.6
Standard Oil Indiana	0.9	Nomura Securities	1.0	Dresdner Bank	2.7
Standard Oil California	0.9	Chubu Electric Power	1.0	Volkswagenwerk	2.6
Procter & Gamble	0.8	Daiichi Kangyo Bank	0.9	Commerzbank	2.3
Total Top Ten	20.1	Total Top Ten	14.5	Total Top Ten	40.6

France	% of Total	Switzerland	% of Total	Netherlands	% of Total
Elf Aquitaine Snea	4.5	Nestlé	12.0	Royal Dutch Petroleum	38.5
Michelin	3.7	Schweiz Bankgesell UBS	9.6	Philips	9.8
Saint-Gobain-P.A.M.	2.8	Schweiz Bankverein SBS	9.1	Unilever	8.2
Dassault-Breguet	2.2	Hoffmann-La Roche	8.6	Algemene Bank	3.9
Peugeot-Citroen	2.2	Ciba-Geigy	6.1	Amro Bank	3.6
Air Liquide	2.0	Schweiz Kreditanstalt	6.0	Nationale-Nederlanden	3.2
Francaise Petroles	1.7	Oerlikon-Buhrle	4.9	Heineken	2.7
Suez	1.6	Sandoz	3.5	Akzo	1.9
Carrefour	1.6	Schweiz Ruckversicherung	2.1	Nedmiddenstandsbank	1.7
Pechiney Ugine Kuhlmann	1.4	Zurich Versicherung	2.0	K L M	1.3
Total Top Ten	23.7	Total Top Ten	63.9	Total Top Ten	74.8

Airlines, and Sony Corp.). In fact, a number of foreign enterprises have listed their securities on the New York Stock Exchange or the American Stock Exchange. However, listings are often limited by the listing requirements of these exchanges which require, among other things, audited and consolidated statements and a minimum level of disclosure. Often foreign firms are either not willing to make these kinds of disclosures and/or foreign standards of accounting do not meet exchange or SEC standards.

There is an active over-the-counter market for foreign securities. Market makers take positions, long or short, in the securities they trade and they buy or sell securities abroad to satisfy needs of the U.S. market.

The direct purchase or sale of securities abroad involves a transaction in a foreign currency, purchase or sale of the necessary foreign exchange, and physical transfer of the securities. The transaction tends to entail a number of steps that may require specialized knowledge of the markets and that are often done more efficiently through the market makers in the United States.

AMERICAN SHARES AND DEPOSITORY RECEIPTS

Shares traded in the United States are generally handled in two forms. The first are the so-called *American shares.* These are security certificates issued in the United States by a transfer agent acting on behalf of the foreign issuer. *American Depository Receipts*

(ADR's) are certificates of ownership issued by a U.S. bank as a convenience in lieu of the underlying shares it holds in custody. The principal difference between these two forms is that American shares are issued on behalf of and under the sponsorship of the foreign issuer who may absorb part of the handling costs involved, while the ADR's can be issued by U.S. banks at their sole initiative. The shareholder absorbs the handling costs through higher transfer expenses and a handling charge deducted from corporate dividend payments.

INTERNATIONAL MUTUAL FUNDS

Perhaps the most convenient method of achieving management and broad diversification of holdings in international securities is through the purchase of one of many international mutual funds. The list of funds available includes those offered in the U.S. and those offered abroad for investment in specific markets.

Included in this list of funds are the Japan Fund, Templeton World Fund, Scudder International Fund, and the Australian Capital Fund, to name a few. Chapter 22 will present useful information on mutual funds and where information can be located regarding their availability and performance records.

Summary

In this chapter we saw how capital market theory, building upon the fundamentals of risk diversification through portfolio management, establishes a linear relationship between the expected return and total risk on all efficient portfolios. Such portfolios include only those composed of varying percentages of a risk-free asset and the market portfolio. From here we turned to the capital asset pricing model that uses the results of capital market theory to derive a linear relationship between the expected return and systematic risk on all assets.

Expanding the universe of assets to include securities outside the United States was seen as a way of extending diversification. But, extending diversification to include non-United States securities affords benefits as well as potential problems. The low level of correlation between securities from different countries was seen as the principal benefit of international diversification. However, the obstacles that exist include currency and political risk as well as a lack of liquidity in certain foreign markets. Additionally, difficulties in obtaining reliable information in a timely fashion and higher transaction costs in foreign markets auger against the benefits of international diversification.

Questions and Problems

1. Point out the differences between the efficient frontier under capital market theory and under the Markowitz approach.

2. What does it mean to assume that all investors have homogeneous expectations? Why is this assumption necessary to capital market theory?

3. What is the relationship between borrowing and lending rates in the "real" world? How does this real world relationship affect the shape of the capital market line and the identification of the optimal portfolio?

4. What is meant by the security market line? Explain the rationale behind the security market line.

5. Assume the assets below are correctly priced according to the security market line. Derive the SML. What is the expected return on an asset with a beta of 2?

$$R_1 = 6\% \qquad\qquad \beta_1 = 0.5$$
$$R_2 = 12\% \qquad\qquad \beta_2 = 1.5$$

6. Assume the SML is given as $R_i = 0.04 + 0.08\beta$ and the estimated betas on two stocks are $\beta_x = 0.5$ and $\beta_y = 2.0$. What must the expected return on the two securities be in order to feel that they are a good purchase?

7. Capital market theory and the capital asset pricing model (CAPM) are based on certain specific assumptions; and the CAPM suggests rather specific things about asset pricing.

  a. What are the basic assumptions underlying capital market theory?
  b. What happens to the capital market line and the choice of an optimal portfolio if the borrowing rate is allowed to exceed the lending rate?
  c. What assets lie on both the security market line and the capital market line? What assets should never lie on the capital market line?
  d. What specifically should a "true believer" in the CAPM do with his money if he sought to hold a portfolio with a beta of 1.25?

8. The following data are available to you as a portfolio manager:

Security	Expected Return	Beta	Standard Deviation
Blue	.32	1.70	.50
White	.30	1.40	.35
Orange	.25	1.10	.40
Grey	.22	.95	.24
Black	.20	1.05	.28
Brown	.14	.70	.18
NYSE composite index	.12	1.00	.20
T-bills	.08	0	0

  a. In terms of a security market line, which of the securities listed above are undervalued? Why?
  b. Assume that a portfolio is constructed using equal portions of the six stocks listed above:
    (1) What is the expected return and risk on such a portfolio?
    (2) What would the expected return and risk be if this portfolio were margined at 40 percent with the cost of borrowing at 8%?

9. Based on the principles of portfolio theory, a number of observers have suggested that a major source of diversification should be international securities.

  a. Indicate why foreign securities, in general, should be good diversification candidates. Describe the characteristics of foreign securities that qualify them as good diversification candidates.
  b. Briefly discuss why there are differences in the relationships of rates of return for stocks in the United States and other countries.

10. Briefly discuss the major problems involved with international diversification that would be greatest for individual investors.

11. Examine a convenient source on international statistics. Compare the percentage changes in a recent year for the following economic date for Japan, Canada, and Italy: (a) inflation; (b) output (GNP); (c) business profits; (d) money supply growth. Which country differed the most from the United States over the same time period?

12. Consult a recent issue of *Barron's*. Examine the weekly percentage change in stock price indexes for Japan, Canada, Italy, and the United States. For each of three weeks, identify which series moved closest with the U.S. market and which was the most divergent. What does this indicate to you regarding international diversification?

13. Examine the latest financial statement information available in *Moody's Manuals,* or elsewhere, on Sony Corporation and KLM Royal Dutch Airlines. What items, if any, appear different to you from standard financial statements you have seen of U.S.-based companies. What does this imply about the ability of investors to analyze foreign securities?

14. Consider the following returns:

Period	USA	United Kingdom	Exchange Rate
1	.10	.05	$3.00
2	.15	−.05	2.50
3	−.05	.15	2.50
4	.12	.08	2.00
5	.06	.10	1.50

What is the average return in each market from the point of view of a U.S. investor and of a British investor?

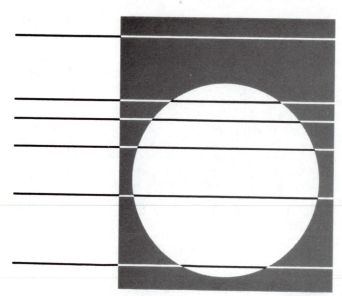

TWENTY-ONE

Portfolio Revision
Techniques

Timing has long been a problem that has challenged investors. Buying at prices that are too high limits the return that can be obtained. Likewise, selling out at low prices will often result in losses. But stock prices do fluctuate, and the natural tendencies of investors often cause them to react in a way opposite to one that would enable them to benefit from these fluctuations. Ideally, investors should buy when prices are low, and then sell these securities when their prices rise to higher limits of their fluctuations. But investors are hesitant to buy when prices are low for fear that prices will fall lower, or for fear that prices won't move upward again. When prices are high, investors are hesitant to sell because they want to maximize their profits, and feel that the price may rise further. It requires discipline to buy when stock prices are low and pessimism abounds, and to sell when stock prices are high and optimism prevails!

Most investors have the discipline to carry out such a course of action *if* they know the course of the future fluctuations. But these fluctuations have proved very difficult, if not impossible, for most investors to forecast. Mechanical portfolio-management techniques have been developed to ease the problem of timing and minimize the emotions involved in investing. These techniques are referred to as *formula plans*.

Formula plans assume that stock prices fluctuate up and down in cycles. Empirical evidence does seem to show that cycles exist and that cycles are closely related to movements in economic activity.[1] Formula plans further assume that investors cannot forecast the direction of the next fluctuation. If an investor merely buys a stock and remains

[1]Richard A. Brealey, *An Introduction to Risk and Return from Common Stocks* (Cambridge, Mass.: MIT Press, 1969), pp. 31-32.

indifferent to fluctuations in its price, he is merely ignoring them. Formula plans are an attempt to exploit these fluctuations and make them a source of profit to the investor. This chapter will examine (1) constant-dollar-value, (2) constant-ratio, and (3) variable-ratio formula plans, as well as another mechanical investment plan, dollar averaging.

Introduction

Formula plans are efforts to make the decisions on timing automatic. They consist of predetermined rules for *when* purchases and sales will be made and *how large* the purchases and sales will be. Formula plans eliminate the emotions that surround timing decisions, such as pessimism and optimism, since the rules and plan of action are predetermined. The rules will often call for specified action that is contrary to what the investor would otherwise do, and contrary to what the majority of the investors in the market are doing. The *selection* of a formula plan and the determination of the appropriate ground rules cause the investor to consider and outline his investment objectives and policies. The *implementation* of a formula plan relieves the pressures on the investor to forecast fluctuations in stock prices.

Formula plans are not, however, a royal road to riches without any weaknesses. First, as an effort to solve the timing problem of investing, they make no provisions for *what securities* should be selected for investment. Such selection is made by analyzing securities within the E-I-C framework. Second, a formula plan by its very nature must be inflexible, thus imposing the necessary action on the investor. This inflexibility makes it difficult to know if and when to adjust the plan to new conditions present in the investment environment. Third, formula plans need a long period to work optimally, and the longer the period required, the more risk there is of substantial changes in the investment environment or in the investor's position. Finally, some formula plans do not free the investor from making forecasts but only require that he make forecasts of a different kind.

Basic Ground Rules

Formula plans call for the investor to divide his investment funds into two portfolios, one aggressive and one conservative (defensive). The aggressive portfolio, usually consisting of stocks, must be more volatile than the conservative portfolio, which often consists of bonds because stability is its most important requirement. The volatility of the aggressive portfolio should ensure that it rises more rapidly and to a greater extent than the conservative portfolio in times when the fluctuation is upward, and that it falls more quickly and more severely when the fluctuation is downward. Generally, the larger the difference between the movements of the two portfolios, the larger the profit the formula plan can yield.

The pursuit of this maximum difference in the movement of the two portfolios is one of the major reasons that high-grade bonds have been advocated as the optimum investment for the conservative, defensive portfolio. High-grade bonds have a high degree of safety and stability, and they also provide steady current income. But in addition, bonds' prices are apt to fall during periods of prosperity, owing to rising interest rates, while stock prices are rising. The opposite situation is likely to appear in unfavorable economic climates. This opposite movement of the two portfolios would be advantageous to formula plans that specify predesignated rules for the transfer of funds from the aggressive into the conservative portfolio as the value of the aggressive portfolio rises. These formula plans also designate that funds be transferred from the conservative to the aggressive portfolio when the value of the aggressive portfolio falls. This automatically causes the investor to sell stocks when their prices are rising and to buy stocks when their prices are falling. If the prices of bonds are moving in the opposite direction to the prices of stocks, this will yield higher profits than if the conservative portfolio's value remains completely stationary.

The facts available from observation, however, show that the fluctuations of stock prices and bond prices do not run in opposite directions at all times. The turning points of trends in stock prices and interest rates do not always coincide, and to the extent that they do not, the bond and stock prices will be moving in the same direction; therefore, the difference between their movements, which the formula plan capitalizes on, will be less than if the conservative portfolio's value had remained stationary. The existence of this coincident movement in bond and stock prices, which sometimes decreases the profits under a formula plan, has led some writers to advocate the use of cash or a savings account for the funds in the conservative portfolio. The stationary value of cash or a savings account would yield a bigger difference between the movements of the two portfolios.

Stock Portfolio

Common stocks are nearly always recommended as the appropriate investment medium for the aggressive portfolio. The selection of the appropriate common stocks is, as stated earlier, not dealt with by the formula plan. The securities that are most appropriate for use in a formula plan are in general no different from those appropriate for investment otherwise, with the one possible exception of *volatility*.

Since maximum profits result from formula plans when the difference between the fluctuations of the two portfolios is the largest, one would expect that the more volatility in the aggressive portfolio, the better. The amount of volatility that any person using a formula plan will seek will depend on his risk-and-return preferences. If the investor seeks a higher level of capital safety and more current income from the aggressive portfolio, he will, of course, choose less volatile stocks than will the investor who is willing to bear more risk in seeking higher capital growth and less current income. The investor employing the formula plan more conservatively will still benefit from its use.

Along with volatility, investors in formula plans must also seek *quality* and *growth* in the stocks they choose. Even though the formula plan seeks to profit from the fluctuations in a stock's price, the investor is taking an ownership position in the stock, and if the general trend that is expected (aside from the fluctuations that the formula plan seeks to exploit) is level or upward, it is better for the investor than if the trend is downward. Also, as we shall see, the formula plan requires that stocks undergo complete price cycles in order to obtain the most favorable results. Stocks of inferior quality or with negative growth trends may never rebound from downward fluctuations.

As one can see, the selection of securities for formula planning may be more difficult than ordinary security selection, since the optimum security has all the qualifications of any otherwise acceptable investment and also a higher degree of volatility than other securities. To select securities with higher levels of volatility, investors must use the past history of a stock's movement compared with the movement of various indexes as a measure. This measure of volatility is actually a beta value, as mentioned in Chapter 18. Even though there does seem to be empirical evidence that the volatility of a stock will tend to persist over time,[2] the volatility characteristic of a stock in the past may or may not materialize in the future. When the aggressive portfolio contains many stocks, however, the volatility of the portfolio as a whole is much more predictable than it is for individual stocks.

Three basic types of formula plans will be discussed here. They are all different in their provisions for transferring funds from an aggressive to a conservative portfolio, or vice versa. The prespecified provisions work automatically to force the investor to sell stocks as their value rises and to buy stocks as their value falls. Each of these plans has many modifications, but if the basic plan is grasped, the modifications are easily understood. The different basic plans are closely related. Some overcome disadvantages of the others while adding complexity and sometimes other shortcomings.

Constant-Dollar-Value Plan

The constant-dollar-value plan specifies that the dollar value of the stock portion of the portfolio will remain constant. Thus, as the value of the stocks rises, the investor must automatically sell some of the shares in order to keep the value of his aggressive portfolio constant. If the prices of the stocks fall, the investor must buy additional stock to keep the value of the aggressive portfolio constant. By specifying that the aggressive portfolio will remain constant in dollar value, the plan also specifies that the remainder of the total fund will be invested in the conservative fund. The constant-dollar-value plan's major advantage is its simplicity. The investor can clearly see the amount that he needs to have invested. However, the percentage of his total fund that this constant amount will represent in the aggressive portfolio will vary at different levels of his stock's values.

The investor must choose predetermined action points—sometimes called *revaluation points*. The action points are the times at which the investor will make the transfers called for to keep the constant dollar value of the stock portfolio. Of course, the portfolio's value cannot be *continuously* the same, since this would necessitate constant attention by the investor, innumerable action points, and excessive transaction costs. In fact, the portfolio will have to be allowed to fluctuate to some extent before action is taken to readjust its value. The action points may be set according to prespecified periods of time, percentage changes in some economic or market index, or—most ideally—percentage changes in the value of the aggressive portfolio.

The timing of action points can have an important effect on the profits the investor obtains. Action points placed too close together cause excessive costs that reduce profits. If the action points are too far apart, however, the investor may completely miss the opportunity to profit from fluctuations that take place between them. For example,

[2]Ibid., pp. 42-46.

assume that action points are set by the percentage change in the value of the aggressive portfolio, such as whenever the value changes by 20 percent. The investor will make no changes, no matter how many fluctuations take place, if the fluctuations are within a range of plus or minus 20 percent of the last valuation of the portfolio. So the setting of action points in this formula plan involves the trade-off between costs and profitability.

The constant-dollar-value plan does not require forecasting the extent to which upward fluctuations may reach. A forecast of the extent of downward fluctuations is necessary, however, since the conservative portfolio must be large enough so that funds are always available for transfer to the stock portfolio as its value shrinks. This step requires a knowledge of how low stock prices might go. Then the required size of the conservative portfolio can be determined. If the investor can start his constant-dollar fund when the stocks he is acquiring are not priced too far above the lowest values to which they might fluctuate, he can obtain better overall results from a constant-dollar-value plan.

Examples will help to clarify the implementation of formula plans. All the plans discussed will be examined as they apply to a single common stock over an identical and complete cycle, thereby facilitating comparison of the plans under various conditions. Although the examples refer to the investment in one stock, the concepts are identical for a portfolio of many stocks, as the portfolio's total value changes. The stock or portfolio of stocks can be changed whenever the investor finds a selection that he feels more appropriately meets his requirements. But the value of investment is regulated by the formula plan. The example covers a full cycle because this is the most appropriate test of the formula plans. A full cycle includes both an upward and a downward fluctuation and ends at the beginning price. We will use fractional shares and ignore transaction costs to simplify the examples.

Example of Constant-Dollar-Value Plan

An investor with $2,000 for investment decides that the constant dollar value of his stock portfolio will be $1,000. The remaining $1,000 of his fund at this time makes up the conservative portfolio. He purchases 40 shares of stock selling at $25 per share. He also determines that he will take action to revalue the fund each time its value reaches 20 percent above or below the constant $1,000 value. Table 21-1 indicates the positions and actions of the investor during the cycle of the stock's price. Also shown is the value of a comparative strategy, where $2,000 is invested only in stocks—80 shares at $25— that are simply held. Column 1 of the table shows various prices of the stock during one cycle of fluctuation. Notice the revaluation actions (represented by boxed areas) taken when the price fluctuated to 20, 24, and 28.8, since the value of the stock fund became 20 percent greater or less than the goal of a constant $1,000 value. Notice, also, that the investor using the constant-dollar-value formula plan has increased the total value of his fund to $2,070 after the complete cycle, while the buy-and-hold strategy yielded only $2,000.

TABLE 21-1

EXAMPLE OF A CONSTANT-DOLLAR-VALUE FORMULA PLAN

(1) Stock Price Index	(2) Value of Buy-and-Hold Strategy (80 Shares X Col. 1)	(3) Value of Conservative Portfolio (Col. 5 − Col. 4)	(4) Value of Stock Portfolio (Col. 7 X Col. 1)	(5) Total Value of Constant-Dollar Portfolio (Col. 3 + Col. 4)	(6) Revaluation Action	(7) Total Number of Shares in Stock Portfolio
25	$2,000	$1,000	$1,000	$2,000		40
22	1,760	1,000	880	1,880		40
20	1,600	1,000	800	1,800		40
20	1,600	800	1,000	1,800	Buy 10 Shares at 20*	50
22	1,760	800	1,100	1,900		50
24	1,920	800	1,200	2,000		50
24	1,920	1,000	1,000	2,000	Sell 8.33 Shares at 24	41.67
26	2,080	1,000	1,083	2,083		41.67
28.8	2,304	1,000	1,200	2,200		41.67
28.8	2,304	1,200	1,000	2,200	Sell 6.95 Shares at 28.8	34.72
25	2,000	1,200	870	2,070		34.72

*To restore the stock portfolio to $1,000, $200 is transferred from conservative portfolio and used to purchase ten shares at $20 per share.

Constant-Ratio Plan

The constant-ratio formula plan specifies that the ratio of the value of the aggressive portfolio to the value of the conservative portfolio will be held constant. This automatically forces the investor to sell stocks as their value rises, in order to keep the ratio of their value to the conservative portfolio constant. Likewise, as the value of the stocks falls, the investor is forced to transfer funds from the conservative portfolio to purchase common stocks.

Since, under this plan, the aggressive portfolio is kept at a constant proportion of the total value of the fund, there will always be funds in the conservative portfolio to be transferred to the aggressive portfolio to purchase stocks if the stocks continue to fall in value. This means that, unlike the constant-dollar-value plan, the constant-ratio plan requires no forecast of the lowest level to which stock prices might fluctuate. The constant-dollar-value plan does, however, call for a consistent level of aggressiveness in transfer to and from the stock portfolio; the very nature of the constant-ratio relationship causes the purchase of stocks to become *less aggressive* as the prices continue to fall, since the constant ratio is applied to a total fund that is *decreasing* in value. Likewise, the constant-ratio plan calls for less aggressive sales as the prices of stocks go up. This is because the total value of the fund grows, and the constant ratio allows a larger dollar value for the stock portfolio.

This phenomenon of the constant-ratio plan—that the most aggressive sales of stocks take place just above the middle range of a fluctuation and the most aggressive purchases just below the middle range of fluctuation—causes it to function suboptimally when the fluctuations of stock prices are characterized by relatively long swings upward and downward. To perform more optimally, as the variable-ratio plan does, a formula plan should sell more aggressively as the stock prices fluctuate further and further above the middle range of the fluctuation and buy more aggressively as the prices move lower and lower below the middle range of the fluctuation. To implement the more optimal strategy, however, requires forecasting a great deal more about the fluctuations that will take place. But decreasing the dependency on forecasts was one of the alleged attributes of formula plans, and the constant-ratio plan calls for no forecasting at all.

The constant-ratio plan will result in higher profits than either the constant-dollar-value plan or the variable-ratio plan during a sustained rise or a sustained fall by itself, since the ratio automatically puts the investor into a more optimal position (that is, larger investment during a rise and lower investment during a fall). However, over the entire cycle of a fluctuation (both up and down), the constant-ratio plan performs less satisfactorily than the other two plans. This is because the constant-ratio plan calls for funds to be transferred into and out of the stock portfolio most aggressively near the median of the fluctuation rather than near its turning points.

The selection of action points for a constant-ratio plan is subject to the same considerations as under the constant-dollar-value plan. Here the action point is determined by the percentage that we allow the constant ratio to fluctuate within before we readjust to its value. If we allow the range of fluctuation of the ratio to be very small, then we will be forced to make many and smaller transactions. If we allow the range of fluctuation of the ratio to be quite large, we will have fewer transactions, but we will not benefit from fluctuations that are too small to cause adjustment action to take place.

Example of a Constant-Ratio Plan

Our example of a constant-ratio plan divides an initial $2,000 fund into equal portfolios. The starting point and other information are the same as in the previous example. The ratio set is:

$$\frac{\text{Value of stock portfolio}}{\text{Value of conservative portfolio}}$$

Equal allotment gives a ratio of 1.00. A constant-ratio plan that placed one-third in the stock portfolio would yield a ratio of .33/.66, or .50. The portfolios will be revalued when the ratio of the value of the stock portfolio to the conservative portfolio becomes plus or minus .10 from the desired ratio of 1.00.

In Table 21-2 the offset rows, shown in boxes, exhibit the actions taken to readjust the value of the portfolios to reobtain the desired ratio. For example, when the stock reaches $27, funds are transferred from the aggressive portfolio into the conservative portfolio by selling stocks. Notice that this constant-ratio plan calls for more trans-

TABLE 21-2
EXAMPLE OF CONSTANT-RATIO FORMULA PLAN

(1) Stock Price Index	(2) Value of Buy-and-Hold Strategy (80 Shares X Col. 1)	(3) Value of Conservative Portfolio (Col. 5 − Col. 4)	(4) Value of Stock Portfolio (Col. 8 X Col. 1)	(5) Total Value of Constant-Ratio Portfolio (Col. 3 + Col. 4)	(6) Ratio (4) : (3)	(7) Revaluation Action	(8) Total Number of Shares in Stock Portfolio
25	$2,000	$1,000	$1,000	$2,000	1.00		40
23	1,840	1,000	920	1,920	.92		40
22.5	1,800	1,000	900	1,900	.90		40
22.5	1,800	950	950	1,900	1.00	Buy 2.22 Shares at 22.5*	42.22
20.25	1,620	950	854	1,804	.90		42.22
20.25	1,620	902	902	1,804	1.00	Buy 2.37 Shares at 20.25	44.59
20	1,600	902	891	1,793	.99		44.59
22.4	1,792	902	992	1,894	1.10		44.59
22.4	1,792	947	947	1,894	1.00	Sell 2.01 Shares at 22.4	42.58
24.6	1,992	947	1,043	1,990	1.10		42.58
24.6	1,992	995	995	1,990	1.00	Sell 1.95 Shares at 24.6	40.63
27.0	2,160	995	1,095	2,090	1.10		40.63
27.0	2,160	1,045	1,045	2,090	1.00	Sell 1.85 Shares at 27.0	38.78
28.8	2,304	1,045	1,117	2,162	1.07		38.78
27.0	2,160	1,045	1,045	2,090	1.00		38.78
25	2,000	1,045	967	2,012	.93		38.78

*To restore the ratio from .90 to 1.00, total value of the fund, $1,900, is simply split in two equal segments of $950; and $950/$950 = 1.00. The $50 transferred from the conservative portfolio will buy 2.22 shares at the prevailing price of $22.50.

actions that the constant-dollar-value plan did, but this plan's purchases and sales are less aggressive. Therefore the constant-ratio plan yielded a smaller increase in total value after the entire cycle, $2,012. It did, however, outperform the buy-and-hold strategy after the complete cycle.

Variable-Ratio Plan

The variable-ratio formula plan specifies that the ratio of the value of the aggressive portfolio to the value of the conservative portfolio will decrease as the value of the aggressive portfolio rises, and increase as the value of the aggressive portfolio decreases. This forces the selling of stocks and the buying of bonds as stock prices rise, and the buying of stocks and selling of bonds as stock prices fall.

The plan specifies a predetermined schedule of the appropriate proportions for various levels of stock prices. If the plan is started at a price that is considered a median around which future fluctuations will move, then the appropriate proportion for the aggressive portfolio would be the proportion of the total fund that the investor can risk in common stocks. From this median proportion, the complete schedule can be determined by the investor. The plan, therefore, calls for a forecast as to whether the current price is a true median. It also requires forecasts of the range of fluctuations both above and below the median to establish the varying ratios at different levels of stock prices. If these forecasts of the range of fluctuations are not correct, the investor may find himself completely in stocks while the prices continue to fall or completely out of stocks while the prices continue to rise, if his schedule of ratios allows either portfolio to become 100 percent. Clearly, variable ratios demand more forecasting than the other formula plans discussed.

Varying the ratio causes the purchases and sales of stocks to become more aggressive as the prices move further below or above the median of their fluctuation. This enables the investor using the variable-ratio plan to profit more from the fluctuations that formula plans are designed to exploit than he can with the other plans. The more extensive forecasts that must be made to implement variable-ratio plans seem to be their only disadvantage. The dependency on forecasting means that incorrect forecasts subject the investor to more risk.

There are many variable-ratio plans that allow for the norm, and thus the whole schedule of ratios, to be changed when new conditions evolve in the investment environment. The most common of these variations is one that calls for the norm to be adjusted along a growth trend that is anticipated for the common stock. This enables the plan to exploit fluctuations around the long-term trend more efficiently, since this growth component of the value change is anticipated by the changing norm. Changing the norm requires even more forecasting.

Other variable-ratio plans call for the ratios to vary according to economic or market indexes rather than the value of the stock portfolio. Some use moving averages of indicators. This means that the indicator that is chosen is considered a better forecaster of the true trend of stock prices than the stocks in the aggressive portfolio. As more and more of these variations of variable-ratio plans are introduced, increased complications are injected. Beyond a point, it might become questionable as to whether the highly complicated variable-ratio plan is more satisfactory or yields higher profits than the extensive analysis and forecasting that it was supposed to replace.

Example of a Variable-Ratio Plan

Our example of a variable-ratio plan assumes that the investor forecasts that the present price of $25 is the median price, and therefore the initial division of the total fund will be into two equal portfolios. The stock-portfolio value is 50 percent of the total portfolio. The plan further states that if the value of the stock portfolio rises 20 percent from the median, the appropriate percentage of the total value of the fund for the stock portfolio will be 30 percent. Likewise, if the value of the stock portfolio decreases by 20 percent from the median, its appropriate percentage of the total fund's value will be 70 percent. Again, other facts are the same as in the original example.

TABLE 21-3
EXAMPLE OF VARIABLE-RATIO FORMULA PLAN

(1) Stock Price Index	(2) Value of Buy-and-Hold Strategy (80 Shares X Col. 1)	(3) Value of Conservative Portfolio (Col. 5 − Col. 4)	(4) Value of Stock Portfolio (Col. 8 X Col. 1)	(5) Total Value of Variable- Ratio Portfolio (Col. 3 + Col. 4)	(6) Value of Stock as % of Total Fund (Col. 4 ÷ Col. 5)	(7) Revaluation Action	(8) Total Number of Shares in Stock Portfolio
25	$2,000	$1,000	$1,000	$2,000	50%		40
22	1,760	1,000	880	1,880	47%		40
20	1,600	1,000	800	1,800	44.5%		40
20	1,600	540	1,260	1,800	70%	Buy 23 Shares at 20	63
22	1,760	540	1,386	1,926	72%		63
25	2,000	540	1,576	2,116	74.5%		63
25	2,000	1,058	1,058	2,116	50%	Sell 20.7 Shares at 25	42.3
26	2,080	1,058	1,100	2,058	53%		42.3
28.8	2,304	1,058	1,218	2,276	54%		42.3
25	2,000	1,058	1,058	2,116	50%		42.3

In Table 21-3, notice that action was taken to readjust the value of the portfolios at $20 and $25, since they are 20 percent shifts from the median. For example, at $20, funds were transferred from the conservative portfolio into the stock portfolio to achieve a new ratio (70 percent). The profits under this plan are $116 after the complete cycle. The higher profits relative to other plans discussed are due to the more aggressive purchases and sales of shares during the cycle, even though there were fewer trades. It should be noted that fluctuations of less than 20 percent from the median were ignored.

Modifications of Formula Plans

There are many modifications of basic formula plans. The most common modification is to *delay action points*. If the investor feels that the trend that has caused the action point to be reached is going to continue, then he can increase his profits by waiting until the trend continues before he takes his action to revalue the portfolio according to the provisions of the plan. This requires forecasting whether or not the trend will continue, and it therefore goes against the unemotional and automatic advantages associated with the nature of formula plans. Many other modifications represent similar efforts to put more flexibility into formula plans. As stated earlier, the inflexibility of formula plans gives them some of their best attributes, but it can also be a disadvantage. Whether or not the investor feels he needs the inflexibility will determine how appropriate modifications are for his use.

It is difficult to generalize on the effectiveness and usefulness of formula plans. Some plans used have often been greatly modified, or they have been used over periods that have not permitted fair tests of their worth. The intrinsic worth of formula plans lies in their taking the investment decision-making process outside the emotions of the investment environment. However, investors must make their predetermined plans on the basis of certain assumptions. They assume that stock prices will fluctuate, and they base this assumption on historical data. The level of success that formula plans achieve will be dependent on the closeness to which actual future behavior resembles the pattern that the formula plan anticipates. Formula plans are, therefore, possibly useful in some cases, but they are not a foolproof method for achieving profits.

Dollar-Cost Averaging

Another mechanical investment technique, which is not technically a formula plan, is dollar averaging. It is very similar to formula plans in that it forces investors to make trades automatically that they might otherwise be averse to making. Dollar averaging requires that investors invest a constant-dollar sum in a specified stock or portfolio of stocks at periodic dates, regardless of the price of the stocks. This technique is especially appropriate for investors who have periodic sums to invest or who are otherwise in the process of *building a fund*. The formula plans discussed earlier dealt with the investment of an *already-accumulated fund*.

Dollar averaging helps the investor avoid buying securities at high levels. If dollar averaging is executed over a complete cycle of stock prices, the investor will obtain his shares at a lower average cost per share than the average price per share of the stock over that same period. This phenomenon results from the fact that the constant-dollar sum purchases more shares at lower prices than at higher prices.

Dollar-averaging plans can vary according to the length of intervals between investments. The size of the dollar sum invested must be large enough to keep the percentage of commission costs relatively low if possible, and this may require the intervals between investments to be fairly long. For best results from the plan, however, the shorter the interval the better. The shorter interval makes it less likely that the investor will miss the opportunity to purchase stocks at low prices resulting from downward fluctuations.

The capacity of the dollar-averaging plan to achieve a lower average cost per share works most dramatically shortly after the program is started, when the fund is still small. As the program continues for long periods of time and the total fund becomes very large, the incremental addition of each new investment at various prices is averaged over many shares, and the effect on the average cost per share is greatly diluted. This is the reason that it is sometimes better for an investor to switch to one of the other formula plans when his fund becomes large.

Table 21-4 shows purchases of shares in the lower range of a fluctuation of the same size (50 to 40). However, as the total size of the fund grows, the new shares purchased lowers the average cost per share by a smaller amount (from 50 to 48.2, versus from 50 to 44.4). As the total size of the fund becomes even larger, this effect will become even smaller.

Dollar averaging does not aid the investor in selecting the appropriate securities. As with formula plans, the investor must still seek quality and growth potential to obtain

TABLE 21-4
EXAMPLE OF CHANGING EFFECTS OF DOLLAR AVERAGING
AS FUND SIZE INCREASES

Date	Dollar Value of Investment	Total Value of Investment	Price of Stock	Number of Shares Purchased	Total Shares	Average Cost per Share
1/69	$1,000	$ 1,000	$50	20	20	$50
1/70	1,000	2,000	40	25	45	44.4
.	.	.	.	.	.	.
.	.	.	.	.	.	.
.	.	.	.	.	.	.
1/79	1,000	11,000	50	20	220	50
1/80	1,000	12,000	40	25	245	48.2

the best possible results. The fact that dollar averaging enables investors to acquire the shares below their average price is not as important as the growth of the value of the shares over the long term (see Table 21-5). Dollar-averaging programs are generally considered most useful over long terms, such as five to fifteen years, periods enabling stock prices to complete numerous cycles and to achieve the long-term growth that is anticipated. Higher volatility leads to higher profits in a dollar-averaging plan over entire cycles, but advocating high volatility seems questionable, particularly concerning the application of dollar averaging for savings plans, in which investors would seek low levels of risk. Dollar averaging is not advocated for use by anyone who might need to withdraw funds from his investment program on short notice. Such a situation can lead to losses if the investor has to liquidate his holdings at low prices. If an investor can meet these requirements, dollar averaging can obtain favorable results if the proper stocks are chosen and timing of liquidation is successful.

Dollar-Cost Averaging with HIA Shares

Table 21-6 displays the results of a hypothetical dollar-cost-averaging program using Holiday Inns stock. The example assumes quarterly investments of $250 from December 1973 through March 1977. For the period considered, the average cost per share is lower than the average market value of a share in March 1977. As indicated in

TABLE 21-5
EXAMPLE OF DOLLAR-COST AVERAGING

Install-ment (1)	Regular Invest-ment (2)	Price of Stock (3)	Shares Purchased (2) ÷ (3) = (4)	Total Shares Owned Σ(4) = (5)	Total Amount Invested Σ(2) = (6)	Total Value of Investment (3)(5) = (7)	Average Price per Shares [Σ(3)] ÷ (1) = (8)	Average Cost per Share (6) ÷ (5) = (9)
1	$1,000	$25	40	40	$1,000	$1,000	$25	$25.0
2	1,000	20	50	90	2,000	1,800	22 1/2	22.2
3	1,000	20	50	140	3,000	2,800	21 2/3	21.4
4	1,000	30	33 1/3	173 1/3	4,000	5,200	21 3/4	23.0
5	1,000	25	40	213 1/3	5,000	5,320	24	23.5
6	1,000	30	33 1/3	246 2/3	6,000	7,400	25	24.3
7	1,000	30	33 1/3	280	7,000	8,400	25 5/7	25.0

TABLE 21-6

DOLLAR-COST AVERAGING WITH HOLIDAY INNS STOCK

(A) Installment Number	Installment (Quarter ending)	(1) Regular Investment	(2) Price of Stock	(3) Shares Purchased (1) ÷ (2)	(4) Total Shares Owned Σ (3)	(5) Total Amount Invested Σ (1)	(6) Total Value of Investment (2) × (4)	(7) Average Price per Share Σ (2) ÷ (A)	(8) Average Cost per Share (5) ÷ (4)
1	December 1973	$250.00	$13.13	19.0	19.0	$ 250.00	$ 250.00	$13.13	$13.13
2	March 1974	250.00	12.13	20.6	39.6	500.00	480.00	12.63	12.62
3	June 1974	250.00	11.00	22.7	62.3	750.00	685.00	12.08	12.03
4	September 1974	250.00	7.50	33.3	95.6	1,000.00	717.00	14.58	10.46
5	December 1974	250.00	5.13	48.7	144.3	1,250.00	740.00	12.22	8.66
6	March 1975	250.00	10.63	23.5	167.8	1,500.00	1,784.00	9.92	8.93
7	June 1975	250.00	13.13	19.0	186.8	1,750.00	2,453.00	10.37	9.36
8	September 1975	250.00	10.63	23.5	210.3	2,000.00	2,235.00	10.41	9.51
9	December 1975	250.00	14.38	17.4	227.7	2,250.00	3,274.00	10.85	9.88
10	March 1976	250.00	17.13	14.6	242.3	2,500.00	4,150.00	11.48	10.31
11	June 1976	250.00	14.38	17.4	259.7	2,750.00	3,734.00	11.74	10.58
12	September 1976	250.00	12.00	20.8	280.5	3,000.00	3,366.00	11.76	10.69
13	December 1976	250.00	13.13	19.0	299.5	3,250.00	3,932.00	11.86	10.85
14	March 1977	250.00	11.38	22.0	321.5	3,500.00	3,659.00	11.83	10.88

our earlier explanation of dollar-cost averaging, these favorable results are a function of the cycle in HIA shares over the period under consideration and the somewhat modest total investment of only $3,500.00.

Summary

The mechanical investment plans discussed in this chapter are valuable to some investors in aiding their investment timing, but they do not help the investor in the selection of appropriate securities. The plans force investors to sell stocks as their prices rise and to buy stocks as their prices fall. The success of formula plans is determined by the closeness to which the pattern of the securities held approximates the pattern anticipated by the formula plan. Dollar averaging seems most appropriate for the investor accumulating an investment fund who might otherwise purchase stocks only at inflated prices.

Questions and Problems

1. It has been said the formula plans aid the investor in overcoming his emotional involvement with the timing of purchases and sales of stock. Why is this said?

2. Do formula plans aid the investor in selecting appropriate securities? If so, how? If not, what do they do?

3. What are some disadvantages of formula plans?

4. Since the defensive portfolio will probably have a low yield, how does it aid the investor using a mechanical formula plan?

5. What kind of security do you think you would select for your aggressive portfolio, and why?

6. What are the strengths and weaknesses of the constant-dollar-value plan? Constant-ratio plan? Variable-ratio plan? Which do you prefer? Why?

7. How are action points chosen?

8. If you were using a constant-dollar-value plan and started with a conservative portfolio worth $2,000 and a stock portfolio consisting of 40 shares of a $50 stock, at what points up and down would you first take action in both portfolios? Assume that you have set your action points at 10 percent above and below the $2,000 initial value of the stock portfolio.

9. Is dollar-cost averaging a formula plan? What exactly is it?

10. Why is it believed that the average cost per share of shares purchased under a dollar-cost-averaging plan will be lower than the average price per share of the same stock during the period of the plan's usage? Is this always true?

11. At what point in the building of a portfolio is the impact of dollar-cost averaging greatest? Why? Prove this by making up an example of your own.

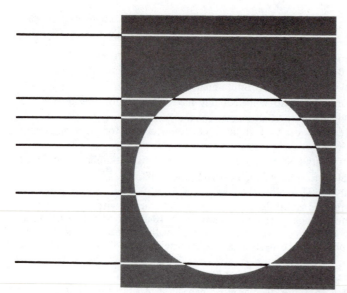

TWENTY-TWO

Managed Portfolios and Performance Measurements

In this chapter we will discuss various types of managed portfolios, looking at broad categories as well as at differences among portfolios in each category. To do this, we will need to specify measures of portfolio performance. These will include the relative merits of return criteria and risk criteria, the adherence of the portfolio's management to publicly stated investment objectives, or some combination of these factors. Finally, we will examine sources of information on various types of managed portfolios.

Classification of Managed Portfolios

Investment Companies

CLOSED-END COMPANIES

A closed-end investment company is so named because its basic capitalization is limited, or "closed." That is, these firms sell shares much as a regular industrial company does. Closed-end firms can also use leverage by selling senior securities—bonds and preferred stocks. Instead of using proceeds from the stock sale to purchase land, equipment, and inventory, the closed-end investment company uses the proceeds to purchase securities of other firms.

The closed-end company is different from the open-end company in how its shares are traded after the initial offering.[1] The closed-end companies' shares are traded on organized exchanges, like those of any other company. Thus, when an investor buys shares in a closed-end investment company, he must generally buy them from another person. The buyer pays the normal commission on such a purchase.

The shares of a closed-end company can sell above or below the net asset value of the shares. *Net asset value* is the total market value of the fund's portfolio minus any liabilities, divided by the total number of shares outstanding. Reasons that closed-end investment companies sell at a discount are the investor's attitude concerning the abilities of the fund's management, lack of sales effort (brokers earn less commission on closed-end fund shares than on open-end fund shares), the riskiness of the fund itself, or the riskiness associated with the lack of marketability of the fund's shares because of a thin float (that is, a small number of shares outstanding).[2] Nonetheless, when these funds sell at unusually large discounts (relative to their historical discounts), they can present interesting investment opportunities.

DUAL FUNDS

The dual fund is a special type of closed-end investment company. As its name implies, it has two types of stock: income shares and capital shares. When the investor purchases shares in a dual fund, he specifies which class of stock he wants. The holders of the capital shares receive all the capital gains earned on all the shares of the fund. The holders of the income shares receive all the interest and dividends earned on all the shares of the fund. Thus it can be seen that the investments of the dual fund's managers are divided into securities that promise a sizeable dividend return and securities that promise substantial capital appreciation. The income investor enjoys leverage to the extent that he receives income on all the shares owned by the fund, and conversely the capital investor enjoys leverage to the extent that he receives capital gains on all the shares owned by the fund.

Potential problems can arise if management is unable to balance its investments properly. That is, if too large a share of the portfolio is invested in stocks with large capital gain potential, there is likely to be too little dividend income earned. Conversely, as too large a share of the portfolio is invested in high-dividend-yielding securities, there is likely to be little capital appreciation.[3]

[1]When the closed-end company desires to raise more capital, it can do so just as any other company can, through the sale of additional shares.

[2]For an interesting discussion of closed-end investment company discounts, see Eugene J. Pratt, "Myths Associated with Closed-End Investment Company Discounts," *Financial Analysts Journal*, July-August 1966, pp. 79-82.

[3]See John P. Shelton, Eugene F. Brigham, and Alfred E. Hofflander, Jr., "An Evaluation and Appraisal of Dual Funds," *Financial Analysts Journal*, May-June 1967, pp. 131-39; and James A. Gentry and John R. Pike, "Dual Funds Revisited," *Financial Analysts Journal*, March-April 1968, pp. 149-57.

OPEN-END COMPANIES

The open-end investment company, more commonly referred to as a mutual fund, is characterized by the continual selling and redeeming of its shares. In other words, the mutual fund does not have a fixed capitalization. It sells its shares to the investing public whenever it can at their net asset value per share, and it stands ready to repurchase these shares directly from the investment public for their net asset value per share. In the case of a "no-load" mutual fund, the investment company sells its shares by mail to the investor. Since no salesman is involved, there is no sales commission (load). In the case of a "load" fund, the shares are sold by a salesman. His entire selling commission (load) is added to the net asset value, and a portion of the investor's equity is removed as the "load" at the beginning of the contract to purchase shares. This process is called "front-end loading," and thus the name "load fund." The load charge or commission is generally about 8 percent of the sale price.

In addition, both the closed-end and open-end funds charge a management fee to defray the costs of operating the portfolios—including such expenses as brokerage fees, transfer costs, bookkeeping expenses, and analysts' salaries. In the case of a load fund, a share with a net asset value of $10 would cost $10.80 if the load fee were 8 percent. If this fund were a no-load, the cost would be only the $10 net asset value. In the newspaper listings of mutual-fund shares, therefore, the bid and asked prices are equal for the no-load shares; the load funds have higher asked prices.

Mutual funds state specific investment objectives in their prospectuses. For example, the main types of objectives are growth, balanced income, and industry-specialized funds. Growth funds typically possess diversified portfolios of common stocks in the hope of achieving large capital gains for their shareholders. The balanced fund generally holds a portfolio of diversified common stocks, preferred stocks, and bonds with the hope of achieving capital gains and dividend and interest income, while at the same time conserving the principal. Income funds concentrate heavily on high-interest and high-dividend-yielding securities. The industry-specialized mutual fund obviously specializes in investing in portfolios of selected industries; such a fund appeals to investors who are extremely optimistic about the prospects for these few industries, and are willing to assume the risks associated with such a concentration of their investment dollars.

MONEY MARKET FUNDS

In 1974 and 1975 high yields prevailed in U.S. government securities, particularly in issues of short-term maturities. In addition to government securities of short-term duration, similar high returns prevailed in other types of short-term issues known as *money market instruments*. Frequently, large dollar amounts are required as minimum purchases for these types of issues. For example, the minimum dollar amount of U.S. Treasury bills that can be purchased is $10,000. Therefore, because of these high yields and because of the often-times large initial investment required, substantial interest developed in mutual funds that invested entirely in such issues. Total net assets of these money market funds amounted to over $140 billion in late 1981.

These money-market funds represent still another variety of open-end company which the mutual-fund industry has brought to the investor's attention. The industry has continually been on the lookout for new types of funds to market.

MUNICIPAL BOND FUNDS

Municipal bond funds invest in a portfolio consisting entirely of tax-exempt bonds. Therefore, the earnings that are passed on to the investor are totally tax free to the investor. Prior to 1976, because of the existing tax laws in the United States, these municipal bond funds took the form of so-called *unit trusts*. These unit trusts do not make continuous offerings as do the open-end funds. The units can either be purchased as new funds are formed or they can be purchased in the over-the-counter market after the initial offering of these units is completed. Normally, these units sell on issuance at $1,000 per unit plus accrued interest. The interest on these units is usually paid monthly. The portfolio comprising the unit trust is fixed; that is, it is purchased before the units are sold to the public.

The Tax Reform Act of 1976 changed the previous tax law and allowed an open-end type of company such as a municipal bond fund to pass its income on to the shareholder in a tax-free manner. This permitted municipal-bond funds that are set up as regular open-end companies to come into existence. The only difference between the municipal-bond fund and the traditional stock open-end company is the portfolio composition. Namely, the portfolio of the municipal bond fund is comprised totally of tax-exempt municipal bonds. At the end of 1980 there was close to $20 billion of municipal unit trusts outstanding. Table 22-1 lists the tax-exempt unit investment trusts offerings for 1961-80. Statistics on these unit trusts are not included in industry totals of the mutual fund industry because the unit trusts are considered different than the normal managed investment company. Statistics on the traditional managed investment companies are given later in this chapter.

INDEX FUNDS

Partly because of the overall poor performance of managed funds, and the market in general during the late 1960s and early 1970s, and because of a growing awareness of the efficient market hypothesis and the random-walk theory as outlined in Chapter 17, a new type of fund has become increasingly popular. This new type of fund is called an *index fund*. An index fund consists of a portfolio designed to reflect the composition of some broad-based market index. It does so by holding securities in the same proportion as the index itself. Frequently these index funds are constructed along the line of the S&P 500 Index—that is, the portfolio of the index fund is constructed in exactly the same proportion with respect to dollars involved as the S&P 500 Index. Therefore, by definition, the index fund is constructed to have a beta of 1.0 with respect to the S&P 500 Index if that is the index being emulated. In fact, an ideal index fund would be one holding all available common stocks in exact proportion to their outstanding market value. However, such an ideal fund would actually be impossible to construct and manage. Therefore it is hoped that an S&P 500 Index Fund will be a good surrogate for this ideal type of fund.[4]

There are two other main reasons for the growing interest in index funds. First, the expenses involved in administering index funds are considerably lower than those in-

---

[4]Walker R. Good, Robert Ferguson, and Jack Treynor, "Investor's Guide to the Index Fund Controversy," *Financial Analysts Journal*, November-December 1976, pp. 27-36.

TABLE 22-1

TAX-EXEMPT UNIT INVESTMENT TRUSTS OFFERINGS, 1961-1980

	Year First Offered	Series Offered in 1980		Total Series Offered	
		No.	$ Amount (millions)	No.	$ Amount (millions)
American Tax-Exempt Bond Trust	1974	6	18.0	46	169.9
Brown Exempt Securities Trust	1980	1	6.0	1	6.0
California Tax-Exempt Bond Fund	1972	—	—	2	11.0
Cardinal Tax-Exempt Bond Trust	1975	3	12.0	16	81.9
Empire State Tax-Exempt Bond Trust	1977	7	97.5	23	343.8
F & M Tax-Exempt Bond Fund	1973	—	—	3	10.5
First Trust of Insured Municipal Bonds	1974	11	225.5	58	717.8
Harris Upham Tax-Exempt Fund	1973	—	—	6	47.5
E.F. Hutton Tax-Exempt Fund:					
California Series	1970	—	—	7	40.0
National Series	1971	5	82.0	49	674.0
New York Series	1970	2	10.0	15	73.0
Investors Municipals — Income Trust	1976	11	263.5	44	997.4
Investors' Municipals Pennsylvania Unit Trust	1979	2	17.5	4	45.5
Investors National Trust Group Tax-Exempt Bond Trust	1979	—	—	1	16.5
Investors Quality Tax-Exempt Trust	1978	6	77.8	8	97.8
Kemper Tax-Exempt Income Trust	1980	7	101.0	17	233.3
Maryland Tax-Exempt Trust	1979	2	8.7	4	16.6
Massachusetts Municipal Bond Trust	1978	—	—	1	10.0
Massachusetts Tax-Exempt Unit Trust	1977	10	58.4	22	135.4
Michigan Fund Tax-Exempt Municipal Investment Trust	1972	—	—	2	11.0
Michigan Municipal Bond Fund	1974	—	—	2	13.5
Michigan Tax-Exempt Bond Fund:					
Long-Term Series	1968	—	—	12	44.3
Insured Series A	1975	—	—	1	4.0
Minnesota Tax-Exempt Income Trust	1976	1	2.2	12	38.4
Multiple Maturity Tax-Exempt Bond Trust	1975	—	—	9	105.8
Municipal Bond Trust:					
Long-Term Series	1972	17	240.0	76	973.5
Multi-State Series	1979	1	12.0	5	67.5
Municipal Exempt Trust — New York Series	1978	—	—	3	26.5
Municipal Income Fund — First Insured Discount Trust	1975	—	—	1	44.0
Municipal Investment Trust Fund:					
Monthly Payment Series	1961	38	1,290.0	158	6,422.7
California Series	1979	—	—	1	12.0
Florida Series	1965	—	—	2	10.0
Michigan Series	1971	—	—	2	18.0
Minnesota Series	1978	—	—	2	16.5
New York Series	1971	7	111.0	31	475.3
Pennsylvania Series	1962	1	10.0	15	149.5
Intermediate Series	1976	—	—	26	478.0
Short-Term Series	1979	—	—	1	15.0
Municipal Securities Trust	1979	5	50.0	7	66.0
National Municipal Trust:					
Long-Term Series	1973	8	104.0	45	445.5
Special Trusts:					
Discount Series	1976	—	—	1	4.5
Intermediate Series	1976	—	—	2	16.5
Multi-State Series	1978	—	—	4	38.5
National Tax-Exempt Bond Trust	1974	—	—	1	10.0
New Jersey Tax-Exempt Income Trust	1979	—	—	1	5.0
New York Municipal Trust	1978	6	61.0	14	134.5
North Carolina Tax-Exempt Bond Fund	1979	—	—	1	5.0

TABLE 22-1 (cont.)

	Year First Offered	Series Offered in 1980		Total Series Offered	
		No.	$ Amount (millions)	No.	$ Amount (millions)
Nuveen Tax-Exempt Bond Fund:					
Long-Term Series	1961	29	970.0	170	3,820.0
Medium-Term Series	1976	—	—	10	132.0
Multi-State Series	1979	9	130.0	15	247.0
PBT Tax-Exempt Bond Fund	1972	—	—	6	24.5
Penn State Tax-Exempt Investment Trust	1977	—	—	1	7.0
Pennsylvania Fund Tax-Exempt Municipal Investment Trust	1972	—	—	1	5.0
Pennsylvania Insured Municipal Bond Trust	1975	3	28.0	11	126.0
Puerto Rico Total Tax-Exempt Income Trust	1979	—	—	1	10.0
Quaker State Investment Trust, Pennsylvania Municipal Tax-Exempt Trust	1974	—	—	1	3.0
Southeast Tax-Exempt Income Trust	1979	3	13.0	4	17.0
Stephens Arkansas Tax-Exempt Bond Fund	1977	—	—	1	2.3
Tax-Exempt Bond Fund of Virginia	1978	—	—	3	16.5
Tax-Exempt Environmental Bond Fund	1973	—	—	1	25.0
Tax-Exempt Income Fund	1965	—	—	4	19.2
Tax-Exempt Municipal Trust:					
National Series	1975	2	19.0	30	344.0
National Non-Insured Series	1979	—	—	2	19.5
New York Exempt Series	1977	—	—	3	29.5
New York Series	1975	—	—	1	10.0
Tax-Exempt Securities Trust:					
Intermediate-Term Series	1977	—	—	2	25.0
Long-Term Series	1975	14	229.0	45	957.0
Multi-State Series	1979	2	30.7	3	47.7
Tax-Exempt Trust for Pennsylvania Residents 1st Series—Combined:					
Investors Municipal Pennsylvania Unit Trust—3rd Series	1979	—	—	1	6.0
Pennsylvania Insured Municipal Bond Trust—9th Series	1979	—	—	1	5.0
Texas-Southwestern Municipal Bond Fund	1973	—	—	1	5.0
Weeden Tax-Exempt Bond Trust:					
Intermediate Series	1977	—	—	1	20.0
Long-Term Series	1976	—	—	10	165.0
Dean Witter Tax-Exempt Trust:					
Intermediate-Term Series	1977	—	—	1	7.5
Long-Term Series	1974	—	—	37	353.0
Total		219	4,278.8	1,131	19,827.6

SOURCE: *Investment Companies* (New York: Arthur Wiesenberger Services, 1981).

volved in handling a truly managed portfolio because the construction of the index-fund portfolio is entirely based upon maintaining proportions of the index being followed. As such, there would be considerably lower transaction costs involved because fewer purchases and sales of securities would take place. Furthermore, there would be much less need for expensive batteries of security analysts and portfolio managers. Thus, the overall administrative expenses would also be reduced. Second, with the passage of the new pension reform law, the investment trust laws surrounding the liability of portfolio managers of pension funds have changed with regard to the risk and return of the portfolio they manage. A discussion of the main changes as they affect portfolio managers is the subject of our next section.

Pension-Fund Management and ERISA

A *pension-fund* is a plan whereby an employer puts aside funds to provide for periodic payments to employees after they retire. Pension-fund assets represent an extremely large and fast-growing pool of institutional capital. At the end of 1975 the Securities and Exchange Commission estimated that pension-fund assets exceeded $400 billion. Of this amount, over one-half consisted of private pension-fund reserves. The remainder consisted of funds of various governmental agencies.

In 1974 the federal government passed the Employee Retirement Income Security Act, ERISA. This act has many far-reaching ramifications. Here we are primarily concerned with the impact on pension-fund institutional managers. Many critics have stated that this complex piece of legislation will greatly influence the behavior of institutional portfolio managers, and especially pension-fund managers. This act creates a federal standard for the legal fiduciary responsibility of the pension-fund manager. It expressly states that the fiduciary must act with care, skill, prudence, and diligence under the circumstances then prevailing that a prudent man acting in a like capacity and familiar with such matters would use in the conduct of an enterprise of a like character and with like aims. The act goes on to say that the fiduciary will be personally liable to make good to the plan any losses resulting from the breach of these responsibilities. The courts have ruled thus far that the fiduciary must produce a reasonable income and must preserve the capital of the fund. In fact, the preservation of capital is the key responsibility. It seems logical, therefore, that an index fund might well be sought after by pension-fund managers in order to escape liability under ERISA. This is because the pension-fund manager might argue that his fund did as well or no worse than the market as a whole performed over the period in question.

Trust Agreement

Commercial banks frequently offer their services as trustees for the management of an individual's portfolio. The fee charged for this service is generally a percentage of the size of the fund, decreasing with the size of the portfolio.

Generally, the trustee (or trustees) exercises complete discretion over the investments of the fund in a very conservative manner. Complete discretion means that the trustee selects which stocks to buy, at what prices, and the quantity he thinks appropriate, on his own, without consulting the person whose money he is managing. The legal statutes generally apply a "prudent-man" rule to judge whether proper management has occurred.

A special type of trust, which has become popular, is the common trust. Common trusts are essentially similar to mutual funds, except that the minimum investment in a common trust is substantially higher than that required in a mutual fund. In a common trust administered by a bank, the monies of a number of investors are commingled and are used to purchase a diversified portfolio of securities. A basic advantage of the common trust is that there is more of a personal relationship between the bank and the investor. Furthermore, a common trust is an alternative available to smaller investors, since it requires less cost and principal investment than the usual trust arrangement does.

Professional Investment Counsel

The investor who uses a professional investment counsel hires the services of either a bank or an outside investment consultant to advise him on his investment policy. Typically, the investor discusses his objectives with the counsel, and as a result the investment counselor suggests alternative investment possibilities to the client. (In some cases, the counselor may even have total discretion.) The range of services can vary considerably under this type of arrangement, and consequently, so do the costs; however, the minimum cost of such a personal service is so high as to preclude this investment route for the typical small investor.

Alleged Advantages of Managed Portfolios

Frequently, investors feel insecure in managing their own investments, because they consider themselves inadequate to perform this delicate task successfully. Oftentimes the investor feels he lacks the education, background, time, foresight, resources, and temperament to carry out the proper handling of his portfolio. When this occurs, the logical step is to turn the job over to a professional portfolio manager. Most often the source chosen takes the form of a mutual fund, or open-end investment company.

The main reasons for selecting an open-end investment company involve the management, diversification, and liquidity aspects of this organization form. Management trained in the ways of security analysis devotes full time to the carrying out of the fund's investment objectives as specified in its prospectus. This permits a constant monitoring of the securities comprising the portfolio. Furthermore, large amounts of money entrusted to the fund enable it to diversify its investments across industry and security types (that is, common stocks with various prospects, preferred stocks, and bonds) to an extent not possibly achieved by the average investor. Furthermore these institutions are able to obtain lower brokerage commissions than an individual small investor. This diversification evolves as a result of stated objectives of the fund.

In Table 22-2, we see that 64 percent of the total assets held by mutual funds are in the hands of only sixty-six funds, or 10 percent of the number of funds. Funds specializing in growth and in growth and income common stocks hold 26 percent of the assets, and another 6 percent are held by those that stress common stocks with maximum capital gains. The investor can shop for a fund whose objectives are most in line with his own.

Finally, open-end companies represent a liquid type of investment. That is, shares can be readily converted into cash, for the company stands ready to redeem its outstanding shares.

Let us examine the record to determine if these alleged advantages have in fact accrued to investors. Since most of the theory surrounding performance measurement, as well as the actual empirical work that has been conducted, has been connected with mutual funds, we will place our emphasis in this area. However, it should be noted that the notion of performance measurement is not something applicable only to open-end investment companies. Performance evaluation is necessary in *all* kinds of portfolios, whether individually or professionally managed.

TABLE 22-2

CLASSIFICATION OF MUTUAL FUNDS BY SIZE AND TYPE
AS OF DECEMBER 31, 1980

Size of Fund	Number of Funds	Combined Assets (000)	Percent of Total
Over $1 billion	30	$ 66,148,100	47.6
$500 million-$1 billion	36	24,575,900	17.7
$300 million-$500 million	33	12,580,400	9.1
$100 million-$300 million	128	22,066,400	16.0
$50 million-$100 million	98	6,961,400	5.1
$10 million-$50 million	205	5,423,300	4.0
$1 million-$10 million	117	571,400	0.5
Under $1 million	12	6,200	0.0
Total	659	$138,333,100	100.0
Type of Fund			
Common Stock:			
Maximum Capital Gain	98	$ 8,252,700	6.0
Growth	139	19,110,100	13.5
Growth and Income	85	16,994,300	12.2
Specialized	19	2,045,400	1.5
Balanced	26	3,502,300	2.6
Income	128	9,875,300	7.2
Bond & pfd stock	11	1,454,400	1.1
Money market	101	71,992,900	52.1
Tax-exempt municipal bonds	43	3,269,100	2.4
Tax-free money markets	9	1,836,600	1.4
Total	659	$138,333,100	100.0

SOURCE: *Investment Companies* (New York: Arthur Wiesenberger Services, 1981).

Management-Performance Evaluation

We are interested in discovering if the management of a mutual fund is performing well. That is, has management done better through its selective buying and selling of securities than would have been achieved through merely "buying the market"—picking a large number of securities randomly and holding them throughout the period?

One of the most popular ways of measuring management's performance is by comparing the yields of the managed portfolio with the market or with a random portfolio. The portfolio-yield formula parallels the holding-period-yield formula for stocks that was presented in Chapter 4, and is

$$\frac{NAV_t + D_t}{NAV_{t-1}} - 1 \tag{22.1}$$

where:

NAV_t = per-share net asset value at the end of year t

D_t = the total of all distributions—both income and capital gains—per share during year t

NAV_{t-1} = per-share net asset value at the end of the previous year

Thus, if $NAV_t = \$11, D_t = \$1$, and $NAV_{t-1} = \$10$, the yield will be:

$$\frac{11 + 1}{10} - 1 = \frac{12}{10} - 1 = 1.2 - 1 = .2, \text{ or } 20\%$$

The two yields (managed portfolio and unmanaged portfolio) calculated by Equation 22.1 are then compared. The portfolio with the highest one-year holding-period yield is by this criterion deemed the better portfolio.[5]

This evaluation implies something about the management of the various portfolios under examination. In Table 22-3, we see the returns on a sample of thirty-nine mutual funds during the period 1951-60. It is of interest that fewer than half these sample funds were able to earn returns in excess of the 14.7 percent earned by the market (as measured by the New York Stock Exchange Average). In addition, note how inconsistent the funds' relative rankings were from year to year. However, merely measuring and comparing the returns on a managed and unmanaged portfolio is not enough.

First, if the managed portfolio did better than the unmanaged portfolio, the investor in the mutual fund should not rejoice too soon. He had to pay a management fee as well as suffer a reduction in equity equal to the loading charge (in the case of a load fund). So he must determine if the excess return is sufficient to cover these added expenses he has incurred by purchasing a mutual fund rather than purchasing a diversified portfolio on his own and paying the commissions (assuming he has this option). Second, the investor must determine the relative riskiness of the portfolio under analysis. It is entirely possible that the managed portfolio has achieved higher returns than the market or the unmanaged portfolio by taking on considerably more risky investments. It is not surprising under such circumstances for higher returns to occur, for higher returns *should* go along with higher risks. Only after the relative risks of the portfolios have been considered is a comparison of returns meaningful.

Sharpe's Performance Measure for Portfolios

William Sharpe has attempted to get a summary measure of portfolio performance.[6] His measure properly adjusts performance for risk. The Sharpe Index is given by

$$S_t = \frac{\overline{r}_t - r^*}{\sigma_t} \qquad (22.2)$$

where:

S_t = Sharpe Index

$\overline{r}_t$ = average return on portfolio t

r^* = riskless rate of interest

σ_t = standard deviation (risk) of the returns of portfolio t

---

[5]This is the general formula used by the Arthur Wiesenberger Services, New York. Representative reproductions from this excellent investment service will be presented in a later section of this chapter.

[6]William F. Sharpe, "Mutual Fund Performance," *Journal of Business, Supplement on Security Prices,* January 1966, pp. 119-38.

TABLE 22-3

YEAR-BY-YEAR RANKING OF INDIVIDUAL FUND RETURNS

Fund	Return on Net	1951	1952	1953	1954	1955	1956	1957	1958	1959	1960
Keystone Lower Price	18.7	29	1	38	5	3	8	35	1	1	36
T. Rowe Price Growth	18.7	1	33	2	8	14	15	2	25	7	4
Dreyfus	18.4	37	37	14	3	7	11	3	2	3	7
Television Electronic	18.4	21	4	9	2	33	20	16	2	4	20
National Investors Corp.	18.0	3	35	4	19	27	4	5	5	8	1
De Vegh Mutual Fund	17.7	32	4	1	8	14	4	8	15	23	36
Growth Industries	17.0	7	34	14	17	9	9	20	5	6	11
Massachusetts Investors Growth	16.9	5	36	31	11	9	1	23	4	9	4
Franklin Custodian	16.5	26	2	4	13	33	20	16	5	9	4
Investment Co. of America	16.0	21	15	14	11	17	15	23	15	15	15
Chemical Fund Inc.	15.6	1	39	14	27	3	33	1	27	4	23
Founders Mutual	15.6	21	13	25	8	2	20	16	11	13	28
Investment Trust of Boston	15.6	6	3	25	3	14	26	31	20	29	20
American Mutual	15.5	14	13	4	22	14	13	16	25	25	4
Keystone Growth	15.3	29	15	25	1	1	1	39	11	13	38
Keystone High	15.2	10	7	3	27	23	36	5	27	25	11
Aberdeen Fund	15.1	32	23	9	25	9	7	10	27	7	30
Massachusetts Investors Trust	14.8	8	9	14	16	9	15	20	18	32	28
NYSE Market Average*	14.7										
Texas Fund, Inc.	14.6	3	15	9	32	23	26	5	27	37	7
Eaton & Howard Stock	14.4	14	9	4	17	20	15	13	37	29	17
Guardian Mutual	14.4	21	26	25	34	31	29	13	20	15	2
Scudder, Stevens, Clark	14.3	14	23	14	19	27	15	29	9	15	30
Investors Stock Fund	14.2	8	28	21	22	27	20	23	5	29	23
Fidelity Fund, Inc.	14.1	21	26	25	34	31	29	13	20	15	23
Fundamental Investment	13.8	14	15	31	16	9	11	31	18	25	30
Century Shares	13.5	14	28	35	25	3	20	23	31	34	2
Bullock Fund Ltd.	13.5	29	9	21	19	14	9	20	34	34	20
Financial Industries	13.0	26	15	31	13	19	29	34	20	9	35
Group Common Stock	13.0	38	8	25	27	27	33	8	20	34	17
Incorporated Investors	12.9	14	13	37	6	3	13	37	11	18	39
Equity Fund	12.9	14	27	21	32	31	33	13	31	18	23
Selected American Shares	12.8	21	15	21	31	23	20	23	15	32	30
Dividend Shares	12.7	32	7	14	34	20	32	4	37	37	11
General Capital Corp.	12.4	10	28	9	38	35	39	23	34	13	23
Wisconsin Fund	12.3	32	26	4	37	35	38	10	34	18	7
International Resources	12.3	10	37	39	22	35	1	37	39	1	11
Delaware Fund	12.1	36	23	25	27	39	26	29	9	23	30
Hamilton Fund	11.9	38	28	9	34	35	36	10	31	18	17
Colonial Energy	10.9	10	15	35	39	20	4	36	20	39	10

*The NYSE market average represents what a tax-exempt investor could have expected to earn by randomly picking (for example, with a dart) a large number of stocks listed on the NYSE and holding them 10 years while reinvesting the dividends. The data were published by L. Fisher and J. Lorie, "Rates of Return on Investments in Common Stock," *Journal of Business*, January 1964, pp. 1-21.

SOURCE: Eugene F. Fama, "The Behavior of Stock Market Prices," *Journal of Business*, January 1965 (Chicago: The University of Chicago Press, January 1965), p. 93.

Thus the Sharpe Index measures the risk premiums of the portfolio (where the risk premium is the excess return required by investors for the assumption of risk) relative to the *total* amount of risk in the portfolio.

Graphically, the index, S_t, measures the slope of the line emanating from the riskless rate outward to the portfolio in question. (See Figure 22-1.) Thus the Sharpe

FIGURE 22-1
GRAPHICAL REPRESENTATION OF THE SHARPE INDEX, S_t

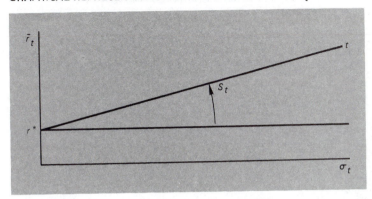

Index summarizes the risk and return of a portfolio in a single measure that categorizes the performance of the fund on a risk-adjusted basis. The larger the S_t, the better the portfolio has performed. For example, assume that portfolio A has an average return of 10 percent with a standard deviation of 2 percent, and portfolio B has an $\bar{r}_B$ of 12 percent and σ_B of 4 percent. Further assume that $r^* = 5$ percent. Then the Sharpe Index (by Equation 22.2) for A equals

$$\frac{.10 - .05}{.02} = 2.5$$

and for B,

$$\frac{.12 - .05}{.04} = 1.75$$

Thus A ranked as the better portfolio because its index is higher $(2.5 > 1.75)$, despite the fact that portfolio B had a higher return $(12\% > 10\%)$. The Sharpe Index and the Treynor Index, which we are about to discuss, have yielded very similar results in actual empirical tests.[7]

Treynor's Performance Measure for Portfolios

A key to understanding Treynor's portfolio-performance measure is the concept of a characteristic line.[8] In Figure 22-2 we see the graphical representation of a characteristic line of an ideal mutual fund.[9] More accurately, this linear representation is an approximation of what is probably more frequently a curvilinear relationship. This curvilinear

[7]Ibid., p. 129.

[8]Jack L. Treynor, "How to Rate Management of Investment Funds," *Harvard Business Review*, January-February 1965, pp. 63-75.

[9]This discussion parallels a comment on Treynor's paper that appears in Kalman J. Cohen and Frederick S. Hammer, *Analytical Methods in Banking* (Homewood, Ill.: Richard D. Irwin, 1966), pp. 374-78.

FIGURE 22-2
TREYNOR'S CHARACTERISTIC LINE OF AN IDEAL FUND

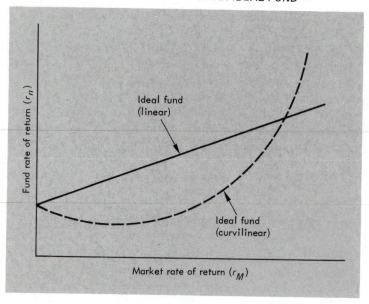

representation is the dashed line in Figure 22-2. If a line were added to this graph that intersected the origin at a 45° angle, it would represent a portfolio return that was equivalent to the return of the market portfolio. The ideal fund lies above and to the left of the imaginary 45° line. Its return is at all times superior to the one earned on the market portfolio. When the market portfolio earns a low or negative return, the ideal portfolio still earns a positive return; and when the market portfolio earns a positive return, the ideal fund earns an even higher return. To put it more succinctly, the *characteristic line* relates the market return to a specific portfolio return without any direct adjustment for risk. This line can be "fitted" via a least-squares regression such as that involving a single index of a market portfolio. The Sharpe model we discussed in Chapter 18 was a single-index idea.

The slope of the characteristic line is the beta coefficient, a measure of the portfolio's systematic risk. Some people view systematic risk as a type of volatility measure. Thus, by comparing the slopes of characteristic lines, the investigator gets an indication of the fund's volatility. The steeper the line, the more systematic risk or volatility the fund possesses. Treynor has proposed incorporating these various concepts into a single index to measure portfolio performance more accurately. This index is given by the following equation:

$$T_n = \frac{\bar{r}_n - r^*}{\beta_n} \qquad (22.3)$$

where:

T_n = Treynor Index

$\bar{r}_n$ = average return on portfolio n

r^* = riskless rate of interest

β_n = beta coefficient of portfolio n

Thus the Treynor Index measures the risk premium of the portfolio, where risk premium equals the difference between the return of the portfolio and the riskless rate. This risk premium is related to the amount of *systematic* risk assumed in the portfolio. So the Treynor index sums up the risk and return of a portfolio in a single number, while categorizing the performance of the portfolio. Graphically, the index measures the slope of the line emanating outward from the riskless rate to the portfolio under consideration. This is shown in Figure 22-3.

FIGURE 22-3
GRAPHICAL REPRESENTATION OF THE TREYNOR INDEX, T_n

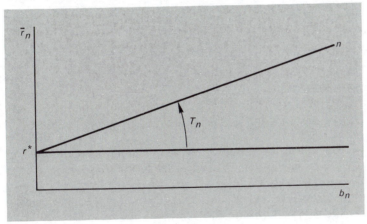

Note the differences in the axes of Figures 22-1 and 22-3. For example, if we assume the same two hypothetical portfolios, A and B, from the previous section, and furthermore assume that the beta coefficients are .5 and 1.0, then the Treynor Index (by Equation 22.3) for A equals

$$\frac{.10 - .05}{.5} = .10$$

and for B,

$$\frac{.12 - .05}{1.0} = .07$$

Again portfolio A performed better than B. Both the Sharpe and Treynor Indexes ranked A higher than B despite B's higher return.

Jensen's Performance Measure for Portfolios

The Treynor and Sharpe Index Models provide measures for ranking the *relative performances* of various portfolios, on a risk-adjusted basis. Jensen attempts to construct a measure of *absolute performance* on a risk-adjusted basis—that is, a definite standard against which performances of various funds can be measured. [10] This standard is based on measuring the "... portfolio manager's *predictive ability*—that is, his ability to earn returns through successful prediction of security prices which are higher than those which we could expect, *given* the level of riskiness of his portfolio. . ."[11] In other words, we are attempting to determine if more than expected returns are being earned for the portfolio's riskiness.

A simplified version of his basic model is given by

$$\overline{R}_{jt} - R_{Ft} = \alpha_j + \beta_j (\overline{R}_{Mt} - R_{Ft}) \tag{22.4}$$

where:

$\overline{R}_{jt}$ = average return on portfolio j for period t

R_{Ft} = riskless rate of interest for period t

α_j = intercept that measures the forecasting ability of the portfolio manager

β_j = a measure of systematic risk

$\overline{R}_{Mt}$ = average return of a market portfolio for period t

The reader should note the similarity between this model and the basic Sharpe and Treynor models. An implication of forms of the Sharpe-Treynor Model is that the intercept of the line is at the origin. In the Jensen Model, the intercept can be at any point, *including* the origin. For example, in Figure 22-4, the upper line represents a case of superior management performance. In fact, α_j = a positive value represents the average superior extra return accruing to that particular portfolio because of superior management talent. The line $\alpha_j = 0$ indicates neutral performance by management; that is, management has done as well as an unmanaged market portfolio or a large, randomly selected portfolio managed with a naive buy-and-hold strategy. The lower line, $\alpha_j = a$ negative value, indicates inferior management performance, because management did not do as well as an unmanaged portfolio of equal systematic risk. This situation could arise in part because portfolio returns were not sufficient to offset the expenses incurred in the selection and managing process.

---

[10]The discussion in this section closely parallels the development found in Michael C. Jensen, "The Performance of Mutual Funds in the Period 1945-1964," *Journal of Finance*, May 1968, pp. 389-416.

[11]Ibid., p. 389.

FIGURE 22-4
GRAPHICAL REPRESENTATIONS OF JENSEN'S MEASURE OF MANAGEMENT ABILITY

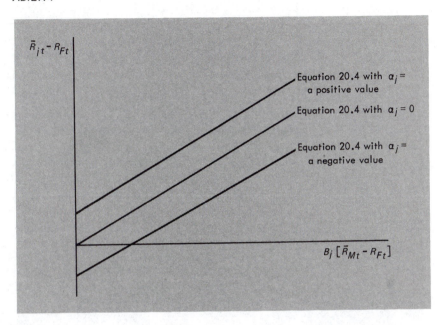

The intercept may be interpreted in this fashion by examining Equation 22.4. This occurs because if the portfolio manager is performing in a superior fashion, his intercept will have a positive value because it will indicate that his portfolio is consistently over performing the overall market. This would happen if either he had superior ability in selecting undervalued securities or had superior ability in recognizing turning points in the market. Conversely, if the intercept were negative, it would indicate that the manager consistently underperformed the overall market. That is, the risk-adjusted returns of his portfolio were consistently lower than the risk-adjusted returns of the market over the same period of time. Figure 22-5 shows an application of the Jensen approach that has been reported by a major Wall Street brokerage firm.[12]

Other Observations on Performance Measures

Up to this point in our discussion we have discussed only three different approaches to measuring portfolio performance, which all utilize a risk-adjusted return measurement. However, it should be observed that prior to the development of these measures, portfolio managers' performance was measured essentially by observing the rates of return they were able to earn over time. It was necessary for them to demonstrate that their rates of return equaled or exceeded the returns of an unmanaged portfolio—that is, a

[12]G. Gordon Biggar, Jr., *Risk-Adjusted Portfolio Performance: Its Investment Implications* (New York: Smith, Barney & Co., 1971).

FIGURE 22-5
*ILLUSTRATION OF AN APPLICATION OF THE JENSEN APPROACH
CONDUCTED BY SMITH, BARNEY & CO.* *

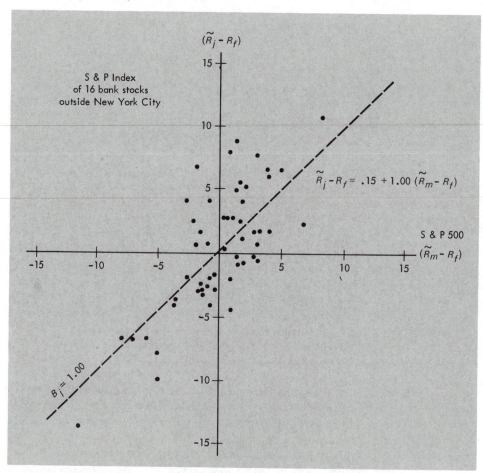

*Scatter diagram comparing the volatility of monthly investment returns (less the
return on Treasury bills R_f) of the S&P Index of 16 Bank Stocks Outside New York
City (vertical axis) and the S&P 500 Stock Index (horizontal axis) during the period
January 1967-September 1971. The slope (B_j) of the dashed line measures the
degree of volatility of the S&P Bank Stock Index in relation to that of the S&P 500.
SOURCE: G. Gordon Biggar, Jr., *Risk-Adjusted Portfolio Performance: Its Investment Implications* (New York: Smith, Barney & Co., 1971), p. 20.

portfolio constructed either by random choice or a portfolio that represented the returns
of the market as a whole and then was held for the duration of the test period. Another
possible measurement of portfolio performance is to check if the manager was successful
in obtaining a beta for the invested portfolio which was consistent with the objectives of
the investor for his individual portfolio. That is, was the level of risk assumed by the
portfolio manager consistent with the level of risks that the investor wished to assume?
Another factor to consider in portfolio management is to evaluate the portfolio manager's

ability to completely diversify away unsystematic risk. Since this nonmarket risk can be completely diversified away in a properly constructed portfolio, an efficient market will pay only for the market or systematic risk. In fact, several of the performance measurement techniques discussed earlier in this chapter incorporated this belief. Several studies subsequent to those already reported have criticized these models because it was felt that they introduced various types of bias into the results. However, no clear-cut resolution of the problems has been reached and we feel that some combination of the models already discussed will yield effective portfolio performance measurement techniques.

Empirical Tests of Mutual-Fund Performance

We have thus far examined various proposals that have been put forward for mutual-fund performance evaluation. In this section we will examine the results of a number of key empirical tests that have been conducted, to answer such questions as "Can mutual funds do better for me than I can do by myself?" "Are the management and selling fees that mutual funds charge worth the price?" and "Do managed funds adhere to their stated investment objectives?"

We have already seen in Table 22-3 that the answer to the first question above is negative. That is, mutual funds contained in this particular sample did not, on the average, outperform the returns that could be earned by following a naive strategy over the sample period. Because of the growing importance of investment companies in the United States, the Securities and Exchange Commission engaged the Wharton School of Finance and Commerce to conduct a study of mutual funds.[13] The investigation found no relationship between the performance of the mutual funds studied and the management fees and sales charges that these funds levied. "The fact that the analysis does not reveal a significant relation between management fees and performance indicates, in other words, that investors cannot assume the existence of higher management fees implies that superior management ability is thereby being purchased by the funds. . . ."[14] The study reached a similar conclusion with regard to sales charges.[15]

Jensen concluded that the funds in his study ". . . were *on average* not able to predict security prices well enough to outperform a buy-the-market-and-hold policy, but also that there is very little evidence that any *individual* fund was able to do significantly better than that which we expected from mere random chance. . . ." The reader can observe this by noting the preponderance of negative alphas in Figure 22-6. Here we see the frequency distribution of the alphas. These are the intercept values by which Jensen measures the ability of professional fund management. It should be noted that this distribution is skewed to the left. This indicates the preponderance of alphas less than

[13]Irwin Friend, F. E. Brown, Edward S. Herman, and Douglas Vickers, *A study of Mutual Funds*, prepared for the Securities and Exchange Commission by the Wharton School of Finance and Commerce, Report of the Committee on Interstate and Foreign Commerce, 87th Cong., 2nd sess., August 28, 1962.
[14]Friend et al., "Summary and Conclusions," ibid., as reprinted in Hsiu-Kwang Wu and Alan J. Zakon, *Elements of Investments* (New York: Holt, Rinehart and Winston, 1965), p. 384.
[15]This latter conclusion would seem to imply that the investor might be better advised to invest in a no-load fund than in a load fund.

FIGURE 22-6
FREQUENCY DISTRIBUTION OF ESTIMATED INTERCEPTS

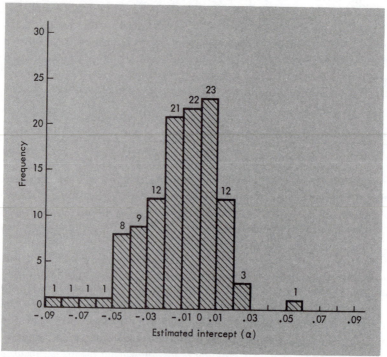

SOURCE: Michael C. Jensen, "The Performance of Mutual Funds in the Period 1945-1964," *Journal of Finance*, May 1968, pp. 389-416.

zero—an indication of negative management worth.[16] Sharpe reached a similar conclusion by comparing the Sharpe Index, the ratio of risk premium to risk, of a number of mutual funds with that of the Dow Jones Industrial Average.[17] Perhaps these findings are in part responsible for the growing popularity of funds, such as the Stagecoach Fund, that are constructed in the same proportions as some market index, such as the S&P 500 (an index fund). These funds would perform as well as the market.

The Securities and Exchange Commission as part of its Institutional Investor Study found some evidence that, in its sample, mutual funds outperformed the market by very small amounts. The SEC study was carried out on a risk-adjusted basis. However, a perhaps more enlightening finding of this same study was that there was no consistency with respect to which funds provided the investor with superior performance. Specifically, during the five-year period 1960-64 the least volatile funds in the sample tended to provide the strongest performance, while during the five-year period 1965-69 the more volatile funds in the sample provided the best performance. Thus the mutual funds in this

[16]Jensen found that the funds earned (net of expenses) "about 1.1% less per year (compounded continuously) than they should have earned given their level of systematic risk . . . ." Jensen, "Performance of Mutual Funds," p. 405.

[17]Sharpe, "Mutual Fund Performance," p. 125.

study demonstrated a considerable lack of consistency in terms of which type of funds provided superior performance on a regular basis.[18]

In general, empirical investigations have found that fund managers are able to assess properly the risks and potential returns associated with alternative investment opportunities and have thus been able to meet their investment objectives fairly well.[19]

Extended Example of Performance Measurement

In Chapters 18 and 19 we introduced a group of stocks from which feasible portfolios were generated. A single "best" portfolio was chosen for holding, unmanaged, for a forward period. Table 22-4 is a listing of the subsequent results for the portfolio, and the Standard & Poor's 500 Stock Index, a representation of the market portfolio. The data represent the standing of both portfolios at the end of eight subsequent quarters (two years).

The quarterly returns on the two portfolios suggest that the "best" portfolio had an average quarterly return of 5.68 percent; the S & P Index showed an average return of 2.24 percent. At first blush it appears that the "best" portfolio outperformed the "market" by a difference of 3.44 percent per quarter. Let us see how these portfolios rank using the Sharpe, Treynor, and Jensen approaches to portfolio evaluation.

The reader should note that our calculation of returns uses only price changes. Dividends are not taken into consideration. The Treasury bill rate (r^*) on a quarterly return basis averaged 1.75 percent over the performance evaluation period.

Sharpe Model

The only inputs needed for the Sharpe model are:

r_t = average return on the "best" portfolio

r_m = average return on the market portfolio

σ_t = standard deviation of returns on the "best" portfolio

σ_m = standard deviation of returns of the market portfolio

For this particular example, the input values can be extracted from Table 22-4. Simply substituting these values into the model we have:

$$S_t = \frac{5.68 - 1.75}{15.23} = .26$$

$$S_m = \frac{2.24 - 1.75}{4.92} = .10$$

[18]*Institutional Investors Study Report of the Securities and Exchange Commission* (Washington, D.C.: Government Printing Office, 1971), Vol. II.

[19]However, the actual volatility of the portfolio proved to be a better appraisal of the funds' ultimate performance than did the words of management as expressed in their prospectuses. See Irwin Friend, Marshall Blume, and Jean Crockett, *Mutual Funds and Other Institutional Investors* (New York: McGraw-Hill, 1970), p. 150; and Donald E. Farrar, *The Investment Decision under Uncertainty* (Englewood Cliffs, N.J.: Prentice Hall, 1962), p. 73.

TABLE 22-4
COMPARATIVE PORTFOLIO PERFORMANCE

Quarter	S&P 500 Stock Index	Percentage of Return	"Best" Portfolio	Percentage of Return
1	98.35	—	100.0	—
2	106.94	8.7	130.1	30.1
3	111.39	4.2	153.1	17.6
4	103.42	−7.2	119.3	−22.0
5	111.32	7.6	132.8	11.2
6	111.83	0.4	138.8	4.5
7	114.77	2.6	139.9	0.7
8	114.07	−0.6	136.6	−2.3
Average		2.24%		5.68%
σ		4.92		15.23
Beta		1.00		2.83

The higher reading for the "best" portfolio suggests that it achieved superior excess return-to-risk relative to the market portfolio.

Treynor Model

The Treynor model and that of Sharpe differ only in that Treynor replaces the standard deviation in the denominator with beta. The beta value of the market is, of course, 1.00. The beta coefficient for the "best" portfolio is calculated by performing a simple regression procedure using the returns on the "best" portfolio as the dependent variable and the returns on the market portfolio as the independent variable. This results in a beta for the "best" portfolio of 2.83. The Treynor results are:

$$T_n = \frac{5.68 - 1.75}{2.83} = 1.39$$

$$T_m = \frac{2.24 - 1.75}{1.00} = 0.49$$

Again, the "best" portfolio outranks the market portfolio.

Jensen Model

The implementation of the Jensen model requires that we regress the quarterly differences between portfolio returns and the Treasury bill rate for the "best" portfolio. This gives us the return earned on the portfolio in excess of the risk-free rate. The equation that results for the "best" portfolio is:

$$(r_t - r^*) = 2.55 + 2.83\,(r_m - r^*)$$

where alpha is equal to 2.55 and beta is 2.83.

The alpha coefficient is the key. This 2.55 percent represents a measure of the bonus performance owing to superior portfolio management.

The equation for the security market line in Chapter 20 is helpful here as a more direct approach to an answer. The equation was:

$$R_i = R_F + \beta_i(R_M - R_F)$$

Using the data at hand we have:

$$R_i = 1.75 + 2.83\,(2.24 - 1.75)$$
$$= 3.13$$

This is the *expected* return from the portfolio, given the risk-free rate, the portfolio beta, and the return on the market portfolio. Since the actual return on the "best" portfolio was 5.68 percent, the excess earned over the expected return is 2.55 percent (5.68 − 3.13). This is also our alpha from above.

Mutual Funds as an Investment

Before we leave the subject of mutual funds, several closing remarks are in order. The fact that many of the studies just cited concluded that mutual funds have not performed very admirably does not lead to the seemingly obvious conclusion that mutual funds represent a bad investment outlet. What the studies concluded were that, *on average,* mutual funds included in the various samples did not perform better than a market portfolio or a large randomly selected portfolio bought and held by the investor; however, exceptions to these summary conclusions were found in all cases.[20] Therefore, profitable investment opportunities existed in both the load and no-load areas. Furthermore, it is *impossible* for many investors to assemble a large, diversified portfolio of the kind that seems to do better than or as well as the managed portfolios, because of capital limitations and higher commissions which have to be paid. Indeed, mutual funds may represent the only opportunity many investors have for investing in an intelligent, diversified fashion in the securities of U.S. corporations.[21]

Sources of Investment-Company Information

One of the best sources of investment-company information available to the investor is Wiesenberger's *Investment Companies*, issued annually. Figures 22-7, 22-8, and 22-9 show the types of information provided by this service. Figure 22-7 is typical of the pages that capsulize information about individual funds. As can be seen, the summary contains a history of the fund, statement of objectives, something about its portfolio composition, key statistical data, and the result of a hypothetical $10,000 investment in the fund over a ten-year period. Figure 22-8 shows the performance of net asset value on a yearly basis

[20]It is interesting to note that the mediocre performance of mutual funds in general was apparently accomplished with considerably varying portfolios. For an interesting discussion of this, see Lawrence J. Marks, "In Defense of Performance," *Financial Analysts Journal,* November-December 1962, pp. 135-37.

[21]The reader will recall the advantages of proper Markowitz diversification, as explained in Chapter 18. In addition, it should be pointed out that mutual funds may in fact overdiversify, as pointed out in Chapter 19.

FIGURE 22-7
SAMPLE PAGE FROM WIESENBERGER'S INVESTMENT COMPANIES

TEMPLETON GROWTH FUND, LTD.

Templeton Growth Fund was incorporated in Canada in 1954. It is a diversified investment company under the U.S. Investment Company Act of 1940. For several years shares of the fund were not offered in the United States, but became available to U.S. investors again in 1974. The fund's investments are diversified among securities issued by different companies and governments. No more than 5% of total assets may be invested in any single company.

The fund's primary objective is long-term capital growth. The investment policy is flexible and investments may be made in all types of securities issued by companies or governments anywhere. At the end of the 1980 fiscal year, the fund had the major proportion of its investments in the U.S., Canada and Japan, with smaller holdings in England, France, Sweden, The Netherlands, Hong Kong, South Africa, and Australia.

At the close of 1980, the fund had 87.2% of its assets in common stocks, of which the major proportion was concentrated in five industry groups: oil & gas (15.8% of assets), insurance (13.2%), banking & finance

(10.6%), mining & metals (8%), and electric & electronics (7.2%). The five largest individual common stock holdings were Alcan Aluminum (4.8% of assets), Royal Dutch Petroleum (3.7%), Nu-West Group "A" (3.4%), Hitachi (3.1%), and Phillips NV (3%). The rate of portfolio turnover during the latest fiscal year was 21.2% of average assets. Unrealized appreciation was 27.5% of calendar year-end assets.

Special Services: An open account arrangement serves for accumulation and automatic dividend reinvestment. Dividends are invested at net asset value. Minimum initial investment is $500 except under payroll deduction or other plans calling for regular monthly investments of $25 or more. Payments may be made by way of preauthorized checks. A withdrawal plan is available for owners of $10,000 or more of shares; withdrawals of a fixed or variable amount may be received monthly or quarterly. Shares of the fund may be exchanged for those of Templeton World Fund, or the independently-managed Reserve Fund, for a $5 fee.

Statistical History

							% of Assets in							
Year	Total Net Assets ($)	Number of Share-holders	Net Asset Value Per Share ($)	Offer-ing Price ($)	Yield (%)	Cash & Equiv-alent	Bonds & Pre-ferreds	Com-mon Stocks	Income Div-idends ($)	Capital Gains Distribu-tion ($)	Expense Ratio (%)	Offering Price ($) High	Low
1980	557,514,524	57,240	7.59	8.30	1.4	11	2*	87	0.12	0.38**	0.78	7.84	5.81
1979	340,460,731	37,990	6.51	7.11	1.1	8	2*	90	0.08	0.09**	0.80	7.31	5.81
1978	164,854,299	20,000	5.29	5.78	0.7	5	3*	92	0.043	0.02**	0.70	6.45	4.66
1977	82,261,382	8,500	4.49	4.91	1.0	10	7*	83	0.053	0.237	0.89	4.49	3.94
1976	42,470,473	3,500	4.01	4.38	0.9	7	4*	89	0.04	0.037	1.00	4.38	3.09
1975	19,484,382	1,900	2.80	3.07	1.5	7	9*	84	0.048	0.01	0.99	3.12	2.29
1974	13,628,104	1,700	2.08	2.27	1.6	13	9*	78	0.038	0.05†	1.07	2.95	2.22
1973	16,767,068	1,500	2.44	2.68	0.7	22	7	71	0.02	0.265†	0.93	3.51	2.56
1972	16,984,925	750	2.98	3.26	0.8	22	12	66	0.023	0.05	1.18	3.26	2.00
1971	7,882,658	650	1.82	1.99	1.3	13	20	67	0.025	0.03	1.30	1.99	1.70
1970	6,526,253	550	1.55	1.69	1.5	26	18	56	0.025		1.16	1.87	1.59

* Includes a substantial proportion in convertible issues.   ** Includes $0.015 short-term gains in 1978; $0.028 in 1979; $0.01 in 1980.
Note: Figures adjusted for 5-for-1 stock split in 1971 and 3-for-1 split in 1979.
† Includes $0.038 representing 1½% stock dividend in 1974 and $0.228 representing 8% stock dividend in 1973.

Directors: John M. Templeton, Pres.; H. Lloyd Blatchford; James W. Bradshaw; William F. James; Harry G. Kuch; Leroy C. Paslay; Archibald D. Russel; John M. Templeton, Jr.; Dennis O. Yorke.
Investment Adviser: Templeton Investment Counsel, Ltd. Compensation to the Adviser is at an annual rate of ½ of 1% of average daily net asset value, paid quarterly.
Custodian: New England Merchants National Bank, P.O. Box 1447, Boston, MA 02106.
Shareholder Service Agent: Securities Fund Services, Inc., P.O. Box 3942, St. Petersburg, FL 33731.
Transfer Agent: Applied Financial Systems, Inc., 155 Bovet Road, San Mateo, CA 94402.
Distributor: Securities Fund Investors, Inc., P.O. Box 3942, St. Petersburg, FL 33731, is the principal underwriter. Moss, Lawson

& Co. Ltd., 48 Yonge St., Toronto, Canada, is the exclusive distributor in Canada.
Sales Charge: Maximum is 8½% of offering price; minimum is 0.5% at $2 million. Reduced charges begin at $10,000 and are applicable to subsequent purchases on a permanent basis. Minimum initial purchase is $500.
Dividends: Income dividends and capital gains, if any, are paid annually in June.
Shareholder Reports: Issued semi-annually. Fiscal year ends April 30. The 1980 prospectus was effective in August.
Qualified for Sale: In all states, DC and PR.
Address: 155 University Ave., Toronto, Ontario M5H 3B7.
Telephone: (416) 364-4672.

An assumed investment of $10,000 in this fund, with capital gains accepted in shares and income dividends reinvested, is illustrated below. The explanation on Page 155 must be read in conjunction with this illustration.

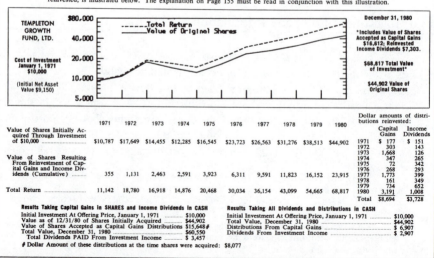

	1971	1972	1973	1974	1975	1976	1977	1978	1979	1980
Value of Shares Initially Acquired Through Investment of $10,000	$10,787	$17,649	$14,455	$12,285	$16,545	$23,723	$26,563	$31,276	$38,513	$44,902
Value of Shares Resulting From Reinvestment of Capital Gains and Income Dividends (Cumulative)	355	1,131	2,463	2,591	3,923	6,311	9,591	11,823	16,152	23,915
Total Return	11,142	18,780	16,918	14,876	20,468	30,034	36,154	43,099	54,665	68,817

Dollar amounts of distributions reinvested:

	Capital Gains	Income Dividends
1971	$ 177	$ 151
1972	303	143
1973	1,668	126
1974	347	265
1975	72	342
1976	268	293
1977	1,773	399
1978	161	349
1979	734	652
1980	3,191	1,008
Total	$8,694	$3,728

Results Taking Capital Gains in SHARES and Income Dividends in CASH
Initial Investment At Offering Price, January 1, 1971	$10,000
Value as of 12/31/80 of Shares Initially Acquired	$44,902
Value of Shares Accepted as Capital Gains Distributions	$15,648#
Total Value, December 31, 1980	$60,550
Total Dividends PAID From Investment Income	$ 3,457

Results Taking All Dividends and Distributions in CASH
Initial Investment At Offering Price, January 1, 1971	$10,000
Total Value, December 31, 1980	$44,902
Distributions From Capital Gains	$ 6,907
Dividends From Investment Income	$ 2,907

\# Dollar Amount of these distributions at the time shares were acquired: $8,077

SOURCE: *Investment Companies 1980* (New York: Wiesenberger Investment Companies Service, 1981).

and on a cumulative basis for a number of growth funds. (The formula utilized was given in Equation 22.1.) Figure 22-9 examines the price volatility of these same growth funds. (The explanation of the volatility measure is contained in the table.)

It is interesting to note that the Wiesenberger Service appears to recognize the importance of both return and risk considerations; however, these measures are presented separately, as can be seen in Figures 22-8 and 22-9, but are not brought together in a summary measure as has been done by others, such as Sharpe and Treynor. In fact, the volatility factor that the Wiesenberger Service calculates might be thought of as a crude measure of the beta factor in Equation 22.4. Figure 22-8 is on pages 610-611 and Figure 22-9 is on pages 612-13.

Forbes, an investment magazine published twice a month, annually rates the performance of investment companies. Its system attempts to incorporate in a summary measure both return and risk considerations. Basically, the approach used is to compare the fund's performance with that of the general market during periods of rising and falling markets. Funds that perform exceptionally well on a consistent basis when compared with the market in up markets receive an A+ rating; those that do not do as well receive ratings down to a possible low of D–. In a similar fashion, *Forbes* compares the relative performance of individual funds with the market portfolio in declining markets. Thus each fund receives two ratings—one in up markets, and one in down markets.

From these ratings, the investor gets a rough indication of the potential risks of investing in a given fund, both when investment conditions are favorable and when they are unfavorable. Furthermore, an investor can choose a fund whose performance is in line with his risk preferences. For example, the investor who is very risk-averse will prefer a fund that has performed consistently well in both kinds of markets (probably betas of one or less). On the other hand, a less risk-averse person or a more aggressive investor might prefer a fund that has done exceptionally well in up markets, even if it means assuming exceptional risk should a down market occur (betas greater than one). Needless to say, it is an ideal portfolio whose performance excels in both rising and falling markets.

Summary

In this chapter we have examined a number of alternative types of managed portfolios available to the investor. These have included closed-end investment companies, open-end investment companies or mutual funds, dual funds, money markets funds, municipal bond unit trusts and funds, index funds, pension funds, ERISA, trust agreements, common trusts, and professional investment counsel. We discussed the characteristics of these alternative investment opportunities, as well as the alleged advantages of such professionally managed portfolios. We analyzed a number of alternative measures of performance evaluation, including the Sharpe, Treynor, and Jensen approaches. Then we reported the results in summary fashion of a number of key empirical studies of mutual fund performance. Finally, we concluded with a survey of key sources of information on investment companies.

FIGURE 22-8
SAMPLE PAGE FROM WIESENBERGER'S INVESTMENT COMPANIES

Approximate Per Cent Change in Net Assets per Share With

RECORDS FOR INDIVIDUAL YEARS

ANNUAL RESULTS

	1980	1979	1978	1977	1976	1975	1974	1973	1972	1971
I. GROWTH FUNDS										
A. Maximum Capital Gain										
Able Associates Fund	56.7	79.1	7.7	6.4	68.4	25.7	—40.6	—24.6	— 2.9	
Acorn Fund	31.0	50.4	16.9	17.9	65.2	30.6	—27.7	—23.7	8.6	31.2
Afuture Fund	37.5	40.3	20.0	3.6	19.3	63.7	—42.0	—35.2	19.2	67.5
Alpha Fund	18.0	24.0	10.5	— 4.2	22.8	22.5	—28.2	—32.0	27.5	28.5
**American General Comstock Fund (1975)	32.7	47.7	13.7	13.9	34.2	64.5	—17.2	—16.9	— 1.3	12.4
**American Gen'l Enterprise Fund (1978)	72.9	51.2	21.5	— 6.8	14.8	33.5	—31.1	—20.6	6.3	23.7
American General Venture Fund	28.5	48.0	24.2	25.9	25.3	86.8	—40.9	—38.8	28.8	61.1
American Investors Fund	47.4	63.4	1.6	5.1	34.8	17.9	—29.7	—15.3	10.8	5.6
American National Growth Fund	18.6	29.9	19.9	13.8	38.2	38.2	—16.7	—37.4	3.0	28.3
Columbia Growth Fund	39.9	40.6	8.1	— 0.4	31.1	42.5	—22.5	—25.6	5.9	36.8
Constellation Growth Fund	74.5	76.8	21.2	— 3.5	23.3	40.0	—26.6	—16.3	5.8	2.0
Delta Trend Fund	28.9	29.3	2.7	6.0	29.5	31.3	—37.8	—33.8	— 7.9	21.4
Dreyfus Leverage Fund	36.6	41.2	10.8	7.5	25.2	25.9	—26.3	—15.5	12.6	28.8
**Eaton & Howard Special Fund (1979)	34.6	45.9	7.4	13.0	19.3	27.3	—40.8	—32.3	3.8	28.9
Evergreen Fund	48.1	46.3	38.0	25.4	48.8	60.1	—21.4	—26.2	10.1	
Explorer Fund	55.4	33.8	20.6	28.1	16.8	22.8	—35.4	—25.8	21.1	24.8
Fairfield Fund	60.3	28.9	10.7	— 8.5	33.6	40.5	—25.6	—28.2	5.2	20.2
Fidelity Contrafund	29.9	26.1	6.1	—10.9	36.8	40.5	—14.1	—10.2	16.2	9.0
Fidelity Growth Associates	55.7	86.1	— 2.3	3.7	24.9	59.5	—40.4	—39.7	23.9	33.0
Financial Dynamics Fund	21.9	42.4	6.2	7.8	31.4	38.3	—35.2	—15.4	17.6	13.3
First Investors Discovery	9.8	34.8	9.0	— 3.3	34.2	41.5	—36.9	—37.7	— 3.4	15.5
First Investors Fund for Growth	40.1	23.8	13.4	0.1	18.4	24.7	—29.9	—29.5	6.4	29.9
44 Wall Street Fund	36.4	73.6	32.9	16.5	46.5	184.1	—52.2	—46.8	— 5.4	71.8
Founders Growth Fund	50.5	36.4	11.9	— 4.7	7.4	30.1	—21.9	—24.9	16.3	24.5
Founders Special Fund	51.7	53.5	6.9	14.0	16.9	0.7	—19.9	—19.1	25.3	35.5
Franklin Dynatech Series	37.4	34.1	13.3	4.5	22.0	32.1	—33.8	—35.4	16.0	25.6
Fund of America	35.0	41.7	4.4	— 3.2	21.2	14.9	—27.9	—17.8	10.3	6.1
Hamilton Growth Fund	36.0	34.1	3.9	0.0	26.9	45.8	—31.6	—30.2	5.5	16.0
Hartwell Growth Fund	70.0	40.6	18.9	16.8	25.4	30.9	—24.7	—34.7	— 9.5	37.7
Hartwell Leverage Fund	93.9	55.4	11.3	16.6	34.6	34.5	—23.7	—17.8	—20.7	35.6
IDS New Dimensions Fund	55.6	33.5	9.1	1.8	14.7	28.5	—34.7	—28.4	27.0	48.6
IDS Progressive Fund	38.5	18.3	9.1	0.2	16.1	30.8	—37.7	—28.4	11.7	44.1
ISI Growth Fund	9.3	38.6	5.5	5.0	12.6	12.8	— 4.5	— 7.3	16.0	8.6
Ivest Fund	33.6	18.1	16.2	1.2	14.5	30.7	—33.4	—32.3	11.8	21.5
Janus Fund	51.5	34.6	15.8	3.5	20.2	13.4	— 6.9	—16.0	33.9	41.4
Kemper Summit Fund	45.7	42.3	18.8	12.6	32.6	56.5	—33.9	—27.5	6.9	26.1
Keystone S-4 (Lower Priced)	60.9	47.1	19.9	8.8	32.5	36.8	—44.0	—40.5	13.0	35.2
Lexington Growth Fund	31.9	26.4	30.8	11.6	47.6	46.2	—23.5	—43.9	13.6	27.2
Lord Abbett Developing Growth Fund	35.8	30.3	34.6	13.1	19.6	38.9	—35.7			
Mathers Fund	40.3	46.6	15.1	14.2	44.4	57.1	—30.6	—37.2	16.1	19.8
Mutual Shares Corporation	19.3	42.8	18.1	15.6	55.2	34.1	8.1	— 8.1	0.5	22.3
Neuwirth Fund	49.1	25.2	10.1	— 2.0	17.9	25.1	—22.0	—30.3	— 2.7	26.5
New York Venture Fund	44.0	38.9	19.4	4.5	20.8	23.2	—20.1	—24.1	22.2	28.0
Nicholas Fund	35.6	31.0	25.6	20.5	22.7	47.9	—33.5	—52.7	28.1	85.5
Omega Fund	37.6	37.7	7.6	0.3	51.4	12.8	—20.4	—18.1	43.9	21.7
Oppenheimer A.I.M. Fund	62.0	50.5	13.4	— 0.2	19.7	29.3	—33.1	—22.0	12.5	33.8
Oppenheimer Fund	41.9	38.6	8.4	—10.4	15.8	27.3	—25.9	—24.8	10.0	18.5
Oppenheimer Special Fund	46.4	43.3	21.5	23.9	49.0	93.1	—16.3			
Oppenheimer Time Fund	41.4	41.8	19.4	15.1	33.1	58.8	—44.1	—43.9	21.8	
**Pace Fund (1975)	44.9	45.4	23.5	28.6	27.8	34.2	—15.4	—42.5	18.0	43.6
**Partners Fund (1975)	34.1	42.9	16.3	7.0	31.2	18.1	3.3	—26.5	— 8.4	13.6
**Pennsylvania Mutual Fund (1972)	25.7	35.5	16.4	23.8	49.0	121.1	—46.0	—48.5	3.4	5.7
Phoenix-Chase Growth Fund Series	30.3	24.7	8.0	— 6.0	10.6	36.4	—36.6	—31.4	5.6	28.8
Pilot Fund	35.5	27.5	4.4	— 1.8	23.8	23.6	—20.0	— 9.5	4.6	21.7
**PLITREND Fund (1971)	33.4	48.1	23.7	17.5	36.3	36.8	—32.3	—17.7	13.5	14.9
T. Rowe Price New Horizons Fund	57.6	35.5	20.9	12.7	11.1	39.6	—38.7	—41.9	21.7	54.0
Putnam Vista Fund	29.9	31.8	18.0	— 2.5	22.7	32.8	—26.1	—24.6	36.5	20.4
Putnam Voyager Fund	41.3	37.2	13.9	6.0	28.5	41.5	—25.2	—16.7	41.0	33.8
Quasar Associates, Inc.	57.7	65.7	27.4	17.0	46.0	42.2	—43.4	—23.2	35.4	36.2
Research Equity Fund	35.2	30.2	7.4	9.7	14.2	13.3	—27.4	—22.8	18.1	18.8
Revere Fund	30.3	31.2	1.7	— 3.8	32.4	7.5	—25.1	—45.8	1.0	19.0
**Schuster Fund (1979)	28.5	28.3	17.3	14.5	31.0	19.7	—32.9	—33.5	2.6	17.2
Scudder Development Fund	46.6	29.9	29.9	25.2	22.8	77.9	—47.1	—46.1	31.0	
Scudder Special Fund	32.2	26.5	20.9	7.8	24.1	30.9	—33.5	—36.5	13.4	20.1
Security Ultra Fund	72.3	58.9	23.7	3.0	54.9	48.4	—26.4	—41.7	19.2	49.5

Questions and Problems

1. Distinguish between closed-end and open-end investment companies.

2. What are the alleged advantages of professionally supervised portfolios? Have empirical tests offered support for these contentions?

3. How can one measure the holding-period yield on a market portfolio?

Capital Gains Accepted in Shares and Income Dividends Reinvested

FOR PERIODS OF TWO TO TEN YEARS ENDED DECEMBER 31, 1980

	2 Years From 1/1/79	3 Years From 1/1/78	4 Years From 1/1/77	5 Years From 1/1/76	6 Years From 1/1/75	7 Years From 1/1/74	8 Years From 1/1/73	9 Years From 1/1/72	10 Years From 1/1/71	Funds Less Than 10 Years Old % Change in Net Asset Value	Funds Less Than 10 Years Old Total Income†	Funds 10 Years Old % Change in Net Asset Value	Funds 10 Years Old Total Income†
I. GROWTH FUNDS													
A. Maximum Capital Gain													
Able Associates Fund	180.6	202.2	221.5	441.4	580.6	304.0	204.7	195.7		195.7	0.0		
Acorn Fund	97.0	130.4	171.6	348.7	485.7	323.7	223.1	251.0	360.6			294.6	66.0
Afuture Fund	92.8	131.5	139.7	185.9	368.2	171.5	76.0	109.7	251.2			235.6	15.6
Alpha Fund	46.4	61.7	54.9	90.3	133.2	67.5	13.9	45.2	86.7			53.2	33.4
**American General Comstock Fund (1975)	96.1	122.9	153.8	240.6	460.4	364.0	285.6	280.4	327.6			226.2	101.5
**American Gen'l Enterprise Fund (1978)	161.4	217.5	195.8	239.7	353.5	212.6	148.2	164.0	226.5			164.8	61.7
American General Venture Fund	90.3	136.4	197.7	272.9	596.6	312.0	152.1	224.7	423.2			381.1	42.0
American Investors Fund	140.9	144.7	157.3	246.9	309.1	187.8	143.7	169.9	184.9			156.9	28.0
American National Growth Fund	54.1	84.7	110.1	190.4	301.4	234.3	109.4	115.6	176.7			117.8	58.9
Columbia Growth Fund	96.6	112.6	111.8	177.6	295.6	206.5	127.9	141.4	230.3			184.6	45.7
Constellation Growth Fund	208.5	273.7	260.5	344.5	522.3	356.7	282.4	304.5	312.7			281.9	30.8
Delta Trend Fund	66.6	71.1	81.2	134.7	208.1	91.7	26.9	16.9	41.9			23.1	18.8
Dreyfus Leverage Fund	92.9	113.7	129.9	187.9	262.4	167.1	125.7	154.3	227.4			174.1	53.3
**Eaton & Howard Special Fund (1979)	96.4	110.9	138.3	184.3	261.8	114.1	45.0	50.4	93.9			71.1	22.8
Evergreen Fund	116.6	199.0	274.9	457.9	793.2	602.2	418.4	470.8		461.1	9.8		
Explorer Fund	107.9	150.8	221.2	275.3	361.0	197.9	121.1	167.7	234.1			203.2	30.9
Fairfield Fund	106.5	128.6	109.3	179.6	292.9	192.4	109.9	120.8	165.4			118.7	46.7
Fidelity Contrafund	63.8	73.8	54.8	111.8	197.5	155.7	129.5	166.7	190.8			125.2	65.6
Fiduciary Growth Associates	189.8	183.3	193.9	267.1	485.4	248.9	110.3	160.6	246.4			223.4	23.1
Financial Dynamics Fund	73.6	84.4	98.8	161.2	261.2	134.1	98.0	132.8	163.7			103.1	60.7
First Investors Discovery	48.0	61.3	56.0	109.4	196.3	86.8	16.3	12.3	29.7			21.9	7.8
First Investors Fund for Growth	73.5	96.8	96.9	133.2	190.7	103.9	43.7	52.8	98.4			73.7	24.7
44 Wall Street Fund	136.8	214.8	266.6	436.9	1,425.4	628.6	287.4	266.4	529.3			529.3	0.0
Founders Growth Fund	105.3	129.7	118.8	135.1	205.7	138.7	79.3	108.5	159.5			98.8	60.7
Founders Special Fund	132.8	149.0	184.0	232.0	234.2	167.7	116.7	171.4	267.8			183.4	84.4
Franklin Dynatech Series	84.3	108.9	118.2	166.3	251.6	132.8	50.3	74.3	119.0			93.3	25.7
Fund of America	91.4	99.8	93.3	134.2	169.2	94.1	59.4	75.9	86.6			33.0	53.6
Hamilton Growth Fund	82.4	89.5	89.5	140.5	250.7	139.9	67.4	76.6	104.9			68.8	36.2
Hartwell Growth Fund	139.1	184.3	232.1	316.5	445.1	310.3	167.8	142.4	233.8			233.8	0.0
Hartwell Leverage Fund	201.4	235.5	291.2	426.4	608.0	440.5	344.0	252.1	377.3			377.3	0.0
IDS New Dimensions Fund	107.7	126.6	130.7	164.5	239.9	122.0	58.9	101.8	199.9			163.0	36.9
IDS Progressive Fund	63.8	78.7	79.0	107.8	171.8	69.3	21.2	35.4	95.1			56.1	39.0
ISI Growth Fund	51.4	59.7	67.7	88.8	112.9	103.2	88.4	118.6	137.5			65.4	72.1
Ivest Fund	57.8	83.3	85.5	112.3	177.5	84.9	25.2	40.0	70.1			41.2	28.9
Janus Fund	104.0	136.3	144.5	193.9	233.4	210.5	160.7	249.0	393.6			327.4	66.2
Kemper Summit Fund	107.3	146.2	177.3	267.7	475.4	280.2	175.7	194.8	271.6			220.9	50.8
Keystone S-4 (Lower Priced)	136.6	183.7	208.8	309.3	460.1	213.9	86.7	110.9	185.2			163.1	22.1
Lexington Growth Fund	66.7	118.1	143.4	259.2	425.3	301.9	125.5	156.1	225.8			209.3	16.4
Lord Abbett Developing Growth Fund	76.9	138.2	169.5	222.2	347.6	187.9				176.1	11.8		
Mathers Fund	105.6	136.6	170.2	290.0	512.6	325.0	167.1	210.2	271.6			193.3	78.3
Mutual Shares Corporation	70.3	101.2	132.6	261.0	384.1	423.5	381.2	383.8	491.5			385.1	106.4
Neuwirth Fund	86.7	105.4	101.4	137.3	196.9	131.7	61.4	57.0	98.5			62.9	35.7
New York Venture Fund	100.0	139.0	149.8	201.6	271.7	197.0	125.6	175.7	253.0			202.2	50.7
Nicholas Fund	77.6	123.1	168.8	229.8	387.7	224.5	53.4	96.5	264.5			227.9	36.6
Omega Fund	89.5	104.0	104.6	209.8	249.5	178.0	127.7	227.7	298.9			218.5	80.4
Oppenheimer A.I.M. Fund	143.9	176.5	176.0	230.4	327.1	185.9	123.0	150.8	235.5			184.0	51.5
Oppenheimer Fund	96.6	113.1	91.0	121.2	181.5	108.6	56.8	72.5	104.4			55.6	48.8
Oppenheimer Special Fund	109.7	154.7	215.5	370.2	807.7	660.0				614.6	45.4		
Oppenheimer Time Fund	100.6	139.4	175.5	266.7	482.3	225.8	82.9	122.9		107.6	15.2		
**Pace Fund (1975)	110.8	160.3	234.7	327.8	474.0	385.9	179.5	229.7	373.5			343.5	30.0
**Partners Fund	91.7	122.9	138.4	212.7	269.4	281.5	180.4	156.9	191.9			133.4	58.5
**Pennsylvania Mutual Fund (1972)	70.3	98.2	145.4	265.6	708.3	336.2	124.8	117.0	129.4			118.5	10.9
Phoenix-Chase Growth Fund Series	62.4	75.5	65.0	82.4	148.9	57.9	8.4	14.4	47.3			15.1	32.2
Pilot Fund	72.8	80.4	77.2	119.4	171.2	117.0	96.3	105.4	150.0			110.4	39.5
**PLITREND Fund (1971)	97.6	144.3	187.0	291.2	435.3	262.4	200.2	240.6	291.3			225.6	65.7
T. Rowe Price New Horizons Fund	113.5	158.1	190.9	223.2	351.1	176.4	60.7	95.5	201.0			172.0	29.0
Putnam Vista Fund	71.2	102.0	96.9	141.6	220.9	137.1	78.7	143.9	193.8			143.7	50.1
Putnam Voyager Fund	94.0	120.8	134.1	200.8	325.5	218.3	165.0	273.5	399.6			349.4	50.1
Quasar Associates, Inc.	161.3	232.8	289.2	468.4	708.3	357.9	251.7	376.2	548.7			547.0	1.7
Research Equity Fund	76.0	89.0	107.3	136.7	168.1	94.5	50.2	77.4	110.8			67.7	43.1
Revere Fund	70.9	73.9	67.2	121.4	138.1	78.3	−3.4	−2.4	16.2			1.5	14.8
**Schuster Fund (1979)	64.9	93.4	121.4	190.0	247.2	133.0	55.0	59.2	86.4			61.8	24.5
Scudder Development Fund	90.5	147.4	209.6	280.2	576.4	257.7	92.9	152.7		137.9	14.7		
Scudder Special Fund	67.3	102.2	118.0	170.6	254.3	135.5	49.5	69.4	103.5			64.6	38.9
Security Ultra Fund	173.7	238.5	248.6	440.0	701.1	489.8	244.1	310.2	513.3			486.5	26.8

SOURCE: *Investment Companies 1980* (New York: Wiesenberger Investment Companies Service, 1981).

4. Many people advocate mutual funds for small investors. They suggest that the best strategy for small investors is to buy shares in a good mutual fund and put them away. What do you think of this advice?

5. What is the essential difference between the Sharpe and Treynor Indexes of portfolio performance? Which do you think is preferable? Why?

6. How can the elements of the Sharpe Index be calculated?

FIGURE 22-9

SAMPLE PAGE FROM WIESENBERGER'S INVESTMENT COMPANIES

PRICE VOLATILITY OF MUTUAL FUND SHARES

Because of varying investment objectives and portfolio policies, it is normal for the prices of some mutual fund shares to reflect rises and declines in the general stock market to a greater degree than do others. The relationship between percentage changes in a fund's asset value per share and the corresponding fluctuations in a broad index of common stock prices provides a measure of a fund's relative "volatility."

In the table below, price changes of leading funds—adjusted for capital gains distributed—are related to changes in the New York Stock Exchange Index of all common stocks listed on the Exchange, to provide a rough indication of volatility. The results are expressed as "factors." A volatility factor of 1.00 would mean that adjusted asset value of a fund experienced a percentage change equal to that of the NYSE Common Stock Index between the same dates; a lower factor indicates a smaller rise or decline; a factor above 1.00 shows an advance or decline in excess of the index.

Note: For the first time since this tabulation was first published, a major group of funds has recorded a "counter trend (CT)" for any period studied. This occurred in the period December 31, 1976 through February 28, 1978, when the price changes for a sizable number of Maximum Capital Gains Funds resulted in an average figure that was counter to the NYSE Composite Index.

The percentage changes in the NYSE Common Stock Index (composite) during the eight periods shown below were as follows:

July 15, 1975 to October 1, 1975 .... −14.2%
October 1, 1975 to December 31, 1976 .... +31.7%
December 31, 1976 to February 28, 1978 ...... −16.3%
February 28, 1978 to September 11, 1978 ...... +24.7%
September 11, 1978 to November 14, 1978 .... −14.9%
November 14, 1978 to October 5, 1979 .... +23.4%
October 5, 1979 to March 27, 1980 .... −12.8%
March 27, 1980 to January 6, 1981 .... +43.1%

Volatility is not a measure of management performance. It can be used chiefly in estimating the relative extent of risk in declining periods and of gain potentials in shorter-term rising markets. Management performance, in contrast, is a long-term concept. Chapter XI discusses this aspect of investment company selection.

	Declining Period 7/15/75 to 10/1/75	Rising Period 10/1/75 to 12/31/76	Declining Period 12/31/76 to 2/28/78	Rising Period 2/28/78 to 9/11/78	Declining Period 9/11/78 to 11/14/78	Rising Period 11/14/78 to 10/5/79	Declining Period 10/5/79 to 3/27/80	Rising Period 3/27/80 to 1/6/81
NYSE Common Stock Index (Composite)	1.00	1.00	1.00	1.00	1.00	1.00	1.00	1.00

I. GROWTH FUNDS
A. Objective: Maximum Capital Gains

Able Associates	1.67	2.33	0.19	2.56	2.34	3.53	0.75	2.06
Acorn Fund	1.27	2.14	CT	1.61	1.41	2.44	0.96	1.21
Afuture Fund	0.93	0.94	0.15	1.51	0.92	2.30	0.37	1.30
Alpha Fund	1.34	1.00	0.81	1.23	1.03	1.12	0.83	0.77
American General Comstock	1.18	1.53	CT	1.43	1.12	1.88	0.20	0.97
American General Enterprise	0.96	0.65	0.82	1.91	1.78	2.48	0.85	2.43
American General Venture Fund	1.72	1.58	CT	2.14	1.14	2.12	1.22	1.18
American Investors Fund	1.60	1.10	0.07	1.45	1.81	2.79	1.87	2.28
American National Growth Fund	1.04	1.53	CT	1.78	1.41	1.68	1.30	0.78
Chase Frontier Capital Fund of Boston	1.36	0.26	0.20	1.41	1.40	2.03	0.69	1.54
Chase Special Fund of Boston	1.02	0.57	0.50	1.23	1.38	2.08	0.72	1.73
Columbia Growth Fund	1.08	1.30	0.58	1.56	1.55	1.85	0.77	1.49
Constellation Growth Fund	1.34	1.06	0.72	2.96	2.20	3.25	0.44	2.48
Delta Trend Fund	1.21	0.99	0.13	2.00	2.25	1.57	0.71	0.93
Directors Capital Fund	0.61	0.48	0.42	0.68	2.18	0.31	2.29	CT
Dreyfus Leverage Fund	0.70	0.73	CT	1.18	1.50	2.06	0.78	1.09
Eaton & Howard Special Fund	1.39	0.58	CT	1.94	2.08	2.10	0.99	1.46
Evergreen Fund	1.32	1.96	CT	2.63	1.74	2.94	0.59	1.58
Explorer Fund	1.52	0.51	CT	1.86	1.57	1.81	0.55	1.71
Fairfield Fund	1.01	1.44	1.06	1.50	1.51	1.31	1.01	2.09
Fidelity Contrafund	0.96	1.17	1.33	1.53	1.18	1.07	1.25	1.16
Financial Dynamics Fund	1.23	0.89	CT	0.79	1.26	1.44	0.37	0.69
First Investors Discovery	1.75	1.34	0.72	2.27	1.93	0.75	2.19	1.24
First Investors Fund for Growth	1.20	0.81	0.61	1.60	1.27	1.02	0.92	1.52
44 Wall Street Fund	1.88	2.15	CT	3.04	2.51	1.85	2.32	2.32
Founders Growth Fund	0.96	0.37	0.80	1.22	1.06	1.51	0.48	1.41
Founders Special Fund	1.15	0.43	CT	1.35	1.59	2.17	0.75	1.69
Franklin DynaTech Series	1.45	0.98	0.44	2.51	1.93	1.68	1.21	1.44
Fund of America	0.93	0.76	0.67	0.96	1.33	1.76	0.95	1.17
Hamilton Growth Fund	0.92	1.06	0.47	1.15	1.43	1.26	0.50	0.99
Hartwell Growth Fund	1.06	0.95	CT	2.10	1.59	2.92	0.69	2.29
Hartwell Leverage Fund	1.23	2.73	CT	2.62	2.23	2.52	1.13	3.27
Herold Fund	0.83	0.67	0.55	1.17	0.92	0.53	0.35	1.04
IDS New Dimensions Fund	1.23	0.63	0.55	1.48	1.31	1.46	0.58	1.55
IDS Progressive Fund	1.01	0.55	0.55	1.62	1.47	1.11	1.37	1.24
Industries Trend Fund	0.94	0.61	0.83	0.98	1.16	0.61	1.23	0.94
ISI Growth Fund	0.87	0.11	CT	0.80	1.07	1.26	1.36	0.74
Ivest Fund	1.06	0.56	0.58	1.51	0.98	0.92	0.97	1.14
Janus Fund	0.98	0.88	CT	1.64	1.45	1.47	1.56	1.82
Kemper Summit	0.89	1.15	CT	1.85	1.51	1.91	0.84	1.52
Keystone International Fund	1.21	0.48	0.39	0.99	1.45	1.30	0.81	0.66
Keystone (S-4) Special Common	1.59	1.21	CT	2.42	1.97	1.00	0.87	1.97
Lexington Growth Fund	1.27	1.87	CT	2.45	1.88	1.86	0.72	1.34
Lord Abbett Developing Growth	1.15	0.62	0.86	2.19	1.56	3.32	1.10	1.36
Mathers Fund	1.26	1.64	CT	1.16	1.04	1.88	0.76	1.38

CT   Counter Trend.

PRICE VOLATILITY OF MUTUAL FUND SHARES (Continued)

	PRICE VOLATILITY							
	Declining Period 7/15/75 to 10/1/75	Rising Period 10/1/75 to 12/31/76	Declining Period 12/31/76 to 2/28/78	Rising Period 2/28/78 to 9/11/78	Declining Period 9/11/78 to 11/14/78	Rising Period 11/14/78 to 10/5/79	Declining Period 10/5/79 to 3/27/80	Rising Period 3/27/80 to 1/6/81
NYSE Common Stock Index (Composite)	1.00	1.00	1.00	1.00	1.00	1.00	1.00	1.00

I. GROWTH FUNDS (Cont'd)
A. Objective: Maximum Capital Gains (Cont'd)

Mutual Shares Corporation	0.65	1.91	CT	1.03	0.94	1.68	0.84	0.79
Naess & Thomas Special Fund	1.15	0.87	CT	1.41	1.50	1.13	1.09	1.52
Neuwirth Fund	0.90	0.69	0.49	1.15	1.24	1.23	1.62	1.88
New York Venture Fund	1.25	0.91	0.20	1.69	1.27	1.59	0.38	1.44
Nicholas Fund	1.30	1.02	CT	1.64	1.42	1.82	1.18	1.35
Omega Fund	1.07	1.36	0.64	1.11	1.58	2.77	2.05	1.78
Oppenheimer AIM Fund	1.30	0.96	0.53	1.44	1.38	2.21	0.62	1.92
Oppenheimer Fund	0.96	0.64	1.24	1.31	1.26	1.55	0.77	1.46
Oppenheimer Special Fund	0.95	2.96	CT	1.76	1.37	2.55	0.35	1.32
Oppenheimer Time Fund	1.67	1.57	CT	1.79	1.41	1.98	0.43	1.34
Pace Fund	1.03	1.34	CT	1.62	1.25	1.70	0.85	1.96
Partners Fund	0.87	1.04	CT	1.15	0.84	1.66	0.11	0.96
Pennsylvania Mutual Fund	1.26	2.00	CT	1.92	1.92	2.20	1.84	1.56
Phoenix Chase Growth Fund Series	0.91	0.34	0.79	0.87	0.94	0.91	0.41	0.85
Pilot Fund	1.07	0.67	0.49	1.68	1.80	0.95	1.14	1.57
PLITREND Fund	0.94	1.16	CT	1.78	0.95	2.15	1.81	1.36
Rowe Price New Horizons	1.39	0.58	CT	2.09	1.64	1.71	0.81	1.91
Putnam Vista Fund	1.47	0.93	0.68	1.52	0.98	1.25	0.80	1.20
Putnam Voyager Fund	1.47	1.32	0.10	1.53	1.35	1.50	0.65	1.25
Rainbow Fund	0.99	1.23	CT	1.39	1.45	1.66	1.15	0.90
Research Equity Fund	1.45	0.62	0.18	1.62	1.36	1.13	0.77	1.24
Revere Fund	1.29	1.12	0.64	1.12	1.58	1.87	1.20	1.20
Schuster Fund	1.42	1.11	CT	1.77	1.47	1.59	0.76	1.01
Scudder Development Fund	1.63	1.21	CT	2.28	1.61	1.64	1.08	1.68
Scudder Special Fund	1.28	1.03	0.01	1.94	1.44	1.45	0.84	1.08
Security Ultra Fund	1.62	1.96	0.21	2.76	2.26	3.21	1.38	2.84
Selected Special Shares	1.07	0.58	1.03	0.98	1.28	1.38	1.32	1.06
Sequoia Fund	0.85	2.45	CT	1.51	0.77	1.19	1.48	0.78
Sherman, Dean Fund	1.34	0.69	CT	1.06	1.96	2.55	0.33	1.00
Sigma Capital Shares	1.29	1.44	0.27	1.38	1.30	1.49	1.19	1.25
Steadman American Industry	1.04	0.08	0.44	1.07	1.92	1.92	1.12	1.32
Steadman Oceanographic Fund	0.87	0.10	0.50	0.49	1.04	1.90	0.58	1.30
Tudor Fund	1.31	1.20	CT	2.20	1.59	1.49	0.98	1.31
Twentieth Century-Growth Fund	1.41	2.46	CT	4.15	2.30	2.00	0.05	2.52
Union Capital Fund	1.01	1.12	0.20	1.74	1.43	1.76	0.26	1.33
United Vanguard Fund	1.50	0.90	0.18	1.43	1.51	1.66	0.27	1.40
Value Line Leveraged Growth	1.74	1.70	CT	2.59	1.73	1.73	0.58	1.21
Value Line Special Situations	1.49	1.65	CT	2.11	2.02	2.26	0.91	2.00
Vance Sanders Special Fund	1.20	1.23	CT	2.11	1.57	1.69	0.92	1.40
Weingarten Equity Fund	1.20	0.66	CT	2.45	1.87	2.36	0.02	2.03
AVERAGES	1.20	1.11	CT	1.68	1.50	1.80	0.92	1.46

I. GROWTH FUNDS
B. Objective: Long-Term Growth—Income Secondary

AMCAP Fund	1.24	1.15	CT	1.88	1.39	2.15	0.63	1.09
American Birthright Trust	0.53	0.98	0.16	0.38	0.79	1.42	1.00	1.30
American General Growth Fund	1.17	1.44	0.18	2.12	1.68	3.67	0.81	2.52
American Growth Fund	1.03	1.01	CT	0.79	0.96	1.60	CT	0.45
American Leaders Fund	0.55	0.70	0.98	0.57	0.58	0.48	0.66	0.59
Anchor Growth Fund	0.93	0.60	0.75	1.23	1.12	1.16	1.14	0.83
Armstrong Associates	0.91	1.83	0.32	2.21	1.41	1.18	0.87	1.65
Axe-Houghton Stock Fund	0.69	0.65	1.13	1.11	0.84	0.81	0.59	1.19
Babson Investment	1.07	0.54	1.07	1.18	0.89	0.77	0.84	0.89
Beacon Growth Fund	0.70	0.56	0.66	0.45	0.63	0.73	0.59	0.83
Beacon Hill Mutual Fund	0.73	0.52	0.34	1.17	1.08	0.62	0.91	0.97
BLC Growth Fund	1.26	0.97	0.36	1.48	1.34	1.23	1.18	1.45
Boston Mutual Fund	0.92	0.66	1.34	1.37	1.03	0.38	0.84	0.33
Bridges Investment Fund	0.67	0.88	0.96	0.92	0.95	0.75	0.89	0.78
Brown Fund	1.08	0.88	0.73	1.07	1.26	1.19	0.39	1.17
Capital Shares	1.13	1.28	0.12	1.57	1.82	2.36	0.99	1.85
Cardinal Fund	0.90	1.33	0.27	1.21	0.90	0.95	0.87	0.77
CG Fund	1.07	0.86	1.01	1.11	0.83	1.07	0.98	1.17
Charter Fund	1.02	1.35	0.37	2.24	1.33	1.53	CT	0.99
Chemical Fund	1.11	0.44	1.02	1.27	1.06	1.03	0.67	1.06
Colonial Growth Shares	1.06	0.57	1.18	0.98	0.97	1.34	0.43	1.30
Common Stock Fund of St. Bd. & Mtge.	1.05	0.99	1.28	1.29	1.10	0.85	0.87	0.96
Continental Mutual Investment	0.61	0.46	0.84	1.13	2.04	1.60	0.90	0.85
Country Capital Growth	1.09	0.68	0.86	0.80	1.05	0.75	0.76	1.12
deVegh Mutual Fund	0.97	0.62	0.82	0.82	0.84	0.89	1.22	0.43	1.14
Drexel Burnham Fund	0.98	0.82	0.77	1.13	0.96	1.05	0.69	0.98
Dreyfus Fund	0.91	1.02	0.74	1.47	1.22	1.14	0.91	1.09
Dreyfus Number Nine Fund	0.79	1.66	CT	2.11	1.51	2.19	0.42	1.61
Dreyfus Third Century Fund	0.65	0.81	CT	1.45	1.57	2.23	CT	1.33
Eagle Growth Shares	1.14	1.25	0.68	1.72	1.40	1.66	1.52	0.71

CT   Counter Trend.

SOURCE: *Investment Companies 1981* (New York: Wiesenberger Investment Companies Service, 1982).

7. What is a characteristic line? How can it be determined?

8. What is the meaning of the alpha value in the Jensen Model?

9. What are the implications, if any, of the results of studies of mutual-fund performance for the random-walk theory?

10. Why may Sharpe's and Treynor's measures of performance give conflicting performance rankings?

11. Management Capital, Inc. (MCI), manages four mutual funds of American Investors Group (AIG). The funds are : Balanced, Investment Growth, Fixed Income, and Variable Growth. The data below include annual total return for each fund followed by key statistical measures. The average return on riskless securities during the measurement period was 5 percent per annum.

	Bal.	Growth	F.I.	V. Growth	DJIA
19X9	−.085	−.117	−.001	.141	−.116
19X8	.028	.032	.056	.035	.077
19X7	.100	.201	.030	.255	.190
19X6	−.093	−.117	−.014	−.101	−.156
19X5	.032	.083	.032	.153	.142
19X4	.096	.123	.045	.113	.187
19X3	.118	.142	.066	.134	.206
19X2	−.072	−.139	.054	−.170	−.076
19X1	.166	.235	.071	.240	.224
Return	.0282	.0403	.0373	.0798	.0654
Variance	.009	.020	.001	.021	.023
Beta	.6207	.9127	.1379	.6991	
Rho	.65	.94	.96	.82	

a. Rank the performance of these portfolios using the Sharpe and Treynor techniques.

b. Consider the Jensen method of ranking portfolios relative to the market. What is the overall performance of each fund relative to the market?

c. Which funds had the most unsystematic risk during the evaluation period? Explain.

12. Suppose that seven portfolios experienced the following results during a ten-year period:

Portfolio	Average Annual Return (%)	Standard Deviation (%)	Correlation with the Market
A	15.6	27.0	.81
B	11.8	18.0	.55
C	8.3	15.2	.38
D	19.0	21.2	.75
E	−6.0	4.0	.45
F	23.5	19.3	.63
G	12.1	8.2	.98
Market	13.0	12.0	
T-bills	6.0		

a. Rank these portfolios using (1) Sharpe's method, and (2) Treynor's method.

b. Compare the rankings in part (a) and explain reasons behind any differences noted.

c. Did any portfolios outperform the market? Why or why not?

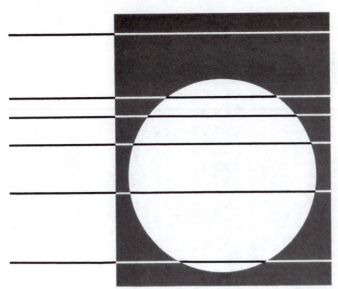

APPENDIX

Interest Tables

On the following pages are tables an analyst or investor would find useful in performing many of the calculations discussed throughout this text. These tables are elaborations of tables 4-1, 4-2, 4-3, and 4-4 on pages 83-85.

TABLE A-1
COMPOUND SUM OF $1 AT THE END OF n PERIODS: $FVIF_{k,n} = (1 + k)^n$

Period	1%	2%	3%	4%	5%	6%	7%	8%	9%	10%	12%	14%	15%	16%	18%	20%	24%	28%	32%	36%
1	1.0100	1.0200	1.0300	1.0400	1.0500	1.0600	1.0700	1.0800	1.0900	1.1000	1.1200	1.1400	1.1500	1.1600	1.1800	1.2000	1.2400	1.2800	1.3200	1.3600
2	1.0201	1.0404	1.0609	1.0816	1.1025	1.1236	1.1449	1.1664	1.1881	1.2100	1.2544	1.2996	1.3225	1.3456	1.3924	1.4400	1.5376	1.6384	1.7424	1.8496
3	1.0303	1.0612	1.0927	1.1249	1.1576	1.1910	1.2250	1.2597	1.2950	1.3310	1.4049	1.4815	1.5209	1.5609	1.6430	1.7280	1.9066	2.0972	2.3000	2.5155
4	1.0406	1.0824	1.1255	1.1699	1.2155	1.2625	1.3108	1.3605	1.4116	1.4641	1.5735	1.6890	1.7490	1.8106	1.9388	2.0736	2.3642	2.6844	3.0360	3.4210
5	1.0510	1.1041	1.1593	1.2167	1.2763	1.3382	1.4026	1.4693	1.5386	1.6105	1.7623	1.9254	2.0114	2.1003	2.2878	2.4883	2.9316	3.4360	4.0075	4.6526
6	1.0615	1.1262	1.1941	1.2653	1.3401	1.4185	1.5007	1.5869	1.6771	1.7716	1.9738	2.1950	2.3131	2.4364	2.6996	2.9860	3.6352	4.3980	5.2899	6.3275
7	1.0721	1.1487	1.2299	1.3159	1.4071	1.5036	1.6058	1.7138	1.8280	1.9487	2.2107	2.5023	2.6600	2.8262	3.1855	3.5832	4.5077	5.6295	6.9826	8.6054
8	1.0829	1.1717	1.2668	1.3686	1.4775	1.5938	1.7182	1.8509	1.9926	2.1436	2.4760	2.8526	3.0590	3.2784	3.7589	4.2998	5.5895	7.2058	9.2170	11.703
9	1.0937	1.1951	1.3048	1.4233	1.5513	1.6895	1.8385	1.9990	2.1719	2.3579	2.7731	3.2519	3.5179	3.8030	4.4355	5.1598	6.9310	9.2234	12.166	15.916
10	1.1046	1.2190	1.3439	1.4802	1.6289	1.7908	1.9672	2.1589	2.3674	2.5937	3.1058	3.7072	4.0456	4.4114	5.2338	6.1917	8.5944	11.805	16.059	21.646
11	1.1157	1.2434	1.3842	1.5395	1.7103	1.8983	2.1049	2.3316	2.5804	2.8531	3.4785	4.2262	4.6524	5.1173	6.1759	7.4301	10.657	15.111	21.198	29.439
12	1.1268	1.2682	1.4258	1.6010	1.7959	2.0122	2.2522	2.5182	2.8127	3.1384	3.8960	4.8179	5.3502	5.9360	7.2876	8.9161	13.214	19.342	27.982	40.037
13	1.1381	1.2936	1.4685	1.6651	1.8856	2.1329	2.4098	2.7196	3.0658	3.4523	4.3635	5.4924	6.1528	6.8858	8.5994	10.699	16.386	24.758	36.937	54.451
14	1.1495	1.3195	1.5126	1.7317	1.9799	2.2609	2.5785	2.9372	3.3417	3.7975	4.8871	6.2613	7.0757	7.9875	10.147	12.839	20.319	31.691	48.756	74.053
15	1.1610	1.3459	1.5580	1.8009	2.0789	2.3966	2.7590	3.1722	3.6425	4.1772	5.4736	7.1379	8.1371	9.2655	11.973	15.407	25.195	40.564	64.358	100.71
16	1.1726	1.3728	1.6047	1.8730	2.1829	2.5404	2.9522	3.4259	3.9703	4.5950	6.1304	8.1372	9.3576	10.748	14.129	18.488	31.242	51.923	84.953	136.96
17	1.1843	1.4002	1.6528	1.9479	2.2920	2.6928	3.1588	3.7000	4.3276	5.0545	6.8660	9.2765	10.761	12.467	16.672	22.186	38.740	66.461	112.13	186.27
18	1.1961	1.4282	1.7024	2.0258	2.4066	2.8543	3.3799	3.9960	4.7171	5.5599	7.6900	10.575	12.375	14.462	19.673	26.623	48.038	85.070	148.02	253.33
19	1.2081	1.4568	1.7535	2.1068	2.5270	3.0256	3.6165	4.3157	5.1417	6.1159	8.6128	12.055	14.231	16.776	23.214	31.948	59.567	108.89	195.39	344.53
20	1.2202	1.4859	1.8061	2.1911	2.6533	3.2071	3.8697	4.6610	5.6044	6.7275	9.6463	13.743	16.366	19.460	27.393	38.337	73.864	139.37	257.91	468.57
21	1.2324	1.5157	1.8603	2.2788	2.7860	3.3996	4.1406	5.0338	6.1088	7.4002	10.803	15.667	18.821	22.574	32.323	46.005	91.591	178.40	340.44	637.26
22	1.2447	1.5460	1.9161	2.3699	2.9253	3.6035	4.4304	5.4365	6.6586	8.1403	12.100	17.861	21.644	26.186	38.142	55.206	113.57	228.35	449.39	866.67
23	1.2572	1.5769	1.9736	2.4647	3.0715	3.8197	4.7405	5.8715	7.2579	8.9543	13.552	20.361	24.891	30.376	45.007	66.247	140.83	292.30	593.19	1178.6
24	1.2697	1.6084	2.0328	2.5633	3.2251	4.0489	5.0724	6.3412	7.9111	9.8497	15.178	23.212	28.625	35.236	53.108	79.496	174.63	374.14	783.02	1602.9
25	1.2824	1.6406	2.0938	2.6658	3.3864	4.2919	5.4274	6.8485	8.6231	10.834	17.000	26.461	32.918	40.874	62.668	95.396	216.54	478.90	1033.5	2180.0
26	1.2953	1.6734	2.1566	2.7725	3.5557	4.5494	5.8074	7.3964	9.3992	11.918	19.040	30.166	37.856	47.414	73.948	114.47	268.51	612.99	1364.3	2964.9
27	1.3082	1.7069	2.2213	2.8834	3.7335	4.8223	6.2139	7.9881	10.245	13.110	21.324	34.389	43.535	55.000	87.259	137.37	332.95	784.63	1800.9	4032.2
28	1.3213	1.7410	2.2879	2.9987	3.9201	5.1117	6.6488	8.6271	11.167	14.421	23.883	39.204	50.065	63.800	102.96	164.84	412.86	1004.3	2377.2	5483.8
29	1.3345	1.7758	2.3566	3.1187	4.1161	5.4184	7.1143	9.3173	12.172	15.863	26.749	44.693	57.575	74.008	121.50	197.81	511.95	1285.5	3137.9	7458.0
30	1.3478	1.8114	2.4273	3.2434	4.3219	5.7435	7.6123	10.062	13.267	17.449	29.959	50.950	66.211	85.849	143.37	237.37	634.81	1645.5	4142.0	10143.
40	1.4889	2.2080	3.2620	4.8010	7.0400	10.285	14.974	21.724	31.409	45.259	93.050	188.88	267.86	378.72	750.37	1469.7	5455.9	19426.	66520.	*

TABLE A-2
PRESENT VALUE OF $1: PVIF = $1/(1 + k)^t$

Period	1%	2%	3%	4%	5%	6%	7%	8%	9%	10%	12%	14%	15%	16%	18%	20%	24%	28%	32%	36%
1	.9901	.9804	.9709	.9615	.9524	.9434	.9346	.9259	.9174	.9091	.8929	.8772	.8696	.8621	.8475	.8333	.8065	.7813	.7576	.7353
2	.9803	.9612	.9426	.9246	.9070	.8900	.8734	.8573	.8417	.8264	.7972	.7695	.7561	.7432	.7182	.6944	.6504	.6104	.5739	.5407
3	.9706	.9423	.9151	.8890	.8638	.8396	.8163	.7938	.7722	.7513	.7118	.6750	.6575	.6407	.6086	.5787	.5245	.4768	.4348	.3975
4	.9610	.9238	.8885	.8548	.8227	.7921	.7629	.7350	.7084	.6830	.6355	.5921	.5718	.5523	.5158	.4823	.4230	.3725	.3294	.2923
5	.9515	.9057	.8626	.8219	.7835	.7473	.7130	.6806	.6499	.6209	.5674	.5194	.4972	.4761	.4371	.4019	.3411	.2910	.2495	.2149
6	.9420	.8880	.8375	.7903	.7462	.7050	.6663	.6302	.5963	.5645	.5066	.4556	.4323	.4104	.3704	.3349	.2751	.2274	.1890	.1580
7	.9327	.8706	.8131	.7599	.7107	.6651	.6227	.5835	.5470	.5132	.4523	.3996	.3759	.3538	.3139	.2791	.2218	.1776	.1432	.1162
8	.9235	.8535	.7894	.7307	.6768	.6274	.5820	.5403	.5019	.4665	.4039	.3506	.3269	.3050	.2660	.2326	.1789	.1388	.1085	.0854
9	.9143	.8368	.7664	.7026	.6446	.5919	.5439	.5002	.4604	.4241	.3606	.3075	.2843	.2630	.2255	.1938	.1443	.1084	.0822	.0628
10	.9053	.8203	.7441	.6756	.6139	.5584	.5083	.4632	.4224	.3855	.3220	.2697	.2472	.2267	.1911	.1615	.1164	.0847	.0623	.0462
11	.8963	.8043	.7224	.6496	.5847	.5268	.4751	.4289	.3875	.3505	.2875	.2366	.2149	.1954	.1619	.1346	.0938	.0662	.0472	.0340
12	.8874	.7885	.7014	.6246	.5568	.4970	.4440	.3971	.3555	.3186	.2567	.2076	.1869	.1685	.1372	.1122	.0757	.0517	.0357	.0250
13	.8787	.7730	.6810	.6006	.5303	.4688	.4150	.3677	.3262	.2897	.2292	.1821	.1625	.1452	.1163	.0935	.0610	.0404	.0271	.0184
14	.8700	.7579	.6611	.5775	.5051	.4423	.3878	.3405	.2992	.2633	.2046	.1597	.1413	.1252	.0985	.0779	.0492	.0316	.0205	.0135
15	.8613	.7430	.6419	.5553	.4810	.4173	.3624	.3152	.2745	.2394	.1827	.1401	.1229	.1079	.0835	.0649	.0397	.0247	.0155	.0099
16	.8528	.7284	.6232	.5339	.4581	.3936	.3387	.2919	.2519	.2176	.1631	.1229	.1069	.0930	.0708	.0541	.0320	.0193	.0118	.0073
17	.8444	.7142	.6050	.5134	.4363	.3714	.3166	.2703	.2311	.1978	.1456	.1078	.0929	.0802	.0600	.0451	.0258	.0150	.0089	.0054
18	.8360	.7002	.5874	.4936	.4155	.3503	.2959	.2502	.2120	.1799	.1300	.0946	.0808	.0691	.0508	.0376	.0208	.0118	.0068	.0039
19	.8277	.6864	.5703	.4746	.3957	.3305	.2765	.2317	.1945	.1635	.1161	.0829	.0703	.0596	.0431	.0313	.0168	.0092	.0051	.0029
20	.8195	.6730	.5537	.4564	.3769	.3118	.2584	.2145	.1784	.1486	.1037	.0728	.0611	.0514	.0365	.0261	.0135	.0072	.0039	.0021
25	.7798	.6095	.4776	.3751	.2953	.2330	.1842	.1460	.1160	.0923	.0588	.0378	.0304	.0245	.0160	.0105	.0046	.0021	.0010	.0005
30	.7419	.5521	.4120	.3083	.2314	.1741	.1314	.0994	.0754	.0573	.0334	.0196	.0151	.0116	.0070	.0042	.0016	.0006	.0002	.0001
40	.6717	.4529	.3066	.2083	.1420	.0972	.0668	.0460	.0318	.0221	.0107	.0053	.0037	.0026	.0013	.0007	.0002	.0001	*	*
50	.6080	.3715	.2281	.1407	.0872	.0543	.0339	.0213	.0134	.0085	.0035	.0014	.0009	.0006	.0003	.0001	*	*	*	*
60	.5504	.3048	.1697	.0951	.0535	.0303	.0173	.0099	.0057	.0033	.0011	.0004	.0002	.0001	*	*	*	*	*	*

*The factor is zero to four decimal places.

TABLE A-3

COMPOUND SUM OF AN ANNUITY OF $1 PER PERIOD FOR n PERIODS:

$$FVIFA_{k,n} = \sum_{t=1}^{n}(1+k)^{t-1} = \frac{(1+k)^n - 1}{k}$$

Number of Periods	1%	2%	3%	4%	5%	6%	7%	8%	9%	10%	12%	14%	15%	16%	18%	20%	24%	28%	32%	36%
1	1.0000	1.0000	1.0000	1.0000	1.0000	1.0000	1.0000	1.0000	1.0000	1.0000	1.0000	1.0000	1.0000	1.0000	1.0000	1.0000	1.0000	1.0000	1.0000	1.0000
2	2.0100	2.0200	2.0300	2.0400	2.0500	2.0600	2.0700	2.0800	2.0900	2.1000	2.1200	2.1400	2.1500	2.1600	2.1800	2.2000	2.2400	2.2800	2.3200	2.3600
3	3.0301	3.0604	3.0909	3.1216	3.1525	3.1836	3.2149	3.2464	3.2781	3.3100	3.3744	3.4396	3.4725	3.5056	3.5724	3.6400	3.7776	3.9184	4.0624	4.2096
4	4.0604	4.1216	4.1836	4.2465	4.3101	4.3746	4.4399	4.5061	4.5731	4.6410	4.7793	4.9211	4.9934	5.0665	5.2154	5.3680	5.6842	6.0156	6.3624	6.7251
5	5.1010	5.2040	5.3091	5.4163	5.5256	5.6371	5.7507	5.8666	5.9847	6.1051	6.3528	6.6101	6.7424	6.8771	7.1542	7.4416	8.0484	8.6999	9.3983	10.146
6	6.1520	6.3081	6.4684	6.6330	6.8019	6.9753	7.1533	7.3359	7.5233	7.7156	8.1152	8.5355	8.7537	8.9775	9.4420	9.9299	10.980	12.135	13.405	14.798
7	7.2135	7.4343	7.6625	7.8983	8.1420	8.3938	8.6540	8.9228	9.2004	9.4872	10.089	10.730	11.066	11.413	12.141	12.915	14.615	16.533	18.695	21.126
8	8.2857	8.5830	8.8923	9.2142	9.5491	9.8975	10.259	10.636	11.028	11.435	12.299	13.232	13.726	14.240	15.327	16.499	19.122	22.163	25.678	29.731
9	9.3685	9.7546	10.159	10.582	11.026	11.491	11.978	12.487	13.021	13.579	14.775	16.085	16.785	17.518	19.085	20.798	24.712	29.369	34.895	41.435
10	10.462	10.949	11.463	12.006	12.577	13.180	13.816	14.486	15.192	15.937	17.548	19.337	20.303	21.321	23.521	25.958	31.643	38.592	47.061	57.351
11	11.566	12.168	12.807	13.486	14.206	14.971	15.783	16.645	17.560	18.531	20.654	23.044	24.349	25.732	28.755	32.150	40.237	50.398	63.121	78.998
12	12.682	13.412	14.192	15.025	15.917	16.869	17.888	18.977	20.140	21.384	24.133	27.270	29.001	30.850	34.931	39.580	50.894	65.510	84.320	108.43
13	13.809	14.680	15.617	16.626	17.713	18.882	20.140	21.495	22.953	24.522	28.029	32.088	34.351	36.786	42.218	48.496	64.109	84.852	112.30	148.47
14	14.947	15.973	17.086	18.291	19.598	21.015	22.550	24.214	26.019	27.975	32.392	37.581	40.504	43.672	50.818	59.195	80.496	109.61	149.23	202.92
15	16.096	17.293	18.598	20.023	21.578	23.276	25.129	27.152	29.360	31.772	37.279	43.842	47.580	51.659	60.965	72.035	100.81	141.30	197.99	276.97
16	17.257	18.639	20.156	21.824	23.657	25.672	27.888	30.324	33.003	35.949	42.753	50.980	55.717	60.925	72.939	87.442	126.01	181.86	262.35	377.69
17	18.430	20.012	21.761	23.697	25.840	28.212	30.840	33.750	36.973	40.544	48.883	59.117	65.075	71.673	87.068	105.93	157.25	233.79	347.30	514.66
18	19.614	21.412	23.414	25.645	28.132	30.905	33.999	37.450	41.301	45.599	55.749	68.394	75.836	84.140	103.74	128.11	195.99	300.25	459.44	700.93
19	20.810	22.840	25.116	27.671	30.539	33.760	37.379	41.446	46.018	51.159	63.439	78.969	88.211	98.603	123.41	154.74	244.03	385.32	607.47	954.27
20	22.019	24.297	26.870	29.778	33.066	36.785	40.995	45.762	51.160	57.275	72.052	91.024	102.44	115.37	146.62	186.68	303.60	494.21	802.86	1298.8
21	23.239	25.783	28.676	31.969	35.719	39.992	44.865	50.422	56.764	64.002	81.698	104.76	118.81	134.84	174.02	225.02	377.46	633.59	1060.7	1767.3
22	24.471	27.299	30.536	34.248	38.505	43.392	49.005	55.456	62.873	71.402	92.502	120.43	137.63	157.41	206.34	271.03	469.05	811.99	1401.2	2404.6
23	25.716	28.845	32.452	36.617	41.430	46.995	53.436	60.893	69.531	79.543	104.60	138.29	159.27	183.60	244.48	326.23	582.62	1040.3	1850.6	3271.3
24	26.973	30.421	34.426	39.082	44.502	50.815	58.176	66.764	76.789	88.497	118.15	158.65	184.16	213.97	289.49	392.48	723.46	1332.6	2443.8	4449.9
25	28.243	32.030	36.459	41.645	47.727	54.864	63.249	73.105	84.700	98.347	133.33	181.87	212.79	249.21	342.60	471.98	898.09	1706.8	3226.8	6052.9
26	29.525	33.670	38.553	44.311	51.113	59.156	68.676	79.954	93.323	109.18	150.33	208.33	245.71	290.08	405.27	567.37	1114.6	2185.7	4260.4	8233.0
27	30.820	35.344	40.709	47.084	54.669	63.705	74.483	87.350	102.72	121.09	169.37	238.49	283.56	337.50	479.22	681.85	1383.1	2798.7	5624.7	11197.9
28	32.129	37.051	42.930	49.967	58.402	68.528	80.697	95.338	112.96	134.20	190.69	272.88	327.10	392.50	566.48	819.22	1716.0	3583.3	7425.6	15230.2
29	33.450	38.792	45.218	52.966	62.322	73.639	87.346	103.96	124.13	148.63	214.58	312.09	377.16	456.30	669.44	984.06	2128.9	4587.6	9802.9	20714.1
30	34.784	40.568	47.575	56.084	66.438	79.058	94.460	113.28	136.30	164.49	241.33	356.78	434.74	530.31	790.94	1181.8	2640.9	5873.2	12940.	28172.2
40	48.886	60.402	75.401	95.025	120.79	154.76	199.63	259.05	337.88	442.59	767.09	1342.0	1779.0	2360.7	4163.2	7343.8	22728.	69377.	*	*
50	64.463	84.579	112.79	152.66	209.34	290.33	406.52	573.76	815.08	1163.9	2400.0	4994.5	7217.7	10435.	21813.	45497.	*	*	*	*
60	81.669	114.05	163.05	237.99	353.58	533.12	813.52	1253.2	1944.7	3034.8	7471.6	18535.	29219.	46057.	*	*	*	*	*	*

TABLE A-4

PRESENT VALUE OF AN ANNUITY OF $1 PER PERIOD FOR n PERIODS: $\text{PVIFA} = \sum_{t=1}^{n} \dfrac{1}{(1+k)^t}$

$$= \dfrac{1 - \dfrac{1}{(1+k)^n}}{k}$$

Number of Payments	1%	2%	3%	4%	5%	6%	7%	8%	9%	10%	12%	14%	15%	16%	18%	20%	24%	28%	32%
1	0.9901	0.9804	0.9709	0.9615	0.9524	0.9434	0.9346	0.9259	0.9174	0.9091	0.8929	0.8772	0.8696	0.8621	0.8475	0.8333	0.8065	0.7813	0.7576
2	1.9704	1.9416	1.9135	1.8861	1.8594	1.8334	1.8080	1.7833	1.7591	1.7355	1.6901	1.6467	1.6257	1.6052	1.5656	1.5278	1.4568	1.3916	1.3315
3	2.9410	2.8839	2.8286	2.7751	2.7232	2.6730	2.6243	2.5771	2.5313	2.4869	2.4018	2.3216	2.2832	2.2459	2.1743	2.1065	1.9813	1.8684	1.7663
4	3.9020	3.8077	3.7171	3.6299	3.5460	3.4651	3.3872	3.3121	3.2397	3.1699	3.0373	2.9137	2.8550	2.7982	2.6901	2.5887	2.4043	2.2410	2.0957
5	4.8534	4.7135	4.5797	4.4518	4.3295	4.2124	4.1002	3.9927	3.8897	3.7908	3.6048	3.4331	3.3522	3.2743	3.1272	2.9906	2.7454	2.5320	2.3452
6	5.7955	5.6014	5.4172	5.2421	5.0757	4.9173	4.7665	4.6229	4.4859	4.3553	4.1114	3.8887	3.7845	3.6847	3.4976	3.3255	3.0205	2.7594	2.5342
7	6.7282	6.4720	6.2303	6.0021	5.7864	5.5824	5.3893	5.2064	5.0330	4.8684	4.5638	4.2883	4.1604	4.0386	3.8115	3.6046	3.2423	2.9370	2.6775
8	7.6517	7.3255	7.0197	6.7327	6.4632	6.2098	5.9713	5.7466	5.5348	5.3349	4.9676	4.6389	4.4873	4.3436	4.0776	3.8372	3.4212	3.0758	2.7860
9	8.5660	8.1622	7.7861	7.4353	7.1078	6.8017	6.5152	6.2469	5.9952	5.7590	5.3282	4.9464	4.7716	4.6065	4.3030	4.0310	3.5655	3.1842	2.8681
10	9.4713	8.9826	8.5302	8.1109	7.7217	7.3601	7.0236	6.7101	6.4177	6.1446	5.6502	5.2161	5.0188	4.8332	4.4941	4.1925	3.6819	3.2689	2.9304
11	10.3676	9.7868	9.2526	8.7605	8.3064	7.8869	7.4987	7.1390	6.8052	6.4951	5.9377	5.4527	5.2337	5.0286	4.6560	4.3271	3.7757	3.3351	2.9776
12	11.2551	10.5753	9.9540	9.3851	8.8633	8.3838	7.9427	7.5361	7.1607	6.8137	6.1944	5.6603	5.4206	5.1971	4.7932	4.4392	3.8514	3.3868	3.0133
13	12.1337	11.3484	10.6350	9.9856	9.3936	8.8527	8.3577	7.9038	7.4869	7.1034	6.4235	5.8424	5.5831	5.3423	4.9095	4.5327	3.9124	3.4272	3.0404
14	13.0037	12.1062	11.2961	10.5631	9.8986	9.2950	8.7455	8.2442	7.7862	7.3667	6.6282	6.0021	5.7245	5.4675	5.0081	4.6106	3.9616	3.4587	3.0609
15	13.8651	12.8493	11.9379	11.1184	10.3797	9.7122	9.1079	8.5595	8.0607	7.6061	6.8109	6.1422	5.8474	5.5755	5.0916	4.6755	4.0013	3.4834	3.0764
16	14.7179	13.5777	12.5611	11.6523	10.8378	10.1059	9.4466	8.8514	8.3126	7.8237	6.9740	6.2651	5.9542	5.6685	5.1624	4.7296	4.0333	3.5026	3.0882
17	15.5623	14.2919	13.1661	12.1657	11.2741	10.4773	9.7632	9.1216	8.5436	8.0216	7.1196	6.3729	6.0472	5.7487	5.2223	4.7746	4.0591	3.5177	3.0971
18	16.3983	14.9920	13.7535	12.6593	11.6896	10.8276	10.0591	9.3719	8.7556	8.2014	7.2497	6.4674	6.1280	5.8178	5.2732	4.8122	4.0799	3.5294	3.1039
19	17.2260	15.6785	14.3238	13.1339	12.0853	11.1581	10.3356	9.6036	8.9501	8.3649	7.3658	6.5504	6.1982	5.8775	5.3162	4.8435	4.0967	3.5386	3.1090
20	18.0456	16.3514	14.8775	13.5903	12.4622	11.4699	10.5940	9.8181	9.1285	8.5136	7.4694	6.6231	6.2593	5.9288	5.3527	4.8696	4.1103	3.5458	3.1129
25	22.0232	19.5235	17.4131	15.6221	14.0939	12.7834	11.6536	10.6748	9.8226	9.0770	7.8431	6.8729	6.4641	6.0971	5.4669	4.9476	4.1474	3.5640	3.1220
30	25.8077	22.3965	19.6004	17.2920	15.3725	13.7648	12.4090	11.2578	10.2737	9.4269	8.0552	7.0027	6.5660	6.1772	5.5168	4.9789	4.1601	3.5693	3.1242
40	32.8347	27.3555	23.1148	19.7928	17.1591	15.0463	13.3317	11.9246	10.7574	9.7791	8.2438	7.1050	6.6418	6.2335	5.5482	4.9966	4.1659	3.5712	3.1250
50	39.1961	31.4236	25.7298	21.4822	18.2559	15.7619	13.8007	12.2335	10.9617	9.9148	8.3045	7.1327	6.6605	6.2463	5.5541	4.9995	4.1666	3.5714	3.1250
60	44.9550	34.7609	27.6756	22.6235	18.9293	16.1614	14.0392	12.3766	11.0480	9.9672	8.3240	7.1401	6.6651	6.2402	5.5553	4.9999	4.1667	3.5714	3.1250

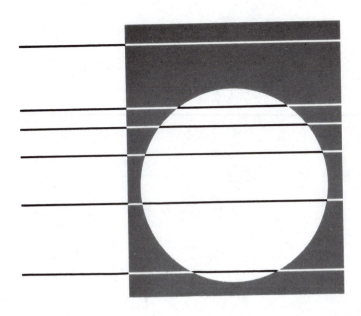

INDEX

and past sales, 172-74, 176, 177
in present-value theory, 95
and stock prices, 108-9, 134-35
Earnings after taxes (EAT), 263, 266
Earnings before interest and taxes (EBIT), 113,
115, 261-62, 343-46, 348
Earnings before taxes (EBT), 115, 259-60, 263
Earnings-coverage ratios, 343-46
Earnings forecasting:
independent forecasts, 253, 270-73, 275-79
market share-profit margin approach, 253,
267-70, 271, 272
return-on-investment approach (ROI), 253,
265-67, 273-75
Earnings growth, in fast-food industry, 176-79
Earnings model, 253-67, 270, 273-75
Earnings per share (EPS):
calculation, 208-10, 263-64
decision trees, 292, 293, 294
forecasting, 265-67, 268, 272
simulation, 297, 298, 299, 300
trend analysis, 284, 285, 289-90
Eclectic theory of the yield curve, 336
Econometric model building, 158-59
Economic analysis, 132-33, 137-64
anticipatory surveys, 142-45
barometric or indicator approach, 145-54
diffusion indexes, 154-58
econometric model building, 158-59
example, 162-64
money supply, 158
opportunistic model building, 159-61
short-term vs. long-term, 139-40
sources of data, 143-44
Economic indicators (*see* Indicators)
Economic-industry-company (EIC) approach,
132-34, 137-38
Economic model, 327-28
Economies of scale, 175
Effective interest rate, 257
Efficiency locus, 514-15, 524-25
Efficient frontier, 515, 524-25, 529, 530n, 531,
538, 539, 557-61
Efficient market theory, 454, 480-97 (*see also*
Random-walk theory)
defined, 4, 79, 80-81
fundamental analysis and, 80, 81, 480-81
semi-strong form, 454, 482-83, 491-93
strong form, 454, 483-84
technical analysis and, 80, 81, 480-81
weak form, 454, 482, 484-91
Either/or order, 58
Empirical tests:
mutual-fund performance, 603-5
random walk theory, 484-93
Employment, and bond yields, 328
Employment Retirement Income Security Act
(ERISA), 592
End-of-holding-period price, formula for, 135
Endogenous variables, 159

End-use analysis, 182-86
Equipment trust certificates, 11
Equity:
and balance sheet, 211-12
in capitalization, 346-47
defined, 11, 47
direct investment, 12-14
and earnings, 261-62
individual ownership, 17-19
via institutions (indirect), 11-12
principal suppliers of, 16
return on, 20-21
U.S. totals, 15
Equity method of accounting, 216, 217
ERISA, 592
Evans, John L., 526
Exchange rates, and portfolio selection, 565-66
Exercise price, 408
Exogenous variables, 159
Expansion stage (industry life cycle), 180
Expectations theory of the yield curve, 335
Expected returns:
in active bond management, 387-89
calculation, 118-21, 137
Expected risk (*see* Earnings forecasting; Risk)
Expected wealth ratio, 378-79
Expenses, forecasts of:
independent, 253, 270-73, 275-79
with regression analysis, 283-90, 301
External information, 198, 223-34
Extramarket covariance, 544-45
Extraordinary gains and losses, 202-3, 213

F

Face value, 8
Fall, Carol L., 125
Fama, Eugene F., 492
"Favorite fifty" securities, 194, 195
Federal government:
attitude toward industry, 174, 176-77
securities (*see* U.S. government securities)
as source of information for industry analy-
sis, 188
Federal Home Loan Banks, 9
Federal National Mortgage Association, 9
Federal personal income tax (*see* Taxes)
Federal Reserve Bank of New York, 34
Federal Reserve Bank of Philadelphia, 161
Federal Reserve Bank of Richmond, 161
Federal Reserve Bank of St. Louis, 323
Federal Reserve Board, 47
Federal Reserve Board Index of Industrial Pro-
duction, 184
Federal Reserve Bulletin, 144, 172, 188, 465
Federal Reserve System, 47, 329, 331, 381
FIFO (first in, first out), 205-6
Fill or kill order, 58
Filter tests, 489-91
Financial Accounting Standards Board (FASB),
199, 218, 222, 347n